Hil...
Tramping in New Zealand

Northland, Auckland & Coromandel
p54

Tongariro, Urewera & Central North Island
p84

Abel Tasman, Kahurangi & Nelson Lakes
p165

Taranaki, Whanganui & Around Wellington
p110

West Coast
p237

Queen Charlotte & Marlborough
p144

Canterbury, Arthur's Pass & Aoraki/Mt Cook
p202

Fiordland & Stewart Island/Rakiura
p285

Mt Aspiring National Park & Around Queenstown
p258

THIS EDITION WRITTEN AND RESEARCHED BY

Sarah Bennett & Lee Slater,

Jim DuFresne

May 2014

Contents

PLAN YOUR TRIP

Welcome to New Zealand. . 4

New Zealand Map 6

New Zealand's
Nine Great Walks 8

Need to Know 14

If You Like. 16

Itineraries 20

Outdoor Pursuits 28

New Zealand's Birds. . . . 34

Safety in the Outdoors. . 38

Clothing, Equipment &
Food 45

Regions at a Glance. . . . 50

STEVE CLANCY PHOTOGRAPHY / GETTY IMAGES ©

BOTTLENOSE DOLPHIN P29

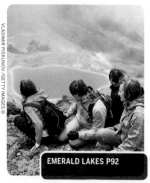

VLADIMIR PISKUNOV /GETTY IMAGES ©

EMERALD LAKES P92

ON THE TRACK

NORTHLAND, AUCKLAND & COROMANDEL 54

Te Paki Coastal Track 56
Rangitoto Island Loop 61
Aotea Track 64
Hillary Trail. 69
Kauaeranga Kauri Trail . . . 75
Towns & Facilities. 80
Auckland 80
Kaitaia 81
Tryphena 82
Thames 83

TONGARIRO, UREWERA & CENTRAL NORTH ISLAND 84

Tongariro National Park. . 86
Tongariro
Northern Circuit 89
Kaimanawa Forest Park. . 93
Umukarikari-Urchin
Circuit. 94
**Te Urewara
National Park 96**
Lake Waikaremoana
Great Walk 98
Ruapani Circuit 101
**Whirinaki Te Pua a
Tane Conservation Park. . 103**
Whirinaki Track 104
Towns & Facilities. 107
Whakapapa Village. 107
National Park 107
Turangi 108
Murupara 108
Wairoa 109

TARANAKI, WHANGANUI & AROUND WELLINGTON 110

Egmont National Park . . 112
Pouakai Circuit 115
Pouakai Crossing 118
Around the
Mountain Circuit 119

Mt Taranaki Summit 121
**Whanganui
National Park 121**
Matemateaonga Track . . . 123
Mangapurua &
Kaiwhakauka Tracks 126
Ruahine Forest Park. . . 129
Rangiwahia &
Deadmans Loop 130
Tararua Forest Park . . . 132
Mt Holdsworth-Jumbo
Circuit. 134
Holdsworth-Kaitoke
Track. 136
Towns & Facilities. 139
New Plymouth 139
Stratford 140
Whanganui. 140
Palmerston North 141
Masterton 142
Wellington 142

QUEEN CHARLOTTE & MARLBOROUGH . . . 144

Queen Charlotte
Track. 146
Nydia Track 152
Pelorus Track 154
Kaikoura Coast Track. . . . 159
Towns & Facilities. 162
Picton. 162
Havelock 163
Kaikoura. 164

ABEL TASMAN, KAHURANGI & NELSON LAKES . . . 165

**Abel Tasman
National Park 168**
Abel Tasman
Coast Track 169
**Kahurangi
National Park 174**
Heaphy Track 175
Wangapeka Track 180
Tableland Circuit 184

Contents

**Nelson Lakes
National Park** **187**
Lake Angelus Track 191
Travers-Sabine
Circuit. 193
St Arnaud Range
Track. 196
Towns & Facilities. 197
Nelson 197
Motueka. 198
Marahau. 199
Takaka 199
Karamea 200
St Arnaud 201

**CANTERBURY,
ARTHUR'S PASS &
AORAKI/MT COOK. . 202**
Banks Peninsula
Track. 204
Mt Somers Track 208
St James Walkway 212
**Arthur's Pass
National Park** **216**
Avalanche Peak 218
Goat Pass Track 220
Harper Pass 222
Cass-Lagoon
Saddles Track 226
**Aoraki/Mt Cook
National Park** **228**
Mueller Hut Route 230
Towns & Facilities. 232
Christchurch. 232
Akaroa 233
Methven. 234
Hanmer Springs. 234
Arthur's Pass 235
Mt Cook Village. 235

WEST COAST. 237
The Old Ghost Road
Track. 240
Paparoa National Park. . 243
Inland Pack Track. 244
Croesus Track. 247

**Westland Tai Poutini
National Park** **250**
Welcome Flat 251
Towns & Facilities. 254
Westport 254
Punakaiki. 255
Greymouth 255
Franz Josef Glacier. 256
Fox Glacier. 256

**MT ASPIRING NATIONAL
PARK & AROUND
QUEENSTOWN 258**
Routeburn Track. 261
Greenstone Caples
Track. 265
Mavora–Greenstone
Walkway. 269
Rees-Dart Track 272
Matukituki
Valley Tracks 275
Gillespie
Pass Circuit. 278
Towns & Facilities. 282
Queenstown 282
Glenorchy 283
Wanaka. 283

**FIORDLAND & STEWART
ISLAND/RAKIURA. . 285**
Fiordland National Park. . 287
Milford Track 290
Hollyford Track 295
Kepler Track 300
Hump Ridge Track 303
**Stewart Island/
Rakiura. 307**
Rakiura Track 308
North West Circuit 312
Towns & Facilities. 316
Te Anau 316
Tuatapere. 317
Invercargill. 317
Oban. 318

UNDERSTAND

New Zealand
Today 322
History 324
Environment 334

SURVIVAL
GUIDE

Directory A–Z 342
Transport 354
Glossary. 361
Index. 364
Map Legend. 375

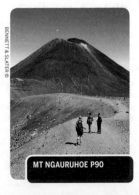

MT NGAURUHOE P90

Welcome to New Zealand

With spectacular scenery, amazing trails, a unique hut network and a rich tramping culture, New Zealand is the ultimate destination for immersing yourself in the great outdoors.

A Freaky Field Trip

Cast adrift from Gondwanaland and dragged to the edge of civilisation by powerful geological forces, NZ boasts a staggering array of landforms – from uplifted mountains and glaciated valleys to rainforests, dunelands and an otherworldly volcanic plateau. Unusual plant life abounds, from mighty 2000-year-old kauri trees to delicate alpine herb fields. In their midst is a veritable menagerie of strange creatures, such as the kiwi, large carnivorous snails, and the tuatara – the 'living fossil' as old as the dinosaurs. There's never a dull moment on a tramp through the NZ wilderness.

Trampers' Territory

Whether Maori on hunting forays or gathering greenstone, or colonial explorers surveying for settlements, early New Zealanders showed an aptitude for journeying through this wild new land. To follow in their footsteps today is to encounter a network of tracks and huts that is the envy of the world. In the wild – where wrong turns can be fatal, ferocious storms are common, and rivers can turn torrential within an hour – such prior knowledge is king. How welcome it is, then, to encounter an emphatic signpost, a splendid suspension bridge, or a Department of Conservation ranger. You're in good company.

Easy Going

It may be one of the world's most popular tramping destinations, but outside of major tracks in peak season there is plenty of room in lodges, huts and campsites, and mile upon mile of empty track. Yet despite this, the shuttle bus driver will still pick you up in the middle of nowhere, probably just 10 minutes late. The logistics of NZ tramping are pretty easy, with plenty of well-oiled operators ready to get you where you need to go – even if it means they have to go out of their way.

Sheer Beauty

You've seen the photographs: soaring peaks, turquoise lakes, golden sands and majestic forest. It's even more amazing in real life, at close range. Strange moss hangs off branches, jewel-like river stones glow in a shaft of sunlight, a raft of age-old forest logs lies piled up on a wild, windswept beach... There *will* be climbing, for this is the land of the lookout. Whether a very low saddle from one beach to the next, or a 1000m grind to an alpine pass, scenic surprises lie around every corner, over every hill. These are the *wow!* moments, and there are many of them.

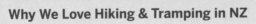

Why We Love Hiking & Tramping in NZ

By Sarah Bennett & Lee Slater, Authors

Welcome to our 'happy place' – a place where our everyday cares disappear, replaced by the need to reach the hut before nightfall, and dry our socks before dawn. Slumbering senses awaken: eyes fix on faraway peaks, ears tune in to songbirds, noses twitch at the scent of honeydew. We relax, open up, see things in a different light. But this could happen anywhere, right? Maybe. But maybe there's magic in the wilderness here – something in the air, in the mountains, in the rivers and beaches. Something in the sparkling night skies. Something that says *it's good to be alive*.

For more about our authors, see page 376.

Above: Hikers at Mackinnon Pass (p294) on the Milford Track

Hiking & Tramping in New Zealand

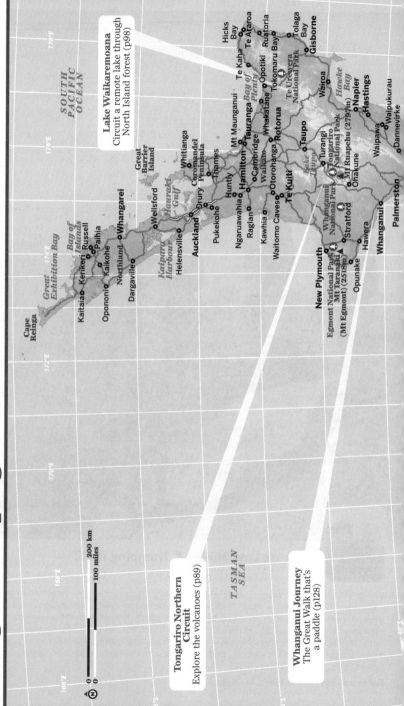

Lake Waikaremoana
Circuit a remote lake through North Island forest (p98)

Tongariro Northern Circuit
Explore the volcanoes (p89)

Whanganui Journey
The Great Walk that's a paddle (p128)

Abel Tasman Coast Track
Postcard-perfect beaches and azure waters (p169)

Heaphy Track
The longest and most diverse of the Great Walks (p175)

Routeburn Track
Wondrous, popular alpine crossing (p261)

Milford Track
Glaciated valleys, waterfalls and alpine splendour (p290)

Kepler Track
Lofty loop track on the fringes of Fiordland (p300)

Rakiura Track
Bird-lover's paradise on NZ's 'third island' (p308)

ELEVATION

2000m
1500m
1250m
1000m
750m
500m
250m
0

SOUTH PACIFIC OCEAN

TASMAN SEA

Cook Strait

Pegasus Bay

Golden Bay *Abel Tasman* *Marlborough Sounds*
Tasman Bay

Collingwood Takaka Motueka
Kahurangi National Park
Karamea
Mt Owen (1875m) Richmond Nelson
Murchison
Westport Lake Rotoiti
Paparoa National Park St Arnaud
Reefton Nelson Lakes National Park
Punakaiki Arthur's Pass National Park
Greymouth Arthur's Pass
Hokitika Mt Murchison (2400m)
Ross
Westland Tai Poutini National Park Whataroa
Franz Josef Glacier Mt Cook (3754m)
Fox Glacier Aoraki/Mt Cook National Park
Jackson Bay Lake Pukaki
Haast Lake Tekapo
Haast Pass Twizel
Mt Aspiring National Park Lake Ohau
Wanaka Omarama
Milford Sound Glenorchy Arrowtown
Milford Cromwell
Fiordland National Park Queenstown Clyde Alexandra
Lake Wakatipu
Te Anau
Lake Te Anau Manapouri
Lake Manapouri Lumsden
Tuatapere Winton Gore
Catlins Conservation Park
Invercargill Balclutha
Foveaux Strait Bluff
Rakiura National Park Oban
Stewart Island (Rakiura)

Picton Blenheim
Kaikoura
Hammer Springs
Christchurch Lyttelton
Banks Peninsula
Akaroa
Ashburton
Mt Hutt Methven
Temuka Timaru
Waimate
Oamaru
Palmerston
Otago Peninsula
Dunedin
Milton

Levin Masterton
Upper Hutt Lower Hutt
Porirua Wellington
Cape Palliser

42°S

44°S

46°S

New Zealand's Nine Great Walks

Abel Tasman Coast Track

1 Routinely touted as NZ's most beautiful Great Walk, it is also the country's most popular (p169), located in its smallest national park. Great weather, granite cliffs, golden sands and a bushy backdrop are just part of its allure, so packed is this track with delightful surprises. Spot seals and birds, explore fascinating estuaries, hidden inlets and freshwater pools, study strange rock formations and significant trees... but it's equally acceptable to just laze around on your beach towel. Water taxis and kayak trips offer endless options for maximising enjoyment.

Bottom: Onetahuti Beach (p173), Abel Tasman National Park

Tongariro Northern Circuit

2 The dynamic, dramatic features of Tongariro National Park are celebrated in its status as a Unesco World Heritage Area. The park also proved a fitting backdrop for *The Lord of the Rings*, with its volcanoes taking a starring role. You, too, can get in on the action on this circuit (p89), which sports nonstop views, not only of crazy craters, steaming vents, glacial valleys, native forest, alpine meadows and surreal lakes, but also of Mt Taranaki, standing solitarily in the west. This is big-picture stuff.

Right: Taranaki Falls (p93), Tongariro National Park

Lake Waikaremoana Great Walk

3 Remote, immense and shrouded in mist, Te Urewera National Park encompasses the largest tract of virgin forest on the North Island. The park's highlight is Lake Waikaremoana ('Sea of Rippling Waters'), a deep, 55-sq-km crucible of water encircled by the Lake Waikaremoana Track (p98). Along the way it passes through ancient rainforest and reedy inlets, and traverses gnarly ridges, including the famous Panekiri Bluff, from where there are stupendous views of the lake and endless forested peaks and valleys.

Whanganui Journey

4 The Great Walk that's actually a canoe or kayak trip (p128) takes paddlers along a 145km stretch of the Whanganui River, NZ's longest navigable river. It is one of the country's great wilderness adventures, a magical journey from highlands to lowlands – through sheer gorges and over quick, bouncy rapids, amid dense native forest aquiver with bird life, including NZ's national icon, the kiwi. Along the way it passes the abandoned Bridge to Nowhere, numerous bush campsites and a *marae* (Maori meeting house) that is now a Great Walk Hut.

Heaphy Track

5 A historic crossing from Golden Bay to the wild West Coast, this Great Walk (p175) dishes up the most diverse scenery of any NZ tramp – from dense forest, tussock-covered downs, caves, secluded river valleys, and beaches dusted in salt-spray, fringed by nikau palms. A mighty wilderness this may well be, but you will not be alone. Among the many critters calling this place home are up to 60 native bird species (including great spotted kiwi), creepy cave weta, weird beetles, leggy spiders and giant, ancient snails.

Top: Kohaihai Beach (p180), Kahurangi National Park

Kepler Track

6 One of three Great Walks within Fiordland, the Kepler (p300) was built to take pressure off the Milford and Routeburn. Many trampers say it rivals them both. This alpine crossing takes you from the peaceful, beech-forested shores of lakes Te Anau and Manapouri to high tussock-lands and over Mt Luxmore. Eye-popping sights include towering limestone bluffs, razor-edged ridges, panoramas galore and crazy caves. The Kepler is a truly spectacular way to appreciate the grandeur of NZ's finest and most vast wilderness.

Rakiura Track

7 Following the Foveaux Strait coast and shore of Paterson Inlet on tranquil Stewart Island, this leisurely loop (p308) offers a rewarding combination of waterside scenery, notable native trees and ferns, and historic relics of bygone days. Bird-watchers in particular will love it here, with a diverse range of species to be seen and heard. These include big-winged coastal birds such as sooty shearwaters and mollymawks, as well as little blue penguins; beaky waders in the inlet such as dotterels, herons and godwits; and forest birds such as kiwi, bellbirds, parakeets, kereru, kaka and tomtits.

Top left: Mason Bay (p315)

Routeburn Track

8 NZ's second-most-popular Great Walk (p261) traverses the mighty Southern Alps linking Mt Aspiring and Fiordland National Parks. It passes through ice-carved valleys and beech forests on its way, and although there is plenty of decent climbing to be done, a well-benched and -graded track enables trampers of average fitness to achieve significant summits. Harris Saddle, Conical Hill and Key Summit offer unforgettable vistas, although close-range sights such as thundering waterfalls, weird rock formations, alpine tarns and peculiar plant life will likely stir your spirits just as much.

Bottom left: Lake Harris (p264)

Milford Track

9 A fitting flag-bearer for NZ's wilderness tramps, the Milford (p290) is every bit as special as you ever heard it was. It delivers everything you want in a mountain-region tramp: a boat trip across a glacier-gouged lake, riverside ambles, a wetland boardwalk and an achievable climb to an unforgettable pass that opens not only a door to sheer peaks and a whole new valley, but a window on the era of the pioneer explorers. Then there's the Sutherland Falls, and Milford Sound itself. The Milford Track equals magic.

Top right: Mackinnon Pass (p294)

Need to Know

For more information, see Survival Guide (p341)

Currency
New Zealand dollar ($)

Language
English, Maori and New
Zealand Sign Language

Visas
Citizens of Australia,
the UK and 56 other
countries don't need
visas for NZ (length-of-
stay allowances vary);
see www.immigration.
govt.nz.

Money
ATMs are widely avail-
able, especially in larger
cities and towns. Credit
cards accepted in most
hotels and restaurants.

Mobile Phones
European phones will
work on NZ's network,
but not most American
or Japanese phones. Use
global roaming or a local
SIM card and prepaid
account.

Driving
Drive on the left; the
steering wheel is on the
right side of the car
(...in case you couldn't
find it).

When to Go

Northland/Auckland
TRAMP Year-Round

Central North Island
TRAMP Nov–Apr

Nelson/Marlborough
TRAMP Year-Round

Arthur's Pass National Park
TRAMP Nov–Mar

**Mt Aspiring/Fiordland
National Parks**
TRAMP Nov–Apr

High Season
(Dec–Feb)

➡ Normally the
best, most-settled
weather.

➡ Tramping high
season starts just
before Christmas.

➡ Huts and tracks
can get busy.

Shoulder
(Oct–Nov &
Feb–Apr)

➡ Tracks are less
busy.

➡ Fine weather
lingers into April.

➡ Most low-level
tracks can be walked
October through
April.

Low Season
(Jun–Aug)

➡ Weather at its
coldest and wettest;
river levels high.

➡ Many high-
altitude tracks closed
because of avalanche
danger.

➡ Some low-level
walks possible, with
solitude guaranteed.

Typical Tramping Costs

Lodges, huts & campsites: Free–$100

➜ Private lodge: $30–100

➜ Great Walk hut: $15–52

➜ Backcountry hut: free–$15

➜ Campsite: free–$18

Track transport $25–250

➜ Shuttle bus, one way up to an hour: $25–50

➜ Shuttle bus, longer return-trip: $90–130

➜ Boat transfer: $45–100

➜ Flight: $160–250

Guided trips & private tracks: $150-plus

➜ Day tramp: $150–330

➜ Private track (2–3 nights): $170–285

➜ Great Walk (3–4 nights): $1400–2100

Useful Websites

Department of Conservation (DOC; www.doc.govt.nz) Parks, reserves, tramps, huts, camping and conservation.

Mountain Safety Council (www.mountainsafety.org.nz) Staying safe in NZ's outdoors.

Federated Mountain Clubs of NZ (www.fmc.org.nz) Umbrella organisation for tramping and mountaineering clubs.

100% Pure New Zealand (www.newzealand.com) Official tourism site.

Lonely Planet (www.lonely planet.com/new-zealand) Advice from travellers who've actually been there.

MetService (www.metservice.com) Weather forecasts and warnings.

Te Ara (www.teara.govt.nz) The 'Encyclopedia of NZ'.

Exchange Rates

Australia	A$1	NZ$1.12
Canada	C$1	NZ$1.15
China	Y10	NZ$1.99
Euro zone	€1	NZ$1.63
Japan	¥100	NZ$1.21
Singapore	S$1	NZ$0.97
UK	UK£1	NZ$1.96
US	US$1	NZ$1.21

For current exchange rates see www.xe.com.

Track Standards

NZ's tracks literally range from easy strolls in the park to full-on, multiday adventures across untamed, unmarked mountainous terrain. Our authors adhere to the following guidelines:

Easy A walk on flat terrain or with minor elevation changes, usually over short distances on well-travelled tracks with no navigational difficulties.

Moderate A walk with challenging terrain, often involving longer distances and steep climbs.

Demanding A walk with long daily distances and difficult terrain with significant elevation change. May involve challenging route-finding and high-altitude travel.

Each track is also graded in accordance with the official DOC (www.doc.govt.nz) categories:

Walking Track Gentle walking from a few minutes to a day on mostly well-formed tracks.

Great Walk/Easy Tramping Track Comfortable multiday tramping on mostly well-formed tracks.

Tramping Track Challenging day or multiday tramping on mostly unformed tracks. Backcountry skills and experience required.

Route Challenging multiday tramping on unformed tracks. Navigation and high-level backcountry skills and experience required.

The NZ Hut System

➜ DOC maintains more than 950 huts in its national parks, conservation areas and reserves. While many were purpose-built for trampers and climbers, others stand as a legacy to industries such as forestry, farming, mining and deer culling. Today they form a network that offers cheap, character-filled accommodation in the most unlikely places, a unique and highly treasured feature of the NZ back country.

➜ Huts come in all shapes and sizes. The flashest specimens are generally Great Walk Huts, large multiroomed buildings equipped with such comforts as solar lighting, kitchen sinks, gas cookers, flush toilets and a hut warden. But even at the bottom end of the scale – in bivvies and basic huts – you'll still get a mattress, some kind of water supply, a toilet (possibly a long drop) and a fireplace, all going well.

➜ The majority of huts operate on a first-come, first-served basis, paid for with DOC's Backcountry hut passes or hut tickets. Popular huts, however, must be booked in advance during peak season.

➜ Often imbued with history, providing ready access to deeper wilderness, and offering shelter from the elements, NZ's huts are also special for their sociable atmosphere. An evening spent in a hut – in the company of strangers who share similar passions and have the stories to prove it, huddled together around the fire – is a quintessential NZ tramping experience.

For information on **getting around**, see p354

PLAN YOUR TRIP NEED TO KNOW

If You Like...

Volcanoes

Straddle the collision boundary of two major tectonic plates and you're bound to get some fallout. Actually, this is less fall, more steam, spurt, bubble and burst forth, often with a very hot head.

Rangitoto Island Loop It's an easy day-trip from Auckland to the volcanic island of Rangitoto, blanketed in 600-year-old black lava, best seen from its crater summit. (p61)

Mt Taranaki Summit At the centre of Egmont National Park is a 'slumbering' volcano with a near-perfect cone. A challenging but achievable 1572m climb reaches its 2518m summit. (p121)

Tongariro Northern Circuit This spectacular four-day epic circumnavigates Ngauruhoe; an optional side scramble affords views into Its creepy crater. (p89)

Banks Peninsula Track The peninsula's rolling hills and picturesque bays might not look like the eroded remains of twin volcanoes. Geology lesson, anyone? (p204)

Wildlife

Due to its isolation, New Zealand is a veritable menagerie of unique animals, which evolved in spectacular ways without the interference of mammalian predators. Brace yourself for freaky critters!

St Arnaud Range Track See and hear the feathery fruits of 15 years' labour by the Rotoiti Nature Recovery Project, which include kaka, bellbirds, tomtits, robins, riflemen and kiwi. (p196)

Kaikoura Coast Track Spot landward-flying riflemen, bellbirds, grey warblers, long-tailed cuckoos and hawks, among others. Look seaward for dolphins, seals and soaring seabirds. (p160)

Heaphy Track Get thee to Kahurangi for a freaky field trip featuring giant snails, bats, cave-dwelling weta, leggy spiders, weird beetles and 60 native bird species. (p175)

Rakiura Track Stewart Island contains the largest and most diverse bird populations in NZ. The tokoeka (kiwi) population alone is estimated to be around 20,000. (p308)

Camping

The endless pleasures of NZ camping far outweigh any negatives. Negatives, you say? Bring a raincoat, sunscreen, sensible shoes, insect repellent, duct tape and a sense of humour.

Te Paki Coastal Track Warm weather, great beaches, grassy pitches – what's not to like? Oh, and there aren't any huts on the track, so you don't have much choice. (p56)

Kauaeranga Kauri Trail The forested and stream-lined Kauaeranga Valley has one very popular hut, and eight campsites. You do the math. This is camping territory, through and through. (p75)

Abel Tasman Coast Track NZ's most popular Great Walk offers coastal camping at its best, in 19 camping grounds offering at least *some* solitude. (p169)

Queen Charlotte Track The joys of camping (sea breezes, lapping waves, starry nights) while your fellow trampers are cooped up in luxurious lodges. You win. (p146)

Climbs

Once you get a couple of good hills under your belt, you'll be away laughing, which is good because NZ's back country offers up some lofty but achievable summits.

Mueller Hut Route Yes, it's a 1040m climb, but this is a quintessential alpine experience, packing in geological wonders, fascinating plant life and an amazing hut. (p230)

Lake Angelus Track Yes, the zigzag up Pinchgut Track is a bit of a rude awakening, but the views along Mt Robert Ridge last the rest of the day. (p191)

Tableland Circuit OK, so maybe it is an 855m climb from the car park to Mt Arthur's bald peak, but the epic panorama from Tasman Bay to the Southern Alps is worth every step. (p184)

Avalanche Peak Granted, it is a pretty grunty 1093m clamber up to the peak, but these Arthur's Pass views rival those of Tongariro Alpine Crossing – *still* NZ's best day walk? (p218)

Rivers

NZ's rivers are in the spotlight, sometimes looking a sorry sight and at other times stealing the show. Whichever way you look at it, NZ's rivers define the land, and its people.

Whanganui Journey This 'Great Walk' is actually a 145km paddle down NZ's longest navigable river, through the deep wilds of Whanganui National Park. (p128)

Pelorus Track So scenic it starred in *The Hobbit,* the gorgeous Pelorus – a boulder-lined gorge with deep green pools – is followed for two days of this three-day tramp. (p154)

Wangapeka Track This remote wilderness tramp follows the Wangapeka, Karamea, Taipo and Little Wanganui Rivers through the forested southern reaches of Kahurangi. (p180)

Greenstone Caples Track This return trip follows two contrasting rivers valleys – the wide, open tussocky Greenstone, and the narrower, more heavily forested Caples. (p265)

(Top) Mt Taranaki, seen from the Pouakai Tarns (p117)
(Bottom) Surfers on Ninety Mile Beach (p58)

Mountain Passes

Early Maori found routes through the mountains, commonly in search of food or *pounamu* (greenstone). Many more have since been found, but most remain passable only on foot.

Travers-Sabine Circuit Grassy river flats, beech forest, an alpine saddle and a side trip to the world's clearest freshwater lake fill up this five-day adventure. (p193)

Cass-Lagoon Saddles Track This Arthur's Pass crossing takes in not one but two alpine saddles as it traverses typical high-country river valleys. (p226)

Gillespie Pass Circuit This popular yet lightly used track crosses a 1500m pass overlooked by towering peaks. (p278)

Milford Track A memorial cairn, tarns, a shelter, and breathtaking views all sit high on Mackinnon Pass. (p290)

Routeburn Track The view from 1255m-high Harris Saddle is spectacular enough; detour to 1515m Conical Hill and have your socks blown off. (p261)

Beaches & Bays

With more than 15,000km of coastline, NZ boasts more bays and beaches than you can shake a stick at. They're less bikini-clad golden sands, more...um... *windswept* and *interesting*.

Te Paki Coastal Track The vast expanse of Ninety Mile Beach gets the glory, but just around the corner are beautiful whitesand beaches backed by grassy camping flats. (p56)

Hillary Trail If you're looking for a bit of ocean drama, you can't beat a wild west coast beach... unless you tag on another, and another, and another. (p69)

Abel Tasman Coast Track No need to Photoshop this postcard paradise. These golden sands, blue bays and verdant hills are for real. (p169)

Queen Charlotte Track This track offers beautiful bays and beaches from the get-go at Ship Cove. We recommend taking a swim via the jetty jump. (p146)

Waterfalls

Waterfalls? It certainly does, especially in the mountains where the gauge can top 11,000mm annually. That's a lot of falling water...

Tongariro Northern Circuit Tumbling 20m over an old lava flow, Wairere ('Quick Water') stream plunges headlong over Taranaki Falls into a boulder-ringed pool. (p89)

Mt Somers Track Maidens Relief, the Water Caves, Spa Pool, Emerald Pool, Howden Falls – there'll hardly be a dry eye in the house. (p208)

Matukituki Valley Tracks Pray for rain so you can see the Brides Veil in full flow; detour

to Rob Roy Glacier to see more following suit. (p275)

Routeburn Track This truly great track boasts some truly great falls, the eponymously named Routeburn Falls. (p261)

Milford Track NZ's top drop and indeed one of the loftiest waterfalls in the world, Sutherland Falls hop, skip and jump 580m in all. (p290)

History

To quote historian James Belich, 'NZ's history is not long, but it is fast.' In the back country this generally involved gold-mining, logging and plenty of 'Number 8 wire'.

Aotea Track This track follows routes laid down by loggers who came to Great Barrier Island in a quest for kauri trees, leaving relics in their wake. (p64)

Hollyford Track A typically hair-brained scheme of the era, the settlement of Jamestown was always a long shot. Cue: colourful characters and a dash of drama. (p295)

The Old Ghost Road Track The completion of this track will finish a job started by 19th-century gold-miners, some of whom left some stuff (and their spirits?) behind. (p240)

Croesus Track Regarded as one of the best surviving 'pack tracks' in NZ, the gold-miners who built it left behind many fascinating landmarks. (p247)

Loop Walks

There's so much satisfaction in a loop walk: making it all the way back to where you started, without the complication of transport

Hiker on the Avalanche Peak track (p218)

connections or the déjà vu of backtracking.

Ruapani Circuit This easy two-day loop to peaceful Lake Waikareiti offers the opportunity to take a rowboat out on the lake. (p101)

Pouakai Circuit This two-day circuit features spectacular views from the top of the Pouakai Range, an area of rugged ridges with an amazing swamp and interesting plants. (p115)

Kepler Track A Fiordland Great Walk often said to rival Routeburn and Milford, this memorable alpine crossing takes in eye-popping sights such as towering bluffs, razor-edged ridges and crazy caves. (p300)

North West Circuit Stewart Island's legendary tramp is a coastal epic around a remote and natural coastline featuring isolated beaches, huge sand dunes and birds galore. (p312)

Mountain Biking

A combination of better bikes, cycling advocacy and trail funding has seen a dramatic increase in off-road cycling, on purpose-built tracks and walking tracks converted to dual use.

Queen Charlotte Track This long-time favourite of Kiwi mountain bikers now numbers among the New Zealand Cycle Trail's 'Great Rides'. (p150)

Heaphy Track After a successful trial, this Great Walk is now officially open to riders in winter.

More will follow this landmark precedent. (p175)

The Old Ghost Road Track Trampers are set to benefit from this purpose-built New Zealand Cycle Trail, one of the network's most ambitious projects. (p240)

Tableland Circuit Biking up Mt Arthur Summit is definitely a bridge too far, but the Flora Track is totally doable, heading through to Golden Bay. (p184)

Mangapurua & Kaiwhakauka Tracks This byway forms part of the 317km Mountains to Sea Cycle Trail, destined to become a classic NZ ride. (p126)

> ### IF YOU LIKE... SHORTCUTS
> Hop aboard a jetboat for a memorable tramping shortcut along the Wilkin River on the Gillespie Pass Circuit (p278) or Dart River on the Rees-Dart Track (p272).

Itineraries

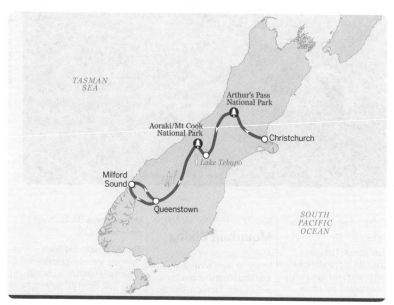

 Southern Highlights

Wing into resurgent **Christchurch** and stock up on supplies before tramping some of the South Island's best tracks. Dive in at the deep end in **Arthur's Pass National Park** by summiting Avalanche Peak, a strenuous but rewarding day walk rivalling the best in the land.

Take the Inland Scenic Route south to **Lake Tekapo**, arriving in time to tour the night skies at Mt John Observatory. The views here are just as impressive during the daytime, too. Get up early and drive to **Aoraki/Mt Cook National Park**, allowing you time to tramp in to Mueller Hut, one of New Zealand's highest.

Make your way south to buzzy **Queenstown**, stopping to sample Central Otago wines and perhaps do a bungy jump at Kawarau Bridge along the way. Soak up some hospitality before setting off the following day for the Routeburn Track, NZ's second-most-popular Great Walk. Having traversed the Southern Alps, take a day off and ogle **Milford Sound** on a boat trip or scenic flight. Return to Queenstown on foot via the Greenstone or Caples Tracks, two distinctly different river valleys that meet near the shores of Lake Wakatipu.

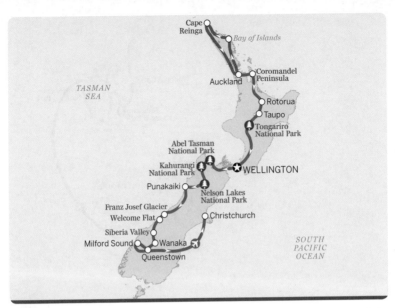

The Grand Tour

Kick off your tramping bonanza in metropolitan **Auckland**. Warm up with a day tramp on the volcanic island of Rangitoto, before driving north via the beautiful **Bay of Islands**. Pilgrimage to NZ's northernmost point, **Cape Reinga**, on Te Paki Coastal Track.

Head south to the sun-soaked **Coromandel Peninsula**, to explore its myriad attractions as well as venturing in to Kauaeranga Valley to scale the Pinnacles. Travel south, pit-stopping at **Rotorua** and **Taupo** to marvel at geothermal wonders and Maori culture. The volcanic landscapes of **Tongariro National Park** could burn up a week; make a beeline for the Northern Circuit, or if time is tight, traverse the Tongariro Alpine Crossing – arguably the world's finest day walk.

Head to **Wellington** and interact in the national museum, Te Papa Tongarewa, then savour the city's great restaurants and bars. Having crossed Cook Strait and cruised the Marlborough Sounds, stop in at vibrant Nelson on the way to **Abel Tasman National Park** and its golden beaches and turquoise waters. Walk, kayak or sail your way around. Two more national parks – **Kahurangi** and **Nelson Lakes** – lie nearby. Tramp the Heaphy or Lake Angelus, on your way to the wild West Coast. Follow the stunning Tasman Sea coast road past Paparoa National Park, pausing at **Punakaiki's** pancake rocks. Walk the half-day Pororari River Loop if you can't fit in the whole Inland Pack Track.

Keep on trucking south towards glacier country. Call in at the West Coast Wildlife Centre in **Franz Josef Glacier** to coo over the kiwi chicks, before tramping into **Welcome Flat** for a well-earned soak in the hot springs. Having cleared Haast Pass, the **Siberia Valley** awaits. Go in on foot, plane, jetboat, or even all three. Don't miss pretty lakeside **Wanaka**, from where you can head into Mt Aspiring National Park via the Matukituki Valley, then head over the Crown Range to adrenaline capital, **Queenstown**. Take your pick from some of NZ's most fabulous walks – the Routeburn, Greenstone Caples and Rees-Dart. Head round to postcard-perfect **Milford Sound**, arriving by car through the Homer Tunnel or on foot via the Milford Track, NZ's most famous Great Walk. Fly or drive to **Christchurch** from Queenstown and you're done.

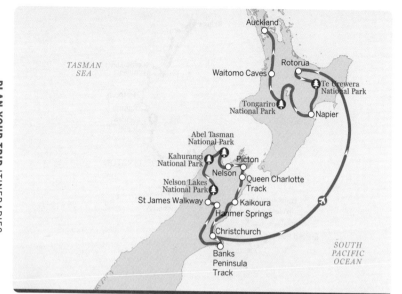

The Gentle Option

4 WEEKS

Ease into things with a couple of days in **Christchurch**, before taking in dramatic coastlines, secluded bays and remnant forest on the private **Banks Peninsula Track**. Head inland to the hot pools of **Hanmer Springs**, priming yourself for the five-day **St James Walkway** through subalpine river valleys and over two easy mountain passes. Continue through Lewis Pass to **Nelson Lakes National Park**, a wonderful place for low-level nature walks if you don't fancy the Mt Robert or St Arnaud Range climbs. Meander through the Motueka Valley, popping in to the Tableland within **Kahurangi National Park**, before hitting **Abel Tasman National Park**, exploring the idyllic coast by boat, kayak or on foot. Or all three.

Indulge in **Nelson's** fine local food and wine, then wind your way eastwards to **Picton** via the scenic Queen Charlotte Drive. Cruise through the Marlborough Sounds, then hit the **Queen Charlotte Track** while your bags are ferried ahead of you by water taxi. Take a restorative tour of Marlborough's world-class wineries. Complete your loop back to Christchurch via **Kaikoura**, where you can whale-watch, bird-watch and swim with seals and dolphins, before embarking on your last South Island tramp, the Kaikoura Coast Track.

Fly to **Rotorua** to soak up some Maori culture and a good dose of sulphur at the region's many geothermal delights, then venture into mystical **Te Urewera National Park** to complete the Lake Waikaremoana Great Walk. Be sure to take time to row on pristine Lake Waikareiti if at all possible. Head southwards to art deco **Napier** in sunny Hawke's Bay. Gorge yourself on the region's ample produce, then burn off the calories on its flat (!) cycling trails. Onward to Taupo, the lakeside resort just a stone's throw from **Tongariro National Park** and the legendary Tongariro Alpine Crossing. Check out the twinkling glowworms of **Waitomo Caves** before heading to **Auckland**, where day tramps abound – out to volcanic Rangitoto Island or Great Barrier Island in the Hauraki Gulf, or the Hillary Trail on the rugged east coast just an hour from downtown.

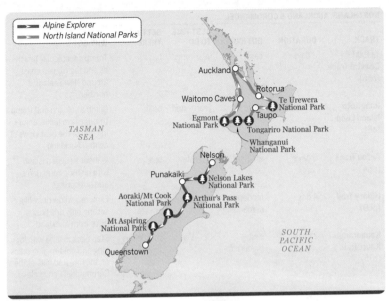

Alpine Explorer
North Island National Parks

2 WEEKS Alpine Explorer

Start in vibrant **Nelson** before heading on this lofty tour along the spine of NZ's Southern Alps. Drive to St Arnaud, gateway to **Nelson Lakes National Park**, where the Lake Angelus Track climbs up Robert Ridge for panoramic views of the Southern Alps.

Wend your way through the wild Buller Gorge to the West Coast and take in **Punakaiki's** Pancake Rocks, before heading east to **Arthur's Pass National Park**. Tackle your first mountain saddle, either Goat Pass or Cass-Lagoon Saddles Track. Top this off with one of the country's best day walk, Avalanche Peak. Through the pass, stick close to the mountains on the Inland Scenic Route through to Tekapo and **Aoraki/Mt Cook National Park**, where you can climb to Mueller Hut for views of NZ's highest mountain.

Epic scenery abounds southwards to Central Otago and the lakeside town of Wanaka. Tramp high above the Matukituki Valley in **Mt Aspiring National Park** on Cascade Saddle and French Ridge. Finally, knock off another pass on the Routeburn, a popular Great Walk, before taking in the razzle-dazzle of **Queenstown**.

2 WEEKS North Island National Parks

From glitzy **Auckland**, head south to the unique geothermal hot spot of **Rotorua**, where geysers, bubbling mud, steaming vents and authentic Maori performances await. Venture into the densely forested **Te Urewera National Park** and complete the Lake Waikaremoana Great Walk, before driving to **Taupo** to leap out of a plane, raft a river or catch a trout.

Nearby is volcanic **Tongariro National Park**, home to the Northern Circuit Great Walk. One of its sections is the Tongariro Alpine Crossing, one of the world's most famous day tramps. Next up is the Great Walk that is actually a river paddle: the 145km Whanganui Journey through the North Island's largest lowland wilderness, **Whanganui National Park**.

Truck west to **Egmont National Park** and the near-symmetrical cone of Mt Taranaki, which can be explored on a network of high-altitude tracks. Loop back to Auckland via **Waitomo Caves** where you can ogle upwards at glowworms or, if you're game, don a wetsuit and explore deep into subterranean labyrinthine passages and caverns.

NORTHLAND, AUCKLAND & COROMANDEL

TRACK	DURATION	DIFFICULTY	BEST TIME TO GO	GETTING THERE	WHY GO?
Te Paki Coastal Track (p56)	3 days	easy	year-round	bus	Tramp spectacular beaches and the rugged coast around New Zealand's northern tip
Rangitoto Island Loop (p61)	4–5 hours	easy	year-round	boat	Climb a volcano and tramp through lava fields, enjoying one of the best views of central Auckland
Aotea Track (p64)	3 days	moderate	Oct–May	bus	Wander a rugged island with historic kauri dams and hot springs
Hillary Trail (p69)	4 days	moderate–demanding	year-round	bus, train, private	Explore a wilderness-like setting only one hour's drive from Auckland
Kauaeranga Kauri Trail (p75)	2 days	easy–moderate	Oct–May	shuttle bus	Step back in time with logging and gold-mining relics on the forested hills of the Coromandel Peninsula

TONGARIRO, UREWERA & CENTRAL NORTH ISLAND

TRACK	DURATION	DIFFICULTY	BEST TIME TO GO	GETTING THERE	WHY GO?
Tongariro Northern Circuit (p89)	4 days	moderate	Dec–Mar	shuttle bus	Tramp past volcanoes and through a spectacular thermal area on this Great Walk
Umukarikari-Urchin Circuit (p94)	2 days	moderate	Nov–Apr	bus, shuttle bus	View the Tongariro volcanoes from a neighbouring forest park
Lake Waikaremoana Great Walk (p98)	4 days	easy–moderate	Nov–Apr	shuttle bus, boat	Enjoy beaches, swimming and fishing on this Great Walk
Ruapani Circuit (p101)	2 days	easy–moderate	Nov–Apr	no transport	Follow a remote river route with plenty of fords and fishing opportunities
Whirinaki Track (p104)	2 days	easy	Nov–Apr	shuttle bus	Explore a lush forest with caves and an impressive gorge

TARANAKI, WHANGANUI & AROUND WELLINGTON

TRACK	DURATION	DIFFICULTY	BEST TIME TO GO	GETTING THERE	WHY GO?
Pouakai Circuit (p115)	2 days	moderate	Oct–May	shuttle bus	Beat the elements and explore the bush while circuiting a stunning volcano
Pouakai Crossing (p118)	1 day	moderate	Oct–May	shuttle bus	As above
Around the Mountain Circuit (p119)	5 days	moderate–demanding	Oct–May	shuttle bus	As above
Mt Taranaki Summit (p121)	1 day	moderate–demanding	Jan–Mar	shuttle bus	As above
Matem-ateaonga Track (p123)	4 days	easy–moderate	Oct–May	shuttle bus, boat	Wander along an isolated wilderness track, ending with a thrilling jetboat ride on the Whanganui River
Mangapurua & Kaiwhakau-ka Tracks (p126)	3 days	easy–moderate	Oct–May	shuttle bus, boat	Pass through the sites of old settlers' farms and grassy flats with small stands of exotic trees
Rangiwahia & Deadmans Loop (p130)	3 days	moderate–demanding	Jan & Feb	shuttle bus, private	Explore lightly used ridges and valleys in Ruahine Forest Park
Mt Holdsworth-Jumbo Circuit (p134)	3 days	moderate–demanding	Oct–May	private, taxi	Stay in scenic huts and admire views from an alpine ridge in Tararua Forest Park
Holdsworth-Kaitoke Track (p136)	3 days	moderate	Oct–May	private, train, taxi	Follow pleasant river valleys through the Tararua Range

QUEEN CHARLOTTE & MARLBOROUGH

TRACK	DURATION	DIFFICULTY	BEST TIME TO GO	GETTING THERE	WHY GO?
Queen Charlotte Track (p146)	4 days	moderate	Nov–Dec & Feb–Apr	boat, shuttle bus	Treat yourself to beautiful coastal scenery and interesting accommodation options
Nydia Track (p152)	2 days	easy	Nov–Dec & Feb–Apr	boat, shuttle bus	Cross two saddles and explore a sheltered shoreline
Pelorus Track (p154)	3 days	moderate	Oct–Apr	shuttle bus	Tussle with trout or take a dip in the deep green pools of the Pelorus River
Kaikoura Coast Track (p159)	3 days	easy–moderate	Dec–Mar	bus	Enjoy following the Pacific coast by day and staying at farms by night

ABEL TASMAN, KAHURANGI & NELSON LAKES

TRACK	DURATION	DIFFICULTY	BEST TIME TO GO	GETTING THERE	WHY GO?
Abel Tasman Coast Track (p169)	5 days	easy	year-round	boat, shuttle bus	Explore a series of beautiful beaches and bays on this Great Walk
Heaphy Track (p175)	5 days	moderate	Nov–Apr	shuttle bus, plane	Follow in historic footsteps and enjoy a stunning variety of scenery on this Great Walk
Wangapeka Track (p180)	5 days	moderate	Nov–Apr	shuttle bus	Climb two 1000m saddles and wander beech-forested valleys
Tableland Circuit (p184)	3 days	moderate	Nov–Apr	shuttle bus	Combine great trout fishing with the dramatic scenery of an earthquake-torn valley
Lake Angelus Track (p191)	2 days	moderate	Nov–Apr	shuttle bus, boat	Climb a challenging alpine pass, tempered by the beauty of Blue Lake
Travers-Sabine Circuit (p193)	5 days	moderate–demanding	Nov–Apr	shuttle bus, boat	Explore grassy river flats, beech forests and two alpine saddles
St Arnaud Range Track (p196)	1 day	moderate	Nov–Apr	no transport	Take in views on this popular day walk, ascending through beech forest to the range top

CANTERBURY, ARTHUR'S PASS & AORAKI/MT COOK

TRACK	DURATION	DIFFICULTY	BEST TIME TO GO	GETTING THERE	WHY GO?
Banks Peninsula Track (p204)	4 days	easy–moderate	Oct–Apr	shuttle bus	Take in wonderful seascapes and wildlife on this private track
Mt Somers Track (p208)	2 days	moderate	Nov–Mar	shuttle bus	Tramp the subalpine areas around Mt Somers, soaking in refreshing pools at night
St James Walkway (p212)	5 days	easy–moderate	Nov–Apr	bus, shuttle bus	Cross two low passes while enjoying fine mountain scenery
Avalanche Peak (p218)	1 day	moderate	Nov–Mar	no transport	Climb high above Arthur's Pass on the South Island's most scenic day tramp
Goat Pass Track (p220)	2 days	moderate	Nov–Mar	shuttle bus	Spend a night high above the bushline in Goat Pass Hut
Harper Pass (p222)	5 days	moderate	Nov–Mar	bus, shuttle bus	Follow a historic gold-mining route over a low pass
Cass-Lagoon Saddles Track (p226)	2 days	moderate	Nov–Feb	bus, shuttle bus, train	Admire spectacular views from two alpine saddles
Mueller Hut Route (p230)	2 days	demanding	Nov–Mar	none	Climb steeply to spend a night among the spectacular peaks of Aoraki/Mt Cook National Park

WEST COAST

TRACK	DURATION	DIFFICULTY	BEST TIME TO GO	GETTING THERE	WHY GO?
The Old Ghost Road Track (p240)	5 days	moderate	Nov–May	bus, shuttle bus	Traverse native forests, river flats and valleys with stunning views of Mokihinui Gorge
Inland Pack Track (p244)	2 days	moderate	Dec–Mar	shuttle bus, private	Admire an unusual karst landscape and stay in one of NZ's largest rock bivvies
Croesus Track (p247)	2 days	moderate	Nov–Mar	shuttle bus	Retrace history on a subalpine track loaded with mining relics
Welcome Flat (p251)	3 days	easy–moderate	Nov–Apr	bus, shuttle bus	Follow the Karangarua River to spectacular hot springs

MT ASPIRING NATIONAL PARK & AROUND QUEENSTOWN

TRACK	DURATION	DIFFICULTY	BEST TIME TO GO	GETTING THERE	WHY GO?
Routeburn Track (p261)	3 days	moderate	Oct–Apr	shuttle bus	Explore one of NZ's best alpine crossings on this Great Walk
Greenstone Caples Track (p265)	4 days	moderate	Nov–Apr	shuttle bus	Enjoy moderate tramping and legendary fishing
Mavora-Greenstone Walkway (p269)	3 days	easy	Nov–Apr	shuttle bus, plane	Savour the solitude, impressive alpine scenery and trout fishing of the Mavora Valley
Rees-Dart Track (p272)	4 days	moderate	Dec–Apr	shuttle bus, jetboat	Cross an alpine pass dividing two splendid valleys
Matukituki Valley Tracks (p275)	2–5 days	easy–demanding	Dec–Mar	shuttle bus	Experience the beauty of the Matukituki Valley's private farmland and beech forest flats
Gillespie Pass Circuit (p278)	3 days	moderate–demanding	Dec–Mar	jetboat, plane	Savour superb views and scenic beech-forested valleys

FIORDLAND & STEWART ISLAND/RAKIURA

TRACK	DURATION	DIFFICULTY	BEST TIME TO GO	GETTING THERE	WHY GO?
Milford Track (p290)	4 days	moderate	Oct–Apr	shuttle bus, boat	Experience lush rainforests, an alpine pass and waterfalls along the 'finest walk in the world'
Hollyford Track (p295)	5 days	easy–moderate	Oct–May	shuttle bus, jet-boat, plane	Tramp to the rugged coast and explore the wildlife of Martins Bay
Kepler Track (p300)	4 days	moderate	Oct–Apr	shuttle bus, boat	Spend a full day surrounded by alpine beauty on this Great Walk
Hump Ridge Track (p303)	3 days	moderate	Nov–Apr	shuttle bus	Explore a spectacular coast and intriguing logging relics
Rakiura Track (p308)	3 days	moderate	Oct–Apr	boat, plane	Follow sheltered shores and beautiful beaches
North West Circuit (p312)	11 days	demanding	Oct–Apr	boat, plane	Slog through mud to wild Mason Bay; admire beaches and birdlife

Outdoor Pursuits

New Zealand's natural assets encourage even the laziest lounge lizards to drag themselves outside and get active, whether it's casting about for trout or taking to the trails on two wheels. Here we bring you a range of readily accessible outdoor activities that will complement your hikes and tramps.

Best Mountains, Rivers & Seas

Top Five Mountain-Biking Areas

Redwoods Whakarewarewa Forest, Rotorua

Mountains to Sea Central Plateau, Whanganui

Makara Peak Mountain Bike Park, Wellington

Queenstown & Wakatipu Basin Queenstown

Alexandra Otago

Top Five White-Water Rafting Trips

Buller River Murchison

Tongariro River Taupo

Kawarau River Queenstown

Kaituna Cascades Rotorua

Shotover Canyon Queenstown

Top Five Surfing Spots

Manu Bay Raglan

Tauranga Bay Westport

Waikanae Beach Gisborne

St Clair Beach Dunedin

Mount Beach Mt Maunganui

Bird-Watching

A diverse and fascinating array of birds may be seen in the wild, with many resident (or regularly returning) populations well protected and indeed promoted by high-profile visitor attractions. Examples include the Royal Albatross Centre on the Otago Peninsula; the godwits of Farewell Spit in Golden Bay; and the kotuku (white heron) sanctuary at Whataroa on the West Coast.

NZ does a great line in island sanctuaries, and increasingly 'mainland islands' – reserves encircled by predator-proof fences. Such enclaves include Tiritiri Matangi island near Auckland, Ulva Island near Stewart Island, Kapiti Island near Wellington, and Motuara Island in the Marlborough Sounds. Visitor-friendly 'mainland islands' include Maungatautari near Hamilton, and Zealandia in Wellington.

Another opportunity to gain insight into NZ bird species and their conservation is at numerous captive breeding facilities, including the West Coast Wildlife Centre in Franz Josef Glacier, where rowi – the rarest of all kiwi species – are hatched. Another such kiwi hatchery is Rainbow Springs, in Rotorua.

For a selection of some of the wonderful birds you may encounter on the tracks and elsewhere, refer to our bird-spotting guide (p34).

Fishing

Introduced in the 19th century, brown and rainbow trout have thrived in NZ's lakes and waterways and attract keen anglers from around the world. Many walking tracks follow rivers or skirt lakes, giving trampers ample opportunity to catch supper. Lake Waikaremoana, the Leslie-Karamea and Caples Greenstone are memorable places to try your luck. Licences (daily adult/youth $23/7, whole season adult/youth $100/24) are essential and can be bought at outdoor/fishing shops, visitor centres or online at Fish and Game New Zealand (www.fishandgame.org.nz), where you'll also find information on when, where and how to fish.

Sea-fishing options are bountiful too, whether casting off the beach or rocks, or reeling fish in from a kayak or chartered boat. Delicious snapper, cod, tarakihi and groper are all on the menu, but know your limits and release all undersize fish. Fishing rules and guidelines are available from www.fish.govt.nz, while www.fishing.net.nz can hook you up with charters and guides, as will i-SITE visitor centres nationwide.

Horse Trekking

Unlike some other parts of the world, where beginners get led by the nose around a paddock, horse trekking in NZ lets you loose in the countryside. Expect to saddle up on farms, in forests, along beaches, and up into the hills amid *Hobbit*-worthy scenery. Rides range from one-hour jaunts (from around $50) to fully catered overnight and multiday treks.

Used to transport people, carry goods and work the land, horses were an integral part of early NZ life and have left a legacy of horse-loving folk offering equine adventures all over the country. For info and operator listings, search 100% Pure New Zealand (www.newzealand.com) or pop into the local visitor centre.

Kayaking

With over 15,000km of coastline NZ is a paddler's haven, and sea kayaking is a fantastic way to see the coast and get close to wildlife you'd otherwise never see.

There are endless great spots for kayaking, readily identifiable by the presence of the ubiquitous boat-hire kiosk. Notable areas include the Hauraki Gulf (particularly off Waiheke and Great Barrier Islands), the Bay of Islands and Coromandel Peninsula on the North Island; and the Marlborough Sounds, Te Anau, Milford Sound, Doubtful Sound and Manapouri on the South Island. The ultimate kayak adventure is an overnight trip on the azure waters of Abel Tasman National Park, camping on secluded, white sandy beaches unreachable on foot. Information on guided trips and freedom rentals can be found at www.newzealand.com.

Marine Mammal–Watching

Kaikoura, on the northeast coast of the South Island, is NZ's nexus of marine mammal–watching. The main attraction here is whale-watching, but this is dependent on weather conditions, so don't expect to be able to just rock up and head straight out on a boat for a dream encounter. The sperm whale, the largest toothed whale, is pretty much a year-round resident, and depending on the season you may also see migrating humpback whales, pilot whales, blue whales and southern right whales.

On NZ's coastal tracks you are likely to spot New Zealand fur seals (kekeno) and several species of dolphin, including the playful dusky that frolics in pods of up to 500, and the pint-sized Hector's dolphin, one of the world's smallest and rarest.

Mountain Biking

NZ is laced with quality mountain-biking opportunities. Recent developments include the creation of the New Zealand Cycle Trail/Nga Haerenga (www.nzcycletrail.com), a network of more than 20 rides nationwide that will eventually cover almost 2500km of track. Construction was well underway at the time of writing, and most trails were open to cyclists to some extent (if not actually complete), providing two-wheeled access to some of the country's most impressive landscapes. See the website for info and updates. Generally graded 1 (easy) to 3 (intermediate), these multiday rides are suitable for most levels of rider, and can generally be split into half- and full-day sections should you not want to overnight along the way.

Some traditional tramping tracks are also open to mountain bikes, including the 71km Queen Charlotte Track and the Heaphy Track. Other excellent dedicated mountain-biking tracks can be found in Rotorua's Redwoods (www.redwoods. co.nz), at Makara Peak (www.makarapeak. org; South Karori Rd, Karori; admission by donation) in Wellington, along the West Coast, and around Queenstown, Alexandra and Wanaka. In recent years the Central Plateau has emerged as one of the country's great cycling destinations.

Mountain bikes can be hired and repaired in major towns, and most definitely in adventure-sports centres like Queenstown, Wanaka, Nelson and Taupo. You will also find supporting bike shops and shuttle operators in smaller gateway towns close to the trails. These shops are normally great sources for the latest track information, as are the local mountain-biking clubs (www.mtbnz.org).

Other useful resources include Classic New Zealand Mountain Bike Rides (www. kennett.co.nz), which details short and long rides all over NZ, and the bimonthly magazine *New Zealand Mountain Biker* (www.nzmtbr.co.nz).

Mountaineering

NZ has a proud mountaineering history – this was, after all, the home of Sir Edmund Hillary (1919–2008), who, along with Tenzing Norgay, was the first to reach the summit of Mt Everest. When he came back down, Sir Ed famously uttered to friend George Lowe, 'Well, George, we knocked the bastard off!'

The Southern Alps are studded with impressive peaks and challenging climbs. The Aoraki/Mt Cook region is outstanding; other mountaineering areas extend along the spine of the South Island from Tapuae-o-Uenuku (in the Kaikoura Ranges) and the Nelson Lakes peaks in the north to the rugged southern mountains of Fiordland. Another area with climbs for all levels is Mt Aspiring National Park.

The Christchurch-based New Zealand Alpine Club (www.alpineclub.org.nz) proffers excellent climbing information and publishes *The Climber* magazine quarterly. Professional outfits for training, guiding and advice can be found in Wanaka, Queenstown, Aoraki/Mt Cook, Lake Tekapo, and Fox and Franz Josef Glaciers.

Rock Climbing

Time to chalk up your fingers and don some natty little rubber shoes. On the North Island, popular rock-climbing, sport-climbing and bouldering areas include Auckland's Mt Eden Quarry; Whanganui Bay, Kinloch, Kawakawa Bay and Motuoapa near Lake Taupo; Mangatepopo Valley and Whakapapa Gorge on the Central Plateau; Humphries Castle and Warwick Castle on Mt Taranaki; and Piarere and Wharepapa South in the Waikato.

On the South Island, there's world-class bouldering at Kura Tawhiti (Castle Hill) on the road to Arthur's Pass, while west of Nelson, the marble and limestone mountains of Golden Bay and Takaka Hill boast prime climbing. Other options include Hospital Flat (west of Wanaka), Long Beach (north of Dunedin), and Mihiwaka and Lovers Leap on the Otago Peninsula.

Climb New Zealand (www.climb.co.nz) and Freeclimb (www.freeclimb.co.nz) have the lowdown on the gnarliest overhangs around NZ, plus maps and details on access and where to learn.

Scuba Diving

NZ is prime scuba territory, with warm waters up north, brilliant sea life and plenty of interesting sites.

Up north, get wet at the Bay of Islands Maritime and Historic Park, Hauraki Gulf Maritime Park, the Bay of Plenty, Great Barrier Island, Goat Island Marine Reserve, the Alderman Islands, Te Tapuwae o

Top: Cyclist on the Otago Central Rail Trail, part of the New Zealand Cycle Trail/ Nga Haerenga (p29)

Bottom: Skier on Mt Hutt, near Methven (p234)

BO TORNVIG / GETTY IMAGES ©

Rongokako Marine Reserve near Gisborne, and Sugar Loaf Islands Marine Park near New Plymouth. The Poor Knights Islands near Whangarei are reputed to have the best diving in NZ (with the diveable wreck of the Greenpeace flagship *Rainbow Warrior* nearby). Stay tuned to see whether the MV *Rena*, grounded off Tauranga in 2011, will become a dive site.

Down south, the Marlborough Sounds Maritime Park hosts the *Mikhail Lermontov,* the largest diveable cruise-ship wreck in the world. In Fiordland head for Dusky Sound, Milford Sound and Doubtful Sound, which offer amazingly clear pseudo-deepwater conditions not far below the surface. Invercargill, with its Antarctic waters, also has a diving club.

Expect to pay anywhere from $180 for a short, introductory, pool-based scuba course to around $600 for a four-day, PADI-approved, ocean dive course. One-off organised boat- and land-based dives start at around $170. Useful resources include Dive New Zealand (www.divenewzealand.com) and Scuba Dive New Zealand (www.scubadive.net.nz).

Skiing & Snowboarding

NZ is a prime southern-hemisphere destination for snow bunnies, with downhill skiing, cross-country (Nordic) skiing and snowboarding all passionately pursued. Heliskiing is popular, too, making good use of a wide off-piste area along the Southern Alps. The NZ ski season is generally June to October, though it varies con-

---

EXTREME SPORTS

We're not sure if it's something that has evolved to lure tourists, or if it's something innate in the Kiwi psyche, but extreme activities (skydiving, bungy jumping, paragliding etc) are part and parcel of the modern NZ adventure experience.

Bungy jumping was made famous by Kiwi AJ Hackett's 1986 plunge from the Eiffel Tower, after which he teamed up with champion NZ skier Henry van Asch to turn the endeavour into a profitable enterprise. And now you can get crazy too! Queenstown is a veritable spiderweb of bungy cords, including the original 43m jump off the Kawarau Bridge, a 47m leap from a ledge at the top of a gondola, and the big daddy, the 134m **Nevis Bungy** (www.bungy.co.nz). On the North Island, you can make the leap in Taupo, Taihape, Auckland and Rotorua. Varying the theme, try the 109m-high **Shotover Canyon Swing** (☑03-442 6990, 0800 279 464; www.canyonswing.co.nz; per person $199, additional swings $39) or **Nevis Swing** (www.bungy.co.nz) in Queenstown; both are seriously high rope swings. You might think this is easier on the nerves than a bungy, but just wait until you try it. A bungy jump will cost $150 to $200, with frequently available combo deals luring you into other adventures with irresistible discounts.

If bungy jumping seems a bit tame, why not leap out of a perfectly good aeroplane? There are numerous skydiving opportunities around NZ, including in Taupo on the North Island, with fantastic views of the lake and volcanoes. In Motueka you can ogle three different national parks with **Skydive Abel Tasman** (☑03-528 4091, 0800 422 899; www.skydive.co.nz; Motueka Aerodrome, College St; jumps 13,000ft/16,500ft $299/399). **Skydive Franz** (☑0800 458 677, 03-752 0714; www.skydivefranz.co.nz; Main Rd, Franz Josef Glacier) claims NZ's highest jump at 19,500ft and 90 seconds of freefall. With Aoraki/Mt Cook in your sights, this could be the most scenic leap you ever do, providing you can keep your eyes open. Tandem jumps involve training with a qualified instructor and cost around $300/400/550/650 for a 12,000/15,000/18,000/19,500ft jump; extra for a DVD/photographs.

Paragliding – sitting in a harness with your instructor under a modified parachute canopy – is a thrilling yet serene way to take in NZ's mountains and lakes. Leap off lofty spots in Hawkes Bay, Nelson, Queenstown and Wanaka and soar like a bird. Tandem paragliding costs from around $180 for 20 minutes, while introductory courses are around $250.

siderably from one ski area to another, and can run as late as November.

The variety of locations and conditions makes it difficult to rate NZ's ski fields in any particular order. Some people like to be near Queenstown's party scene or Mt Ruapehu's volcanic landscapes; others prefer the quality high-altitude runs on Mt Hutt, Treble Cone's steep slopes or quieter club skiing areas.

Most fields have dedicated websites, while visitor information centres can also make bookings and organise packages. Brown Bear (www.brownbearski. co.nz) and snow.co.nz are useful online resources covering all of NZ's ski areas. Lift passes at the main resorts cost from around $95/55 per adult/child per day; ski and snowboard equipment rental starts at around $40 a day (less for multiday hire). Heliskiing is cheaper than in North America and costs around $825 to $1450 for three to eight runs.

Surfing

With swells hitting the shores of NZ from all points of the compass, there's good surfing to be found *somewhere* in NZ at any time of the year.

Surf.co.nz has the lowdown on many great surf spots, although unsurprisingly local knowledge is king for some of the best and more remote spots. Newbies can learn to hang ten at surf schools at most of the well-known breaks and beaches; visit www.surfingnz.co.nz for some recommendations. Two hours of group tuition will cost around $80 per person; expect to pay around $120 for a one-on-one lesson.

Raglan's Manu Bay has NZ's most famous wave, but the Auckland area (Piha, Muriwai), Gisborne (Waikanae Beach, among many others), Mount Beach at Mt Maunganui, Taranaki (Greenmeadows Point, Stent Road, Fitzroy Beach), Tauranga Bay near Westport, and Dunedin (including St Clair) attract surf dudes from all over.

White-Water Rafting & Canoeing

There are almost as many white-water rafting and canoeing possibilities as there are rivers in the country, and there's no shortage of companies to get you into the rapids. Rivers are graded from I to VI, with VI meaning 'unraftable'. On the rougher stretches there's usually a minimum age requirement of 12 or 13 years.

Popular South Island rafting rivers include the Shotover Canyon and Kawarau River (Queenstown), Rangitata River (Christchurch), Buller River (Murchison/Westport), Karamea River (Westport) and the Arnold and Waiho Rivers on the West Coast. On the North Island try the Rangitaiki, Wairoa, Motu, Mokau, Mohaka, Tongariro and Rangitikei Rivers. There are also the Kaituna Cascades near Rotorua, the highlight of which is the 7m drop at Okere Falls.

Canoeing is so popular on the North Island's Whanganui River that it's been designated one of NZ's 'Great Walks'! You can also dip your paddle into northern lakes such as Lake Taupo and Lake Rotorua, as well as freshwater lakes on the South Island. Many backpacker hostels close to canoe-friendly waters have Canadian canoes and kayaks for hire (or free loan), and loads of commercial operators run guided trips. The New Zealand Rafting Association (www.nz-rafting.co.nz) is a good place to start.

New Zealand's Birds

New Zealand is a great country for bird-spotting, with all sorts of weird and wonderful creatures in its midst. Here are just a few that you may encounter, as chosen by our authors and Forest & Bird (www.forestandbird.org.nz), NZ's largest conservation group. Also check out the excellent Digital Encyclopaedia of New Zealand Birds (www.nzbirdsonline.org.nz).

1. Silvereye/Tauhou
One of NZ's most prevalent birds, this small, agile creature is easily recognised by its white eye-ring and inclination to sing.

2. Kereru
If you can hear heavy wingbeats overhead, it'll be the kereru. NZ's handsome native pigeon is widespread through the country and fond of powerlines and branches.

3. Bellbird/Korimako
Sounding less like a bell and more like Adele, this enchanting songbird sounds big but is a small, green slip of a thing, fond of nectar and found on both islands.

4. Fantail/Piwakawaka
This little charmer will entrance you up close, but in truth it cares not a jot about you, merely the insects you displace.

5. Grey Warbler/Riroriro
NZ's most widely distributed endemic bird species is also one of its smallest. Tending to hide in dense vegetation, the featherweight affirms its presence by warbling its jolly head off.

6. Woodhen/Weka
Often mistaken by visitors to NZ as a kiwi, this large flightless bird has a keen nose for lunch crumbs and will often appear at well-frequented picnic spots.

7. Pukeko
Often seen pecking about in paddocks or crossing the road in front of high-speed traffic. Territorial, highly social and easily recognised, it looks like a smooth blue chicken with a red forehead.

8. Paradise Shelduck
This colourful, conspicuous and honking waterfowl could be mistaken for a small goose as it hangs out in wild wetlands, river flats, sportsfields and other open grassed areas.

9. Rifleman/Tititi Pounamu
NZ's smallest bird, this hyperactive forest-dweller produces a characteristic 'wing-flicking' while moving through the canopy and foraging up and down tree trunks.

10. Kiwi
A national icon with an onomatopoeic name, at least for the male which cries 'kiwi!' The females make an ugly sound, a bit like someone with a sore throat. There are five different species.

11. Robin
Inhabiting forest and scrub, the distinct North Island and South Island robins stand leggy and erect, sing loud and long, and will often approach very closely.

12. Tomtit/Miromiro
Widespread inhabitants of forest and shrubland, the tomtit is often reclusive and hard to see, but occasionally moves in for a closer look.

13. Kea
Resident only in the South Island, this is the world's only true alpine parrot. Kea appear innately curious, but this is simply a pretence to peck destructively at your possessions.

14. Falcon/Karearea
The NZ falcon is a magpie-sized bird of prey found in both forest and open habitats such as tussocklands and roughly grazed hill country.

15. Kaka
This screechy parrot flaps boldly across the sky and settles in a wide variety of native forest including podocarp and beech forest, and in Wellington city near Zealandia.

16. Tui
Common throughout town and country, up close the 'parson bird' is metallic bluey-green with white throat tufts. Sometimes tuneful, and sometimes cacophonous, it is always an aerobatic flapper.

17. Morepork/Ruru
You'll probably hear this small, nocturnal owl rather than see it ('more-pork' call; peculiar screeches), although it may eyeball you from a low branch in both native and exotic forests.

18. Blue Duck/Whio
Mostly confined to clear, fast-flowing rivers in the mountains, this darling little bird issues a shrill 'whio' whistle above the noise of turbulent waters.

19. Kakariki
Also known as the red- or yellow-crowned parakeets and now reasonably rare on the mainland, these birds will most likely be seen in tall forest, or on islands such as Tiritiri Matangi and Ulva.

Plan Your Trip
Safety in the Outdoors

Tramping mishaps are a frequent occurrence in the New Zealand wilderness. The majority are caused by underestimating track and weather conditions, compounded by bad preparation. Venturing into the back country should not be taken lightly. It is extremely important to understand the risks involved, and to be prepared for them.

New Zealand Outdoor Safety Code

Plan Your Trip

Seek local knowledge and plan the route you will take and the amount of time you can reasonably expect it to take.

Tell Someone

Tell someone your plans and leave a date for when to raise the alarm if you haven't returned.

Be Aware of the Weather

NZ's weather can be highly unpredictable. Check the forecasts and expect weather changes.

Know Your Limits

Challenge yourself within your physical limits and experience.

Take Sufficient Supplies

Make sure you have enough food, equipment, clothing and emergency rations for the worst-case scenario. Take an appropriate means of communication.

Trip Planning

Choosing Your Tramp

Select a tramp that suits your level of fitness and experience. Tramps are graded within this guidebook and on the Department of Conservation (DOC) website to help you choose the most suitable ones for you. Talking to people who have recently completed the tramp is also a great source of information.

Many of NZ's most famous tracks are located in mountainous regions, and in winter these will be off limits to all but the most experienced and well-equipped trampers. There are, however, tracks that can be completed in shoulder seasons or even all year round. Choose the right tramp for the right time of year.

If it's your first tramp or you've just arrived in the country, the Great Walks (p8) are an ideal introduction. Not only incredibly scenic, they are also well signposted and maintained, and monitored by hut wardens who will pass on weather reports, track condition updates, and helpful advice. Another way to ease yourself into it is to start with day hikes or go on a guided trip.

Go With Those in the Know

If possible, tramp with someone else or within a group. Not only is there safety in numbers, it's usually more fun. Hiking companions can be found by reading noticeboards, lingering around DOC visitor centres, or online through sites such as Meetup (www.meetup.com) or the Federated Mountain Clubs (www.fmc.org.nz).

Another great source of knowledge on the NZ tramping experience is the Mountain Safety Council (www.mountainsafety.org.nz). It produces the excellent *Bushcraft* manual as well as other helpful guides such as *Plan to Survive, Preventing Hypothermia* and *Outdoor Communications*. It also runs regular courses at local branches throughout NZ.

Clothing, Equipment & Food

You need the right kit for the job, and nothing less will do. Staying warm and dry is essential, so pack quality clothing layers and a spare set of dry clothes to change into. The rest of your kit will be dictated by your trip length and location, but prioritise the inclusion of a first-aid kit, wet-weather gear, warm clothes and a means of communication.

You will expend far more energy than normal when tramping. Fuelling up on the right types of food and staying hydrated will keep you rational, and smiling. See the Clothing, Equipment & Food chapter (p45) for more details.

Intentions

Tell someone your plans and set a date and time for raising an alarm if you haven't returned. The New Zealand Outdoors Intentions process is the most widely supported and endorsed system for registering your trip plans. It's best to do it before you set off: online, by email, or by manually completing a form via AdventureSmart (www.adventuresmart.org.nz). Just remember to inform your trusted contact that you have returned safely.

When you're on the track write in the hut logbooks even if you're not staying there, as this will help would-be rescuers find you more quickly.

Get the Latest Information

Before you set off, check in at the nearest DOC office for the latest track and weather information.

Navigation

Stay on Track

With the exception of remote and lightly used backcountry tracks, NZ's track network is very well signposted with marker posts, permolats (metal disks), orange plastic triangles, orange tipped poles and clear junction signage.

The main challenge to navigation is bad weather, where tree-fall or track washout might encourage you to deviate from the signposted route, or an enveloping mist leaves you without any sense of direction. The art of navigation is an essential tramping skill, and one you shouldn't leave home without. Not only will it ensure you know where you are and where you need to go, reading a map and using a compass will help you see the bigger picture, including having an awareness of the surrounding area and possible escape routes, distances and types of terrain. It can also help you apply weather information such as wind direction from a weather forecast to your area. See p40 for more tips on navigation.

If you do get lost, remember the following basic rules:

➡ Stop, stay calm and carefully plan what to do.

➡ If you think you can retrace your route then do so, marking your spot (in case you have to start again) and your route as you move. Otherwise, stay put or move to an open area such as a clearing or a riverbank. The last thing you want to do is wander hopelessly in the bush.

➡ If you have to spend a night in the open, find or make a shelter, put on extra clothes and build a fire.

➡ Help searchers find you by building arrows or cairns out of rocks and wood, laying out brightly coloured items that can be easily seen from the air, and by burning green wood and leaves to produce smoke.

Maps

An up-to-date topographic map is recommended for all but the shortest of day walks. The most commonly used maps are the NZTopo50 map series (1:50,000) produced by Land Information New Zealand (www.linz.govt.nz), which cover the whole country. Hard copies are available from most good outdoor gear shops, while digital maps can be viewed and downloaded from the LINZ website and www.topomap.co.nz.

Park maps are good for planning and may be adequate for some tramps, including the Great Walks. However, many of these have gone out of print; ask at the local DOC office or outdoor gear shop what is available. A great alternative is the New-Topo (www.newtopo.co.nz) map series, of varying scales, which logically cover popular tramping areas previously covered by multiple maps. Whichever hard-copy maps you use, they're best laminated or placed in a clear plastic sleeve to protect them from the elements.

A good computer program for NZ is MapToaster Topo (www.maptoaster.com), which features a search tool for places and road names, integrated aerial photography and GPS compatibility. Don't rely solely on electronic versions if you are using a GPS; batteries can go flat!

Plot Your Progress

When planning your trip, estimate how long each leg will take based on suggested track times. Make allowances for the fitness of you and your group, and for regular breaks. Set off early enough so that you complete your day's walk with plenty of daylight to spare, factoring in stopping to smell the roses.

When you're on the track check your times against those indicated on the DOC signposts and adjust your estimates ac-cordingly. Always stick a torch in your pack even on short day walks, in case of unforeseen delays.

Navigation Equipment

Maps & Compass

Always carry a good topographical map and know how to read it properly. Before the tramp, ensure that you understand the contours and the map symbols, plus the main ridge and river systems in the area. Familiarise yourself with the north–south directions, and the general direction you are heading in. On the trail, identify major landforms (mountain ranges, gorges etc) and find them on the map. This will give you a better understanding of the local geography.

Buy an adjustable-dial compass and learn how to use it. A compass in NZ will point through the earth towards magnetic north, so the needle needs to be specially weighted to keep it horizontal. Northern hemisphere compasses should not be used in NZ. Magnetic north in NZ is between 18° and 25° east of grid north; using a variation of 21° is adequate for most back-country navigation around the middle of NZ, but check the map for local variation.

Learn How to Use a Compass

Once you've got your compass, make sure you know how to use it. Learn to orient your map, take bearings and then be able to follow them. The Safety Tips section of the Mountain Safety Council website (www.mountainsafety.org.nz) is a good place to start, although one of its courses will be even better. Once you've mastered the basics, practise on short walks.

GPS

Global Positioning System (GPS) has been a significant navigational development. Hand-held receivers are cheap, compact, easy to use and, in the right conditions, able to identify your location down to around 20m. On many models, you can input waypoints, mark your route, measure your altitude, record your progress and overlay maps. They are, however, no substitute for sound navigational skills and a

---

THE MAPS IN THIS BOOK

The maps within this book are designed as a reference guide when reading the text, not to be used for navigation on the track! They are no substitute for the detailed topographical maps recommended for each walk.

compass and map. Batteries go flat, units get dropped and you can't always get a good satellite signal under forest canopies, below high cliffs or in snow or hail.

Altimeter

Altimeters determine altitude by measuring air pressure, which can fluctuate with temperature at any given elevation. Calibrate altimeters regularly at known elevations such as spot heights and passes. Use the altimeter in conjunction with other navigation techniques to fix your position. For instance, taking a back bearing to a known peak or river confluence, determining the general direction of the track and obtaining your elevation should give you a pretty good fix on your position.

Altimeters can also provide a general idea of barometric pressure trends and are useful for indicating changing weather conditions. If the altimeter shows increasing elevation while you are not climbing, it means the air pressure is dropping and a low-pressure weather system may be approaching.

Watch the Weather

Expect the Unexpected

The Crowded House song 'Four Seasons in One Day' is a popular adage for NZ's unpredictable and occasionally extreme weather.

AVALANCHES

Avalanche conditions are most likely to occur between winter and spring, but avalanche paths can be active any time of the year that there are unseasonable snowfalls. If you are heading above the bushline or into alpine territory you should check the NZ Avalanche Centre (www.avalanche.net.nz) and the local DOC office for the latest conditions and safest routes. If you visit avalanche-prone areas, do not tramp alone, bear in mind that avalanches occur most commonly on 30° to 45° slopes, and be cautious on sunny slopes, particularly later in the day.

The usual weather pattern in NZ is a cycle of high-pressure systems (anticyclones or ridges) followed by low-pressure systems (troughs or depressions), travelling west to east. Anticyclones normally pass the northern portions of the country at intervals of three to seven days, bringing fine weather with light or moderate winds. In between are depressions of rain, strong winds and lower temperatures.

Because most of the country's mountain ranges run roughly north–south, they make their own weather. It is not uncommon to have rain on the windward (western side) of a range, fine weather on the lee side, and miserable conditions of heavy wind and rain along the ridge tops.

Check the Forecast

Always check the weather forecast before you set off. In a country obsessed with weather reports, it is not hard to find one. DOC and i-SITE visitor centres are a reliable source of short- and long-range forecasts, as is the MetService (www.metservice.com), which produces detailed five-day forecasts for 24 national park locations (also available as a mobile app). You are also bound to get varying predictions from accommodation providers, shuttle drivers and the lady at the pie shop. None of these are a substitute for official, up-to-date reports, but they may provide some sage local knowledge.

If things are looking dicey, delay your trip or seek advice from local experts on alternative routes or other options.

Reading the Weather

Once on the track, keep an eye on the skies. Given sufficient warning you can put your foot on the gas to out-tramp an oncoming storm, know when to wait it out at a hut, or slow down to a snail's pace to maximise a slot of sunshine. The key thing to remember, though, is that NZ's weather can change extremely quickly, especially in the mountains.

Two early signs of approaching bad weather are an increase in wind speed and the appearance of high cloud sheets. These sheets, often stacked on top of one another or looking like flying saucers, are known as lenticular or hog's back clouds and are the outriders of northwesterly storms. As the depression moves onto the country, the wind changes direction, often quite suddenly, and a weather change results.

The wind is the key to reading the weather in the bush. As a general rule, northwesterlies bring wet weather and storms, while southerlies are a sign of a cool frontal change, often followed by clear conditions. Northeasterlies may also signal good weather approaching, whereas southwesterlies are normally associated with cool, rain-laden winds.

The higher you are, the more severe the weather can be, with significantly lower temperatures, stronger winds and rain that can quickly turn to snow. Snowfall and blizzards can occur at any time of the year in alpine areas, so you must be properly equipped.

If heavy storms move in once you are on the track, the best idea is to stay in a hut and take a day off, especially if you are in an alpine area. Be patient and don't worry about missing a bus or lift at the end of the tramp.

From One Extreme to the Other

Hypothermia

Hypothermia occurs when your body is unable to maintain its core temperature, leading to a loss of normal function and, in severe cases, possibly death. Indeed, it is one of the greatest risks to those venturing into the NZ outdoors, and the cause of tramper deaths every year.

Good clothing is critical in preventing hypothermia. Dress in layers (preferably wool, fleece or synthetics), covered with a sturdy waterproof outer layer, and wear a hat. Stay fuelled up with regular intakes of nourishing foods and liquids. Early signs of hypothermia include the inability to perform fine movements (such as doing up buttons), shivering, and a bad case of the 'umbles' (fumbles, mumbles, grumbles, stumbles, tumbles).

The treatment for hypothermia is to get warm again. Stop, find shelter, replace wet clothing with dry, and get into a sleeping bag. Another fully clothed person inside the bag will help to raise the patient's core temperature gently, as will warm sweet drinks if they are conscious. In severe hypothermia, shivering may stop; this requires immediate action to warm the patient, followed by evacuation.

Sunburn & Heatstroke

Trampers spend a great deal of time outdoors and are therefore at high risk of sunburn, heat exhaustion, heatstroke, and, in the long term, of developing skin cancer. You get sunburnt surprisingly quickly in NZ, as the ozone layer is among the thinnest in the world.

Reduce the risk of sunburn by covering up, even when it's cloudy, and especially when you are at high altitude. Protect your eyes with good-quality sunglasses, particularly near water, sand or snow, and use 30+ SPF sunscreen on exposed skin. A full-brimmed hat will set your tramping wardrobe off nicely and keep the sun's rays (and some sandflies) at bay. Choose well-shaded spots for rest stops and lunch breaks.

Long, continuous periods of exposure to high temperatures and insufficient fluid intake can leave you vulnerable to heatstroke. Symptoms include feeling nauseous, minimal sweating and a high body temperature (above 39°C). In severe cases sweating may cease and the skin can become flushed. Headaches and a lack of coordination may also occur, and the patient may be confused or aggressive. Eventually the victim will become delirious and/or suffer convulsions. Evacuation to a hospital is essential for heatstroke sufferers. While waiting for evacuation get the patient out of the sun, remove his or her clothing, cover them with wet clothing or a wet sheet or towel, then fan them continuously. Also administer fluids if they are conscious.

River Crossings

Where & When

Most rivers and major streams are bridged at key crossing points, while smaller streams usually only require an ankle-deep wade to reach the other side. However, it is essential to carefully consider all but the most short and shallow of crossings. What looks like a good crossing point might actually conceal a deeper channel: even knee-deep water can often be too difficult to cross without the mutual support of several people. Also, if you can't keep pace with a floating stick while walking next to the river, this is a good indication that the river is flowing too fast for you to cross.

During and immediately after heavy rain is a particularly dangerous time to ford. It doesn't take long – sometimes less than an hour – to turn a mountain creek into an impassable torrent of white water.

If you are not certain you can cross a river or stream safely, check your map for a safe alternate route where there is a bridge, take shelter and wait, or head back to the last hut or camp and sit it out. Remember, you do *not* have to cross that river: *if in doubt, stay out.* Streams and rivers rise quickly, but return to their normal levels almost as fast. If you wait a day, or even an afternoon, the water will often subside enough for you to ford safely.

How to Cross

If you decide that it is safe to cross, look for an area where the river is braided into several shallow channels, or where the water is flowing over an even riverbed. Avoid large boulders and uneven areas of the riverbed. Cross the river at an angle moving with the current.

If you are alone, use a 2m-long pole as a 'third leg' to ensure you always have two contact points with the riverbed when moving. If you're in a group, link arms around waists by inserting arms between your neighbour's pack and back and grab either their hip belt or pack strap on the furthest side. If your companions aren't wearing packs you can grasp their trouser tops or belts in the same manner. Cross at the same time, walking parallel to the opposite bank, with the strongest person at the upstream end of the line.

Never attempt to cross if the water is discoloured, when there is the sound of rolling boulders or if debris and trees are being carried along in the current. You also need to select a good exit point and make sure there is sufficient recovery area if you decide to back out and retreat to the bank. Check what's downriver and avoid areas just upstream of waterfalls, rapids and dead trees that could cause you problems.

Wear your pack when crossing rivers. Unfasten the chest strap, loosen the shoulder strap and keep the hip belt done up. Practise releasing the hip belt, although don't take your pack off while crossing unless it becomes trapped. Your pack can act as a buoyancy aid and if you get swept away you'll want your gear when you make it back to shore. If you fall, manoeuvre yourself feet first and use your arms and feet for control and to move you to the nearest bank, or float to a shallow area to exit.

Emergencies, Rescue & Communication

Emergencies & Rescue

Things can go wrong for even the most well-prepared and experienced trampers. If you find yourself in an emergency, the STAR model will help you make the right decision:

Stop Take a breath, sit down and remain calm

Think Look around you; listen and brainstorm options

Assess Evaluate the options and their potential consequences

Respond Make the best decision

If someone in your group is injured or falls ill and can't move, you may decide to seek help. If you have a mobile phone, satellite phone or mountain radio you should be able to get a message out. If not, leave somebody with that person while another person or two (preferably) goes for help. If the only option is to leave the injured person while you go for help, leave them with as much warm clothing, food and water as it is sensible to spare, plus a whistle and torch.

Help rescuers find you: mark your position by building arrows or cairns out of rocks and wood, laying out brightly coloured items or tying them to trees so they can be easily seen from the air, and by burning green wood and leaves to produce smoke. If you have a personal locator beacon (PLB), and you're in a life-threatening situation, activate it so rescuers know you're in trouble and can pinpoint your location. This can save precious time, and lives.

In NZ, many search-and-rescue evacuations are done by helicopter. Find or create a clearing approximately 25m by 25m with a flat area for the helicopter to land that is at least 6m by 6m. Where no landing area is available, a person and harness might be lowered. When the chopper arrives, indicate wind direction to the pilot by standing with your back to the wind and your arms pointed ahead of you. Make sure there are no loose items around and await the pilot's instructions. Never approach a helicopter unless directed to, and always from the front. Avoid high ground, keep low and follow the instructions of the pilot and crew.

Communication

There are five ways that NZ trampers equip themselves to communicate with Police Search and Rescue in an emergency. The main methods for two-way communications are mountain radios or satellite phones. Mobile phones should not be relied upon as there is very little coverage in NZ's back country. If you do have a signal and have an emergency, dial ⤴111. Keep the phone switched off to save batteries, and stowed in a waterproof plastic bag.

The Mountain Radio Service (www.mountainradio.co.nz) comprises volunteer organisations providing backcountry radio communication including regular 'scheds' to relay weather forecasts, locations and intended routes. You can rent radio sets cheaply (from $5 per day) from the organisations and some outdoor gear shops. It's an excellent way of keeping in touch and although not all areas are monitored 24/7, there is usually someone listening in on one of the frequencies. Satellite phones can be also used anywhere there is a view of a satellite. They're expensive to buy and operate, but they can be hired for around $30 per day.

When activated, personal locator beacons (PLBs) emit a radio distress signal that is picked up by satellite or aircraft and relayed to the Rescue Coordination Centre of New Zealand. They are lightweight, require no set-up and could save your life. They are also cheap to hire (from $5 per day) and readily available from outdoor gear shops and some visitor centres and DOC offices. Only activate your PLB in life-threatening situations; see www.beacons.org.nz for more details.

Also available are emergency satellite instant messenger devices, such as SPOT (www.findmespot.com) and inReach (www.inreachdelorme.com). These allow you to send and receive text messages but signal strength is generally less than a PLB.

If no other emergency communications are available, use the internationally recognised emergency alert: six short blasts of a whistle at 10-second intervals (yell or use a torch if you haven't got a whistle), followed by a minute's rest. Repeat the sequence until you receive a response, which should be three signals at 20-second intervals, followed by a one-minute pause and then a repetition of the sequence.

First Aid

At least one person in your group should possess adequate first-aid knowledge and know how to apply it. If possible, attend a course before heading into the outdoors or at least do some reading; MSC's *Outdoor First Aid* manual ($35) is comprehensive and NZ-relevant, as is the St John (www.stjohn.org.nz) online *First Aid Library*. A first-aid kit is a must for any tramp.

Plan Your Trip
Clothing, Equipment & Food

Careful planning will help you determine what clothing, equipment and food is indispensable, and what will prove a burden in your already brimming backpack. Make sure you devote adequate time to this phase of trip planning, and sample your pack-load before you set off.

Clothing

When buying clothes for tramping consider their weight, warmth, fit, breathability and, for outer layers, their ability to keep you dry. Never underestimate the wide range of daily temperatures that can occur in New Zealand, particularly in alpine country where you can easily wake to brilliant sunshine and go to bed in a snowstorm. Always be prepared for bad weather.

Layering

Layering your clothes will trap air between layers – which is the best way to conserve body heat – and allow you to add or remove clothing to suit conditions.

Choose your undergarments carefully as they have to deal with sweat, which in cool conditions can reduce your ability to keep warm. Merino wool, polypropylene, polyester or merino-synthetic mixes are good options; cotton is not. Ultrafine merino can be expensive and does take longer to dry than synthetic materials, but is soft and comfortable and won't smell even after a few days on the trail. Polypropylene and polyester are excellent at wicking moisture away from the skin but they do tend to retain odours.

Tips for Packing Light

➡ Consider weight when purchasing your hiking clothes and equipment.

➡ Take only the food and fuel you need, plus one or two days spare in case you are delayed by bad weather.

➡ Plan your water fills, accounting for availability en route.

➡ Beyond a sensible set of clothing for daytime and night, you need not take anything more.

➡ Don't take jeans: they're heavy, especially when wet.

➡ Limit your toiletries (miniature travel packs are ideal); weight obsessives have even been known to snap their toothbrushes in half!

➡ Repackage all foodstuffs into lightweight plastic.

➡ Share gear – if you're tramping in a pair or a group, share your stove, food, toothpaste, first-aid kit... everything you can.

An insulating midlayer provides essential additional warmth; many trampers use a jersey or jacket of pile or fleece fabric, such as Polartec, or merino wool. Avoid cotton hooded sweatshirts, as they will not insulate when wet and take forever to dry. Also toss into your backpack some woollen mittens and a wool or fleece hat. The body loses most of its heat through its extremities, particularly the head.

A common and practical uniform for the track is thermal leggings under a pair of baggy hiking shorts, giving maximum freedom of movement while providing protection from cold weather, light rain, excessive sun, and bugs. If you prefer long trousers (pants), they should preferably be of stretch nylon, synthetic pile or light merino, never denim.

Waterproof Shell

Your jacket should be made of a breathable waterproof fabric, with capacious pockets, a good-quality heavy-gauge zip protected by a storm flap, and a hood roomy enough to cover headwear but which still affords peripheral vision. Make sure the sleeves extend well down the wrist, and that the overall body length allows you to sit down without getting a mossy bottom.

Although restrictive, overtrousers are essential if you're tramping in wet and cold conditions. Choose a style with slits for pocket access, and long ankle zips so that you can pull them on and off over your boots.

Footwear

Many trampers now opt for lightweight nylon boots made by many sporting-shoe companies. Designed for for trail hiking, easy terrain and carrying light loads, such boots are fine for benched tracks like the Kepler, Milford, Routeburn and Greenstone.

For trickier tracks and alpine routes, sturdy leather walking boots are a much wiser choice, offering more support with a stiff leather upper, durable sole and protective shanks. Many also feature a high-tech waterproof lining. When choosing new boots, do your research and purchase the best quality and most comfortable you can afford, and break them in before you go on your tramp.

Most trampers also carry a pair of 'camp shoes' such as thongs (flip-flops, jandals) or sport sandals, to wear around the huts and give some welcome relief to achy feet.

Gaiters

If you will be tramping through snow, deep mud or scratchy scrub, consider using gaiters or puttees to protect your legs and keep your socks dry. The best are made of strong synthetic fabric – with a robust zip protected by a flap – and have an easy-to-undo method of securing around the foot.

Socks

The best tramping socks are made of a hard-wearing mix of wool (70% to 80%) and synthetic (20% to 30%) material, and are free of ridged seams in the toes and heels. Socks with a high proportion of wool are more comfortable when worn for several successive days without washing. On any trip longer than two days you should have at least three pairs of socks.

Equipment

Backpack

For day tramps a 30L to 40L day-pack should suffice, but for multiday tramps you'll need a backpack of between 45L and 90L. The required capacity will depend on the destination, whether you plan to camp or stay in huts, and the duration of your tramp. It should be big enough for your gear without the need to strap additional items to the outside.

Assemble the kit you intend to take and try loading it into a pack to see if it's big enough. Keep in mind that as your pack's weight increases, your enjoyment decreases, so think twice about taking unnecessary items.

A good backpack should have an adjustable, well-padded harness, and a chest strap to evenly distribute the weight between your shoulders and hips. External pockets are good for quick access to water bottles, snacks and maps. Finally, even if the manufacturer claims your pack is waterproof, use a heavy-duty plastic liner to ensure everything stays dry. The best liner (the one you'll see most New Zealanders using) is a large bright-yellow plastic sack with outdoor tips on it, produced by the NZ Mountain Safety Council and sold at Department of Conservation (DOC) offices, outdoor gear shops and visitor information centres.

Sleeping Bag & Mat

Down bags are warm, lightweight and compact but useless if they get wet. Synthetic bags are cheaper and better wet, but generally bulkier. Mummy-shaped designs prove best for weight and warmth but can be claustrophobic. The rating (–5°C, for instance) is the coldest temperature at which a person should feel comfortable in the bag. For extra warmth, purchase a liner. Most huts have mattresses and are warm enough that a medium-weight bag of synthetic fibres is more than sufficient.

Self-inflating sleeping mats provide comfort and insulate from the cold. Foam mats are cheap but less comfortable. If you're planning to stay in huts you most likely won't need a sleeping mat. However, if you're tramping a popular track during high season, the hut might be full when you arrive, in which case a sleeping mat will make a night on the floor much more pleasant.

Stove & Fuel

Before your trip, check whether the huts you intend to stay at have gas cookers. Even if they do, carrying your own stove means you won't have to fight for space on the hob, and you can prepare hot food or a cup of tea on the track, providing warm relief on wet and cold days

When buying a stove, choose one that is lightweight and easy to operate. Butane stoves are the easiest to operate. Multifuel stoves are versatile but need pumping, priming and lots of cleaning. In general, liquid fuels are efficient and cheap; look for high-performance, cleaner-burning fuel. Gas is more expensive, cleaner and a reasonable performer. When using canisters be sure to pack yours out. Fuel can be found at outdoor gear shops, hardware stores (white gas) and some supermarkets.

Airlines prohibit flammable materials and may well reject empty liquid-fuel bottles or even the stoves themselves.

Tent

A tent is obviously a necessity on tracks without huts, such as the Te Paki Coastal Track, but they can also come in handy on popular tracks when huts might be full, snorers keep you awake, or you just want to enjoy the outdoors in solitude.

A three-season tent will suffice in most conditions. Because of the amount of climbing usually done in NZ, weight is a major issue, with most trampers selecting tents of around 2kg to 3kg that will sleep two or three people. The floor and the fly should be waterproof, have taped or sealed seams and covered zips to stop leaks. Make sure the tent has good bug netting to keep pesky sandflies out. Dome- and tunnel-shaped tents handle blustery conditions better than flat-sided tents.

Walking Poles

In NZ, tramping with walking poles is popular, especially on tracks and routes above the bushline. A pair of lightweight telescopic poles will help you balance, give you an added push when climbing steep ridges and slopes, and ease the jarring on your knees during descents.

Equipment Checklist

This list is a general guide to the things you might take on a tramp. Your personal list will vary depending on the type and length of your tramp, whether you're camping or staying in huts and lodges, and on the terrain, weather conditions and time of year.

Clothing

➡ sturdy walking boots and spare laces

➡ gaiters/puttees

➡ warm hat or balaclava, scarf and gloves/mittens

➡ overtrousers (waterproof)

➡ waterproof rain jacket with hood

➡ footwear for hut use: sandals or thongs (flip-flops, jandals)

➡ shorts and trousers or skirt (quick-drying)

➡ wool socks

➡ underwear

➡ sunhat

➡ sweater or fleece jacket

➡ thermal top and bottom

➡ T-shirt and long-sleeved shirts (quick-drying)

Equipment

➡ backpack with waterproof liner

➡ first-aid kit

➡ food and snacks (high energy) and one day's emergency supplies

➡ tent, pegs, poles and guy ropes (if not staying in huts)

➡ sleeping bag and bag liner/inner sheet

➡ sleeping mat (if not staying in huts)

➡ portable stove, fuel and pan(s)

➡ cooking, eating and drinking utensils

➡ insect repellent

➡ map (in clear plastic cover) and compass

➡ communication device (mobile phone and satellite phone/mountain radio/PLB)

➡ torch (flashlight) or headlamp, spare batteries and bulb

➡ water bottle or bladder

➡ pocket knife

➡ sunglasses

➡ sunscreen and lip balm

➡ survival bag or blanket

➡ toilet paper and trowel

➡ plastic bags (for carrying rubbish)

➡ whistle (for emergencies)

➡ dishwashing kit (pot scrubber & detergent)

➡ matches and lighter and candle(s)

➡ sewing/repair kit

➡ spare cord

➡ toiletries

➡ small towel

➡ water purification tablets, iodine or filter

➡ notebook/paper and pen/pencil

Optional Items

➡ GPS receiver

➡ altimeter

➡ backpack cover (waterproof and slip-on)

➡ binoculars

➡ book

➡ camera

➡ day-pack

➡ groundsheet

➡ mosquito net

➡ swimming costume

➡ walking poles

➡ bandana (they keep the sun off and make a fine flannel!)

➡ deck of cards

Buying & Hiring Locally

Most major towns in NZ will have at least one outdoor gear shop specialising in tramping and camping supplies, but prices are noticeably higher than in Australia or North America. One of our favourite outfitters with stores across the country is Bivouac Outdoor (www.bivouac.co.nz), which has an excellent range of local and international brands. These and other dependable stores are detailed in each of the destination chapters.

Outdoor gear shops in popular tramping areas such as Queenstown, Te Anau and Nelson will often hire a variety of gear for a daily or weekly charge. Prices vary but generally you can count on paying around $15 a day for a two-person tent, sleeping bag, backpack and jacket, and $5 to $10 for a stove. Overseas travellers who want to tramp more than one track should plan on bringing all their own gear, or at least the major items such as boots, backpack, sleeping bag and stove. If a tent is needed for an easy tramp, such as the Abel Tasman Coast Track, hire one or you could get away with purchasing an inexpensive one for under $50.

Food

Having enough of the right food is a tramping essential and can enhance your trip substantially. A hearty and tasty meal at the end of the day or a square of chocolate or a delicious snack on the track helps keep energy levels and morale high.

Food should be lightweight and nutritious. A good overall ratio is 1:1:4 for proteins (meats, cheese, eggs, milk powder, nuts), fats (cheese, chocolates, cured meats) and carbohydrates (sugar, bread, rice, pasta, sweets, dried fruit). If it's a short tramp of only two or three days you can take fresh foods like steak and even a bottle of booze (decanted into plastic, of course), but for longer trips, save weight and space by taking more dehydrated foods and ready-made meals such as those

produced by Back Country Cuisine (www.
backcountrycuisine.co.nz).

Plan what to take well ahead of your departure and always include spares for that
unscheduled extra day on the track due to
bad weather or an emergency.

Water

Tap water is clean and safe to drink in NZ.
Water in lakes, rivers and streams will look
clean and may be OK, but since the
diarrhoea-causing *Giardia lamblia* parasite has been found in some waterways,
water from any of these sources may need
treating before drinking. The protozoan
cryptosporidium (crypto) has also been
found in some feral animals and livestock
(mainly possums and cows). DOC can
advise on the occurrence of giardia and
crypto in national parks and forests, and
along tracks it administers. Most huts
are equipped with a rainwater tank that
provides water safe for drinking without
being treated.

If you are unsure about water quality
treat it before drinking it. Boiling is the
simplest method; around three minutes
should do it, although at high altitude
water boils at a lower temperature, so boil
it for a little longer just in case.

Filtering is also acceptable with giardia-
rated filters, which are widely available
from outdoor gear retailers and will also
remove crypto. Compact battery-powered
purifiers are also available that kill most
waterborne bacteria and viruses using UV
light.

If you can't boil, filter or purify water
it should be treated chemically. Iodine is
effective and is available in tablet form,
but follow the directions carefully and
remember that too much iodine can be
harmful. Iodine should be avoided by
pregnant women and people with thyroid
complaints.

Regions at a Glance

Northland, Auckland & Coromandel

Forests
Beaches
History

Forests
Explore extensive tracts of remnant native forest on a multitude of tracks in Northland, the Coromandel's Kauaeranga Valley and on Great Barrier Island. Stars of the show are the ancient kauri giants that can live for more than 2000 years.

Beaches
With Northland, Auckland, the Hauraki Gulf and the Coromandel all lined with beautiful beaches, water-lovers really are spoilt for choice.

History
New Zealand's oldest surviving buildings can be found in Kerikeri, while nearby is the country's 'birthplace' where the Treaty of Waitangi was signed. Coromandel Town and Thames show their goldrush roots in streets lined with historic wooden buildings, while the whole region is littered with pioneer relics.

p54

Tongariro, Urewera & Central North Island

Volcanoes
Lakes
Outdoor action

Volcanoes
The three steaming, occasionally erupting volcanoes at the heart of the North Island are a beguiling sight. Centrepieces of Tongariro National Park, they can be skied in winter and tramped the rest of the year.

Lakes
In Taupo, NZ's mightiest river is born from its greatest lake. Aquatic pursuits such as kayaking, sailing and fishing abound. In remote Te Urewera National Park, the magical, mystical lakes of Waikaremoana and Waikareiti are waiting to be explored.

Outdoor Action
Skydiving, bungy jumping, whitewater rafting, jetboating, mountain biking, wakeboarding, parasailing, skiing – you want thrills, you got 'em.

p84

Taranaki, Whanganui & Around Wellington

National parks
Coastal scenery
Capital city

National Parks
Steeped in Maori lore, lush Whanganui National Park is one of NZ's most isolated, interesting parks. Mt Taranaki (Egmont National Park) is picture-perfect with fabulous tramping.

Coastal Scenery
Hit Surf Hwy 45 south of New Plymouth for black-sand beaches and gnarly breaks. Whanganui offers remote and storm-buffeted beaches; the Horowhenua District has acres of empty brown sand.

Capital City
Compact, cool and creative, Wellington is home to Te Papa museum and the internationally flavoured City Gallery. It's also NZ's most hospitable city with scores of hip cafes and restaurants and a revolutionary craft beer scene.

p110

Queen Charlotte & Marlborough

The Sounds
Wildlife tours
Wineries

The Sounds

A popular playground for lovers of the great outdoors, these labyrinthine waterways can be explored by boat or on foot or bike via a network of trails from beach to peak, including the Queen Charlotte Track.

Wildlife Tours

The top of the South Island is home to myriad creatures, both in the water and on the wing. Motuara Island in the Sounds is a birdspotting paradise, while Kaikoura is a great one-stop shop to spot a whale or swim with dolphins and seals.

Wineries

Bobbing in Marlborough's sea of sauvignon blanc, riesling, pinot noir and bubbly are barrel-loads of quality cellar-door experiences and some fine regional food.

p144

Abel Tasman, Kahurangi & Nelson Lakes

National parks
Beaches
Geology

National Parks

Not satisfied with just one national park, the Nelson region has three: Nelson Lakes, Kahurangi and Abel Tasman. Explore sun-kissed coastlines, remote river valleys and mountain ranges.

Beaches

Abel Tasman is lined with dozens of secluded golden beaches accessible only by boat, kayak or on foot. Kahurangi's West Coast beaches are equally appealing for a walk on the wild side.

Geology

A smorgasbord of geological delights, from Abel Tasman's rocky outcrops of granite, limestone and marble, to karst landscapes etched with caves, arches and bluffs in Kahurangi, and glaciated valleys and alpine basins of the Nelson Lakes.

p165

Canterbury, Arthur's Pass & Aoraki/Mt Cook

Mountains
Night skies
History

Mountains

River valleys, soaring Southern Alps peaks, glaciers, mountain passes, the highest spot in the land and some of NZ's finest high-country tramps.

Night Skies

The night skies above Lake Tekapo are so clear and the stars so bright that they have been designated as the Aoraki Mackenzie Dark Sky Reserve. Visit Mt John Observatory and enjoy the show.

History

Akaroa and the Banks Peninsula celebrate their French heritage, while inland lie the historical riches of the pioneering prospectors in alpine passes to the West Coast. Aoraki/Mt Cook was where Sir Edmund Hillary learned the ropes.

p202

West Coast

Coast
Wildlife
History

Coast

From Kohaihai at the end of the Heaphy Track, to Jackson Bay in the south, stretches around 600km of wild and woolly coastline, sculpted by the elements into crazy rock formations such as Punakaiki's Pancake Rocks.

Wildlife

With around 90% of its land lying within the conservation estate, the West Coast is a haven for wildlife, especially birds. Highlights include the white heron sanctuary at Whataroa and cute kiwi chicks in Franz Josef's West Coast Wildlife Centre.

History

Explore old mining and milling routes like Charming Creek Walkway and Mahinapua Walkway, and watch the coast's pioneering history come to life at places like Denniston, Shanty Town and Jackson Bay.

p237

Mt Aspiring National Park & Around Queenstown

Mountains
Lakes
Adrenaline

Mountain Scenery

Queenstown's photogenic combination of Lake Wakatipu and the soaring Remarkables is a real jaw-dropper, as is the wilderness around Glenorchy and Mt Aspiring National Park, stars of *Lord of the Rings* and *The Hobbit*.

Lakes

With Wakatipu, Wanaka, the Mavora Lakes and dozens of mountain tarns, this is Southern Lakes country. Boat on them, hike and bike around them, or freeze off your extremities with a swim.

Adrenaline

Nowhere on earth offers so many adventurous activities. Bungy jump, whitewater raft, skydive and mountain bike and you will have only scratched the surface.

p258

Fiordland & Stewart Island/ Rakiura

National parks
Epic scenery
Bird life

National Parks

Rugged Fiordland National Park is the country's biggest, and one half of Te Wahipounamu – Southwest New Zealand World Heritage area. Smaller Rakiura National Park still takes up around 85% of Stewart Island.

Epic Scenery

The jewel in the crown is remarkable Milford Sound, but take your time exploring the Eglinton Valley on your way to Milford and enjoy the remote appeal of Stewart Island.

Bird Life

Stewart Island is home to a rich bird population boasting more than 100 species including a flotilla of seabirds. It's also your best chance of seeing a kiwi (or at least hearing one) in the wild.

p285

On the Track

Northland, Auckland & Coromandel
p54

Tongariro, Urewera & Central North Island
p84

Abel Tasman, Kahurangi & Nelson Lakes
p165

Taranaki, Whanganui & Around Wellington
p110

Queen Charlotte & Marlborough
p144

West Coast
p237

Canterbury, Arthur's Pass & Aoraki/Mt Cook
p202

Fiordland & Stewart Island/Rakiura
p285

Mt Aspiring National Park & Around Queenstown
p258

Northland, Auckland & Coromandel

Includes ➡

Te Paki
Coastal Track 56
Rangitoto Island
Loop. 61
Aotea Track. 64
Hillary Trail 69
Kauaeranga
Kauri Trail 75

Best Landforms

➡ Cape Reinga (p60)

➡ Ninety Mile Beach (p58)

➡ Rangitoto (p61)

➡ Hirakimata
(Mt Hobson, p68)

➡ Whatipu Scientific
Reserve (p73)

➡ The Pinnacles (p79)

Best Historical Sites

➡ Cape Reinga
Lighthouse (p60)

➡ Rangitoto (p61)

➡ Aotea Track
Kauri Dam (p68)

➡ Kauaeranga Kauri
Trail (p75)

Why Go?

Drawn southwards by stories of New Zealand's legendary national parks and in particular the spectacular Southern Alps, visiting trampers often overlook the northern North Island. This is a mistake. This lush, warm and diverse part of NZ is packed with natural and historical wonders.

The region's most famous landmark is Te Rerenga Wairua (Cape Reinga), the country's northernmost point and a popular pilgrimage. Te Paki Coastal Track affords an opportunity to traverse this coast, taking in the epic Ninety Mile Beach. Closer to Auckland, however, are numerous rewarding tramps including the multiday Hillary Trail accessed just an hour from downtown, and many through the isolated islands of the beautiful Hauraki Gulf. On the Coromandel Peninsula east of Auckland, the Kauaeranga Forest Park affords fascinating insights into the history of NZ's forests and the people who would change them forever.

When to Go

The northern part of the North Island boasts a mild climate with long dry periods in summer. Temperatures range from almost tropical around the northern tip at Cape Reinga, to an average closer to 20°C around Auckland in summer. The islands northeast of Auckland are often a degree or two warmer, averaging 25°C from December to February and sometimes climbing to 30°C. Winters are moist, with most of the rain falling in June and July. Weather on the Coromandel Peninsula may differ between the east and west coats due to the mountain range through the interior. Generally, though, the weather during the summer is good, with temperatures reaching as high as 31°C. Torrential rain, however, can occur at any time, especially during winter.

Background Reading

There is a wealth of tramping guides and natural history books that cover the far north in detail, such as *A Field Guide to Auckland: Exploring the Region's Natural and Historic Heritage* (Ewen Cameron, ed). A worthy companion for visitors to the city, it features 150 interesting sites and details their natural features such as rock formations, plants and animals, as well as history. Another handy companion is *Day Walks of Northland and Greater Auckland* (Gavalas & Janssen) – just one in an eight-strong series of regional day-walking guides published by Penguin Books.

While you're in the bookshop, pick up a copy of *New Zealand Geographic* magazine. This is a stellar bi-monthly, with well-written, in-depth features and stunning photography.

DON'T MISS

It's a long way to the northernmost point of Aotearoa, but what a fitting end it is: Cape Reinga (Te Rerenga Wairua) – 'the leaping place of the spirits' – so named by Maori who believe that the souls of the dead depart from this point on their journey from Aotearoa to their homeland, Hawaiki.

The Cape isn't, however, the northernmost point of the North Island. This honour actually belongs to Surville Cliffs, further east. But no matter. Cape Reinga is undoubtedly the point of pilgrimage, reached 108km (around two hours) from the base of the Aupouri peninsula.

The legend of the leaping and other stories are well told in excellent interpretive displays along the path from a grand gateway to the lighthouse. There are various other ambles around the promontory, taking in expansive views over the flaxy, sandy landscape and the seemingly boundless waters where the Tasman Sea meets the Pacific Ocean. This *does* feel like the end of the line.

DOC Offices & Field Centres

➡ **DOC Auckland Information Centre** (☎ 09-379 6476; www.doc.govt.nz; 137 Quay St, Princes Wharf; ☻ 9am-5pm Mon-Sat)

➡ **DOC Kaitaia Area Office** (☎ 09-408 6014; www.doc.govt.nz; 25 Matthews Ave; ☻ 8am-4.30pm Mon-Fri)

➡ **DOC Great Barrier Field Centre** (☎ 09-429 0044; www.doc.govt.nz; Port Fitzroy; ☻ 8am-4.30pm Mon-Fri)

➡ **Arataki Visitor Centre** (☎ 09-817 0077; www.avc.govt.nz; 300 Scenic Drive; ☻ 9am-5pm Sep-Apr, 10am-4pm Mon-Fri, 9am-5pm Sat & Sun May-Aug)

➡ **DOC Kauaeranga Visitor Centre** (☎ 07-867 9080; www.doc.govt.nz; Kauaeranga Valley Rd; ☻ 8.30am-4pm)

GATEWAY TOWNS

➡ Auckland (p80)
➡ Kaitaia (p81)
➡ Tryphena (p82)
➡ Thames (p83)

NORTHLAND, AUCKLAND & COROMANDEL

Fast Facts

➡ Ninety Mile Beach is a historical misnomer, thought to be overestimated by missionaries travelling along the sand on horseback; its length is in fact just under 90km.

➡ Northland is home to the largest kauri alive today, Tane Mahuta, with a diameter of 4.6m and height of 52m. It is estimated to be between 1200 and 2000 years old.

➡ Only 5% of the Coromandel's original kauri forests remain unlogged, mostly in the Manaia Forest Sanctuary.

Top Tip

Come summer, there's a strong chance of sunshine and high temperatures along these exposed, northern tramps. A long-sleeved shirt, hat and sunscreen are essential to avoid sunburn and heatstroke.

Resources

➡ www.northlandnz.com
➡ www.aucklandnz.com
➡ www.greatbarriernz.com
➡ www.thamesinfo.co.nz

Te Paki Coastal Track

Duration 3 days

Distance 42.5km (26.4 miles)

Track Standard Tramping track

Difficulty Easy

Start Te Paki Stream

End Kapowairua

Nearest Town Kaitaia (p81)

Transport Bus

Summary A scenic tramp along the sweeping Te Paki coastline, encompassing coastal forest, the semitropical sands of seven beaches, and iconic Cape Reinga (Te Rerenga Wairua).

The top of NZ is a place pounded by the seas, whipped by winds and bathed in sunshine. It's a wild and powerful place, where the strong and unforgiving currents of the Tasman Sea and Pacific Ocean sweep along the shorelines, before meeting in a fury of foam just west of Cape Reinga.

Providing trampers with a front-row seat to nature's beauty and drama here is Te Paki Coastal Track, a meander between spectacular beaches, coastal forest, wetlands, towering dunes and NZ's longest beach. Once described as a 'desert coast', Ninety Mile Beach is almost concrete-hard below the high-tide line – which makes for easy tramping – and is bordered much of the way by sand dunes up to 6km wide and rising in places to 143m in height. The tramp then climbs to Cape Reinga, site of the famous lighthouse, but also one of the Maori's most sacred sites, before following clifftops and descending to idyllic, sandy beaches.

The walkway lies entirely in the Te Paki Recreation Reserve and is managed by the Department of Conservation (DOC), which maintains four camping grounds along the track. The tramp can be extended by starting in Ahipara, 83km south of Te Paki Stream at the southern end of Ninety Mile Beach, adding three or four days to the journey. You can also join it at Waipapakauri (69km south of Te Paki Stream), Hukatere (51km) or the Bluff (19km); the 32km portion from Hukatere to the Bluff (a famous spot for surf fishing) is ruler-straight. Keep in mind, however, that you'll encounter cars and tour buses daily on Ninety Mile Beach until you pass Te Paki Stream.

History

Maori were already well established in NZ's far north by the time Europeans arrived, and Cape Reinga had long been regarded by Maori as the departure point of the spirit after death. Only the village of Te Hapua remains from the once-thriving settlements. However, ancient *pa* (fortifications), middens and relics of gardens and food storage pits remain to remind us of a different era in Te Paki's history.

In 1642 Dutch explorer Abel Tasman sailed past and named Cape Maria van Diemen, a point southwest of Cape Reinga. Captain James Cook also sailed by during his first visit to NZ in 1769, but arrived during a storm. He sat tight and refused to leave until he had recorded, with remarkable accuracy, the position of the cape. In 1941 a lighthouse was erected at Cape Reinga. Originally sited at nearby Motuopao Island, it was one of the first in the country to be automated by electric power provided by a diesel generator, and it shines a warning signal 49km out to sea.

Environment

Because of its isolation from mainland NZ for millions of years, Te Paki is described as an ecological treasure trove, with many plants and animals unique to the area. Te Paki is home to a large number of rare insects, plants and trees, including one of the world's rarest trees: the Rata Mochau or Bartlett's rata, which once numbered only five trees in the wild. There are impressive stands of native bush, containing giant kauri and pohutukawa trees, around Sandy Bay, Pandora and Tapotupotu Bay.

The wildlife most trampers will encounter includes coastal birds such as oystercatchers, NZ dotterels, pied stilts, terns, gulls and the occasional white-faced heron. A meandering boardwalk across the Waitahora Lagoon between Kapowairua and Pandora offers trampers a chance to enjoy a dynamic dune lake environment. The area is best known for its high numbers of native land snails, including many colonies of the threatened pupuharakeke (flax snail). Make sure to pack your snorkel gear and take the plunge into crystal-clear, aquamarine water teaming with life.

ℹ Planning

WHEN TO TRAMP

This is an excellent tramp for any time of the year. However, during summer the region has

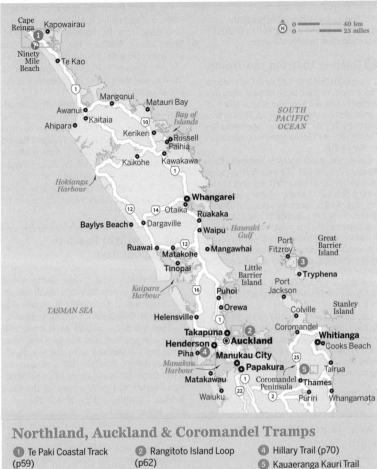

Northland, Auckland & Coromandel Tramps

1 Te Paki Coastal Track (p59)

2 Rangitoto Island Loop (p62)

3 Aotea Track (p66)

4 Hillary Trail (p70)

5 Kauaeranga Kauri Trail (p76)

long spells of dry weather, with temperatures hot enough to be considered almost tropical, and a very intense sun. As there are river crossings on this tramp, you will need to check tide times in advance at Metservice (www.metservice.com)

WHAT TO BRING

As there are no huts on this tramp, you will need a tent. The track is exposed so ensure you have sunscreen, a wide-brimmed hat, long-sleeved shirt and a large-capacity water bottle. Treat all water by either filtering or boiling it. Because of the extreme fire risk in summer, fires are prohibited, so pack a stove.

MAPS & BROCHURES

The track is covered by maps NewTopo *Cape Reinga* 1:75,000 and NZTopo50 AT24 (Cape Reinga).

HUTS & CAMPING

Backcountry campsites (www.doc.govt.nz; free) are located at Twilight Beach and Pandora (both with toilets). There are also two **Standard campsites** (www.doc.govt.nz; $6) at Kapowairua (Spirits Bay) and Tapotupotu Bay. They have fresh water, cold showers and toilets, but no electricity.

INFORMATION SOURCES

DOC Kaitaia Area Office (p55) has all the necessary information on walking Te Paki Coastal Track and other Northland tramps.

Getting to/from the Tramp

It's around 111km from Kaitaia to Cape Reinga. There's no scheduled bus transport along this section of SH1, but a number of local tour companies offer drop-off and pick-up. The key access points are Te Paki Stream and Tapotupotu Bay. The logistics are trickier from Kapowairua as it's further off SH1.

Kaitaia-based tour operator **Harrisons Cape Runner** (☑ 0800 227 373; www.harrisonscapereingatours.co.nz) has scheduled daily tours departing 9am from Kaitaia, returning by 5pm. For the price of a $50 tour you're dropped off and picked up any day you wish, as long as there is an empty seat on the bus – outside the high season of mid-December to mid-January that's usually not a problem. If you want to guarantee a seat on the return trip it's another $50. Based 13km east of Kaitaia at Ahipara, **Sand Safaris** (☑ 09-408 1778, 0800 869 090; www.sandsafaris.co.nz) also offers trailhead drop-offs as part of its $50 tour.

Olly Lancaster (☑ 09-409 7500) offers on-demand transport to all trailheads including Kapowairua for $70 per person (cheaper for more people) from his base in Paua, around 30km shy of the cape. Secure vehicle storage and basic accommodation is also available.

The Tramp

Day 1: Te Paki Stream to Twilight Beach

3½–4 HOURS, 12KM

Te Paki Stream (Kauaeparaoa) marks the southern border of Te Paki Recreation Reserve, but is more famous for being a 'quicksand stream'. If your bus drops you off at the Te Paki Stream Rd car park, rather than at the stream mouth, it's an additional 45 minutes of wet trekking through the stream.

From the end of the stream head northwest along the wide, flat expanse of Ninety Mile Beach, flanked by sand dunes on the east and the pounding surf of the Tasman Sea to the west. After an hour you pass a campsite and come to Waitapu Stream, which may or may not be dry. The track then leaves the beach and begins a steep climb – via steps, thankfully – to the southern side of Scott Point. Cross a small gully then resume climbing steeply before topping out to good views of Ninety Mile Beach below.

On Scott Point the track moves into scrub and then joins a 4WD track to arrive at a good area for backcountry camping. There are no facilities, but the grassy site sits high above the pounding surf; you can see over to Cape Maria van Diemen during the day, and the glow of its lighthouse is visible at night.

The track continues across Scott Point, well marked by orange posts to guide you through the maze. It takes 1½ hours to cross the point and descend onto Twilight Beach (Te Paengarehia), which is named after a schooner that sank here in 1871. Twilight Campsite, near the southern end of the beach, has composting toilets and water from a tank, the safety of which cannot be guaranteed.

Day 2: Twilight Beach to Tapotupotu Bay

6 HOURS, 13KM

It's a 45-minute walk to the northern end of the beach, where there's a small stream and a signposted route to the Te Werahi gate along Cape Reinga Rd, a 1½-hour walk away.

Head left along an old 4WD track that skirts a swamp and then climbs a ridge that separates the wetland from the sea. Heading northwest through flax and manuka scrub there are great views of Cape Maria van Diemen and even a peek of the Cape Reinga Lighthouse. Having left the ridge and headed into sand dunes, the track reaches a signposted junction one hour from Twilight Beach. Turn west (left) to continue onto Cape Maria van Diemen. This side trail follows the coast for 40 minutes, providing excellent views most of the way to the lighthouse that was built after the one on nearby Motuopao Island closed in 1941.

There are two ways to reach Te Werahi Beach from the end of Cape Maria van Diemen. Most trampers backtrack and head north (left) at the junction to follow the high-level track around Herangi Hill (159m). Going this way takes 45 minutes to one hour to walk to the southern end of Te Werahi Beach.

At low tide, more adventurous souls can follow the rocky shoreline. If you have any concerns about the tide or your timing, take the high-level track. The tracks meet at Te Werahi Stream, which should be crossed near low tide.

From the stream it takes 45 minutes to one hour to tramp along the long, sweeping

Te Paki Coastal Track

10 km
5 miles

Cape Reinga (Te Rerenga Wairua)

Tarawamaomao Point

Motuopao Island

Cape Maria van Diemen

Te Kohatu Point

Te Werahi Beach

Herangi Hill (159m)

Hiriki Pa

Cape Reinga Walkway

Te Werahi Gate

Te Werahi Stream

Day 3

Sandy Bay (Ngataeawhiti)

SOUTH PACIFIC OCEAN

Tapotupotu Bay

Darkies Ridge

Tirikawa Pa (285m)

Tohureo

Pandora Campsite

Pandora Bay

Pandora Point

Te Paki (310m)

Gate

Kauri Bush

Watarihi Stream

Te Paki Recreation Reserve

Hooper Point (Ngataea)

END Kapowairua

Pandora Track

Te Horo Beach

Waitahora Stream

Kawanui Stream

95m

Old Earth Well

Spirits Bay (Piwhane Bay)

Spirits Bay Rd

Te Hapua Rd

Pd

Parengarenga Harbour

Paua Rd

Te Hapua

Waitiki Landing

Far North Rd

Karatia (Thoms Landing)

Kaitaia (85km)

The Big Lake

Kohuronaki (292m)

Papawiri Hill (124m)

Te Paki

Keene Hill (115m)

Lake Ngakeketa

START

Te Paki Stream (Kauaparaoa)

Bluff (19km); Hukatere (51km); Ahipara (83km)

Sand dunes

Waitapu Stream

Ninety Mile Beach

Far North Rd

Tupotupotu Stream

Cape Reinga Rd

Te Werahi Stream

Twilight Beach (Te Paengarehia)

Tehepouto Point

Pitokuku Point

Maungatiketike Point

Twilight Campsite

Day 2

Pukekarea (120m)

Scott Point

TASMAN SEA

Te Werahi Beach to Tarawamaomao Point at the northern end. At high tide you'll get your boots wet, as the cliffs close in at the northern end before the track climbs sharply away from the beach. Continue along steep clifftops where on clear days you're rewarded with spectacular views of sandy beaches, Cape Maria van Diemen and Motuopao Island.

Within an hour of the ascent from Te Werahi Beach, the walkway emerges at Cape Reinga. The lighthouse is a 10-minute stroll away.

Reinga means 'place of leaping' in Maori. On the headland, perched above a turbulent eddy of swirling kelp, is a solitary pohutukawa tree. Maori spirits were said to have descended to the underworld by sliding down a root into the sea, emerging on Ohaua – the highest point of the Three Kings Islands – to bid farewell before returning to their ancestral homeland, Hawaiki.

The Three Kings Islands are visible on a clear day. A nature reserve, they are home to a number of rare and endangered trees, as well as a rich abundance and variety of marine life.

Interpretive signage provides an insight into the natural and human history of this magnificent site, one of NZ's most photographed spots. The swirling seas where the Pacific Ocean and Tasman Sea meet is utterly mesmerising, and keeping an eye on the waters may reward you with sightings of the pods of dolphins that round the cape in feeding forays.

There are flash flush toilets at the cape, which cater to the hordes of tourists who make the popular pilgrimage here.

The walkway resumes in the car park and heads east, sidling a hill, then descending to Sandy Bay (Ngatangawhiti), a pretty spot with a freshwater stream and grassy flats beneath pohutukawa trees. It is reached 30 minutes from the lighthouse. On the other side of the small bay the track begins a steep climb to a coastal ridge, turns inland for a spell, then returns to the clifftops and good views, from where it descends sharply towards Tapotupotu Bay, 2½ hours from Cape Reinga.

Tapotupotu is one of the most scenic beaches in the far north, a horseshoe of white sand and light-green seas enclosed by forested cliffs. There's a freshwater stream here and a road-accessible and therefore well-populated DOC campsite with a shelter, cold showers, toilets and drinking water.

Day 3: Tapotupotu Bay to Kapowairua

7–8 HOURS, 17.5KM

Many trampers pass up this rewarding section of track due to the difficulty of arranging transport out of Kapowairua. This leg of the journey can be extended into two days by an overnight stop at tranquil Pandora Bay, where a small backcountry campsite nestles among burgeoning pohutukawa. The first part of the day is along old ridgetop farm tracks, the second is through stunning Pandora Bay and Te Horo Bay.

At Tapotupotu Bay, begin by walking to the end of the campsite and cross the stream via a boardwalk and small bridge. The track resumes at the end of the bridge and leads into a bush-clad hill and makes a 200m climb to the top of the coastal ridge. For the next 40 minutes to one hour there are spectacular views of Tapotupotu Bay and all the way back to Cape Reinga, before the track descends inland.

You then climb over Tirikawa Pa (285m) and traverse Darkies Ridge to reach the Pandora Track, an old metalled road, at a signposted junction within two hours of the campsite.

Just south along the Pandora Track, 15 minutes from the junction, is a sidetrack to Te Paki (310m), the highest point in the area. Plan an hour for the return trip to the summit, where you can see the remains of a wartime radar station and a spectacular panorama of the coastline.

Pandora Track heads northeast and leads down to secluded Pandora Bay, reached one hour from the junction or four to five hours (9km) from Tapotupotu Bay. Pandora Campsite, which has composting toilets and tank water, sits on the grassy flats alongside the beach, surrounded by fruit trees and the remains of an old tourist camp from the 1920s. It's the perfect spot to strip down to your nothings and jump into the sea. A snorkel and mask will prove welcome here.

If you hit the beach near low tide you can reach Spirits Bay by the seaward route, around the rocky shoreline. Otherwise, follow the orange posts that mark the high-tide route, as it climbs a pair of headlands divided by Wairahi Stream.

Once on the bay you can follow Te Horo Beach to Kapowairua at the eastern end of the beach, a three-hour (8.5km) trek from Pandora. After the rock-hard surface of

Ninety Mile Beach, many trampers find the soft sand of Te Horo to be exhausting work. The alternative is to tramp behind the sand dunes along an old vehicle track marked by orange poles. The walking is easier and the wetlands you skirt are an interesting change from the pounding sea.

For either route you must first cross Waitahora Lagoon, which is where **Waitahora Stream** flows into the ocean. A boardwalk provides safe passage and a close-up experience of this dynamic wetland environment. Look out for flowering native hibiscus in the late summer.

Rangitoto Island Loop

Duration 4–5 hours

Distance 10km (6.2 miles)

Track Standard Walking track

Difficulty Easy

Start/End Rangitoto Wharf

Nearest Town Auckland (p80)

Transport Boat

Summary Tramp to the summit of Rangitoto Volcano and then along the coast of the island it created 600 years ago. The views of Auckland are among the best in the region.

Even if you only have a day to spare in Auckland before moving on, seriously consider warming up your tramping legs with this easy yet fascinating walk in Rangitoto Island Scenic Reserve. Part of the Hauraki Gulf Marine Park, this 23-sq-km island is only 10km northeast of the city, and features several kilometres of tramping tracks that wind through the black lava fields and around the summit crater of its volcano.

Rangitoto (www.rangitoto.org) is connected to Motutapu Island by a causeway and, if you take a tent and sleeping bag, you can turn this tramp into a two-day adventure. At the head of Islington Bay you pick up the Motutapu Walkway on the east side of the causeway, and follow it to the DOC camping ground at Home Bay, a tramp of 1½ hours across farmland and clifftops. The next day is a 2½-hour tramp back to Islington Bay along farm roads via Administration Bay. The extended Rangitoto–Motutapu Circuit is expected to be formalised in 2014, making for a three-day adventure with hut-style accommodation along the way.

TE ARAROA – NEW ZEALAND'S TRAIL

In a nation of trampers, the idea of a track the length of NZ – from Cape Reinga on the northern point of the North Island, to Bluff on the southern tip of the South Island – has always been an appealing one. The idea was first proposed in 1967 by the Federated Mountain Clubs (FMC), and was on the agenda in 1976 when the New Zealand Walkways Commission (NZWC) was established.

After putting in more than 100 small trails, the NZWC was dissolved in 1989, without having progressed the long-trail concept. That goal was revived in 1994 when Geoff Chapple wrote a piece for the *Sunday Star-Times* urging the construction of Te Araroa – New Zealand's Trail. Support poured in, resulting in the establishment of the Te Araroa Trust (www.teararoa.org.nz), with Sir Edmund Hillary as a patron. The trust opened its first trail – a 22km section between Waitangi and Kerikeri – in 1995. From small acorns...

Officially launched in 2011, having been driven by Chapple and many volunteers, Te Araroa today is a continuous trail from Cape Reinga to Bluff. It's 3000km long, more than double the distance from NZ's top to tail as the crow flies. The expected completion time is anywhere from 100 to 150 days, but it can walked any way you like, taking anything from a few hours, a few days, to a week or more.

The trail is a mixture of existing tracks and new, traversing many of NZ's most famous landscapes. Forty percent crosses conservation land, with the remainder linking towns and cities across the map, doing so with an aim of 'encouraging social and economic transactions ... for *marae* stays and other cultural experiences, also food and accommodation. The track corridor showcases a wide variety of NZ experiences – natural, cultural, and historic.'

Geoff Chapple stood down as Te Araroa Trust CEO in 2012, having committed 18 years to the project. His efforts were honoured with a gong in the 2012 Queens Birthday Honours.

The official guidebook – *Te Araroa: A Walking Guide to New Zealand's Long Trail* – provides an overview of the route; the website is excellent for trip planning.

Rangitoto Island Loop

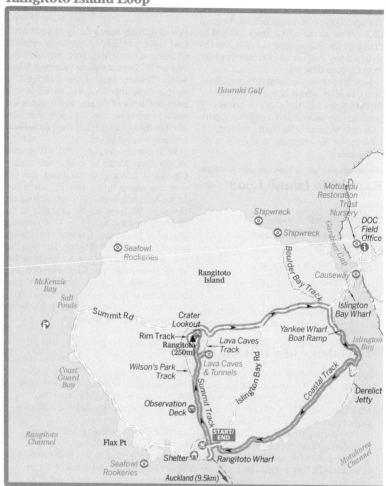

History

Rangitoto is a relatively young volcano, having emerged from the sea in a series of fiery eruptions only 600 years ago. Maori were living on neighbouring Motutapu Island at the time of the eruptions and Rangitoto's dramatic appearance ensured it would always have an important place in their history and mythology. The island's name is derived from the Maori phrase *Te Rangi totongia a Tama-te-kapua* (the day the blood of Tama-te-kapua was shed). Tama-te-kapua was chief of one of the canoes that brought the early Polynesian settlers. He

arrived about 1350 and then lost a major battle with the Tainui at Islington Bay, which lies between Rangitoto and Motutapu Islands.

The Crown purchased Rangitoto in 1854 from the Maori, and during the 1920s and 1930s prisoners built 19km of hard-packed roads and trails on the island, some of which are still in use. During WWII Rangitoto was a base for harbour defence and a radar station. A handful of the old cement huts and foundations can still be seen along the tracks.

heats to very high temperatures. Still, plants and bush are slowly covering the open lava fields. Moss, lichen and algae were the first plants to colonise, followed by pohutukawa trees. Rangitoto now has the largest remaining pohutukawa forest in NZ. The island is also home to more than 250 species of native trees and flowering plants, including 40 kinds of fern and several species of orchid. The new forest does not support many land birds, but seabirds are common along the shoreline, and the population includes a black-backed gull colony.

ⓘ Planning

WHEN TO TRAMP

You can tramp year-round on Rangitoto Island, though it can be a hot and dry place during summer, often a degree or two warmer than Auckland. From December through February the temperature is usually around 25°C, and at times can reach 30°C. When the sun and heat reflect off the lava fields, it feels like you're tramping through an oven. Christmas and Easter holidays can be very busy, and with so many people heading for the Rangitoto summit it's like a pilgrimage. Once you are away from the Summit Track, however, you will encounter far fewer trampers, and possibly none at all on the Coastal Track.

WHAT TO BRING

As these are offshore islands with no available supplies, you will need to bring everything with you. Sunscreen and a wide-brimmed hat are advisable, as are strong walking shoes, if not boots.

MAPS & BROCHURES

The track is covered by NewTopo map *Rangitoto–Motutapu* 1:42,000, as well as NZ-Topo50 BA32 (Auckland).

HUTS & CAMPING

There are no huts or other accommodation on Rangitoto Island. On Motutapu Island there is a **Standard campsite** (www.doc.govt.nz; $6) at Home Bay, with water, toilets and showers. Bookings are essential.

INFORMATION SOURCES

DOC Auckland Information Centre (p55) supplies information and handles bookings for tracks nationwide.

ⓘ Getting to/from the Tramp

Rangitoto is reached on a 30-minute ferry ride from Auckland, departing from the pier at the bottom of Queen St. There are several services daily (leaving Auckland 9.15am, 10.30am and

Environment

Rangitoto, the largest of the 50 volcanic cones and craters in the Auckland area, is the only one of its kind in NZ. The black basaltic lava that erupted and now constitutes much of the island makes Rangitoto one of the few basalt shield volcanoes in the world, and a miniature version of the great volcanoes of Hawaii. Although Rangitoto is thought to be extinct, the Auckland volcano field is regarded as only dormant – that is, 'resting' but potentially active.

The lava rock is an inhospitable environment for plant life, as it is highly porous and

12.15pm; returning 12.45pm and 3.30pm; additional services at weekends) run by **Fullers** (📞 09-367 9111; www.fullers.co.nz; Ferry Bldg, 99 Quay St).

🥾 The Tramp

4–5 HOURS, 10KM

At the new Rangitoto Wharf there is a large day shelter in which to escape the sun, an outdoor saltwater swimming pool and toilets. There is also drinking water here; fill up your bottles as this is the only source of safe water on the island.

The Summit Track is well marked and heads north into bush, but within 10 minutes breaks out into a lava field, a jumbled mass of black rocks. In the middle of it is an observation deck with interpretive displays. From here the track continues climbing at a very gentle rate, passing a signposted junction to Wilson's Park Track (left) before reaching the Lava Caves Track (right), 45 minutes from the wharf. Follow this sidetrack for 15 minutes to a series of caves and tunnels, formed when the outer surface of the lava cooled after an eruption (when the liquid inner lava drained, the outer shell remained as a cave).

Return to the Summit Track and continue upwards. The trail steepens for the final 15 minutes to the crater rim, but is never what anybody could consider strenuous. About 2km from the wharf you reach Crater Lookout, a large wooden deck. The Rangitoto crater is 60m deep and 200m wide. The inner edge is dotted with tall pohutukawa, while in the crater itself there's a thicket of manuka and kanuka.

Head west at the deck to follow the Rim Track, which immediately climbs a long stairway to the highest point on Rangitoto; the 259m summit is marked by a large trig on the edge of the crater. There are great views here, including a fine panorama of downtown Auckland. Also located here is a cement hut that served as a fire command post during WWII.

Continue along the Rim Track to return to the Crater Lookout in 10 minutes. You never see the crater from the trail, but a few minutes from the trig you pass a view of the west side of Rangitoto Island, taking in the lighthouse in McKenzie Bay. Just beyond it is another cement hut that served as a wireless radar room.

Back at Crater Lookout, follow the long set of stairs that descends to the northeast

and ends at Summit Rd, used by Fullers to drive visitors up from McKenzie Bay. Head east on the narrow gravel road as it gently descends through more lava fields. Within 30 to 40 minutes of the stairs on Summit Rd, you'll arrive at the signposted intersection with Islington Bay Rd. Continue heading east towards Islington Bay, and in 30 minutes you'll reach a signposted junction with Boulder Bay Track (left). This track is a 1½-hour return walk to Boulder Bay on the north side of the island. The bay was once used as a wrecking ground for old ships, and in its first cove are four wrecks – though none can be seen from the island.

Another 15 minutes from the Boulder Bay Track junction, or 5km from the wharf, you reach a signposted junction; the road to the left continues to Islington Bay Wharf and the causeway to Motutapu Island. Take the road to the right, marked as the Coastal Track, heading south along the shoreline of Islington Bay. If it's a holiday or weekend the bay will be filled with boats at anchor.

The gravel road ends at the Yankee Wharf boat ramp, and from here the Coastal Track continues along the shoreline for another 10 minutes before heading inland. For the next 1½ hours the track stays away from the shoreline and it is a moderately difficult tramp over a path of loose lava rock. This can be hot and tiring, heading through bush with little to look at.

Eventually the track emerges at a large lava field, crossing it to return to the shoreline. The final 30 to 40 minutes to the Rangitoto Wharf is a well-beaten path along the shoreline, where you can search for seabirds or view Auckland on the horizon. The Coastal Track joins Islington Bay Rd just before you reach the day shelter and swimming pool at Rangitoto Wharf.

Aotea Track

Duration 3 days

Distance 25km (15.5 miles)

Track Standard Tramping & easy tramping

Difficulty Moderate

Start/End Whangaparapara Rd

Nearest Town Tryphena (p82)

Transport Bus

Summary Explore the rugged interior of Great Barrier Island, via a climb to the island's highest peak, a soak in a natural hot spring and a visit to one of the best-preserved kauri dams in the country.

Great Barrier Island (Aotea) is 88km northeast of Auckland, set within the Hauraki Gulf Marine Park. It features numerous long sandy beaches on its eastern side, deep sheltered inlets on its west, and in the middle a rugged area of steep ridges rising to a high point of 621m at Hirakimata (Mt Hobson).

Of the island's 285 sq km, 220 sq km is conservation land, with the central mass – known as the Great Barrier Forest – under DOC management. A network of tracks through wild bush combines with old logging roads and tramways to provide numerous tramping opportunities. Natural hot springs, towering kauri trees, rock formations, the relics of kauri dams and sweeping views of the Hauraki Gulf are the most interesting features of the area; the island's relaxing, get-away-from-it-all aura is a bonus.

This track loops around the central mountainous area and is an easily manageable adventure for reasonably fit beginner or experienced trampers. It can be walked in either direction, and although the route described here starts and ends at Whangaparapa Rd, there are two other access points. From the east, it is possible to reach Mt Heale Hut (in three to 3½ hours) starting at **Windy Canyon**, and tramping Palmers and South Fork Tracks, accessed from Aotea Rd at the top of Whangapoua Hill. This is a short and easy option with superb views. Trampers can also set off from **Port Fitzroy**, the island's other main harbour. Port Fitzroy, one hour's drive from Tryphena, is serviced by ferries, has a store for provisions, and Akapoua campsite lies to the south.

History

The Hauraki Gulf was one of the first places in NZ settled by Polynesians. Captain Cook sighted and named Great Barrier Island (it seemed to bar the entrance to Hauraki Gulf) in 1769. As happened elsewhere in the far north, it was Great Barrier Island's natural riches that led Europeans to settle there. The first European settlement was a village established by Cornish miners in 1842 at Miners Cove in the island's northwest corner, and whalers often worked the waters offshore in the 1800s.

It was, however, the kauri tree and its natural by-product – gum – that was the most sought-after and longest-lasting resource. By the 1930s logging had devastated the land. Timber drives, using kauri dams and large amounts of water to flush the logs out to sea, had been especially destructive, and quickly eroded valleys and stream beds, leaving a broad silt flat at river mouths. In 1946 the New Zealand Forest Service began rehabilitating the forest and, in 1973, it was declared a forest recreation reserve. When DOC was established in 1987 it took over administration of the Crown land.

Environment

Great Barrier Island is predominantly volcanic rock, the eroded remnants of a line of andesitic and rhyolitic volcanoes that erupted more than three million years ago. The result is a rugged landscape, and one of the last wilderness areas in the Auckland region. The heart of the island is a regenerating 80-sq-km kauri forest, crowned by Hirakimata (Mt Hobson). On the west coast, steep forested ridges extend to the sea, where they merge into a flooded coastal landscape and a maze of bays and harbours, making Great Barrier a popular destination for kayakers. The east coast is gentler, featuring sweeping white beaches and alluvial flats.

The island is a haven for a long list of rare and endangered birds. More than 60% of NZ's entire brown teal population lives on Great Barrier, and they can often be seen in the Whangapoua and Okiwi Estuaries. The island also serves as a stronghold for the North Island kaka and banded rail. There are also some spotless crakes and fernbirds.

Lower to the ground you might spot a lizard: Great Barrier Island has one of the most diverse populations in the country. The 13 species recorded include the large and rare chevron skink, which is found only on Great Barrier and Little Barrier Islands.

🛈 Planning

WHEN TO TRAMP

Tramping takes place year-round, although the wet winters can quickly turn the tracks to mud. The peak season is mid-December to mid-January. However, because of the cost of getting to Great Barrier Island, the tracks and huts, although busy, are not overrun. Visitors begin thinning out after January, and many believe the best time to explore the island is March to May, when temperatures are still warm but the rainy season has yet to set in.

Aotea Track

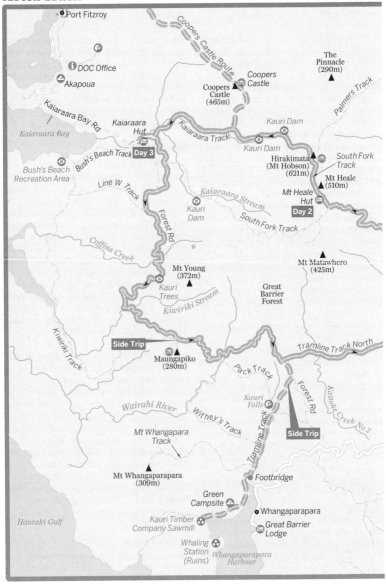

WHAT TO BRING

There is no reticulated water on the island, but freshwater is available from various sites. While most water is considered safe to drink, the parasite giardia may be present. All water should be boiled or treated before drinking. Fires are not permitted at any campsites, so bring a stove if you plan to camp.

There's also no mains power on the island and no streetlights, so bring a torch (flashlight). Food is available, but it is more expensive than on the mainland and shop hours are limited, so it's wise to bring all supplies from Auckland.

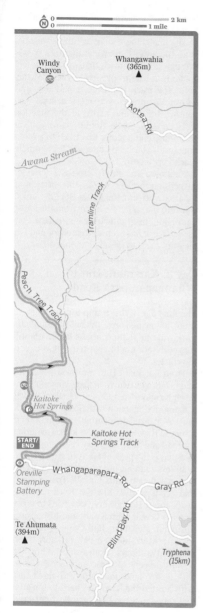

MAPS & BROCHURES

NZTopo50 map AY34 (Claris) covers this tramp, as does NewTopo *Aotea Great Barrier* 1:90,000. DOC's *Aotea Track* and *Great Barrier Island* brochures are also helpful.

HUTS & CAMPING

There are two **Serviced huts** (www.doc.govt. nz; $15) on Great Barrier Island, one of which is the new Mt Heale Hut that has gas cookers; the other, Kaiaraara, has a wood stove. Backcountry hut passes and tickets are not valid in these two huts. There are also five **Scenic campsites** (www.doc.govt.nz; $10).

Huts and campsites should be booked online before you head out to the island, particularly in December and January, as camping is not allowed outside of designated camping grounds, and the number of campers at each site is also restricted. If the huts and camping grounds are full, you may have no alternative but to return to the mainland.

INFORMATION SOURCES

For information before you set off from the mainland, call in at DOC Auckland Information Centre (p55). On the island, there is a small information counter at the airport that is attended during the high season. You can pick up leaflets and brochures about the track from here and **DOC Great Barrier Field Centre** (☑ 09-429 0044; www.doc.govt.nz; Port Fitzroy; ☺ 8am-4.30pm Mon-Fri), which is a 20-minute walk south of the ferry landing. Call in for brochures, maps and weather information, and to sign the intentions book for longer walks.

❶ Getting to/from the Tramp

This loop track begins and ends on the Kaitoke Hot Springs Track on Whangaparapara Rd, 4km west of Claris. **Great Barrier Travel** (☑ 09-429 0474; www.greatbarriertravel.co.nz) offers airport and accommodation transfers and can hook you up with shuttle services and rental cars. **GBI Shuttle Buses** (☑ 09-429 0062; www.greatbarrierisland.co.nz) offers on-demand transport services around the island.

🚶 The Tramp

Day 1: Whangaparapara Road To Mt Heale Hut

3–4 HOURS, 8KM, 480M ASCENT

The trailhead is indicated at Whangaparapara Rd by a large display sign and a toilet. Your first leg is along **Kaitoke Hot Springs Track**, which is easy and flat as it crosses Kaitoke Wetlands, where you should look out for birds. You may hear the rare fernbird around this area.

It takes around 40 minutes to reach **Kaitoke Hot Springs,** the best of which are half-hidden in a canopy of trees. Not only are some of them too hot, they may also contain amoebic parasites, so *do not immerse your* *head in the hot water.* You could have a soak here, although you could also wait until day three, when you're on your way out again.

After a brief but steep climb, you join Tramline Track North and turn right. Along this wide, old tramline are relics of the logging era, when the Kauri Timber Company used to haul kauri logs out of the forest.

Peach Tree Track soon appears on the left, which you should follow to climb steadily through the regenerating forest to reach Mt Heale Hut. There are spectacular views from here, especially on clear evenings when there are striking sunsets over Little Barrier Island (Hauturu).

Day 2: Mt Heale Hut To Kaiaraara Hut

3 HOURS, 6KM, 227M ASCENT, 627M DESCENT

From Mt Heale Hut, it's a steep 40-minute climb north along South Fork Track to the junction with Kaiaraara Track, which descends towards Kaiaraara Hut. Before starting the descent, however, be sure to take the five-minute sidetrack leading to the summit of Hirakimata (Mt Hobson; 621m).

The peak has a wooden platform with a large trig and views of both sides of Great Barrier Island, as well as the outer islands in the Hauraki Gulf. It is also the site of several rare species, being a spot favoured by the tomtit, black petrel and recently reintroduced North Island robin, and it's also frequented by kakariki and kaka. The beautiful endemic Great Barrier tree daisy and tiny sundews like it here as well.

You will encounter a mix of steep paths, stairways and bridges as you descend the steep west slope of the mountain, ending just before you arrive at the upper kauri dam. All that remains of the dam is a stack of large logs and rusting cables, but the view of the sheer rock walls of the gorge below is stunning.

Around 40 minutes from the Hirakimata (Mt Hobson) summit you'll see a two-minute side track to NZ's best-preserved kauri driving dam, built in the 1920s along with six smaller dams upstream. This lower kauri dam is truly impressive: a massive, wooden structure held in place across the gorge by huge kauri logs. When this dam was tripped, the force of water sent the logs all the way to Kaiaraara Bay, where they were held in huge booms until being floated to sawmills in Auckland. These dams were constructed in 1926 and amazingly, after all the work to build them, were used for only three years.

The intriguing scenery continues just beyond the lower dam, when the track passes through a nikau grove that makes you feel you're in a true tropical wilderness. At this point the track improves remarkably, and within 15 minutes you cross a large suspension bridge and arrive at the junction with Coopers Castle Route (right) – it's a 45-minute climb along this track to a lookout, and if you keep going you'll eventually reach Port Fitzroy.

Kaiaraara Track (left) crosses a series of suspension bridges across this branch of Kaiaraara Stream. Kaiaraara Hut (28 bunks) is just to the right (1½ hours from the lower dam). Built in 1973 by the New Zealand Forest Service, it has been well cared for and is a pleasant place to spend an evening.

Day 3: Kaiaraara Hut to Whangaparapara Road

4 HOURS, 11KM

The final day of this tramp is an easy grade route, following Forest Rd, built in the 1950s to provide firefighters access to the island's rugged interior, although today it is closed to vehicles.

From Kaiaraara Hut, return to Forest Rd and head right. The road takes you on a gentle climb and within 15 minutes (1km) passes a signposted junction with South Fork Track (left). You need to continue climbing, and soon you'll see an impressive kauri tree along the road and then, high above, the stone fortress that is the peak of Mt Young (372m).

In less than an hour you reach the signposted junction with Line W Track (right) that heads west to Kiwiriki Track (25 minutes). Forest Rd, however, descends to cross Coffins Creek, with a dark and lush grotto upstream, and then climbs to a signposted spur track leading to a pair of kauri trees, reached two hours (5km) from the hut. It's a short descent to these impressive giants, with one so large four people couldn't link arms around the trunk. It's hard to imagine that at one time most of Great Barrier Island was covered with trees like these.

The road descends to cross Kiwiriki Stream and then makes the longest climb of the day, a steady 30-minute (1.5km) march towards Maungapiko (280m). You top out near Kiwiriki Track (right) and a short spur track to Maungapiko Lookout. This rocky outcrop is a 20-minute side trip to fine views of the island's west coast. Forest Rd descends to reach a junction with **Pack Track** (right), 30 minutes from the lookout.

Continue along Forest Rd to the junction of the **Tramline Track**, which leads south to Green Campsite, an hour or so away.

Should you decide to skip the side trip to Green Campsite, continue on Tramline Track North towards Kaitoke Hot Springs Track. The wide track drops steeply through the rugged terrain to Kaitoke Creek No 2, ascends on the other side, and then descends again to a tributary of Kaitoke Creek No 1. It follows the stream, gradually dropping towards the eastern side of the island, until it arrives at a signposted junction for Kaitoke Hot Springs Track.

Head right (southeast) on Kaitoke Hot Springs Track, which immediately crosses Kaitoke Stream. It then climbs steadily to a ridge, where there are excellent views of Kaitoke Swamp, the surrounding ridges and the crashing surf of Kaitoke Beach to the east.

Before long you will reach the Whangaparapara Rd trailhead, thus closing the loop. Before you go, be sure to check out the massive stone walls of the **Oreville stamping battery**, above and below Whangaparapara Rd. They are an impressive reminder of the mining period.

SIDE TRIP: GREEN CAMPSITE
2–3 HOURS, 6KM RETURN

From the junction of Forest Rd and the Tramline Track, head south on the latter towards Green Campsite. On the way, you can detour to **Kauri Falls**, where a 3m waterfall empties into a swimming pool.

Continue on the Tramline Track right (southwest), crossing bridges over several small streams and passing signposted junctions to Withey's Track and the Mt Whangaparapara Track. Within 30 minutes you arrive at a fenced paddock. Step over the fence and arrive at a junction just before a footbridge.

To reach the secluded Green Campsite, on the western shore of the harbour, follow **Old Mill Track**, signposted at the junction. It's an easy 15-minute walk to the grassy meadow, where the DOC camping ground offers a view of the harbour, a shelter, sinks, display panels and toilets.

From the campsite, a rough track continues west, climbing steeply over two ridges to reach the site of the **Kauri Timber Company sawmill**, the largest in the southern hemisphere in 1910. Today, all that remains

are the concrete foundations, some pilings, and an old steam traction engine.

At low tide you can continue around the shore of a small bay for 30 minutes to the ruins of an old **whaling station**.

Hillary Trail

Duration 4 days

Distance 75km (46.6 miles)

Track Standard Tramping track

Difficulty Moderate to demanding

Start Arataki Visitor Centre

End Muriwai Beach

Nearest Town Auckland (p80)

Transport Bus, train, private transport

Summary Opened in 2010 in the name of NZ's most famous mountaineer, this trail traverses the rugged Waitakere Ranges, offering a multiday wilderness tramp on the doorstep of Auckland.

Bordering Auckland's wild west coast is the Waitakere Ranges Regional Park, a largely rugged and remote wilderness surprisingly close to NZ's largest city. The gateway to the Waitakere Ranges, Arataki Visitor Centre, is only 25km from downtown Auckland.

Managed by the Auckland Council, the Waitakere Ranges Regional Park is one of the most popular wilderness areas in the country. Each year it attracts more than one million visitors to its rainforest, black-sand beaches and coastal settlements.

The park is criss-crossed by around 240km of tracks, many of which link to form the signature Hillary Trail, formally opened in January 2010. This 75km track starts at Arataki Visitor Centre and skirts around the Manukau Harbour before following the coast to finish at Muriwai. A side branch, which shortens the last day, heads inland to finish at Swanson Railway Station.

In creating the Hillary Trail, the Auckland Council both celebrates the achievements of NZ's most famous adventurer, and hopes that urban Aucklanders will get outdoors and experience the wilderness on their doorstep. And so they should – the trail has much to recommend it to residents and visitors alike, including lush, sub-tropical forest, rolling farmland, waterfalls, sandy beaches backed by dunes and cliffs, and splendid lookouts taking in a diverse range of views in every direction.

Hillary Trail

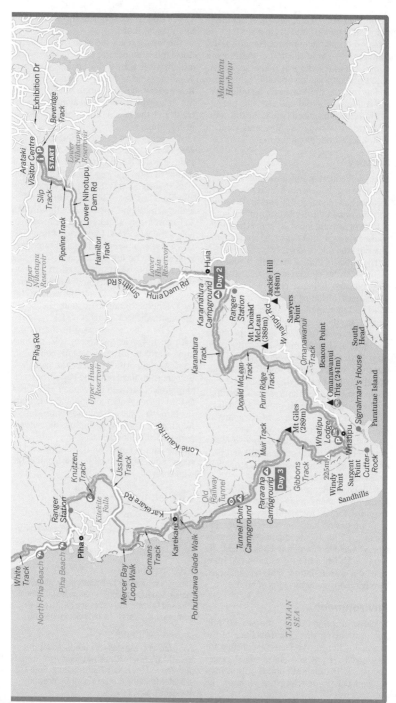

The trail can be completed in either direction, and is divided into distinct sections. As it passes through a number of small coastal communities along the route, there are a number of entry and exit points and alternative accommodation options – which also means that the trail can easily be tailored to suit tramping abilities and available time.

The option described here is the full, four-day option, staying at Auckland Council camping grounds along the route.

History

Maori settlement in this area dates back 700 to 800 years. Te Kawerau a Maki people lived between the Manukau Harbour in the south and Muriwai in the north, living off the bounty from ocean and forest. This *iwi* (tribe) still holds strong spiritual ties to the land and has inherited the role of *kaitiaki* (guardians).

The arrival of Europeans in the 1830s led to the most visible change in the area. The logging industry, and later farm clearance, saw native trees (including most accessible kauri) felled and thousands of hectares of forest destroyed. Bushmen dammed streams to float logs to the coast. They built several tramlines, including a 14km tramline down the coast from Piha to Whatipu, which was used to transport kauri logs to a wharf at Paratutae Island. Remains of the tramline can be seen on the coast between Karekare and Whatipu.

The park is home to numerous historic sites, from Maori *pa* sites to remnants of the logging industry. Water was, and still is, a valuable resource in the area. Five major reservoirs were built between 1910 and 1970 and these continue to supply metropolitan Auckland with water today.

Waitakere Ranges Regional Park was formed over many years dating from 1900, when the former Auckland City Council began purchasing land for water supply and because of its scenic qualities. Originally named Auckland Centennial Memorial Park, it was established in 1940 to mark 100 years since the city's founding. This was enlarged through many generous gifts of land.

Environment

Volcanic eruptions under the sea 20 million years ago formed the backbone of the Waitakere Ranges, and are responsible for its rugged terrain and sharp-edged ridges and peaks. The highest point is only 474m – Te Toiokawharu, northwest of Huia on the Twin Peaks Track – but trampers will find many steep climbs.

The ranges guard the western flank of the Auckland isthmus, and the prevailing westerlies have, in turn, created a rainforest from Whatipu as far north as Te Henga (Bethells Beach). Few stands of virgin timber remain, but regrowth is vigorous along the west coast and the regenerating forest is now a lush setting.

A century after being decimated by logging, kauri in the ranges is again at risk. Kauri dieback is a fungus-like disease that is unique to kauri and kills trees of all ages and sizes. Nearly all infected kauri will eventually die. The disease is present in the Waitakere Ranges and spreads mainly through soil movement. Visitors to the ranges can help save NZ's iconic trees by cleaning their shoes and equipment before and after they visit, staying on formed tracks and keeping off kauri roots when in forested areas. Footwear cleaning stations and kauri dieback information can be found throughout the park. Find out more about kauri dieback at www.kauridieback.co.nz.

The bird life is also good in the ranges, with such species as kereru (NZ pigeon), grey warbler, tui and fantail commonly seen. At the northern end of the park, volunteers from the Ark in the Park, a partnership project between the council and Forest & Bird, have created a mainland sanctuary for birds and have begun to reintroduce a number of species, including the endangered North Island kokako.

The park is famed for its beaches and its rocky outcrops and cliffs overlooking the wild coast.

ℹ Planning

WHEN TO TRAMP

This track can be enjoyed year-round. However, in winter months and during heavy rains, be aware of rapidly rising creeks and slippery track surfaces.

WHAT TO BRING

Campers will need to be entirely self-sufficient, although some food supplies can be found at Huia, Piha and Muriwai. Make sure you pack a wide-brimmed hat, sunscreen and insect repellent.

MAPS & BROCHURES

Two excellent resources are produced for this trail: the *Waitakere Ranges Regional Park Recreation Map* and the *Hillary Trail* brochure. Both are available from the Arataki Visitor Centre and Auckland Council.

CAMPING GROUNDS, LODGES & BOOKINGS

There are no huts on the trail. Many camping grounds can be found along the route, including **Auckland Council camping grounds** ($6) at Barn Paddock, Karamatura Valley, Whatipu Caves, Tunnel Point, McCreadies Paddock and Craw. Each has composting toilets and water (which will need treatment).

Three basic **Auckland Council baches** (per night $96) lie near the trail route: Quaint Barr Cottage at Little Huia, Craw Homestead alongside the camping ground, and secluded Keddle House.

For bach and camping ground availability and bookings, contact either the Arataki Visitor Centre or Auckland Council.

There are also plenty of private accommodation options along the way including lodges, holiday parks, backpackers and B&Bs. These are listed on the Auckland Council website, or enquire at the Arataki Visitor Centre.

INFORMATION SOURCES

The gateway to Waitakere Ranges Regional Park is 6km east of Titirangi, at the **Arataki Visitor Centre** (☑ 09-817 0077; www.arc.govt.nz; 300 Scenic Dr; ☺ 9am-5pm). Housed in a beautiful building, it features Maori carvings, interpretive displays, a theatre screening a video on the Waitakere Ranges, and a shop that sells books and maps. Outside is a series of short nature walks. Visitor centre staff can provide advice on tracks and planning your trail. Trail information and bookings are also available in downtown Auckland at **Auckland Council** (☑ 09-301 0101; www.aucklandcouncil.govt.nz; off Aotea Sq; ☺ 7.30am-5pm Mon-Fri).

ℹ Getting to/from the Tramp

The trail officially starts at the Arataki Visitor Centre on Scenic Dr. If you are catching public transport to Titirangi, you can walk 6.6km from there to Arataki via Exhibition Dr and the Beveridge Track. The trail can be started and finished at a number of points along the way including Cascade Kauri and the Swanson Railway Station.

Titirangi and Swanson are well serviced by public transport, for which you should contact **Auckland Transport** (☑ 09-366 6400; www.at.co.nz), which covers buses and trains and has an excellent trip-planning feature.

🏃 The Tramp

Day 1: Arataki Car Park to Karamatura Campground

4–5 HOURS, 11.5KM, 374M ASCENT, 570M DESCENT

Drop in to the Arataki Visitor Centre first to check on weather and track conditions, then head for the big Hillary Trail informa-tion board next to the car park. From there, set out along **Slip Track**, climbing through bush up a small hill to a clearing at the top. Detour a minute or so to the lookout that has great views of the southern Waitakere Ranges and the Manukau Harbour.

Slip Track descends past the historic tram-line, which you cross. The track continues to slope steeply into the junction with **Pipeline Track**. This 900m section of track is narrow-er, and after around 200m you will have to clamber down and up a small gully, crossing a stream. At the end of Pipeline Track you come to an intersection with the gravelled **Lower Nihotupu Dam Road**, which winds for around 1km uphill before coming to the **Hamilton Track**. Early on along this track there are some nice waterfalls and a spec-tacular kauri knoll.

Hamilton Track emerges on to a grassy 4WD track named Crusher Pipe Track and after 100m you hit gravelled **Smiths Road**. Cross the bridge over the dam and then a short climb to join the wider gravel road, **Huia Dam Road**. Follow this all the way past Lower Huia Dam towards Huia Beach. There are some toilets on the left of the road, a little more than 100m from the bottom of the dam. The track then meets a road junc-tion between Huia Dam Rd and Huia Rd.

If the tide is low, go straight ahead at this junction along a grassy track and down concrete stairs to **Huia Beach**. Follow the coastline towards the stream in the dis-tance. Cross the stream and follow it inland through the trees. You will soon reach the Huia Settlers Museum car park. Cross the road and go up the driveway to the Ka-ramatura car park, where you will pick up the start of **Karamatura Track**; follow the markers to the Karamatura Campground.

If the tide is high, turn right and follow Huia Rd up the hill to the driveway for the Karamatura Farm. Follow this gravel drive-way up the hill to the top to Barn Paddock Campground or continue across the farm to Karamatura Campground.

Day 2: Karamatura Campground to Pararaha Valley Campground

8–9 HOURS, 15KM, 862M ASCENT, 789M DESCENT

Follow the Karamatura Track alongside the stream and up the valley, climbing very steeply to Karamatura Forks. Take **Donald McLean Track** onward towards **Mt Donald McLean** (389m), one of the highest points in the area. It is worth a short 15-minute

NORTHLAND, AUCKLAND & COROMANDEL HILLARY TRAIL

detour to the summit for sweeping views of the area. The trail then follows **Puriri Ridge Track**, which has stunning views of the Whatipu Valley along its 2km stretch.

Cross Whatipu Rd to the start of **Omanawanui Track**. This track, which is steep at times and can be slippery after rain, is perhaps one of the most dramatic and stunning stretches on the trail. Halfway along, the track skirts the edge of the cliffs (watch your footing) and you're rewarded with more views, each better than the last. Pause at the top of **Omanawanui Trig**; to the south you'll see the towering cliffs of the South Head of the Awhitu Peninsula, while to the north and east is the rugged interior of the Waitakere Ranges.

The final section of Omanawanui Track takes you on a quick descent to **Whatipu**. You will pass a signposted junction for the Signal House Track; it is a 20-minute return walk along the ridge to the site of **Signalman's House** above Paratutae Island and a great view of the mouth of Manukau Harbour. In 1863 this wild and treacherous harbour claimed 259 lives when the HMS *Orpheus* hit the Manukau bar and sank, resulting in NZ's worst maritime tragedy.

In the late 1800s Whatipu was a booming timber centre and the terminus for Piha Tramways. Today, it is as wild and remote a place as any in the greater Auckland area. Historic **Whatipu Lodge** includes many heritage buildings from this era.

The Hillary Trail continues along **Gibbons Track**, which begins by climbing in earnest with only occasional relief but rewarding trampers with sweeping views of the extensive and precious **Whatipu Scientific Reserve**. After 3.5km the track reaches a junction with Muir and Walker Ridge Tracks. Take **Muir Track**, which starts flat then descends more steeply towards the Pararaha Valley.

After a decent descent, including a brief rock scramble, the track reaches a clearing and the Pararaha Campground. The Pararaha Stream is around 300m further down the hill.

Day 3: Pararaha Valley Campground to Craw Campground

8–9 HOURS, 21KM, 869M ASCENT, 1099M DESCENT

Head down the valley and cross Pararaha Stream. The trail includes a section of boardwalk through wetlands, which can be submerged at times.

Follow the markers through the extensive sand dunes that form part of the Whatipu Scientific Reserve and enjoy the area's unique flora and fauna.

You will soon come to the **Old Railway Tunnel**, the site of Tunnel Point Campground. The track continues, emerging at the beach. Follow the wild black sandy coastline until you reach the cliffs at the southern end of **Karekare Beach** and head inland via the **Pohutukawa Glade Walk**. Once on Karekare Rd, cross the wooden bridge and pass alongside the beach reserve, where you'll find toilets and a picnic area. Turn onto Watchman Rd and get back onto the trail at Comans Track. This section climbs along the cliff edge, looking down on the beach known the world over due to the movie *The Piano*.

After the summit the track drops to the junction with **Ahu Ahu Track**; turn left and head along this track for a few minutes to the junction with **Mercer Bay Loop Walk**. This is a nice wide track through flax bushes with views from atop the highest sea cliffs in Auckland down into Mercer Bay and along the full sweep of the west coast.

The track emerges at Log Race Rd, which takes you inland. Log Race Rd quickly turns into Te Ahu Ahu Rd, finishing at a T-junction with the main Piha Rd. Turn right, and cross the road, onto the grass verge. Piha Rd can be very busy: watch out for cars and stick to the verge as much as possible.

Just before the junction with Karekare Rd, turn left onto **Ussher Track**, which meets up with Winstone Track, which you follow to the junction with Kauri Grove Track. Cross onto the **Connect Track**, head down the hill, and follow **Knutzen Track** to reach the beautiful **Kitekite Falls**.

Cross the stream to the stone steps and carry on to meet Kitekite Track, which leads to Glen Esk Rd and Wai o Kahu, where there are toilets and water.

Walk to the end of Glen Esk Rd and turn onto Seaview Rd, continuing past the Piha Store and Piha Cafe. Step onto the beach (near Lion Rock) and head north.

When you see the surf lifesavers tower at United North Piha Surf Club, turn inland through the dunes to the Les Waygood car park. Follow the road to the right for around 100m to the start of Marawhara Walk. Follow this track to a clearing and take **Whites Track**. Follow Whites Track until it meets the gravelled **Anawhata Road**, where you turn right and follow the road gently uphill. Note the signpost to the Kuataika Track, to which you will return the next day.

To reach Craw Campground, continue along Anawhata Rd and follow the signs.

Day 4: Craw Campground to Muriwai Beach

12 HOURS, 27.5KM

At the time of writing there was no council camping ground at Te Henga (Bethells Beach), but there were plans to construct one. Check for updates as it is recommended that this final day be broken at Bethells.

Return to the junction of **Kuataika Track**. The trail takes you across Anawhata Farm before passing through a gate into the bush. It descends steeply to the beautiful Anawhata Stream before climbing equally steeply back out. Take time to visit the Kuataika Trig Lookout, a welcome spot for a break after a steep climb.

Continue to the signposted four-way junction of Kuataika, Smyth Ridge, Houghton and Wainamu Bush Tracks. Here you can branch off on to the Smyth Ridge Track for a shorter finish at Swanson, or continue on to Muriwai.

To finish at Muriwai, take **Houghton Track**, which descends to Lake Wainamu Track. This track skirts the lake and passes a lovely waterfall before emerging alongside the extensive Wainamu Dunes. Follow the stream around to meet **Bethells Road**.

Cross the road to the start of the **Te Henga Walkway**, which climbs out of Bethells before skirting behind O'Neills Beach and a steep climb to the top of Raetihinga Point.

From here the walkway follows the clifftops to emerge onto Constable Rd. Watch your footing as it can be slippery in places, but the views are outstanding. Follow Constable Rd onto Oaia Rd and then onto Edwin Mitchelson Track. Follow the Lookout and Quarry Tracks as you descend into Muriwai. The final part of the trail takes in Otakamiro Point and gannet colony, where hundreds of these majestic birds nest and fledge from August to March. The official Hillary Trail finish is at the noticeboard opposite the Muriwai beachfront cafe.

Alternative End: Swanson

7½–8½ HOURS, 18.5KM

At the signposted four-way junction of Kuataika, Smyth Ridge, Houghton and Wainamu Bush Tracks, continue along Smyth Ridge Track to Long Road Track. Follow **Long Road Track** until you meet **Upper Kauri Track**, which drops down into **Cascade Kauri**, the region's largest area of unspoilt kauri forest and home to the 'Ark in the Park' conservation project, which aims to restore native flora and fauna through pest control.

You are now at Falls Rd, 10km from Craw Campground, where you can finish the track if you can arrange a pick-up. Otherwise, continue on the **Auckland City Walk** before climbing steeply out of the valley on **Anderson Track**. Cross Scenic Dr and take **Peripatus Track** steeply downhill to meet **Swanson Pipeline Track** to Tram Valley Rd.

Follow Tram Valley Rd to Christian Rd and then Swanson Rd to reach the Swanson Railway Station.

Kauaeranga Kauri Trail

Duration 2 days

Distance 14km (8.7 miles)

Track Standard Tramping and easy tramping tracks

Difficulty Easy to moderate

Start/Finish Kauaeranga Valley Rd

Nearest Town Thames (p83)

Transport Shuttle bus

Summary A tramp up the popular Kauaeranga Valley, featuring a large number of logging and gold-mining relics, plus a side trip to the lofty Pinnacles.

The 719 sq km of rugged, forested reserves that make up the Coromandel Forest Park are spread across the Coromandel Peninsula. The highest point in the park is Mt Moehau (892m), located near the northern tip of the peninsula; Table Mountain (846m) is the highest point around Kauaeranga Valley.

There are more than 30 tramps through Coromandel Forest Park, covering the area from Karangahake Gorge (near Paeroa) to Cape Colville. The most popular region is the Kauaeranga Valley, which cuts into the Coromandel Range behind Thames.

A logging boom took place in the Coromandel Range during the late 19th century, when stands of massive kauri were extracted. Today, like Great Barrier Island, the Kauaeranga Valley is filled with deteriorating reminders of its lumbering past:

Kauaeranga Kauri Trail

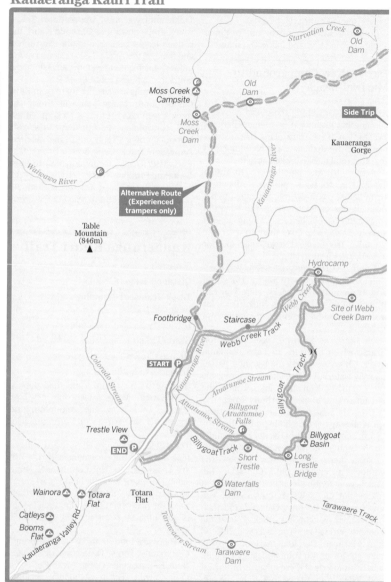

packhorse trails, tramway clearings and many old kauri dams, including Tarawaere, Waterfalls, Dancing Camp, Kauaeranga Main, Moss Creek and Waterfalls Creek.

Due to the valley's popularity and proximity to Auckland, DOC has upgraded the tracks and added campsites to what is now called the Kauaeranga Kauri Trail. For the more adventurous it is possible to hike from Pinnacles Hut to the Moss Creek campsites, and then to Kauaeranga Valley Rd for a three-day circuit. This is a demanding tramp

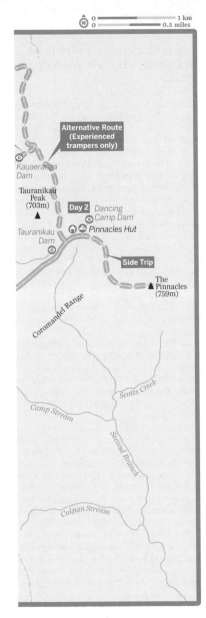

that involves steeper climbs and considerable mire.

History

It is thought that the crews of canoes carrying early Polynesian settlers to NZ rested on the Coromandel Peninsula during their epic journey. In 1769 Captain Cook sailed into a rugged little inlet on the eastern shore of the peninsula. He raised the British flag over NZ for the first time and named the spot Mercury Bay (after the planet that appeared in the sky that night). The peninsula, however, takes its name from the HMS *Coromandel,* which visited in 1820, bringing with it the missionary Samuel Marsden.

Full-scale kauri logging began in the mid-1850s, and by the 1880s there were timber millers within the Kauaeranga Valley. It was the gold rush at Thames that gave impetus to the local logging efforts, because of the sudden demand for building materials in the boomtowns.

Kauri logging ended in 1928, and the state forest was declared in 1938, along with a program to re-establish the native bush.

Environment

Before it was logged, the Coromandel Peninsula had a rich variety of forest flora, which was unmatched by any other area of comparable size in the country. Now, much of the park is busy regenerating native bush, including kauri and rata – with the latter noted for its brilliant orange-red flowers. The Kauaeranga Valley and its surrounding ridges are covered with podocarps and hardwoods, a few scattered pockets of kauri, and areas of bracken, fern and scrub. The predominant species around here are rimu and tawa, but you can also find miro, matai and kahikatea.

The peninsula's wildlife consists of many of the usual native NZ birds – tui, bellbirds, kiwi, kereru (NZ pigeon) and fantails – and introduced mammals, such as pigs, possums, goats, cats and mustelids (stoats, ferrets and weasels).

Various kinds of jaspers, petrified wood, rhodonite and agate are found in or near most streams, which makes this place an excellent source of rare rocks and gemstones. (Permits are not required for mineral collecting, but interested rock-hounds should make themselves aware of where the activity is allowed. No more than 2kg of rock can be removed per person, per day.)

🛈 Planning

WHEN TO TRAMP

The forest park is only a two-hour drive from Auckland, so it can be busy much of summer. On weekends, Pinnacles Hut may be full.

On weekdays from October to December and February to April, school and scout groups frequent the area. If possible, go elsewhere during public holidays, or book a space in the hut or a campsite.

MAPS & BROCHURES

Most tramps in the Kauaeranga Valley are covered by NZTopo50 maps BB35 (Hikuai), with BB34 (Thames) covering the western fringe. NewTopo map *Coromandel Peninsula* 1:75,000 may prove useful for trip planning. DOC's *Kauaeranga Valley Recreation* brochure details all significant walks in the park.

HUT & CAMPING

Pinnacles Hut is the only hut in the valley. This modern **Serviced hut** (www.doc.govt.nz; $15) has gas stoves, solid fuel heater, running water, mattresses, a barbecue and solar-powered lighting. The old hut is now used as a residence for a permanent hut warden. This popular hut must be booked in advance; DOC hut passes and tickets are not valid.

There are, however, eight self-registration **Scenic campsites** (www.doc.govt.nz; $10), all in appealing settings with water supply and toilets. There are also **Backcountry campsites** (www.doc.govt.nz; free) near Pinnacles Hut, at Billy-goat Basin and Moss Creek.

INFORMATION SOURCES

The **DOC Kauaeranga Visitor Centre** (☎ 07-867 9080; www.doc.govt.nz; Kauaeranga Valley Rd; ☺ 8.30am-4pm) is in the Kauaeranga Valley. It has interesting historical displays, dispenses maps, brochures and advice, and handles hut and campsite bookings (which can also be made online, inside the centre).

GUIDED TRAMPS

Walking Legends (☎ 07-312 5297, 0800 925 569; www.walkinglegends.com) offers a four-day package of Coromandel day tramps, which includes the Pinnacles in Kauaeranga Valley (for $1490).

🛈 Getting to/from the Tramp

The DOC Kauaeranga Visitor Centre is 14km off SH25; it's a further 9km along a gravel road to the start of the trails. **Sunkist Backpackers** (☎ 07-868 8808; www.sunkistbackpackers.com) provides a shuttle service into the valley three days a week (Tuesday, Thursday and Saturday; other days on demand) departing Thames at 8am, returning from the valley at 4.30pm (per person $35, minimum two people).

🛉 The Tramp

Day 1: Kauaeranga Valley Road to Pinnacles Hut via Webb Creek Track

3 HOURS, 7KM, 380M ASCENT

The tramp begins at the far end of **Kauaeranga Valley Road** (9km beyond the visitor centre), where you will see a large display sign offering directions. Follow the main track north, as it almost immediately crosses a swing bridge over the **Kauaeranga River**.

The main track then skirts the true left (east) bank of the river for 20 minutes, going through an impressive forest of rata, ferns and nikau palms. Just before **Webb Creek** is a signposted junction, with the fork leading to Moss Creek. Take the right fork (the main track), heading east towards Hydrocamp. This historic packhorse route was used by kauri bushmen in the 1920s to reach logging sites further up the valley.

After crossing Webb Creek you will climb a staircase cut into rock to make the journey easier for the packhorses. Care is required in places as the rocks can be slippery.

At the top of the climb up Webb Creek, the remains of a skidded road are visible beside the track. Skidded roads were made from small logs laid lengthwise with cross pieces forming the 'skids'. Logs were pulled along the skids by teams of bullocks or steam haulers.

The **Hydrocamp**, reached 1½ to two hours from the trailhead, is a clearing built in the late 1940s by workers erecting power lines from Thames to Whitianga. It is also the major junction for those walking back to Kauaeranga Valley Rd via Billygoat Track.

Take the left fork towards Pinnacles Hut, a continuation of the old packhorse track. It climbs onto an open ridge, where there are superb views of the Coromandel Peninsula's east coast and the rugged **Kauaeranga Valley**. The track remains on the ridge for 45 minutes and eventually you're rewarded with a view of the Pinnacles forming a skyline straight ahead.

One hour beyond Hydrocamp you reach a signposted junction. Take the right fork east towards the Pinnacles to arrive at the huge **Pinnacles Hut** (80 bunks) in 10 minutes. Nearby, but out of view, are the warden's quarters and campsite.

From the hut it's a five-minute walk down a side trail to **Dancing Camp Dam**. This was the second-largest kauri dam in the valley when it was built in 1921. It's also one of the best preserved after it was partially restored in 1994 with kauri timber that had washed downriver in a flash flood the previous year.

SIDE TRIP: THE PINNACLES
1½–2 HOURS, 3KM RETURN

From the hut a track swings southeast, becomes a marked route and in 45 minutes reaches the jagged summit of the **Pinnacles** (759m). The route to the top is steep but well signposted, and has ladders bolted in the rock face in some sections to assist you. The views from the summit are among the best in the area; you can see the entire Coromandel Peninsula, from Mt Moehau to Mt Te Aroha.

SIDE TRIP: KAUAERANGA GORGE
1½–2 HOURS, 3KM RETURN

Another interesting side trip from Pinnacles Hut is to view Kauaeranga Gorge and Dam. To get there, head back to the Pinnacles Hut track junction on the main ridge track and head north. Within about 45 minutes you descend steeply into the Kauaeranga Valley and reach the river. When the river is low it's possible to hike down to **Kauaeranga Gorge** by departing from the track and heading past **Kauaeranga Dam**, 10 to 15 minutes downstream.

Built in 1912, the Kauaeranga was the largest dam constructed in the valley, but all that remains today is the floor and a few supporting beams. There are good swimming pools near the dam. Travel in the gorge should never be attempted when the river is swollen, and even at normal water levels it will involve tramping through waist-deep pools.

Day 2: Pinnacles Hut to Kauaeranga Valley Road via Billygoat Track
4 HOURS, 7KM, 380M DESCENT

Backtrack to Hydrocamp, an hour's tramp from Pinnacles Hut. At the signposted junction take the left fork to follow **Billygoat Track**, beginning with a 30-minute climb to a saddle, where there are excellent views down the Kauaeranga Valley to the Hauraki Plains.

A little further on, a knoll overlooks the Billygoat Basin. The first attempt to log this basin was made in the 1880s but was abandoned within a few years, as driving logs down the Billygoat Falls proved too destructive. The basin was successfully logged in

the 1920s after the construction of the Billygoat incline to bypass the falls, and the use of a steam hauler.

Drop down into **Billygoat Basin** and cross Billygoat Stream before passing through a clearing with basic camping facilities. A few minutes further on, a 50m sidetrack overlooks the collapsed remains of the **Long Trestle bridge**, which at one time was 160m long and 11m high.

The main track swings northwest and follows the route of the Billygoat tramway down past the Tarawaere Track junction and the remains of **Short Trestle**, a bridge built for the tramway. Near here you'll enjoy some spectacular views of **Billygoat (Atuatumoe) Falls** below you. Billygoat Track ends with a steep descent to the Kauaeranga River, which is crossed to reach Kauaeranga Valley Rd and the Tarawaere car park, about 1km down the valley from the end of the road. There is a swing bridge here for use during floods. From Hydrocamp, the tramp back to the road takes three hours.

Alternative Route: Pinnacles Hut to Kauaeranga Valley Road via Moss Creek
2 DAYS, 12KM

It's possible to return to Kauaeranga Valley Rd by way of **Moss Creek**. This is a more demanding route for experienced trampers only, as the track is not as well maintained and graded as Webb Creek or Billygoat Tracks and involves considerable mud at times. The route should be broken in half with a night at Moss Creek Campsite, otherwise it makes it a very long day (nine to 12 hours of walking).

From Pinnacles Hut, return to the ridge and head north, as per the Kauaeranga Gorge side trip. This track runs along a power transmission line and eventually reaches Rangihau Rd, which leads to Coroglen.

Head west towards Moss Creek. The track can be muddy and slippery as it passes through regenerating forest, but atones with good views of the Upper Kauaeranga Valley. It also passes the site of an old logging camp and kauri dam.

Around three hours from the Rangihau Rd junction you will reach Moss Creek Campsite, located in another old dam site.

The final leg is a three- to four-hour descent from Moss Creek to a junction with the Webb Creek Track. This stretch is steep at times and, depending on the weather, muddy. Continue southwest along the Webb Creek Track, retracing your steps from day one to the start of the tramp.

TOWNS & FACILITIES

Auckland

🏃 09 / POP 1.4 MILLION

NZ's largest city is a good spot to ready oneself for tramping adventures, or recover afterwards. Not only is it vibrant, cosmopolitan and crammed with multifarious supplies, Auckland is also lush, leafy, and surrounded by ocean and islands. It's a rewarding walking destination in its own right.

🛏 Sleeping & Eating

Auckland International YHA   HOSTEL $

(📞 09-302 8200; www.yha.co.nz; 5 Turner St; dm $32-36, r $98-110; 🅿 @ 🛜) Clean and brightly painted, this 170-bed YHA has a friendly vibe, good security, a games room and lots of lockers. In short, it's your typical, well-run YHA.

Verandahs   HOSTEL $

(📞 09-360 4180; www.verandahs.co.nz; 6 Hopetoun St; dm $27-31, s $55, d $72-88, tr $92; 🅿 @ 🛜) Ponsonby Rd, K Rd and the city are an easy walk from this grand hostel, housed in two neighbouring villas overlooking the mature trees of Western Park. It's easily Auckland's best backpackers.

THE MIGHTY KAURI

The mighty kauri (*Agathis australis*) is an outsize member of the conifer family and one of the world's most massive trees. It can live for over 2000 years, reach 50m in height and boast an impressive girth of up to 16m.

When the first humans arrived in NZ, kauri forest covered large areas of Northland, the Coromandel and Great Barrier Island. The trees played an important role in many aspects of early Maori culture; integrated in creation mythology, rituals, war, art and everyday life. Some large trees were given names and revered as chiefs of the forest. On special occasions giant trunks were used to carve out large *waka taua* (sea/war canoes). Kauri gum had many valuable functions: burned as an insecticide in kumara plots, wrapped in flax to make torches for night-fishing, and used as chewing gum. Resin was also burnt and mixed with fat to create the ink for *moko* (facial tattooing).

It didn't take long for European settlers to cotton on. Prizing the excellent timber and useful gum, they went about decimating these magnificent forests. The first kauri stands to be felled were close to the sea, and on rolling country where bullock teams could easily haul logs out. But as demand for timber increased, it became necessary to log more rugged locations, such as the headwaters of the Kauaeranga Valley. The problem of transporting logs to mills was overcome by the creation of reusable kauri dams.

The first dams were built before the 1850s and they remained the main feature of logging until 1930. The massive wooden structures were built across the upper portions of streams to trap water. Trees were cut and positioned in the creek bed, either above or below the dam catchment, and when the water was high enough, a loose-plank gate in the middle of the dam was tripped. The sudden flood swept the timber through the steep and difficult terrain to the rivers below.

Of the 70 dams that were built in the Kauaeranga Valley, remnants of one-quarter of them can still be seen, including six on the Kauaeranga Kauri Trail. You can spot the odd giant kauri here too, but the best places to view mature trees are Northland's protected pockets of remnant forest such as Waipoua and Trounson Kauri Park.

Saved from the lumberjacks, the kauri are now under threat from a fungus-like disease known as kauri dieback, which has killed thousands of the trees. Visitors to areas where kauri grow need to do their bit to prevent the spread of spores, which infect the roots of the trees. For a starter, stick to defined tracks, and keep well away from kauri tree roots. Any footwear or equipment that comes into contact with soil should be cleaned both before and after you leave the area. See www.kauridieback.co.nz for more information.

Elliott Hotel
APARTMENT $$

(☑09-308 9334; www.theelliotthotel.com; cnr Elliott & Wellesley Sts; apt $139-219; P) Housed in a grand historic building (1880s), this apartment-style hotel is much plusher than the price implies. Rooms may not be huge but the high ceilings let your spirits rise.

Food Alley
FOOD HALL $

(9 Albert St; mains $7-13; ☉10.30am-10pm) There's Chinese, Indian, Thai, Vietnamese, Turkish, Malaysian, Korean and Japanese on offer at this large, no-frills (but plenty of thrills) food hall. Our pick of the bunch is Indonesian, Wardani, hidden in the back corner.

L'Assiette
FRENCH $

(www.lassiette.co.nz; 9 Britomart Pl, Britomart; breakfast & lunch $10-19, dinner $28-33; ☉breakfast & lunch daily, dinner Thu-Sat) Fresh and bright, this little cafe is a popular coffee-and-pastry stop for harried office workers. By night it morphs into a fully-fledged bistro, serving a delicious but limited menu of French classics at reasonable prices.

Depot
MODERN NZ $$

(www.eatatdepot.co.nz; 86 Federal St; dishes $14-32; ☉7am-late) Owned by one of NZ's 'real deal' celebrity restaurateurs, Depot offers first-rate comfort food in informal surrounds. Dishes are divided into 'small' and 'a little bigger', although there are also freshly shucked oysters and simple but delicious breakfast options.

🔒 Supplies & Equipment

If you need to purchase equipment or high-tech clothing, the best option is to head to Queen St, which has a selection of outdoor gear specialists.

Bivouac
OUTDOOR EQUIPMENT

(210 Queen St) The unparalleled Bivouac is staffed by people who walk the talk.

Countdown
SUPERMARKET

(76 Quay St; ☉24hr) For city-centre convenience, head to handy Countdown at the bottom of town.

New World
SUPERMARKET

(2 College Hill, Freemans Bay; ☉7am-midnight) A handy supermarket by Victoria Park.

ℹ Information

One of the two city-centre i-SITEs shares the DOC Information Centre's premises: **Princes**

Wharf i-SITE (☑09-307 0612; www.aucklandnz.com; 137 Quay St; ☉9am-5.30pm). The other is **SkyCity i-SITE** (☑09-363 7182; www.aucklandnz.com; SkyCity Atrium, cnr Victoria & Federal Sts; ☉8am-8pm)

ℹ Getting There & Away

Auckland International Airport (AKL; ☑09-275 0789; www.aucklandairport.co.nz; Ray Emery Dr, Mangere), 21km (35 minutes) south of the city centre, is the main gateway to NZ and a hub for domestic flights, most of which are operated by **Air New Zealand** (☑0800 737 000; www.airnewzealand.co.nz).

InterCity (☑09-623 1503; www.intercitycoach.co.nz) buses depart from the **SkyCity Coach Terminal** (☑09-913 6220; 102 Hobson St). Major routes, with multiple daily departures, include Rotorua (four hours), Taupo (five hours), New Plymouth (six hours) and Wellington (11 hours). Other coach companies depart from 172 Quay St, opposite the Ferry Building on the waterfront, including **Naked Bus** (☑0900 62533; www.nakedbus.com), which travels north to Kerikeri (four hours) and as far south as Wellington (12 hours), as well as heading to Tauranga (3½ hours) and Napier (seven hours).

KiwiRail Scenic (☑0800 872 467; www.kiwirailscenic.co.nz) runs the *Northern Explorer* train between Auckland and Wellington, stopping at seven towns through the middle of the North Island.

Auckland is the best place in NZ to hire a car long-term, with a swag of outlets conveniently grouped together along Beach Rd and Stanley St close to the city centre. As well as many major companies are smaller outfits with older cars, such as **A2B Rentals** (☑0800 310 510; www.a2brentals.co.nz) and **Escape** (☑0800 216 171; www.escaperentals.co.nz; 39 Beach Rd), which hire out small, affordable campervans.

Kaitaia

☑09 / POP 5200

Kaitaia is about 80km from the start of the Te Paki Coastal Track and serves as the main departure point for most trips and tours to Ninety Mile Beach and Cape Reinga.

🛏 Sleeping & Eating

Most of Kaitaia's cafes and restaurants are on or very near Commerce St.

Mainstreet Lodge
HOSTEL $

(☑09-408 1275; www.mainstreetlodge.co.nz; 235 Commerce St; dm $27-34, s $55-70, d $64-78; @🛜) Maori carvings abound at this groovy old cottage, which has a modern purpose-built wing facing the rear courtyard. The friendly owners know the area inside out.

Loredo Motel MOTEL $$
(☑09-408 3200; www.loredomotel.co.nz; 25 North Rd; units $130-210; 🅿🖥) Opting for a breezy Spanish style (think stucco walls and terracotta tiles), this tidy motel has well-kept units set among palm trees and lawns. It's not quite Benidorm, but there is a swimming pool.

Beachcomber RESTAURANT $$
(www.beachcomber.net.nz; 222 Commerce St; lunch $17-33, dinner $27-35; ⊘lunch & dinner Mon-Sat) Easily the best place to eat in town, with a wide range of seafood and meatier fare, all deftly prepared, and a well-stocked salad bar.

🔧 Supplies & Equipment

Riders Sports Depot OUTDOOR EQUIPMENT
(☑09-408 0240; 73 Commerce St) Stop here for maps, stove fuel and freeze-dried meals.

Hunting & Fishing OUTDOOR EQUIPMENT
(www.huntingandfishing.co.nz; 147 Commerce St) Worth a try for equipment.

Pak 'n Save SUPERMARKET
(11 North Rd) Stock up on all (and we mean all) your food for the trail at this gigantic supermarket.

ℹ️ Information

Far North i-SITE (☑03-408 0879; www.topofnz.co.nz; Te Ahu Community Centre, South Rd) Travel information and DOC brochures on the region. Also books accommodation, tours and transport to Cape Reinga, and serves as the major bus stop in town.

ℹ️ Getting There & Away

InterCity (☑09-623 1503; www.intercitycoach.co.nz) links Kaitaia to Auckland, along with stops en route and beyond. Book at the i-SITE, where you'll find the bus stop.

Kaitaia does have an airport serviced by Air New Zealand, but the price of airfares to such small NZ towns usually proves off-putting.

Tryphena
☑09

Tryphena is Great Barrier Island's main settlement, 4km from the ferry wharf. Strung out along several kilometres of coastal road, it consists of a few dozen houses and a handful of shops and accommodation.

🛏️ Sleeping & Eating

Unless you're camping, Great Barrier isn't a cheap place to stay, although rates drop considerably in the off-season. Self-caterers will find small stores in Tryphena, Claris, Whangaparapara and Port Fitzroy.

Crossroads Lodge HOSTEL $
(☑09-429 0889; www.xroadslodge.com; 1 Blind Bay Rd; dm/s/d $30/50/75; @🖥) This low-key backpackers is close to forest walks and hot springs, and has mountain bikes for hire.

Medlands Beach Backpackers HOSTEL $
(☑09-429 0320; www.medlandsbeach.com; 9 Mason Rd; dm $35, d/units from $70/120) Chill out in the garden of this house on the hill, overlooking beautiful Medlands Beach. The backpackers area is simple, with a little double cabin for romantic budgeteers at a slight remove from the rest.

Shoal Bay Lodge APARTMENT $$
(☑09-429 0890; www.shoalbaylodge.co.nz; 145 Shoal Bay Rd; apt $150-240) Hidden among the trees, these comfy self-contained apartments offer sea views, birdsong, solar power and environmentally friendly cleaning products.

Wild Rose CAFE $
(☑09-429 0905; Blackwell Dr; mains $5-18; ⊘8.30am-4pm) This relatively cosmopolitan cafe keeps the locals happy with the likes of toasted sandwiches and burgers, made from free-range, organic and local produce where possible.

Currach Irish Pub PUB $$
(☑09-429 0211; Blackwell Dr; mains $14-28; ⊘from 4pm) This lively pub has a changing menu of seafood, steak and burgers, and is the island's social centre. Rub shoulders with local musos on jam nights.

Tipi & Bob's RESTAURANT $$$
(☑09-429 0550; www.waterfrontlodge.co.nz; 38 Puriri Bay Rd; mains $32-33; ⊘breakfast & dinner) Serving simple but satisfying meals in large portions, this popular haunt has an inviting deck overlooking the harbour. There's a cheaper pub menu in the bar.

🔧 Supplies & Equipment

Stonewall Store SUPERMARKET
(www.stonewallvillage.co.nz; 82 Blackwell Dr) In the heart of Tryphena, this well-stocked grocery shop doubles as the bakery, gift shop and post office.

❶ Information

Great Barrier Island i-SITE (www.greatbarrier nz.com; Claris Airport; ⊙11am-noon Mon, Wed & Fri, 8am-2.30pm Sat, extended in summer) Stocks brochures including its own *Great Barrier Island* pamphlet, which is full of useful information and has a handy map.

❶ Getting There & Away

Great Barrier Island (Aotea Island) can be reached by boat or plane.

Ferries to Great Barrier Island stop at both Tryphena and Port Fitzroy. **SeaLink** (☑09-300 5900, 0800 732 546; www.sealink.co.nz) is the main ferry provider, with sailings three to four times a week according to season (return $85 to $120, 4½ hours). **Fullers** (☑09-367 9111; www.fullers.co.nz; Ferry Bldg, 99 Quay St) runs a seasonal high-speed catamaran during summer (return $147, two hours).

Two airlines fly several times daily from Auckland's domestic airport to Claris: **Great Barrier Airlines** (☑09-275 9120, 0800 900 600; www.greatbarrierairlines.co.nz) and **FlyMySky** (☑09-256 7025, 0800 222 123; www.flymysky. co.nz). Fares range around $180 to $250 return.

Thames

☑07 / POP 6800

A former gold-rush town sprinkled with dinky wooden buildings, Thames serves as the Coromandel Peninsula's western gateway and the main service centre for people touring the peninsula.

🛏 Sleeping & Eating

Pollen St, one of the longest straight shopping streets in NZ, has plenty of takeaways and cafes.

Sunkist Backpackers   HOSTEL $
(☑07-868 8808; www.sunkistbackpackers.com; 506 Brown St; dm $26-29, d $70; @ 🖥) This down-home hostel in a character-filled 1860s heritage building has spacious dorms and a garden. The owners also run shuttle services into the Kauaeranga Valley ($35 return).

Gateway Backpackers   HOSTEL $
(☑07-868 6339; overend@xtra.co.nz; 209 Mackay St; dm $25-27, s $50, d $62-72; @) Generations of Kiwis grew up in state houses just like this, giving this relaxed, friendly hostel a homely feel. Bathrooms are in short supply but there are pleasant rooms, a nice garden and free laundry facilities.

Sola Cafe   VEGETARIAN $
(720b Pollen St; mains $9-13; ⊙8am-4pm; 🖥🖍) Bright and friendly, this meat-free cafe is first-rate. Expect excellent coffee and a range of vegan, dairy-free and gluten-free options that include heavenly salads.

Nakontong   THAI $$
(☑07-868 6821; 728 Pollen St; mains $16-20; ⊙lunch Mon-Fri, dinner daily; 🖍) This is the most popular restaurant in Thames by a country mile. Although the bright lighting may not induce romance, the tangy Thai dishes will provide a warm glow.

🔒 Supplies & Equipment

Hunting & Fishing   OUTDOOR EQUIPMENT
(www.huntingandfishing.co.nz; 26 Kopu Rd; ⊙7am-5pm Mon-Fri, 7am-noon Sat) Head here for camping supplies.

Pak 'n Save   SUPERMARKET
(Mary St; ⊙8am-8pm) Stock up on food supplies.

❶ Information

Thames i-SITE (☑07-868 7284; www.thames info.co.nz; 206 Pollen St; ⊙9am-5pm) Dispenses regional information and doubles as the InterCity bus depot.

❶ Getting There & Away

Thames is serviced by **InterCity** (☑09-623 1503; www.intercitycoach.co.nz). **Go Kiwi** (☑07-866 0336; www.go-kiwi.co.nz) offers a daily shuttle between Auckland and major Coromandel centres including Thames, Tairua and Whitianga. From mid-December to Easter it also runs down to Rotorua and Tauranga. Other Coromandel routes are serviced by **Tairua Bus Company** (TBC; ☑07-864 7194; www. tairuabus.co.nz).

Tongariro, Urewera & Central North Island

Includes ➡

Tongariro Northern
Circuit 89

Umukarikari-Urchin
Circuit 94

Lake Waikaremoana
Great Walk. 98

Ruapani Circuit 101

Whirinaki Track. 104

Best Sights

➡ Ngauruhoe Summit (p90)

➡ Emerald Lakes (p91)

➡ Urchin Trig (p96)

➡ Lake Waikareiti (p102)

➡ Lake Waikaremoana (p96)

➡ Whirinaki Track Glowworm
Cave (p106)

Best Huts

➡ Old Waihohonu Hut (p93)

➡ Mangatepopo Hut (p90)

➡ Panekire Hut (p99)

Why Go

From the spare, volcanic landscape of Tongariro National Park to the dense, mountainous forests of Te Urewera, the central region of the North Island contains diverse and rewarding tramping terrain.

Relatively close as the crow flies, two national parks and two forest parks offer visitors an opportunity to tick off many classic New Zealand wilderness experiences: summit a bald, volcanic peak rent with steaming vents, then stride down a scree slope; visit a historic tramping hut, now converted into a mini-museum; traverse an open ridge with nonstop views, then loop back through a valley following an ever-changing river bed; spend several days skirting a bluff-lined lakeshore, deep in an untouched wilderness; row a boat across a pristine lake, to a hut where you can spend the night; explore ancient forest, internationally recognised for its unique ecological make-up; and see the landscape through the eyes of both Maori and Pakeha, whose stories are retold along the way.

When to Go

With plenty of mountains in their midst, the tramping areas in the North Island's centre-east are prone to unpredictable weather patterns. What is predictable, however, is heavy rain appearing at some point or another, which often renders river crossings impassable. Alpine areas may also be snowbound as late as the start of summer. Strong winds on peaks and ridges are an added hazard.

The substantial alpine sections of Tongariro's Northern Circuit and Alpine Crossing mean they are best attempted November to March. This is also the most pleasant time to complete other tracks in this region, although they can be completed at any time of year in favourable conditions.

Background Reading

NZ's oldest backcountry hut, Old Waihohonu, can be found in Tongariro National Park. Built in 1904 and now a listed heritage building, it is but one of many splendid examples in NZ's unparalleled hut network. A deserved winner in the 2013 NZ book awards, *Shelter from the Storm* is a handsome illustrated history of the huts and the people who built them, written by long-time tramping writers Shaun Barnett, Rob Brown and Geoff Spearpoint. 'On one level, huts are simple structures that provide shelter in a country with a tempestuous climate; but on another level they act as repositories of our backcountry history, with many fascinating stories invariably surrounding them.'

DON'T MISS

A road trip between Tongariro and Te Urewera National Parks will most likely require you to pass through Taupo and Rotorua, two lakeside tourist towns with some very steamy attractions. We're talking about volcanic activity here – an eye-popping collection of bubbling mud pools, shooting geysers and multicoloured silica pans, along with a strong smell of sulphur in the air.

In Taupo, get an introduction at the **Volcanic Activity Centre** (www.volcanoes.co.nz; Karetoto Rd; adult/child $10/6; ⊙ 9am-5pm Mon-Fri, 10am-4pm Sat & Sun), which has displays on the region's geothermal and volcanic activity, including a live seismograph and earthquake simulator. Nearby is the **Craters of the Moon** (www.cratersofthemoon.co.nz; Karapiti Rd; adult/child $8/4; ⊙ 8.30am-5.30pm), a geothermal area where you can get close to the action along a 45-minute perimeter loop walk.

Between Taupo and Rotorua, **Orakei Korako** (☑ 07-378 3131; www.orakeikorako.co.nz; adult/child $36/15; ⊙ 8am-5pm) is arguably the best thermal area left in NZ, with a boardwalk around colourful silica terraces, geysers, and a cave complete with deep green pool.

Rotorua is even steamier still, with numerous geothermal attractions including **Te Whakarewarewa**, the town's main drawcard famous for Maori cultural performances and displays, more than 500 springs, and a couple of very dramatic geysers.

DOC Offices

→ **DOC Tongariro National Park Visitor Centre** (☑ 07-892 3729; www.doc.govt.nz; Whakapapa Village; ⊙ 8am-5pm)

→ **Turangi i-SITE** (☑ 07-386 8999; www.greatlaketaupo.com; Ngawaka Pl; ⊙ 8.30am-5pm)

→ **DOC Te Urewera National Park Visitor Centre** (☑ 06-837 3803; www.doc.govt.nz; Aniwaniwa; ⊙ 8am-4.45pm)

→ **DOC Murupara Visitor Centre** (☑ 07-366 1080; www.doc.govt.nz; SH38; ⊙ 9am-5pm Mon-Fri)

GATEWAY TOWNS

→ Whakapapa Village (p107)

→ National Park (p107)

→ Turangi (p108)

→ Murupara (p108)

→ Wairoa (p109)

Fast Facts

→ Tongariro National Park was the country's first national park, founded in 1887.

→ The largest active volcano in NZ, Ruapehu is also considered one of the world's most active.

→ The Tongariro Alpine Crossing is NZ's most popular day walk, completed by more than 60,000 trampers each year.

→ Te Urewera contains the largest untouched native forest on the North Island.

Top Tip

Tramping in Tongariro National Park is not a winter activity. If you want to see it blanketed in snow, don skis and hit the slopes, or hire an experienced guide to take you on the Alpine Crossing.

Resources

→ www.greatlaketaupo.com

→ www.nationalpark.co.nz

→ www.teurewera.co.nz

→ www.visitwairoa.co.nz

TONGARIRO NATIONAL PARK

Tongariro National Park (797 sq km) lies in the heart of the North Island. Its landmark features are its active volcanoes. Three of them – Mts Ruapehu, Ngauruhoe and Tongariro – form the 'top of the roof' for the North Island.

These mountains are the southern end of a volcanic chain that extends northwest through the heart of the North Island, past Taupo and Rotorua, to finally reach Whakaari (White) Island. The volcanic nature of the region is responsible for Tongariro's hot springs, boiling mud pools, fumaroles and craters.

Ruapehu, at 2797m, is the highest mountain on the North Island and its snowfields are the only legitimate ski area north of Wellington. Northeast of Ruapehu is the almost symmetrical cone of Ngauruhoe (2287m), and Tongariro (1967m), the lowest in height and northernmost of the three peaks.

Since its establishment in 1887, the park has been developed for recreational use. It now contains the famous Chateau hotel, a golf course, various ski fields and a network of tracks, many of which pass through bare lava fields and tussock, making Tongariro the best alpine tramping area in the North Island.

The variety of scenery and recreational activities make Tongariro the most popular national park in NZ. Many come to ski, but more than 200,000 people arrive each summer to tramp up, down and around the mountains. The park can get busy, most noticeably on the popular day walks, but most visitors consider this a small price to pay for the chance to experience its magic.

The most popular tramps in the park are the Northern Circuit and the Alpine Crossing, but there are plenty more besides. These range from short ambles to excellent day walks such as the Whakapapa Valley and Tama Lakes tracks, both of which begin from the national park visitor centre at Whakapapa. There are also various challenging routes that should only be attempted by the fit, experienced and well equipped. One of these is the Round-the-Mountain Track, a remote 71km, four- to six-day tramp circuiting Mt Ruapehu.

History

It is the powerful Maori history of Tongariro that has earned the national park an unusual dual World Heritage status – it is cited on both natural and cultural grounds.

To the Maori the volcanoes of Tongariro were *tapu* (sacred) and they sought to prevent anybody from climbing them. They believed Ngatoro-i-rangi, high priest of the Ngati Tuwharetoa tribe of Lake Taupo, arrived in the Bay of Plenty and travelled south to claim the volcanic plateau for his people. He climbed Ngauruhoe to view the land but, upon reaching the top, suddenly found himself in the middle of a raging snowstorm. It was something the high priest had never experienced and he cried out to priestess sisters in the north to send him warmth.

The sisters responded by sending fire from the earth. It burst from the ground, creating the craters of Ngauruhoe and Tongariro, thus saving Ngatoro-i-rangi. He slew a female slave, then climbed to the newly formed crater and tossed the body in to give his prayer more strength, claiming the surrounding land for his people.

The volcanoes, especially Tongariro, have been sacred to Maori ever since. They often travelled to Ketetahi Hot Springs to bathe, but were forbidden to go any further. Europeans were also discouraged from visiting the area. In 1839 John Bidwill, a botanist and explorer, became the first Pakeha to scale Ngauruhoe.

For the next 12 years the local tribe was successful in keeping intruders from its sacred grounds. However, in 1851, Ruapehu fell to a climber's passion when Sir George Grey ascended one of the volcano's peaks and then hid from his Maori guides to avoid their discontent. In 1879 George Beetham and JP Maxwell became the first Europeans to scale Ruapehu and see Crater Lake.

During the mid- to late 1880s the local *iwi* (tribe) was under considerable pressure to relinquish the lands to farmers, loggers and rival tribes. Horonuku Te Heuheu Tukino IV, paramount chief of Ngati Tuwharetoa, came up with a solution: on 23 September 1887 he gifted the sacred volcanoes of Tongariro, Ngauruhoe and Ruapehu to the people of New Zealand.

An Act of Parliament formally established Tongariro National Park in 1894 and it was gazetted as such in 1907. The original gift area of 2360 hectares has been increased over the years by government purchase of surrounding land to create a national park of 797 sq km.

More recently, the park's fame has been bolstered by starring roles in Peter Jackson's *Lord of the Rings* and *The Hobbit* movies. Mt Ngauruhoe was most noticeably transformed into fiery Mt Doom of Mordor, while numerous locations around Ruapehu, including the Mangawhero Falls and River, make magical appearances.

Environment

Geologically speaking, the Tongariro volcanoes are relatively young. Both Ruapehu and Tongariro are less than 300,000 years old. They were shaped by a mixture of eruptions and glacial action, especially in the last ice age. At one time, glaciers extended down Ruapehu to below 1300m, leaving polished rock far below their present snouts.

Ngauruhoe is even younger. Its first eruptions are thought to have occurred 2500 years ago. Until 1975 Ngauruhoe had erupted at least every nine years, including a 1954 eruption that lasted 11 months and disgorged six million cubic metres of lava.

Ruapehu is one of the world's most active volcanoes. One eruption began in March 1945 and continued for almost a year, spreading lava over Crater Lake and sending

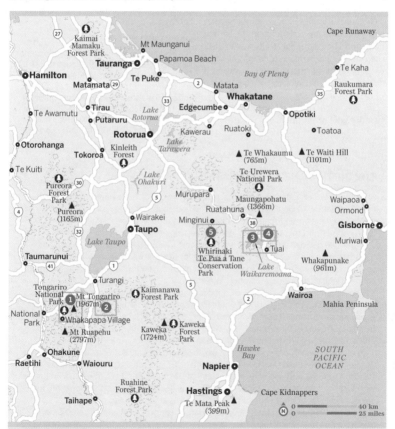

Tongariro, Urewera & Central North Island Tramps

1 Tongariro Northern Circuit (p90)

2 Umukarikari-Urchin Circuit (p95)

3 Lake Waikaremoana Great Walk (p100)

4 Ruapani Circuit (p102)

5 Whirinaki Track (p105)

huge dark clouds of ash as far away as Wellington. Ruapehu rumbled again in 1969 and 1973, but its worst disaster was on Christmas Eve 1953, when a crater lake lip collapsed. An enormous lahar (mudflow) swept down the mountainside, taking everything in its path, including a railway bridge. Moments later a crowded train plunged into the river, killing 151 people; it was one of NZ's worst tragedies.

Ruapehu hasn't let up, with significant eruptions occurring with suspicious frequency. In 2007 a primary school teacher had a lucky shave when a rock was propelled through the roof of Dome Shelter. He survived, but his leg was crushed.

Ongoing rumbles are reminders that these volcanoes are very much in the land of the living. The last major event was in 2012 when Mt Tongariro gave a couple of good blasts from its northern craters, causing a nine-month partial closure of the famous Alpine Crossing track.

To see video of recent eruptions, visit www.doc.govt.nz/eruption.

ℹ Planning

WHEN TO TRAMP

The safest and most popular time to tramp in the national park is December to March, when the tracks are normally clear of snow and the weather is more settled. In winter many of the tracks become full alpine adventures, requiring alpine experience, an ice axe and crampons.

WHAT TO BRING

This is a highly changeable, alpine environment, so appropriate clothing is paramount. Think wool, and several layers of it, topped with a waterproof jacket. Gloves and a hat are good too, even in summer. And don't even think about wearing anything other than sturdy boots. Bring plenty of water and sunscreen, especially on hot days.

MAPS & BROCHURES

The best map for planning a tramp in Tongariro National Park is the 1:80,000 Parkmap 273-04 (Tongariro), which shows Mt Ruapehu summit and the Tongariro Alpine Crossing at 1:50,000. Tongariro is also covered by NZTopo50 BH34 (Raurimu), BH35 (Turangi), BJ34 (Ruapehu) and BJ35 (Waiouru), and by NewTopo maps *Mount Ruapehu* 1:40,000; *Tongariro Northern*

THE BIRTH OF NZ'S FIRST NATIONAL PARK

After the New Zealand Wars (Land Wars), during which Ngati Tuwharetoa chief Horonuku Te Heuheu Tukino IV aided the rebel Te Kooti, those tribes loyal to the Crown wanted the land around Tongariro redistributed. In 1886, at a schoolhouse in Taupo, the Native Land Court met to determine the ownership of land.

Horonuku pleaded passionately with the court to leave the area intact. At one point, he turned to the rival chiefs who were longing for the land and asked: 'Where is your fire, your *ahi ka*? You cannot show me for it does not exist. Now I shall show you mine. Look yonder. Behold my fire, my mountain Tongariro!'

The forcefulness of his speech dissuaded Maori from dividing up the sacred land, but Horonuku was equally worried about Pakeha, who were eyeing the area's tussock grassland for grazing. 'If our mountains of Tongariro are included in the blocks passed through the court in the ordinary way, what will become of them? They will be cut up and sold, a piece going to one Pakeha and a piece to another.'

The chief saw only one solution that would ensure the land's everlasting preservation. Before the Native Land Court, on 23 September 1887, Horonuku presented the area to the Crown for the purpose of a national park, the first in NZ and only the fourth in the world. With incredible vision for a man of his time, the chief realised that Tongariro's value lay in its priceless beauty and heritage, not as another sheep paddock.

An Act of Parliament created Tongariro National Park in 1894, but its development was slow. The main trunk railroad reached the region in 1909. By then there were huts at Waihohonu, in the east, with a track leading to them and to Ketetahi Hot Springs. The railroad brought a large number of tourists to the western side of the park, and by 1918 a track and hut were built at Mangatepopo for skiers on Ngauruhoe.

Development of the park mushroomed in the 1950s and 1960s as roads were sealed, tracks cut and more huts built. Today the park receives around 200,00 visitors per annum.

Circuit 1:60,000; and *Tongariro Alpine Crossing* 1:30,000.

Department of Conservation (DOC) brochures covering the area include *Tongariro Northern Circuit* and *Tongariro Alpine Crossing* as well as the extensive and helpful *Walks in and around Tongariro National Park*, which features 30 walks and tramps.

HUTS, CAMPING & BOOKINGS

The Tongariro Northern Circuit is a Great Walk. Between mid-October and 30 April the three DOC huts – Mangatepopo, Oturere and Waihohonu – are designated **Great Walk huts** ($32). Each hut has gas cookers, heating, cold running water and good old long-drop loos, along with communal bunk rooms with mattresses. Campsites are located next to the huts; the $15 fee allows campers use of the hut facilities.

Great Walk hut tickets must be obtained in advance, either from the Tongariro National Park Visitor Centre, **Great Walks Bookings** (☑ 0800 694 732; www.greatwalks.co.nz), or DOC visitor centres nationwide. It will pay to book early during the Great Walk season.

In the off-season the huts become **Standard huts** (www.doc.govt.nz; $15), the gas cookers are removed, and fees can be paid with backcountry hut passes and tickets.

INFORMATION SOURCES

The DOC information hub is **Tongariro National Park Visitor Centre** (☑ 07-892 3729; www.doc.govt.nz; Whakapapa Village; ☉ 8am-5pm), which has interesting exhibits and displays on the park's geological history – enough to keep you occupied for at least half a rainy day.

Turangi i-SITE (p108) is also a DOC agent, and can therefore supply information and maps on Tongariro National Park and other reserves in the area.

GUIDED TRAMPS

Walking Legends (☑ 07-312 5297, 0800 925 569; www.walkinglegends.com) runs small-group, fully catered, guided three-day tramps on the Tongariro Northern Circuit ($890), and one-day Tongariro Alpine Crossing (from $330).

❶ Getting To/From the Tramp

The national park is well serviced by shuttle operators, including Taupo-based **Tongariro Expeditions** (☑ 0800 828 763; www.tongariroexpeditions.com), Turangi-based **Turangi Alpine Shuttles** (☑ 0272 322 135, 07-386 8226; www.turangirentals.co.nz) and Whakapapa Village–based **Roam** (☑ 021 588 734, 0800 762 612; www.roam.net.nz). Some other shuttle operators are offshoots or affiliates of accommodation providers so it might pay to ask when you book your stay.

Note that the Base Camp, on the SH47 between Turangi and National Park, is a popular pick-up point where you can either park for the day, or stay overnight at the pleasant **Tongariro Family Holiday Park** (☑ 07-386 8062; www.thp.co.nz; sites from $18, cabins $60-160; ☎), although you can only use its facilities if you are staying there.

Sample shuttle prices are $35 from Turangi to Whakapapa, and $35 to $40 return for the Tongariro Alpine Crossing (from Base Camp or Whakapapa to Mangatepopo and return from Ketatahi). Be sure to book your shuttle in advance to avoid being stranded.

Tongariro Northern Circuit

Duration 4 days

Distance 50km (31 miles)

Track Standard Great Walk

Difficulty Moderate

Start/End Whakapapa Village

Nearest Towns National Park (p107), Whakapapa Village (p107), Turangi (p108)

Transport Shuttle bus

Summary The spectacular alpine Northern Circuit winds its way around the crazy volcanic slopes of Mt Ngauruhoe, on the way taking in the famous Tongariro Alpine Crossing, often lauded as NZ's best one-day walk.

Circumnavigating Ngauruhoe, this track is a Great Walk for a number of good reasons. The route can be easily walked in four days from Whakapapa Village, Mangatepopo Rd or Ketetahi Rd, all regularly serviced by shuttle services. Although there is some moderate climbing, the track is well marked and well maintained, putting it within the ability of people of medium fitness and tramping experience.

But, most of all, the Northern Circuit includes the most spectacular and colourful volcanic areas that have earned the park its status as a Unesco World Heritage Area.

The traditional place to start and finish the tramp is Whakapapa Village, the site of the park's visitor information centre. However, many trampers begin at Mangatepopo Rd to ensure they have good weather for the tramp's most dramatic day. This reduces it to a three-day tramp, with stays at Oturere and Waihohonu Huts, ending at Whakapapa Village.

Tongariro Northern Circuit

TONGARIRO, UREWERA & CENTRAL NORTH ISLAND TONGARIRO NORTHERN CIRCUIT

🥾 The Tramp

Day 1: Whakapapa Village to Mangatepopo Hut

3–5 HOURS, 8.5KM

Many trampers skip this first day of the circuit, because, in the past, the **Mangatepopo Track** had a reputation for being uninteresting and extremely muddy. The scenery has not changed but the track has certainly improved over the years with the addition of boardwalk and bridges. That said, it may take all of five hours in bad weather.

From 100m below the Tongariro National Park Visitor Centre (p85), head up Ngauruhoe Pl to the signposted Mangatepopo Track on your left. The tramp begins here, along a well-maintained track that wanders through tussock grass and a few stands of beech for 1.5km. At Wairere Stream it passes a signposted junction with a track that leads to Taranaki Falls, and eventually to the Tama Lakes.

Within 3km of the start are impressive views of the volcanic cones of **Ngauruhoe** and **Pukekaikiore** to the northeast. Straight ahead is the small cone of Pukeonake, formed by a continuous eruption of scoria – small pebbles of lava that have erupted from within.

After a few more stream crossings the track swings eastward around Pukekaikiore, and you quickly climb a ridge from which you can see Mangatepopo Hut (20 bunks), 2km in the distance.

The hut sits at 1180m in a pleasant spot. On clear evenings you can enjoy fine sunsets over Mt Taranaki, around 140km away, and by looking in the other direction you can study the climb to South Crater, the destination for the next day. The campsite is situated next to the hut.

To the west of the hut is a track that after 30 minutes reaches the car park and shelter at the end of Mangatepopo Rd, which connects to SH47. This is where the **Tongariro Alpine Crossing** day hike begins.

Day 2: Mangatepopo Hut to Oturere Hut

5–6 HOURS, 12.8KM, 706M ASCENT, 536M DESCENT

This is the day you complete the Tongariro Alpine Crossing, one of the most spectacular tracks in NZ. It's not unusual in foul weather for trampers to walk from one hut to the next in three hours, but if the weather is clear plan on spending the whole day on and around the track to marvel at the amazing volcanic scenery.

Brace yourself for encounters with hordes of day hikers, who will start stampeding past the hut soon after daybreak. They will almost certainly want to maintain a faster pace than you do, so take your time and let them steam on ahead.

The day begins with an easy tramp up Mangatepopo Valley and over a succession of old lava flows. Within an hour you pass a spur track to **Soda Springs** (an easy 15-minute return trip), which, if the wind is right, might be smelt before they are seen. Look out for pretty yellow buttercups here.

The main track continues up the valley and quickly begins a well-marked climb to the saddle between Ngauruhoe and Tongariro. The ascent among the lava rocks is steep, but well marked with stacks of steps and marker poles. After 45 minutes to one hour you reach the top, passing the signposted route to Mt Ngauruhoe Summit.

Follow the poles as they continue past the junction and cross **South Crater**, an eerie place when the clouds are low, and a huge walled amphitheatre when the weather is clear. The walk through the crater is flat,

---

TONGARIRO ALPINE CROSSING

This legendary crossing is often lauded as NZ's finest one-day walk. It's certainly the most popular, with 60,000 to 70,000 trampers completing it every year.

It's no wonder. Very few day walks can offer such thrilling scenery. Among its highlights are steaming vents and springs, crazy rock formations and peculiar moonscape basins, impossible scree slopes and vast views in almost every direction.

This is a fair-weather tramp. In poor conditions it is little more than an arduous up-and-down, with only orange-tipped poles to mark the passing of the day. Should strong winds be blowing on top, you'll be practically crawling along the ridge of Red Crater, the high point of the trek.

This *is* an alpine crossing, and it needs to be treated with respect. You need not only a reasonable level of fitness, you should be prepared for all types of weather. Shockingly ill-equipped trampers are legendary on this route – stupid shoes, wafer-thin rainjackets, blue jeans soaked to the skin – we've seen it all.

As well as proper gear, you'll need plenty of water, as there is none available between Mangatepopo and Ketetahi.

The most crowded times on the track are the first nice days after Christmas and Easter, when there can easily be more than 1000 people strung out between the two road-ends. Your average Kiwi tramper will complain that it's far too busy, but in reality it's hardly Piccadilly Circus. It pays to remember that most of these people have come here for the same reason you have: to experience nature at its most primal and spectacular. Be patient, pick your gap, and rejoice in a journey shared with like-minded people.

Starting at the Mangatepopo Rd carpark, it takes seven to eight hours to make the 19.4km journey through to Ketetahi Rd, although this will vary significantly if you decide to take side trips up to the summits of Ngauruhoe or Tongariro.

with the slopes of Ngauruhoe to the right and the Tongariro summit to the left.

Once across the crater, the track – now a poled route – resumes climbing the ridge, and at the top you can see Oturere Valley and the Kaimanawa Range to the east.

Having slogged up the rocky ridge, you will reach a signposted junction to a route up to Mt Tongariro Summit (1967m, two hours return). To the right is the gaping **Red Crater**, around which you sidle to the highest point on the track (1886m). It's essential to have favourable weather when traversing it, and if you're lucky enough to get a clear day you will enjoy stupendous views that might even include Taranaki to the west and Mt Tauhara, Mt Putuaki and Mt Tarawera to the north.

The track begins its descent along the side of Red Crater, where you will get your first view of the surreal **Emerald Lakes**. These three old explosion pits feature brilliant colouring, thanks to minerals washing down from Red Crater.

The track then drops steeply into **Central Crater**. Be careful along this stretch of track, which begins as loose scree but turns into a hard, packed surface with loose stones that act like marbles. Many trampers have injured themselves here.

Trampers wishing to exit the tramp via Ketetahi Rd should stick with Tongariro Alpine Crossing walkers, and follow the **Ketatahi Track** towards **Blue Lake** and onward around the flanks of **North Crater**. Eventually the track dips below the bushline into lush podocarp forest. So many trampers depart at Ketetahi Rd that there is usually a vendor selling drinks and sandwiches. There is also a shelter and a toilet, but no drinking water. It's a 700m descent over 6.5km, taking two to three hours.

Those continuing around the circuit should turn off at the junction signposted to Oturere Valley, where there are views of the Kaimanawa Ranges and Rangipo Desert. A barren landscape of reddish sand with small clumps of tussock, this unique desert landscape is the result of two million years of volcanic eruptions – especially the Taupo eruption about 2000 years ago, which coated the land with thick deposits of pumice and destroyed all vegetation.

The track weaves through a moonscape created by early eruptions from Red Crater. Oturere Hut (26 bunks) nestles on the eastern edge of these flows. Don't forget to check out the waterfall over the ridge in front of the hut.

SIDE TRIP: MT NGAURUHOE SUMMIT
3 HOURS RETURN, 781M ASCENT

The near-perfect cone of Ngauruhoe (2287m) is a tantalising proposition, but as will be obvious when you eyeball it, this is not a climb for the faint-hearted. It should only be attempted by fit, strong, sensible people.

Follow the poled route to the foot of the ridge near the centre of the northern slope. From here the route is not marked, but climbs a band of scoria to the summit. It gets increasingly difficult the higher you climb, with the last 100m or so a near-spirit-breaking two steps forward, one step back. The views from the top are undeniably worth it – in good weather, that is. In bad weather don't even think about it. Keep an eye out for untoward volcanic activity, and your nose turned on to overpowering gases.

The descent is best made via the scree slope, which you can clamber over to once you've negotiated the first stretch of red scoria. Take large, carefully planted strides and be very wary of what's happening above you. Other people can dislodge large rocks that will then chase you down the mountain.

Day 3: Oturere Hut to Waihohonu Hut
3 HOURS, 7.5KM, 240M ASCENT, 400M DESCENT

This relatively short day's tramp will leave you plenty of time to take in a couple of leisurely side trips.

From Oturere Hut the track swings southwest through open country as it skirts the eastern flanks of Ngauruhoe. It descends straight towards Ruapehu, working its way across numerous streams, before a lengthy 120m descent bottoms out at a bridge over the upper branch of **Waihohonu Stream**, 1½ to two hours from Oturere Hut.

On the other side, climb through a beech-clad valley, topping out on the 1269m crest of an open ridge before making a final descent to Waihohonu Hut (28 bunks) in the next valley. The hut, the third to be built in this area, is in a pocket of beech trees near a branch of the Waihohonu Stream; nearby are camping sites.

The first hut is still standing and makes for an interesting side trip after you drop your pack. Another short side trip is to follow the **Round-the-Mountain Track** south to **Ohinepango Springs**, a 20-minute walk from Waihohonu Hut. The springs are cold and they bubble up from beneath an old lava flow. A huge volume of water discharges into the Ohinepango Stream.

Day 4: Waihohonu Hut to Whakapapa Village

5½–6 HOURS, 16KM

The final day begins with the track crossing a bridge over a branch of Waihohonu Stream. On the other side is a signposted junction. The Round-the-Mountain Track continues south along the slopes of **Ruapehu** (www.mtruapehu.com), and the Waihohonu Track (not part of the Tongariro Northern Circuit) heads east towards Desert Rd (1½ hours).

Turn right at the junction, following the Waihohonu Track west. The track follows the upper branch of Waihohonu Stream, dropping and climbing out of several streams that have eroded the thin covering of tussock grass. The walking is tiresome at times, but beautiful if the weather is clear; Ngauruhoe's perfect cone is on one side and Ruapehu's snowcapped summit is on the other. Eventually the track rises gently to **Tama Saddle**, between the two volcanoes, and in another 1.5km arrives at a junction to **Tama Lakes**. The lower lake is a short trip up the side track, but it's 45 minutes along an exposed ridge to the upper lake.

The main track continues west, working down and across another six streams until it descends to **Wairere Stream** where there are two routes returning to Whakapapa Village. To the right the track passes **Taranaki Falls**, where the Wairere Stream spills over a 20m rock face into a boulder-ringed pool, and then merges into Mangatepopo Track 1.5km from its start on Ngauruhoe Pl. To the left the track makes a steady descent to Whakapapa Village, passing through grasslands and small patches of beech forest. It's 30 to 45 minutes to the village along either route.

KAIMANAWA FOREST PARK

Just to the east of Tongariro National Park is Kaimanawa Forest Park, a 773-sq-km conservation park dominated by the Kaimanawa Range and the beech forest that covers much of the area. The park contains the upper catchments of four major rivers: the Mohaka, the Rangitikei, the Ngaruroro and the Tongariro.

For trampers, Kaimanawa is a complete contrast to Tongariro National Park: one is well known, well used and easily accessible;

OLD WAIHOHONU HUT

Old Waihohonu Hut is NZ's oldest mountain hut, and it's certainly one of the most beloved among Kiwi trampers.

The hut was built in 1904 by the Tourist and Health Resorts Department as a stop-off for stagecoaches on the Grand Tourist Route from Wanganui to Taupo, through what is now Whanganui and Tongariro National Parks. After the main trunk railway was opened on the other side of the park in 1908, Waihohonu Hut became the base for the first recreational skiing in NZ in 1913. Later it served as shearers' quarters before becoming popular with trampers. Tongariro's oldest hut was finally retired in 1968, and was eventually declared a historical structure.

The fact that it has endured a century of extreme weather is testament to the Kiwi ingenuity of its builders. The hut was constructed from pit-sawn totara wood beams, and clad with corrugated iron, with all materials being carried up by men or horses. Workers then filled the wall cavities with pumice stones to insulate the hut and protect it from fire. The hut was so well designed that it has survived the foul weather buffeting the slopes of Ruapehu, occasional trampers' mishaps with stoves, and even a few volcanic eruptions.

Today, the classic red structure, the oldest example of an early two-room alpine hut in the country, is a museum with an interesting series of displays of early equipment and photos. But the hut also serves as a monument to NZ's passion for mountain recreation and adventure. The fact that this museum has to be reached on foot seems totally appropriate.

the other is little known, little used and difficult to reach by public transport. In Tongariro, tracks are benched and well marked; in Kaimanawa, you need good bushcraft and river-crossing skills to travel from hut to hut.

History

Although there was scant Maori settlement in Kaimanawa, the area was widely travelled with some evidence of camps. Its name is derived from the words of Hape-ki-tuarangi, who was asked by Ngatoro-i-rangi why he was in such cold and barren country, to which he replied: 'My breath *(manawa)* is my food *(kai)*.'

Europeans began exploring and surveying the area from the mid-1880s. Following in their footsteps were goldminers who searched for gold in the rivers and streams. The exploitation continued with the burning of forest to make way for farmland, a largely unsuccessful venture, after which the timber industry tried its luck. From the late 1930s to the 1970s more than 4500 hectares of red and silver beech were logged, mainly for fence posts. That's *a lot* of fence posts.

The commercial hunting and culling of deer during the 1950s and '60s laid the foundation of the current track system. In 1965 the *Forest Amendment Act* was passed to protect sections of forest as parks. Kaimanawa was gazetted in 1969.

Environment

Kaimanawa can be divided into two general regions. The central and southern portions of the park are mountainous, with forested valleys, extensive scrublands and alpine grasslands. In contrast, the area to the north and east is less rugged and almost entirely forested – making it easier for tramping.

Most of the park is covered in beech forest, with red and silver beech dominating in the north and east, and mountain beech in the south and interior valleys. Towards the west, including along the Umukarikari-Urchin Circuit, podocarps (rimu, matai and totara) are encountered more frequently. The bushline lies between 1160m and 1370m, and marks the point where the forest is replaced by tussock grassland and sub-alpine vegetation.

Sika (Japanese deer) and red deer mean hunters flock here during the roar (mating season) in late March and April. Native birds include the kereru (NZ pigeon), the rifleman, the karearea (NZ falcon*)*, fantails,

bellbirds, whiteheads, fernbirds, kiwis and sometimes whio (blue ducks).

The Kaimanawa area is known for its trout, and is one of the best spots on the North Island for trampers with a rod and reel. Most rivers in the park contain trout. Some (Rangitikei, Mohaka and Ngaruroro) have brown and rainbow trout; the Waipakihi, on the Umukarikari-Urchin Circuit, has only rainbow trout.

Umukarikari-Urchin Circuit

Duration 2 days

Distance 32km (20 miles)

Track Standard Tramping track and route

Difficulty Moderate

Start Umukarikari car park

End Urchin car park

Nearest Town Turangi (p108)

Transport Bus, shuttle bus

Summary The most popular tramp in the lightly used Kaimanawa Forest Park features exposed sections across the tops, and a pretty river valley.

As well as its scenic attractions, this tramp is one of the easiest to reach in the forest park. It includes tramping through the Waipakihi River Valley, down an unmarked route along a riverbed which allows some liberating following of your nose. The circuit can be tramped in either direction, but is described here starting at the Umukarikari Track, and looping around in a clockwise direction.

ⓘ Planning

WHEN TO TRAMP

Summer and autumn are the best times. In November and early December heavy rain and low clouds can make travel difficult. Be aware that river levels can rise rapidly, so be prepared to wait things out or turn back if the Waipakihi River starts cranking.

WHAT TO BRING

The weather in the park is extremely changeable, so trampers should be prepared for wet, cold weather whenever they visit. You will also need a cooker. As giardia may be present, bring sufficient fuel to boil your drinking water, or some other form of purifier.

Umukarikari-Urchin Circuit

N 0 ————————— 4 km
   0 ————————— 2 miles

MAPS & BROCHURES

The best map for this tramp is NZTopo50 BH36 (Motutere).

HUTS & CAMPING

There are four **Standard huts** (www.doc.govt. nz; $5) in the park, including Waipakihi Hut. All are first-come, first-served, equipped with a wood burner, and can be paid for with DOC backcountry hut passes and hut tickets. Fuel is supplied but you are encouraged to use it sparingly.

Campsites are located next to Waipakihi Hut, although there are also plenty of lovely **Backcountry campsites** (www.doc.govt.nz; free) along the Waipakihi River. A **Standard campsite** (www.doc.govt.nz; $6) is also located near the start of the Urchin Track.

INFORMATION SOURCES

Turangi i-SITE (p108) is the local DOC agent, and can therefore supply information and maps on the Kaimanawa Forest Park and other reserves in the area.

ℹ Getting to/from the Tramp

Most of the tracks in the Kaimanawa Forest Park are isolated and difficult to reach without a vehicle. The Umukarikari-Urchin Circuit is the exception, being located not far off SH1, 15km south of Turangi.

From SH1, head east on Kaimanawa Rd. From the highway turn-off it's 6km to the Umukarikari car park, and 8km to the Urchin car park. It's 6km from one trailhead to the other.

Turangi-based Turangi Alpine Shuttles (p89) offers track transport (return $45) as well as secure vehicle storage.

InterCity (☎ 06-835 4326; www.intercity. co.nz) will drop you off at the start of Kaimanawa Rd, but you have to clear it with the driver first and purchase the full fare for Turangi to Waiouru.

🥾 The Tramp

Day 1: Umukarikari Car Park to Waipakihi Hut

6–8 HOURS, 14KM, 911M ASCENT, 500M DESCENT

Most of this day is spent tramping along the open ridges of the **Umukarikari Range**. Pay homage to the weather gods – sacrifice a bag of scroggin if you have to – because if they smile on you with clear weather conditions, this is an outstanding tramp with panoramic views.

From the Umukarikari car park, the track sets off nice and easy before beginning a fairly steady climb through beech forest dotted with some impressive rimu. Having emerged from the treeline you are greeted by views of Tongariro National Park's skyline.

The track continues for the best part of several hours along Umukarikari's western flank, over **Sharp Cone** (1480m), and then **Umukarikari Trig**, the high point of the entire tramp at 1591m. From this flat peak there are views all around, particularly of the grassy plains and river valleys of Kaimanawa Forest Park to the east.

From the trig the track descends easily over a wide, open ridge, before plunging more knee-jarringly down to the head of the **Waipakihi Valley**. Having crossed the river, you reach Waipakihi Hut (12 bunks) on a grassy terrace.

Day 2: Waipakihi Hut to Urchin Car Park

6–8 HOURS, 18KM, 569M DESCENT, 436M ASCENT

The first part of this tramp follows the Waipakihi River flats, through which there is no defined track. It's easy walking, though, the key being to ford the river when necessary (and often), and make use of grassy flats and forested terraces.

From the hut, the journey begins with around 6km of river-walking before meeting a small gorge. Re-emerging, the track continues and, in all, it takes around four to five hours to reach the **Urchin Track**, signalling a climb up and out of the Waipakihi Valley. You've got two to three hours to go before you reach the car park at the end of the track.

It's a fairly steep 1km climb through the forest before you emerge above the bushline on to the Urchin ridge. It takes around an hour to pass across the tussocky crest, following a poled route. Shortly before the final descent you will reach the high point of the ridge, **Urchin Trig** (1392m), where you are rewarded with views in all directions. What captures the eye, however, is the volcanic trio of Ruapehu, Ngauruhoe and Tongariro to the west.

It's a long way down from here – nearly 600m in fact. A slight undulation follows the trig, after which it is a steady descent all the way to the Urchin car park.

TE UREWERA NATIONAL PARK

Shrouded in mist and mysticism, Te Urewera National Park is the North Island's largest, encompassing 2127 sq km of virgin forest cut with lakes and rivers. The highlight is Lake Waikaremoana ('sea of rippling waters'), a deep, 55-sq-km crucible of water encircled by the Lake Waikaremoana Track, one of NZ's Great Walks. Rugged bluffs drop away to reedy inlets, the lake's mirror surface disturbed only by mountain zephyrs, waterbirds taking to the skies and the occasional pleasure boat.

The name Te Urewera still has the capacity to make Pakeha New Zealanders feel slightly uneasy – and not just because it translates as 'The Burnt Penis'. There's something primal and untamed about this wild woodland, with its rich history of Maori resistance. The local Tuhoe people – prosaically known as the 'Children of the Mist' – never signed the Treaty of Waitangi and it was only in June 2013 that the *iwi* (tribe) and the Crown signed a deed of settlement to provide redress for historical land confiscations.

Remote, rugged, and immense – it's not surprising that Te Urewera became a stronghold for Maori. Even today it remains a relatively infrequently visited area, with the main road through it, SH38, largely unsealed as it winds its way through the park's mountainous interior.

History

Maori legend says human settlement in Te Urewera began when Hine-Pokohu-Rangi (the Mist Maiden) married Te Maunga (a mountain), producing the fierce Tuhoe tribe (the Children of the Mist). Genealogical evidence places the arrival of the Tuhoe at around AD 1350.

Tuhoe settled the rugged interior of Te Urewera, but not around Lake Waikaremoana. That was home to another coastal tribe, Ngati Ruapani.

With life determined by the practical demands of food gathering, Te Urewera nurtured an industrious, resilient people with links to the land. No part of the forest was left unexplored.

Missionaries were the first Pakeha to explore the area, when Reverend William Williams travelled through in November 1840 and came across Lake Waikaremoana. Naturally suspicious of any intrusion, Tuhoe closely guarded Te Urewera's isolation and joined other tribes in the 1860s to war against government troops.

The tribes had just suffered a severe defeat when, in 1868, Tuhoe destiny took a strange turn. In that year Te Kooti, a charismatic Maori leader, escaped from a Chatham Island prison and sought refuge in Te Urewera. Te Kooti and Tuhoe formed a pact that led to a three-year running battle with government troops. The soldiers applied a scorched-earth policy in an effort to eliminate Tuhoe food supplies and flush the tribe from the woods.

Te Kooti used unique military manoeuvres to score victories and to stage successful raids on towns, including Rotorua. However, Tuhoe, with their limited resources, were no match for the government troops. Te Kooti narrowly escaped several times, helped once by a premature gunshot that warned him off. By 1871 disease and starvation had overtaken the Tuhoe and eroded their morale. The tribe finally ended its involvement in the war by agreeing to swear allegiance to the Crown. Te Kooti, however, refused and the rebel leader escaped once more to the King Country, around Waitomo.

With a continuing distrust of Pakeha, Tuhoe turned to another self-proclaimed prophet, Rua Kenana, who presided over the isolated farming settlement of Maungapohatu from 1905 until his politically motivated 1916 arrest. This effectively erased the last bastion of Maori independence in the country.

The open hostility against the government surveyors and construction workers trying to build a road through Te Urewera eased, with Tuhoe finally convinced that such a road would bring them trade and agricultural benefits. Troops were needed to protect government workers and the road was not completed until 1930.

Tuhoe remain proud of their identity and traditions, with around 40% still speaking *te reo* (the language) on a regular basis.

The idea of preserving the forest as a watershed was first promoted in 1925. After WWII, support for turning the area into a national park grew. In early 1954 Tuhoe approved the name Te Urewera National Park, and the new park was officially gazetted later that year.

Environment

One of NZ's largest national parks, Te Urewera also contains the largest untouched native forest on the North Island. It is a rugged land that rises to 1400m and forms part of the mountainous spine stretching from the East Cape to Wellington. The forests form a blanket over the mountains so thick that barely a peak or ridge can be seen.

Lake Waikaremoana was formed by a landslide that dammed the Waikaretaheke River around 2200 years ago. The lake filled up to a maximum depth of 248m, but was lowered 5m in 1946 by a hydroelectric development.

There is a diverse selection of trees in the park's forests, ranging from tall and lush podocarp and tawa forests in the river valleys, to stunted, moss-covered beech in the higher ranges. The major change in forest composition occurs around 800m, where the bush of rimu, northern rata and tawa is replaced by beech and rimu. Above 900m only beech is usually found. It is estimated that 650 types of native plant are present in the park. The park's remoteness has preserved much of its wildlife, with a full complement of North Island native forest birds being found within its confines, with the exception of weka.

Te Urewera's rivers and lakes offer some of NZ's finest rainbow trout fishing. There is good fly fishing for brown trout from the shore on the Lake Waikaremoana Great Walk. Fishing with both fly and spinning gear is allowed in most areas.

ℹ Planning

WHEN TO TRAMP
Because of the mountainous nature of the area, trampers would be wise to expect rain at any time of year, with the annual average rainfall of 2500mm swept in by prevailing northwesterly and southerly winds. In winter, this can turn to snow at higher altitudes.

That said, the Lake Waikaremoana Great Walk and Ruapani Circuit can be tramped throughout the year. They are particularly popular at Easter and during the summer school holidays from mid-December until the end of January. In summer, trampers can generally expect regular spells of fine, dry weather.

MAPS & BROCHURES
The Great Walk and Ruapani Circuit are covered by NZTopo50 BG40 (Waikaremoana) and BG39 (Ruatahuna). The whole area is covered by NewTopo *Lake Waikaremoana* 1:55,000. DOC's *Lake Waikaremoana* brochure includes a useful directory of local visitor services.

HUTS, CAMPING & LODGES
DOC has more than 43 huts within the park. All of these are either are **Standard huts**

(www.doc.govt.nz; $5) or **Basic huts** (www.doc. govt.nz; free), with the exception of the huts along the Lake Waikaremoana Great Walk, and Sandy Bay Hut, which is a **Serviced hut** (www. doc.govt.nz; $15).

There are also numerous **Backcountry campsites** (www.doc.govt.nz; free) and **Standard campsites** (www.doc.govt.nz; $6) throughout the park including at Mokau Landing, 10km northwest of the National Park Visitor Centre, and another near Hopuruahine at the northern end of the Great Walk.

On Lake Waikaremoana, **Waikaremoana Holiday Park** (☏ 06-837 3826; www.lake.co.nz; SH38; sites from $15, cabins $55, units $90-160) is a good base for tramping in the national park. It has chalets and cabins, campsites, and a shop full of essentials such as hot pies, chocolate and a swarm of fishing flies. The camp can also hook you up with water taxis, shuttles and petrol, and offers gear and car storage.

INFORMATION SOURCES

Situated in the hub of the park near the lakeshore, Te Urewera National Park Visitor Centre (p85) has weather forecasts, accommodation information and hut/camping passes for the Lake Waikaremoana Great Walk and other tracks.

Another port of call is the DOC Murupara Visitor Centre (p85), 1.8km south of Murupara centre, which sells hut tickets, maps, books and brochures about the forest park's tracks.

GUIDED TRAMPS

Whakatane-based **Walking Legends** (☏ 07-312 5297, 0800 925 569; www.walkinglegends.com) run small-group, fully catered, guided four-day tramps on the Lake Waikaremoana Great Walk (from $1390), as does **Te Urewera Treks** (☏ 07-366 6055, 0800 873 937; www.teureweratreks. co.nz), based in Rotorua ($1345).

❶ Towns & Facilities

The nearest town to the start of the Lake Waikaremoana Great Walk is Tuai, a small hamlet with a couple of accommodation options and a very small, unreliable store. Nearby is the **Big Bush Holiday Park** (☏ 06-837 3777, 0800 525 392; www.lakewaikaremoana.co.nz; SH38; sites from $15, s/d $30/60), 3.5km from the Onepoto car park.

To the west, 49km from the Aniwaniwa Visitor Centre and 113km from Rotorua on SH38, Ruatahuna is a similar size. It offers little more than a general store with fuel.

For a decent range of facilities you will need to head to Wairoa (p109), in the east, while to the west is Murupara (p108), which will meet modest needs.

❶ Getting to/from the Tramps

Waikaremoana can be approached from two directions via SH38, which links Wairoa and the East Coast with the central North Island. The highway has a gravel surface for about 90km between Murupara and Aniwaniwa. There are well-marked side roads to the main boat ramps, campsites and walk entrances.

Both ends of the track are easily accessible off SH38. The southern end is at Onepoto, 10km south of the national park visitor centre; the northern end is near Hopuruahine Landing, 15km northwest of the visitor centre.

Shuttle buses and water taxis provide transport to both trailheads. Visitors with vehicles would be wise to use these services so that their cars can be stored at the car park at the visitor centre or Waikaremoana Holiday Park. **Home Bay Water Taxi & Shuttles** (☏ 06-837 3857; www.waikaremoana.com) runs boats from the holiday park to stops all around the lake (trailhead $60 return), and also runs a shuttle through to Wairoa ($80 for four people).

Vehicle storage, shuttles to Wairoa and water-taxi services are also offered by **Big Bush Water Taxi** (☏ 0800 525 392; www.lakewaikaremoana. co.nz). Return-trip trailhead transport is $45, with hut-to-hut pack transfers for the less gungho. It also runs shuttles to and from Wairoa ($45 one way).

Servicing the park from the west is **Te Urewera Shuttle** (☏ 07-366 6055, 0800 873 937; www.teureweratreks.co.nz), which runs through from Rotorua twice a week (Thursday and Sunday) with return-trip track transport costing $175 per person.

Lake Waikaremoana Great Walk

Duration 4 days

Distance 46km (28.6 miles)

Track Standard Great Walk

Difficulty Easy to moderate

Start Onepoto

End Hopuruahine Landing

Nearest Towns Wairoa (p109), Murupara (p108)

Transport Shuttle bus, boat

Summary One of the most popular multiday tramps on the North Island, this track follows most of the shoreline of Lake Waikaremoana, the largest lake in Te Urewera National Park.

Built in 1962 as a volunteer project by boys from 14 secondary schools, the Lake Waikaremoana Great Walk is indeed a great walk, with spectacular views from Panekiri Bluff, deep green forest, numerous beaches and swimming holes.

Due to increasing popularity, in 2001 the track was designated a Great Walk requiring advance bookings, which eliminate overcrowded huts. Around 15,000 trampers now tackle the walk annually.

The track, which is well benched and easy to follow, can be completed in either direction, although by starting from Onepoto you put the steep climb up the spectacular Panekiri Bluff behind you in the first few hours. Walking in the opposite direction you'll need an extra hour from Waiopaoa Hut to Panekire Hut, but then it will take less time from Panekire Hut to the end of the trail at Onepoto.

ℹ Planning

HUTS, CAMPING & BOOKINGS

The Lake Waikaremoana Track has five **Great Walk huts** ($32) along the track: Panekire, Waiopaoa, Marauiti, Waiharuru and Whanganui. Each has a wood-burning stove, water supply, cooking benches and vault toilets as well as bunks with mattresses. Note there are no cooking facilities so you need to bring a stove.

There are five designated **Great Walk campsites** ($14): one at Waiopaoa and Waiharuru huts, as well as Korokoro, Maraunui and Tapuaenui. These have grassy sites, cooking shelters, water supply and vault toilets. Camping on the track is only permitted at these campsites.

Note that for both huts and campsites, water supply is rainfall-dependent. Furthermore, it is recommended that you boil or treat all drinking water.

As this is a Great Walk, you need to book your huts or campsite in advance through Great Walks Bookings (p89), or DOC visitor centres nationwide, including the one at Aniwaniwa. Backcountry hut passes and hut tickets are not valid.

🥾 The Tramp

Day 1: Onepoto to Panekire Hut

4–6 HOURS, 9KM, 532M ASCENT

The beginning of the track is signposted 500m from SH38, next to the day shelter (where there is track information). Before setting out, make sure you fill your water bottle as there is no water available along this first leg.

There is little time to warm up at this end of the track because it immediately begins a steep climb up the sandstone cliffs of **Pane-kiri Bluff**. Plan on 2½ to three hours to ascend 532m over 4km to **Pukenui Trig**, one of the highest points of the trip at 1181m. From there you begin the second half of the day's tramp, following the track along an undulating ridge of knobs and knolls, from which you're rewarded with spectacular views of Lake Waikaremoana, 600m below.

Continue along the ridge through mixed beech forest for almost 4km, until you suddenly break out at a sheer rock bluff that seems to bar the way. Closer inspection reveals a staircase and wire up the bluff, where the bush has been cleared.

Panekire Hut (36 bunks) is 100m further on, at **Puketapu Trig** (1185m). Only 10m from the edge of the bluff, this hut offers the park's best panorama, encompassing most of the lake, **Huiarau Range** and sometimes even the coastal town of Wairoa. A rainwater tank is the sole water source at the hut.

Day 2: Panekire Hut to Waiopaoa Hut

3–4 HOURS, 8KM, 580M DESCENT

Continue southwest and follow the main ridge for 3km, gradually descending around bluffs and rock gullies until the track takes a sharp right swing to the northwest. If the weather is good there will be panoramas of the lake and forest. At this point the gradual descent becomes steep, with the track heading off the ridge towards Wairaumoana (the Wairau Arm of the lake), and at one section it drops 250m in about 1km. Trampers are aided here by a staircase.

On the way down there is an interesting change in vegetation as the forest moves from the beech of the high country to tawa and podocarp, with a thick understorey of ferns. The grade becomes more gentle as you approach the Wairaumoana and, eventually, you arrive at the Waiopaoa Hut (36 bunks) and campsite, near the shoreline. The hut is a short stroll from a sandy bay with good spots for fishing and swimming.

Day 3: Waiopaoa Hut to Marauiti Hut

4–5 HOURS, 12KM

Start the day early to take advantage of the many places where you can linger and while away the afternoon. The track turns inland from Waiopaoa Hut to cross Waitehetehe and Waiopaoa Streams, then follows the lakeshore across grassy flats and terraces of

Lake Waikaremoana Great Walk

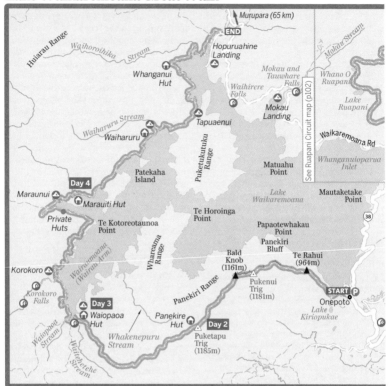

kanuka. In the first hour you'll encounter a number of streams that are bridged.

The signposted junction to **Korokoro Falls** is 3.5km from Waiopaoa Hut, a 1½-hour walk for most trampers, and makes for a scenic diversion. It's 15 minutes to the falls, which drop 20m over a sheer rock face in one of the most impressive displays of cascading water in the park. Korokoro Campsite is 200m past the swing bridge and makes for a very scenic place to pitch a tent.

The main track continues around the lake, rounding **Te Kotoreotaunoa Point** then dropping into Maraunui Bay. It's 30 to 40 minutes along the southern shore of the bay, past a Maori reserve and private huts, to Te Wharau Stream, a popular fishing spot. Located at the stream, around 2½ hours from the Korokoro Falls junction, is Maraunui Campsite. From here the track climbs over a low saddle in the Whakaneke Spur and, in 1.7km, dips to Marauiti Bay and

the 200m side track to Marauiti Hut (26 bunks) on the lakeshore.

Day 4: Marauiti Hut to Hopuruahine Landing

4–5 HOURS, 14KM

Return to the main trail and immediately cross the stream at the head of Marauiti Bay. The track follows the northern side of the bay before swinging northeast to skirt Te Kopua Bay, 30 minutes from Marauiti Hut. This is one of the most isolated and beautiful bays on the lake.

The track leaves the bay, climbs to a low saddle in the Te Kopua headland and descends to Te Totara Bay. It then passes **Patekaha Island**, no longer a true island, and hugs the shoreline, which is dotted by a number of small sandy beaches. It's 1.5km from the island to Waiharuru Hut (40 bunks), a two-hour walk from Marauiti Hut.

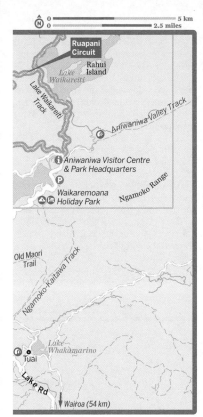

This is largest hut on the track, with a deck with lake views. Next to it is the Waiharuru Campsite.

The track swings inland to cross Waiharuru Stream, then returns to the shoreline and climbs over a saddle, returning to the lakeshore at Tapuaenui Bay in the Whanganui Inlet, 1½ hours from Waiharuru Hut. Tapuaenui Campsite is located here. For the next hour follow the shoreline (with a short diversion up Tapuaenui Stream) until it reaches Whanganui Hut, on a grassy flat between two streams, close to a nice beach.

The last leg of the trip begins with a scenic walk around the lakeshore and through a short section of bush to the **Waihoroihika Stream**. Once across the bridge, the track continues up through the grassy flats on the northwestern side of the Hopuruahine Stream to a point opposite the access road. Thanks to a swing bridge, trampers no long-

er have to ford the river or endure an extra 30-minute walk to a road bridge on SH38.

Camping is allowed along the access road, and there are usually a few tents and caravans among the grassy sites because the Hopuruahine Stream and its mouth are popular fishing spots. It's 1km up the gravel access road to SH38 if you haven't arranged for a water taxi or shuttle collection from Hopuruahine Landing.

Ruapani Circuit

Duration 2 days

Distance 24km (15 miles)

Track Standard Tramping track

Difficulty Easy to moderate

Start/End Aniwaniwa

Nearest Towns Wairoa (p109), Murupara (p108)

Transport None required

Summary Conveniently setting off and finishing at the National Park DOC Visitor Centre, this fascinating loop takes in a dense forest pocked with wetlands, and a beautiful hidden lake dotted with islands.

This track partially follows the most popular short walk in the park, the two-hour return walk to Lake Waikareiti. The whole Ruapani Circuit can be completed in a day (six hours), but with just a few hours' extra walking – or a row across the lake – an overnight stop in this beautiful place is there for the taking.

The forest along the way is consistently lovely, especially the profusion of neinei (pineapple scrub, *Dracopyhllum latifolium*), and NZ's tallest species of tree, the kahikatea. There's also plenty of bird life in the midst, including kaka, kakariki, and the inquisitive North Island robin.

The Ruapani Circuit Track can be completed in either direction, although it is most traversed anti-clockwise, starting on Waikareiti Track, just northwest of DOC's National Park Visitor Centre at Aniwaniwa.

🛈 Planning

HUTS, CAMPING & BOOKINGS

The only hut on this track is Sandy Bay, a Serviced hut with a wood-burning stove, water supply (if rainfall is sufficient), cooking benches and vault toilets as well as bunks with mattresses. As it is considered a Great Walk hut, you need

TONGARIRO, UREWERA & CENTRAL NORTH ISLAND RUAPANI CIRCUIT

to book it in advance through Great Walks Bookings (p89), or DOC visitor centres nationwide, including the one at Aniwaniwa. Backcountry hut passes and hut tickets are not valid.

While camping is permitted, it is an uncertain prospect, with grassy areas in short supply. It is therefore not recommended.

🥾 The Tramp

Day 1: Aniwaniwa to Sandy Bay Hut

3–4 HOURS, 10KM

From the DOC visitor centre, follow the signs to **Waikareiti Track**. It's an hour of gentle climbing (300m in all) to walk the 3km to the shores of **Lake Waikareiti**. The lake lies at 892m above sea level and 300m above the level of Lake Waikaremoana, which lies to its southwest.

Lake Waikareiti was formed by a massive landslide that took place about 18,000 years ago. The lake – home to numerous islands – is free of pollution and all introduced aquatic plants, and has remarkable water clarity. It's fine, pebbly bottom is conducive to a paddle, or indeed even a full-immersion swim.

The Waikareiti day shelter lies on the lakeshore, alongside the boatshed from where you can launch your pre-booked rowing boat for a jaunt across the lake (see box on opposite page).

Trampers should continue following the track through the forest, which affords occasional lake views. Half an hour beyond the day shelter, a left fork takes you onto the **Ruapani Circuit Track**, back to the road and visitor centre. For Sandy Bay Hut, take the right fork, which sets out along the shore of **Tawari Bay**, from where there is a different perspective of the lake's islands. Having reached the end of the bay, the track heads inland, and away from the lake edge, meeting it again only when it reaches Sandy Bay Hut (18 bunks), which lies idyllically on the

Ruapani Circuit Track

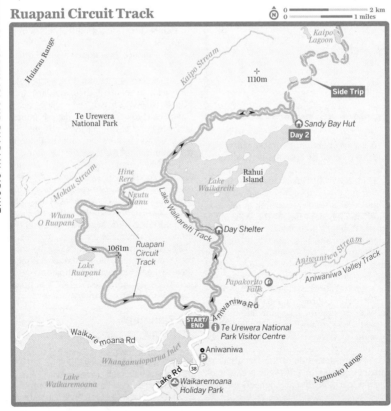

ROW YOUR BOAT ASHORE

The tramp to Lake Waikareiti offers the opportunity to embark on one of NZ's classic 'multisport' adventures, combining a traditional bush tramp with a spot of leisurely boating.

In the boatshed alongside the Lake Waikareiti day shelter, DOC has dinghies available for hire (four hours $20). Pay for and pick up a boatshed key at the DOC visitor centre. The boats hold three people with packs, or four without.

A popular outing is to **Rahui Island**, situated in the middle of the lake, where there's a boat landing and a short walk to another lake – that's a lake on an island in a lake. You may also see rare mistletoes blooming with red and orange flowers, which flourish on the islands in Lake Waikareiti due to an absence of pesky possums.

Many people take the dinghies out for a few hours, but overnight hire is also permitted, allowing you to row across the lake to Sandy Bay Hut and stay overnight. Located at the northern end of the lake, it's a 1½-hour row in calm conditions.

shores of a shallow bay with brilliant white sand. It's 4km from the Ruapani Circuit Track junction to the hut.

Ten minutes before you reach the hut a track leads to **Kaipo Lagoon**. If you want to see what an untouched 11,000-year-old peat bog looks like, a two-hour side trip will satisfy this urge.

Day 2: Sandy Bay Hut to Aniwaniwa

4–5 HOURS, 14KM

From Sandy Bay Hut, return along the same track you previously came up. At the junction beyond Tawari Bay, take the right fork and follow the Ruapani Circuit Track back out to the road – a distance of 10km taking around 3½ hours.

The track passes through a forest dominated by red and silver beech with the occasional mighty rimu emerging above the canopy. It also passes by several wetlands and little lakes, including Lake Ruapani, the track's namesake. On the descent from this lake, the final body of water en route, there is an enticing glimpse of Lake Waikaremoana, Panekiri Bluff and Hawke's Bay in the distance.

WHIRINAKI TE PUA A TANE CONSERVATION PARK

Forming a boundary between the commercial pine plantations of the Kaingaroa plains and the vast forests of Te Urewera National Park, the 549-sq-km Whirinaki Te Pua a Tane Conservation Park is an internationally recognised enclave of native forest. Lauded for its biodiversity and ecological values, it is a dense and magisterial landscape similar to the forests that blanketed Gondwana in the Jurassic period, more than 150 million years ago. For this reason Whirinaki is often referred to as the 'dinosaur forest'.

History

From the beginning of their recorded history, the Ngati Whare, a *hapu* (clan) of the Tuhoe tribe, lived in harmony with the forest of Whirinaki, and plenty of evidence of their occupation remains.

Intense logging of the area's native bush began in the 1930s, and by the mid-1970s more than 130 people were employed in the forest industry at Whirinaki, harvesting up to 30,000 cu metres of native trees annually. The land became a heated battlefield in 1978 and 1979, when conservation groups challenged government policy on managing the forests. What most irked conservationists was the practice of removing native trees and replacing them with fast-growing exotic species.

The result of the bitter conflict was an effort to preserve the remaining native bush. The forest park was formed in 1984, and a year later all logging of native trees officially ended.

Environment

The northern half of the forest park is relatively low, its tree-covered hills and gullies rising from 360m to only 730m. The southern half is steep, rugged greywacke country, which tops off at 1373m at Maungataniwha, the highest point in the park.

The most striking feature of Whirinaki is its unique podocarp forest. Dominating the forest are towering kahikatea, totara, matai, rimu, miro and tawa. Podocarps are slow-growing species; many of the trees in the park are 500 to 700 years old, and some have been dated at more than 1000 years. The size of the trees along the first half of the Whirinaki Track is truly amazing. If you don't know a rimu from a miro, there are some tree-identification signs at the beginning of the track, along with a few interpretive displays on podocarp forests.

The dense podocarps support a diverse bird population, including North Island kaka, red- and yellow-crowned kakariki (parakeet), kereru (NZ pigeon) and the endangered karearea (NZ falcon) and whio (blue duck). The other animal that thrives here is trout; there is good fishing in the Whirinaki, Rangitaiki and Whaeo Rivers.

❶ Planning

WHEN TO TRAMP

Whirinaki shares Te Urewera National Park's climate, with decent rainfall and snow on higher peaks during winter. However, the Whirinaki Track is a well-cut path with no difficult fords. Beyond this, track conditions vary, and are subject to the vagaries of unpredictable weather. Visitors should be prepared for cold, wet spells even at the height of summer, as well as rising river levels. In summer, trampers can generally expect regular spells of fine, dry weather.

MAPS & BROCHURES

The Whirinaki Track is covered by NZTopo50 BG38 (Wairapukao), with the remainder of the park covered by BG39 (Ruatahuna). DOC's brochure *Walks in Whirinaki Forest* details walks of varying lengths, from 15 minutes to five days.

HUTS & CAMPING

Central Whirinaki Hut is a **Serviced hut** (www.doc.govt.nz; $15) with heating, but no cooking facilities. All other huts in the park are **Standard huts** (www.doc.govt.nz; $5).

Free camping is permitted throughout the park. In addition, there are two **Backcountry campsites** (www.doc.govt.nz; free) south of Minginui: Sanctuary and Mid Okahu. To the north of Minginui, Mangamate Waterfall campsite is a **Standard campsite** (www.doc.govt.nz; $6) in an excellent location on the banks of the Whirinaki River, overlooking the beautiful waterfall.

INFORMATION SOURCES

DOC Murupara Visitor Centre (p85), 1.8km south of Murupara centre, sells hut tickets, maps, books and brochures about the forest park's tracks. You can also leave your intentions here.

GUIDED TRAMPS

Walking Legends (☑ 07-312 5297; www.walkinglegends.com) provides guiding services in Whirinaki Te Pua a Tane Conservation Park, as does **Te Urewera Treks** (☑ 07-366 6055, 0800 873 937; www.teureweratreks.co.nz).

❶ Towns & Facilities

The former sawmilling town of Minginui is just a dot on the map, less than 7km from the northern entrances to the forest park. Typical of small-town NZ, however, it manages to provide sufficient services and hospitality to make wilderness adventures possible.

A couple of outfits provide affordable, homely accommodation with shuttle services as a sideline. **Jailhouse** (☑ 07-366 3311; www.jailhousefarmstay.co.nz; 283 Minginui Road; s/d $95, $20 per extra person) offers self-contained farmstay accommodation and transport to the northern end of Whirinaki Te Pua a Tane Conservation Park; continental breakfast is available by request. **Whirinaki Forest Holidays** (☑ 07-366 3235; www.whirinakiforestholidays.co.nz; Farm Rd; s/d $95, $25 per extra person), 1km along Minginui Rd from Te Whaiti Rd, has a backpacker lodge, basic motel rooms and meals.

That's pretty much where Minginui begins and ends. There's no shop, so you'll need to bring all your own supplies.

Whirinaki Track

Duration 2 days

Distance 25km (15.5 miles)

Track Standard Tramping track

Difficulty Easy

Start River Rd car park

End Plateau Rd car park

Nearest Town Minginui

Transport Shuttle bus

Summary An all-weather track offering an easy tramp along the scenic Whirinaki River; it's so level it uses a tunnel through a hill.

This track is a surprisingly easy walk, which is ideal for families, novice trampers and those unfamiliar with NZ backcountry tramping. While Whirinaki lacks the dramatic alpine and volcanic features many trampers come to NZ to see, it is still an interesting tramp, with highlights such as Te

Whirinaki Track

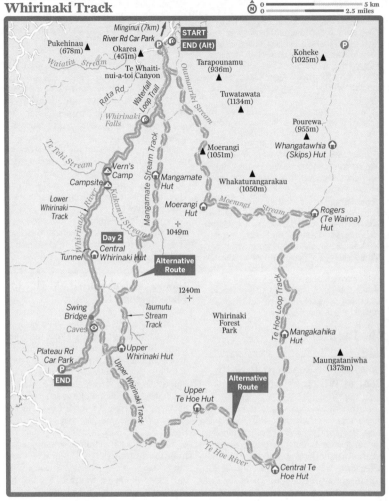

Whaiti-nui-a-toi Canyon, thundering Whirinaki Falls and the caves near the southern end of the track. Best of all, this is one of the few places in NZ where you will encounter trees of such size and density.

Although the one-way Lower Whirinaki Track is the park's most popular option, there are many other choices, including the three-hour **Waterfall Loop**, a good option for day-trippers wanting a taste of the park.

Extended multiday trips are also possible, many of which form a loop and may involve stream crossings. From the southern end of the Whirinaki Track, for example, it's possi-

ble to return to the River Rd car park via Mangamate Stream passing Upper Whirinaki Hut (nine bunks), then heading north to Mangamate Hut (nine bunks) and out to the car park – a trip of three or so days.

The **Te Hoe Loop Track** is even longer (five to six days): it continues from Upper Whirinaki Hut to Upper Te Hoe Hut (nine bunks), along the **Pukahunui Ridge Track** to Central Te Hoe Hut (15 bunks) and Rogers (Te Wairoa) Hut (six bunks), and out via Moerangi Hut (nine bunks) back to the River Rd car park. This option is a much more demanding outing than the others.

❶ Getting to/from the Tramp

Whirinaki Te Pua a Tane Conservation Park is 90km southeast of Rotorua. The northern end of the track is 7km from Minginui, near the end of River Rd, which is picked up west of the village. It's a 1½- to two-hour walk along River Rd from Minginui. Hitching may be possible because the popular Waterfall Loop day walk begins at the car park.

The southern end of the track is at the end of Plateau Rd, which is accessible either by forest roads from Minginui or from SH5 (Napier–Taupo Rd), 2.5km south of Iwitahi. From SH5, turn north onto Pohokura Rd. After 1.5km turn left onto Waipunga Rd and follow it for 19km, then turn right at the signposted intersection and follow the signs for 'Whirinaki Track'.

Two Minginui-based shuttle companies offer transport to and from the trailheads. **Jailhouse Shuttles** (⌖ 07-366 3311; www.jailhousefarm stay.co.nz) services the River Rd car park (and the Okahu Rd car park, on the northeastern edge of the park) for $50 minimum charge. Whirinaki Forest Holidays (p104) offers transport to all the park's main entrances, as well as car storage. If you have your own wheels, it's $100 per vehicle to be dropped off at River Rd car park from Minginui and then picked up at Plateau Rd.

 The Tramp

Day 1: River Road Car Park to Central Whirinaki Hut

5 HOURS, 16KM

The River Rd car park sets the scene for this tramp, being surrounded by huge podocarps. Pick up the track, clearly signposted, and in less than 1km the track passes the return track of the Waterfall Loop and then descends to a bridge over the impressive **Te Whaiti-nui-a-toi Canyon**, where the river cuts through an ancient lava flow. From here you follow the true right bank of the **Whirinaki River** for the rest of the day, on the **Lower Whirinaki Track**.

Thirty minutes from the car park you pass a junction with the track to Moerangi Hut (nine bunks), five hours (13km) away. In another 30 minutes the track crosses Upper Mangamate Stream and then passes a signposted junction to Mangamate Hut (nine bunks), which is 2½ hours (4.5km) away.

From here it's a 200m detour to **Whirinaki Falls** where cascading water drops 8m into a large pool in the river, an impressive sight that can be viewed from several angles.

Return to the Whirinaki Track, which remains in view of the river, often sidling the steep bluffs above it. About 3km from the junction with the Whirinaki Falls track you reach Vern's Camp. The site of a former track-cutters' camp, this grassy spot makes an excellent campsite with its upgraded shelter and stream water. In another 1.5km the track makes one of the few descents of the day, passes a noticeable campsite on the edge of the river and arrives at the signposted **Kakanui Stream**. Along this stretch keep an eye out for the rare whio (blue duck).

Once over the stream the track stays just above the river for nearly two hours, passing intriguing deep pools along the way. About 20 minutes before Central Whirinaki Hut the track passes through a short and unusual tunnel.

Central Whirinaki Hut (24 bunks) is in a small, grassy clearing near the river. Hut wardens are regularly in residence in summer.

Day 2: Central Whirinaki Hut to Plateau Road Car Park

2½–3 HOURS, 9KM

Follow the signpost to the track heading south. The tramp resumes along the bluffs above the river, and in around 45 minutes arrives at **Taumutu Stream** and a junction with a track to Upper Whirinaki Hut (nine bunks). From the stream there is a long but gradual ascent before the track descends back to the river. An hour from the hut you reach a swing bridge across Whirinaki River.

A major track junction is well signposted from the eastern side of the bridge. Cross the bridge to reach the end of Plateau Rd, or to see the **caves**; trampers heading for Upper Whirinaki Hut or Upper Te Hoe Hut should continue along the eastern bank of the river.

To reach the caves, turn south once you've crossed the bridge and follow the track for about 70m. When the main track begins to ascend, look for a partially obscured track that continues along the river – it will quickly lead to the main cave. The huge cavern is interesting and at night it is possible to see glowworms. The track is wide and it's an easy night-time excursion from Central Whirinaki Hut if you take a torch.

The main track climbs the ridge above the river and then heads southwest to the car park at the end of Plateau Rd.

TOWNS & FACILITIES

Whakapapa Village

📍 07

This tiny resort town is the trailhead for many Tongariro National Park tramps, and home to the national park visitor centre. It has limited accommodation and eating options, with National Park Village and Ohakune offering a greater range. That said, outside of winter this hillside village is sleepy and a bit leafy and a good spot for quiet contemplation.

🛏 Sleeping & Eating

Whakapapa Holiday Park　　HOLIDAY PARK $
(📞 07-892 3897; www.whakapapa.net.nz; sites from $19, dm $25, units $69-149; 🛜) This popular DOC-associated park has a wide range of accommodation options, including bushy campsites and a backpackers lodge. The camp store stocks basic groceries.

Skotel Alpine Resort　　HOSTEL $
(📞 07-892 3719, 0800 756 835; www.skotel. co.nz; Ngauruhoe Pl; s/tw/tr without bathroom $40/55/75, r with bathroom $110-185, cabin $185; 🛜) If you think of it more as a hostel than a hotel, you'll excuse the odd bit of stained carpet or cheap lino, and enjoy the timber-lined alpine ambience and hotelesque facilities such as a sauna, spa pool, restaurant and bar.

Chateau Tongariro　　HOTEL, RESTAURANT $$$
(📞 07-892 3809, 0800 242 832; www.chateau. co.nz; r from $155; @) With its sublime setting and manor-house grandeur, the Chateau promises much but delivers just enough. Of most interest to trampers is the elegant on-site restaurant (mains $36 to $38), Pihanga Cafe (mains $20 to $27, serves lunch and dinner) and bar.

Fergusson's Cafe　　CAFE $
(⊙ breakfast & lunch; 🛜) This is your classic tiny-town tearoom, with lashings of home-baking, decent espresso, and tables in the sun.

ⓘ Getting There & Away

The national park area is well serviced by shuttle operators, including Taupo-based Tongariro Expeditions (p89) and Turangi-based Turangi Alpine Shuttles (p89), both good options if you're coming from the north. Other than local shuttle operators, your best bet for getting to

Whakapapa Village is with **Naked Bus** (📞 0900 62533; www.nakedbus.com), which offers a link from its National Park drop-off.

National Park

📍 07 / POP 460

This small settlement is on the intersection of SH4 and SH47, 15km from Whakapapa Village. National Park services trampers in the summer and skiers in the winter. There is no visitor information centre here, but the website of the National Park Village Business Association (www.nationalpark.co.nz) is very useful.

🛏 Sleeping & Eating

Plateau　　LODGE, HOSTEL $
(📞 07-892 2993; www.plateaulodge.co.nz; 17 Carroll St; dm $30, d $70-110, apt from $160; @ 🛜) Cosy rooms, some with en suite and TV, and an attractive communal lounge, kitchen and hot tub make Plateau an attractive option. It also has its own shuttle bus.

Howard's Lodge　　LODGE $
(📞 07-892 2827; www.howardslodge.co.nz; 43-45 Carroll St; dm from $26, s/d from $60/75; 🛜) Not only a comfortable place with a variety of rooms, a spa, a comfortable lounge and a large kitchen, Howard's also has its own shuttle service and tramping gear hire.

Mangahuia Campsite　　CAMPSITE $
(www.doc.govt.nz; SH47; $6) Between National Park and the SH48 turn-off to Whakapapa Village, this basic DOC campsite has cold water and pit toilets.

The Station　　CAFE $$
(www.stationcafe.co.nz; Findlay St; lunch $9-16, dinner $29-36; ⊙ lunch daily, dinner Wed-Mon) Count your blessings ye who find this little railway station along the line. It's a lovely old dear, carefully restored and now serving eggy brunch, pies, coffee and cakes, plus an impressive à la carte evening menu.

Schnapps　　PUB $$
(www.schnappsbarruapehu.com; Findlay St; meals $14-28; ⊙ noon-late) This popular pub serves better-than-average grub and has a handy ATM.

National Park Service Station　　GAS STATION
(📞 07-892 2879; cnr SH4 & SH47; ⊙ 7.30am-7pm) You'll find limited grocery supplies here along with hot pies and coffee.

TONGARIRO, UREWERA & CENTRAL NORTH ISLAND WHAKAPAPA VILLAGE

❶ Getting There & Away

Daily bus services are run by InterCity (p95), north to Auckland (five hours) via Hamilton (three hours), and south to Palmerston North (four hours). The buses arrive and depart outside **Ski Haus** (📞07-892 2854; www.skihaus. co.nz; cnr Carroll & McKenzie Sts), which sells tickets, and those for the **TranzScenic** (www. tranzscenic.co.nz) train, which passes through on its way between Auckland and Wellington.

Naked Bus (p107) services a similar network.

Turangi

📞07 / POP 3500

Once a service town for the nearby hydro-electric power station, sleepy Turangi's claim to fame nowadays is as the 'Trout Fishing Capital of the World' and as one of the country's premier white-water-rafting destinations. Set on the Tongariro River, the town is a shortish hop for Tongariro National Park trampers.

🛏 Sleeping & Eating

There are a handful of places to eat in or near the Turangi Shopping Mall.

Turangi Holiday Park   HOLIDAY PARK $
(📞07-386 8754; www.turangiholidaypark.co.nz; 13 Te Reiti Tamara Grove; sites from $18, cabins s/d $40/55) Near the centre of town, this place is cabin-central and sprawls over extensive grounds.

Extreme Backpackers   HOSTEL $
(📞07-386 8949; www.extremebackpackers.co.nz; 22 Ngawaka Pl; dm $25-27, s $46-56, d $62-72; @🛜) This craftily constructed backpackers has a climbing wall, a cafe and a sunny courtyard, as well as four- to eight-bed dorms and pricier en suite rooms. The operators also run national park shuttles.

Parklands Motor Lodge   MOTEL $
(📞07-386 7515; www.parklandsmotorlodge.co.nz; 25 Arahori St; sites from $17, units $110-140; 🛜❄) On SH1 but set back beyond an epic front lawn, Parklands offers a small but functional area for campervans and a splay of well-presented units. There's a swimming pool and play area for the kids.

Grand Central Fry   FAST FOOD $
(8 Ohuanga Rd; meals $3-8; ⊘11am-8.30pm) This local legend serves top fish and chips, plus burgers and anything else fryable.

Licorice   CAFE $
(57 SH1, Motuoapa; mains $9-17; ⊘8am-4pm Mon-Sat, 9am-3pm Sun) Look for the giant licorice allsort on the roof of this roadside cafe, 8km north of Turangi. It's better than any of the cafes in the town itself.

🔒 Supplies & Equipment

It's best to pick up any necessary tramping equipment and supplies in Turangi, as National Park and Whakapapa Village have very limited offerings.

Sporting Life   OUTDOOR EQUIPMENT
(www.sportinglife-turangi.co.nz; The Mall; ⊘8am-5.30pm Mon-Sat) This small outdoor gear shop stocks tramping essentials such as wool clothing and dehydrated food.

New World   SUPERMARKET
(19 Ohuanga Rd; ⊘8am-8pm) Centrally located right next to the i-SITE.

❶ Information

Turangi i-SITE (📞07-386 8999; www.great laketaupo.com; Ngawaka Pl; ⊘8.30am-5pm; 🛜) A good stop for information on Tongariro National Park, Kaimanawa Forest Park, trout fishing, and snow and road conditions. It issues DOC hut tickets, ski passes and fishing licences, and makes bookings for transport, accommodation and activities.

❶ Getting There & Away

Turangi is a stop on the routes of both InterCity (p95) and Naked Bus (p107), which stop at the i-SITE.

Murupara

📞07 / POP 1900

Murupara is to the west of Te Urewera National Park, on SH38 62km southeast of Rotorua and 93km from the park visitor centre. However, if you're heading into the park from the west, you'd be wise to stock up on your essentials before you hit Murupara, the last sizeable (ahem!) stop before you enter the park. Murupara offers food, lodging and other services, but choices are few. There is no information centre other than the DOC office, and no place to purchase tramping equipment.

🛏 Sleeping & Eating

Murupara Hotel   HOTEL, PUB $
(📞07-366 5871; Pine Dr; s/d $30/50) This decidedly back-blocks pub has rooms, but can be loud and smoky due to the adjoining tavern. It also does basic bar meals ($18 to $20).

Murupara Motel   MOTEL $
(✆ 07-366 5583; www.flaxylodge.co.nz; 990 SH38;
s/d $80/90) A small, simple but serviceable
motel complex in Murupara township.

Cocomo Cafe   CAFE $
(Murupara Shopping Centre, cnr Oregon & Pine Drs;
⊙ 4.30am-2pm Mon-Fri) Has pies, sandwiches
and light meals.

Four Square   SUPERMARKET $
(cnr Oregon & Pine Drs; ⊙ 7.30am-6pm) Located
in the shopping centre, the town's one and
only supermarket stocks all the basics.

ℹ Getting There & Away

You can get to Murupara from Rotorua on
Tuesday, Thursday and Saturday (55 minutes)
on services run by **Bay Bus** (✆ 0800 422 928;
www.baybus.co.nz).

Wairoa
♪ 06 / POP 5228

At the intersection of SH2 and SH36, Wairoa
serves as the eastern gateway to Te Urewera.
This is your last decent opportunity to stock
up on supplies before you head into Te Urewera National Park.

🛏 Sleeping & Eating

Pickings can be slim on the eating front
come sundown.

Riverside Motor Camp   HOLIDAY PARK $
(✆ 06-838 6301; www.riversidemotorcamp.co.nz;
19 Marine Pde; sites per person $16-20, dm $27-30, d
$65-70; @) This compact and peaceful, park-
like camping ground is conveniently located
and offers tidy communal facilities as well as
a bunk room and basic cabins.

Three Oaks Motel   MOTEL $$
(✆ 06-838 8204; www.threeoaksmotel.co.nz; cnr
Clyde Rd & Campbell St; d $105-140; 🛜 ✉) A short
walk from town, this tidy motel complex will
do the trick with its pool, pleasant gardens,
and evening meals by arrangement.

Cafe Jafa   CAFE $
(182 Marine Pde; ⊙ 7am-6pm Mon-Sat, 8am-5pm
Sun) Overlooking the river, this homely cafe
dishes up hearty, good-value country fare
such as all-day breakfast, burgers and fresh
seasonal seafood such as scallops and white-
bait. Good cakes and great coffee.

Osler's Bakery   BAKERY $
(Marine Pde; ⊙ 4.30am-5pm Mon-Fri, 5am-3pm Sat
& Sun) A testament to its excellent product –
including memorable meat pies – this is the
most happening spot in Wairoa. Solid hot
meals.

🛍 Supplies & Equipment

Angus Gemmell   OUTDOOR EQUIPMENT
(176 Marine Pde; ⊙ 8am-5pm Mon-Fri) Your best
bet for camping equipment and fuel.

New World   SUPERMARKET
(41 Queen St; ⊙ 7am-7pm) Saves the day on the
grocery front.

ℹ Information

Wairoa i-SITE (✆ 06-838 7440, 0800 924 762;
www.visitwairoa.co.nz; cnr SH2 & Queen St;
⊙ 8am-5pm Mon-Fri) Has information on Te
Urewera National Park and sells DOC passes.
The centre also serves as the bus station for
InterCity and the national park shuttle services.

ℹ Getting There & Away

InterCity (✆ 09-583 5780; www.intercity.co.nz)
buses stop at the Wairoa i-SITE on their way
between Gisborne (1½ hours) and Napier (2½
hours).

Taranaki, Whanganui & Around Wellington

Includes ➡

Pouakai Circuit 115
Pouakai Crossing 118
Around the Mountain
Circuit 119
Mt Taranaki
Summit 121
Matemateaonga
Track 123
Mangapurua &
Kaiwhakauka Tracks . . 126
Rangiwahia &
Deadmans Loop 130
Mt Holdsworth-
Jumbo Circuit 134
Holdsworth-
Kaitoke Track 136

Best Huts

➡ Pouakai Hut (p117)

➡ Syme Hut (p120)

➡ Rangiwahia Hut (p131)

➡ Jumbo Hut (p135)

Best Views

➡ Mt Taranaki Summit (p121)

➡ Pouakai Tarns (p117)

➡ Mangapurua Trig (p127)

➡ Mt Holdsworth (p135)

Why Go?

Trampers often overlook the southern half of the North Island. This may be because its most dramatic feature – the near-perfect cone of Mt Taranaki – is well off the beaten track, as is the largely impenetrable Whanganui National Park. Another highlight, the Tararuas, have a reputation for being wet and challenging. In these places, however, lie the roots of New Zealand tramping. Egmont National Park was NZ's second national park, created in 1900, and the country's first tramping club was formed in Wellington in 1919.

The tracks across these regions are well established and diverse, from alpine, lowland, wetland and forest. Most are also lightly used, which means solitude is pretty much guaranteed.

In this chapter we present just a few of the region's tramps, in the most high-profile locations. Other worthy wilderness areas to explore include Rimutaka and Aorangi Forest Parks, and amazing Kapiti Island, where you can enjoy day tramps among prolific bird life.

When to Go

The weather in the southern half of the North Island varies greatly, but one common trait across the region is the possibility of ugly weather. In the high-altitude areas of Egmont National Park, the Ruahines and the Tararuas the weather can change in a matter of hours, with blue skies obliterated by raging storms that can bring white-outs and freezing temperatures. If you want to explore the peaks, aim to visit between November and April, although be prepared for bad weather at any time of year.

Whanganui National Park has a mild climate with few extremes, and an occasional dusting of frost and snow on high ridges in winter. It can therefore be tramped at any time of year.

Background Reading

In *Ask That Mountain,* author Dick Scott vividly captures a seminal period in early Maori–Pakeha relations. From the mid-1860s Parihaka, a small Maori settlement at the foot of Mt Taranaki, became the centre of a peaceful resistance movement. In response to the surveying of confiscated tribal lands, Maori – led by Te Whiti-o-Rongomai and Tohu Kakahi and wearing the movement's iconic white feather in their hair – obstructed development by ploughing troughs across roads, erecting random fences and pulling survey pegs. Despite many Maori being arrested and held without trial, the protests continued and intensified. Finally, in November 1881 the government sent a force of more than 1500 troops to Parihaka in a quest to quash the resistance.

DON'T MISS

Sitting at a lofty altitude of 946m, North Egmont Visitor Centre is the highest national park visitor centre in New Zealand. Here's your chance to get a considerable way up the side of a volcano without running out of puff.

The centre is a pleasant 35-minute drive (29km) from downtown New Plymouth. The Egmont Rd section is particularly picturesque as it passes through farmland before winding up the mountain's lower slopes, covered with dense podocarp/broadleaf rainforest. Large rimu and rata trees can be seen. As it climbs higher it passes through wetter and cooler montane forest with kamahi, mosses, liverworts and ferns.

Located at the road's end, the centre dispenses all the usual DOC (Department of Conservation) information and has displays on the natural and human history of the park. It also has a small cafe and souvenir shop.

Nearby is a viewing platform offering stunning views of Mt Taranaki, the surrounding countryside, the Taranaki coast and the volcanic mountain peaks of the central North Island. There are also plenty of short walks should your itinerary allow.

DOC Offices

➡ **DOC Dawson Falls Visitor Centre** (☑ 443 0248; www.doc.govt.nz; Manaia Rd, Kaponga; ⊘ 9am-4pm Thu-Sun, daily during school holidays)

➡ **DOC New Plymouth Area Office** (☑ 759 0350; www.doc.govt.nz; 55a Rimu St; ⊘ 8am-4.30pm Mon-Fri)

➡ **DOC North Egmont Visitor Centre** (☑ 06-756 0990; www.doc.govt.nz; Egmont Rd, Inglewood; ⊘ 8am-4.30pm)

➡ **DOC Wairarapa Area Office** (p133)

➡ **DOC Wellington Visitor Centre** (p133)

➡ **DOC Whanganui Area Office** (☑ 06-349 2100; www.doc.govt.nz; 34-36 Taupo Quay; ⊘ 8am-4.30pm Mon-Fri)

GATEWAY TOWNS

➡ New Plymouth (p139)

➡ Stratford (p140)

➡ Whanganui (p140)

➡ Palmerston North (p141)

➡ Masterton (p142)

➡ Wellington (p142)

Fast Facts

➡ The Whanganui is NZ's longest navigable river, meandering for 290km from Mt Tongariro to the Tasman Sea.

➡ At 2518m, Mt Taranaki is the North Island's second-highest mountain.

➡ Tararua Forest Park is the largest DOC-managed conservation park on the North Island, covering a whopping 1165 sq km.

Top Tip

This region has some rugged, wild and weather-beaten tracks. It is essential to obtain current forecasts and updates on conditions. If the weather looks dicey, delay your tramp.

Resources

➡ www.taranaki.co.nz

➡ www.whanganuinz.com

➡ www.manawatunz.co.nz

➡ www.wairarapanz.com

➡ www.wellingtonnz.com

TARANAKI, WHANGANUI & AROUND WELLINGTON

EGMONT NATIONAL PARK

A classic 2518m volcanic cone dominating the landscape, Mt Taranaki catches the eye like a magnet. Geologically, Taranaki is the youngest, largest and only active volcano in a chain of four large volcanoes in an area including Paritutu and the Sugar Loaf Islands, and the Kaitake and Pouakai Ranges. Its last significant eruption was over 350 years ago and experts say that the mountain is overdue for another go. But don't let that put you off, because this mountain is an absolute beauty, and from it there are magnificent views of patchwork dairy farms, the stormy Tasman Sea and the rugged Tongariro peaks.

The entire mountain, along with the Kaitake and Pouakai Ranges, lies in Egmont National Park. The park includes 335 sq km of native forest and bush, more than 145km of tracks and routes, and scattered huts and shelters. There are three main roads into the park; two take motorists to 900m and the other up to 1140m.

History

Maori believe Taranaki once resided with the mountains of the central North Island. After a dispute with Mt Tongariro over the maiden Pihanga (a small volcano near Lake Taupo) he fled his ancestral home, gouging a wide scar in the earth (now the Whanganui River) on his journey to the west coast. He remains here in majestic isolation, hiding his face behind a cloud of tears.

Taranaki is a sacred place to Maori – a place where the bones of chiefs are buried and a place of refuge against marauding enemies. The legendary Tahurangi was said to be the first person to climb to the summit; when he lit a fire on it he claimed the surrounding land for his *iwi* (tribe).

It was Captain Cook who named the mountain Egmont, after the Earl he sought to flatter at that particular time. Cook would later write that it was 'the noblest hill I have ever seen'. Two years after Cook's visit, Mt Taranaki was the first thing French explorer Marion du Fresne saw of NZ. Both Cook and du Fresne recorded seeing the fires of Maori settlers, but never made contact with the people. Naturalist Ernest Dieffenbach did, however, in 1839. While working for the New Zealand Company, which had been awarded large tracts of land and was responsible for the English settlement of them, Dieffenbach told the local Maori of his plans to climb to the summit. The native tribes tried passionately to dissuade him, but Dieffenbach set off in early December. Although the first attempt was unsuccessful, the naturalist set out again on 23 December and, after bashing through thick bush, he finally reached the peak.

The volcano soon became a popular spot for trampers and adventurers. Fanny Fantham was the first woman to climb Panitahi (also known as Te Iringa and Rangitoto, depending on the *iwi*) – the cone on Mt Taranaki's southern side – in 1887, and it was quickly renamed Fanthams Peak in her honour. A year later the summit route from the plateau (Stratford Plateau) was developed. In 1901, Harry Skeet completed the task of surveying the area for the first topographical map. Tourism boomed.

To protect the forest and watershed from settlers seeking farmland, the Taranaki provincial government set aside an area of roughly 9.5km radius from the summit. The national park was created in October 1900.

Mt Taranaki eventually reclaimed its name, although the name Egmont has stuck like, well, egg. The mountain starred as Mt Fuji in *The Last Samurai* (2003), the production of which caused near-hysteria in the locals, especially when Tom Cruise came to town.

Environment

Volcanic activity began building Mt Taranaki around 130,000 years ago and it last erupted around two centuries ago. It's estimated that significant activity occurs approximately every 340 years, leading vulcanologists to conclude that, rather than Mt Taranaki being extinct, the near perfectly symmetrical cone you see today can be described as a slumbering active volcano.

It won't be like this forever though. Even if volcanic rumblings peter out to the odd puff of smoke and belch of ash, Taranaki will eventually be worn down by rain, wind and ice, as has happened to the deeply eroded stumps of the Kaitake and Pouakai volcanoes that now form the ranges to the northwest.

The very high rainfall, and Taranaki's isolation from NZ's other mountainous regions, have created a unique vegetation pattern. Species such as tussock grass, mountain daisy, harebell, koromiko and foxglove have developed local variations, and many common NZ mountain species are not found here; in particular, trampers will notice the complete absence of beech.

The lush rainforest that covers 90% of the park is predominantly made up of broadleaved podocarps. At lower altitudes you will find many large rimu and rata. Further up, around 900m, kamahi (often referred to as 'goblin forest' because of its tangled trunks and hanging moss) becomes dominant.

ℹ Planning

WHEN TO TRAMP

Mt Taranaki's high altitude means that trampers can be exposed to strong winds, low temperatures and foul weather at any time of year. Changes are often sudden. Most tracks in Egmont National Park should be walked during the traditional tramping season of October to May, with January to April the best time to climb to the Mt Taranaki summit. Trampers must always go prepared for bad conditions, taking with them a warm hat, gloves and good rain gear – no matter how things look when they set off.

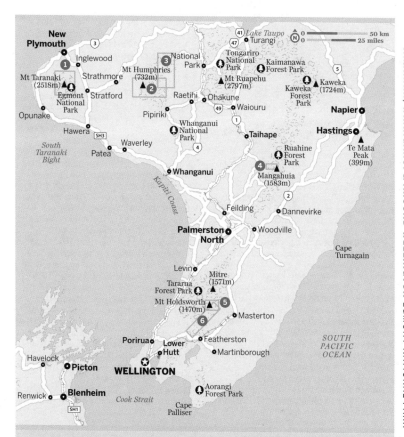

Taranaki, Whanganui & Around Wellington Tramps

1 Mt Taranaki Tramps (p116)

2 Matemateaonga Track (p124)

3 Mangapurua & Kaiwhakauka Tracks (p127)

4 Rangiwahia & Deadmans Loop (p130)

5 Mt Holdsworth-Jumbo Circuit (p134)

6 Holdsworth-Kaitoke Track (p136)

ℹ EMERGENCY EXITS

Mt Taranaki is famous for its trickery, giving visitors a false sense of safety that results in numerous accidents each year. The high altitudes reached by road put inexperienced trampers within easy reach of icy slopes and unpredictable conditions, including massive rain dumps and subsequent rising river levels. A good number of rivers and streams are not bridged and may become impassable after heavy rain. Usually it's simply a case of waiting it out – once the rain stops the rivers recede almost as quickly as they rise. From Kahui or Pouakai Huts it is possible to exit the park along tracks not requiring river crossings, such as Kahui and Puniho tracks for Kahui Hut and Mangorei track for Pouakai Hut.

MAPS & BROCHURES

The park is covered by NZTopo50 BJ29 (*Egmont National Park*), as well as NewTopo map *Taranaki Mt Egmont* 1:65,000. Three brochures, *Pouakai Circuit*, *Around the Mountain Circuit* and *Mt Taranaki Summit Climb* provide similar detail to this guide.

HUTS & LODGES

Six of the eight huts in the park are **Serviced Huts** (www.doc.govt.nz; $15): Holly, Lake Dive, Maketawa, Pouakai, Waiaua Gorge and Waingongoro. They all have woodburners, unlike the two **Standard Huts** (www.doc.govt.nz; $5), Kahui and Syme. You'll need to carry a stove for all huts. Purchase hut tickets at the North Egmont Visitor Centre, Dawson Falls Visitor Centre and other DOC visitor centres nationwide. Hut tickets can also be bought at the region's i-SITES.

Behind North Egmont Visitor Centre you'll find the **Camphouse** (☑ 278 6523; www.mttaranaki.co.nz; Egmont Rd; dm/d $35/80), a historic bunkhouse complete with gun ports in the walls and endless horizon views from the porch.

Further south on the road up to the Stratford Plateau (the highest road in the park) is the **Stratford Mountain House** (☑ 06-765 6100; www.stratfordmountainhouse.co.nz; Pembroke Rd; r $155), an upbeat lodge with motel-style rooms and an on-site cafe and restaurant.

Near the Dawson Falls Visitor Centre is the Swiss-style **Dawson Falls Romantic Hotel** (☑ 765 5457; www.dawson-falls.co.nz; Manaia Rd; s/d $100/150), which has meals available. Nearby is **Konini Lodge** (☑ 06-756 0990; www.doc.govt.nz; Manaia Rd, Dawson Falls; dm $25), a DOC-managed 38-bed bunk-room accommodation with a full kitchen and good views of the mountain from an outdoor deck.

INFORMATION

DOC operates two visitor information centres on the mountain, providing maps and other information, including the latest weather forecasts and track conditions. North Egmont Visitor Centre (p111) is the closest to New Plymouth, and the major departure point for trampers. The centre also houses displays and the **Mountain Cafe** (meals $10-18), which serves, among other things, ice-cold beer – something to keep in mind when you're finishing a long tramp.

On the southeastern side of the mountain is Dawson Falls Visitor Centre (p111).

GUIDED TRAMPS

The reassuringly named and vastly experienced Ian McAlpine of **Mt Taranaki Guided Tours** (☑ 441 7042; www.mttaranakiguidedtours.co.nz) runs guided trips to the summit and around the park year-round.

ℹ Getting Around

More than 30 roads go to or near the national park, and from most of them a track leads into the park. Three roads – Egmont, Pembroke and Manaia – take you up the mountain. These roads are the most common access points.

Many trampers access the park along Egmont Rd, because it's the closest entrance to New Plymouth; 13km southeast of New Plymouth it turns off SH3, then it's another 16km to the North Egmont Visitor Centre. Those without transport may hitch to Egmont Village, the turn-off to Egmont Rd on SH3, but it will prove harder to get a ride up the mountain from there.

Pembroke Rd extends for 18km from Stratford to the Plateau (1140m), on the eastern side of the volcano. Manaia Rd is 15km southwest of Stratford, on the Opunake Rd just north of Kaponga, and it runs for 8km to Dawson Falls.

There is no scheduled public transport to Egmont National Park but several local transport operators will take you there, including **Kiwi Outdoors Centre** (☑ 03-758 4152; www.outdoorgurus.co.nz), which specialises in tramper transport and charges $50 return to North Egmont (less for more people) and $55 to Dawson Falls (minimum four people).

Cruise NZ Tours (☑ 497 3908, 0800 688 687) runs a daily service that departs New Plymouth at 7.30am and returns from North Egmont Visitor Centre at 4.30pm (one-way/return $30/45). It also runs on demand for the Pouakai Crossing. **Eastern Taranaki Experience** (☑ 06-765 7482; www.eastern-taranaki.co.nz) provides transport from Stratford to North Egmont ($80) and Dawson Falls ($50). **Taranaki Tours** (☑ 0800 886 877) also provides park service, given sufficient advance notice.

Pouakai Circuit

Duration 2 days

Distance 25km (15.5 miles)

Track Standard Tramping track

Difficulty Moderate

Start/End North Egmont

Nearest Town New Plymouth (p139)

Transport Shuttle bus

Summary Considerable upgrades have seen this short circuit emerge as Egmont National Park's classic tramp, passing through diverse forest, tussock and swamp, and offering spectacular views.

The Pouakai Circuit features spectacular views from the top of the Pouakai Range, which at one time was a volcano of similar size to Mt Taranaki. Natural erosion has reduced it to a rugged area of high ridges and rolling hills of subalpine bush.

The track also passes through the mighty Ahukawakawa Swamp, a unique wetland formed around 3500 years ago. It is home to many plant species, some of which are found nowhere else on the planet. Sedges, sphagnum moss, herbs and red tussock are all common here, along with small orchids and other flowering plants.

This loop can be tramped in either direction, but trampers can also leave the route at Pouakai Hut and follow the Mangorei Track, a 2½-hour tramp, to the end of Mangorei Rd. This road leads to New Plymouth, a mostly downhill walk of 15km (there is usually very little traffic this far up).

🏃 The Tramp

Day 1: North Egmont to Pouakai Hut

5–6 HOURS, 12KM, 348M ASCENT, 200M DESCENT

The tramp begins along **Holly Hut Track**, signposted near the Camphouse. The track climbs steadily up steps, gaining 240m and passing the Ambury Monument on the way to a trig (1181m), where, if the day is clear, you are rewarded with spectacular views of Mt Taranaki and the valleys below. The track continues beyond the trig and up the narrow Razorback ridge, ascending another 100m, before leaving the lava flow and sidling around the slope. Within an hour (3km) of leaving the Camphouse you reach

a signposted junction. The left turn takes you via the Around the Mountain Circuit to Stratford Plateau.

The Pouakai Circuit continues past the junction and follows the well-marked Holly Hut Track as it climbs around the headwaters of the Waiwhakaiho River and along the base of the **Dieffenbach Cliffs**, which rise above you. Enjoy views of New Plymouth while skirting the mountain's northern flanks for the next hour or so.

The track descends slightly to the headwaters of Kokowai Stream and cuts across **Boomerang Slip**. Extreme care must be used when tramping across this slide of loose rocks and dirt. From the slip the track works around the head of Kokowai Stream, and then gently climbs a prominent ridge to the junction with the signposted Kokowai Track. From this point you will be able to view Ahukawakawa Swamp and much of the track up the Pouakai Range.

Head west (left), following the track as it descends 244m over 2.5km to the junction with the **Ahukawakawa Track** (the right fork). Turn left to reach Holly Hut (32 bunks), five minutes away across the unbridged Minarapa Stream. This is a popular place to spend a night, with Mt Taranaki looming behind and good views of the Pouakai Range from the veranda.

If you have spare time, consider going the extra distance from Holly Hut to the spectacular 31m-high **Bells Falls**, around 30 minutes away. From the hut follow the sign to Bells Falls. The track heads across Holly Flats before swinging north around the Dome and descending towards the Stony River. At the signposted junction turn right to Bells Falls and follow the track upstream to the base of the falls.

Trampers continuing to Pouakai Hut should return from Holly Hut to the Ahukawakawa Track, and follow it. Within 500m the track reaches an elaborate viewing platform and then descends to the southwest end of **Ahukawakawa Swamp**. This remarkable sphagnum moss swamp is crossed via 1km of boardwalks, including an unusual arched bridge over Stony River.

On the northern side of the swamp the track begins a long climb along a forested ridge. The 304m ascent to the junction with the Pouakai Track is a one- to 1½-hour effort, with the first 20 to 30 minutes the steepest part. The track then levels briefly, before continuing at a more gentle incline. If the day is nice, views of the swamp and Mt

Mt Taranaki Tramps

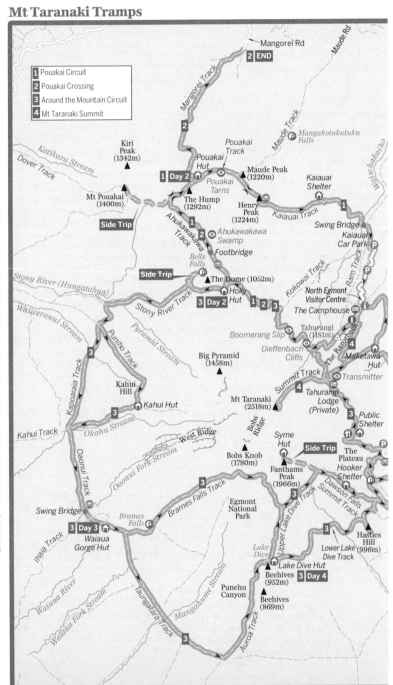

1 Pouakai Circuit
2 Pouakai Crossing
3 Around the Mountain Circuit
4 Mt Taranaki Summit

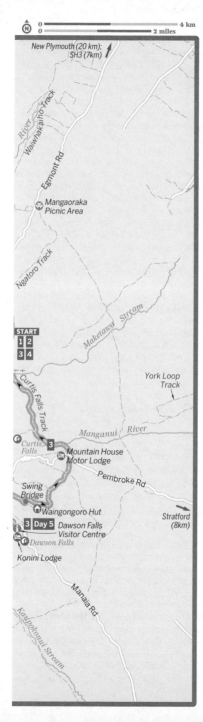

Taranaki rising above it are well worth the knee-bending effort. If it's raining, this can be a bit of a slog, even with all the steps that have been installed.

Two hours from Holly Hut you top out at a saddle that opens up to views of New Plymouth, and reach **Pouakai Track** at a signposted junction. Head northeast (right), as the track sidles around the north side of the **Hump** (1292m) and then makes a short descent to a signposted junction with Mangorei Track. Those with sharp eyes will see a corner of Pouakai Hut 15 to 20 minutes before reaching it.

Pouakai Hut (16 bunks) is just five minutes down Mangorei Track (left), about 2½ hours from Holly Hut. Nestled on the west side of the ridge, it has grand views from its veranda over the curved coastline and New Plymouth. The sunsets can be spectacular from this perch, followed by the city lights of New Plymouth gradually flickering on.

Mangorei Track is a good exit off the mountain in bad weather, and the final leg of the Pouakai Crossing.

SIDE TRIP: MT POUAKAI

2 HOURS, 6KM RETURN, 200M ASCENT

Pouakai Hut is in such a scenic location that you may be tempted to spend a spare day here. If so, use part of it to climb to the summit of **Mt Pouakai** (1400m) for even better views of the Taranaki region. To get there, head back up to the Pouakai Track junction and turn right. It's a one-hour (3km) climb from here along a route that marches straight to the top of the peak.

Day 2: Pouakai Hut to North Egmont

5–7 HOURS, 13KM, 744M ASCENT, 966M DESCENT

Keep your fingers crossed for clear weather as you traverse the backbone of the Pouakai Range because the views are superb.

Return to the Pouakai Track and head northeast (left) to follow the tussocky ridge for a level and scenic stretch, with New Plymouth on one side of you and Mt Taranaki on the other. Within 1km of the hut you reach the **Pouakai Tarns**. On a clear and windless day, Mt Taranaki will be reflected in the surface of the tarns, making for the classic photograph of the national park.

The track sidles around **Maude Peak** (1220m) then drops southeast into a low saddle at the base of Henry Peak,

45 minutes from Pouakai Hut. The 152m climb to the top of **Henry Peak** (1224m) looks more daunting than it is, with most trampers reaching the observation deck within 20 minutes. It's well worth the modest effort for the 360-degree view.

From the peak the track begins a long, steady descent on a series of steps. Within an hour you emerge at the edge of Kai Auahi Stream, where you can peer into its gorge. The track skirts the gorge for another 30 minutes before arriving at Kaiauai Shelter.

This three-sided shelter was built for trampers to wait in when the stream is too flooded to ford. In normal conditions you can cross it and barely get your boots wet. It's a short, steep descent into the stream bed and a climb out the other side. There is a proposal to put a bridge across this stream sometime in the future.

For the next hour the track climbs in and out of a couple of small gorges and two major ones, with recent track work improving what used to be quite a slog.

Less than 1½ hours from the shelter you reach a signposted junction with Kokowai Track, which heads southwest up the mountain. You head south (left) and in five minutes arrive at a swing bridge across the **Waiwhakaiho River**.

On the other side is a junction with Waiwhakaiho Track (left fork), which heads northeast. You're now less than 30 minutes from North Egmont Rd. Continue south (right) on **Kaiauai Track** as it climbs out of the gorge, passes a signposted junction with Ram Track (right fork) and then breaks out on to asphalt at the Kaiauai car park.

North Egmont is 2km – a good 30-minute walk – up the road. The alternative is to follow Ram Track back to North Egmont, a two-hour walk from its junction with the Kaiauai Track. Most trampers take the road, knowing they are that much closer to a cold beer at the Mountain Cafe.

Pouakai Crossing

Duration 1 day

Distance 17km (10.6 miles)

Track Standard Tramping track

Difficulty Moderate

Start North Egmont

End End of Mangorei Rd

Nearest Town New Plymouth (p139)

Transport Shuttle bus

Summary Take the major highlights of Egmont National Park, pack them into a day tramp, and you've got a crossing that just *might* challenge Tongariro for NZ's top-day-walk crown.

This increasingly popular day tramp packs plenty of panoramic punch without the need to lug a heavy pack filled with overnight gear. It's also a great option for those based in New Plymouth, allowing you a grand day out with a debrief under the bright lights of the city. Its relatively low altitude means it can also be completed around 320 days of the year.

Starting at the North Egmont Visitor Centre, the track follows the first day of the Pouakai Circuit as far as Pouakai Hut before heading down Mangorei Track to the road's end, where you can be collected by shuttle bus for the return trip to town. Along the way it takes in a spectacular array of the national park's highlights, including Dieffenbach Cliffs, Bells Falls, the primeval Ahukawakawa Swamp and the Pouakai Tarns. It's a full-on day, but a hugely satisfying one.

Local shuttle operators and tramping guides will gladly get you to and from trailheads.

🥾 The Tramp

8–10 HOURS, 17KM, 952M ASCENT, 1385M DESCENT

Follow the route for Day 1 of the Pouakai Circuit, from North Egmont to Pouakai Hut (p115). If you're a steady tramper you should have no trouble factoring in the side trips to Holly Hut and on to Bells Falls.

From Pouakai Hut there are other side trips that should not be missed if you can help it: the two-hour return trip to Mt Pouakai (1400m), and the part of the track towards Henry Peak as far as the Pouakai Tarns, where you should break out the camera for the obligatory snapshots. You'll need to allow another hour if you wish to head up and down Henry Peak (1224m) with its 360-degree panorama.

The way home is via **Mangorei Track**, which departs from Pouakai Hut and heads steadily downhill on a stepped boardwalk for 1½ to two hours to reach the road's end. This recently upgraded track is very popular with locals due to its proximity to New Plymouth.

After a short downhill stretch through low shrub the track partially circumnavigates the knoll known to locals as Photographic Peak (1232m). Look out for the historic graffiti carved in rock on the left as you descend, and be sure to pause to appreciate the views of northern Taranaki and coastline before you drop below the bushline.

The last area of low shrub is known as Graylings Clearing, where pioneering summit parties would graze their horses and pick up a fresh mount. Growing in this area is the unusual parasitic plant *Dactylanthus taylorii,* otherwise known as wood rose.

From here the track continues its constant descent through rainforest broken only by one of the last stands of mature rimu and miro to escape the last eruption of Mt Taranaki. Around 30 minutes later you will emerge at a gravel road; follow it for five minutes to reach the road end and transport pick-up point.

Around the Mountain Circuit

Duration 5 days

Distance 49–53km (30–33 miles)

Track Standard Tramping track

Difficulty Moderate to demanding

Start/End North Egmont

Nearest Towns New Plymouth (p139), Stratford (p140)

Transport Shuttle bus

Summary Around the Mountain Circuit (AMC) is a backcountry track for experienced trampers through stunted subalpine forest and spectacular volcanic scenery. Circumnavigating Mt Taranaki, you're spoiled for views up, down and around the mountain, with options for side trips to waterfalls, a historic hut and the 2518m peak itself.

The track can be started at either North Egmont or Dawson Falls. The tramp is described here in an anticlockwise direction beginning at North Egmont. Trampers starting at Dawson Falls often travel clockwise and go directly to Waiaua Gorge Hut via the upper level tracks on Day 1. Note that high- and low-level tracks exist for some sections. Generally trampers take the high road in good weather, the low road in bad.

🚶 The Tramp

Day 1: North Egmont to Holly Hut

3–4 HOURS, 8KM, 348M ASCENT, 200M DESCENT

Follow Day 1 of the Pouakai Circuit (p115) as far as Holly Hut.

Day 2: Holly Hut to Waiaua Gorge Hut

7–9 HOURS, 13KM

The track crosses Holly Flats then swings north around the **Dome** (1052m) and steadily descends on steps to the Stony River. The 30-minute detour to view the spectacular **Bells Falls** is worthwhile.

Continue in a generally westerly direction beside – and sometimes along the river bed of – **Stony River**, taking care as it is severely eroded. You will need to look carefully for marker poles.

Around 4km from Holly Hut the entrance to the **Kapoaiaia Track** is on the true left of the river. Follow this track across two badly eroded stream beds to reach **Puniho Track**. From here there are two options, each going their own way for around two hours before meeting again.

For the high track, turn left and follow Puniho Track uphill into subalpine forest and around to Kahui Hut, then continue down **Kahui Track** to turn left at the Oaonui Track junction.

For the low track, continue along Kapoaiaia Track through the forest, crossing many streams to the junction with the Kahui and Oaonui Tracks.

Both options then follow the **Oaonui Track** about two hours, climbing in and out of numerous gullies. Finally you meet **Ihaia Track**; turn left and follow it to Waiaua Gorge Hut, being careful to look for markers along the open riverbed section.

Built in 1984, the hut is situated on the cliffs above the deep Waiaua Gorge and provides excellent views of Taranaki's western slopes.

Day 3: Waiaua Gorge Hut to Lake Dive Hut

7–8 HOURS, 10KM, 340M ASCENT

Follow **Brames Falls Track** into the Waiaua Gorge, via an aluminium ladder and a steep track, then climb out again to the Taungatara Track junction, which you will reach about 45 minutes from the hut. There are two options from here, both of which take around seven hours.

For the high track, continue up the Brames Falls Track, climbing steeply to the rock bluffs of Bobs Ridge. Carefully follow the poled route through eroded rocky sections and across tussock slopes before descending to the Lake Dive Track junction. Take the right fork for a 45-minute tramp down to Lake Dive Hut. The left fork leads directly to Dawson Falls (2½ hours). This high track can be impassable due to snow in wintery conditions.

For the low track, turn right and follow the **Taungatara Track** approximately 6km through forest, until reaching the Auroa Track junction. Turn left and ascend the **Auroa Track** to Lake Dive Hut. This track can be muddy and has many stream crossings.

Lake Dive Hut, built in 1980, is situated at the eastern end of the lake, and on a windless day a reflection of Fanthams Peak graces the water in front of it. If you're contemplating a swim after a hot day above the bushline, keep in mind that the water is very cold and the bottom very muddy.

Day 4: Lake Dive Hut to Dawson Falls

3–4 HOURS, 7KM

Although it is possible to tramp all the way to North Egmont in one day, splitting the remaining distance into two days will allow sufficient time to take the rewarding side trip to Fanthams Peak, which can be reached by taking the Upper Lake Dive Track, as opposed to the Lower.

The high track offers excellent views but is very exposed and requires mountaineering experience in winter conditions. It climbs steeply from the hut up **Upper Lake Dive Track** to the junction with the Brames Falls Track. Turn right to continue along the Upper Lake Dive Track, heading across tussock slopes to the Fanthams Peak Track junction. Turn right to descend to Dawson Falls, or left for the side trip to Fanthams Peak and Syme Hut.

The low-level option follows **Lower Lake Dive Track**, undulating through forest and crossing many unbridged streams and dipping into gorges on its way to Dawson Falls. When the track eventually reaches the junction with the Fanthams Peak Track, turn right and descend through 'goblin forest' to Dawson Falls, where you can stay at either

Konini Lodge (bookings required), or continue to Waingongoro Hut (16 bunks), 1½ hours from Dawson Falls.

SIDE TRIP: FANTHAMS PEAK

6–7 HOURS RETURN, 10KM, 1066M ASCENT

When the weather is kind this is a worthy side trip with splendid views of Taranaki and to the coastline far below. From the Dawson Falls Visitor Centre take the **Fanthams Peak Track** and follow it up past the Hooker Shelter before ascending a steep staircase to the junction with Upper Lake Dive Track.

From here it's around 1½ hours following a poled zigzagging route up precipitous scoria slopes to **Syme Hut** (10 bunks) and **Fanthams Peak** (1966m). The hut, at 1950m, is the second highest on the North Island. Soak up the lofty views before heading back down the same route you came up, or settle into the hut if you've been game enough to lug your pack up with you.

The track is very exposed along its upper parts and is best avoided in winter and inclement conditions unless parties are appropriately experienced and equipped with ice axes and crampons.

Day 5: Dawson Falls to North Egmont

HIGH TRACK 4–5 HOURS, 11KM, 614M ASCENT; LOW TRACK 7–8 HOURS, 14.5KM

Again there are low- and high-track options. The high track is the more direct route, achievable in fine weather. In bad weather it is very exposed, and may be impassable due to snow/ice in winter conditions.

The high track follows the well-benched **Wilkies Pools Track**, which climbs northwest away from the car park. The tramp begins in forest, and within 30 minutes arrives at **Wilkies Pools**, an interesting series of small pools and cascades gouged out of a lava flow by the stream.

From Wilkies Pools cross the river and continue until you reach a track junction; from here follow signs to **Stratford Plateau**.

Once you reach the Stratford Plateau car park follow signs to the Manganui Ski Field. This track will take you through a small tunnel, and down into the Manganui Gorge before climbing to the ski field area. Follow the markers across the tussock slope to continue on the track to privately owned Tahurangi Lodge, reached around 1½ hours after leaving the Stratford Plateau. From the lodge turn downhill and follow the 4WD track to North Egmont Visitor Centre, passing the giant TV transmission tower on your descent.

For the low track from Dawson Falls, follow signs for Waingongoro Hut. Before reaching the hut, take the left at the track junction and cross the swing bridge before following the track to the Te Popo car park.

The route continues across Pembroke Rd as **Curtis Falls Track**. It's a difficult three- to four-hour tramp to Maketawa Hut, and includes climbing in and out of five gorges and crossing many unbridged streams. Although most trampers push on to North Egmont, a nice option is to stay at Maketawa Hut (16 bunks), which includes a large kitchen, wood fire and an outdoor deck where you can sit and admire views of Mt Taranaki. This is also a great base if you want to scale the summit. The final leg to North Egmont from the hut is a 1½-hour tramp along a forested track.

Mt Taranaki Summit

Duration 8 to 10 hours

Distance 12.6km (7.8 miles)

Track Standard Tramping track

Difficulty Moderate to demanding

Start/End North Egmont

Nearest Town New Plymouth (p139)

Transport Shuttle bus

Summary Completing the challenging climb to the 2518m pinnacle of this slumbering volcano is likely to be a major highlight of your NZ tramping adventures.

The majestic Mt Taranaki is the central point of the 335-sq-km Egmont National Park. Approximately 130,000 years old, it is the park's most recent volcanic peak. It last erupted around 200 years ago – the mountain has been quiet for a while but is not considered extinct.

Under ideal weather conditions in the summer, most fit trampers can make it to the top of Mt Taranaki, the most-climbed mountain in NZ. But you need to be prepared – a long list of people have been killed on its slopes.

Because of sudden weather changes it is essential that you have the right gear and supplies (including plenty of water as there are no streams). You must check the fore-

cast, and be prepared to turn tail and retreat if the weather deteriorates.

The best time of year for nonmountaineers to climb is during January to March, when the mountain is often clear of snow and ice other than in the crater.

🏃 The Tramp

8–10 HOURS, 12.6KM RETURN, 1572M ASCENT

From North Egmont, follow the **Summit Track** signs and head up the 4WD Translator Rd. This 1½-hour walk is a good warm up, with one section aptly named 'the Puffer'. There's a small public day shelter under the privately owned Tahurangi Lodge, and public toilets just below the giant TV tower.

From the lodge a track continues to Hongi Valley then climbs up a heap of steps to 1950m where you move onto the scree slope of North Ridge. Follow the poles as they zigzag up the loose gravel to the ridge known as the Lizard (2134m). Be mindful of falling rocks here.

The poles up the Lizard lead to the north, or summer, entrance of the crater, where you will encounter snowfields and icy rocks. Once in the crater, at 2450m, it is a walk across the ice and snow to the west rim and a clamber up the rocks to the **summit**, around four hours from Tahurangi Lodge.

The area is sacred to Maori, and visitors are asked to respect the mountain by not standing directly on the summit peak, by not camping or cooking on or around the summit area and by removing all rubbish.

You return down along the ascent route. It will take three to four hours, so allow yourself plenty of time to descend safely before nightfall.

WHANGANUI NATIONAL PARK

The 742-sq-km Whanganui National Park – lying between Egmont National Park to the west, and Tongariro National Park to the east – is the North Island's largest lowland wilderness. The park's dominant feature is the Whanganui River, which winds 290km from its source on Mt Tongariro to the Tasman Sea. It is NZ's longest navigable river, a fact that's been shaping its destiny for centuries, with rich Maori history an important part of the park experience.

The river remains the main byway through the park, well utilised by travellers in kayaks and canoes lured through the national park stretch by the promise of clear, green waters bounded by high-sided gorges buttressing dense native forest. This waterborne wilderness adventure is now known as the Whanganui Journey, the Great Walk that isn't actually a walk.

This is a national park not particularly easy to access on foot. But the walks that do exist are popular, well bedded down and maintained. Two of these, the Kaiwhakauka and Mangapurua Tracks, form part of the 317km **Mountains to Sea Cycle Trail**, part of the **Nga Haerenga/New Zealand Cycle Trail** (www.nzcycletrail.com). This four- to six-day mountain biking epic from Tongariro National Park through to Whanganui town will undoubtedly grow in popularity, as will many of NZ's wilderness trails now being converted to dual use.

History

In Maori legend the Whanganui River was formed when Mt Taranaki, after brawling with Mt Tongariro over the lovely Mt Pihanga, fled the central North Island for the sea, leaving a long gouge behind him. He turned west at the coast, finally stopping at his current address. Mt Tongariro sent cool water to heal the gouge and, thus, the Whanganui River was born.

Maori arrived permanently in this area around 1350. They flourished in pre-European days because food in the valley was plentiful – it included produce from cultivated terraces, and eels caught in sophisticated weirs on river channels. At each bend of the river, *kaitiaki* (guardians) ensured preservation of the *mauri* (life force) of the place. Many *kainga* (villages) were located in the rugged hill country. The numerous steep bluffs and ridges made suitable sites for *pa* (fortified villages), which were needed because intertribal warfare was common in this well-populated region.

Europeans arrived in the 1840s. The Church of England's Reverend Richard Taylor was the most influential minister to travel up the Whanganui River, and numerous churches and missions were built along its banks. At Maori request, Taylor bestowed new names on many of their settlements: Koriniti (Corinth), Hiruharama (Jerusalem), Ranana (London) and Atene (Athens) survive today. The ministers persuaded the tribes to abandon their *pa* and begin cultivating wheat, especially near the lower reaches of the Whanganui River, where several flour mills were established.

NZ's contemporary tourism leviathan was seeded here. Internationally advertised trips on the 'Rhine of Maoriland' became so popular that by 1905, 12,000 tourists a year were making the trip upriver from Whanganui to Pipiriki or downriver from Taumarunui, on a fleet of 12 riverboats. The engineering feats and skippering ability required on the river became legendary.

From 1918 land upstream of Pipiriki was granted to returning WWI soldiers. Farming here was a major challenge, with many families struggling for years to make the rugged land productive. Only a few endured into the early 1940s. The completion of the railway from Auckland to Wellington and the improving roads ultimately signed the river transport's death warrant; 1959 saw the last commercial riverboat voyage. Today, just one old-fleet vessel cruises the river – the *Waimarie*.

In 1912 the Whanganui River Trust was established, and by 1980 it covered an area of 350 sq km. A national-park assessment began in 1980 and Whanganui National Park, the country's 11th national park, was gazetted in 1986.

Environment

The hilly Whanganui lowlands are marked by myriad streams cutting between flat-topped ridges carpeted in thick native forest.

The park contains extensive stands of podocarp-hardwood lowland forest, an ecosystem under-represented in the NZ conservation estate. Kamahi and tawa are a common canopy species, while the understorey is rich in ferns. Large podocarps include rimu, miro and totara on ridges and faces, while kahikatea and matai predominate in the river terraces and flats, as does the unmistakable nikau palm. Large northern rata throughout the park put on a spectacular display in mid-summer, and there are also various species of beech. Steep riverbanks are a haven for some of the park's more vulnerable plants, such as hutu, fuchsia and the rare daisy *Brachiglottis turneri.*

The park's isolated centre, in particular, is a notable haven for bird life. Common species that can be seen include fantails, grey warblers, silvereyes, tomtits, robins, bellbirds, kereru, tui and whitehead. Migratory cuckoos are heard in spring and early summer. You may be lucky enough to see kakariki or kaka along the Matemateaonga Track, and perhaps also the rifleman and NZ falcon. The park is home to the largest population of North Island brown kiwi, with several thousand birds present. The whio (blue duck) inhabits the clean fast-flowing river habitats in the park, with the most significant populations on rivers bordering the park.

🛈 Planning

WHEN TO TRAMP
Whanganui National Park has a mild climate with few extremes, and an occasional dusting of frost and snow on high ridges in winter. This means that the tramps in this park can be done year round, but will be best enjoyed from October to May.

INFORMATION
Maps and information about the park are available at DOC's Whanganui Area Office (p111). There are also the **Pipiriki DOC Field Base** (☑ 06-385 5022; Owairua Rd, Pipiriki) and **Taumarunui DOC Field Base** (☑ 07-895 8201; Cherry Grove Domain, Taumarunui), but these offices are not always staffed.

Matemateaonga Track

Duration 4 days

Distance 43km (26.7 miles)

Track Standard Tramping track

Difficulty Easy to moderate

Start Kohi Saddle

End Whanganui River

Nearest Towns Stratford (p140), Whanganui (p140)

Transport Shuttle bus, boat

Summary Penetrating deep into the wilderness and emerging at the mystical Whanganui River, this is the classic Whanganui National Park tramp.

This track follows an old Maori trail and a settlers' dray road across the broken and thickly forested crests of the Matemateaonga Range, at altitudes between 400m and 730m. There are vantage points offering impressive views of the rugged countryside and glimpses of the peaks of Tongariro National Park. The main interest, however, is lush native forest.

Surprisingly, the tramp is easier than the rugged nature of the countryside sug-

gests, because the old graded road reduces the amount of steep climbing. Although it lacks the alpine appeal of many other tracks, especially those in Tongariro National Park, when its isolated nature is combined with a jetboat tour of the Whanganui River at the end, the Matemateaonga Track becomes one of NZ's great bush adventures.

A return day walk from Kohi Saddle to Omaru Hut (four hours total) provides an excellent sampler of the track, with fantastic views, interesting plant life and a pleasant lunch spot at the hut.

🛈 Planning

MAPS & BROCHURES
The tramp is covered by *NZTopo50 BJ31* (Strathmore) and *BJ32* (Pipiriki). A simplified map is included in DOC's *Matemateaonga Track* brochure, but this is not suitable for navigation.

HUTS, CAMPING & LODGES
The Matemateaonga Track sports four **Serviced Huts** (www.doc.govt.nz; $15) – Omaru, Pouri, Ngapurua and Puketotara – none of which have cooking facilities. Free camping is permitted throughout the park, but particularly encouraged at sites where DOC has provided toilets.

Across the river from the Tieke Kainga *marae*, 21km upriver from Pipiriki, the **Bridge to Nowhere Lodge** (☑ 0800 480 308; www.bridgetonowhere.co.nz; campsites from $15, dm $45) makes a pleasant alternative to spending your final night at Puketotara Hut. It has a range of accommodation, a licensed bar, home-cooked meals, as well as jetboat services, and canoe and mountain-bike hire.

🛈 Getting to/from the Tramp

The traditional start of the Matemateaonga Track is at Kohi Saddle, 55km from Stratford. Take SH43 northeast to Strathmore, and then head east along Brewer Rd to Makahu. The trailhead is well signposted, and is reached at the upper end of Upper Mangaehu Rd, about 15km east of Makahu.

The track start can also be reached via shuttle bus from Stratford or Whanganui. **Eastern Taranaki Experience** (☑ 06-765 7482; www.eastern-taranaki.co.nz) provides round-trip transport from Stratford to Kohi Saddle, and return from Pipiriki for $240 per person (minimum four people), which includes the jetboat. **Whanganui Tours** (☑ 027 201 2472, 06-345 3475; www.whanganuitours.co.nz) runs on-demand shuttle services to Kohi Saddle, departing Whanganui ($380 for minimum three people; $25 per extra person).

Matemateaonga Track

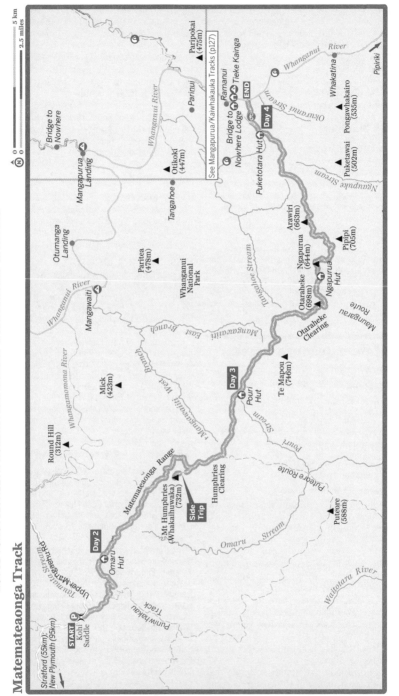

The track ends at Tieke Reach, an isolated bend on the Whanganui River, 25km upriver from Pipiriki. Apart from retracing your steps, a 30-minute ride on a commercial jetboat is the only way out. The jetboat is run by **Whanganui River Adventures** (☑0800 862 743; www.whanganuiriveradventures.co.nz), who will pick up or drop off trampers ($75). For $130 the company will also include you on its Bridge to Nowhere Tour, a four-hour trip into the spectacular upper river where you can tramp in to the famous bridge and enjoy a few 'Hamilton turns' (360-degree spins) before heading to Pipiriki.

From Pipiriki, you can either head out 28km east to Raetihi, Ohakune or National Park; Whanganui River Adventures runs shuttles to all three. Otherwise, you can return to Whanganui, 79km south. This route is serviced by the mail run courtesy of Whanganui Tours, which leaves Pipiriki around 4pm. It also runs transport in the other direction, from Whanganui, leaving 7am, to Pipiriki (one way/return $30/63).

🥾 The Tramp

Day 1: Kohi Saddle to Omaru Hut
2 HOURS, 5.6KM

At the Kohi Saddle car park, a large sign marks the beginning of the track. Begin by climbing through regenerating bush along a spur, towards the crest of the **Matemateaonga Range**. Within 30 minutes you move into a thick forest of kamahi and tawa, the dominant feature for the rest of the tramp.

The track eventually becomes a 3m-wide trail as it follows the remains of the original dray road that was cut all the way to Pouri Hut. Sidle the narrow Tanawapiti Valley and follow it to the signposted junction with **Puniwhakau Track** (right), 1½ hours from the car park.

At the junction the Matemateaonga Track reaches the crest of the range. It continues east (left fork), then north, descending easily for 30 minutes. The track levels out at a small saddle, where Omaru Hut is in a clearing. The hut, featuring mattresses, a wood-burning stove and rainwater tank, is surrounded by forest near the source of the Omaru Stream.

Day 2: Omaru Hut to Pouri Hut
5 HOURS, 13.3KM

The track heads southeast from the hut and continues in this direction practically the whole day. At first it follows the southwestern slopes of the Matemateaonga Range,

through thick forest. After two hours you cross to the northern flank of the range; if the day is clear there is an occasional glimpse of the three Tongariro National Park volcanoes through the trees. The track, which is muddy in places, continues through the forest until it reaches a junction with the trail (right) to the summit of Mt Humphries, 3½ hours from Omaru Hut. This makes a good side trip if you have the time.

The track continues roughly southeast from the junction, and after 30 minutes or so passes through **Humphries Clearing**, the site of the former Humphries Hut, an animal-control hut that was removed in 2000. It's another hour or so from this junction to Pouri Hut (12 bunks), in a large clearing at the end of the dray road.

SIDE TRIP: MT HUMPHRIES
1½ HOURS, 2KM RETURN, 100M ASCENT

Known to Maori as Whakaihuwaka – 'made like the prow of a canoe' – 732m **Mt Humphries** is a rewarding side trip. From the top are excellent views of the King Country around Waitomo to the north and Mt Taranaki to the west. On a clear day you can see three national parks: Egmont to the west, Tongariro to the north and Whanganui at your feet.

Day 3: Pouri Hut to Puketotara Hut
7 HOURS, 22KM

This is the longest leg of the trip, but it is an easy tramp along a well-graded track, passing through the most pristine forest in the national park. Before leaving Pouri Hut make sure your water bottle is full, because the only water source along the ridge is the water tank at Ngapurua Hut.

For most of the day the track remains on the crest of the ridge, at an altitude of about 640m, so there is very little climbing. You begin in a tawa and mixed podocarp forest and then move into a predominantly kamahi forest.

After around two hours, the track descends to **Otaraheke Clearing**. If you're not ready for a break it's less than one hour to Ngapurua Hut (10 bunks), built in this clearing in 2010.

Near **Pipipi Peak** (705m), 30 minutes beyond the hut, it's possible to see fossilised shells embedded in the track. At this point the track swings northeast. Within 1½ hours it begins the final descent towards Puketotara Hut. It takes one hour to descend the 200m to the ridge-top clearing where the hut is located, and here the bush is rich with bird life, including kereru, parakeets and long-tailed cuckoos. Puketotara Hut (12 bunks) is a fitting place for a final night on the track – just beyond it are sweeping views of the Whanganui River, while the volcanoes of Tongariro National Park crown the skyline to the east.

If you're planning on spending a night at Bridge to Nowhere Lodge, follow the track from Puketotara Hut. You'll find it behind the hut, heading past the water tanks; it is well signposted. It takes one to 1½ hours to reach the lodge, perched high above the river. Rooms have balcony views of the water or the thick native bush.

Day 4: Puketotara Hut to Whanganui River

1 HOUR, 2KM

A short final day is welcome if you are meeting a jetboat for the trip back to civilisation. You must make sure you reach the river well before the jetboat does; there are pickups throughout the day during summer, but only by prior arrangement. The track quickly drops 100m to a lookout along the crest of a spur. It then descends steeply another 250m, reaching the Matemateaonga Track sign above the sandy banks of the Whanganui River. The jetboat pick-up point is well signposted.

Mangapurua & Kaiwhakauka Tracks

Duration 3 days

Distance 40km (25 miles)

Track Standard Tramping track

Difficulty Easy to moderate

Start Whakahoro

End Mangapurua Landing, Whanganui River

Nearest Town Whanganui (p140)

Transport Shuttle bus, boat

Summary Following two tributaries of the Whanganui River, this verdant tramp passes through the sites of old settlers' farms, grassy flats with small stands of exotic trees, and over a historic bridge.

The Mangapurua and Kaiwhakauka are tributaries of the Whanganui River. Parcels of land throughout these valleys were offered to returned soldiers following WWI.

These pioneer settlers cleared the land of much of its virgin native forest and transformed it into farmland. At the peak of settlement there were 30 farms in the Mangapurua and 16 in the Kaiwhakauka. Old chimneys, fruit trees and roses indicate the original house sites. Problems such as poor access, erosion and falling stock prices during the Depression years forced most of the settlers to abandon their farms; the last remaining farmers left the valley in 1942. Their endeavours account for not only the unique historic qualities of these two tracks, but also the largest degree of modification within Whanganui National Park.

The Mangapurua and Kaiwhakauka Tracks are sections of the Nga Ara Tuhono/Mountains to Sea Cycle Trail (www.mountainstosea.co.nz), which is part of the Nga Haerenga/New Zealand Cycle Trail (www.nzcycletrail.com). The Mangapurua and Kaiwhakauka Tracks are also part of Te Araroa (www.teararoa.org.nz), a walking trail from Cape Reinga to Bluff. New shelters and campsites are being developed to cater to the resulting increase in visitors.

There is an alternative entry point to this track, via the Ruatiti Rd end, which requires a four- to five-hour walk to pick up the Mangapurua. This alternative route skips the Kaiwhakauka section.

ℹ Planning

MAPS & BROCHURES

The tramp is covered by *NZTopo50 BJ32* (Pipiriki), *BH33* (Retaruke) and *BJ33* (Raetihi). A simplified map is included in DOC's *Mangapurua/Kaiwhakauka Tracks* brochure, but this is not suitable for navigation.

CAMPING & LODGES

There are no huts along these tracks but there are plenty of campsites, with Whakahoro the only one you need to pay for ($10).

At Whakahoro you will also find **Blue Duck Station** (www.blueduckstation.co.nz; s/d from $45/95; ☎), a wildlife-focused outfit with a cafe.

If you fancy spending another night or two on the river, with a roof over your head, the Bridge to Nowhere Lodge (p123) can oblige, situated downstream on the way to Pipiriki. Your jetboat operator can drop you off.

ⓘ Getting to/from the Tramp

Whakahoro is reached by road from SH4, turning off at either Owhango or Raurimu.

National Park (p107) is a good base for setting off from for both Whakahoro or Ruatiti, as it is well serviced with lodging and shuttle-bus services.

From the end of the track at Mangapurua Landing, you can jetboat out to Pipiriki with Whanganui River Adventures (p125). Blue Duck Station also runs **Wild Journeys** (www.wildjourneys.co.nz), a jetboat service that can collect you and return you to Whakahoro ($160 per person; minimum three people).

From Pipiriki you can either head out 28km east to Raetihi, Ohakune or National Park; Whanganui River Adventures runs shuttles to all three. Otherwise, you can return to Whanganui, 79km south. This route is serviced by the mail run courtesy of **Whanganui Tours** (www.whanganuitours.co.nz), which leaves Pipiriki around 4pm. It also runs transport in the other direction, from Whanganui, leaving 7am, to Pipiriki (one way/return $30/63).

🥾 The Tramp

Day 1: Whakahoro to Mangapurua Trig

6–7 HOURS, 16KM

From Whakahoro, the **Kaiwhakauka Track** begins along a farm road through private Retaruke Station following the true right of the **Kaiwhakauka Stream** to a large stock and pedestrian swing bridge. Care should be taken to leave gates as found and not to disturb stock.

The bridge is built over the original Depot Bridge, the last remaining truss bridge of its type in the district. Off to the right is the original depot where deliveries from riverboat services were stored for the valley settlers. The track leads up the valley through a mixture of regenerating bush and farmland, and two hours from the start of the track you will reach the national park boundary.

From the park boundary it is a steady 1½-hour climb to the site of the Mosley Homestead near the **Waione Stream**, where an open clearing lends itself well to camping.

Continue towards Cootes Homestead; on the way the track crosses many small bridged side streams, and passes just a few small, open flats. The old Tobin Homestead, marked by an old chimney stack, can be

Mangapurua & Kaiwhakauka Tracks

seen on the right of the track. From here the steep climb to the junction passes through relatively undisturbed mixed tawa/podocarp forest, reaching the junction of the old Kaiwhakauka and Mangapurua Rds around 2½ hours from Mosley.

Continue heading west towards the Whanganui River. After around 30 minutes you will reach Mangapurua Trig Campsite, an excellent camping spot with spring water and toilets. A side track leads up to the **Mangapurua Trig** (663m), from which there are sweeping views of Tongariro National Park to the east and Mt Taranaki to the west on fine days.

Day 2: Mangapurua Trig to Hellawell's

5–6 HOURS, 14.8KM

From Mangapurua Trig the track heads steadily downhill, passing the only uncut section of forest in the Mangapurua Valley. As you move down the valley, the track crosses the grassy clearings that were created by the early settlers, and many of the papa bluffs are named after settlers who farmed the surrounding land. The names of these settlers also live on in the wooden signs installed along the track marking the location of the original house sites. You may also notice rows of exotic trees that mark the road and the house sites.

The first swing bridge in the valley crosses **Slippery Creek** and after a further 1.5km you reach **Johnson's**, named after the farmer Edward Johnson who collected the mail twice a week from the Mangapurua Landing and distributed it through the valley. Two hours into your journey from the trig, the large camping flat makes for a pleasant stop.

The track continues down the valley road to the abandoned **Tester House**, which was the location of the first school in the valley, started in 1926 with seven children. There are a number of large flats in the upper valley, and a whole lot of Himalayan honeysuckle, an introduced weed that acts as a nursery plant for natives in much the same way as gorse.

It's 1¼ hours from Johnson's to the site of **Bettjeman's house**, easily identified by the straight row of poplars that line the old road. The Bettjeman family were among the first settlers to arrive and last to leave when the valley was abandoned in 1942. In its heyday, the homestead included a family house, a bunk room built of split totara shingles

and a tennis court. All that remains today is the old chimney stack and exotic plants such as holly and cotoneaster.

Around 1.5km from Bettjeman's is **Bartrum's swing bridge**, from which point the valley becomes very narrow as the track sidles around a series of steep bluffs, some as high as 70m. Of particular note is the long bluff up-valley of **Cody's House**. It is sometimes called Currant Bun Bluff because of the rounded boulders set into the cliffs.

A short distance further down the valley is Waterfall Creek, with **Hellawell's** on the southern side, 1½ hours from Bettjeman's. This was the location of many community picnics and hockey games. A 1.5km side trip up the true left of the creek provides views of the waterfall.

Day 3: Hellawell's to Mangapurua Landing

2–3 HOURS, 8.4KM

The track continues to follow the true left of the Mangapurua Stream before descending towards the Bridge to Nowhere, with more rows of exotic trees marking the road and the house sites as you head through the valley.

About an hour from Hellawell's is **Battleship Bluff**, named for a feature across the Mangapurua Stream, resembling the prow of an old battleship. The bluff posed the greatest difficulty for the early road builders: two years were spent terracing the bluff from the top using gelignite.

WHANGANUI JOURNEY – THE GREAT WALK THAT'S A PADDLE

One of NZ's nine Great Walks, the Whanganui Journey is in fact a river journey, although there are welcome opportunities to disembark your vessel and stretch the legs on dry land.

The 145km journey from Taumarunui to Pipiriki takes around five days. It is one of NZ's great river adventures, wending from highlands to lowlands, through the heart of Whanganui National Park. It's a journey of natural beauty, history and cultural interest. Along the way are two huts, a bunk house and 11 campsites.

The level of effort and skill required is largely dictated by the river flows. When the river is slow, be prepared to paddle for hours. Frequent rapids are generally gentle and fun, but you will need water confidence, paddling skills and good general fitness – this is, after all, a long journey through the middle of nowhere.

Local companies are geared up to set you on your way, and fully guided trips are available if you don't want to tackle it on your own. For more information and bookings, which are essential all year round, contact **Great Walks Bookings** (☑ 0800 694 732; www.greatwalks.co.nz) or any Department of Conservation (DOC) Visitor Centre (www.doc.govt.nz). A good potted summary is also compiled in DOC's brochure *Whanganui Journey*, downloadable from its website.

Continue along the track as it dips and climbs, crossing streams and small bridges down the valley. Almost out of nowhere you will turn the corner onto the historic Bridge to Nowhere. This large concrete bridge was completed in 1936, and now stands abandoned in bush in the middle of nowhere. By the time the bridge was constructed, the lower valley had been abandoned by the settlers. From the concrete bridge you can see the remains of the old suspension bridge used between 1920 and 1936. This old bridge and its two predecessor wire cages were vital to the initial settlers for the transport of all supplies.

It's a 40-minute walk to Mangapurua Landing, along a well-formed walking track frequented by day visitors venturing to the Bridge to Nowhere. The Mangapurua Landing was the main access point to the Mangapurua Valley during the early years of settlement when the paddle steamer provided the only transport option. The landing is now used by jetboaters and canoeists.

RUAHINE FOREST PARK

Located a 35km drive from Palmerston North, Ruahine Forest Park spans 936 sq km, from the Manawatu Gorge north to the Taruarau and Ngaruroro Rivers, which form its boundary with Kaweka Forest Park. Ruahine is long (95km), narrow (only 8km wide at its southern end) and very rugged. It encompasses the main Ruahine Range, as well as the Mokai Patea, Hikurangi, Whanahuia and Ngamoko Ranges.

The park is laced with tracks and poled routes, and within its boundaries are 60 DOC and club huts available to trampers. East–west crossings over the Ruahines are popular, but the area is not well served by public transport, making it twice as hard for trampers to arrange a drop-off on one side of the mountains and a pick-up on the other.

But the lack of transport leads to the park's most endearing quality – a lack of other trampers. If you're looking for an alpine adventure, where it's possible to spend an afternoon tramping alone along a ridge and through tussock, then the Ruahines are well worth the effort needed to reach the tracks.

History

There has been human activity in and around the park area for almost 1000 years, beginning with the Maori. In pre-European times the forests and streams were a good source of food for the descendants of the Rangitane, Ngati Apa and Ngati Kahungungu people.

The first European to explore the Ruahine Range was Reverend William Colenso. After arriving in NZ in 1834, Colenso became a travelling missionary and crossed the range seven times. He was a skilled botanist whose observations became the basis of the first botanical records of the area. Eventually the Maori track he used became known as Colenso's Track.

In the early 1900s the forests in the Ruahine foothills were cleared for farms and milling. Red deer were released in the mid-1920s for game hunting, but their numbers increased so rapidly their browsing caused extensive forest destruction. That resulted in the New Zealand Forest Service (NZFS) building many of the park's tracks and huts in the 1960s for deer cullers.

Ruahine's most famous hut, Rangiwahia, was originally a shepherd's shelter, built in 1930 just above the bushline on the western side of the range. It became the focal point of a ski hill in 1938, after a group of young men drinking pints in the Rangiwahia Hotel formed the Rangiwahia Ski Club – only the second ski club to be incorporated in NZ. The skiers winched a bulldozer up the valley to level out the slopes, built a towrope that used an engine from an Indian motorcycle and added a wing to the hut.

The club's membership peaked with 80 skiers, but sadly it was disbanded during WWII and never reformed. In 1967 the NZFS rebuilt Rangiwahia Hut, and the classic corrugated-iron structure served trampers for almost two decades, finally being replaced in 1984. Sitting at almost 1300m, on the edge of a vast alpine area, 'Rangi Hut' (as most locals refer to it) is still an important gateway into the Ruahine Range for trampers, deer hunters and the occasional skier.

Environment

The Ruahine Range forms part of the North Island's main divide. The dividing range traps moisture carried by prevailing westerly winds, causing heavy rainfall and a damp climate on the west and a rainshadow effect on the east, where there are drier conditions. The southern end of the range is generally lower than the northern

Rangiwahia & Deadmans Loop

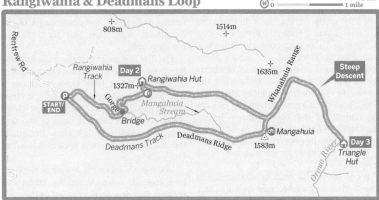

TARANAKI, WHANGANUI & AROUND WELLINGTON RANGIWAHIA & DEADMANS LOOP

end, which includes Mangaweka – the highest point in the park at 1733m. The range is geologically young, and is still uplifting, which combined with the dramatic weather precipitates high rates of erosion. In general the terrain is steep and rugged, and features sharp-crested ridges.

The forests within the park extend to 1100m. Broad-leaved podocarp is found on the lower slopes, while beech, kamahi and pahautea dominate higher altitudes. Above the forest, leatherwood and subalpine vegetation take over, giving way to tussock and alpine herb fields.

A number of common native birds can be found in the park, including the tui, korimako (bellbird), piwakawaka (fantail), popokotea (whiteheads), kereru, titipounamu (rifleman) and riroriro (grey warbler). If you're lucky you'll see whio (blue ducks), kakariki (parakeets), karearea (falcons) and hear kiwi and kaka.

Rangiwahia & Deadmans Loop

Duration 3 days

Distance 24.5km (15.2 miles)

Track Standard Tramping track and route

Difficulty Moderate to demanding

Start/End Rangiwahia car park

Nearest Town Palmerston North (p141)

Transport Shuttle bus, private

Summary This tramp takes you on an exploration of the little-visited but beautiful Ruahine Forest Park. It includes sections of tramping above the bushline and excellent views on clear days.

The 4km walk to Rangiwahia Hut, at the start of this tramp, is one of the more popular tracks in Ruahine Forest Park. The track zigzags up and around an old slip, then meanders up through montane forest and subalpine scrub to Rangiwahia Hut, set among the tussock and alpine herbs on the open tops.

If you are unsure about your tramping ability, plan on just a 15km return tramp to Mangahuia, staying two nights at Rangiwahia Hut; the extension into Oroua Valley involves a steep descent that is dangerously exposed and difficult in bad weather, and the second half of the loop along Deadmans Ridge can be demanding.

🛈 Planning

WHEN TO TRAMP
The season is from late November to April, but because of the rain and strong winds that often occur in the Ruahines, the best time to undertake this tramp is January and February.

WHAT TO BRING
Good rain gear is essential. In places the track and poled routes can be muddy, making gaiters handy. You should also pack a stove; in Rangiwahia Hut there is a gas stove but in Triangle Hut there is only a wood stove.

MAPS & BROCHURES
The tramp is covered by *NZTopo50 BL36* (Norsewood). DOC's *Western Ruahine Forest Park*

brochure is also helpful as it details other walks in the area.

HUTS

Rangiwahia is a **Serviced Hut** (www.doc.govt.nz; $15), while Triangle is a **Standard Hut** (www.doc.govt.nz; $5). Obtain hut tickets from Palmerston North i-SITE (p141) or DOC Visitor Centres nationwide.

INFORMATION

The very helpful Palmerston North i-SITE can supply information about the Ruahines, help arrange transport and sell hut tickets.

ⓘ Getting to/from the Tramp

From Palmerston North head northwest on SH3 and then northeast on SH54. At the hamlet of Rangiwahia turn right onto Te Parapara Rd. Within 4km turn left on Renfrew Rd and follow it for 5km to its eastern end, where there is a car park and information board.

There is no regular public transport to Ruahine Forest Park, but you shouldn't have too much trouble hooking up with a ride. Palmerston North–based **Pathfinder Tours** (☑ 0275 827 113, 0800 766 623; www.pathfindertours.co.nz; min 2 people $160) services the Rangiwahia trailhead. Failing that, enquire at the i-SITE.

The Tramp

Day 1: Rangiwahia Car Park to Rangiwahia Hut

3 HOURS, 4KM, 470M ASCENT

A well-benched track departs the car park and begins ascending through beech forest, passing some impressive red beech along the way. Within 10 minutes you're walking along the side of the steep Mangahuia Valley, enjoying views of the Whanahuia Range.

Around 2km from the car park, an impressive arched wooden bridge crosses a deep narrow gorge. This is the third bridge to have been constructed over the gorge. An earlier one, dating from the 1930s, can be seen dangling from the sides of the gorge below.

Beyond the bridge the ascent becomes steep, and occasionally you have to scramble over large boulders and grab tree roots. The track climbs to the head of a gully marked by a beautiful waterfall cascading into a small pool. From here the track moves into leatherwood and then tussock, reaching Rangiwahia Hut (12 bunks) 10 minutes from the waterfall.

Rangiwahia Hut, or 'Rangi Hut' as is posted above its door, is a great place to spend a night or even two. The large hut has two sleeping rooms, a gas stove, wood burner and water. Located just above the bushline, its L-shaped veranda gives a panoramic view of the expansive farm country below, while on the horizon are the volcanoes of Tongariro National Park.

Day 2: Rangiwahia Hut to Triangle Hut

3–4 HOURS, 8KM, 335M ASCENT, 775M DESCENT

The track heads east towards Mangahuia and is rutted to begin with. The tramp up this broad alpine tussock ridge is easy, though, and if the weather is clear the views of the surrounding peaks and ridges are excellent. Within 30 minutes you climb to a flattish high point at 1400m, cross it, descend briefly and then begin climbing again. Snow poles appear here and, about 30 minutes from the flattish high point, you reach a marked junction. The route south is to the top of Mangahuia (a 20-minute climb), and then along Deadmans Track back to the car park.

The route to Triangle Hut (left) is marked by snow poles, and descends north from the junction for 1.5km towards Maungamahue (1660m). At times you're tramping along the edge of some steep cliffs and can see the red roof of Triangle Hut far below. About 40 minutes from the junction the poled route swings east and begins to descend a side ridge into Oroua Valley. This section involves a steep descent that is dangerously exposed and difficult in bad weather.

For the first 20 or 30 minutes you descend through tussock, until you arrive at a marked track at the bushline. Next is one of the most difficult sections; a wide swath cuts through the leatherwood and you must use roots as handholds to descend. The track eases up for a bit but then resumes its steep descent until you reach Oroua River. Triangle Hut is on the other side of the river, an easy ford when water levels are normal. From the junction it takes one to two hours to reach the river, depending on the weather and your fitness.

Built in 1966 to aid deer cullers, Triangle Hut (six bunks) overlooks the upper waters of the Oroua River from the bottom of a deep, narrow valley. You feel as if you're in the heart of the Ruahines, isolated from the rest of the world...and for all practical purposes you are. This hut is in good shape and has a wood stove; water is from the river.

Day 3: Triangle Hut to Rangiwahia Car Park

5–7 HOURS, 12.5KM, 723M ASCENT, 753M DESCENT

Return to the track junction. Most trampers do not find this stretch so daunting the second time; you are hitting it first thing in the morning, while you are fresh and, as is so often the case, climbing the steep track is easier than descending it. Still, if it took you two hours to descend to the hut, plan on three hours to climb back to the junction.

At the junction, continue south along a poled route, and after 20 minutes climb easily to Mangahuia Trig (1583m). If the weather is clear this is a great spot for lunch, with views in every direction – including east to the Sawtooth Ridge and northward to the Hikurangi Range.

Snow poles lead west from Mangahuia, along Deadmans Track, a route that begins as a steady descent off the high point and then skirts a very steep edge of Deadmans Ridge. In poor weather and whiteout conditions this section is dangerous, and well worthy of its name, but in good conditions it's an amazing place to tramp. You can see more than 700m straight down into a steep-sided valley. At the bottom is a stream that flows into the rugged interior of the Ruahines.

From the edge of the ridge you descend to a saddle with a tarn just off the route. There are a number of these small pockets of water in the area, and for the most part they are the only source of water above the bushline.

You climb 60m out of the saddle and follow snow poles along the crest of the ridge, remaining in the tussock for 1km and then dropping into leatherwood for the next 2km. At one point the ridge is so narrow you can easily peer into the valleys on both sides. As might be expected, the views are excellent on a clear day.

About 4km from Mangahuia Trig you reach the bushline, where Deadmans Track enters the forest. It's a gentle descent at first, then a rapid one as you drop 300m in the final 2km. Steps assist you much of the way, and less than one hour after entering the trees you bottom out at Rangiwahia Track, only a few minutes east of the car park.

TARARUA FOREST PARK

North of Wellington is a place where the wind whips along the sides of mountains and the fog creeps silently in the early morning. It's a place where gales blow through steep river gorges, snow falls on sharp, greywacke (grey sandstone) peaks and rain trickles down narrow ridges. This is Tararua Forest Park, the largest conservation park managed by DOC on the North Island.

The park is centred on the Tararua Range, which stretches 80km from the Rimutaka Saddle in the south, north to the Manawatu Gorge, a natural gap that separates the Tararuas from the Ruahine Range. The tallest peak is Mitre (1571m), but there are many other peaks close to that height throughout the park. The ridges and spurs above the bushline are renowned for being narrow, steep and exposed.

Only 50km from Wellington, the park used to be popular largely with weekend trampers from the windy city. Today, trampers from around the country are attracted to the Tararuas' broken terrain and sheer features, which present a challenge to even the most experienced.

The park has an extensive network of tracks, routes and huts, most accessible from the main gateways of Otaki Forks in the west (off State Hwy 1), and Holdsworth and Waiohine Gorge on the eastern, Wairarapa side.

These tracks are not as well formed as those in most national parks so it's easy to lose them; they are mostly of 'tramping track' and 'route' standard. On the open ridge tops there are rarely signposts or poles marking the routes, only the occasional cairn. The tramps described in this section are less demanding than most routes through the Tararuas, and are therefore undertaken by a greater number of trampers.

History

Although the range was probably too rugged for any permanent Maori settlements, the local Maori did establish several routes through it to the west coast. It was Maori guides who led JC Crawford to the top of Mt Dennan in 1863, the first recorded European ascent in the range. From the 1860s to the late 1880s, prospectors struggled over the ridges and peaks in search of gold, but little was ever found.

The Tararua Tramping Club, the first such club in NZ, was formed in 1919 by Wellington trampers keen to promote trips into the range. Independent trampers had been visiting the range since the 1880s.

When the New Zealand Forest Service was established in 1919, a move began to reserve a section of the Tararua Range, but it was not until 1952 that the government set aside the area as NZ's first forest park. It was gazetted in 1967 and now covers 1165 sq km.

Environment

The sediments that would later form the Tararua Range were laid in a deep-sea basin 200 million years ago. Earth movements along a series of faults that extended through the Upper Hutt Valley and the Wellington region then resulted in a complicated uplifted mass of folded and faulted rock. This mass was subsequently eroded by wind, rain and ice, resulting in the rugged Tararuas.

There are a good variety of plants in the park, and many species reach their southern limits here. Cover is predominantly verdant rainforest, and podocarp tawa and kamahi forest in the lowlands scattered with rimu and northern rata. Silver beech is the species along the bushline in the south, while above 1200m the forest gives way to open alpine tussock, snow grass and herb fields.

The Tararuas were one of the last known refuges of the huia, with the last official sighting recorded in 1903 on the Mt Holdsworth Track. Clearing of lowland forest habitats and predation by introduced pests have also meant the disappearance of whio, kiwi, North Island robin and kokako from the range. But there are still plenty of birds in the park: on the river flats you're likely to encounter honking paradise shelducks,

WARNING

Wind, fog and rain are the park's trademarks: the Tararuas are exposed to westerly winds that funnel through the gap between the North and South Islands. The range is often the first thing the airstreams hit, which they do with full force, smacking against the high ridges and peaks. At times it's almost impossible to stand upright in the wind, especially with a backpack on. On average, the summits and peaks are fogbound two days out of three.

Storms arrive with little warning and have dumped more than 300mm of rain in a single day. Trampers must be prepared to spend an extra day in a hut if such storms blow in, because they quickly reduce visibility in the uplands and cause rivers to flood dangerously.

while in the forests there are riflemen, grey warblers, tomtits and whiteheads, all easier to hear than spot.

Planning

MAPS

The Tararuas are covered by *NewTopo Tararua Tramps 1:55,000*.

INFORMATION

In downtown Wellington, DOC's **Visitor Centre** (04-384 7770; www.doc.govt.nz; 18 Manners St; 9am-5pm Mon-Fri, 10am-3.30pm Sat) handles bookings, passes and information for national and local parks and tracks. Closer to the park, the **Wairarapa Area Office** (06-377 0700; www.doc.govt.nz; 220 South Rd; 9am-5pm Mon-Fri) provides detailed information on the Tararua Forest Park and sells hut tickets.

Getting Around

Holdsworth Lodge, in the Mt Holdsworth recreation area, is reached from SH2 by turning west onto Norfolk Rd, just south of Masterton. Norfolk Rd leads into Mt Holdsworth Rd, which ends at the recreation area, 15km from SH2.

If you don't have your own vehicle, getting to Holdsworth Lodge can be a bit tricky. **Masterton Radio Taxi** (06-378 2555) charges around $65 for the trip. Or you can call the Holdsworth Lodge caretaker and see if you can arrange a lift if they are coming into town. Then there's hitching. The roads aren't quite the hitchhiker's nightmare they appear to be on the map – there are a number of farms along the way, and between the farmers and day visitors to the park, you can usually pick up a ride if you're patient. See our info on hitching (p360).

The Kaitoke trailhead is a 30-minute walk down Marchant Rd off SH2 north of Upper Hutt. The Tranz Metro (p143) train passes this way between Wellington and the Wairarapa, with the closest stop Maymorn, north of Upper Hutt, but it's still a 12km trek to the Kaitoke car park. Unless you want to leg it, your best bet for a transfer will be **Hutt & City Taxis** (☑ 570 0057; www.huttcitytaxis.co.nz).

Mt Holdsworth-Jumbo Circuit

Duration 3 days

Distance 24km (15 miles)

Track Standard Tramping track and route

Difficulty Moderate to demanding

Start/End Holdsworth Lodge

Nearest Town Masterton (p142)

Transport Private, taxi

Summary An old favourite of local trampers, this circuit includes nights at two scenic huts above the bushline, and a day following alpine ridges.

The Holdsworth recreation area, where the Lodge is located, is a beautiful spot to begin any tramp in the forest park. It is surrounded by rugged hills and graced by the rushing waters of Atiwhakatu Stream, which has brisk but brilliant swimming holes.

Although you can cover this route in two days, it is probably a better idea to schedule three, just in case bad weather intervenes and forces you to sit out a day in one of the alpine huts.

🛈 Planning

WHEN TO TRAMP

Attempting this tramp out of season is not recommended – the season is October through to May.

MAPS

The walk is covered by *NZTopo50 BP33* (Featherston) and *BP34* (Masterton).

LODGES & HUTS

Located in the recreation area at the start of the track is **Holdsworth Lodge** (☑ 06-377 0700; www.doc.govt.nz; dm $25), a large, roomy lodge popular with school groups and tramping clubs but also available to individual trampers passing through. You need to book in advance. There is a caretaker at the lodge, whose office serves as a visitor information centre. The extensive fields

Mt Holdsworth-Jumbo Circuit

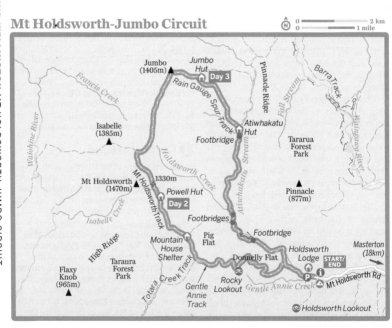

of the recreation area make for excellent camping ($6), serviced with toilets and water supply.

The huts on this track include Powell and Jumbo, both of which are which are **Serviced Huts** (www.doc.govt.nz; $15) and should be booked online in advance from 1 October to 30 April. Outside of this period you can stay with hut tickets purchased from the i-SITE or DOC Area Office in Masterton, or DOC centres nationwide.

🏃 The Tramp

Day 1: Holdsworth Lodge to Powell Hut

3–4 HOURS, 6KM, 880M ASCENT

The track departs the lodge heading west on a wide gravel path, crosses a footbridge over **Atiwhakatu Stream** and passes a track (left) to Holdsworth Lookout (30 minutes away). Another junction lies 200m further.

Follow the well-graded **Gentle Annie Track** southwest (left fork), climbing steadily towards Mountain House shelter. Approximately one hour from Holdsworth Lodge you reach **Rocky Lookout**, from where there are good views of Powell Hut and, for those with sharp eyes, the trig on Mt Holdsworth.

The track sidles around to the junction with Totara Creek Track (the route of the Holdsworth-Kaitoke Track), approximately 45 minutes from Rocky Lookout. Continue north (signposted) to Pig Flat, and cross to a track leading to Mountain House shelter, which has historic displays and a long-drop toilet nearby.

Beyond the shelter, the well-marked track begins with a steep climb and in 45 minutes emerges from the bushline into subalpine scrub. Follow the track along the ridgeline up to **Powell Hut** (28 bunks).

Originally built in 1939, rebuilt in 1981 and then burnt to the ground in 1999, the hut was rebuilt again within a year because it is one of the most popular spots in the park to spend a night. The hut has gas stoves and, more importantly, excellent views of the surrounding mountains and valleys from its veranda. If the night is clear you can watch the lights of Masterton appear after sunset.

Day 2: Powell Hut to Jumbo Hut

3½–4 HOURS, 7KM, 270M ASCENT, 260M DESCENT

The rest of the climb to Mt Holdsworth is technically a route, with very few markers or cairns, but the trip is so popular that a track has been worn to the peak and most of the way to Jumbo Hut. Fill your water bottle

before leaving Powell Hut, because there is little water along the ridge.

Heading northwest, climb steeply for 15 to 20 minutes until you reach a small knob at 1330m with a battered sign on top. Below is Powell Hut; above, in good weather, you can see the trig on Mt Holdsworth. It takes another 30 to 45 minutes of tramping along the ridge to reach the trig. From the summit of **Mt Holdsworth** (1470m) there are excellent views of Mt Hector, the main Tararua Range, and the small towns along SH2.

Three ridges come together at Mt Holdsworth. The track from Powell Hut follows one ridge, while another is marked by an obvious route that heads first northwest, then west towards Mid Waiohine Hut (two hours). Those heading to Jumbo Hut (signposted) need to go east. You almost have to backtrack a few steps from the trig to pick up the partially worn track that drops quickly to the ridge below.

Once on the ridge it takes 1½ to two hours to reach Jumbo Hut. The route climbs a number of knobs: the first is marked with a rock cairn near the top, the second involves working around some rock outcrops on the way up, and the third, **Jumbo** (1405m), is really a pair of knobs with several small tarns between them. As a side trip you can continue along the main ridge to Angle Knob, about 40 minutes away, where there are some good views.

Jumbo peak's southern knob has a small cairn at one side; a track running along the east-sloping ridge begins here, and it's a steady 30-minute descent to Jumbo Hut. Within 20 minutes you come to a spot on the ridge where it's possible to see the hut far below. **Jumbo Hut** (20 bunks) has excellent views from its veranda. At night you can see the lights of Masterton, Carterton and Greytown, and if you get up early on a clear morning the sunrise is spectacular.

It's a reasonably short tramp from Powell Hut to Jumbo Hut, so an enjoyable afternoon can be spent exploring the ridges to the north and viewing prominent features such as Broken Axe Pinnacle or the Three Kings.

Day 3: Jumbo Hut to Holdsworth Lodge

3–4 HOURS, 9KM, 890M DESCENT

Just south of the hut is a benched track heading southeast. This is the beginning of the descent along **Rain Gauge Spur**. The track is well marked though steep and

Holdsworth-Kaitoke Track

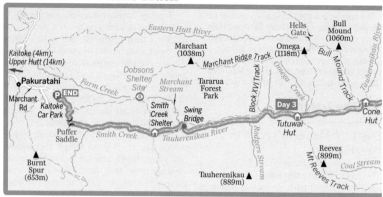

slippery, especially during wet weather. It should take about one hour to reach the valley and the recently upgraded Atiwhakatu Hut (28 bunks).

The track from the hut to Holdsworth Lodge is well defined and level. Jumbo Creek and Holdsworth Creek used to pose problems in wet weather – in fact they were downright dangerous. Nowadays they are bridged, making for an all-weather track. Soon after the bridge across Holdsworth Creek, you come to a junction. The trail you can see climbing to the west (right) rises steeply to Mountain House shelter (one to 1½ hours).

Stay on the main track, which is well formed and runs along the stream, past a small gorge, to Donnelly Flat. This wooded camping area is 1km from Holdsworth Lodge. A 15-minute loop track at the flat passes through tall stands of podocarp forest – rimu, matai and kahikatea. The walk from Donnelly Flat to Holdsworth Lodge backtracks along the starting route for part of the way. It's about 15 minutes to the lodge from the junction with Gentle Annie Track.

Holdsworth-Kaitoke Track

Duration 3 days

Distance 36km (22 miles)

Track Standard Tramping track

Difficulty Moderate

Start Holdsworth Lodge

End Kaitoke car park

Nearest Towns Masterton (p142), Wellington (p142)

Transport Private, train, taxi

Summary This classic Tararua tramp involves no arduous alpine crossings and follows peaceful river valleys most of the way.

Tararua Forest Park dishes up plenty of rugged and genuinely dangerous tramping territory, but this track is perfect for less-experienced trampers who may be unsure about crossing open, unmarked, alpine ridge routes. Following the Waiohine and Tauherenikau rivers between Holdsworth and Kaitoke, this low-level tramp gains a maximum of 740m in altitude along a track that is well marked and signposted at every junction.

Although it can be tramped in either direction, it is most commonly started at Holdsworth.

ℹ Planning

WHEN TO TRAMP

This tramp can be done year-round.

MAPS

This tramp is covered by *NZTopo50 BP33* (Featherston) and *BP34* (Masterton).

HUTS & CAMPING

Huts en route are Totara Flats and Tutuwai, both of which are **Serviced Huts** (www.doc.govt.nz; $15), although note that neither has a gas cooker. Sayers is a **Standard Hut** (www.doc.govt.nz; $5); Cone is a **Basic Hut** (www.doc.govt.nz; free). Camping is permitted near the huts ($5), and at suitable sites along the tracks such as Totara Flats, for free.

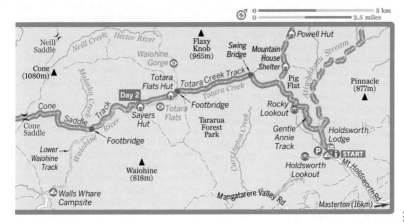

0 ——————————————————— 5 km
0 ——————————————————— 2.5 miles

 The Tramp

Day 1: Holdsworth Lodge to Totara Flats Hut

4–5 HOURS, 12KM

The track departs the lodge west, on a wide gravel path, crosses a footbridge over **Atiwhakatu Stream** and passes a track (left) to Holdsworth Lookout (30 minutes away). Another junction lies 200m further on.

Follow the well-graded **Gentle Annie Track** southwest (left fork), climbing steadily towards Mountain House shelter. Approximately one hour from Holdsworth Lodge you reach **Rocky Lookout**, from where there are good views of Powell Hut and Mt Holdsworth.

The track sidles around to the signposted junction to Totara Flats. Take the left fork (south), which begins with a steep descent along a well-worn track – so worn in places it looks like a gully. Follow the track along a spur to a high point (575m) and continue along the track heading down towards **Totara Creek**. Follow the creek on the true left to the swing bridge, then continue downstream on the true right.

About 30 minutes (2.5km) from the creek crossing, the track reaches the confluence of Totara Creek and the **Waiohine River**. Crossing the swing bridge here, the track continues for 100m, arriving at **Totara Flats Hut** (26 bunks). The hut is a pleasant and popular place to stay, and is often attended to by a warden. It has sweeping views of the flats, Mt Holdsworth to the north, and the foothills you'll soon be

climbing over to the south. For an interesting side trip, tramp up the Waiohine River Gorge – best done in the water when the river is at a normal level.

The track descends near the river and then emerges onto **Totara Flats**, a 2km-long grassy area, easily the largest clearing in the Tararuas, and a nice place to camp. If Totara Flats Hut is too crowded, there's always Sayers Hut (six bunks), on the opposite side of the river, halfway down the flats. It's an older hut with an interesting interior, but it's easy to miss.

Day 2: Totara Flats Hut to Tutuwai Hut

4½–5 HOURS, 12KM

Cut across the grassy area, past Sayers Hut. Before reaching a high bluff, swing away from the river, following the track up a steep, short climb onto a high river terrace and continue to the river.

You will soon encounter a large slip. Either follow the all-weather track over the slip (30 minutes), or travel downstream on the river terrace to **Makaka Creek**, although this is only possible when the river is low. Cross the Makaka Creek bridge and climb up the bank to the marked junction.

On top of the embankment, the track swings right and climbs again to reach a signposted junction with the **Cone Saddle Track** (southwest) and the track to Walls Whare campsite (which continues south along the river terraces).

Cone Saddle Track (right fork) begins with a steep climb of 300m to a roundish knob, and then sidles down to Clem Creek; the track reappears on the other side of the creek and is marked by a large cairn. It then makes a gentle ascent to **Cone Saddle** and a signposted junction of four tracks.

Continue southwest towards the **Tauherenikau River**, following the track down a steep, 240m-descent over the next 30 minutes. The path arrives at Cone Hut (six bunks), a historic slab hut still used occasionally by those who like to reminisce about tramping in days gone by. There are excellent campsites just a short way downriver.

The last segment of the day is a 3km tramp across grassy flats. Most of the time the track remains just below the bushline, but it's easy to make your own way across the flat for a much more scenic tramp. Eventually a sign points to a hut on a terrace above the river (one hour from Cone Hut). Tutuwai Hut (20 bunks), often attended by a warden, enjoys a nice view of the river flats.

Day 3: Tutuwai Hut to Kaitoke Car Park

5–6 HOURS, 13KM

Note that slips and washouts across this section may add an hour or two to your day, depending on their current condition. Take care in these areas.

Around two hours from Tutuwai Hut, you arrive at a swing bridge across the Tauherenikau River. The track follows the true right of the river to Marchant Stream. The stream is easily identified by the cable strung across it to assist trampers during flooded conditions. When the water level is normal you can cross it without getting your boots wet. Smith Creek Shelter, 10 to 15 minutes from the stream, is not suitable for overnight stays.

The track from the shelter is a popular day walk. It's a wide path most of the way, and soon passes a track (right) to the former Dobsons Shelter site (the hut was removed in 1994). It crosses a tributary of Smith Creek after one hour, and then begins a steep climb to **Puffer Saddle**, reached

TARARUA BISCUITS

It would be impossible to pinpoint the birthplace of tramping in NZ, but the Tararuas have as much right to claim the title as anywhere else. Interest in cutting a track dates back to 1895, and by 1917 the famed 'Southern Crossing' route had been marked and had two huts built along it. In 1919, NZ's first tramping club, the Tararua Tramping Club, was formed in Wellington. Within a few years there were several others in the Hutt Valley, Masterton and at Victoria University.

The rugged range was also responsible for a bit of unique Kiwi cuisine: the Tararua biscuit. Loaded with rolled oats and sugar, these biscuits were hard, heavy and practically indestructible. Trampers loved them; they were packed with calories, never lost their shape in the bottom of a backpack and were still edible months after they were baked. How hard are they? At one time mothers used them for teething their babies.

These days you rarely see Tararua biscuits in a hut, and some Kiwi trampers don't even know the history behind them, much less ever consume one. But if you are a patron of the past and want to make a batch before your next tramp, here is one recipe:

➡ 1 cup of butter

➡ 1 cup of sugar

➡ 1 tablespoon of molasses

➡ 2½ cups of rolled oats

➡ 1½ cups of flour

➡ half a teaspoon of salt

Cream the butter and mix with the other ingredients. Add enough water to make a stiff, non-sticky dough. Roll out on a flour-dusted board to a thickness of 10mm. Cut into 50 round biscuits (which some trampers claim are better at resisting breakage), or square ones (which are easier to pack). Bake at 180°C for 10 to 15 minutes, or until golden but not brown.

after the track sidles the ridge for the last few hundred metres. From the saddle there are impressive views of the sheep stations and farms in the Hutt River Valley.

From here it's a 30-minute descent, with good views, to the car park. You'll also pass the signposted Southern Crossing Track (right) to **Marchant Ridge** and Alpha Hut.

TOWNS & FACILITIES

New Plymouth

📞 06 / POP 52,500

Dominated (in the best possible way) by Mt Taranaki and surrounded by lush farmland, New Plymouth is a vibrant small city, with a bubbling arts scene, good hospitality and shopping, and a rootsy, outdoorsy vibe humming along between the national park and some fab beaches.

🛏 Sleeping & Eating

Devon St is the place to head for food and drink.

Belt Road Holiday Park HOLIDAY PARK **$**
(📞 758 0228, 0800 804 204; www.beltroad.co.nz; 2 Belt Rd; campsites from $18, cabins $65-125) This environmentally attuned, pohutukawa-covered holiday park sits atop a bluff overlooking the interesting Lee Breakwater area, about a 10-minute walk from town. The half-dozen best cabins have million-dollar views.

Seaspray House HOSTEL **$**
(📞 759 8934; www.seasprayhouse.co.nz; 13 Weymouth St; dm/s/d $30/50/74; @📶) A big old house with gloriously high ceilings, relaxed and affordable Seaspray features retro and antique furniture. Fresh and arty, it's a rare bunk-free backpackers with no TV (conversation is encouraged). Closed July and August.

Fitzroy Beach Motel MOTEL **$$**
(📞 06-757 2925; www.fitzroybeachmotel.co.nz; 25 Beach St; s/d $130/150, units $190; 📶) This quiet, old-time motel (just 160m from Fitzroy Beach) has been spruced up beautifully with quality carpets, double glazing and lovely bathrooms. There are free bikes, too. Beaut!

Petit Paris BAKERY **$**
(www.petitparis.co.nz; 34 Currie St; lunches $8-15; ⏰7.30am-3.30pm) Flying the tricolor with pride, this boulangerie and patisserie turns

out crispy baguettes and *tart au citron* (lemon tart), alongside the likes of omelette and *croque monsieur*.

Arborio MEDITERRANEAN **$$**
(www.arborio.co.nz; Puke Ariki, 1 Ariki St; mains $13-34; ⏰breakfast, lunch & dinner) Housed in Puke Ariki, the region's museum, this airy, arty modern restaurant boasts sea views and smart service. The menu ranges from pork-belly pizza to pasta, risotto and barbecued-chilli squid. Quality NZ wine selection.

India Today INDIAN **$$**
(📞 06-758 4634; 40 Devon St E; mains $17-19; ⏰lunch & dinner; 📶) A sumptuous gold-walled room draped with bolts of silk, India Today wafts with spicy aromas and serves classic and creative curries.

🛒 Supplies & Equipment

Kiwi Outdoors Centre OUTDOOR EQUIPMENT
(📞 758 4152; www.outdoorgurus.co.nz; 18 Ariki St; ⏰9am-5pm Mon-Fri, 9.30am-2.30pm Sat) The town's outstanding outdoor gear shop, run by people who walk the talk, run shuttles, sell hut tickets and hire out necessary gear.

Fresha DELICATESSEN
(www.fresha.net.nz; cnr Devon & Morley Sts) Stocks an array of super-tasty tramping treats.

New World SUPERMARKET
(78 Courtenay St) One of many major supermarkets; centrally located.

ℹ Information

New Plymouth i-SITE (📞 06-759 6060; www.taranaki.co.nz; Puke Ariki, 1 Ariki St; ⏰9am-6pm Mon-Tue & Thu-Fri, to 9pm Wed, to 5pm Sat & Sun) This excellent centre provides tramping and general travel information for the region.

ℹ Getting There & Away

Air New Zealand (📞 0800 737 000; www.airnewzealand.co.nz) has daily direct flights to/from Auckland, Wellington and Christchurch, with onward connections.

The bus centre is on the corner of Egmont and Ariki Sts. **InterCity** (📞 583 5780; www.intercitycoach.co.nz) services all major NZ towns and smaller dots in between, as does **Naked Bus** (📞 0900 625 33; www.nakedbus.com). The Naki Bus, operated by **Dalroy Express** (📞 759 0197; www.dalroytours.co.nz), runs daily to/from Auckland via Hamilton and south to Hawera via Stratford.

Stratford

☎06 / POP 5330

Almost all street names in town are inspired by Shakespearian characters; the town was named after William Shakespeare's birthplace of Stratford-upon-Avon in England. Stratford is on SH3, about 40km southeast of New Plymouth and 18km from the Plateau on Mt Taranaki.

🛏 Sleeping & Eating

The highway, passing right through town, is home to plenty of fast-food joints.

**Stratford Top Town
Holiday Park** HOLIDAY PARK $
(☎06-765 6440; www.stratfordtoptownholiday-park.co.nz; 10 Page St; campsites/dm/cabins from $14/22/40; @🐾) A trim caravan park offering one-room cabins, motel-style units and backpackers' bunks.

Amity Court Motel MOTEL $$
(☎06-765 4496; www.amitycourtmotel.co.nz; 35 Broadway N; d $120, apt $140-160; @🐾) A relatively new kid on the Stratford block, upping the town's accommodation standings 100% with its stone-clad columns, jaunty roof angles, timber louvres and muted cave colours.

Casa Pequena CAFE $$
(☎06-765 6680; 280 Broadway; snacks $3-5, meals $12-28; ⊙6am-4pm Mon-Fri, 7am-1.30pm Sat) This disarmingly retro, trapped-in-a-timewarp tearoom dishes up classics such as bangers and mash, and hot beef-and-gravy sandwiches.

🔒 Supplies & Equipment

Stratford Leisure OUTDOOR EQUIPMENT
(☎06-765 7580; 420 Broadway; ⊙8.30am-5pm Mon-Fri, 9am-noon Sat) Stocks camping gear.

New World SUPERMARKET
(124 Regan St) For food supplies, head to this supermarket.

ℹ Information

Stratford i-SITE (☎06-765 6708, 0800 765 6708; www.taranaki.co.nz; Prospero Pl, Broadway S; ⊙8.30am-5pm Mon-Fri, 10am-3pm Sat & Sun) A helpful visitor centre with heaps of brochures on the town and the national park. It can assist you with transport, the options for which are the same as for New Plymouth.

Whanganui

☎06 / POP 39,700

Halfway between Wellington and New Plymouth, Whanganui is a raggedy historic town on the banks of the Whanganui River.

🛏 Sleeping & Eating

Whatever you're craving for dinner can be found on, or near, Victoria Ave.

Anndion Lodge HOSTEL $
(☎0800 343 056, 343 3593; www.anndion-lodge.co.nz; 143 Anzac Pde; s/d/f/ste from $75/88/105/130; @🐾🏊) Hell-bent on constantly improving and expanding their fabulous hyper-hostel, hosts Ann and Dion go to enormous lengths to make things homey: stereo systems, big TVs, spa, swimming pool, barbecue area, restaurant, bar, courtesy van etc.

Tamara Backpackers Lodge HOSTEL $
(☎347 6300; www.tamaralodge.com; 24 Somme Pde; dm $31, s from $54, d & tw with/without bathroom $86/72; @) This photogenic, mazelike two-storey heritage house has a wide balcony, lofty ceilings, kitchen, TV lounge, free bikes and a leafy, hammock-hung back garden. Ask for one of the beaut doubles overlooking the river.

**Whanganui River Top 10
Holiday Park** HOLIDAY PARK $
(☎0800 272 664, 343 8402; www.wrivertop10.co.nz; 460 Somme Pde; campsites/cabins/units from $21/72/135; @🐾🏊) Sitting on the Whanganui's west bank 6km north of Dublin Bridge, this place has prodigious facilities spread around the grassy riverbank.

Cracked Pepper CAFE $
(21 Victoria Ave; mains $5-18; ⊙7am-4.30pm; 🐾) At Whanganui's best cafe, spot-on staff serve great coffee and food, including plenty of vegetarian options. The 1890s building is a beauty.

Stellar CAFE, BAR $$
(www.stellarwanganui.co.nz; 2 Victoria Ave; mains $15-35; ⊙3pm-late Mon, 9am-late Tue-Sun; 🐾) Stellar lives up to its name with its convivial family atmosphere. In fact, it's the town's pride and joy with its leather couches, bar snacks, gourmet pizzas and surf 'n' turf fare, along with frequent bands, DJs and quiz nights.

🛒 Supplies & Equipment

Eides Sports World OUTDOOR EQUIPMENT
(☑ 345 5391; 184 Victoria Ave; ⊙ 8.30am-5pm Mon-Fri, 9am-12.30pm Sat) Tramping equipment, including stove fuel, can be found here.

New World SUPERMARKET
(www.newworld.co.nz; 374 Victoria Ave; ⊙ 7am-9pm) For food supplies.

ℹ️ Information

Whanganui i-SITE (☑ 349 0508, 0800 926 426; www.whanganuinz.com; 31 Taupo Quay; ⊙ 8.30am-5pm Mon-Fri, 9am-3pm Sat & Sun) Can provide general assistance from its impressive riverside building.

ℹ️ Getting There & Away

Whanganui has an airport, serviced by **Air New Zealand** (☑ 06-348 3500, 0800 737 000; www.airnewzealand.co.nz; 133 Victoria Ave; ⊙ 9am-5pm Mon-Fri), which provides extensive nationwide connections.

Buses operate from the **Whanganui Travel Centre** (☑ 345 7100; 160 Ridgeway St; ⊙ 8.15am-5.15pm Mon-Fri), including **InterCity** (☑ 09-583 5780; www.intercitycoach.co.nz), which links towns and cities nationwide. **Naked Bus** (☑ 0900 625 33; www.nakedbus.com) departs from Whanganui i-SITE to most North Island centres.

Palmerston North

☑ 06 / POP 82,400
Located on the banks of Manawatu River, and in the shadow of Wellington, this city can fulfil any tramper's needs before or after a walk.

🛏️ Sleeping & Eating

Palmerston North Holiday Park HOLIDAY PARK $
(☑ 358 0349; www.palmerstonnorthholidaypark.co.nz; 133 Dittmer Dr; campsites/cabins/units from $16/45/80; 🛜) Off Ruha Pl and next to Esplanade Park; a pleasant and shady camping ground 2km from the city centre.

Peppertree Hostel HOSTEL $
(☑ 06-355 4054; www.peppertreehostel.co.nz; 121 Grey St; dm/s/d $28/53/70; @) This endearing 100-year-old house is the best budget option in town, and downright homely with its piano and wood fire.

Plum Trees Lodge LODGE $$
(☑ 358 7813; www.plumtreeslodge.co.nz; 97 Russell St; s/d incl breakfast from $135/150; 🛜) This se-cluded lodge features recycled timber, raked timber ceilings punctuated with skylights, and a balcony set among swaying boughs. Sumptuous breakfast hampers boast fruit, croissants, jam, eggs, cheese, coffee and juice.

Moxies CAFE $
(67 George St; meals $6-20; ⊙ 7am-5pm Mon-Sat, 7.30am-5pm Sun; 🖋) This chipper corner cafe is a real George St fixture, colourfully decked out and offering a top-value all-day menu.

Halikarnas Cafe TURKISH $$
(15 Fitzherbert Ave; mains $16-20; ⊙ lunch Tue-Fri, dinner daily) Angling for an Ali Baba and the Forty Thieves vibe, with magic carpets, brass hookahs and funky trans-Bosphorus beats, Halikarnas plates up generous Turkish delights, from lamb shish kebabs to felafels and kick-arse Turkish coffee.

🛒 Supplies & Equipment

Bivouac Outdoor OUTDOOR EQUIPMENT
(www.bivouac.co.nz; 99 The Square; ⊙ 9am-5.30pm Mon-Fri, 9am to 4pm Sat, 10am-4pm Sun) The best spot for tramping gear, including hire, along with hut tickets and maps.

Pak 'n Save SUPERMARKET
(335 Ferguson St; ⊙ 7am-11pm) Head here to restock the tramping larder.

ℹ️ Information

Palmerston North i-SITE (☑ 0800 626 292, 06-350 1922; www.manawatunz.co.nz; The Square; ⊙ 9am-5pm Mon-Fri, 10am-2pm Sat & Sun; 🛜) A super-helpful source of tourist information; free wi-fi throughout the Square.

ℹ️ Getting There & Away

Palmerston North has an airport, serviced by **Air New Zealand** (☑ 06-351 8800; www.airnewzealand.co.nz; 382 Church St; ⊙ 9am-5pm Mon-Fri), which provides extensive nationwide connections.

Buses operate from the **Palmerston North Travel Centre** (☑ 355 4955; cnr Main & Pitt Sts; ⊙ 8.45am-5pm Mon-Thu, 9am-7.45pm Fri, 9am-2.45pm Sat, 9am-2.45pm & 4-7.15pm Sun), including **InterCity** (☑ 09-583 5780; www.intercitycoach.co.nz), which links towns and cities nationwide. **Naked Bus** (www.nakedbus.com) runs similar services from the same departure point.

You can also reach Palmerston North on the long-haul **KiwiRail Scenic** (☑ 0800 872 467; www.kiwirailscenic.co.nz) *Northern Explorer* between Wellington and Auckland, which stops at seven towns through the middle of the North Island.

Masterton

📞 06 / POP 19,500

Masterton is the rural Wairarapa's utilitarian hub, an unselfconscious town getting on with its business. Of particular interest to trampers is the DOC-run Pukaha Mount Bruce National Wildlife Centre (www.pukaha.org.nz; ⊙ 9am-4.30pm) 30km north, a 1000-hectare breeding ground for endangered birds.

🛏 Sleeping & Eating

Mawley Holiday Park   HOLIDAY PARK $
(📞 378 6454; www.mawleypark.co.nz; 5 Oxford St; sites from $15, cabins $25-60) Mawley Holiday Park is a pleasant, clean camping spot across mature grounds on the banks of the Waipoua River.

Cornwall Park Motel   MOTEL $$
(📞 378 2939, 0508 267 692; www.cornwallparkmotel.co.nz; 119 Cornwall St; d $115-125; @ 🛜 ♿) Within walking distance of the town centre, this lovely motel complex has handsome gardens, warm and comfortable rooms, and excellent facilities, including a swimming pool.

Ten O'Clock Cookie   CAFE $
(180 Queen St; ⊙ 7am-4.30pm Mon-Fri, 8am-2.30pm Sat) This bakery-cum-cafe is utterly splendid. Since you're tramping, you can get away with a pie (or two), and a packet of those amazing toffee biscuits to take with you.

New World   SUPERMARKET $
(cnr Queen & Bruce Sts; ⊙ 7am-9pm) This supermarket will hit the spot for self-caterers and tramping-trip stock-ups.

ℹ Information

Masterton i-SITE (📞 370 0900; www.wairarapanz.com; cnr Dixon & Bruce Sts; ⊙ 9am-5pm Mon-Fri, 10am-4pm Sat & Sun) Has DOC brochures and hut tickets, as well as general tourist information.

ℹ Getting There & Away

Regular region-wide bus services, and train services to and from Wellington, are run through Tranz Metro.

Wellington

📞 04 / POP 199,200

NZ's capital is windy, wonderfully arty and wall-to-wall with restaurants, cafes and bars. It's also green and hilly, which will be welcome news to visiting trampers, and is a major travel crossroads, being the northern port of interisland ferry services.

🛏 Sleeping & Eating

There's no shortage of good accommodation in the downtown area, including at the budget end, where a few good hostels keep things keenly priced. There's plenty of great food, too – head to Cuba St and Courtenay Place for the highest density.

Nomads Capital   HOSTEL $
(📞 978 7800, 0508 666 237; www.nomadscapital.com; 118 Wakefield St; dm $28-36, d with bathroom $95-105; @ 🛜) Smack-bang in the middle of town, Nomads has good security, spick-and-span rooms, an on-site cafe-bar, and heritage features such as an amazing stairwell.

YHA Wellington City   HOSTEL $
(📞 801 7280; www.yha.co.nz; cnr Cambridge Tce & Wakefield St; dm $29-36, d with/without bathroom $120/88; @ 🛜) This happy, helpful hostel sets a high standard, with fantastic communal areas, including a reading room and dedicated movie room. Sustainable initiatives impress, and there's a comprehensive booking service at reception.

Comfort & Quality Hotels   HOTEL $$
(📞 0800 873 553, 04-385 2156; www.hotelwellington.co.nz; 223 Cuba St; d $104-200; @ 🛜 ♿) Two solid, adjoining hotels in the heart of Cuba St offer smaller, cheaper rooms and snazzier ones with modern styling. Both share the in-house bar and dining room (mains $22 to $30).

Pandoro Panetteria   BAKERY $
(2 Allen St; items $3-6; ⊙ 7am-5pm Mon-Fri, to 4pm Sat & Sun; 📶) An excellent Italian bakery with smooth coffee, cakes, pastries and a range of yummy savoury, bready, scrolly, rolly things.

Fidel's   CAFE $
(234 Cuba St; meals $9-20; ⊙ 7.30am-late; 📶) This super-busy Cuba St institution for caffeine-craving, alternative types dishes up eggs any-which-way, pizza and splendid salads, along with Welly's best milkshakes. Revolutionary memorabilia adorns the walls of the funky interior; decent outdoor areas too.

KK Malaysian Cafe   MALAYSIAN $
(54 Ghuznee St; mains $9-14; ⊙ lunch Mon-Sat, dinner daily; 📶) Tiny KK is one of Wellington's

most popular cheap Malaysian joints in a city obsessed with Southeast Asian cuisine. There's scrumptious satay and rendang to put a smile on your face, accompanied by the ubiquitous roti, of course.

🔒 Supplies & Equipment

Bivouac Outdoor   OUTDOOR EQUIPMENT
(www.bivouac.co.nz; 39 Mercer St) There are numerous outdoor gear stores where you can pick up tramping equipment and stove fuel; this is the best.

Unity Books   BOOKS
(57 Willis St) For an excellent range of travel books, visit NZ's best independent bookstore, which sports a huge table piled high with NZ titles.

Moore Wilson Fresh   DELICATESSEN
(cnr College & Tory Sts) This unparalleled minimart is a fantasyland of quality NZ food and drink, perfect for stocking up on proteins and picnic supplies.

New World   SUPERMARKET
(☑04-384 8054; 279 Wakefield St) There are now several supermarkets in and around the city centre; this is the most convenient and comprehensive.

ℹ️ Information

Wellington i-SITE (☑04-802 4860; www. wellingtonnz.com; Civic Sq, cnr Wakefield & Victoria Sts) Can supply tourist information for the region and make bookings for accommodation and transport.

ℹ️ Getting There & Away

Although Wellington airport has an international terminal, it is largely a domestic enterprise. **Air New Zealand** (☑474 8950, 0800 737 000; www.airnewzealand.co.nz; cnr Lambton Quay & Grey St; ☉9am-5pm Mon-Fri, 10am-1pm Sat) offers flights between Wellington and most domestic centres, including Auckland,

Christchurch, Queenstown and Nelson. Flights start as low as $59, booked well in advance or during promotions. **Jetstar** (☑0800 800 995; www.jetstar.com) flies between Wellington and Auckland, Christchurch and Queenstown, with bargain fares available. **Soundsair** (☑520 3080, 0800 505 005; www.soundsair.com) flies frequently between Wellington and Picton, Nelson and Blenheim. **Air2there** (☑904 5130, 0800 777 000; www.air2there.com) flies between Wellington and Blenheim.

Wellington is a bus-travel hub, with connections north to Auckland and all major towns in between. **InterCity** (☑385 0520; www.intercity. co.nz) buses depart from platform 9 at the train station. Tickets are sold at the InterCity ticket window in the train station; there are good savings when booked online. **Naked Bus** (☑0900 625 33; www.nakedbus.com) also services major North Island destinations, with buses departing from opposite the Amora Hotel in Wakefield St, and collecting more passengers at Bunny St opposite the railway station. Book online or at Wellington i-SITE; get in early for the cheapest fares.

Long-haul **KiwiRail Scenic** (☑0800 872 467; www.kiwirailscenic.co.nz) routes include the *Northern Explorer* between Wellington and Auckland (from $129, 10½ hours, Thursday to Sunday May to September), stopping at most major towns through the middle of the North Island.

Two companies ply Cook Strait between the North and South Islands, a journey of around 3½ hours: **Bluebridge Ferries** (☑0800 844 844, 471 6188; www.bluebridge.co.nz; 50 Waterloo Quay) and the **Interislander** (☑0800 802 802, 498 3302; www.interislander.co.nz; Aotea Quay).

Wellington train station (☑0800 801 700; ☉6.30am-8pm Mon-Thu, to 1pm Fri & Sat, to 3pm Sun) has windows selling tickets for Tranz Scenic trains, Interislander ferries and InterCity coaches, as well as local **Tranz Metro** (☑0800 801 700; www.tranzmetro.co.nz) train services.

For local bus information, call **Metlink** (☑0800 801 700; www.metlink.org.nz).

Queen Charlotte & Marlborough

Includes ➡

Queen Charlotte
Track 146
Nydia Track 152
Pelorus Track 154
Kaikoura Coast
Track 159

Best Swimming

➡ Ship Cove (p149)

➡ Mistletoe Bay (p152)

➡ Anakiwa (p152)

➡ Pelorus Bridge Scenic Reserve (p157)

Best Views

➡ Eatwells Lookout (p151)

➡ Onahau Lookout (p152)

➡ Totara Saddle (p158)

➡ Dun Mountain (p158)

➡ Skull Peak (p162)

Why Go?

For many travellers, Marlborough is their introduction to the 'Mainland', with the interisland ferry to Picton offering a tantalising glimpse of the region's beauty.

The Marlborough Sounds are a popular playground for lovers of the great outdoors. A convoluted maze of waterways, its reaches are lined with trails from beach to peak, crossing and following ridges with wondrous views. The Queen Charlotte and Nydia Tracks are classic examples of such tramps.

The Kaikoura Coast Track is another seaside spectacular, with extensive ocean and mountain views from a trio of neighbouring coastal farms.

Inland, the lesser-known and lightly trodden Mt Richmond Forest Park offers plenty of solitude. The park's signature track, the Pelorus, features deep green river pools and rare lowland forest.

As well as sunshine and warm temperatures, this region is well known for world-class wine and whale-watching tours. These attractions work in very well with the rewarding tramps on offer.

When to Go

The forecast is good: the Marlborough region soaks up some of New Zealand's sunniest weather. January and February are the warmest months, with daytime temperatures averaging 22°C, but even in the middle of winter the daily average is a relatively balmy 12°C.

The Marlborough Sounds' tracks and Kaikoura Coast Track are year-round tramping options. From Christmas to mid-February, however, be prepared to jostle with flocks of Kiwi holidaymakers on their summer holidays.

As the Mt Richmond Forest Park sees plenty of rain, the Pelorus Track is best tramped from October to April.

Background Reading

Come high summer you might think the Marlborough Sounds are very well populated, but for the most part these waterways are incredibly sleepy. And so it has always been. Such isolation – particularly in the outer reaches – breeds singular folk with strange stories to tell, such as those collected in books by Don Grady. Another local yarn-spinner is Heather Heberley, storyteller and biographer, and kin to a prominent whaling family. Notable books in the same genre include *Tales of Kenepuru* (Helen Godsiff), *The Lighthouse Keeper's Wife* (Jeanette Aplin) and *Angela* (Gerald Hindmarsh), the remarkable tale of a young Italian immigrant who finds herself living on remote D'Urville Island in the early part of the 20th century.

DON'T MISS

The Pacific coast town of Kaikoura is terrific for wildlife-spotting. Whales, dolphins, NZ fur seals, penguins, shearwaters, petrels and wandering albatross are just some of the interesting creatures that stop in or call this place home. The area is most famous for marine animals, present in abundance due to ocean-current and continental-shelf conditions.

A good place to get to grips with this lively, salty town is at Point Kean, where seals laze around on a craggy reef – and sometimes in the car park. From there you can pick up the Kaikoura Peninsula Walkway, along which you might see various soaring seabirds.

For a fully immersive experience consider a swim with seals or dolphins on regular tours that get rave reviews. The ultimate Kaikoura experience, however, is to go on a whale-watching boat trip with Whale Watch Kaikoura (☑ 0800 655 121, 03-319 6767; www.whalewatch. co.nz; Railway Station; 3hr tour adult/child $145/60), on which you can get up close to the incredible creatures.

DOC Offices

➡ Picton i-SITE (☑ 03-520 3113; www.lovemarlborough.co.nz; Foreshore; ☺ 9am-5pm Mon-Fri, to 4pm Sat & Sun)

➡ Sounds Area Office (☑ 03-520 3002; www.doc.govt.nz; 14 Auckland St, Picton; ☺ 9am-4.30pm Mon-Fri)

➡ Havelock Information Centre (☑ 03-574 2114; www. havelockinfocentre.co.nz; 256 Main Rd; ☺ 9am-4pm)

➡ DOC Nelson Regional Visitor Centre (p198)

➡ Kaikoura i-SITE (☑ 03-319 5641; www.kaikoura.co.nz; West End; ☺ 9am-5pm Mon-Fri, to 4pm Sat & Sun)

GATEWAY TOWNS

➡ Picton (p162)

➡ Havelock (p163)

➡ Nelson (p197)

➡ Kaikoura (p164)

Fast Facts

➡ Queen Charlotte Sound is a classic example of a drowned valley, caused by tilting of the land 15 to 20 million years ago.

➡ Marlborough is NZ's vinous colossus, producing around three-quarters of the country's wine.

➡ The best thing to eat alongside that glass of world-famous sauvignon blanc is a freshly cooked crayfish, a delicacy readily available at roadside stalls around Kaikoura.

Top Tip

The Queen Charlotte Track offers a great opportunity to undertake a multiday walk without the burden of a heavy pack. Take advantage of water taxis that will ferry your bags while you walk from lodge to lodge, or camp to camp.

Resources

➡ www.destination marlborough.com

➡ www.qctrack.co.nz

➡ www.havelockinfocentre. co.nz

➡ www.nelsonnz.com

➡ www.kaikoura.co.nz

QUEEN CHARLOTTE & MARLBOROUGH

History

Maori knew the Marlborough area as Te Tau Ihu o Te Waka a Maui ('The Prow of Maui's Canoe'). The region's many archaeological sites have revealed that *pa* (fortified villages) and the sites surrounding them were not permanently occupied, and that the Maori were highly mobile, moving with the seasons to harness different resources.

The first European to visit the Marlborough region was Abel Tasman, who spent five days sheltering off the east coast of D'Urville Island in 1642, but never landed. It was to be more than a century before the next European, James Cook, turned up, in January 1770. Cook stayed 23 days and made four more visits over the next seven years to Ship Cove and the stretch of water he named Queen Charlotte Sound. In 1827 the French navigator Jules Dumont d'Urville discovered the narrow strait now known as French Pass, and his officers named the island to the north in his honour. In the same year a whaling station was established at Te Awaiti in Tory Channel, which brought about the first permanent European settlement in the district.

In June 1840 Governor Hobson's envoy, Major Bunbury, arrived in the Marlborough Sounds on the HMS *Herald* to gather Maori signatures for the Treaty of Waitangi. It was on 17 June, on the Sounds' Horahora Kakahu Island, that Bunbury proclaimed British sovereignty over the South Island.

Environment

The Marlborough region is diverse. Great swaths of its plains have been given over to agriculture, including the growing of grapes, for which it is renowned. It is also home to the fascinating Molesworth Station, NZ's largest farm, managed by the Department of Conservation (DOC) in line with its notable ecological values.

The east coast around Kaikoura is famous for wildlife. Indeed, there are few places in the world with so much to see: whales, dolphins, NZ fur seals, penguins, shearwaters, petrels and wandering albatross all stop by or call this area home. Marine animals are abundant here due to ocean-current and continental-shelf conditions: the seabed gradually slopes away from the land before plunging to more than 800m where the southerly current hits the continental shelf. This creates an upwelling, bringing nutrients up from the ocean floor into the feeding zone.

The Marlborough Sounds are a mixed bag of habitats, varying from farmland to commercial forestry, regenerating native forest and some that has remained more or less undisturbed. The Queen Charlotte and Nydia Tracks offer opportunities to experience this great diversity. Of particular interest is the remnant podocarp broad-leaved coastal forest, such as that seen on the Nydia Track. Ngawhakawhiti Bay is a good example of this kind of forest, with pukatea, tawa, matai, rimu, miro, beech, nikau palm and a colourful blanket of riotous kiekie. Meanwhile, the Queen Charlotte Track is distinctly divided into three recognisable forest types, with coastal broad-leaved forest at Ship Cove, regenerating forest from Kenepuru to Torea Saddles, and mature beech forest between Mistletoe Bay and Anakiwa. Bird life is prolific. The birds of the forest include tui, bellbird, tomtit and silvereye. In summer you will hear long-tailed and shining cuckoos, and at night moreporks and weka. Waders are prominent in tidal estuaries.

Queen Charlotte Track

Duration 4 days

Distance 71km (44 miles)

Track Standard Easy tramping track

Difficulty Moderate

Start Ship Cove

End Anakiwa

Nearest Town Picton (p162)

Transport Boat, shuttle bus

Summary Tramp around bays and along ridges between Queen Charlotte and Kenepuru Sounds, combining beautiful coastal scenery with accommodation in interesting lodges, hostels and resorts.

The hugely popular, meandering 71km Queen Charlotte Track offers gorgeous coastal scenery on its way from historic Ship Cove to Anakiwa, passing through a mixture of privately owned land and DOC reserves. The coastal forest is lush, and from the ridges you can look into either Queen Charlotte or Kenepuru Sounds.

Queen Charlotte is a well-defined track, suitable for people of average fitness. The full length can be completed in three to five days, with Ship Cove the usual (and recommended) starting point – mainly because it's easier to arrange a boat from Picton to Ship Cove

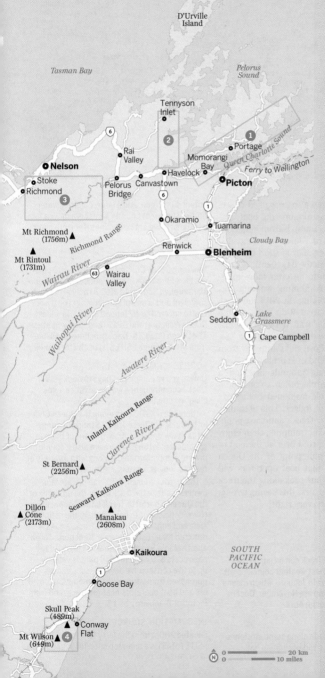

Queen Charlotte & Marlborough Tramps

1 Queen Charlotte Track (p148)

2 Nydia Track (p153)

3 Pelorus Track (p155)

4 Kaikoura Coast Track (p160)

D'Urville Island

Tasman Bay

Pelorus Sound

Tennyson Inlet

2

6

Rai Valley

Portage

1

Momorangi Bay

Queen Charlotte Sound

Nelson

Stoke

Richmond

Pelorus Bridge

Canvastown

Havelock

Picton

Ferry to Wellington

3

6

Okaramio

Tuamarina

Mt Richmond (1756m) ▲

Richmond Range

Cloudy Bay

Mt Rintoul (1731m) ▲

Wairau River

Renwick

Blenheim

63

Wairau Valley

Waihopai River

Seddon

Lake Grassmere

1 Cape Campbell

Awatere River

Inland Kaikoura Range

Clarence River

St Bernard (2256m) ▲

Seaward Kaikoura Range

Dillon Cone (2173m) ▲

Manakau (2608m) ▲

Kaikoura

SOUTH PACIFIC OCEAN

1 Goose Bay

Skull Peak (489m) ▲

Conway Flat

Mt Wilson (649m) ▲ **4**

N

0 —— 20 km
0 —— 10 miles

Queen Charlotte Track

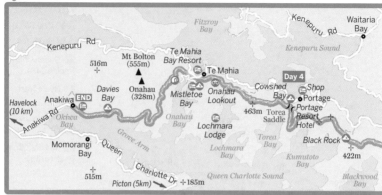

than vice versa. It can also be walked in sections by hopping aboard numerous boat services. A good two-day tramp is from Ship Cove to Punga Cove (27km), while a recommended day walk is from Torea Bay (a short boat ride from Picton) to Mistletoe Bay (9km).

Turn the track into an even more exciting adventure by combining walking legs with kayaking or biking. In 2013 the track was designated a Great Ride track on the New Zealand Cycle Trail network. Bikers, however, are banned from using the section between Ship Cove and Camp Bay from 1 December to the end of February.

Six DOC camping grounds are dotted along the route, while other accommodation ranges from old-fashioned homestays to luxury waterfront lodges. This accounts, in large part, for the track's enduring popularity – spend the day tramping, then enjoy a hot shower and a cold beer at the end of it. Another major plus point of the Queen Charlotte Track is that boat operators will happily transport your pack along the track for you. Trust us: at first this seems wrong, but soon it feels very, very right!

ℹ Planning

WHEN TO TRAMP

The Queen Charlotte Track can be enjoyed all year round. The warmest weather coincides with the NZ school holidays in January, which means the best times to tramp are November, December and February through April.

WHAT TO BRING

There's little or no shade along some stretches of the track, so bring a wide-brimmed hat, potent sunscreen, and a large-capacity water bottle. The sweet Sounds' forest is a mecca for wasps, so bring antihistamines if you are allergic to stings.

MAPS & BROCHURES

NewTopo *Queen Charlotte Track* 1:75,000 covers the entire track in sufficient detail. NewTopo *Marlborough Sounds* 1:130,000 may also prove sufficient and is useful for planning. The track is also covered by *NZTopo50 BQ28* (Havelock), *BQ29* (Waikawa) and *BP29* (Endeavour Inlet). The *Queen Charlotte Track* brochure, available from Marlborough i-SITES, is useful for planning.

LODGES, CAMPING & PASSES

Unless you're camping, it pays to book your track accommodation way in advance, especially in summer.

There are no DOC huts along the Queen Charlotte Track, but there are six **Standard campsites** (www.doc.govt.nz; $6), many of them in spectacular settings. There are also a couple of private camping grounds, along with a variety of resorts, lodges, hostels and guesthouses.

The district council, DOC, and private landowners manage the track under the umbrella of the **Queen Charlotte Track Land Cooperative** (www.qctlc.com). To contribute to the maintenance and enhancement of the track, a pass is required for all users between Kenepuru, Torea and Te Mahia Saddles or Anakiwa (a one-day pass costs $10 while the $18 pass is valid for up to five consecutive days). Passes can be purchased from various accommodation providers and boat operators near the track, and from Picton or Blenheim i-SITES.

INFORMATION SOURCES

Located 200m from the ferry terminal, Picton i-SITE (p145) is a one-stop shop for accommoda-

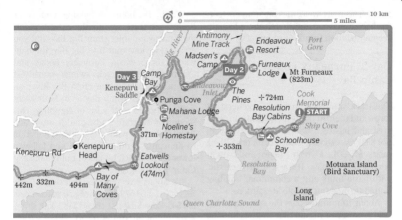

tion and transport bookings, DOC maps and hut tickets, and the Queen Charlotte Track Pass. Picton's DOC Sounds Area Office (p145) is largely a field office and offers only hut tickets and local tramping information.

ℹ Getting to/from the Tramp

The only way to reach the start of the track at Ship Cove is by a 45-minute boat trip. Numerous operators ply this route, depositing you there or various other spots along the track and forwarding your luggage where possible. A track return-trip with luggage transfers is around $100. You'll find operators clustered at Picton's pleasant town wharf.

Arrow Water Taxis (☑ 027 444 4689, 03-573 8229; www.arrowwatertaxis.co.nz)

Beachcomber Fun Cruises (☑ 0800 624 526, 03-573 6175; www.beachcombercruises.co.nz)

Cougar Line (☑ 03-573 7925, 0800 504 090; www.cougarline.co.nz)

Endeavour Express (☑ 03-573 5456; www. boatrides.co.nz)

Picton Water Taxis (☑ 027 227 0284, 03-573 7853; www.pictonwatertaxis.co.nz)

🥾 The Tramp

Day 1: Ship Cove to Furneaux Lodge

4–5 HOURS, 15KM

James Cook anchored at **Ship Cove** five times between 1770 and 1777, as commemorated by the memorial on the grassed picnic area. If time allows, while away an hour or two at this beautiful spot.

The track climbs quite steeply, at first through podocarp and broad-leaved forest of kahikatea, rimu and kohekohe with an understorey of ferns and pigeonwood, and then into beech forest. About 45 minutes up there is a lookout over **Motuara Island**, a bird sanctuary, and outer Queen Charlotte Sound.

It is about 10 minutes from the lookout to a saddle at the top of the ridge, where there is an observation point and sweeping views down to Resolution Bay. The track drops steeply to the bay and then sidles the hill until it comes to a signposted junction. The track to Schoolhouse Bay Campsite is down the left fork, which heads back in the direction of the saddle. No fires are permitted at the campsite. Continue southwest (right fork), reaching **Resolution Bay** two hours from Ship Cove.

The track climbs above Resolution Bay, and in 1½ hours reaches Tawa Saddle between the bay and Endeavour Inlet, where there are toilets and benches. A sit-down is obligatory here, or so would say the cheeky weka that will inevitably pop out of the bush to see what's for lunch. Resist their scampering antics and admire the view.

There are plenty of views of **Endeavour Inlet** on descent, before you bottom out and pass through a cluster of holiday homes and boat sheds known as The Pines. From here the track stays in the forest until it arrives at a signposted spur track to Furneaux Lodge, reached 25 minutes from The Pines, or 1½ hours from the saddle.

Furneaux Lodge (☑ 03-579 8259; www. furneaux.co.nz; dm $38, cabins from $45, units $199-269, meals $20-36) is a Sounds' stalwart, the highlight of which is the historic lodge building and epic lawns throughout the

QUEEN CHARLOTTE & MARLBOROUGH QUEEN CHARLOTTE TRACK

resort. This place welcomes pit-stoppers (coffee, beer, lunch etc), but there's also adequate accommodation to suit most budgets.

Day 2: Furneaux Lodge to Camp Bay

4 HOURS, 12KM

The track wanders through a regenerating forest and then, in 1km, emerges into an open area and passes Endeavour Resort (☑03-579 8381; www.endeavourresort.co.nz; dm $30-40, cabins $75-90), a retro board-and-batten bach-style complex. It's a real Kiwi classic, with basic units and a communal building dotted throughout its hillside gardens.

About 10 minutes past the resort a swing bridge crosses a stream that empties into the inlet. On the other side is a signposted junction. To the north (right) is the Antimony Mine Track, a two-hour return walk to the narrow and dark remains of abandoned antimony mines. The Queen Charlotte Track continues south (left fork) as a grassy corridor that hugs the western side of the inlet.

The track soon climbs away from the shoreline, and for the next 8km passes through regenerating bush as it skirts the western slopes above Endeavour Inlet. The walking is easy, with only gentle climbs and descents.

Within 1½ hours of passing Endeavour Resort, the track rounds the ridge separating Endeavour Inlet from Big Bay and you arrive at a viewpoint into Big Bay, the halfway point between Furneaux Lodge and Camp Bay. The track swings northwest and in 30 minutes you cross Big River on a swing bridge. Camp Bay is an hour away, and is reached after a bit of climbing. This section of the trail can be muddy after rain. Eventually you pass a signposted junction to Kenepuru Saddle. Turn left and follow a lower track, which breaks out of the bush at Camp Bay Campsite.

It's about five minutes to Punga Cove Resort (☑03-579 8561; www.pungacove.co.nz; dm $45, lodge $150-180, chalets $180-450; @ ☎), a rustic but charming resort with a variety of accommodation, including basic dorm rooms. The views easily atone for any rough edges, as do ample facilities (including a pool and spa, and games, kayak and bike hire), plus a restaurant and boatshed bar-cafe (decent local beers and $25 pizza).

Around 10 minutes further along the bay are two other lodging options, the first of which is Mahana Lodge (☑03-579 8373; www.mahanalodge.com; d $195; ☉closed May-Aug). This idyllic waterside property has a purpose-built lodge with en-suite doubles, home-cooked meals available, and an eco-

MOUNTAIN BIKING ON QUEEN CHARLOTTE TRACK

Although it has long been popular with NZ mountain bikers, track improvements in recent years have seen a sharp increase in the number of cyclists on Queen Charlotte Track. You can't really blame them: although the track features some good hills and a few other hazards, it is an achievable ride for a fit, competent cyclist and is now part of Nga Haerenga/New Zealand Cycle Trail (www.nzcycletrail.com).

Bike rental is readily available in Picton; most water taxis will transport the bike to the track for you. A fantastic three-day 'multisport' trip is offered by the Marlborough Sounds Adventure Company (☑0800 283 283, 03-573 6078; www.marlboroughsounds. com), which involves a tramp from Ship Cove to Endeavour Inlet, kayak to Portage Resort Hotel, and mountain bike to Anakiwa. This Ultimate Sounds Adventure is $1025, all inclusive.

To keep both walkers and cyclists happy, an easy-to-follow code of conduct has been developed:

➡ Mountain bikers are allowed on the Kenepuru Saddle to Anakiwa section any time of the year, but only from Ship Cove to Kenepuru Saddle during March to November.

➡ Bikers should give way to walkers; trampers have the right of way at all times.

➡ Bikers need to avoid excessive braking as it can damage the track surface, especially after rain.

➡ Bikers need to control their speed and not surprise trampers from behind; use a bell or give a yell.

➡ Trampers need to respect the bikers' right to be there, and share the track with them.

friendly attitude towards bush regeneration and pest trapping. Keep following the pink arrows and you'll reach **Noeline's Homestay** (☎03-579 8375; dm $30-35), a relaxed place run by 70-something Noeline, 'the Universal Grandma'. It's a friendly arrangement, with cooking facilities, great views and the bonus of home-baked treats.

Day 3: Camp Bay to Portage

8 HOURS, 23KM

This is a tough day's walk, kicking off with a steep climb up to Akerbloms Rd, where signs will command you continue onward and upward. You'll have a good half an hour's warm-up under your belt when you reach **Kenepuru Saddle**, at the intersection of Akerbloms and Titirangi Rds. Follow the signpost directing you south to the Bay of Many Coves.

The track sidles the ridge, and at first you are treated to views of Deep Bay to the east, but most of the time you are gazing down at the head of Kenepuru Sound to the west. Constant climbing and descending is rewarded with ever-changing panoramas of the inlets and sounds on both sides.

Two hours on from the saddle you hit the longest and steepest climb of the day, which tops off at a signposted spur track to **Eatwells Lookout**. This short spur track climbs steadily to 474m, one of the highest points along the Queen Charlotte Track. The climb is worth it. From the lookout you can see both Queen Charlotte and Kenepuru Sounds; 1203m Mt Stokes, the highest mountain in the Marlborough Sounds, is to the north.

From the junction you begin a long descent that bottoms out at **Bay of Many Coves Saddle**, from where it's just another 15-minute climb to the Bay of Many Coves Campsite. Great views, a shelter, water and toilets make this a nice spot for morning tea or lunch. It's not the most sheltered spot for tent pitching should the winds be a-blowing.

From the shelter there is a gentle 40-minute climb to a high point where a signpost indicates the spur track to **Bay of Many Coves Resort** (☎03-579 9771, 0800 579 9771; www.bayofmanycovesresort. co.nz; 1-/2-/3-bedroom apt $620/830/995; ☎☎), a 1½- to two-hour walk downhill. This plush joint has secluded apartments,

upmarket dining options and, most importantly, a hot tub and massage services.

From the ridgeline junction, the Queen Charlotte Track continues relatively level for an hour or so before some more uphill action is required. Around 1½ hours from Bay of Many Coves Campsite, the track skirts the south side of the ridge, and for almost 1km you enjoy a continuous view of Blackwood Bay. The track then dips into the bush and emerges to more great views on the north side. Less than 30 minutes from Black Rock you make a long descent, and then an equally long climb, until you top off at the campsite.

Black Rock Campsite is a six-hour walk from Camp Bay and two hours from Portage. Situated on the south side of the ridge, its shelter affords panoramic views, including a vista of Picton across Queen Charlotte Sound.

From Black Rock the track climbs gently before levelling out, providing great views for the next 30 minutes. You leave the crest of the ridge and descend into beech forest along the south side for the next hour, with the occasional glimpse of Queen Charlotte Sound. For the most part, this last stretch is a gentle and easy descent at the end of what is a long day.

Almost two hours from Black Rock you pop out at a war memorial on **Torea Saddle**. The road here crosses the same route used by Maori to haul their *waka* (canoes) from Queen Charlotte to Kenepuru Sound, thus saving a considerable sea journey. To the south, Torea Rd leads to a jetty on Torea Bay, where it is possible to catch a water taxi to Picton.

Follow Torea Rd downhill northwards to reach Portage, around 15 minutes away. You can reach nearby Cowshed Bay Campsite by this route, too, or take the direct track as signposted. This campsite can be busy in summer.

Portage is home to **Portage Resort Hotel** (☎03-573 4309; www.portage.co.nz; dm $40, d $165-365; ☎☎), complete with restaurant, bar and backpacker wing. Next door is the **Kenepuru Store** (☎03-573 4445; ⏰8am-8pm Oct-Apr, to 4.30pm May-Sep), stocking basic supplies and ice cream. A few minutes' walk up the hill is the homely, family-run, **DeBretts & Treetops** (☎03-573 4522; www. stayportage.co.nz; dm without/with linen $40/45, d $50).

Day 4: Portage to Anakiwa

7–8 HOURS, 21KM

Return to Torea Saddle and head west on the track. This section follows the ridge proper, and involves the ascent of two features that are each more than 400m high. Within 1½ hours of leaving Torea Saddle you reach the fine viewpoint at the top of a 407m knoll. A long descent follows before the track bottoms out in a pasture on private land. You continue on an old bridle trail that gently climbs to a view of Lochmara Bay, and then passes a side trail to Lochmara Lodge (☑ 03-573 4554; www.lochmaralodge. co.nz; Lochmara Bay; units $90-280). Situated in lush surroundings, this wonderful retreat boasts tramper-friendly facilities such as a waterview bathhouse and a restaurant.

You now begin the steady climb towards the 417m knoll, the highest point of the day. The track skirts its northern flank, begins descending and then comes to the Onahau Lookout Track junction. The descent now steepens until you arrive at the junction with James Vogel Track. The walkway is a 20-minute descent to idyllic Mistletoe Bay (☑ 03-573 4048; www.mistletoebay.co.nz; unpowered sites $32, dm $20, cabins $140, linen $7.50; ☒). Surrounded by bushy hills, this sweet spot has simple accommodation and communal facilities, and a jetty just perfect for jumping off. It's a 9km, four-hour walk from Torea Saddle to Mistletoe Bay, making the bay ideal for a lunch break or lazy afternoon.

Just beyond the junction with James Vogel Track, the Queen Charlotte Track arrives at Onahau Rd and Te Mahia Saddle, which heads south to provide vehicle access to Mistletoe Bay, and north to reach Te Mahia Bay Resort (☑ 03-573 4089; www.temahia.co.nz; d $140-248). This pleasant, low-key resort has a range of rooms and an on-site store with pre-cooked meals and pizza.

Turn down Onahau Rd towards Mistletoe Bay for 500m, where you will see the sign back on to the Queen Charlotte Track. Past the road you follow old bridle paths above Onahau Bay, passing through regenerating forest and skirting grazing land for about 1½ hours before a long, gentle descent through beech forest above Bottle Bay. There are wonderful vistas on this section, with Queen Charlotte Sound visible to the Grove Arm.

From Bottle Bay there are views to the water, which sparkles through an understorey of ferns, pittosporums, five-finger, broad-leaved rangiora and tawa. About 2½

to three hours from Mistletoe Bay, you reach the spacious camping area at Davies Bay (Umungata) Campsite.

The last hour of this long journey is one of its best parts. The track passes through Iwituaroa Reserve and its splendid stands of beech, before emerging at the Anakiwa car park where there is a shelter, toilets, and an ice-cream and coffee caravan if you time it right. The local outdoor pursuits school has a jetty here where boat services will pick you up for the trip back to Picton. The jetty's also a good launch pad for a refreshing dip after a sticky day's walking.

At the end of the track is Anakiwa Backpackers (☑ 03-574 1388; www.anakiwabackpackers.co.nz; 401 Anakiwa Rd; dm $33, d $85-105; ☎), a soothing spot to rest for the night, or longer.

SIDE TRIP: ONAHAU LOOKOUT

1 HOUR, 150M ASCENT

Onahau Lookout Track is reached three hours from Torea Saddle. Follow the left fork as it climbs to the lookout, located between Lochmara and Onahau Bays. This is the best viewpoint of the entire trip and a rewarding moment as you look back at the ridge you have traversed all the way from Camp Bay.

Nydia Track

Duration 2 days

Distance 27km (16.8 miles)

Track Standard Tramping track

Difficulty Easy

Start Shag Point

End Duncan Bay

Nearest Town Havelock (p163)

Transport Boat, shuttle bus

Summary This track crosses the Kaiuma and Nydia Saddles and follows the sheltered shoreline of Nydia Bay, the historic site of a long-gone sawmilling settlement.

Completed in 1979, most of the Nydia Track follows old bridle paths through a variety of environments, including virgin forest and farmland. At one point in the early 1900s, steam-powered haulers dragged logs over a saddle into Nydia Bay, the site of a large mill and a 300m wharf. It's two short and easy days to complete this tramp, allowing you plenty of time to pause and appreciate the magnificence of the Marlborough Sounds.

ℹ️ Planning

WHEN TO TRAMP

The Nydia Track can be enjoyed all year round. The warmest weather coincides with the NZ school holidays in January, which means the best times to tramp are November, December and February through April.

MAPS & BROCHURES

The entire track is covered by NZTopo50 *BQ28* (Havelock). NewTopo *Marlborough Sounds* 1:130,000 provides a large-scale overview of the entire area. The Nydia Track brochure can be downloaded from DOC's website.

LODGES & CAMPING

On Nydia Bay, **Nydia Lodge** (☎ 03-520 3002; dm $15, minimum charge $60) is a 50-bed complex of DOC huts, 30 minutes' walk from the main track. Often used by schools and organised groups, individual trampers are welcome to bunk there and make use of the facilities, which include a dining room and kitchen. Bookings must be made online or through the DOC Sounds Area Office (p145).

There is also accommodation at **On the Track Lodge** (☎ 03-579 8411; www.nydiatrack.org. nz; dm $40), a tranquil, ecofriendly place offering everything from packed lunches to evening meals and a hot tub.

Designated **Standard campsites** (www.doc. govt.nz; $6) are located in Nydia Bay and near Harvey Bay.

INFORMATION SOURCES

The Havelock Information Centre (p145) can assist you with transport and accommodation bookings.

ℹ️ Getting to/from the Tramp

The official start of the track is from the side of Kaiuma Bay Rd, 32km north of Havelock by road, and the end is at Duncan Bay, 27km northeast of Rai Valley. Both points can be reached by road, but you can also arrange to be dropped off and picked up by boat operators in Havelock. Most trampers arrange a water taxi to Shag Point, and then walk the 3km to the southern end of the track. Van transport can be booked at Duncan Bay back to either Havelock or Picton.

🚶 The Tramp

Day 1: Shag Point to Nydia Bay

4–5½ HOURS, 15KM

This tramp starts at Shag Point, a rocky promontory that juts into Kaiuma Bay in Pelorus Sound. From here it is 3km to the Nydia Track start. The first 1km winds

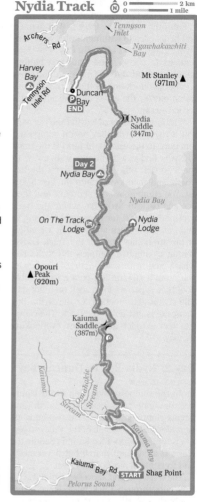

through a grassy paddock and then swings north and begins to climb towards a 490m point above Kaiuma Bay. You move into beech forest and sidle around the point's western flank, and in one hour descend to cross two branches of the Omahakie Stream.

On the other side, the track re-enters beech forest and climbs steadily to Kaiuma Saddle (387m). It's a steady climb, taking the average tramper around one to 1½ hours to reach it from the stream. Halfway up you pass a waterfall that cascades down a rock slide into a small pool. Views from the saddle are somewhat limited, but it's still a pleasant spot to take a break.

From the saddle the track is well defined and benched, and within minutes you're enjoying grand views of Nydia Bay. The track remains in beech forest until you bottom out in farmland and ford a stream. You cross another paddock (follow the track signs and watch out for the cows) and quickly ford a second stream.

Within four hours of leaving the car park you arrive at Nydia Bay and a signposted junction. To the east (right fork) is the track to Nydia Lodge, a 30-minute walk away. To the west (left fork) the track skirts the bay briefly and then swings into the beech forest. You climb above the shoreline and then descend back to Nydia Bay where the track continues to skirt the shoreline, weaving in and out of the bush and passing a handful of private homes and On the Track Lodge. Within 15 minutes you pass the Nydia Bay wharf, and within an hour of the wharf you cross a stream and pass an incredible pool that is perfect for a soak on a hot day. The signposted junction for the Nydia Bay Campsite is just down the track. The campsite has a toilet and pitches overlooking the bay.

Day 2: Nydia Bay to Duncan Bay
4–4½ HOURS, 12KM

From the signposted junction to the campsite, the main track heads left (north) and begins climbing. It's a 1½- to two-hour ascent along the west side of the valley to Nydia Saddle (347m). Like Kaiuma Saddle the climb is a constant march but never steep, and trees block most of the views.

The track passing above Ngawhakawhiti Bay cuts through thick bush. Once again, the bush is worth more than just a cursory upward glance. The forest greenery is predominantly made up of beech, kamahi and ferns, with the odd kahikatea and rimu also on show. A sign near the bay describes the bird life that can be observed along the tramp. The broad-leaved coastal forest here is beautiful, featuring a collection of miro, nikau palm, beech, matai and rimu.

From here the tramp on to Duncan Bay remains level and easy almost the entire way, passing along a track that has been cut into the bluff above the water. It will take you an hour from the saddle to reach Ngawhakawhiti Bay, and another hour to get to Duncan Bay car park, where trampers

are picked up by van transport. No camping is allowed at Duncan Bay, so the nearest facility is now Harvey Bay Campsite, a five- to 10-minute drive – or about an hour's walk – further up Tennyson Inlet Rd.

Pelorus Track

Duration 3 days

Distance 36km (22.4 miles)

Track Standard Tramping track

Difficulty Moderate

Start Maungatapu Rd

End Hacket picnic area

Nearest Towns Havelock (p163), Nelson (p197)

Transport Shuttle bus

Summary This track offers a remote forest experience up the Pelorus Valley at the edge of bustling Nelson. The Pelorus River is noted for its deep green pools, which are the delight of both trout and sore-footed trampers.

Often overlooked by trampers rushing off to Abel Tasman National Park, Mt Richmond Forest Park is right on the doorsteps of Havelock, Picton, Blenheim and Nelson. The Richmond Range forms the backbone of the 1660-sq-km park, which covers most of the steep, bush-clad mountains between Blenheim and Nelson, reaching north to the Tasman Sea near Whangamoa Head.

There are more than 250km of cut and marked tracks in the park, with about 30 huts scattered along them. The tracks range from challenging alpine routes to easy overnight walks suitable for families.

One of the more popular tramps is the Pelorus Track. The Pelorus is renowned for its large trout, which often use the river's deep pools as their hideaways. Trampers will find these pools a delight on hot days on the trail, although accessing them often involves a scurry off-track.

Officially, the western end of the Pelorus Track is the Hacket picnic area, but it is difficult – although not impossible – to arrange transport from there to Nelson. For this reason, an alternative route into Nelson, the Dun Mountain Track, has been included. This track conveniently lands trampers on Brook St on the edge of Nelson, and is the more popular finish. Trampers following this route hike directly from Middy Creek Hut

Pelorus Track

to Nelson, a long seven- to eight-hour day. A better alternative, especially if you get a late start on day one, is to stay the first night at Captain Creek Hut, and hike to Rocks Hut the second night. Rocks Hut, with its mountain views, offers much nicer accommodation than Middy Creek Hut.

There is plenty of other tramping to be had in the Forest Park, including the moderate two-day Wakamarina Track, following an old gold-miners' trail across the Richmond Range from the Wairau Valley to the Wakamarina. Another worthwhile option for experienced alpine trampers is the Mt Richmond Alpine Route, a three- to four-day route along the exposed ridges.

History

Maori had a number of argillite quarries in the Mt Richmond area, where they mined hard mudstone for weapons and tools. The first European visitors were also attracted by minerals – initially copper and chromium. There was a mining company on Dun Mountain as early as 1852, and Hacket Creek chromite was being removed from open shallow-cuts by the 1860s. There are still parts of an old, benched bullock track – the Old Chrome Rd – near Hacket Creek, on the western side of the forest park.

Gold was discovered in the Wakamarina River in 1861, and within three years thousands of canvas tents had sprung up as miners flocked to the prosperous goldfield, which was one of the richest in the country. The township of Pinedale, in the Wakamarina Valley, 8km west of Havelock, earned the nickname Canvastown. However, the boom lasted only until 1865.

When most of the accessible alluvial gold had been mined, quartz reefs were developed. Companies operated in the Wakamarina Valley from 1874 until the 1920s.

Environment

The whole park is covered by forest, with the exception of small patches of alpine tussock around the summits of taller peaks. The bush includes all five species of beech, as well as the podocarp species of rimu, miro, totara, matai and kahikatea. Uncommon birds found in the park include the whio (blue duck), the yellow-crowned parakeet, kaka and, occasionally, weka.

ℹ Planning

WHEN TO TRAMP
The Pelorus and Aniseed valleys receive some of the highest rainfall in Mt Richmond Forest Park, and streams may become impassable in heavy rain. The track is therefore best tramped from October to April.

MAPS & BROCHURES
This track is covered by NZTopo50 *BQ26* (Nelson) and *BQ27* (Rai Valley). The *Pelorus Track* brochure can be downloaded from DOC's website.

HUTS & CAMPING
All huts in Mt Richmond Forest Park are graded **Standard huts** (www.doc.govt.nz; $5), including Captain Creek, Middy Creek, Rocks, Roebuck, Browning and Hacket).

Near the Maungatapu Rd trailhead, camping can be had at Pelorus Bridge Campground and Cafe. At the Dun Mountain Track trailhead is **Brook Valley Holiday Park** (☑03-548 0399; www.brookholidaypark.co.nz; 600 Brook St; campsites per person $17, cabins from $52), in a rural location around 4km from central Nelson.

INFORMATION SOURCES
The two guardian DOC offices are the DOC Sounds Area Office (p145) and DOC Nelson Regional Visitor Centre (p198).

ℹ Towns & Facilities

The most popular area of Mt Richmond Forest Park is Pelorus Bridge Scenic Reserve, 18km west of Havelock, where SH6 crosses the Pelorus River. As well as nature trails and swimming holes, the reserve is home to Pelorus Bridge Campground & Cafe. This fully serviced DOC campsite is a picturesque gem, with hot showers, a smart kitchen and large deck with river views. The cafe has great home-cooked food and basic provisions.

ℹ Getting to/from the Tramp

The start of the track is 13km up the Pelorus River Valley from the Pelorus Bridge Scenic Reserve, along Maungatapu Rd.

The western end of the Pelorus Track is at the Hacket picnic area, at the confluence of Hacket Creek and Roding River, in the Aniseed Valley. This picnic area is 29km from Nelson and is reached by driving 1.5km south of Hope on SH6 and turning east onto Aniseed Valley Rd. If you take the alternative finish to The Brook, which is by far the most popular option, you arrive 4km from the Nelson city centre, so transport will not be a problem.

From Nelson, **Trek Express** (☎ 0800 128 735; www.trekexpress.co.nz) supplies an on-demand shuttle-bus service to the Maungatapu Rd trailhead (per person $50, minimum four people). It will also pick you up at the Hacket picnic area, transporting you back to Nelson (per person $25, minimum four people).

Otherwise, passing bus companies will drop you off at Pelorus Bridge Scenic Reserve, which is on the Picton–Nelson route. Your best bet is **InterCity** (☎ 03-365 1113; www.intercitycoach.co.nz).

Once at Pelorus Bridge, stop in at the cafe and ask about a lift to the trailhead. Often there is somebody who will provide transport for a small fee.

The Tramp

Day 1: Maungatapu Road to Middy Creek Hut

5–6 HOURS, 14KM

The start of the track is just down the road from the car park at the end of Maungatapu Rd, and begins by descending towards the river. In 10 to 15 minutes you arrive at the first of many swing bridges, this one over Scott Creek, near where it empties into a deep pool of the **Pelorus River**. Continue following the true left (west) side of the river to enter the forest park, and one hour (3km) from the start arrive at **Emerald Pool**. A picnic table tips you off that you have arrived at the popular day-walk destination – a great place for a dip if the sandflies aren't swarming.

At this point the track leaves the river and makes a steep 100m climb through a thick forest of rimu, tawa (quite rare in this park), matai and beech. Within 30 minutes you're sidling the river bluff and the walking is easier. You follow the river for one hour (3km), descending sharply twice via switchbacks, the second time right back to the edge of the Pelorus.

The track now swings to the west and in 30 minutes reaches the short side track to Captain Creek Hut (six bunks), located in a clearing just above the river. The hut is a three- to four-hour walk from the car park; it has no rainwater supply. Right in front of the hut is a nice pool for swimming. You may also see the occasional angler in these parts.

From here, the main track continues to follow the river and within 10 minutes crosses **Captain Creek**, a good-sized stream rushing out of the mountains. Exercise extreme care here during or after high rainfall. In another five minutes the track arrives at a swing bridge that spans a tight, rocky gorge high above the Pelorus. If swing bridges make you uneasy, this one will have you gripping its cables all the way across. Once on the true right side (south) of the Pelorus, you climb steeply out of the gorge and then sidle the bluffs until the track descends to a swing bridge across Fishtail Stream, reached one hour (3km) from Captain Creek Hut.

From the creek you climb again, and cross a bush-clad terrace where the Pelorus forms a wide loop. It's another 1km before you pop out at Middy Creek Hut (six bunks), a two-hour (6km) walk from Captain Creek, opposite the confluence of Middy Creek and the Pelorus River. Nearby is a signposted junction with a track that heads south to Conical Knob (1216m) and Mt Fell (1606m). The river is close at hand and there is a very deep pool under the nearby swing bridge. Beware of the ferocious sandflies.

PELORUS BRIDGE SCENIC RESERVE

A pocket of deep green forest tucked away among paddocks of bog-standard pasture, 18km west of Havelock, Pelorus Bridge Scenic Reserve contains one of the last stands of river-flat forest in Marlborough. It survived only because a town planned in 1865 didn't get off the ground by 1912, by which time obliterative logging made this little remnant look precious. The reserve was born, and hats off to that, because now visitors can explore its many tracks, admire the historic bridge, or even take a dip in the limpid Pelorus River (beautiful enough to star in Peter Jackson's *The Hobbit*).

But wait, there's more. Secluded away from the highway, nestled into the forest, **Pelorus Bridge Campground & Cafe** (☎ 03-571 6019; www.doc.govt.nz; unpowered/powered sites per person $12/6) is a magical place to spend a night or two. Not only is it a picturesque gem, it has hot showers, a smart kitchen and a large deck with river views. The cafe has delightful home-baked pies which you can walk off on a nearby nature trail before heading back in for cake.

Day 2: Middy Creek Hut to Browning Hut

7–8 HOURS, 16KM

About 150m west of Middy Creek Hut, a swing bridge crosses the Pelorus River to its true left side. From here you climb sharply to a junction with a track that continues up the spur to Rocks Hut. The Pelorus Track heads southwest (left fork), working its way to a saddle above Rocks Creek and then dropping steeply to the creek some distance upstream from the Pelorus River.

After crossing the creek the tramp becomes more difficult, starting with 4km of thick forest – a mixture of beech, rimu, tree ferns and horopito – with protruding tree roots ready to trip you up.

Eventually the track descends to **Roebuck Creek** and a pair of swing bridges. The first one crosses the creek; the second extends over the Pelorus River, 200m upriver. Roebuck Hut (six bunks), three to four hours from Middy Creek Hut, is on an open terrace directly across from the junction of the creek and the Pelorus, which at normal water levels can be forded here.

Return to the swing bridge over the Pelorus River, where on the true left side the track immediately climbs the ridge that separates Roebuck and Mates Creeks. It's a steep 30-minute climb for the first 150m of ascent, and then the track begins to climb at a more gradual rate to **Totara Saddle** (690m). Before reaching the saddle the track works its way across the slopes of the Roebuck catchment, and has good views of Mt Fell and Mt Richmond.

At the saddle there is a junction with a track heading northwards to Rocks Hut (four hours). The main track (left fork) heads west, dropping 180m in 1km. It traverses an open slip and goes through beech forest on the way to Browning Hut (eight bunks), situated in a large open area on the edge of Browning Stream.

ALTERNATIVE END: THE BROOK VIA DUN MOUNTAIN TRACK

7–8 HOURS, 21KM, 800M ASCENT, 880M DESCENT

This is a long day that begins immediately with its longest climb. An early-morning start is wise and, as water is scarce along this section, carry plenty with you and refill at Rocks Hut.

At the track junction, 20 minutes out from Middy Creek Hut, take the right fork and continue climbing. For the next 4km

it's a steady 600m trudge uphill with a couple of major descents into the bargain. It's basically a three-hour climb with no views. From here you resume climbing, quickly passing moss-covered rock pinnacles, and within 30 minutes arrive at a signposted junction. The left fork is a ridge track that heads southwest to Totara Saddle and then Browning Hut.

The right fork quickly emerges from the bush into subalpine scrub and arrives at Rocks Hut (16 bunks), reached 6km (2½ to three hours) from Middy Creek Hut. This is a very appealing hut overlooking Mt Richmond and Mt Fell. There are few sandflies (if any) and a rainwater supply. If staying at the hut, follow the Browning Hut track for 30 minutes to check out a series of pinnacles known as **The Rocks** (939m).

From the hut the track heads northeast towards Dun Saddle and quickly passes a side track (10 minutes) to an open perch with a view to the west. Within 45 minutes you break out of the trees and stunted scrub for good, and then reach **Dun Saddle** (960m), one hour (2km) from Rocks Hut. It's usually too windy to hang around this spot. **Dun Mountain** (1129m) is 45 minutes away (1.5km) via a poled route that heads right. If the winds are light, consider a side trip to the mountain for excellent views of Nelson and the surrounding region.

You then head left along a barren route, which is not marked nearly as well as the previous section of track (keep an eye out for metal poles and orange triangles on the trees), but the views are great. You briefly re-enter the bush, but within 30 minutes of Dun Saddle you reach **Coppermine Saddle**. This is the start of the old Dun Mountain Railway, NZ's first railway, which was constructed to enable horse-drawn carts to haul chromite ore from the mountain to Nelson.

The walking track resumes by sidling a ridge off Wooded Peak, and in 30 minutes (two hours from Rocks Hut) arrives at **Windy Point**. This exposed tip of the ridge is signposted because the winds here are legendary – so much so that at times it can be hard to stand. Hang onto your hat...with both hands. Just as amazing, walk 15 minutes down the track and the roaring winds are often just steady breezes. Departing from Windy Point is the poled Wells Ridge Route to **Wooded Peak** (1111m), 1½ hours away.

The Dun Mountain Track continues to skirt Wooded Peak, and with every step looks more like the railroad bed that it is. The walking is easy, a pleasant end to a long day for many. You quickly re-enter the beech forest and 1½ hours from Windy Point you reach Third House Shelter. This is strictly a place for a break, as camping is not allowed and there is no water. At this point Brook St is two hours away along a well-signposted trail that still looks like a 4WD track. The final 30 minutes is a rapid descent, ending just north of the Brook Valley Holiday Park (p156), 4km from Nelson's city centre.

Day 3: Browning Hut to Hacket Picnic Area

2 HOURS, 6KM

The track immediately crosses to the true right (north) side of a tributary of **Browning Stream**. For the next hour it's easy walking through forest and across several eroded streambeds. During high water you can follow a steep, alternative track around these streams and slips. Shortly before crossing Browning Stream for the last time, you pass a side track that leads south (left fork) over a low saddle to Hacket Hut (six bunks). The main track crosses the stream after five minutes, near the confluence with Hacket Creek, which is forded immediately.

The other side of Hacket Creek is private farmland, but you don't need permission to walk through it. An easy, benched track follows the creek on its true left (west) side for an hour, almost to the Hacket picnic area. About 1km before the picnic area the track crosses a swing bridge over Hacket Creek, and then joins a 4WD track to a wooden footbridge over the Roding River.

Kaikoura Coast Track

Duration 3 days

Distance 37.3km (23 miles)

Track Standard Easy tramping track

Difficulty Easy to moderate

Start/End Ngaroma

Nearest Town Kaikoura (p164)

Transport Bus

Summary A private track that combines alpine views and a lengthy beach walk with gracious farm hospitality at night.

In 1994, three adjoining farms along the Kaikoura coast – Hawkswood, Medina and Ngaroma – were all searching for a way to diversify their activities while preserving, even expanding, their large areas of native forest and bush. Taking a cue from the Banks Peninsula Track, the country's first private track just down the coast, they formed one of their own, opening up their farms and their homes to a small number of trampers each day.

Kaikoura Coast Track is a three-day tramp that has you traversing tussock tops, climbing Mt Wilson and skirting the Pacific Ocean, keeping an eye out for marine wildlife. A large part of the experience, however, is the farms themselves – scattering sheep as you cut through a paddock, stopping to watch sheepdogs round up a flock, and sipping lemonade made from freshly squeezed, home-grown lemons. It's a tramp through remote and rural NZ, with your hosts each night being the families who work the farms. For many that's as intriguing as the view from Skull Peak.

The track fee includes both comfortable accommodation and the transportation of your luggage and food. That means every night you can enjoy a hot shower and a soft bed, and pack along a few steaks and a bottle of good NZ wine. Without having to haul a backpack, the climbs are easily accomplished by most trampers, who can then recover with a bit of luxury at night before setting out the next day.

History & Environment

The Caverhill and Macfarlane families began farming Hawkswood in 1860, and at its peak the estate covered 24,510 hectares, including all the coastal land between the Conway River and Waiau Rivers. Today the three farms involved with the Kaikoura Coast Track combine for a total of 3935 hectares, with the majority of it being either tussock ridges or paddocks and farm blocks. Several gullies have been fenced off from livestock and turned into conservation areas. These pockets of native bush include ancient remnants of beech forest, giant podocarps such as kahikatea, matai and totara, and a variety of ferns. Don't know your native bush? Not to worry – the families have done an impressive job of labelling trees and plants along the track, and by the end of the tramp you will know the difference between lancewood and pigeonwood.

Most of the wildlife encountered will be a variety of birds in the forested areas – such as riflemen, bellbirds, grey warblers and long-tailed cuckoos – and possibly NZ hawks on the tops. Along the beach, trampers have spotted Hector's and dusky dolphins playing in the surf, and occasionally seals basking on the sand.

ℹ Planning

WHEN TO TRAMP

The season for tramping the track is October to April, with the warmest months being December through March.

WHAT TO BRING

Sun protection (a wide-brimmed hat and sunscreen) is important. So is a bathing suit; there are swimming pools at all three farms, plus the ocean. Many trampers will also use a chilly bin (cooler) to transport their meat and other perishable food between farms.

MAPS & BROCHURES

Every tramper is given a *Kaikoura Coast Track Guide Booklet,* which covers the natural highlights of each section of track and contains a map that is more than sufficient. For more detail, obtain NZTopo50 *BU26* (Parnassus) and *BU27* (Oaro).

HUTS & BOOKINGS

Each farm provides accommodation for trampers along the track, with the first night spent at Ngaroma, the second at Medina, and the third at the Staging Post at Hawkswood Farm. The cost of the accommodation is included in the track booking fee.

The number of trampers on the track is limited to 10 per day, so bookings are wise if you have particular dates you want to walk. The cost is $230 per person, which includes transportation of luggage, accommodation and secured parking. Book through **Kaikoura Coast Track** (☏ 03-319 2715; www.kaikouratrack.co.nz).

ℹ Getting to/from the Tramp

The walk begins and ends at Ngaroma, 7.5km off SH1, 150km north of Christchurch and 45km south of Kaikoura. InterCity and Atomic bus services will drop you off at the Conway River Bridge where you can be collected by arrangement.

The Tramp

Day 1: Ngaroma to Medina

4–5 HOURS, 12KM

The first night is spent in the Loft at **Ngaroma Farm**, which has great views of the Kaikoura Range. It's an easy stroll down to the Pacific Ocean or you can wander around the farm and soak up the bucolic atmosphere.

The tramp begins the next morning. If you hustle, this section could easily take less than four hours, but why hurry? Linger on the beach, scan the ocean for marine life, look for shells in the cliffs and soak in the views.

To set off on the track, head to the beach following a gravel road east from the farmhouse and then cross a bridge and continue south. A track sign will divert you off the road to the greyish, gravelly beach. The darker the sand the better the footing, but overall this is something of a trudge. The scenery is amazing, however, and soon you're skirting the base of towering tan bluffs on one side, with the roar of the Pacific on the other. The endless crashing of waves onto the beach sets a tranquil tone for the rest of the morning.

About 1.8km from Ngaroma you reach the first stumps of the **Buried Forest** – matai, rimu and kanuka that were living trees 8000 years ago, but were eventually covered by sediment and preserved. Now sea erosion has revealed these ancient trees in several locations along a 1km stretch of the beach to **Ploughman's Creek**, a wide gap in the bluffs where you can see a road bridge. Seal Gap and Doug's Gap follow, and one hour from Ngaroma (3.6km) you reach **Big Bush Beach**. Here the sand extends up into a huge gap to form a big beach.

The cliffs turn whitish and layers of shells are easily seen. You pass Dawn's Creek at 4.8km, and 1.2km later (two hours from Ngaroma) reach a track turning inland to Circle Shelter. This lunchtime shelter has loads of character, including a large and very comfortable couch, a 'loo with a view', and a fire pit where you can boil a billy for a cup of tea.

Within 1km of the shelter you reach **The Lookout**, where a bench allows you to enjoy a view of the coastline, with Kaikoura Peninsula 37km to the north and Banks Peninsula 145km to the south. The track then turns inland, cuts through a couple of paddocks and descends into the **Medina Conservation Area**. Protected from livestock grazing since 1984, this gully is rich in native plants and also features several ancient podocarps, including an 800-year-old kahikatea, so large it takes four people to link their arms around it.

Eventually you climb out of the conservation area into open tussock, to reach the **Rest and Reflect Bench** (10.6km from Ngaroma) with its grand view of Medina Farm. From here it's less than 30 minutes to the farm's accommodation, **Medina**, where you will stay in either the Whare or the Garden Cottage. Both offer stunning views of the farm, its livestock and the mountains beyond. There's a pool to recover in, and wine in the refrigerator that can be enjoyed for a fair price.

Day 2: Medina to the Staging Post

4–5 HOURS, 13KM, 589M ASCENT, 549M DESCENT

You can see the first half of the day's tramp, right to the climb of Mt Wilson, before even leaving Medina. The first hour is a gentle climb through open farmland with wonderful views all around, including the ocean behind you. Within 2km you reach a stile, which marks the boundary to **Hawkswood Farm**, the second you'll cross.

The track remains in open country until it descends into a forested gully and crosses Little Dawn Creek. You resume climbing, merge onto a 4WD track, and about 4.5km from Medina, make a sharp right onto another sheep track at a well-signposted junction. This one leads you to open tussock, with a steady ascent that improves the views dramatically. You reach **Mt Wilson Saddle** where, if you peer to the west, you can see the Staging Post, your target for the day. Just up the track, a two-hour (6.8km) walk from Medina, is a large track sign announcing that the top of Mt Wilson is just a two-minute climb to the left, while the Mt Wilson Shelter is 10 minutes to the right, on the back side of the mountain.

You can peer in any direction from the top of Mt Wilson, a 649m rocky knob. From the benches in front of Mt Wilson Shelter you can see west to Mt Tapuae-o-Uenuku (2885m), the highest peak on the South Island outside the Southern Alps. This is the most basic of the three lunch shelters, but there is drinking water and protection from the wind.

Continue the ridge walk to Saddle Shelter, reached at 8km, where there are the final views of the Pacific Ocean. At this point you begin the long descent to Hawkswood Farm. The remaining 5km are all downhill and all along 4WD tracks. The exception is at the very end, when you follow a track into the Chilly Stream gully and are faced with a 10-minute climb out, just before emerging at the farm where you find your accommodation, the Staging Post.

Day 3: The Staging Post to Ngaroma

4–6 HOURS, 12.3KM, 429M ASCENT, 449M DESCENT

The third morning begins with a short van ride taking trampers north on SH1 to the start of the track. The usual departure is 9am, but if it appears you're in for a hot and sunny day you might consider an earlier start. All the uphill walking is completed in the first two hours, which is always easier in the cool of the morning.

From the trailhead you immediately climb through a pine plantation over a ridge but within 1.5km descend into Buntings Bush Gully. This conservation area is a rich forest compared to the farmed pines and features huge podocarps, including one totara big enough to be turned into a Maori war canoe. All too soon, however, you begin the long hike to the tussock tops. Within 3.5km (one hour) of the start you reach Heather's Bench, overlooking the Conway Valley, and after another 1km you're out of the trees for good, arriving at Bruce's Bench. This bench, a huge split log overlooking a mountain panorama, almost commands you to take a break, even if you're not tired.

You're now ridge-walking in the Hawkswood Range, by far the most scenic stretch of the day. With views all around, you reach a saddle and are greeted with the Kaikoura coast on the horizon, and then in another 500m you climb to Skull Peak (489m). At either point you can see the Pacific in one direction and inland mountains in the other. From the peak you can also see Skull Peak

Shelter, 1km and a tussock gully away. The final climb to this delightful lunch spot is gentle, and reached in two to three hours (7.5km) from SH1. Inside the small hut there is water, a gas cooker for tea, and even a couple of mattresses for a post-lunch nap. Outside there are benches and stunning views.

The second half of the day is all downhill. You steeply descend along a 4WD track for more than 1km, losing much of the height you worked so hard to gain before lunch. You return to a walking track at the Back Paddock and, 2.5km from the shelter, re-enter native bush when you descend to Possum Drive, the reason there's a 'Cow Bar' across the track.

Over the final 2km of the day you cross a couple of bridges – one labelled 'Muddy Butt Bridge' because it's at the bottom of a long slippery slope – and cut through several paddocks complete with grazing sheep. Ngaroma is reached two hours (4.8km) from the shelter.

TOWNS & FACILITIES

Picton

☑ 03 / POP 4000

Half asleep in winter, but hyperactive in summer, boaty Picton clusters around a deep gulch at the head of Queen Charlotte Sound. It's the main traveller port for the South Island, and the best place from which to explore the Marlborough Sounds and tackle the Queen Charlotte Track. There's ample accommodation in Picton, including lots of low-budget options. It's also a good spot for stocking up on provisions.

🛏 Sleeping & Eating

Picton Top 10 Holiday Park   HOLIDAY PARK $
(☑ 03-573 7212, 0800 277 444; www.pictontop10.
co.nz; 70 Waikawa Rd; sites from $20, units $70-100;
🛜 🗷) About 500m from town, this compact, well-kept place has modern, crowd-pleasing facilities, including a barbecue area, heated swimming pool and a recreation room.

Tombstone Backpackers   HOSTEL $
(☑ 0800 573 7116, 03-573 7116; www.tombstonebp.
co.nz; 16 Gravesend Pl; dm $28, d with/without
bathroom $81/75; 🛜 🗷) Rest in peace in hotel-worthy dorms, double rooms and a self-contained apartment. Bonuses include

free breakfast, a sunny reading room, a pool table, a DVD library and free ferry pick-up and drop-off.

Villa　　　　　　　　　　　　　HOSTEL $
(✆03-573 6598; www.thevilla.co.nz; 34 Auckland St; dm $26-30, d with/without bathroom $76/67; ☞) This bright backpackers has a blooming garden and sociable outdoor areas, and in-demand en-suite rooms. A real home away from home, with fresh flowers and free apple crumble (fruit supply permitting). Queen Charlotte Track bookings and camping gear for hire.

Picton Village Bakkerij　　　　　BAKERY $
(cnr Auckland & Dublin Sts; items $2-8; ⊗6am-4pm) Dutch owners bake trays of European goodies here, including interesting breads, decent pies and filled rolls, cakes and custardy, tarty treats. Be prepared to queue.

🛍 Supplies & Equipment

Picton Sports & Outdoors　　　　　OUTDOOR EQUIPMENT
(8 High St; ⊗8.30am-5pm Mon-Fri, to 2.30pm Sat, 9.30am-2pm Sun) For tramping equipment or stove fuel.

Fresh Choice　　　　　　　　　　SUPERMARKET
(Mariners Mall, 100 High St; ⊗7am-9pm) Pretty much the only choice as far as groceries go, and actually pretty good.

ℹ Information

Located 200m from the ferry terminal, Picton i-SITE (p145) is a one-stop shop for accommodation and transport bookings, and has a DOC agency on site.

ℹ Getting There & Away

Soundsair (✆520 3080, 0800 505 005; www.soundsair.co.nz) has regular air service across Cook Strait to and from Wellington (adult/child $100/88). A free shuttle bus is provided between Picton and the airstrip in Koromiko, 8km south of town.

Numerous bus operators service Picton, with the most extensive network covered by **InterCity** (✆03-365 1113; www.intercitycoach.co.nz), which runs to Christchurch (from $26, 5½ hours) via Kaikoura (from $17, 2½ hours); Nelson (from $26, 2¼ hours) with connections to Motueka and the West Coast; and to/from Blenheim (from $10, 30 minutes). **Atomic Shuttles** (✆03-349 0697; www.atomictravel.co.nz) is a smaller shuttle operator running from Picton to Christchurch. **Ritchies Transport** (✆03-578 5467; www.ritchies.co.nz) buses traverse the Picton–Blenheim line daily (from $12), departing from the Interislander ferry terminal.

Picton is one of the start/end points of the Coastal Pacific service operated by **KiwiRail Scenic** (✆0800 872 467; www.kiwirailscenic.co.nz), which stops at various stations (including Blenheim and Kaikoura) on its 5¼-hour daily run to Christchurch.

Shuttles (and tours) around Picton and wider Marlborough are offered by **Marlborough Sounds Shuttles** (✆03-573 7122; www.marlboroughsoundsshuttles.co.nz). Between Picton and Havelock (via Anakiwa), you can hitch a van ride with **Coleman Post** (✆027 255 8882; $15).

Departing from the Picton ferry terminal are the **Interislander** (✆0800 802 802; www.interislander.co.nz) and **Bluebridge** (✆0800 844 844; www.bluebridge.co.nz), between them offering around eight sailings in each direction daily. The North–South journey is just over three hours, with fares starting at around $55 per person each way.

Havelock
✆03 / POP 500

Situated at the confluence of the Pelorus and Kaiuma Rivers, 35km from Blenheim and 73km from Nelson, Havelock is the western bookend of the picturesque 35km Queen Charlotte Drive, which goes through to Picton. The self-proclaimed 'Greenshell Mussel Capital of the World' is hardly the most rock-and-roll of NZ towns, but it's your best base for the Nydia Track and a logical one for Pelorus Track, as you'll readily locate most necessities.

🛏 Sleeping & Eating

Havelock Motor Camp　　　　HOLIDAY PARK $
(✆03-574 2339; www.havelockmotorcamp.co.nz; 24 Inglis St; campsites from $30, d $50) Conveniently located near the marina, this workaday place has tent sites and basic cabins.

Blue Moon　　　　　　　　　　　HOSTEL $
(✆03-574 2212; www.bluemoonhavelock.co.nz; 48 Main Rd, Havelock; dm $28, r with/without bathroom $96/76; @☞) This largely unremarkable lodge has homely rooms in the main house (one with en suite), as well as cabins and a bunkhouse in the yard (along with a spa pool). The lounge and kitchen are pleasant and relaxed, as is the sunny barbecue deck. Hosts run shuttle transport servicing the Nydia Track, Queen Charlotte, and surrounds.

QUEEN CHARLOTTE & MARLBOROUGH HAVELOCK

Smiths Farm Holiday Park
HOLIDAY PARK $

(☑ 03-574 2806, 0800 727 578; www.smithsfarm.co.nz; 1419 Queen Charlotte Dr, Linkwater; campsites from $16, cabins $60-130, units $130; @ 🛜) Handily located within walking distance of the Anakiwa end of the Queen Charlotte Track, right on Queen Charlotte Drive, this lovely, rural park has its own nearby waterfall and glowworm dell.

Havelock Garden Motel
MOTEL $$

(☑ 03-574 2387; www.gardenmotels.com; 71 Main Rd; d $115-150) Set in a large, graceful garden complete with dear old trees and a duck-filled creek, these tastefully revamped 1960s units offer homely comfort.

Havelock Four Square
SUPERMARKET $

(☑ 03-574 2166; cnr Main Rd & Neil St) This modest grocery shop is the best option for miles and miles.

ℹ Information

The best place for information is Havelock Information Centre (p145), which can also assist you with transport and accommodation bookings.

ℹ Getting There & Away

InterCity (p157) runs daily from Picton to Havelock via Blenheim ($22, one hour), and from Havelock to Nelson ($23, 1¼ hours). **Atomic Shuttles** (☑ 03-349 0697; www.atomictravel.co.nz) plies the same run. You can travel between Havelock and Picton for $15 via the scenic Queen Charlotte Drive with Coleman Post. Buses depart from the high street in the middle of town – look for the restaurant with the mussels on the roof.

Kaikoura
☑ 03 / POP 3850

The whale-watching capital of NZ and a rewarding stop for lots of other salty activities, Kaikoura is a major tourism town and can cater to most tramping needs.

🛏 Sleeping & Eating

Alpine Pacific Holiday Park
HOLIDAY PARK $

(☑ 03-319 6275, 0800 692 322; www.alpine-pacific.co.nz; 69 Beach Rd; campsites from $40, cabins $75, units & motels $140-180; @ 🛜 ☒) This compact and proudly trimmed park offers mountain views, neat cabins and excellent communal facilities, including a shiny kitchen, resorty pool area and barbecue pavilion.

Dolphin Lodge
LODGE $

(☑ 03-319 5842; www.dolphinlodge.co.nz; 15 Deal St; dm $27, d with/without bathroom $67/60; @ 🛜) This small and slightly tight lodge makes amends with a home-away-from-home feel, a lovely scented garden (hammocks ahoy), fantastic deck, barbecue and spa pool.

Pier Hotel
PUB $$

(☑ 03-319 5037; www.thepierhotel.co.nz; 1 Avoca St; mains $24 to $34 ⊙ 11am-late) Enjoying wide views of the bay and mountains beyond, this creaky, character-filled charmer dishes up honest food (including fresh local fish) and good-value lodgings upstairs.

Cafe Encounter
CAFE $

(96 Esplanade; meals $8-19; ⊙ 7.30am-5pm; ☑) Housed in the Dolphin Encounter complex, this bustling cafe has great coffee and yummy food such as cakes, pastries, bagels, toasties and specials like braised pork belly and fennel slaw. Ocean views from the sunny patio.

🛒 Supplies & Equipment

R&R Sport
OUTDOOR EQUIPMENT

(www.rrsport.co.nz; 14 West End; ⊙ 9am-5.30pm Mon-Sat, 10am-4pm Sun) This good all-rounder can sort you out with supplies, including stove fuel.

New World
SUPERMARKET

(124 Beach Rd; ⊙ 7.30am-9pm) The town's best supermarket, 10 minutes' walk from the town centre.

ℹ Information

Kaikoura i-SITE (☑ 03-319 5641; www.kaikoura.co.nz; West End; ⊙ 9am-5pm Mon-Fri, to 4pm Sat & Sun, extended hours Dec-Mar) Helpful staff make tour, accommodation and transport bookings, and help with DOC-related matters.

ℹ Getting There & Away

InterCity (☑ 03-365 1113; www.intercitycoach.co.nz) buses run between Kaikoura and Nelson (from $49, 3½ hours), Picton (from $17, 2¼ hours) and Christchurch (from $15, 2¾ hours). Smaller shuttle buses running along the same route are **Atomic Shuttles** (☑ 03-349 0697; www.atomictravel.co.nz) and **Naked Bus** (☑ 0900 625 33; www.nakedbus.com). Buses depart from and can be booked at the i-SITE.

The Coastal Pacific service operated by **KiwiRail Scenic** (☑ 0800 872 467; www.kiwirailscenic.co.nz) stops at Kaikoura on its daily run between Picton (2¼ hours) and Christchurch (three hours).

Abel Tasman, Kahurangi & Nelson Lakes

Includes ➡

Abel Tasman
Coast Track.........169
Heaphy Track 175
Wangapeka Track....180
Tableland Circuit 184
Lake Angelus Track .. 191
Travers-Sabine
Circuit 193
St Arnaud Range
Track 196

Best Huts

➡ Anchorage Hut (p172)

➡ Whariwharangi Hut (p174)

➡ Heaphy Hut (p179)

➡ Salisbury Lodge (p186)

➡ Angelus Hut (p192)

Best Views

➡ Separation Point (p173)

➡ James Mackay Hut (p178)

➡ Little Wanganui
Saddle (p183)

➡ Mt Arthur (p185)

➡ St Arnaud Range (p196)

Why Go?

The Nelson region is a trampers' paradise, boasting three national parks – Abel Tasman, Kahurangi and Nelson Lakes. Between them they offer a mind-blowing diversity of landscapes and experiences, from swimming in golden coves or quick plunges in frigid mountain streams, to traversing a plateau strewn with ancient rock formations, tramping across the sands of a wild West Coast beach, or exploring alpine peaks and passes with views as far as the eye can see.

This region has two Great Walks, including New Zealand's most popular, the Abel Tasman Coast Track. The other, the Heaphy Track, is famed for its ecological and geological wonders. There are many other well-established tracks and myriad more-remote and less-frequented options such as the Mt Arthur Tableland Circuit, included in this book for the first time.

When to Go

Sheltered by mountain ranges, Abel Tasman National Park basks in some of NZ's best weather. Particularly pleasant spells occur reliably through summer and autumn, but the park can happily be tramped all year round.

Kahurangi cops the westerly winds that blow off the Tasman Sea, bringing substantial rainfall to mountain areas that in turn lead to river flooding. Snow is also possible at higher altitudes, but Kahurangi can be tramped all year round in favourable conditions.

Nelson Lakes possesses a surprisingly moderate climate for an alpine region. Things can turn pear-shaped very quickly, though, with the arrival of heavy rain or even a blizzard. The odds of good weather are considerably higher from November to April.

GATEWAY TOWNS

→ Nelson (p197)

→ Motueka (p198)

→ Marahau (p199)

→ Takaka (p199)

→ Karamea (p200)

→ St Arnaud (p201)

Fast Facts

→ Abel Tasman National Park is NZ's smallest, covering 227 sq km. But small doesn't mean unpopular...around 30,000 people walk the Abel Tasman Coast Track every year, making it NZ's most popular Great Walk.

→ At the other end of the scale, Kahurangi is NZ's second-largest national park, at 4520 sq km, but only 6500 people a year complete its Great Walk, the Heaphy Track.

Top Tip

Between rivers, lakes and ocean, you can count on getting out on or in the water at some stage during your tramping adventures. Pack a hat, sunscreen and swimsuit (although you'll probably get away with a skinny dip).

Resources

→ www.nelsonnz.com

→ www.motuekaisite.co.nz

→ www.goldenbaynz.co.nz

→ www.heaphytrack.com

→ www.karameainfo.co.nz

→ www.starnaud.co.nz

Background Reading

Golden Bay writer Gerald Hindmarsh has produced several highly readable social-history books in recent years. In *Kahurangi Calling: Stories from the Backcountry of Northwest Nelson,* he describes many of the natural wonders found in Kahurangi and tells the stories of the fascinating characters who have lived there or travelled through, including explorers, miners, graziers, eelers, hermits and trampers. His 2013 book, *Outsiders: Stories from the Fringe of New Zealand Society,* continues in the same vein. Hindmarsh believes that a society is lucky to have people such as those he mentions in his book, that these 'outsiders' offer 'an important counterbalance to the high-pressured, commercialised and urban world that most of us inhabit'.

DON'T MISS

The Abel Tasman Coast Track has long been trampers' territory, but its coastal beauty makes it an equally seductive spot for sea kayaking, which can be combined with walking and camping. The possibilities and permutations for guided or freedom rental trips are vast. You can kayak from half a day up to three days, camping or staying in DOC huts, baches, even a floating backpackers, either fully catered or self-catering. You can kayak one day, camp overnight then walk back, or walk further into the park and catch a water taxi back.

A popular choice if time is tight is to spend a few hours kayaking, followed by a walk on the coastal track, stopping off for a dip or two in the azure waters.

Marahau is the main base for departure, but trips also depart from Kaiteriteri. There are plenty of professional operators ready to float you out on the water, most offering similar trips at similar prices. The Nelson region i-SITEs are well versed in kayak trip planning, recommendations and bookings.

DOC Offices

→ **DOC Nelson Regional Visitor Centre** (☎03-548 2304; www.nelsonnz.com; cnr Trafalgar & Halifax Sts; ⊗8.30am-5pm Mon-Fri, 9am-5pm Sat & Sun)

→ **DOC Motueka Area Office** (☎03-528 1810; www.doc.govt. nz; cnr King Edward & High Sts; ⊗8am-4pm Mon-Fri)

→ **DOC Golden Bay Area Office** (☎03-525 8026; www.doc. govt.nz; 62 Commercial St; ⊗8.30am-4pm Mon-Fri)

→ **Nelson Lakes Visitor Centre** (☎03-521 1806; www.doc. govt.nz; View Rd; ⊗8am-4.30pm, to 5pm in summer)

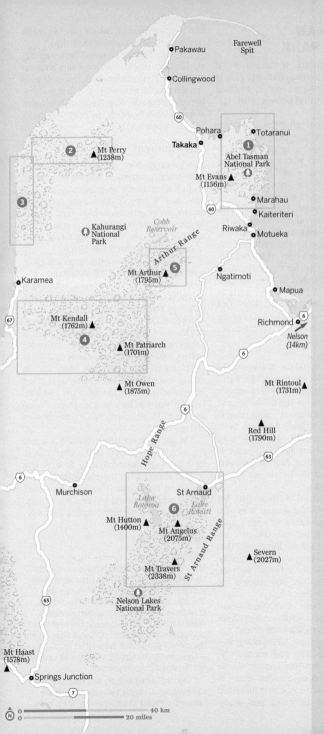

Abel Tasman, Kahurangi & Nelson Lakes Tramps

1. Abel Tasman Coast Track (p170)

2. Heaphy Track (North, p176)

3. Heaphy Track (South, p178)

4. Wangapeka Track (p181)

5. Tableland Circuit (p185)

6. Lake Angelus Track, Travers-Sabine Circuit & St Arnaud Range Track (p188)

ABEL TASMAN NATIONAL PARK

Basking in the sunshine at the top of the South Island, Abel Tasman National Park is renowned for its golden beaches, sculpted granite cliffs and world-famous Abel Tasman Coast Track.

The park is named after the Dutch explorer Abel Janzoon Tasman, who ventured this way in 1642. Despite being NZ's smallest national park and with a high point of just 1156m, it contains a wealth of fascinating natural features – far more than just the picture-postcard arcs of golden sand greeting seas of shimmering blue. Numbering among its many other landmarks are limpid lagoons, marble gorges and a spectacular system of karst caves in its rugged interior.

Hugging the water's edge, the Abel Tasman Coast Track is by far the park's most popular byway, although in high summer there seems as much traffic on the water as off it. Come the Christmas school holidays an armada of NZ boaties make it one of the country's most popular ocean playgrounds.

History

Maori have lived along the shores of the present Abel Tasman National Park for at least 500 years. They had abundant sources of food from both the sea and the forest, and seasonally cultivated kumara (sweet potato).

Maori were in residence when, in 1642, Abel Tasman anchored his ships near Wainui. A skirmish ensued, the upshot of which was the death of four of Tasman's crew without any of the Europeans having ever set foot on land.

Captain Cook stopped briefly in 1770, but recorded little about the coastal area and nothing of its inhabitants. It wasn't until Dumont d'Urville sailed into the area between Marahau and Torrent Bay in 1827 that Europeans met the Maori on peaceful terms. The French navigator made friends with the villagers, studied wildlife, and charted the park's bays and shoreline.

European settlement of the area began around 1855. The new settlers ranged from farmers and fishers to shipwrights and loggers, but by far the most enterprising was William Gibbs. The farm and mansion he built at Totaranui, and the innovations he implemented – such as running water in every bedroom, a glasshouse that furnished grapes and a model dairy that used porcelain pans warmed by copper pipes to make cream rise – were ahead of their time.

The Abel Tasman National Park was created in 1942, much credit for which is due to Nelsonian Perrine Moncrieff, the dedicated conservationist who wrote the first ornithological field guide, *New Zealand Birds and How to Identify Them,* in 1925. We thank you, Ms Moncrieff.

Environment

Nineteenth-century settlers embarked on their usual program of logging, quarrying and clearing forest to make way for pasture, and it was an ultimately successful campaign by conservationists that saw an original block of 15,000 hectares made into a national park. The varying vegetation cover of Abel Tasman reflects this history.

The moist, warm coastal areas are characterised by regenerating shrublands and lush coastal broad-leaved forest, with vines, perching plants, tree ferns and an abundance of the country's national plant, the silver fern. On the drier ridges and throughout much of the park's interior, the bush is predominantly beech forest, with all five NZ species found within its confines.

The more common forest birds, like tui and bellbird (korimako), can be seen along with pukeko around the estuaries and wetlands. Oystercatchers (torea), shags (koau) and little blue penguins (korora) can be seen on the coast.

The park's boundaries formally exclude the estuaries, foreshore and seabed but in 1993 the Tonga Island Marine Reserve was created along part of the Abel Tasman coast. All life in the marine reserve is protected. Native wildlife, natural, cultural and historic features are also protected within the park.

❶ Planning

WHEN TO TRAMP

The top of the South Island enjoys an enviable climate, making Abel Tasman a sparkling jewel at any time of year. Timing your visit for the shoulder season or even winter will avoid the crowds, as Coastal Track trampers number more than 250 a day in January. The best time to visit is from the end of February to May, when the crowds thin out but the weather is still pleasantly warm. Come August, you'll feel like you've got the whole place to yourself.

If you can't avoid January and February, you can keep out of people's way by skipping the huts and camping at smaller campsites. Avoid the main water-taxi and kayak drop-off and pick-up beaches between 9.30am and 10.30am, and 3.30pm and 5pm, when the coming and going of trampers is like rush-hour traffic in Auckland. You can also head to the lesser-used northern end of the park, from Totaranui north to Wainui.

WHAT TO BRING

The main Abel Tasman tracks are so well benched that sneakers are perfectly adequate. They are also easier to pull on and off again as you wade across tidal sections or paddle the shallows. Make sure you pack sunglasses, a swimsuit and a wide-brimmed hat, insect repellent and sunscreen.

Bring a stove, as none of the huts have cooking facilities.

INFORMATION SOURCES

The DOC Nelson Regional Visitor Centre (p198), located within the i-SITE, is the region's primary DOC centre and a good place to get advice, purchase hut tickets and maps, or to book Great Walks huts and campsites.

Information and bookings are also available at **DOC Motueka Area Office** (☑ 03-528 1810; www.doc.govt.nz; cnr King Edward & High Sts; ☉ 8am-4pm Mon-Fri), and over the hill in Golden Bay at both the **DOC Golden Bay Area Office** (☑ 03-525 8026; www.doc.govt.nz; 62 Commercial St; ☉ 8.30am-4pm Mon-Fri) and Golden Bay i-SITE (p200).

Abel Tasman Coast Track

Duration 5 days

Distance 51km (32 miles)

Track Standard Great Walk

Difficulty Easy

Start Marahau

End Wainui car park

Nearest Towns Marahau (p199), Takaka (p199)

Transport Boat, shuttle bus

Summary NZ's most popular tramp, linking a series of beautiful beaches and bays, and offering lots of sunshine.

This is arguably NZ's most beautiful Great Walk – a seductive combination of reliably pleasant weather, sparkling seas, golden sand, quintessential NZ coastal forest, and hidden surprises with intriguing names such as Cleopatra's Pool. That got your attention, didn't it?

You're not alone. Such is the pulling power of this track that it is now the most widely used recreational track in the country, attracting nearly 30,000 overnight trampers and kayakers, who all stay at least one night in the park. By way of comparison, the next most popular is the Routeburn, which draws around 13,000.

Another attraction is the terrain, for this is not a typical, rugged NZ track. It is better serviced than any other track in the country: well cut, well graded and well marked. It's almost impossible to get lost and can be tramped in sneakers.

Leaving the boots behind is a bonus, because you'll probably get your feet wet – and you'll probably *want* to get your feet wet. This is a track with long stretches of beach and crazy tides. In fact the tidal differences in the park are among the greatest in the country, up to a staggering 6m. At Torrent and Bark Bays, it's much easier and more fun to doff the shoes and cross the soggy sands, rather than take the all-tidal track. At Awaroa Bay you have no choice but to plan on crossing at low tide. Tide tables are posted along the track and on the DOC website; regional i-SITEs also have them.

It's a commonly held belief that the Coast Track ends at Totaranui, but it actually extends to a car park near Wainui Bay. Those who continue north of Totaranui will discover the most dramatic viewing point (Separation Point), the least-crowded hut (Whariwharangi) and some of the best beaches (Anapai and Mutton Cove) in the park.

The entire tramp takes only three to five days, although with water-taxi transport you can convert it into an almost endless array of options (particularly if you combine it with a kayak leg). If you can only spare a couple of days, a deservedly popular option is the loop around the northern end of the park, hiking the Coastal Track from Totaranui, passing Anapai and Mutton Cove, overnighting at Whariwharangi Hut (20 bunks), then returning to Totaranui via the Gibbs Hill Track. This will give you a slice of the park's best features (beaches, seals, coastal scenery) and will be far less crowded than any other segment.

Those wishing to explore the interior of the national park might like to consider the Inland Track, a harder and much less frequented path taking three days, which can be combined with the Coast Track to form a five- to six-day loop.

Abel Tasman Coast Track

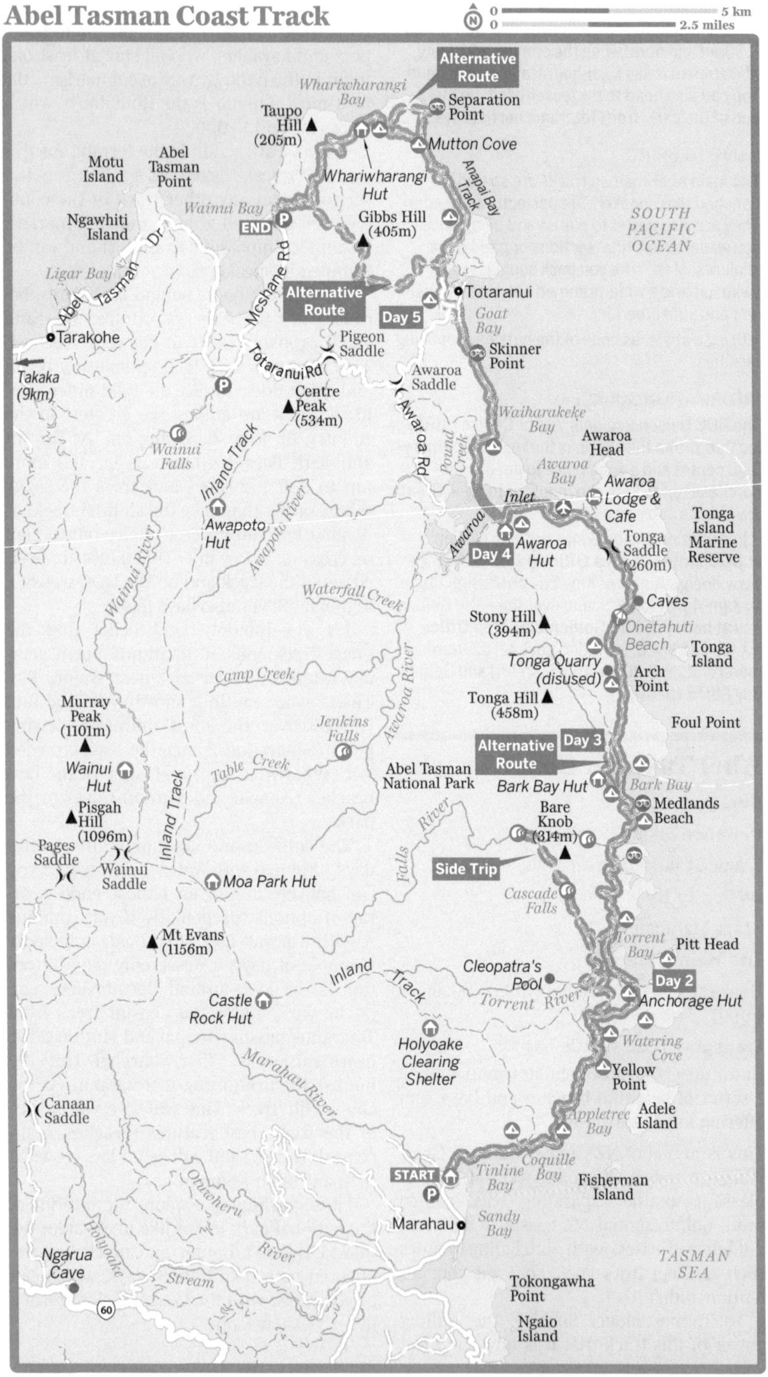

ⓘ Planning

MAPS & BROCHURES

This track is so well trodden that a topographical map isn't essential for navigation. The map within DOC's *Abel Tasman Coast Track* brochure provides sufficient detail. However, NewTopo *Abel Tasman* 1:55,000 will give you the lay of the land.

HUTS, CAMPING & LODGES

There are eight huts in the park. Anchorage, Bark Bay, Awaroa and Whariwharangi lie along the Coast Track and are designated **Great Walk huts** ($32). These have bunks, tables, benches and heating, flush toilets, and washbasins with cold water only. There are no cooking facilities or lighting. There are also 19 designated **Great Walk campsites** (www.doc.govt.nz; $14).

As the Abel Tasman Track is a Great Walk, all huts and campsites must be booked in advance year-round. Bookings can be made online through **Great Walks Bookings** (☑ 0800 694 732; www.greatwalks.co.nz) or at any DOC visitor centre.

DOC hut tickets and annual passes cannot be used on the track, and there is a two-night limit on staying in huts or campsites. The exception is Totaranui, which has a one-night limit for trampers. Penalty fees of up to 100% will apply to those who do not have a valid booking, and you may be required to leave the park.

Moored permanently in Anchorage Bay, **Aqua-packers** (☑ 0800 430 744; www.aquapackers.co.nz; dm/d incl breakfast $70/195) is a specially converted 13m catamaran providing unusual but buoyant backpacker accommodation for 22. Facilities are basic but decent; prices include bedding, dinner and breakfast. Bookings essential.

GUIDED TRAMPS

Abel Tasman Tours & Guided Walks (☑ 03-528 9602; www.abeltasmantours.co.nz; from $220) Small-group, day-long walking tours (minimum of two people). Day tramps, which include packed lunch and water taxis.

Kahurangi Guided Walks (☑ 03-525 7177; www.kahurangiwalks.co.nz) Runs small-group three-day Coast Track tramps ($700).

Wilsons Abel Tasman (☑ 03-528 2027, 0800 223 582; www.abeltasman.co.nz; 265 High St, Motueka; cruise & walk $60-75, kayak & walk $90-195) Offers a wide range of combination tours (walk, kayak, cruise) and owns beachfront lodges at Awaroa and Torrent Bay.

ⓘ Getting to/from the Tramp

The major gateway town to the Abel Tasman is Motueka, one hour's drive from Nelson. From here, it's easy to get to the major entry points of Marahau, the southern gateway, and Totaranui to the north, accessible by driving over Takaka to Golden Bay. Wainui is the official northern trailhead, although it is more common to finish in Totaranui, either skipping the northernmost section or looping back to Totaranui over Gibbs Hill Track. All gateways are serviced by either **Abel Tasman Coachlines** (☑ 03-548 0285; www.abeltasmantravel.co.nz) or **Golden Bay Coachlines** (☑ 03-525 8352; www.gbcoachlines.co.nz).

Trek Express (☑ 027-222 1872, 0800 128 735; www.trekexpress.co.nz) runs on demand (minimum four people) from Nelson to Marahau ($35); and from Wainui back to Marahau or Nelson (both $55).

Unless you wish to retrace your steps, your return transport options from either end are a long drive over Takaka Hill or, much more easily, a water-taxi service which doubles as a scenic cruise. There are numerous regular services departing from either Marahau or Kaiteriteri up to Totaranui (no services are permitted past that point), stopping off at various bays in between at Anchorage, Torrent Bay, Medlands Beach, Bark Bay, Tonga Quarry, Onetahuti, Awaroa and Totaranui. One-way prices start from around $33 (Anchorage, Torrent Bay) and range up to around $46 for Totaranui. These operators are very well versed in tailoring options to suit, including kayak/walk packages for those who want to mix things up a bit. Key operators are **Abel Tasman Aqua Taxi** (☑ 0800 278 282, 03-527 8083; www.aquataxi.co.nz; Marahau-Sandy Bay Rd, Marahau), **Abel Tasman Sea Shuttle** (☑ 0800 732 748, 03-527 8688; www.abeltasmanseashuttles.co.nz; Kaiteriteri), **Wilsons Abel Tasman** (☑ 0800 223 582, 03-528 2027; www.abeltasman.co.nz; 265 High St, Motueka) and **Marahau Water Taxis** (☑ 0800 808 018, 03-527 8176; Abel Tasman Centre, Franklin St, Marahau).

🥾 The Tramp

Day 1: Marahau to Anchorage

4 HOURS, 11.5KM

The track begins at a turn-off 1km north of Marahau, where there is a car park, information kiosk and shelter. From here it crosses the Marahau estuary on an all-tidal causeway, climbs gently to a clearing above Tinline Bay, and then passes Tinline Campsite, one hour (2.5km) from the car park. Just beyond the campsite a sign marks one end of the Inland Track.

The Coast Track continues northeast, skirting around dry ridges, hugging the coast and opening up to scenic views of Adele and Fisherman Islands, and Coquille and Appletree Bays. Signposts indicate side tracks leading down to the beaches where you can enjoy a refreshing swim in the surf. Trampers can pitch a tent at Appletree Bay Campsite, but be aware that this is a popular stop for kayakers.

After passing Yellow Point and its spur track, the trail turns inland, climbing in and out of gullies and along ridges lined with silver ferns. Eventually the trees thin out and you are rewarded with views of Torrent Bay. Here the track branches at a signposted junction. The main track heads east (right fork), passes a spur track (right), descends quickly to Anchorage Beach – 30 minutes away – and goes along the beach to the improved Anchorage Hut (34 bunks), constructed in 2014. Just beyond the hut is the Anchorage Campsite, a large and very popular spot in summer. The whole area is a makeshift marina in that season, with water taxis, yachties and kayakers coming and going, or sitting anchored offshore.

You can escape the crush of humanity around the hut by following the short side track at the eastern end of the beach to Te Pukatea Bay Campsite, or backtracking and taking the signposted spur track to Watering Cove Campsite.

Day 2: Anchorage to Bark Bay

3 HOURS, 9.5KM

This is a short day, and it can easily be combined with the next stage for a seven-hour walk to Awaroa...but then again, why hurry when you could dally along the way or hang out longer at Bark Bay?

From Anchorage Hut, head west along the beach and within 20 minutes climb an easy track over the headland into Torrent Bay. If the tide is right and the water low enough you can zip straight across the bay; usually you have to be within two hours either side of low tide to cross.

If you miss low tide and don't wish to wait, follow the all-tide track at the junction above the tidal crossing on Torrent Bay. It takes around 1½ hours to walk the 3.5km track, which circles the bay through bush, arriving at the bach settlement of Torrent Bay. It's well worth taking the 15-minute side track to beautiful Cleopatra's Pool where the Torrent River gushes over smooth rocks. The cold, fresh water is invigorating after a day in the sun and sea.

Near Torrent Bay Village Campsite you skirt the lagoon in front of a string of beaches, then turn left up the beach and pass yet more without one pang of envy. Or maybe just one. Keep going for 500m before the track heads away from the coast.

Once the main track moves inland it climbs 90m and sidles around Kilby Stream, before reaching a low saddle, where a side track takes you to a lookout. The Coast Track descends to a swing bridge over Falls River and then climbs to a spur track to a second lookout. Take a breather and enjoy the views of Bark Bay to the north and the coastline to the south. From the junction it's a 20-minute descent to Bark Bay.

Bark Bay is now a major access point for the track, with passenger boats coming in and out several times a day. Bark Bay Hut (34 bunks) is on the edge of the lagoon, a short walk from the beach. Like the hut, Bark Bay Campsite is also a large facility, so at times this snug little bay can be overflowing with trampers. But if you don't mind the people, it's a beautiful place to spend a night.

SIDE TRIP: FALLS RIVER TRACK

3 HOURS, 6KM RETURN

Those who want to see the various falls and pools of Tregidga Creek and Falls River should look for the track heading northwest from Torrent Bay Village. An easy track follows Tregidga Creek to the modest Cascade Falls after one hour. Stay on this track to reach Falls River, 15 minutes downstream from its main falls. A boulder-hopping scramble, helped by an occasional marker, will bring you to the impressive cascade.

Day 3: Bark Bay to Awaroa Bay

4 HOURS, 11.4KM

The coast along this section of track is classified as Tonga Island Marine Reserve, home to a seal colony and visiting dolphins. Tonga Island itself is the small island off Onetahuti Beach.

The track follows the spit to its northern end and traverses the tidal lagoon that can be crossed two hours either side of low tide. The all-tide track takes an extra 10 minutes.

Beyond the lagoon the track enters the bush and immediately begins to climb steeply to a low saddle. You then wind over several inland ridges before dropping sharply to Tonga Quarry, 3.5km from Bark Bay. A metal plaque describes the quarry operations that took place here, and several large, squarish stones are nearby. What remains of the wharf can be seen in the sand. Located just off the beach is the Tonga Quarry Campsite.

The most interesting feature of the bay can only be reached 1½ hours either side of low tide. Follow the rocky shore south from the southern end of the beach, and after a 10-minute scramble you come to the sea arches of **Arch Point**, a set of impressive stone sculptures formed by the repeated pounding of the waves.

The Coast Track continues by climbing the headland that separates Tonga Quarry and **Onetahuti Beach**. After a 1km walk you come to a clearing overlooking the graceful curve of the long beach. This is another classic Abel Tasman National Park beach, and Onetahuti Campsite is at the southern end. Near the campsite a sign points the way to the delightfully cold and clear freshwater pools that lie beneath a small waterfall – ideal after a hot day.

The beach is more than 1km long. Follow it to the northern end where a boardwalk and two bridges will stop you from getting your feet wet. The Coast Track leaves the beach by gently climbing above the swamp, providing a nice overview of the area. Within an hour the track climbs to **Tonga Saddle** (260m) and you get a quick glimpse ahead of the beaches in the distance. If you're heading for Awaroa Hut (26 bunks), take the north-west path (left fork). The track descends to a bridge over Venture Creek. Large orange discs lead along the shore for 15 minutes to Awaroa Hut, on a small beach in Awaroa Inlet. Nearby is Awaroa Campsite.

The right fork leads to Awaroa Lodge, where you will find a cafe offering civilised refreshment. From the lodge the path to Awaroa Hut passes an airstrip before reaching Venture Creek, which can only be crossed two hours either side of low tide. Once across the creek follow the orange discs to Awaroa Hut.

Day 4: Awaroa Bay to Totaranui

1½–2 HOURS, 5.5KM

Awaroa Inlet can only be crossed 1½ hours before and two hours after low tide. Check the tide chart in the hut or at the lodge, then plan your day. Cross the bay directly in front of the hut and follow the large orange discs that lead to Pound Creek. The track follows the creek until it passes a signposted junction to Awaroa Rd, then quickly arrives at **Waiharakeke Bay**, another beautiful beach. The Waiharakeke Campsite is a great spot,

only 30 to 40 minutes north of Awaroa. The campsites are 50m south from the point where Waiharakeke Stream emerges onto the beach.

The track climbs away from the beach, across a rocky ridge and then descends into **Goat Bay**. From Goat Bay it's a 30-minute walk over the hill to Totaranui, with a short side track to **Skinner Point Lookout**, which provides an excellent view of the settlement at Totaranui.

To spend the night at Totaranui you need a tent – there are no huts or cabins – and there is a one-night limit for trampers. The next and final hut is at Whariwharangi, three hours away.

Totaranui Campsite (☎03-528 8083; www.doc.govt.nz; summer/winter $15/10) is an extremely popular facility with a whopping capacity (850 campers) and a splendid setting next to the beach backed by some of the best bush in the park. A staffed DOC office has interpretive displays, flush toilets, cold showers and a public phone.

Day 5: Totaranui to Wainui Car Park

4–5 HOURS, 13KM

Follow the tree-lined avenue in front of the camp office and turn north at the intersection, passing the Education Centre. At the end of the road the Anapai Bay Track begins, crossing Kaikau Stream and reaching a junction with the Headlands Track. Take the left fork, climbing to a low saddle and then descending along a forested stream to **Anapai Bay**, which is split in two by unusual rock outcrops. The Anapai Bay Campsite is one hour from Totaranui; it makes for a great place to spend a night, as the sites overlook the scenic beach.

The Coast Track continues up the sandy beach, then heads inland. After 2km it reaches **Mutton Cove** and the Mutton Cove Campsite.

From the campsite, the track – an old farm road – heads inland over a low saddle. Or you can take a one-hour detour along an alternative route that takes in **Separation Point**, the granite headland separating Tasman Bay from Golden Bay. Pick up this track by continuing along the beach at Mutton Cove to the northern end of the second bay. This track climbs to the side trail from the Coast Track and eliminates any backtracking. The views are worth the walk – Farewell Spit is visible to the northwest, and on an exceptionally clear day so is the North Island. The point is also a favourite haunt of migrating fur seals, which are often spotted sunning themselves on the rocks or swimming offshore. Follow the side trail west, and within 30 minutes you return to the true Coast Track at the low saddle between Mutton Cove and Whariwharangi Bay.

From this saddle the track descends through regenerating scrubland. About 2km from Mutton Cove it reaches Whariwharangi Bay, another beautiful, curved beach. Whariwharangi Hut (20 bunks) is at the western end of the bay, 500m inland. This hut is unique; it's a restored two-storey farmhouse built in 1897 that was last permanently occupied in 1926. Nearby is Whariwharangi Campsite.

Those who wish to loop back to Totaranui can follow the Gibbs Hill Track (three hours) beyond Whariwharangi. Otherwise, continue to Wainui by following the Coast Track, which climbs another low saddle capturing views of Wainui Inlet, before descending to the estuary and skirting the shore to reach the Wainui car park, 5.5km (about 1½ hours) from Whariwharangi Bay.

KAHURANGI NATIONAL PARK

Situated due west of Abel Tasman National Park, Kahurangi – 'blue skies' in one of several translations – is the second largest of NZ's national parks. Within its 4520 sq km lie the Tasman Mountains, a chain of steep and rugged ranges, along with a pair of significant ranges (Arthur and Matiri) alongside. The park's highest point is Mt Owen (1875m). Its lowest remains unmeasured, deep underground amid the karst crevices that make up the largest known cave systems in the southern hemisphere.

Five major river systems drain the park: Aorere and Takaka into Golden Bay, Motueka into Tasman Bay, and Karamea and Heaphy into the Tasman Sea.

The best-known walk in Kahurangi is the Heaphy Track, which stretches from the Aorere Valley, near Collingwood, to the West Coast, north of Karamea; the more challenging Wangapeka and remote Leslie-Karamea Tracks are less frequented. These walks form just part of a 650km network of tracks.

History

The legendary moa thrived in the northwest region of the South Island, and were an important food source for the early Maori who settled here from the 14th century. As was so often the case, routes through the area were often laid down in the quest for *pounamu* (greenstone), sourced from the West Coast.

In 1846, Charles Heaphy (a draftsman for the New Zealand Company) and Thomas Brunner became the first Europeans to walk up the West Coast to the Heaphy River. In 1860, James Mackay and John Clark completed the inland portion of the Heaphy Track while searching for pastoral land between Buller and Collingwood. A year later gold was discovered at Karamea, inspiring prospectors to struggle over the track in search of riches. The Wangapeka Valley was also opened up when gold was discovered in the Rolling, Wangapeka and Sherry Rivers in the late 1850s. Dr Ferdinand von Hochstetter is believed to have been the first person to travel the entire Wangapeka Track when, in 1860, he carried out a geological exploration of the valley.

Miners also had a hand in developing the Karamea Track, progressing from gold diggings at Mt Arthur Tableland to the river. By 1878 a benched track had been formed, and diggers were active in the Leslie, Crow and Roaring Lion Valleys.

The Heaphy was improved when JB Saxon surveyed and graded the track in 1888 for the Collingwood County Council. Gold deposits were never found, though, and use of the Heaphy and Wangapeka Tracks declined considerably in the early 1900s.

After the Northwest Nelson Forest Park (which was to become Kahurangi National Park) was established in 1970, the two tracks were improved dramatically, and the New Zealand Forest Service began to bench the routes and construct huts. The Heaphy Track did not become really popular, though, until plans for a road from Collingwood to Karamea were announced in the early 1970s. Conservationists, deeply concerned about the damage the road would do to the environment – especially to nikau palms – began an intensive campaign to stop the work going ahead, and to increase the popularity of the track.

Environment

Kahurangi is the most diverse of NZ's national parks, in landforms and in flora and fauna. Its most eye-catching features are arguably its rock formations, ranging from windswept beaches and sea cliffs to earthquake-shattered slopes and moraine-dammed lakes, and the smooth, strange karst forms of the interior tableland.

There's plenty of room in between for bush to flourish. Around 85% of the park is forested, with beech prevalent, along with rimu and other podocarps particularly on the lower slopes in the western fringes. These fringes have an understorey of broad-leaved trees and ferns, climbers and perching plants. In all, more than 50% of all NZ's plant species can be found in the park, including more than 80% of its alpine plant species.

This ecological wonderment is not just confined to plants, with 60 native bird species flitting about in the confines, including the great spotted kiwi (ambling, rather than flitting), kea, kaka and whio (blue duck). There are rather unattractive cave weta sharing a home with various weird beetles and a huge, leggy spider, and a majestic and ancient snail known as Powelliphanta – something of a (slow) flag bearer for the park's animal kingdom.

If you like a field trip filled with plenty that's new and strange, Kahurangi National Park will make you very happy.

❶ Planning

WHEN TO TRAMP

It's possible to tramp in Kahurangi all year round. Easter is traditionally the most popular time to walk the Heaphy Track, while late February through March is a particularly good time to tackle tracks throughout the park.

INFORMATION SOURCES

The DOC Nelson Regional Visitor Centre (p198), located within the i-SITE, is the region's primary DOC centre. Information and bookings are also available at DOC Motueka Area Office (p169).

Closer to the Golden Bay end of the track, hut tickets, bookings and other track information can be obtained from DOC Golden Bay Area Office (p169) and the friendly little Golden Bay i-SITE (p200), which also has copies of their indispensable yellow tourist map.

At the West Coast end your port of call should be **Karamea Information & Resource Centre** (☑ 03-782 6652; www.karameainfo.co.nz; Market Cross; ☺ 9am-5pm daily Jan-May, 9am-1pm Sat & Sun only Jun-Dec), an excellent, community-owned centre with all necessary

track services (including hut tickets and bookings) and general local low down.

GUIDED TRAMPS

Bush & Beyond (☑ 03-528 9054; www.bushand beyond.co.nz) offers a guided six-day Heaphy Track package ($1749).

Kahurangi Guided Walks (☑ 03-525 7177; www.kahurangiwalks.co.nz) runs small-group, five-day Heaphy tramps ($1500), and popular one-day options ($150).

Heaphy Track

Duration 5 days

Distance 78km (48 miles)

Track Standard Great Walk

Difficulty Moderate

Start Brown Hut

End Kohaihai

Nearest Town Karamea (p200)

Transport Shuttle bus, plane

Summary The Heaphy Track is a historic and beautiful crossing from Golden Bay to the wild West Coast, offering one of the widest ranges of scenery seen on any of NZ's tramps.

It's one of the most popular tracks in the country. A Great Walk in every sense, it traverses diverse terrain – dense native forest, the mystical Gouland Downs, secluded river valleys, and beaches dusted in salt spray and fringed by nikau palms.

Although quite long, the Heaphy is well cut and benched, making it easier than any other extended tramp found in Kahurangi National Park. That said, it may still be found arduous, particularly in unfavourable weather.

By walking from east to west – as the tramp is described here – most of the climbing is done on the first day, and the scenic beach walk is saved for the end, a fitting and energising grand finale.

A strong tramper could walk the Heaphy in three days, but most people choose to take four or five.

Recently, as part of a trial, the track has been opened to mountain bikers from May to September. Factoring in distance, remoteness and the possibility of bad weather, this epic journey is only suited to well-equipped cyclists with advanced riding skills. It takes most cyclists three days to complete it, although you can get a taster by zipping in

ABEL TASMAN, KAHURANGI & NELSON LAKES HEAPHY TRACK

Heaphy Track (North)

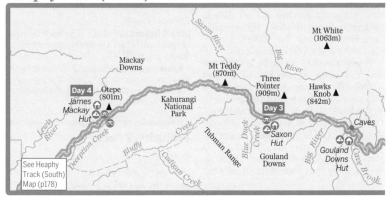

from the West Coast for a day ride or spending a night at Heaphy Hut (32 bunks) and then heading back out the next day. You can hire bikes in Takaka and Westport.

ℹ Planning

WHAT TO BRING
Note that not all huts have gas rings, so check when you make your booking. Pack plenty of insect repellent as without it you'll be toast at the coast.

MAPS & BROCHURES
This tramp is covered by NZTopo50 maps BP23 (Gouland Downs) and BP22 (Heaphy Beach). It is also covered by NewTopo map *Heaphy Track* 1:55 000. DOC's *Heaphy Track* brochure may also prove helpful.

HUTS & CAMPING
Seven designated **Great Walk huts** ($32) lie along the Heaphy Track – Brown, Perry Saddle, Gouland Downs, Saxon, James Mackay, Lewis and Heaphy. These have bunks and a kitchen area, heating, flush toilets and washbasins with cold water. Most but not all have gas rings; a couple have lighting. There are also nine **Great Walk campsites** (www.doc.govt.nz; $14) along the route. The two day shelters are just that; overnight stays are not permitted.

As the Heaphy is a Great Walk, all huts and campsites must be booked in advance year-round. Bookings can be made online through **Great Walks Bookings** (☑ 0800 694 732; www.greatwalks.co.nz) or at any DOC visitor centre. DOC hut tickets and annual passes cannot be used on the track, and there is a two-night limit on staying in huts or campsites.

At the West Coast end of the track is the beachside **Kohaihai Campsite** (www.doc.govt.nz; $6), 15km north of Karamea.

ℹ Getting to/from the Tramp

The two road ends of the Heaphy Track are an almost unfathomable distance apart: 463km to be precise. By far the best way to close the loop is to fly back from Karamea by aeroplane or helicopter – the time saving and scenery go some considerable way to justifying the cost. Aeroplane flights are run by **Adventure Flights Golden Bay** (☑ 03-525 6167, 0800 150 338; www.adventureflightsgoldenbay.co.nz; Takaka Airfield; $185 per person for 3-5 people, $200 per person up to 2 people). The same company offers flights from Takaka to Brown Hut for $50 per person (minimum two people), saving an hour-long shuttle ride. **Golden Bay Air** (☑ 0800 588 885; www.goldenbayair.co.nz; $189 per person for 2-3 people, $169 per person for 4-5 people) plies the same route and offers the additional services of shuttles from Takaka Airfield to Brown Hut ($65 per person for two people, $45 per person for more than three people) and car relocations back to the airfield from Brown Hut ($60). **Helicopter Charter Karamea** (☑ 03-782 6111; www.karameahelicharter.co.nz) can carry up to three people for $750.

The Brown Hut trailhead, a 50-minute drive from Takaka, is serviced each morning by **Golden Bay Coachlines** (☑ 03-525 8352; www.gbcoachlines.co.nz), which stops at Collingwood on the way ($33, one hour).

Scheduled return-trip transport is offered from around 20 November to the end of April by **Heaphy Bus** (☑ 027 222 1872, 0800 128 735; www.theheaphybus.co.nz; from Nelson $130), servicing Brown Hut on Monday and Wednesday, and Kohaihai on Sunday. Out-of-season services are

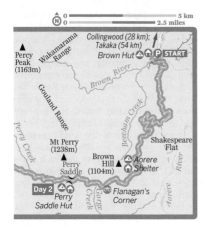

offered on demand through the same company in the guise of **Trek Express** (☎ 027 222 1872, 0800 128 735; www.trekexpress.co.nz; Brown Hut $65, Kohaihai $115, min 4 people). Secure parking (in Mapua) and luggage relocations are also available.

Heaphy Track Help (☎ 03-525 9576; www. heaphytrackhelp.co.nz) offers car relocations ($200 to $300, depending on the direction and time).

The Kohaihai trailhead is 15km from the small town of Karamea. **Karamea Express** (☎ 03-782 6757; info@karamea-express.co.nz) departs from the shelter at 1pm and 2pm for Karamea from October to the end of April ($15). The same service is also offered on demand all year round for $20 per person for two people, $15 for three or more. On-demand shuttle services are also offered by **Karamea Connections** (www.karamea connections.co.nz).

 The Tramp

Day 1: Brown Hut to Perry Saddle Hut

5 HOURS, 17.5KM, 775M ASCENT

The car park at the Heaphy Track's eastern end is now at Brown Hut (16 bunks). The hut was built to enable trampers to get an early start on the first leg of the journey – the climb to Perry Saddle – and has flush toilets and drinking water. Nearby is Brown Hut Campsite.

From the hut the track follows Brown River for 200m before crossing it on a footbridge. On the other side you pass through pasture and then begin the long climb towards Gouland Downs. Beech forest with scattered podocarps and rata surrounds the wide track as it slowly climbs along monotonous switchbacks.

Within 1½ hours the track passes a junction with the **Shakespeare Flat Track**, a route that descends south (left fork) to the **Aorere River**.

The main track swings uphill and about three hours from Brown Hut, after an 11km climb, reaches Aorere Shelter, an ideal spot for lunch or morning tea, complete with a water supply. Nearby is Aorere Shelter Campsite.

Beyond the shelter the track remains wide and continues to climb, but at a more gentle pace. Within one hour, or 3km, you reach **Flanagan's Corner**, the highest point of the tramp at 915m. A five-minute spur track (left) leads to a viewing point that includes the surrounding ridges and Mt Perry.

From Flanagan's Corner it's another 40 minutes (2km) along a level track before you break out of the bush into the open tussock and patches of beech found on **Perry Saddle**. Five minutes away, the brand-spanking new Perry Saddle Hut (28 bunks), at an elevation of 880m, commands views of the Douglas Range across the Aorere Valley. Perry Saddle Campsite is also located here, and nearby is the deep **Gorge Creek**, which is popular for bathing despite its somewhat shocking temperature.

Day 2: Perry Saddle Hut to Saxon Hut

3–4 HOURS, 12.5KM

A well-formed track enters the bush and remains in it for the next hour or so, crossing a handful of streams, three of them bridged. The third one is Sheep Creek, and from here the track opens into the bowl of **Gouland Downs**, a wide expanse of rolling tussock broken by patches of stunted silver beech and pygmy pine. You skirt the upper edge of this basin for more than 1km, and at one point you can look down and see Gouland Downs Hut. The track then begins a long descent, bottoming out at a bridge over **Cave Brook**. On the other side you quickly climb to Gouland Downs Hut (eight bunks) and Gouland Downs Campsite.

Although the small hut is old, it has a large fireplace and a cosy atmosphere. The fireplace is probably the only original part of the hut, built in 1932. Most trampers push on, because the hut is only a two-hour (8km) walk from Perry Saddle.

Heaphy Track (South)

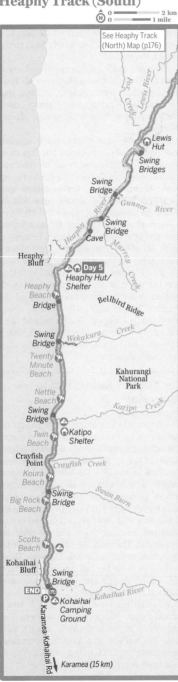

Heading west you immediately enter a scene of eroded **limestone caves** and stone arches, covered by stunted beech and carpeted by a thick moss. It's all rather *Lord of the Rings*. In a few minutes you emerge again onto the red-tussock downs and cross three streams in the next hour: Shiner Brook, **Big River** and Weka Creek. Under normal conditions all can be easily forded, but there are bridges nearby in case of high water.

From Weka Creek the track re-enters the bush and begins climbing. It's a gentle 20-minute climb before the track levels out and, in 10 minutes, reaches Saxon Hut (16 bunks) and Saxon Campsite, 1½ hours (5km) from Gouland Downs Hut. Located on the edge of the downs and with excellent views, Saxon is a very pleasant place to stay overnight, although many trampers push on another three hours and overnight at James Mackay Hut.

Day 3: Saxon Hut to James Mackay Hut

3 HOURS, 12KM

The track begins with 3km of level tramping, crossing **Saxon River** and **Blue Duck Creek** on bridges, and passing the signposted border between DOC's Tasman and Buller Districts.

Welcome to the West Coast! Eventually you enter the bush and begin the final climb to regain the height you lost in the descent to Gouland Downs. One hour from Saxon Hut you get your first glimpse of the Tasman Sea and the mouth of the Heaphy River.

The climb lasts for almost one hour, ascending 100m. When you finally top off you emerge onto the small patches of tussock that make up the **Mackay Downs**. It takes one hour to cross the southern end of the downs. Think of DOC fondly as you pass across the boardwalk, as this section used to be an absolute mudfest.

The track crosses several more streams and then **Deception Creek**, which is bridged and signposted. Within 15 minutes of the river you arrive at James Mackay Hut (26 bunks), which may have been rebuilt by the time you read this. Located on the fringe of the bush, this hut site has expansive views across the Tasman Sea and Gunner Downs. On a clear evening the sunsets are extraordinary, with the sun melting into a shimmering Tasman Sea. Nearby is the James Mackay Campsite.

Day 4: James Mackay Hut to Heaphy Hut

5–6 HOURS, 20.5KM, 710M DESCENT

The track heads southwest, and in 10 minutes passes a spur track that leads to one of the last views down the Heaphy Valley. From here you begin a steady descent towards the coast. Gradually the valley closes in, and within one hour you spy the **Heaphy River** below. In another two hours the 12km descent ends with the trail bottoming out beside your first nikau palms, three of them clustered 100m above the junction of the Lewis and Heaphy Rivers. In all you'll have dropped 600m in little more than two hours. Lewis Hut (20 bunks) is just five minutes away, down a short side trail.

The hut – a three-hour, 13.5km walk from James Mackay Hut (26 bunks) – is perched on a terrace above the Heaphy River. From its veranda there is a nice view of the water. It would be an enjoyable place to sit and relax but the sandflies can be thick at times. Trampers often pass up Lewis Hut for the popular Heaphy Hut, on the Tasman Sea, just 2½ hours away.

Follow the track in front of Lewis Hut 100m upstream to the new, 150m-long **Heaphy River Bridge**. The track now follows the true left (south) bank of the Heaphy, and will remain on this side until it reaches the Tasman Sea. Limestone bluffs keep the track close to the river and occasionally you break out to a view of the water below. Most of the time you're in a rainforest so thick and lush its canopy forms a tunnel around the track.

Within 3km (one hour) of crossing the Heaphy you arrive at another new bridge, over the **Gunner River**, and in another 30 minutes you cross the last swing bridge of the day over **Murray Creek**. In the final hour the track remains close to the river until you skirt a steep bluff, looking at the Heaphy River below and the Tasman Sea just to the west. This is a scenic end to a fine day of tramping. You are now only about 15 minutes from the hut.

The spectacular new **Heaphy Hut** (32 bunks), completed in 2013, is just up from the river in an open, grassy area enclosed by nikau palms and overlooking a lagoon in the Heaphy River where there is good swimming. Swimming in the sea should be avoided as there are vicious undertows. Most trampers are simply content to stroll along the beach to witness its powerful surf and let the sea run through their toes. In this wilderness setting, having a beach like this to yourself is worth every step it takes to reach it.

Also near the hut is the Heaphy River Campsite and a shelter in a grassy clearing. This is the best campsite along the track, and the sandflies seem to agree.

Day 5: Heaphy Hut to Kohaihai Camping Ground

5 HOURS, 16KM

Unquestionably one of the most beautiful sections of track on the South Island, the final segment of the Heaphy Track meanders along the coast, sticking close to the pounding Tasman Sea. The track stays in the bush much of the way, but in many places well-worn paths show where trampers have decided to forgo the track and hike along the beach. Big seas and high tides have eroded short sections of the coastal track, and these are now marked with warning signs indicating that waves could break dangerously over the track. If in doubt, wait it out. Tide times are posted at Heaphy Hut (and also at Kohaihai Shelter).

FAREWELL SPIT

Bleak, exposed and slightly sci-fi, Farewell Spit is a wetland of international importance and a renowned bird sanctuary – the summer home of thousands of migratory waders, notably the bar-tailed godwit (which flies more than 12,000km to get there), Caspian terns and Australasian gannets. The spit is 35km long, and still growing, and features colossal, crescent-shaped dunes, from where panoramic views extend across Golden Bay and a vast low-tide salt marsh. Walkers can explore the first 4km of the spit via a network of tracks, but beyond that point access is via tour only.

The knowledgeable and affable folk at **Farewell Spit Eco Tours** (☑ 03-524 8257, 0800 808 257; www.farewellspit.com; Tasman St, Collingwood; tours $120-155) run trips ranging from two to 6½ hours, taking in the spit, lighthouse, gannets and godwits. Tours depart from Collingwood.

The track departs from Heaphy Hut and, for the first time, heads south. It wends through a grove of nikau palms, occasionally alongside wetlands bordered by a forested bluff.

Within 1km you cross a bridge over Cold Creek and then break out to a view of Heaphy Beach. For the next hour you remain close to the shore, often in view of it. You cross Wekakura Creek on a swing bridge and then arrive at Twenty Minute Beach, where you have the opportunity to bypass the track and walk along the sand.

Orange markers lead you back onto the track and follow Nettle Beach, with the track staying well above the shoreline. At this point you head inland, into a grove of palms. Cross a long swing bridge over Katipo Creek and arrive at Katipo Shelter, the halfway point of the day, 2½ hours from Heaphy Hut. Located here is Katipo Campsite.

To the south the track skirts Twin Beach, fords Crayfish Creek and then arrives at Crayfish Point. Normally you drop to the shore and scramble over the rocks to round it. But if the tide is in, you may have to use the high-tide track that climbs above the shore.

From Crayfish Point, the track dips back into the bush and then climbs the bluff to skirt both Koura Beach and Big Rock Beach, allowing you to look down at the crashing surf. One hour (3km) from Crayfish Point you descend to Scotts Beach Campsite, where you may encounter day walkers who have come in from Kohaihai, just one hour away.

From Scotts Beach the Heaphy Track makes a steady but gentle climb to a saddle. You top off at a spur track to Scotts Hill Lookout, a 10-minute walk to a spectacular view of the coastline, and then descend. The track ends with a big swing bridge over the Kohaihai River that deposits you at Kohaihai, where there is a shelter and campsite.

Wangapeka Track

Duration 5 days

Distance 59km (37 miles)

Track Standard Tramping track and route

Difficulty Moderate

Start Rolling River car park

End Wangapeka Rd car park

Nearest Towns Nelson (p197), Motueka (p198), Karamea (p200)

Transport Shuttle bus

Summary In the shadow of the well-known Heaphy Track, the Wangapeka is a challenging tramp over two 1000m saddles and through the beech-forested valleys of the Wangapeka, Karamea, Taipo and Little Wanganui Rivers.

The Wangapeka Track is a journey across the southern end of Kahurangi National Park. There are no beaches or pounding surf on this tramp, but to many trampers its rugged scenery and isolation make it a more interesting walk than the Heaphy Track.

It was the quest for gold that led to the construction of this track from the 1860s, with fossicking in the area lasting for around 70 years. Farming followed, with sheep grazing the Wangapeka Valley right up to the alpine tops with bags of grass seed tied around their necks. Despite this ingenuity, grazing was eventually abandoned around the time that introduced deer moved in.

This area contains a wide variety of rocks, some of which are the oldest in the country. In 1929 the Murchison earthquake caused considerable collapse of the hillsides in the area. Evidence of the quake's severity is visible in the Little Wanganui Valley, and at the Luna and Taipo slips.

The track can be walked in four days – although most trampers spread it over five – and in either direction. It is described here from east to west, the easiest way to climb the saddles. The track is classified as a tramping track; it's well marked and has bridges over all major streams, but there are still multiple unbridged crossings and the track is not always benched.

Experienced and eager trampers can combine the Wangapeka with the Leslie-Karamea Track, which intersects it. It will add another three to four days of challenging tramping through remote backcountry, connecting the Wangapeka with the Flora car park, to the northeast.

The Wangapeka can also be combined with the Heaphy Track which (although they don't intersect) provides a fulsome Nelson–West Coast return trip.

Wangapeka Track

0 — 5 miles
0 — 10 km

N

Mt Star (1588m)
Skeet Saddle
Mt Sodom (1565m)
Mt Gomorrah (1592m)
Mt Baldy (1542m)
Tapawera; Motueka
Rolling River
Car Park START
i
Swing Bridge
Chummies Track
Gibbs Creek
Track
Gibbs
Rolling River
Swing Bridge
John Reid Hut
Patriarch Creek
Wangapeka Track
Wrights Creek
Little Crow River
Crow River
Crow River
Crow Hut
Taitel Stream
Mt Patriarch (1701m)
Kiwi Saddle Hut
Swing Bridge
Kahurangi National Park
Luna Ridge
Kiwi Stream
Kings Creek Hut
Swing Bridge
Kings
Cecil
Kings Hut
Day 2
Karamea River
Venus Creek
Venus Hut
Satellite Creek
Star Creek
Mt Luna (1630m)
Swing Bridges
Luna Lake
North Branch
Leslie-Karamea Track
Thor Hut
Mt Kendall (1762m)
Trevor Carter Hut
Stone Hut
Nugget Knob (1502m)
Alternative Route
Mercury Creek
Mt Herbert (1507m)
Saxon Falls
Tabernacle Lookout
Biggs Tops (1384m)
Wangapeka Saddle (1009m)
Karamea River
Kakapo Saddle
Lost Valley Track
Swing Bridge
Taipo River
Mt Dean (1462m)
Helicopter Flat Hut
Pike Peak
Day 3
Kakapo River
Kakapo Hut
Black Lakes
Little Wanganui Saddle
Bridge
Swing Bridge
Taipo Hut
Right Branch
Mt Allen (1510m)
Johnson Hut
Lawrence Saddle
Mt Scarlett (1226m)
Mt Lester (1351m)
Mt Brilliant
Wangapeka Bivvy
Mt Zetland (1413m)
Stag Flat Emergency Shelter
Day 4
Left Branch
Johnson River
Lake Phyllis
Lake Marina
Black Rat (1000m)
Scarlett Range
Belltown Manunui Hut
Day 5
Mt Radiant (1305m)
Anaconaa (1196m)
Mt Fugel (1374m)
Mt Johnson (1323m)
Mt Gorgeous
Marris Peak (1313m)
Mt Webb (1350m)
Mt Young
Redant Range
Gilmore Clearing
Little Wanganui River
Shag Tarn
Swampy Tarn
Wanganui Rd
Wanganui (5km); Karamea (23km)
END
Mt O'Connor (1257m)

❶ Planning

WHAT TO BRING

Wasps can be a real problem from January through March, especially in the grassy flats at the eastern end, near the Rolling River car park. Pack antihistamine if you are allergic to their stings.

The huts do not have gas cookers, so carry a stove.

MAPS & BROCHURES

This tramp is covered by NZTopo50 maps BQ22 (Karamea), BQ23 (Wangapeka Saddle) *and* BQ24 (Tapawera), as well as NewTopo *Wangapeka Track* 1:55,000.

HUTS & CAMPING

There are seven huts along the track. Five are **Standard huts** (www.doc.govt.nz; $5): Belltown Manunui, Taipo, Helicopter Flat, Stone Hut and Kings Creek. Cecil King's is a **Basic hut** (www. doc.govt.nz), and there are two emergency shelters either side of Little Wanganui Saddle. There are few flat places suitable for camping (which is free); your best bet is near the huts where there are often clearings and toilet facilities, although note that you will have to pay half the hut fee and make use of the hut facilities during the day only. Backcountry hut tickets or passes can be bought online or from any DOC visitor centre.

❶ Getting to/from the Tramp

Rolling River car park is 31km from the tiny settlement of Tapawera; to get there follow the signposts west to the Wangapeka Valley. About 1km before the trailhead you will find Prices Clearing, where there's an information kiosk and telephone.

The end of the track is a car park on Wangapeka Rd, signposted 18km south of Karamea on SH67. It's 5km from the turn-off to the car park; there's a telephone 500m down Wangapeka Rd from the end of the track.

Trek Express (p177) runs on demand (minimum four people) from Nelson to Rolling River ($50); and Wangapeka Rd to Nelson ($115), but if you're flexible the company can often hook you on to another booked trip.

Karamea Express (p177) offers on-demand pick-ups from Wangapeka Rd to Karamea for $20 per person for two people, $15 for three or more. On-demand shuttle services are also offered by Karamea Connections (p177).

And in the true spirit of Kiwi hospitality, the friendly people at **Little Wanganui Tavern** (☑ 03-782 6752) will pick you up and deposit you at Little Wanganui on SH67.

The Tramp

Day 1: Rolling River to Kings Creek Hut

3½ HOURS, 11.4KM

From the car park, the track crosses a swing bridge over Rolling River just upstream from its confluence with Wangapeka River. The track then begins on the southern bank of Wangapeka River. The water is almost always in sight as the well-defined track winds through river flats of grass and scrub.

Within 3km the track crosses a bridge over Wright Creek and then continues crossing grassy flats. After three hours you cross a swing bridge to the northern bank of the Wangapeka River, passing a signposted junction. The right fork is a side track north to Kiwi Saddle Hut (six bunks), 3½ hours away.

Take the left fork along the main track, which heads southwest and skirts the edge of the river gorge. Within 30 minutes of the junction you reach Kings Creek Hut (20 bunks).

If you arrive with plenty of daylight left and gas in the tank, you might like to embark on a foray to (or even stay at) the historic Cecil King's hut (four bunks), 10 minutes up the track. Mr King built the wooden slab hut in 1935 as part of a Depression-era scheme encouraging unemployed men to prospect for gold. Despite living in Lower Hutt, near Wellington, he spent every summer here, fossicking in the area until 1981. After his passing at age 78 in 1982, his family spread his ashes around the hut, and after an initial restoration in 1991 DOC has continued to preserve it as a precious relic of a bygone era.

Day 2: Kings Creek Hut to Helicopter Flat Hut

6–7 HOURS, 18.7KM, 549M ASCENT, 268M DESCENT

From Cecil King's Hut, just before the junction of the north and south branches of the Wangapeka River, the track continues along the true left (east) side of the north branch and gently climbs towards Stone Hut; it is well benched and makes for easy walking. Much of the time you can peer into the deep gorge cut by the north branch, which dwindles as you climb.

It's a 2½-hour (6.5km) walk to Stone Hut. Thirty minutes before reaching it the track crosses a bridge over Luna Stream, and then immediately crosses a larger one to the true right side of the north branch, where a grassy flat overlooks the confluence with Stone Creek. Here is the pleasant Stone Hut (10 bunks) near which is a signposted route to Mt Luna (1630m).

The track leaves Stone Hut in bush, but soon comes to an open slip, the result of the 1929 Murchison earthquake. Boulder-hop across the slip to emerge at a long gravel bar, featuring a ghost forest of dead, standing trees. In the middle is the Wangapeka River north branch, just a small stream at this point.

The track follows the river to its source, then ascends sharply to Wangapeka Saddle (1009m) along a well-marked route. At the bush-clad top is a signposted junction, with one track heading northwest along a steep, rough route to Biggs Tops (1384m) and Trevor Carter Hut (12 bunks). This is a possible alternative route – the additional climb (around one hour) rewards with spectacular views followed by a steep descent to Trevor Carter Hut and onward to Helicopter Hut via the Lost Valley Track.

The main track from Wangapeka Saddle descends gently and then swings up a narrow valley to arrive at Chime Creek within 30 minutes. There is a series of scenic waterfalls here, as well as a walk-wire 100m upstream, although at most times you can easily ford the creek. Within 2km of the saddle you descend along the creek to the infant Karamea River, fording it in a gravel area with more standing dead trees.

The track crosses several side streams as it follows the true left (south) bank of the Karamea. The river itself is also crossed twice in the final 2km to Helicopter Flat Hut. The fords are easy if the weather is good; if not, there is an alternative, all-weather route (marked with poles) that continues along the true left bank. The flood route takes an extra 20 minutes to walk. The routes rejoin on the southern bank and continue to Helicopter Flat Hut (10 bunks), just past Waters Creek. If the creek is flooded, there is a walk-wire 30m upstream.

The hut has a veranda on which to sit and admire the scenery at the end of a long day of tramping. There is little camping in the area. The only flat space is the helicopter pad, on which you must not pitch your tent.

This hut is located at the junction with the Leslie-Karamea Track, a challenging and remote tramp through the middle of Kahurangi National Park.

Day 3: Helicopter Flat Hut to Taipo Hut

3–4 HOURS, 8.6KM

From Helicopter Flat Hut the track begins by skirting the gorge above the Karamea River, then sidles up through bush away from the river. The track gradually climbs to the Tabernacle Lookout, reached within one hour, far above the deep and rugged gorge. The Tabernacle was the site of an old A-frame shelter, now long gone, that was built in 1898 by Jonathan Brough when he was surveying the original track. The views from here are excellent – you can see most of the Karamea Valley below.

The track leaves the lookout and after 100m passes a side track that descends sharply east (right fork) to Saxon Falls and Trevor Carter Hut. The main track (left fork) heads north then west, and descends steeply for 30 minutes to a suspension bridge over the Taipo River. On the true left (north) side of the river there is a junction with a track heading east (right fork) down the Taipo River to its confluence with the Karamea River. It's possible during fair weather to include the loop from the Tabernacle past Saxon Falls to Trevor Carter Hut, cross the Karamea River and then return to the main track, although this adds more than two hours to the day.

The main track is well marked as it heads west and follows the northern bank of the Taipo. You climb gently for several kilometres and, two hours from the bridge, you reach Taipo Hut (16 bunks). This is a pleasant hut with good campsites below the nearby helicopter pad.

Day 4: Taipo Hut to Belltown Manunui Hut

6–7 HOURS, 10.2KM, 407M ASCENT, 847M DESCENT

Soon after leaving the hut you cross a bridge over Pannikin Creek and then begin a steady climb towards Stag Flat, a tussock subalpine plateau. The climb steepens just before you reach the flats and Stag Flat Emergency Shelter.

After leaving the shelter you sidle around Stag Flat and begin another steep climb towards Little Wanganui Saddle (1087m), an open clearing of snow grass. The climb is a knee-bender, but the views from the top are the best of the trip. The saddle is the highest point of the track and overlooks the Little

Wanganui River to the West Coast and the Taipo River to the east.

The track descends past Saddle Lakes and drops steeply to the valley floor, re-entering bush and finally crossing a bridge over the Little Wanganui River to its true right (north) side. Just before crossing the bridge you pass a signposted side track that leads 150m to Wangapeka Bivvy (four bunks).

Note that despite the western end of the Wangapeka Track having been altered a number of times, the section along the Little Wanganui River can still be hazardous due to erosion and particularly during periods of high water.

After crossing a swing bridge, the track continues to Tangent Creek then climbs above the river and sidles along the gorge, returning to the river at Smith Creek.

A little further downstream the track leads directly to Belltown Manunui Hut (10 bunks). A clearing just downstream from the hut is a good area for camping.

Day 5: Belltown Manunui Hut to Wangapeka Road Car Park

3 HOURS, 10KM

From Belltown Manunui Hut the track immediately crosses Drain Creek and remains on the true right (north) side of the river. Within 2km you use a swing bridge to cross Lawrence Stream, and in another 1km cut through a large grassy area known as **Gilmor Clearing**.

Just beyond the clearing, the track follows an old access road to climb north away from the Little Wanganui for the next 3km, before dropping back to the river. It is a further 4km to the finish of the track, the last section of which crosses private land before reaching Wangapeka Rd car park, where you will find a public telephone.

Tableland Circuit

Duration 3 days

Distance 28km (17.4 miles)

Track Standard Route, tramping track, easy walk

Difficulty Moderate

Start/End Flora car park

Nearest Towns Nelson (p197), Motueka (p198)

Transport Shuttle bus

Summary This loop around the fascinating tableland packs in plenty of eye candy, from freaky alpine plants to twittering forest, odd rock forms and a grand peak, as well as wide open views to lands way, way below.

The Arthur Range is one of three significant mountain ranges in Kahurangi National Park. Its highest peak is Mt Arthur (1795m), the summit of which can be reached by fit trampers without any special equipment in good weather. To the west of the mountain is the great uplifted plateau known as the Mt Arthur Tableland, a fascinating area with strange and ancient rock formations, diverse plant life and relics from the pioneer era.

The tableland is also crossed by the long and remote Leslie-Karamea Track, which heads southwest before connecting with the Wangapeka Track. It also lies adjacent to Cobb Valley – yet more stimulating tramping territory, which is also accessible from Golden Bay.

The gently rolling tableland is a remnant of a once extensive sea-level plain that stretched across NZ over 45 million years ago. As the land sank below sea level, thick quartz gravel and then limestone were deposited on the ancient plain. In the last 14 million years, the plain has been uplifted, mostly buckled and folded into mountains, its limestones and quartz gravels eroded away. But here and there remnants have survived, and can be seen here.

There's something otherworldly – almost magical – about this place, and this three-day adventure is sure to leave you with indelible memories.

Planning

MAPS & BROCHURES

This tramp is covered by NZTopo50 maps BP24 (Takaka) and BQ24 (Tapawera), as well as New-Topo *Mt Arthur, Cobb Valley* 1:55,000. DOC's excellent brochure *Cobb Valley, Mt Arthur, Tableland* details myriad walks in this area.

HUTS & CAMPING

There are four huts along this route, two of which (Mt Arthur and Salisbury Lodge) are recommended overnight stops. Both are **Serviced huts** (www.doc.govt.nz; $15), although only Salisbury has gas cookers, so be sure to carry a stove. There are numerous other huts on and around the tablelands, ranging from Serviced to Basic, along with rock shelters, which are free. Camping is also permitted and is free unless you wish to camp within 50m of a hut – in that case you will have to pay half the hut fee and

Tableland Circuit

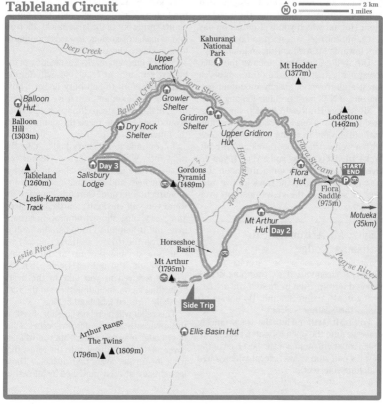

0 — 2 km
0 — 1 miles

make use of the hut facilities during the day only. Backcounty hut tickets or passes can be bought online or from any DOC visitor centre.

GUIDED TRAMPS

Kahurangi Guided Walks (p175) runs small-group, three-day tramps around the tablelands ($450) and Cobb Valley.

Bush & Beyond (p175) offers tailored trips of varying lengths around the tablelands and Cobb Valley, including an all-inclusive two-day Tableland Circuit ($625).

ⓘ Getting to/from the Tramp

Flora car park is 75km from Nelson and 36km from Motueka, reached via the steep and winding Graham Valley Rd, accessed off SH61 running up Motueka Valley. Follow signs from Ngatimoti, where a bridge crosses to West Bank Rd.

Trek Express (p177) provides on-demand transport to Flora car park from Nelson/Motueka (per person $45/40, minimum four people).

The Tramp

Day 1: Flora Car Park to Mt Arthur Hut

1½ HOURS, 3.6KM, 370M ASCENT

This is a short day's tramp, so those with energy, strength and good weather may consider combining it with the challenging but entirely possible climb to the summit of **Mt Arthur**, a three- to four-hour return trip from Mt Arthur Hut. With an early rise, it's also possible to bag the peak on day two, which avoids some backtracking, thus shaving off one to two hours.

Arriving at Flora car park deposits you at an elevation of 940m, where views of Mt Arthur can be had from a shelter complete with interpretive displays.

From the car park a wide gravel path, originally a miners' track, departs into the bush. Within 10 minutes you arrive at **Flora**

Saddle (975m), where there is a signposted junction. Straight ahead lies the track to Flora Hut, on which you will return on day three, but for now you need to take the left fork towards Mt Arthur Hut, an hour away.

The well-graded track follows the ridge towards Mt Arthur, winding through beech forest and groves of shaggy mountain neinei, one of NZ's most peculiar-looking trees.

Mt Arthur Hut (eight bunks) sits on the bushline. It's a classic backcountry hut, with little room to swing a cat but atoning with a well-worn outdoor area and fire pit. Weka are likely to pay you a visit. If you arrive looking to lap up some afternoon sun, it's worth heading up the track for five minutes or so where the views open up even further.

Day 2: Mt Arthur Hut to Salisbury Lodge

4–5 HOURS, 10.4KM, 590 ASCENT, 770 DESCENT

This is a strenuous day's tramping across exposed terrain, even more so if you are factoring in Mt Arthur Summit. Do not set off unless the weather is clear.

From Mt Arthur Hut, the track quickly emerges onto the open tops above the bushline. From here on in, for the best part of the day, it's non-stop views (except when you're watching your feet).

Follow the poled route as it wends first through rock gardens, where tufts of alpine plants spring out of the large cracks, then up and along a grassy ridge towards mountains looming large ahead.

A track junction marks the meeting of the Mt Arthur Summit Track (straight ahead), and a right fork to Salisbury Lodge. Those heading to the summit can leave their packs here, making the steep climb a bit easier. It's around one hour to reach the summit from the junction.

To continue to Salisbury Lodge, take the right fork, which leads across Horseshoe Basin. There is considerable undulation between here and the final assault in the monumental form of Gordons Pyramid. En route you will encounter particularly steep and rocky bits; those tramping in groups may find it helpful to cooperate in hauling packs over the trickier sections.

It is a strenuous climb to the summit of Gordons Pyramid (1489m), but all will be forgiven as you take in the head-swivelling views, including those of the vast, partially forested tableland below.

This relief will be relatively short-lived, as the apparently endless descent begins. Salisbury Lodge may seem close, but you will discover as the track drops into the forest that it's a lot further away than it looks. Those legs already severely punished by Mt Arthur

GOING UNDERGROUND

Keep an eye out for *tomo* (cave) openings as you wander around the Mt Arthur Tableland, because beneath your feet lies a vast subterranean world of abyssal shafts, cathedralesque chambers and endlessly winding passages and waterways.

Over the course of millions of years, water has eroded the limestone and marble heart of the Kahurangi National Park, creating some of the deepest and most intricate cave systems in NZ. Under Mt Arthur's western flank are two of the biggest, Stormy Pot and Nettlebed, which have been explored by an elite team of spelunkers who spend weeks at a time below ground. Climbing, abseiling, clambering, squeezing and sometimes even swimming their way through this labyrinthine underworld, the team has discovered and mapped some 40-odd kilometres of passages.

Armed with gumboots, head torches and a mole-like disregard for claustrophobia, the spelunkers enter into systems through yawns in the karst landscape with evocative names like Big Friendly Giant and Blizzard Pot. Following the flow of water and the draught that blows through the caves, the spelunkers are convinced that the two systems are linked. No connection has been found yet, but surveys show that Nettlebed and Stormy Pot are aligned around two vast chambers dubbed Neverland and Goodbye Yellow Brick Road. The search for NZ's deepest cave continues...

Watch where you tread and don't be tempted to go spelunking yourself: this is one pursuit that should definitely be left to the experts! You can, however, get a safe peak into this subterranean wonderland at Ngarua Caves atop Takaka Hill, or Rawhiti Cave in Golden Bay.

and Gordons Pyramid may enter purgatory as they pick their way down through the forest of stunted beech trees festooned with lichen, the track trip-laden with tree roots.

Eventually you will emerge into the golden, tufty tussock lands known as **Salisbury's Open**. Cross the meadow to **Salisbury Lodge** (22 bunks), a relatively luxurious hut (well, there is solar lighting...) with views out over the golden meadows and the Arthur Range. The lodge is named after Thomas Salisbury, who stumbled across the tableland in 1865. Just east of the lodge is a small cave and some potholes that can be explored.

SIDE TRIP: MT ARTHUR SUMMIT
2–3 HOURS, 10KM RETURN, 245M ASCENT/DESCENT

The summit of Mt Arthur is a truly magnificent viewpoint, one that may elicit a spontaneous outburst of the chorus of the Carpenters' song 'Top of the World' as you survey Tasman Bay, the Richmond Ranges, the nearby Twins, the Southern Alps and then some.

This track should only be scaled by experienced trampers with appropriate equipment and in favourable weather. A well-marked route ascends from Mt Arthur Hut, passing the junction to Gordons Pyramid, and continuing up an exposed ridge to the summit (1795m). Take care around the many bluffs, sinkholes and caves.

Day 3: Salisbury Lodge to Flora Car Park
4 HOURS, 14KM, 190M DESCENT

The last leg of this tramp is a relatively easy amble along a former stock route, passing a series of interesting landmarks along the way.

The track begins in front of Salisbury Lodge and heads north across the open tussock lands towards Upper Junction and Flora Valley. Around 20 minutes into the day, a short side track leads to **Dry Rock Shelter**, an unusual rock bivvy.

The track continues its gentle descent, eventually dropping into the bush alongside Balloon Creek, and passing Growler Shelter, nestled into an overhang.

Having headed east (the right fork) at Upper Junction, the Flora Track levels out and crosses Gridiron Creek. It then ambles through **Gridiron Gulch**, within which you will pass Gridiron Shelter, a rock bivvy burrowed under two mammoth rocks.

Amongst its many admirable features is a sleeping loft.

Upper Gridiron Hut is a little further along, a five-minute detour off the track. This shelter is wedged under a huge rock overhang and features a swing-seat.

Easy walking continues through the Flora Valley. Around two hours into the day you will pass beneath a wooden arch, the gateway to the gulch.

The track climbs gently towards Flora Saddle. Around 15 minutes from the saddle is historic Flora Hut (12 bunks). The grassy clearing it occupies was once the site of Edward's Store, from where provisions were supplied to gold diggers who, unfortunately, never dug up much at all. From here the track continues to Flora Saddle and the track junction, signalling that you have completed the loop. Continue along the main gravel path back down to Flora car park, 10 minutes away.

NELSON LAKES NATIONAL PARK

Most visitors come to Nelson Lakes National Park to see Lakes Rotoiti and Rotoroa. Beyond the lakes, trampers will discover a land of long glaciated valleys, basins, tarns and craggy mountain ranges. Situated at the northern end of the Southern Alps, the park is home to numerous passes and routes that are not nearly as demanding as those found in other alpine national parks such as Arthur's Pass or Mt Aspiring.

If you long to climb a mountain and stroll along an open ridge, Nelson Lakes is a good place to begin adventuring above the bushline. It is a mountainous region, with many peaks above 2000m, but lots of the tramping tracks are benched and most routes are marked with cairns or poles.

A number of return trips are possible in the park, most requiring three to six days of tramping and the climbing of ridges and passes. A favourite for trampers with limited alpine experience is the tramp along Robert Ridge to the grand Lake Angelus cirque basin, returning to St Arnaud via one of two different routes. A more remote and challenging tramp is the Travers-Sabine Circuit, which includes walking over Travers Saddle, not an easy climb but one that is well marked and, in good summer weather, within the capabilities of most fit trampers.

Nelson Lakes National Park

Blenheim (95km)
63
START Tramp 2
Kerr Bay
Tramp 3 Day Walk
Parachute Rocks
St Arnaud Range Track
St Arnaud Range
Mt McRae (1878m)
Black Hill (746m)
St Arnaud
Pinchgut Track
Lake Rotoiti
Lakehead Track
END Tramp 1
Lakehead Hut
Peanter Peak (1880m)
63
Murchison (57km)
START Tramp 1 END Tramp 2
Mt Robert Car Park
Relax Shelter
Mt Robert (1421m)
Paddy's Track
Bushline Hut
Lakeside Track
Coldwater Hut
Swing Bridge
Chandler Stream
Flagtop (1690m)
Julius Summit (1794m)
Robert Ridge
Mt Robert Route
Mt Robert Track
Speargrass Track
Bad Weather Route Tramp 1
Bridge
Speargrass Route
Speargrass Hut
Bad Weather Route Tramp 1
Irakere Stream
Lake Angelus
Angelus Hut
Day 2
Mt Angelus (2075m)
Angelus Ridge
Mt Angelus Cascade Track
Maggie Creek
Maud Creek
Hodgson Stream
Tier Stream
Cedric Stream
Hinapouri Tarn
Sunset Saddle
Open Stream
Speargrass Track
Suspension Bridge
Howard Saddle
Mt Cedric (1532m)
Sabine Hut
Steadnip Creek
Howard River
Howard Valley Rd
Rotoroa Route
Muntz Range
Lake Rotoroa
Sabine D'urville Track
Day 5
D'Urville Hut
Mt Hutton (1400m)
Braeburn Range
Tiraumea Track
Rotoroa
Gowan Valley Rd
Mt Pickering (1241m)
Braeburn Track

1	Lake Angelus Track
2	Travers-Sabine Circuit
3	St Arnaud Range Track

10 km
5 miles
0
0
N

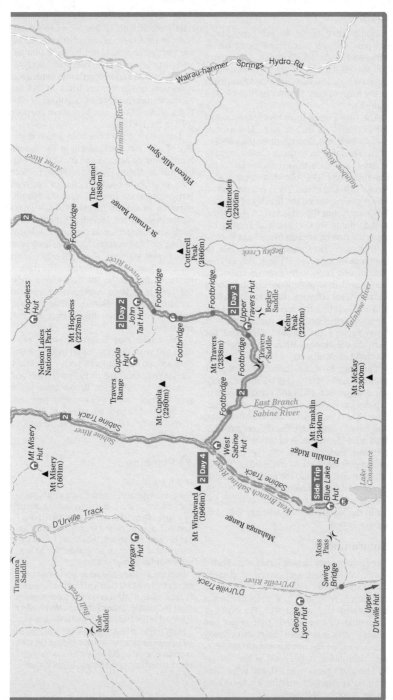

History

Although they rarely settled here, Maori did pass through this region along routes between Nelson, Marlborough, Canterbury and the West Coast in search of *pounamu* (greenstone). The lakes provided *kai* (food) in the form of eels, freshwater mussels and waterfowl.

The first European to visit the area was John Cotterell. In 1842 he and a Maori guide pushed their way through more than 300km of trackless terrain to the Tophouse, near St Arnaud, and then turned southeast to the Clarence River. The following January, Cotterell with his friend Dick Peanter and a Maori guide retraced the first leg of that earlier journey, but this time turned southwest. And in doing so, Cotterell and Peanter became the first Europeans to see Lake Rotoiti.

Three years later, another Maori guide, by the name of Kehu, led William Fox, Charles Heaphy and Thomas Brunner on one of the best-recorded explorations on the South Island. With Heaphy keeping the diary and Fox painting the scenery as they went, the group struggled down to Rotoiti under heavy packs. From the lake, Kehu took the party up the Howard River, where they discovered Lake Rotoroa.

Camping by Lake Rotoiti was popular from the early 1900s, and before long holiday cottages were built and walkers began to explore the surrounding valleys and mountains. The area's significant environmental and scenic worth was officially recognised in 1956 with the gazetting of the Nelson Lakes National Park, centred on the mountain catchments of the two main lakes, Rotoiti and Rotoroa. In 1983, the park significantly increased to its present size, 1017 sq km, with the addition of 430 sq km of beech forest in the Matakitaki and Glenroy Valleys to the southwest.

Environment

The landscape of Nelson Lakes was created by the Alpine Fault and carved by glaciers. The long, curved valleys that characterise the park were formed by a series of glaciers that waxed and waned with the onset of sequential ice-age periods that began two million years ago. When the glaciers finally retreated after the last ice age, 10,000 years ago, deep holes at the head of the Travers and Gowan Valleys were left, and these filled with water from the melting ice to become Lakes Rotoiti and Rotoroa.

The forests of Nelson Lakes are predominantly beech, with all five NZ species found here. In the lower valleys, where conditions are warmer and more fertile, you'll find red and silver beech interspersed with such species as kamahi and southern rata (which has a mass of bright flowers when in bloom). Mountain beech becomes dominant at altitudes above 1050m, or where there are poor soils in the lowlands.

The national park contains a rich diversity of bird life, particularly in the forests located near St Arnaud, the site of the 50-sq-km Rotoiti Nature Recovery Project. More than 15 years of predator control has seen bird populations flourish, and it's not uncommon to see the raucous kaka, a large, native bush parrot. Melodious tui and bellbirds are abundant, and can often be heard calling on the forest tracks. If you keep your eyes peeled you may also spot other birds such as tomtits, robins and NZ's tiniest feathered friend, the rifleman. Great spotted kiwi have been reintroduced and are breeding quite successfully, although you're unlikely to encounter these shy, nocturnal creatures.

The native long-finned eel, some more than 100 years old, are found in large numbers around the jetties in both main lakes. These creatures are fully protected and must not be fished for. Brown trout is the predominant fish species caught here and can be found in both the lakes and the main rivers (Travers, D'Urville, Sabine, Matakitaki and Buller).

ℹ Planning

WHEN TO TRAMP

The overall climate of the national park is pleasantly moderate and is characterised in summer by long spells of settled clear weather. Having said that, a warm, clear day on a mountain pass can become a white-out, with heavy rain or even a blizzard, in no time at all. Above the bushline snow may fall throughout the year.

Both tracks described are in alpine environments that are best tramped from November to April, when weather and snow conditions are most favourable. January through March offers the most settled weather to tackle the tracks.

Many tracks in Nelson Lakes National Park can be safely navigated in winter, although the park is avalanche-prone during winter and spring; check conditions at the Nelson Lakes Visitor Centre.

WHAT TO BRING

It is imperative that you come prepared for sudden weather changes, at any time of year. All trampers should carry warm clothing and good windproof and waterproof gear.

MAPS & BROCHURES

The 1:100,000 Parkmap 273-05 (Nelson Lakes National Park) is good for planning and adequate for many tramps in the park. NZTopo50 maps BR24 (Kawatiri) and BS24 (Mount Robert) cover the Lake Angelus routes and Travers-Sabine Circuit in greater detail. Useful DOC brochures include Angelus Hut Tracks & Routes, Travers-Sabine Circuit and Walks in Nelson Lakes National Park.

HUTS & CAMPING

There are 22 huts within the national park, most dotted at convenient intervals along the main track network. Eight of these are **Serviced huts** (www.doc.govt.nz; $15), equipped with mattresses, water supply, toilets, washbasins, and heating with fuel available. The rest are **Standard huts** (www.doc.govt.nz; $5), **Basic huts** (www.doc.govt.nz; free) or **Bivvies** (www.doc.govt.nz; free). There are no cooking facilities in the huts; all trampers should carry stoves. Hut tickets must be pre-purchased from the Nelson Lakes Visitor Centre.

Backcountry hut tickets and passes are valid at the park's huts, with the exception of the relatively luxurious, serviced Angelus Hut (28 bunks) from late November through to the end of April. During this peak period the hut and the nearby campsites ($10) must be booked in advance online or through DOC visitor centres nationwide.

Camping is permitted throughout the park. There is a fee of one Backcountry hut ticket for camping close to Serviced huts. Camping around Standard/Basic huts and away from huts is free.

A short stroll from St Arnaud and a stone's throw from Lake Rotoiti, DOC's lovely **Kerr Bay Camp** (powered/unpowered site $15/10) has bushy nooks for campervans and decent grass for tenters. It also has hot showers, a cooking shelter and laundry facilities during summer. Further round the lake, DOC's more basic **West Bay Camp** ($6) is open mid-December to Easter. Both camps have to be pre-booked from mid-December through to Easter online or at the Nelson Lakes Visitor Centre.

At the northern end of Lake Rotoroa, DOC's Lake Rotoroa Camp ($6) has toilets, water and ferocious sandflies.

INFORMATION SOURCES

The **Nelson Lakes Visitor Centre** (☎ 03-521 1806; www.doc.govt.nz; View Rd; ☺ 8am-4.30pm, to 5pm in summer) is a five-minute walk from the village centre and has park information, the latest weather forecasts, hut passes and interpretive displays.

ⓘ Getting to/from the Tramps

The Travers-Sabine Circuit begins on the Lakehead Track, which is signposted from the Kerr Bay campsite. The end of the tramp and the start of the Robert Ridge route to Lake Angelus is the Mt Robert car park, 7km from the visitor centre. The very accommodating **Nelson Lakes Shuttles** (☎ 035 476 896; www.nelsonlakesshuttles.co.nz) provides on-demand transport between Mt Robert car park and St Arnaud (per person $15, minimum $30). It is also the primary bus operator between Nelson and the national park.

Rotoiti Water Taxis (☎ 021 702 278; www.rotoitiwatertaxis.co.nz) will ferry trampers between Kerr Bay and the head of Lake Rotoiti (up to four people $100, extra person $25). Many trampers use this as their starting point for the Travers-Sabine Circuit or to end the trip to Lake Angelus, as it shaves off 9km (three hours) of walking and gives you the bonus of seeing the lake and mountains from a different perspective.

Trek Express (☎ 027 222 1872, 0800 128 735; www.trekexpress.co.nz; $50) runs a scheduled Sunday service and an on-demand one (minimum four people) between Nelson and St Arnaud, working in cooperation with Nelson Lakes Shuttles.

Lake Angelus Track

Duration 2 days

Distance 21.5km (13.4 miles)

Track Standard Tramping track and route

Difficulty Moderate

Start Mt Robert car park

End Coldwater Hut

Nearest Towns St Arnaud (p201), Nelson (p197)

Transport Shuttle bus, boat

Summary An epic ridge walk, an alpine lake-filled basin and one of NZ's flashest above-the-bushline huts.

Despite its relative short length, this tramp rates as one of the best in the country, boasting all that's good about Nelson Lakes National Park. In fine weather, the walk along Robert Ridge is spectacular – seldom do tramps afford such an extended period across such open tops. The views will blow your socks off, as they will again as you descend into the extraordinary Lake Angelus basin (1650m), a good base for short forays. A two-night stay at Angelus Hut is highly desirable.

The start of the tramp is 7km from St Arnaud, which will add around two hours and 165m of climbing to the walk. From the Coldwater Hut trailhead you can either catch a boat back across the lake – a nice way to finish – or tramp back to St Arnaud via the Lakeside Track (12km, four hours), or the Lakehead Track (9km, three hours), accessed from Lakehead Hut.

 The Tramp

Day 1: Mt Robert Carpark to Angelus Hut (via Robert Ridge)

6 HOURS, 12KM, 770M ASCENT

Fill your water bottles before embarking on this day's tramping as there is no water along the way.

From the Mt Robert car park it's a steep, zigzagged climb up **Pinchgut Track**. After 30 minutes you'll come to the junction with **Paddy's Track**, part of the **Mt Robert Circuit** – the most popular day walk in the park.

Keep walking beyond the junction and on to the poled route that wends steadily up into the distance. Follow this broad ridge past the second alpine basin, the site of an old ski field, and continue for 1.5km, ascending 160m to **Flagtop** (1690m).

Along the tops, keep an eye out for the karearea (NZ falcon), squawky kea and elusive rock wren. If you don't spot any of these, console yourself by stroking the cushion-like vegetable sheep *(Raoulia eximia)*, a most peculiar plant that has found a foothold among the rocks.

The well-marked route continues climbing gently towards **Julius Summit** (1794m) with the third large tarn-filled basin to your left. Pass under the peak on its western side, then regain the ridge and follow it in a southwesterly direction. Take care along this sharp and rocky section.

When you reach the sign for Speargrass Hut on your right, you are only 30 minutes from Angelus Hut. Follow the track up on to the ridge where you will encounter views over Angelus Basin, then follow the poles down to the lakeside Angelus Hut, built in 2010. Perched on the edge of the lake 1650m above sea level among golden tussock, this hut is a particularly fine specimen, with insulated walls, a capacious common area and large sunny deck.

SIDE TRIP: ANGELUS BASIN/MT ANGELUS

2–3 HOURS RETURN

Many trampers choose to spend two nights at Angelus Hut, allowing them a whole day to explore this beguiling alpine environment without having to carry heavy, full packs. A good half-day option is to circumnavigate along the ridge around the cirque basin overlooking **Lake Angelus**. Gouged out by glaciers over a series of ice ages 10,000 to 20,000 years ago, the basin is made all the more impressive by the 100m-plus high fans of scree and shattered greywacke peaks that almost encircle the lake. Earlier named Rangimarie ('peaceful') by an unknown European, Lake Angelus is known by Maori as Rotomaninitua (the 'glowing white lake', by our translation).

Mt Angelus (2075m) stands sentry to the south and, if it's free of snow, can be scaled with no special equipment or climb-

---

ROBERT RIDGE BAD WEATHER ROUTE

The route along Robert Ridge is spectacular in good weather, requiring little more than a good head for heights and confidence walking over rough terrain as it winds its way along sharp ridges and through vertiginous scree slopes. However, the whole length of the ridge is exposed to winds from the southeast, with few places for shelter on the lee side. In bad weather, with low visibility, it is easy to become disoriented and wander off the route. Check with the Nelson Lakes Visitor Centre for the latest track and weather conditions before you set out and if the weather is poor, do not attempt it.

Should weather conditions prevent you attempting the above route, it may be possible to reach Angelus Hut safely via an alternative route: from Mt Robert car park, walk to Speargrass Hut (three hours) and then take the Speargrass Creek Route (three hours) up to the junction with Robert Ridge, 30 minutes shy of Angelus Hut. If the weather improves, you can always return to St Arnaud along Robert Ridge, rather than taking the Cascade Track.

ing experience required – just a good head for heights, a decent level of fitness and a love of scrambling up loose rock. It will take around three hours to the summit and back from Angelus Hut.

Day 2: Angelus Hut to Coldwater Hut

6 HOURS, 9.5KM, 1030M DESCENT

Retrace the track behind Angelus Hut to the signposted junction where you can pick up **Cascade Track**. This is a steep and rocky, poled route down into the head of the **Hukere Stream** and alongside a series of dramatic cascades.

Take your time and go easy on your knees during the upper section, where there are plenty of trip hazards and the additional danger of slipping when wet or icy. Once you hit the bushline the track descends more gently through lush beech forest and past impressive rock chutes, before reaching the Travers Valley.

Once in the valley, take the bridge across Hukere Stream and then head north along the true left of the **Travers River**. Knees wobbly from the descent will welcome the easy walking along the valley flats, their golden meadows a stark contrast to the shadowy valley from which you have just emerged.

A pleasurable amble of around 1½ hours will see you reach Coldwater Hut (12 bunks) at the head of **Lake Rotoiti**, an ideal spot for a post-tramp dip in the lake before your boat arrives to ferry you back to St Arnaud.

Energetic and thrifty walkers can skip the boat and walk to St Arnaud via the Lakeside Track (12km, four hours), or the Lakehead Track (9km, three hours), accessed from Lakehead Hut (28 bunks).

Travers-Sabine Circuit

Duration 5 days

Distance 80km (50 miles)

Track Standard Tramping track and route

Difficulty Moderate to demanding

Start St Arnaud

End Mt Robert car park

Nearest Towns St Arnaud (p201), Nelson (p197)

Transport Shuttle bus, boat

Summary Grassy river flats, beech forests, a high alpine saddle, and a side trip to the world's clearest freshwater lake are features of this circuit.

An accessible and popular tramping area of Nelson Lakes, the Travers Valley provides easy tramping along good tracks with excellent alpine scenery, tranquil forest, plenty of huts and a bridge almost every time you need one. Combined with the route in the Sabine Valley, via the Travers Saddle, the trip is ideal for those new to NZ's alpine areas. The pass is steep and not to be taken lightly, but on a clear day – and there are usually many such days in February – the panoramic views from the top are spectacular.

The tramp is described here as a five-day expedition, but a different arrangement of legs (power legs or lazy legs) could spread it over anything from four to seven. The day-long side trip to enchanting Blue Lake – a highlight of the park – should be completed if at all possible. More than a dozen huts en (or close to the) route facilitate extended missions.

🥾 The Tramp

Day 1: St Arnaud to John Tait Hut

7–8 HOURS, 25KM, 180M ASCENT

Some trampers make Upper Travers Hut, rather than John Tait Hut, the destination for their first day. Even with boat transport up Lake Rotoiti, this is still a long day (22km), leaving many with sore legs and feet on the eve of crossing Travers Saddle the following day.

The trip begins with the **Lakehead Track** along the eastern side of Lake Rotoiti. You can also take the **Lakeside Track** along the west side, but this is a longer walk.

The Lakehead Track is signposted from the Kerr Bay campsite. For the first 1km, to the junction of the Loop Track, the way is wide and level. Beyond the junction it more resembles a track but remains an easy walk through forest at the edge of Lake Rotoiti. After 4km the track passes a gravel clearing, where there are good views of the northern half of the lake, including the peninsula between the bays. In another 2.5km it passes a second clearing, and this time the southern half of the lake can be seen.

Lakehead Hut (28 bunks) is around two to three hours (9km) from Kerr Bay and is on a grassy bank overlooking the mouth of the Travers River, where there is good trout fishing. Coldwater Hut (12 bunks), which is smaller and older, is about 800m away, across the Travers River on the other side of the lake.

At Lakehead Hut, signposts direct you across Travers River and through a grassy flat to the walking track on the true left (west) side of the river. The alternative during high water is to follow the true right (east) side of the river for 5km, to a footbridge across the Travers. The true left side is more scenic because it swings close to the river in many places.

Once on the track on the true left side, head south and you soon pass a signposted junction for Cascade Track, which leads to Angelus Hut (4½ hours). The main track continues south, meandering between stands of beech and grassy flats until it reaches a swing bridge across the Travers. Stay on the true left side, following the river closely through the forest, to emerge after 3.5km onto another flat, where Mt Travers dominates the view.

Just beyond the end of the flat you arrive at a swing bridge over Hopeless Creek. On the other side is a signposted junction indicating the track to Hopeless Hut (2½ hours). The track now begins to climb gradually.

John Tait Hut (27 bunks), under two hours from the junction, is in a small grassy clearing with good views of the peaks at the head of the valley. Its best feature is an enclosed veranda that allows you to enjoy the views but keeps the sandflies at bay.

Day 2: John Tait Hut to Upper Travers Hut

3 HOURS, 6KM, 510M ASCENT

The track sets off by continuing its climb up the valley. About 20 minutes (1km) from the hut it passes the track junction to the Cupola Hut (2½ hours) before crossing a bridge over Cupola Creek. The climb steepens, and within another 1km the track enters a chasm and passes a side track to Travers Falls, a worthy three-minute detour to the 20m cascade that plunges into a sparkling, clear pool.

Back on the track the gradient eases slightly and after crossing several scree slopes you walk over a bridge to the true right of the Travers River about 1½ hours

from the falls. At this point you begin an even steeper climb to the bushline, passing three signposted avalanche paths along the way. At the edge of the bush, little more than 2km from the bridge, trampers are greeted with good views of the peaks of both the Travers Range and St Arnaud Range.

Upper Travers Hut (24 bunks) overlooks a tussocky flat before the last stand of mountain beech towards the saddle. At 1340m it's a beautiful spot, surrounded by gravel and scree slopes that can be easily climbed for better views, while looming overhead is the east face of Mt Travers.

Day 3: Upper Travers Hut to West Sabine Hut

6–8 HOURS, 8KM, 467M ASCENT, 1117M DESCENT

The route over Travers Saddle is well marked with snow poles, but is still a climb into the alpine zone. If the weather is foul, hold off and wait another day.

The track begins by crossing the river. After 30 minutes or so, the ascent is signalled when you emerge from the final stand of trees and head west into an area of tussock-covered slopes and large scattered boulders. From here you are technically following a route, but because of its popularity a track can be seen most of the way.

The route climbs gently towards the saddle for 1km, until you reach a signpost directing you up a steep scree slope. The zigzagging climb lasts several hundred metres; take your time, stopping often to admire the fine views.

Once at the top of the slope, a 450m ascent from the hut, the final climb to the saddle is easy; you pass two tarns while the sharp-edged Mt Travers (2338m) towers overhead to the north. Travers Saddle (1787m) is reached 1½ hours from Upper Travers Hut and is marked by a huge rock cairn. This is a nice spot, but for a truly awe-inspiring outlook you should scramble to one of the nearby ridges.

From the saddle you begin descending the 1000m to Sabine Forks, passing first through tussock slopes, then heading right over a rockslide before returning to grassland.

Around 1.5km from the saddle there is a superb view of the Mahanga Range, just before you descend into the bushline and return to the track. You remain in the stunted mountain beech only momentarily, because the track quickly swings into a scree-covered gully and embarks on a very rapid descent – 600m over just 3km. This is probably the hardest section of the day and care is required on the steep sections of loose rock. Halfway down, at the tree line, the track returns – with trail markers appearing on the left-hand side of the gully – and you follow it as it levels out next to the gorge of the **East Branch Sabine River**.

Shortly afterwards you cross a small bridge over the deep chasm. Although you won't actually see the water, you will certainly hear it roaring through the narrow rock walls. The best view is from the riverbank upstream.

Once on the other side, the track follows the steep valley for 2km and in many places is a maze of tree roots. The final leg of this long day is a very steep drop down the East Branch of the Sabine. The track swings south to West Sabine Hut (30 bunks).

SIDE TRIP: WEST SABINE HUT TO BLUE LAKE
6–7 HOURS RETURN, 14KM, 520M ASCENT/DESCENT

Enchanting Blue Lake is a national park highlight and well worth the extra day on the track. **Blue Lake Hut** (16 bunks), set above the lake near the edge of the bushline, is a beautiful spot to spend the night if you don't want to return to West Sabine Hut the same day. It's a pretty steep climb to the lake, though, and many trampers visit Blue Lake as a return day trip from West Sabine Hut without their full packs.

From West Sabine Hut, cross the swing bridge to return to the true left (west) side of the West Branch Sabine River and continue south along the track. From the river fork the track climbs over often-slippery beech tree roots, and after two hours the valley opens up at a large slip to a stunning view. In front of you is a theatre of mountains, with Moss Pass an obvious dip to the right. Turn around and you can look back down the valley or at **Mt Cupola** (2260m).

The track dips back into the bush and the climb becomes steeper as you traverse forest and scree slopes, many of them formed by avalanches. At one point you top off at a boardwalk and manicured track though a beautiful garden-like setting, with the river just to the left. Take a break and enjoy the beauty because you still have one more steep, forested hillside to climb in the last 1km before **Blue Lake** finally comes into view.

Just before Blue Lake Hut is a spot where avalanches are funnelled down chutes and across the track from winter well into spring. Conditions are worst between May and November, but the avalanche paths can be active during unseasonable January snowfalls. Do not stop between the warning signs during periods prone to avalanches.

The lake, known to Maori as Rotomairewhenua, is thought to be the clearest natural freshwater lake in the world, with visibility of around 80m. Take care to avoid any contamination of the lake. If you take the track that climbs 1km south through one last stand of stunted beech you'll be rewarded with excellent views of both **Lake Constance** and Blue Lake. This is one of the most scenic spots in the park.

Day 4: West Sabine Hut to Sabine Hut
5 HOURS, 15KM

Five minutes upriver from the hut is the swing bridge over the West Branch Sabine River. Cross to the true left (west) side, following the level route north. This is a very pleasant stretch as the track remains close to the water, and it's an easy start for those with achy legs from the climb over Travers Saddle. The track remains in the wooded fringe of the river for 7km before breaking out onto a grassy flat.

The track crosses the flat for 2km and climbs steeply at its northern end, only to descend onto another flat. At the northern end of this flat is a climb to a small knob that overlooks a deep gorge; this is the steepest ascent of a relatively easy day.

Once the track descends the other side, it follows the river to the junction with the track to D'Urville Hut (10 bunks). Cross the bridge over the impressive deep gorge. It's an easy scramble down to the water, and trampers have even been known to float through the gorge for a refreshing dip on a hot day.

From the bridge the track climbs out of the narrow valley, then spills onto a grassy flat. You are now less than 2km from the hut, reached along a wooded and level path. Sabine Hut (32 bunks) has views of **Lake Rotoroa** and a spacious kitchen-common area. Despite the multitudinous sandflies, you can enjoy excellent sunsets over the lake from the hut's jetty.

Day 5: Sabine Hut to Mt Robert Car Park
(via Speargrass Hut)

7½–9½ HOURS, 27KM

The final leg of the Travers-Sabine Circuit takes you to the Mt Robert car park via Speargrass Hut. However, if you're fit and the weather's fine, you can head up steep Mt Cedric Track to Lake Angelus and spend a night at the stunning Angelus Hut (28 bunks) before returning to St Arnaud via one of three tracks the following day. The different options are described in DOC's *Angelus Hut Tracks & Routes* brochure.

To get to Speargrass Hut from Sabine Hut, take the track north that skirts the lakeshore before angling into beech forest and making a long climb to Howard Saddle. It takes one hour to climb the 350m to the saddle, which is dimpled by a series of small ponds. The track then swings more northeast and contours around the base of Robert Ridge.

Two hours from Sabine Hut is a suspension bridge over Cedric Stream. In the next hour you cross several streams, bridged where necessary. Now, only an hour from Speargrass Hut, the track vastly improves. It's well benched, and at one point follows more than 500m of boardwalk, complete with benches and a fine view of Howard Valley. Botanists may admire the conical shape of the kaikawaka (NZ cedar), or search for the tiny sundew – a plant that survives the lack of nitrogen by catching and devouring insects on its sticky leaves.

Eventually the track makes a steep but short descent to Speargrass Hut (12 bunks), reached four to five hours from Sabine Hut. It is located in a small grassy meadow surrounded by mountains, and is a pleasant way to turn a long tramp into an easy overnighter if you have a spare day.

From the hut the track crosses the flat and within five minutes arrives at a bridge over Speargrass Creek. On the other side is a signposted junction with the Speargrass Creek Route (right fork), which climbs to Lake Angelus (three hours).

Take the left fork along Speargrass Track, which begins with an hour-long descent, sidling the ridge until it bottoms out at Speargrass Creek. Follow the creek for 30 minutes and then begin the final leg, a steady but easy climb that lasts almost one hour and crosses bridges over two streams.

The day ends with a short descent to the Mt Robert car park, 2½ to three hours from Speargrass Hut. Unless you have transport, it's another 7km (1½ hours) of walking into St Arnaud.

St Arnaud Range Track

Duration 5 hours return

Distance 11km (6.8 miles)

Track Standard Tramping track

Difficulty Moderate

Start/End Kerr Bay, St Arnaud

Nearest Towns St Arnaud (p201), Nelson (p197)

Transport None

Summary A popular day walk with a steep ascent through beech forest and above the bushline to the top of the range for a grand panorama at 1650m.

This popular up-and-down day walk provides one of the best viewpoints of Nelson Lakes National Park and beyond, surveyed from the top of the St Arnaud Range. It's around a 1000m ascent from lake to ridge but achy legs will be numbed by the splendour of beech forest – red, silver and mountain – that gradually changes with altitude. Equally diverting is the chatter of native birds whose populations are bolstered by the work of the Rotoiti Nature Recovery Project, through which this track passes.

Above the bushline (1400m) the views are worthy of a sit-down, but don't be content with gawping at the lake and Mt Robert from Parachute Rocks, as many walkers are. Fuel up with some scroggin and conquer the final 30-minute climb through alpine tussock to the ridge (1650m). You won't be disappointed.

🏃 The Tramp

5 HOURS RETURN, 11KM, 1000M ASCENT/DESCENT

The start of this track is an easy stroll from St Arnaud township. You'll find the trailhead in the eastern corner of Kerr Bay, on the lake edge near the campsite toilet block.

To begin it follows three short walks through beech forest – Bellbird Walk, Honeydew Walk and Loop Track – which form part of the 50-sq-km Rotoiti Nature Recovery Project. Keep an eye and an ear out for nectarivorous tui and korimako (bellbirds), and cute fantails, robins and tomtits that may flit around your feet as you kick up insects for them to feed on. Three species of beech mistletoe creep around tree trunks thanks to possum eradication programs, their yellow and red flowers resplendent in December and January.

Shortly after joining the Loop Track in the clockwise direction, the **St Arnaud Range Track** bears left and climbs steadily up and across moraine terraces deposited by glaciers.

Divert your attention from the relentless climb by studying the trees as you ascend, noticing how they have adapted to the changing altitude and environment. At lower elevations red beech is dominant, while higher up silver beech is more apparent and then mountain beech after that. Nearing the bushline (1400m) the trees become more and more stunted.

Free of the forest, you can catch your breath on **Parachute Rocks**, aptly named after the canopy-shaped scree slopes located to the north, and take in the spectacular views down to St Arnaud and across Lake Rotoiti to Mt Robert. From here the gradient doesn't let up but the extra 30 minutes to the ridge through snow tussock and fields of alpine shrubs and herbs is certainly worth the effort. Late spring and early summer the herbs bloom in gloriously gold and white blankets across the steep slopes.

Atop the ridge, on a good day you can see for miles: west to Kahurangi National Park and the Buller Valley, north to Richmond Forest Park, east down the Wairau Valley and south to the heart of the Nelson Lakes National Park. Those with energy to spare might like to explore southwest along the craggy ridge or scramble down to the tarn-filled basins on the eastern side. Return to Kerr Bay via the same route that you came up, pausing often to savour the views before heading back into the forest.

TOWNS & FACILITIES

Nelson

☑ 03 / POP 60,800

This pleasant and active city is a great place from which to set off for tramps, or to recuperate in after finishing tramps. It has plentiful supplies of every description, including an enticing array of excellent local produce such as fruit, wine and craft beer.

🛏 Sleeping

Nelson has a stack of hostels and other budget to midrange accommodation options. Its food scene runs the gamut, and is particularly friendly to self-caterers.

Accents on the Park   HOSTEL $
(☑0800 888 335, 03-548 4335; www.accents onthepark.com; 335 Trafalgar Sq; sites from $15, dm $20-28, d with/without bathroom from $92/60; @⎙) This perfectly positioned hostel has a hotel feel with its professional staff, balconies, groovy cafe-bar (meals around $15), free daily bread, soundproofed rooms, quality linen, fresh bathrooms and bikes for hire. Bravo! (Book early.)

Trampers Rest   HOSTEL $
(☑03-545 7477; 31 Alton St; dm/s/d $29/46/66; @⎙) With just a few beds (no bunks), the tiny but much-loved Trampers is hard to beat for a homely environment. The enthusiastic owner is a keen tramper and cyclist, and provides comprehensive local information and free bikes.

Nelson YHA   HOSTEL $
(☑03-545 9988; www.yha.co.nz; 59 Rutherford St; dm/s/d from $33/66/87, d with bathroom $110; @⎙) A tidy, purpose-built, central hostel with high-quality facilities including two well-organised kitchens and a sunny outdoor terrace. Solid service on tour and activity bookings.

Nelson City Holiday Park   HOLIDAY PARK $
(☑0800 778 898, 03-548 1445; www.nelson holidaypark.co.nz; 230 Vanguard St; sites from $40, cabins & units $60-168; @⎙) The closest option to town: convenient, well-maintained, clean, but cramped (although the motel units are pretty good). Limited campsites by the creek out back.

🍴 Eating & Drinking

Falafel Gourmet   MIDDLE EASTERN $
(195 Hardy St; meals $8-18; ☑) A cranking joint dishing out the best kebabs in town, jam-packed with salad.

DeVille   CAFE $$
(22 New St; meals $13-20; ☺9am-4pm Mon-Sat; ☑) Most of DeVille's tables lie in its walled courtyard, a boho inner-city oasis in which to enjoy very good food – from fresh baked goods to an eggy brunch, Caesar salad or sticky pork sandwich. Open late for live music Friday and Saturday in summer.

Free House
CRAFT BEER

(www.freehouse.co.nz; 95 Collingwood St) Come rejoice at this church of ales. Tastefully converted from its original, more reverent purpose, it now proffers an oft-changing selection of NZ craft beers, simple bar food and pizza delivery from Stefano's, the city's best pizzeria.

Supplies & Equipment

Rollo's Outdoor Centre
OUTDOOR EQUIPMENT

(www.rollos.co.nz; 12 Bridge St; ⊙9am-5.30am Mon-Fri, to 3pm Sat) The most specialised of Nelson's several outdoor gear stores.

Fresh Choice
SUPERMARKET

(69 Collingwood St; ⊙7am-9pm) There are plenty of places to stock up on groceries, including this inner-city supermarket.

Information

Nelson i-SITE (☑03-548 2304; www.nelsonnz. com; cnr Trafalgar & Halifax Sts; ⊙8.30am-5pm Mon-Fri, 9am-5pm Sat & Sun) Loads of information on the area, including lodging and transport, and will book bus and tour tickets.

Getting There & Away

Nelson airport is serviced by **Air New Zealand** (☑0800 737 000; www.airnewzealand.co.nz), which provides extensive nationwide connections including direct flights to Auckland, Wellington and Christchurch. Two small regional airlines, **Soundsair** (☑0800 505 005, 03-520 3080; www.soundsair.com) and **Air2there** (☑0800 777 000; www.air2there.com), fly daily between Nelson and Wellington.

Most bus services operate from **Nelson SBL Travel Centre** (☑03-548 1539; www. nelsoncoaches.co.nz; 27 Bridge St), where you can also book local and nationwide transport services including **Abel Tasman Coachlines** (☑03-548 0285; www.abeltasmantravel.co.nz), **Golden Bay Coachlines** (☑03-525 8352; www. gbcoachlines.co.nz), **InterCity** (☑03-548 1538; www.intercity.co.nz; Bridge St, departs SBL Travel Centre) and interisland ferries.

Departing from (and bookable at) the i-SITE, **Atomic Shuttles** (☑03-349 0697; www. atomictravel.co.nz) runs from Nelson to Picton (2¼ hours), and daily to West Coast centres such as Greymouth (5¾ hours) and Fox Glacier (9½ hours).

Motueka
☑03 / POP 6900

Motueka (pronounced Mott-oo-ecka, meaning 'Island of Wekas') is a bustling town, one which visitors will find handy for stocking up en route to all three of the region's national parks.

Sleeping

Motueka Top 10 Holiday Park
HOLIDAY PARK $

(☑0800 668 835, 03-528 7189; www.motueka top10.co.nz; 10 Fearon St; sites from $40, cabins $55-130, units/motels $99-350; @🛜🏊) Busy it may be, but this place retains plenty of grassy, green charm. All the bells and whistles are in evidence, as you'd expect from a holiday park routinely touted as among the nation's best.

Happy Apple
HOSTEL $

(☑0800 427 792, 03-528 8652; www.happy applebackpackers.co.nz; 500 High St; sites from $15, dm/s/d $26/41/60; @🛜) There's nothing rotten about this apple, which has tidy rooms divided between the house (nice doubles) and dorm wing. The action happens in the backyard, where there's an expansive lawn (camping allowed), gardens, fireplace, lounging areas and spa pool.

Eden's Edge Lodge
HOSTEL $

(☑03-528 4242; www.edensedge.co.nz; 137 Lodder Ln, Riwaka; sites from $17, dm $28, d with/without bathroom $82/76; @🛜🏊) Surrounded by orchards 4km from Motueka, within walking distance of the main highway, this modern lodge with a gleaming kitchen comes pretty close to backpacker heaven.

Eating & Drinking

As far as eating goes, it all happens on High St. If you're around on Sunday, don't miss the **Motueka Sunday Market** (Wallace St; ⊙8am-1pm) behind the i-SITE.

Patisserie Royale
BAKERY $

(152 High St; baked goods $2-8; ⊙6am-4pm Mon-Sat, 6am-2pm Sat & Sun) The best of several Mot bakeries and worth every delectable calorie. Lots of French fancies and a darn good pie.

Simply Indian
INDIAN $$

(130 High St; mains $16-23; ⊙lunch & dinner Mon-Sat, dinner Sun; ☑) As the name suggests, this is no-nonsense curry in a no-frills setting. The food is consistently good and relatively cheap, with takeaway available.

Sprig and Fern
PUB $$

(www.sprigandfern.co.nz; Wallace St; meals $14-19; ⊙2pm-late) The best of Motueka's drinking holes is an offshoot of the Nelson brewery of the same name. It's small but pleasant, with courtyards, 20 beer taps, simple food (burgers, pizza, platters) and occasional live music.

🔒 Supplies & Equipment

Coppins Great Outdoors Centre OUTDOOR EQUIPMENT
(255 High St; ⊗ 8.30am-5.30pm Mon-Fri, 9am-4pm Sat, 10am-2pm Sun) Head here for the widest range of tramping supplies.

New World SUPERMARKET
(271 High St) Ample places to stock up on groceries include this good supermarket.

ℹ️ Information

Motueka i-SITE (✆ 03-528 6543; www. motuekaisite.co.nz; 20 Wallace St; ⊗ 8.30am-5pm Mon-Fri, 9am-4pm Sat & Sun) Book transport, lodging and tours and buy hut passes at this excellent visitor centre.

ℹ️ Getting There & Away

All Motueka bus services depart from the i-SITE. Most ply the route between Nelson, Abel Tasman and Kahurangi National Parks. **Abel Tasman Coachlines** (✆ 03-528 8850; www.abeltasman travel.co.nz) runs several times daily between Motueka and Nelson ($12, one hour), Marahau ($10, 30 minutes), Kaiteriteri ($10, 25 minutes) and Takaka ($26, one hour). In summer these services connect with **Golden Bay Coachlines** (✆ 03-525 8352; www.gbcoachlines.co.nz) through to Collingwood and the Heaphy, Totaranui and other Golden Bay destinations; from May to September all buses run less frequently.

Motueka is also serviced by **Atomic Shuttles** (✆ 03-349 0697; www.atomictravel.co.nz) and **InterCity** (✆ 03-365 1113; www.intercitycoach. co.nz) to destinations further afield.

Marahau

✆ 03 / POP 200

This tiny village, largely comprised of tourism businesses and holiday homes, is 18km north of Motueka and the last bit of civilisation before you enter Abel Tasman National Park. You can easily walk from Marahau to the southern end of the Abel Tasman Coast Track, 1km from town.

🛏️ Sleeping & Eating

Kanuka Ridge HOSTEL $
(✆ 03-527 8435; www.abeltasmanbackpackers. co.nz; Moss Rd, off Marahau-Sandy Bay Rd; dm $29,

d & tw with/without bathroom $89/64; 🛜) Five minutes' drive (3km) from Marahau and the start of the Abel Tasman track, this cottage-style arrangement is set in bushy surroundings. Hosts are willing and able to hook you up to the nature buzz, with mountain bikes, activity bookings and car storage.

Marahau Beach Camp HOLIDAY PARK $
(✆ 527 8176, 0800 808 018; www.abeltasman centre.co.nz; Franklin St; sites from $35, dm $22, cabins $70-80; @) This well-established camping ground is an adequate place to pitch up before or after your Abel Tasman adventure.

Park Cafe CAFE $$
(Harvey Rd; lunch $9-22, dinner $16-30; ⊗ 8am-late mid-Sep–May; 🍴) Sitting at the start (or the end) of the Abel Tasman Coast Track, this breezy, licensed cafe is perfectly placed for fuelling up or restoring the waistline. High-calorie options include the big breakfast, burgers, seafood pasta and homemade cakes.

Fat Tui BURGERS $$
(cnr Marahau-Sandy Bay & Marahau Valley Rds; burgers $13-16; ⊗ noon-8.30pm (Wed-Sun winter); 🍴) This caravan ain't rollin' anywhere fast, thank goodness. Serves superlative burgers, such as the Cowpat (beef), the Ewe Beaut (lamb) and the Sparrow's Fart breakfast burger. Fish and chips, and coffee, too.

ℹ️ Getting There & Away

Marahau is serviced by the Abel Tasman transport providers (see p171).

Takaka

✆ 03 / POP 1230

Despite the distractions of semi-transient yoga-pant-wearing alternative types, good old Takaka gets on with the real business of servicing its rural community and visitors, most of whom are outdoor enthusiasts like you. Although the nearest town to the start of the Heaphy Track (Brown Hut) is actually Collingwood, regular transport services and a much wider range of supplies mean that Takaka is a preferable option.

🛏️ Sleeping

Annie's Nirvana Lodge HOSTEL $
(✆ 03-525 8766; www.nirvanalodge.co.nz; 25 Motupipi St; dm/d $28/66; @ 🛜) It's clean, it's tidy, and it smells good: dorms are in the main

ABEL TASMAN, KAHURANGI & NELSON LAKES MARAHAU

house, four doubles are at the bottom of the secluded courtyard garden. This YHA hostel is lovely and has friendly owners. Free bikes for guests.

Golden Bay Motel　　MOTEL **$$**
(☑03-525 9428, 0800 401 212; www.goldenbay motel.co.nz; 132 Commercial St; d $95-140, extra person $20; ☎) It's golden, all right: check out the paint job. Clean, spacious, self-contained units with decent older-style fixtures and decent older-style hosts. The rear patios overlook a lush green lawn with a playground.

✕ Eating & Drinking

Dangerous Kitchen　　CAFE **$$**
(46a Commercial St; meals $12-28; ☻10am-10pm Mon-Sat) Mellow and laid-back, with a sun-trap courtyard out back and a people-watching patio on the main drag, this popular joint serves largely healthy, good-value fare such as felafel, pizza, burritos, megacake and fresh juice.

Brigand　　CAFE, BAR **$$**
(www.brigand.co.nz; 90 Commercial St; meals $16-35; ☻11am-late Mon-Sat) Beyond the gates you'll find good food such as home-baked cakes, sandwiches, chowder and meaty mains served in a relaxed interior and garden bar. The Brigand is also the mainstay of the local music scene – with luck you'll rock up on a gig night.

Fresh Choice　　SUPERMARKET
(13 Willow St; ☻8am-7pm) Stock up while you can.

❶ Information

Golden Bay i-SITE (☑03-525 9136; www.golden baynz.co.nz; Willow St; ☻9am-5pm Nov-Apr, 10am-4.30pm Mon-Fri, to 4pm Sat & Sun May-Oct) Can furnish you with the indispensible, official *Map of Golden Bay*, and assist with hut passes, bookings and other track information.

❶ Getting There & Away

Takaka is serviced most regulary by **Golden Bay Coachlines** (☑03-525 8352; www.gb coachlines.co.nz) but also by the track transport operators that service the Abel Tasman (p171) and Heaphy (p176) tracks.

Karamea

☑03 / POP 650
At the end of SH67, 100km north of Westport, sweet little Karamea is the closest town to the western ends of the Heaphy and Wangapeka Tracks.

🛏 Sleeping & Eating

Karamea Memorial Domain　　CAMPSITE, HOSTEL **$**
(☑03-782 6069; Waverley St; sites unpowered 1/2 people $12/16, powered $13/18, dm $13) Behind Karamea School, this place offers simple camping over the bank from the river. There are bunks in the old-fashioned but tidy communal building with laundry. Non-staying visitors can also use the showers by paying $3 to the on-site caretaker.

Last Resort　　LODGE **$**
(☑03-782 6617, 0800 505 042; www.lastresort. co.nz; 71 Waverley St; dm $37, d $78-155; @☎) This rambling and rustic resort has simple rooms and warm and welcoming communal areas including a cafe (lunch $9 to $15, dinner $18 to $29) serving simple all-day food like burgers and fish and chips.

Wangapeka Backpackers Retreat & Farmstay　　HOSTEL **$**
(☑03-782 6663; www.wangapeka.co.nz; Atawhai Farm, Wangapeka Valley; campsites from $10, dm $20, s/d $45/75; ☎) This laid-back and friendly farmstay close to the end of the Wangapeka Track and 20km south of Karamea has rustic dorms with clean linen, and meals by arrangement.

Karamea Village Hotel　　PUB, HOTEL **$$**
(☑0800 826 800, 03-782 6800; karameahotel@ xtra.co.nz; cnr Waverley & Wharf Sts; r $110; mains $18-29; ☻11am-11pm) Treat yourself to life's simple pleasures: a game of pool with the locals, a pint of Monteith's Original Ale, and a whitebait-fritter sandwich. Sorted.

Four Square Supermarket　　SUPERMARKET
(103 Bridge St; ☻8.30am-6pm) This place will easily suffice for basic groceries including camping food.

❶ Getting There & Away

Karamea Express (☑03-782 6757; info@ karamea-express.co.nz) links Karamea and Westport ($35, two hours, 7.40am Monday to Friday May to September, plus Saturday from October to April). It also services Kohaihai on the Heaphy Track twice daily during peak summer periods, and runs shuttles to Wangapeka Rd.

Westport is serviced by **InterCity** (☑03-789 7819; www.intercitycoach.co.nz) and **Atomic Shuttles** (☑03-349 0697; www.atomictravel. co.nz), which pass through on their Nelson to Fox Glacier runs.

St Arnaud

🎵 03 / POP 200

This is a small hamlet of resorts and restaurants – plus the DOC area office – all clustered around Kerr Bay at the northern end of Lake Rotoiti.

🛏 Sleeping & Eating

Kerr Bay Camp   CAMPSITE $

(www.doc.govt.nz; unpowered/powered sites per person $10/15) This beautifully situated DOC campsite with hot showers and a laundry is perennially popular with trampers as well as NZ holidaymakers. It's an inspiring base for your adventures, but do book in advance. Overflow camping is available at DOC's nearby West Bay campsite, which is more basic.

Travers-Sabine Lodge   LODGE $

(📋 03-521 1887; www.nelsonlakes.co.nz; Main Rd; dm/d $26/62; @ 🖥) This modern lodge is a short walk to Lake Rotoiti, and is inexpensive, clean and comfortable. The owners are experienced adventurers themselves, so tips come as standard. Tramping equipment and snowshoes are available for hire.

Nelson Lakes Motels   MOTEL $$

(📋 03-521 1887; www.nelsonlakes.co.nz; Main Rd; d $120-135; @ 🖥) These log cabins and newer board-and-batten units offer all the creature comforts, including kitchenettes and Sky TV. Bigger units sleep up to six.

Alpine Lodge   LODGE $$

(📋 03-521 1869; www.alpinelodge.co.nz; Main Rd; d $155-210; @ 🖥) This expansive lodge has a range of accommodation including a separate backpackers (dorm/double $29/69), which is spartan but clean and warm. The snug in-house restaurant and bar has mountain views and dishes up good food (meals $16 to $29).

St Arnaud Alpine Village Store   SUPERMARKET, TAKEAWAYS $

(⊙ 8am-6pm, takeaways 4.30-8pm Fri & Sat, daily Dec-Feb; 🖥) The settlement's only general store sells groceries, petrol, beer, possum-wool socks, tramping food, sandwiches, pies and milkshakes, with the fish and chips cranking up on weekends and daily in peak season ($6 to $10).

❶ Getting There & Away

Nelson Lakes Shuttles (p191) links St Arnaud with Nelson on a scheduled service December to April (Monday, Wednesday and Friday; $45), and on demand the rest of the year (per person $45, minimum four people). It will also collect/drop off at Kawatiri Junction on SH63, to meet other bus services heading between Nelson and the West Coast (per person $25, minimum two people). It also offers services from St Arnaud through to Picton/Blenheim ($50/45).

Canterbury, Arthur's Pass & Aoraki/Mt Cook

Includes ➡

Banks Peninsula
Track 204
Mt Somers Track . . . 208
St James Walkway . . . 212
Avalanche Peak 218
Goat Pass Track 220
Harper Pass 222
Cass-Lagoon
Saddles Track 226
Mueller Hut Route . . . 230

Best Huts

➡ Stony Bay Cottage (p207)

➡ Woolshed Creek Hut (p210)

➡ Goat Pass Hut (p221)

➡ Mueller Hut (p231)

Best Views

➡ Mt John (p203)

➡ Trig GG (p206)

➡ Mt Somers Summit (p212)

➡ Ada Valley (p215)

➡ Avalanche Peak (p218)

➡ Mueller Hut (p231)

Why Go?

New Zealand's largest region, Canterbury comprises vast agricultural plains hemmed in by the Pacific Ocean on one side, and the Southern Alps on the other. As scenic as its epic coastline may be, Canterbury is all about the mountains, and the other fascinating geological landforms – such as Banks Peninsula – that fill in the big picture. And this is big-picture territory, famous for vast horizons on the plains, and bird's-eye views from the peaks of its inland parks and reserves.

The tramps in this region are dominated by the mighty Southern Alps, and they pass through them – in Arthur's Pass and Aoraki/Mt Cook National Park – or close enough to appreciate them from other angles. Between them they offer a diverse range of tramping experiences – taking in farmland, high country, regenerating and native forest, waterfalls and achievable climbs to peaks that will make you feel like you're on top of the world.

When to Go

Lowland Canterbury is one of the driest and flattest areas of NZ. The moisture-laden westerlies from the Tasman Sea hit the Southern Alps and dump their rainfall on the West Coast (an impressive annual 5000mm in places) before reaching Canterbury (which collects a dribble, only 750mm or so).

For the most part, though, you'll be tramping in the midst of the mountains which, when they're not attracting bad weather, are creating it. The Southern Alps have a volatile climate, where you can expect to encounter cold, wind and rain at any time of year. The optimum time to tramp in the South Island mountains is December through April.

Background Reading

Beyond the rural plains, it is the Southern Alps that define the Canterbury region, and within those mountains originate many of its best stories. To find them, look for books by or about NZ mountaineers Graeme Dingle, Sir Edmund Hillary and John Pascoe. A woman's perspective is brought to light in *Wind from a Distant Summit,* by leading lady mountaineer Pat Deavoll.

To navigate your way across the famously clear skies of the South Island back country, seek out astronomer Richard Hall's *How to Gaze at the Southern Stars.* This illuminating little book not only includes a foolproof method for locating the Southern Cross, it is packed with fascinating stories of the constellations, their origins and their role in the survival of humankind.

DON'T MISS

Inland SH8 between Christchurch to Aoraki/Mt Cook National Park is one of NZ's great scenic drives, the highlight of which is Lake Tekapo, an intensely turquoise lake with a backdrop of the Southern Alps. The small township is popular with passersby who stop in for a cuppa and perhaps a look at the historic lakeside church, but in doing so they miss Tekapo's best landmark: Mt John. This, we declare, is one of NZ's best lookout points.

The best way to appreciate this 1029m mountain (which is actually more of a hill) is to sidle up and around its slopes, around three hours return from the town. Conveniently located at the top is the delightful **Astro Cafe** (Mt John Observatory; coffee & cake $4-8, snacks $7-12; ⊘10am-5pm), a glass-walled pavilion with 360-degree views across the entire Mackenzie Basin.

The view, however, is equally as dazzling at night. Thanks to clear skies and an absence of light pollution, the area is known as one of the finest spots on the planet to explore the heavens. To unravel the mysteries of the Southern Hemisphere sky, take a star-gazing tour with **Earth & Sky** (⊘03-680 6960; www.earthandskynz.com; SH1; star-gazing adult/child $105/60), based at Mt John Observatory.

DOC Offices

➽ **Waimakariri Area Office** (p214)

➽ **DOC Arthur's Pass Visitor Centre** (p218)

➽ **Christchurch Visitor Centre** (p214)

➽ **DOC Aoraki/Mt Cook National Park Visitor Centre** (⊘03-435 1186; www.doc.govt.nz; 1 Larch Grove; ⊘8.30am-5pm Oct-Apr, to 4.30pm May-Sep)

GATEWAY TOWNS

➽ Christchurch (p232)

➽ Akaroa (p233)

➽ Methven (p234)

➽ Hanmer Springs (p234)

➽ Arthur's Pass (p235)

➽ Mt Cook Village (p235)

Fast Facts

➽ The beautiful high-country Hakatere Conservation Park, two hours south of Christchurch on the Inland Scenic Route (near Mt Somers), appeared as Edoras in the *Lord of the Rings* films.

➽ The quickest runners complete the 25km-Avalanche Peak Challenge in around 2½ hours. Fit trampers climb to the summit and back down again in about six hours.

➽ Thanks to almost half a century of possum-eradication efforts, the Otira Valley, north of Arthur's Pass, puts on possibly the South Island's best display of blooming rata every summer.

Top Tip

There's a good reason why tramping times in this chapter seem so long for such short distances. Mountainous terrain usually means gruelling climbs and knee-crunching descents. Set off early and stop often for scroggin (trail mix).

Resources

➽ www.christchurchnz.com

➽ www.akaroa.com

➽ www.visithurunui.co.nz

➽ www.visithanmer springs.co.nz

➽ www.arthurspass.com

➽ www.mtcooknz.com

Banks Peninsula Track

Duration 4 days

Distance 35km (21.7 miles)

Track Standard Tramping track

Difficulty Easy to moderate

Start Onuku Farm

End Akaroa

Nearest Towns Akaroa (p233), Christchurch (p232)

Transport Shuttle bus

Summary This tramp takes you through the spectacular coastal scenery of the Banks Peninsula, which abounds with wildlife and is resplendent with remnant tracts of native forest and farmland.

The eroded remains of two old volcanic craters, beautiful Banks Peninsula stands in high relief against the flat Canterbury Plains. Reached from nearby Christchurch via a long and winding road, the main town-

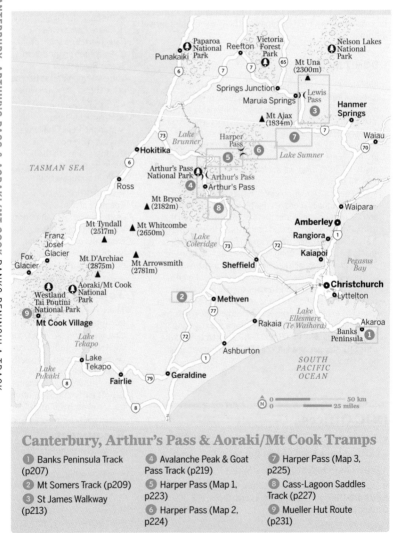

Canterbury, Arthur's Pass & Aoraki/Mt Cook Tramps

1. Banks Peninsula Track (p207)
2. Mt Somers Track (p209)
3. St James Walkway (p213)
4. Avalanche Peak & Goat Pass Track (p219)
5. Harper Pass (Map 1, p223)
6. Harper Pass (Map 2, p224)
7. Harper Pass (Map 3, p225)
8. Cass-Lagoon Saddles Track (p227)
9. Mueller Hut Route (p231)

ship of Akaroa and its beautiful harbour lure in hordes of holidaymakers and cruise-ship passengers, most of whom avail themselves of the town's wine and food and waterside attractions. Relatively few, however, venture on foot into the hills and down into the many tiny inlets. This is a fascinating landscape to explore, but most of it lies beyond the fenceline of the peninsula's many farms.

The first private walk established in NZ, the Banks Peninsula Track takes you across private farmland and forest, and through the remote outer bays of the peninsula. The route takes in a spectacular volcanic coastline, native bush, waterfalls and sandy beaches with two crossings of the crater rim high above Akaroa Harbour.

Other than two steep 600m climbs, this is a leisurely tramp with short daily distances, making it ideal for trampers wishing to take in the marvellous scenery. For the more energetic, cutting the tramp to two days is an option.

History

Maori have occupied the peninsula for centuries. First came the moa hunters, followed by the Waitaha and then the Ngati Mamoe from the North Island. In the 17th century the Ngai Tahu landed at Parakakariki, near Otanerito Bay, and overcame the Ngati Mamoe.

Captain Cook sighted the peninsula in 1770. He named it after naturalist Sir Joseph Banks. Close European contact began in the 1820s, when traders arrived searching for dressed flax, which was used to make sails and rope. In 1836 the British established a whaling station at Peraki.

Two years later French captain Jean Langlois chose the attractive site of Akaroa as a likely spot for French settlement. In 1840 a group of 63 French and six German colonists set out from Rochefort, France, for NZ in the *Comte de Paris*. In 1849 the French land claim was sold to the New Zealand Company and the following year the French were joined by a large group of British settlers. However, the small group of French colonists clearly stamped their mark on this place.

Environment

Banks Peninsula is composed of the remnants of huge twin volcanoes, now attached to the South Island mainland by gravel pushed down from the eroding Southern Alps. It is believed to have once been an island, and was surrounded by a 15km band of swamps and reeds only 150 years ago.

The Lyttelton volcano was already extinct when the Akaroa volcano began to erupt around nine million years ago. Both volcanoes were once much higher; Akaroa is estimated to have peaked at around 1370m. During ice ages, when the sea level was considerably lower, valleys were gouged on the slopes of the volcanoes. When the sea rose, the valleys drowned and the peninsula took its present form, with rugged sea cliffs and skylines studded with basalt plugs.

Once heavily forested, the land has been cleared for timber and farming, making this one of the few areas where trampers pass through paddocks filled with grazing sheep. There is, however, plenty of interesting wildlife to be seen, such as penguins, fur seals and Hector's dolphins. In four days of tramping you could possibly see all three.

Birds of the bush include riflemen, bellbirds, kereru, fantails, tomtits and paradise shelducks. Shore and sea birds are prolific, and include spotted shags, little shags, gulls, terns, oystercatchers, sooty shearwaters and petrels.

ℹ Planning

WHEN TO TRAMP

The season for the track is October to April. The warmest months are December through March, with average temperatures around 21°C maximum and 11°C minimum. A broad-brimmed hat and sunscreen are essential on blue-sky days as it can get very toasty indeed.

MAPS & BROCHURES

As the track is very well signposted, a topographical map is not required. The booklet *Banks Peninsula Track: A Guide to the Route, Natural Features and Human History* (included in the track booking fee) should keep you on course. To get a handle on the entire peninsula, seek out NewTopo *Banks Peninsula* 1:60,000 map.

HUTS, BOOKINGS & INFORMATION

The beauty of this track is that all your accommodation and transport is included in the package. Bookings are essential and should be made through **Banks Peninsula Track** (☑ 06-304 7612; www.banksstrack.co.nz). Tramper numbers are limited, so book early for peak summer and NZ holiday periods.

Accommodation is provided at Trampers' Hut (Onuku Farm), Flea Bay Cottage, track huts at Stony Bay, and a cosy farmhouse at Otanerito Bay.

CANTERBURY, ARTHUR'S PASS & AORAKI/MT COOK BANKS PENINSULA TRACK

The four-day package ($240 to $285) includes transport from Akaroa to Trampers' Hut, hut accommodation, landowners' fees, track registration and a copy of *Banks Peninsula Track: A Guide to the Route, Natural Features and Human History*. A two-day package ($150 to $175) covers the same route, but at a less leisurely pace.

Getting to/from the Tramp

Trampers are picked up from Akaroa old post office at 5.45pm by the Banks Peninsula Track bus. A car park is provided at Mt Vernon Lodge, but you need to allow 30 minutes for the walk to the post office from there.

The Tramp

Day 1: Onuku Farm to Flea Bay Cottage

4–6 HOURS, 11KM

After spending a night in Onuku Farm Trampers' Hut, the day starts near the farm gate, where there is a sign indicating the Banks Peninsula Track. The marked track rises steeply through sheep paddocks, swings east, sidles around a rocky promontory on a ridge and traverses a patch of bush to reach the site of Paradise Farm. Stockyards and exotic trees are all that remain of the farm. From the track there are great views of the harbour and Onuku Farm.

The track swings east, and about 45 minutes from the Onuku Farm gate you come to a prominent track junction on a ridge. To the west is a marked track to a lookout and an alternative route back to Onuku. The main track is indicated by a 'BP Track' sign, which points uphill and to the east. Keep following this track until you come to some park benches overlooking Akaroa Head. There is a side trip from here to a rock-studded knoll on the ridge.

The main track switches back from the benches, crosses an electric fence and aims for the highest point in the area, Trig GG (699m). Observe how the wind has shaped the vegetation here. If you're lucky you may also see Aoraki/Mt Cook 230km away to the west. From the Onuku Farm gate to this point is a solid two-hour climb.

From Trig GG it's a canter down to Eagle's Roost Shelter. The track leads from here to a road junction; Lighthouse Rd goes north to Akaroa, and south to the lighthouse near Akaroa Head. Ignore the road, follow signs to Flea Bay Rd and take that downhill for just over 1km. Watch out for the turn-off (a sharp left fork) to the track, which passes through the Department of Conservation (DOC) Tutakakahikura Scenic Reserve. This patch of remnant red beech has survived the once-extensive logging on this part of the peninsula. Climb the stile where it is signposted and follow the track down a serene gully, eventually joining the main stream, which drains into Flea Bay.

There are a number of signposted cascades and waterfalls along this stretch, all shrouded in tree ferns. About one hour after entering the gully, the track emerges into an open area and drops steeply. Park your backpack here and head off to do some exploring. There is a waterfall that you can walk behind.

The track soon passes through a grove of tree ferns and nikau palms at their southern natural limit. Beyond the palms the track follows the stream on its true left (east) bank for about 1.5km. The track crosses the stream a couple of times before arriving at Flea Bay Cottage, sited within the boundaries of the largest mainland colony of little blue penguins.

Day 2: Flea Bay Cottage to Stony Bay

2½–4 HOURS, 8KM

Head to the beach, then take the road east through the gate and follow the markers up to a stile. Having elegantly negotiated it, you will find yourself heading uphill to circumvent high cliffs on the eastern side of Flea Bay. If you're very lucky you may see Hector's dolphins (one of the world's rarest and smallest) in the waters below.

The track heads southeast to the tip of the headland, rounds it, and then heads northeast to the gully above Island Nook. The remarkable transitions of the tramp now become apparent: one moment there are sheep paddocks, the next ancient forest and then, suddenly, cliffs that seem to form the edge of the world – indeed, the next landfall across the Pacific is South America.

From Island Nook the track sidles along the cliffs to Redcliffe Point, stained by iron oxide. The track heads northeast and crosses a stream before dropping to Seal Cove, about two hours from Flea Bay. The 'Gull and Shag Shelter' here is a good lunch stop with a fantastic view of the great cliff formations and a soundtrack of squealing seabirds and barking fur seals, blubbering around the rocks or curled up asleep in the cave.

Banks Peninsula Track

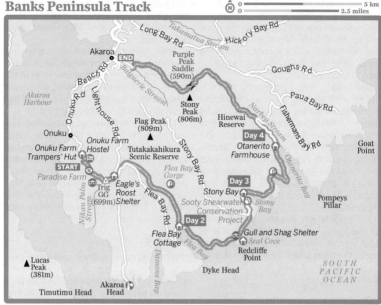

It is quite a steep climb out of Seal Cove to the intersecting ridge between the cave and Stony Bay. From the top of the ridge there are great views across to Pompeys Pillar, on the northern side of Otanerito Bay.

The track passes the **Sooty Shearwater Conservation Project**, protected by a predator-proof fence. This is the last mainland colony of muttonbirds (or titi, as they are known in Maori) in Canterbury; an interpretive display tells the story of this reserve. The track continues past the colony and wends its way steeply down into **Stony Bay**, through coastal scrub.

Idyllic Stony Bay Cottage boasts many welcome features, including two outdoor wood-heated baths, a swing, fresh produce, good hosts and the odd penguin nest. It's a very special spot to spend a night.

Day 3: Stony Bay to Otanerito Farmhouse

2–3 HOURS, 6KM

This is a short day's tramp, but it does involve rounding three prominent headlands on an undulating track.

Immediately after leaving Stony Bay you begin climbing a zigzagging track to avoid the penguin burrows below. The track then sidles southeast to the tip of the headland, rounds it, and then heads down in a northeasterly direction to the stream that empties into Blind Bay.

It repeats this pattern to drop into Sleepy Bay. Where the vehicle track meets the stream it is worthwhile following it upstream for two minutes to view the waterfall.

From the stream the track heads uphill to a point where you can look to the southern side of Sleepy Bay. The track then rounds the third headland of the day. Over the next 2km you descend through a small patch of bush to the beach at the head of **Otanerito Bay** and the old Otanerito Farmhouse.

Day 4: Otanerito Farmhouse to Akaroa

3–5 HOURS, 10KM

Rejoin the track as it leaves the beach to follow the creek northwest up the valley and into Hinewai Reserve. After crossing a road bridge you leave the road, cut over to the true right (west) side of the stream and begin the climb to Purple Peak Saddle.

For nearly the whole climb you are in the 1250-hectare **Hinewai Reserve**, managed privately for the protection and restoration of native vegetation and wildlife. There are more than 30 waterfalls in the reserve's valleys and some can be visited from the track. As you gain altitude the vegetation changes; near its highest point there's a red-beech forest, while lower down there are some ancient kahikatea.

The track is well signposted – which is just as well, because there are a number of alternative routes, especially as you get higher up the valley. You leave the reserve at a stile. Follow the track in a southwesterly direction to **Purple Peak Saddle** (590m), south of Purple Peak and two hours from Otanerito Farmhouse. Stony Bay Peak (806m) is almost due south, Akaroa Harbour is to the west and Otanerito Bay to the southeast.

The track snakes downhill from the saddle and joins a vehicle track before arriving at Mt Vernon, which is the official end of the tramp. Continue along the vehicle track for about 30 minutes, joining Stony Bay Rd into Akaroa.

Mt Somers Track

Duration 2 days

Distance 25.5km (15.8 miles)

Track Standard Easy tramping track

Difficulty Moderate

Start/End Sharplin Falls car park

Nearest Towns Staveley (p209), Mt Somers (p209), Methven (p234)

Transport Shuttle bus

Summary This track circles the subalpine area around Mt Somers, and features great views and refreshing pools to soothe tired legs at the end of the day.

Mt Somers Track is a loop circling Mt Somers (Te Kiekie; 1687m), providing access to the spectacular subalpine country of the Mt Somers Conservation Area. It is only an hour's drive from Christchurch and, best of all, you can now finish where you began without backtracking.

The track officially opened in 1987. It was founded upon the Mt Somers Subalpine Walkway, a popular 17km tramp from Woolshed Creek car park to Sharplin Falls car park built by the Mount Somers Walkway Society. Subsequent additions have included the South Face Route, a high-altitude seven-hour tramp from Woolshed Creek

Hut back to Sharplin Falls, and the 26-bunk Woolshed Creek Hut. Mt Somers Track now qualifies as one of NZ's classic alpine adventures.

Note that the South Face Route is very exposed to cold southerly winds. Be prepared for such weather! The best way to walk the circuit is anticlockwise around the mountain, allowing you to lay over at a hut if bad weather descends on the area.

The Sharplin Falls car park is the best starting point for those planning to tramp the entire circuit. Such a tramp involves two long days of walking, and is recommended for experienced and well-prepared trampers. If you arrive late at Sharplin Falls, plan on a three-day tramp, spending the first night at Pinnacles Hut, a three-hour walk from the car park.

History

Maori came here to hunt moa more than 500 years ago, burning the forest and ground cover as they searched for their prey. The path followed by SH72 near Alford Forest is believed to have been used by these seasonal hunting parties.

There are plenty of signs of modern human occupation and exploitation in this area. Saw milling was instrumental in the development of the Staveley area, with logging teams extracting native trees by bullock cart before milling and transporting them down to the Canterbury settlements for house-building.

From the mid-1800s a number of coalmines sprung up, two of which – McClimonts and Blackburn – are near Woolshed Creek. The latter was the last mine to close, in 1960.

Environment

While much of the mid-Canterbury area is composed of greywacke, Mt Somers betrays its relatively recent volcanic activity through the presence of hard rhyolite rock. Its impressive rock formations include some toothy pinnacles that are irresistible to rock climbers.

A highlight of the walkway is the number of latitudinal plant sequences trampers pass through. Bog species proliferate because of the infertile soil and poor drainage. These are easily seen in Slaughterhouse Gully. Lower down, in both Woolshed Creek and the lower reaches of Bowyers Stream, there are well-preserved remnants of the beech forests that covered mid-Canterbury before

Mt Somers Track

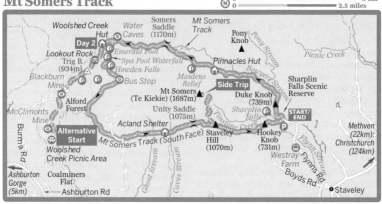

burning, milling and pastoralism. Mountain and black beech are found in Sharplin Falls Scenic Reserve, where there is a sub-canopy of broad-leaved trees and southern rata on the rocky outcrops. The ancient forest in Woolshed Creek is silver beech.

ⓘ Planning

WHEN TO TRAMP

With a good portion of the walking time spent in open alpine country, this track is best tramped from November to March.

MAPS & BROCHURES

Maps for this tramp are NZTopo50 *BX19* (Hakatere) and *BX20* (Methven). The *Mt Somers Track* brochure can be downloaded from DOC's website or obtained from visitor centres.

HUTS

There are two huts on the tramp: Pinnacles Hut is a **Standard hut** (www.doc.govt.nz; $5) and Woolshed Creek Hut is a **Serviced hut** (www.doc.govt.nz; $15). Acland Shelter on the South Face Route is not designed for overnight stays. You can purchase hut tickets at Methven i-SITE, the Staveley Store or Mt Somers General Store.

INFORMATION SOURCES

The **Methven i-SITE** (☑03-302 8955; www.methveninfo.co.nz; 160 Main St; ☉9am-5pm) stocks DOC brochures and hut tickets, and can advise on track transport and local accommodation.

ⓘ Towns & Facilities

The track starting points can be reached from the tiny settlements of Staveley or Mt Somers, 24km and 33km respectively from the nearest decent-sized town, Methven.

Staveley (population 120) is 4km from the Sharplin Falls car park, at the start of this tramp. For information, hut tickets and supplies, head to the **Staveley Store** (☑03-303 0859; SH72; ☉9am-5pm), which also doubles as a cafe with good food.

Mt Somers (population 100) is just off SH72, 13km from Woolshed Creek picnic area. For supplies and hut tickets there's **Mt Somers General Store** (☑03-303 9831; Pattons Rd; ☉8am-6pm Mon-Sat, 9am-5pm Sun). If the store doesn't have what you need, well, you probably don't really need it! **Mt Somers Holiday Park** (☑03-303 9719; www.mountsomers.co.nz; Hoods Rd; sites from $22, cabins $54-79) is small and well maintained. Across the street from the Domain is **Mt Somers Tavern** (☑03-303 9879; Hoods Rd) with meals, a pub and a bottle shop. Mt Somers is little more than a one-hour drive from Christchurch via Methven. There is no public transport to the town.

ⓘ Getting to/from the Tramp

The Sharplin Falls car park is 4km northwest of Staveley at the end of Flynns Rd. The Woodshed Creek car park is closest to Mt Somers: follow Ashburton Gorge Rd for 10.5km and turn right onto Jig Rd.

Methven Travel (☑03-302 8106, 0800 684 888; www.methventravel.co.nz) will drop you off or pick you up at either end of the track from Methven (per person one/two people $55/30).

If you have your own vehicle the best way to arrange transport is a shuttle from Staveley. **Westray Farm** (☑03-303 0809), located only 2km from the Sharplin Falls car park, will shuttle you to the trailhead and return your car to secure parking while you're tramping (per car $30).

🚶 The Tramp

Day 1: Sharplin Falls Car Park to Woolshed Creek Hut

6–7 HOURS, 12KM

From the car park you begin with the sign-posted **Sharplin Falls Track**. Follow it along Bowyers Stream for five minutes, before departing onto **Mt Somers Track** and climbing steeply to **Duke Knob** (739m), a rhyolite outcrop reached in 45 minutes. A short detour from the track leads to the knob and its panoramic views of the beech forest below and the plains further afield.

Beyond Duke Knob, skirt a ridge and then drop steeply to **Bowyers Stream**. Be careful sidling around the slip reached just before crossing **Pony Stream**. On the other side the track passes through a small flat, and then crosses to the true right (south) bank of Bowyers Stream via a swing bridge.

Once on the other side you follow Bowyers Stream, staying on the true right bank (south) while climbing around a number of bluffs. Eventually the track leaves the stream and climbs One Tree Ridge for one hour before reaching Slaughterhouse Gully and Pinnacles Hut (20 bunks), complete with potbelly stove and water supply. The hut is a three-hour tramp and a 470m climb from the car park (or two hours from Somers Saddle for those coming in the opposite direction).

From the hut the track skirts a rocky outcrop and enters subalpine scrub as it gradually works its way closer to the vertical north face of **Mt Somers** (1687m). Within one hour, about halfway to the saddle, you pass beneath a bath-shaped rock pool at the foot of a small waterfall. This is **Maidens Relief**, and it makes for a pleasant place to rest and enjoy the view of Mt Winterslow (1700m) across the valley.

The track continues to the head of the valley, passing through tussock and subalpine scrub, and becoming a 4WD track before rising to Somers Saddle. At 1170m, this is the highest point of the circuit and is reached two hours from Pinnacles Hut. If the weather is clear you are rewarded with vistas of the Mt Winterslow, Old Man and Taylor Ranges, although the saddle is often covered in cloud.

Continue west along the 4WD track as it makes a steady descent. After 1.5km you begin skirting a branch of Morgan Stream and then cross the small creek to its true left (south) side. Within 10 or 15 minutes you pass a side track that can be followed back down to the stream to view the **Water Caves**, impressive rock formations carved by the strong current.

Eventually the 4WD track reaches Morgan Stream and you cross it at a well-marked ford. Just downstream from here is a pleasant spot that is often used as a campsite. On the other side you follow the 4WD track as it climbs a ridge and then descends to Woolshed Creek. Directly across the creek is your hut for the night. Built in 2006, Woolshed Creek Hut (26 bunks) replaced the classic Mt Somers Hut, which had separate sleeping quarters for trampers and musterers.

There are great soaking opportunities nearby. Cross Woolshed Creek and follow the track downstream (south) to **Spa Pool Waterfall**, via a ladder. This impressive cascade drops straight into a deep and wonderful pool at the confluence of Woolshed Creek and Morgan Stream. A little further up Morgan Stream is **Emerald Pool**.

ALTERNATIVE START: WOOLSHED CREEK CAR PARK TO WOOLSHED CREEK HUT

2–3 HOURS, 5KM

The original 17km alpine crossing from Woolshed Creek to Sharplin Falls is an easier tramp than the circuit, and avoids the exposed areas on the southern flanks of Mt Somers. Arranging transport to and from each trailhead is more of a logistical challenge, but you get an opportunity to view the mines and mining artefacts that litter this segment of track.

From the picnic area, the track begins as a level nature walk up the true right (west) side of Woolshed Creek. Within 10 minutes you pass a crumpled coal car still sitting on its rails below the site of **McClimonts Mine**, and 30 minutes from the start you arrive at the area known as the jig. Here you'll find the remains of a jig line and a hopper, which were used to transport coal from Blackburn Mine down the steep hill to wagons on the Mt Somers branch railway. As each full hopper hurtled to the bottom of the jig, the momentum pulled an empty one to the top. Interpretive displays here cover the history of the operation in detail.

Beyond the jig, follow a segment known as Miners Track. The jig was too dangerous for workers to use, so they began each day by climbing to the Blackburn Mine along this track. You climb steeply through the trees for 15 minutes and then break out into a subalpine setting with views of the surrounding mountains. One hour from the car park you arrive at the well-preserved site of **Blackburn Mine**.

From the mine, the track follows Burma Rd briefly then veers off northeast at a well-signposted junction. You climb steeply along an open ridge and, about 40 minutes from Blackburn Mine, reach **Trig R** (934m). The final 15 minutes of this climb is stunning, with panoramic views of distant Arrowsmith Range and Upper Ashburton Gorge. The magnificent vista from the trig includes the Manuka Range, the glaciated U-shaped Stour Valley, and, across to the east, Mt Somers.

Take the signposted track to the north, which leads to another great vantage point known as **Lookout Rock**, where there are views of the new Woolshed Creek Hut on the western bank of Woolshed Creek. From there, it's a fast descent to the stream, passing Spa Pool Waterfall along the way and reaching the hut 30 minutes from Trig R.

Day 2: Woolshed Creek Hut to Sharplin Falls Car Park via South Face Track

7–8 HOURS, 13.5KM

This can be a long day along an exposed route, although the Acland Shelter provides welcome relief around the halfway point. If in doubt about the weather, stay put or tramp out to Woolshed Creek car park.

Begin by crossing the bridge across Woolshed Creek directly in front of the hut, and then follow the track signs to Emerald Pool on Morgan Stream. Cross the stream and continue up a dry ridge with sparse subalpine vegetation, before descending through beech forest to Trifalls Stream. Just after crossing the stream there is a signposted track that heads upstream to **Howden Falls**. This five-minute side trip ends at the highest-elevation falls in the Mt Somers Conservation Area.

From Trifalls Stream, the track steadily climbs a scrub-and-tussock ridge before topping off at the **Bus Stop**. At 1150m, this rock formation of colourful rhyolite has been a welcome sight for many trampers who need a place to wait out bad weather (thus its name). In clear conditions you can linger here, enjoying great views of the upper catchment of Woolshed Creek, the Taylor Range, and even as far west as the Arrowsmith Range.

Make a rapid descent from the Bus Stop to Moses Stream and, after crossing the small creek, climb out of the gully to tussock-covered flats. The nearly flat terrace is an extensive area of fragile red tussock and care must be taken not to leave the track and further damage these wetlands. It takes 30 minutes to cross the flats to the well-signposted junction for the **Mt Somers Track (South Face)**, reached 4km (two to 2½ hours) from Woolshed Creek Hut. The track that heads west (right) is the Rhyolite Ridge Track, which reaches the Woolshed Creek car park within one hour.

The South Face Track continues southeast from the junction and quickly descends to Chapmans Creek. After crossing the creek, you sidle across the valley slope and then cross a low saddle (940m) to merge onto an old 4WD track, reached within an hour of the junction. This track heads downhill for 500m until it reaches the bush edge.

Depart the 4WD track as the South Face Track enters mountain beech forest and descends to cross the first of five gullies, all of which are tributaries of **Ghost Stream** and Stony Creek. Marker poles clearly define the route across the ridges between the forested gullies, where you maintain an altitude of around 900m beneath the impressive south face of Mt Somers. The sight of Acland Shelter will be very welcome during inclement weather.

Finally, one hour from the saddle, you descend to the bush and cross **Caves Stream**. At the stream, a well-formed track climbs steadily through mountain beech forest and in 30 minutes breaks out briefly into subalpine scrub on **Unity Saddle** (1075m). After re-entering the bush the track sidles around a small gully and two avalanche chutes, and then merges into the Mt Somers Summit Track. From this junction it is less than 10 minutes down to Staveley Hill (1070m). It's 2.5km (about a 1½-hour walk) from Caves Stream to Staveley Hill.

On the final leg of the circuit the track steadily descends the ridgeline of Staveley Hill, through subalpine and manuka scrub, and finally reaches a small grass clearing at the bushline, where you enjoy your last view of the Canterbury Plains. You then descend to the bush, pass **Hookey Knob** (731m) and continue a steady descent until you reach the Sharplin Falls car park, 3km (1½ hours) from Staveley Hill.

SIDE TRIP: MT SOMERS SUMMIT
2–3 HOURS, 2KM RETURN, 617M ASCENT

By Staveley Hill is a signposted junction for the Mt Somers Summit Track, a climb to the top of Mt Somers. The summit track is a well-marked and poled track that climbs west through subalpine scrub to quickly reach the tree line. The climb then gets steeper as the track works its way across a scree face, before emerging on a ridge, where a small, flat area makes for an ideal place to catch your breath and enjoy the views.

Track poles continue up the ridge, in what is the steepest part of the climb. Care is essential, especially if conditions are windy. A small flat area is reached at 1500m, and then you endure a final steep climb before reaching the summit ridge. The actual summit is not marked by the trig station at 1687m, but is at the Millennium Marker and plane table – 100m further west on the flat summit – where you can sign your name in the book and enjoy 360-degree views of the peaks shown on the plane table.

If you're coming from the Sharplin Falls car park, the tramp to the summit is a five-hour (5km) trek that climbs 1245m, with a four-hour return. No matter where you begin, this is a demanding climb for physically fit trampers with experience in NZ's mountains. The route is exposed to the south, and cold, wet or snowy weather can sweep in very quickly. Even in fine weather, waterproof clothing must be carried, along with plenty of water, as there is none on the track.

St James Walkway

Duration 5 days

Distance 65km (40 miles)

Track Standard Easy tramping track

Difficulty Easy to moderate

Start Lewis Pass

End Boyle Village

Nearest Towns Hanmer Springs (p234), Christchurch (p232)

Transport Shuttle bus, bus

Summary The first walkway to be established in a subalpine area, this tramp features open river valleys, two passes and great mountain scenery.

Built in 1981, the St James Walkway begins in the Lewis Pass National Reserve, traverses the western side of the St James Conservation Area, and ends in the Lake Sumner Forest Park. Despite being the longest walkway in the country and taking in two mountain passes – Ada Pass (1008m) and Anne Saddle (1136m) – it's not particularly challenging. The climbs are not steep, and the rest of the walk is spent tramping through open river valleys and beech forests.

The walkway follows historic pack tracks, is well benched and has an excellent series of huts. The heart of the track, from Ada River along Anne River to upper Boyle River, runs through St James Conservation Area. Vegetation within the area includes red, mountain and silver beech forests; manuka/kanuka and matagouri scrublands; numerous alpine species; at least five species of tussock; and a vast expanse of valley-floor native grasslands. It is also home to some 430 indigenous species of flora and 30 native bird species.

History

Although this region was only sparsely settled, Maori did pass along a portion of the St James Walkway, it having proven a popular route from the West Coast to Canterbury. Ngati Tumatakokiri, the most powerful tribe to use the route, were constantly warring with a rival tribe, Ngai Tahu. This rivalry peaked in a particularly nasty manner when Ngati Tumatakokiri trapped and massacred a Ngai Tahu party in a gorge along the Maruia River. Hence the name of Cannibal Gorge, a feature of the track.

Opened in November 1981, the St James became the first walkway to be established in a subalpine area; it's named after the historic sheep station through which it runs. Dating back to 1862, St James Station was one of NZ's largest sheep and cattle stations. It was purchased by the government in 2008 to protect its natural, physical and cultural values, and to open it up for recreation. With the exception of a breeding herd of wild horses, all livestock have since been removed.

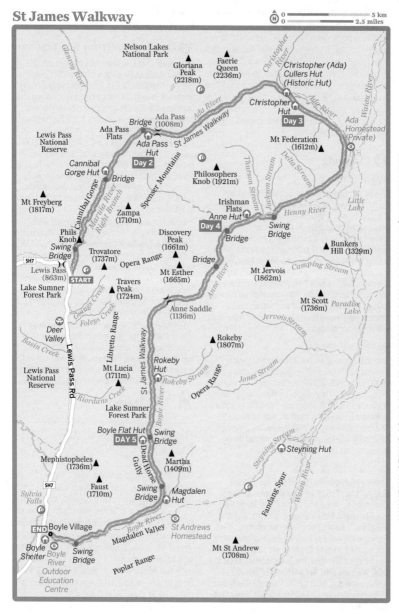

Environment

St James Walkway passes through a mix of flats, forests and subalpine regions. At times you'll be passing through the grassy meadows and rocky paddocks of some of the most remote high-country stations in NZ.

Much of the tramp, however, will be spent in beech forest. Silver and red beech are common up to 950m, and mountain beech, found on higher slopes, is dominant in dry country such as Ada Pass.

The upper Ada Valley is particularly interesting, as it features flats, forests and subalpine areas, all within a few kilometres, which in turn support numerous species of birds. The area is known for its thriving population of South Island robins. Trampers may also spot paradise ducks, tomtits, pipits, long-tailed cuckoos and possibly even kea, among others.

ℹ Planning

WHEN TO TRAMP

The St James traverses a subalpine area on the main divide of the Southern Alps, making it prone to extremely changeable weather, flooding and avalanches. Heavy rain and even snow can occur at almost any time of the year, even in the middle of summer. The best time to tramp the St James is November to April, with the warmest months January and February, and the most settled weather from late February through March. During these periods be sure to bring a wide-brimmed hat and sunscreen, as the track is very exposed in places. Insect repellent will prove handy, too.

MAPS & BROCHURES

The most detailed coverage for this track is provided by NZTopo50 maps *BT23* (Lewis), *BT24* (Ada Flat) and *BU23* (Boyle Village). The tramp is also covered in its entirety by NewTopo *St James Walkway* 1:75,000. There are two DOC brochures available from visitor centres and its website: *St James Walkway*, and *St James Conservation Area*, which detail various other recreational pursuits.

HUTS & LODGES

The walkway has five **Serviced huts** (www. doc.govt.nz; $15): Cannibal Gorge, Ada Pass, Christopher, Anne and Boyle Flats. Magdalen is a **Standard hut** (www.doc.govt.nz; $5) and Rokeby is a **Basic hut** (www.doc.govt.nz; free). During peak holiday periods you might want to carry a tent, in case the huts are full. Hut tickets can be obtained from the Hanmer i-SITE (p235), **DOC Waimakariri Area Office** (☑ 03-313 0820; www.doc.govt.nz; 32 River Rd, Rangiora; ⊙ 8am-5pm Mon-Fri) and the **Boyle River Outdoor Education Centre** (☑ 03-315 7082; www. boyle.org.nz; SH7), which often has backpacker accommodation available ($28).

INFORMATION SOURCES

The **DOC Christchurch Visitor Centre** (☑ 03-341 9113; www.doc.govt.nz; Botanic Gardens, via Armagh St car park; ⊙ 9am-4pm Mon-Fri, 10.15am-4pm Sat & Sun) offers all necessary DOC services and resources, including track bookings, hut tickets, maps and advice.

ℹ Getting to/from the Tramp

Both ends of the walkway are located off SH7, which crosses Lewis Pass from north Canterbury to the West Coast. Transport to and from the track is easy, because bus drivers along the highway are used to dropping off – and being flagged down by – trampers. It's a 15-minute drive between the ends of the track.

East West Coaches (☑ 03-789 6251, 0800 142 622; eastwestcoaches@xtra.co.nz) provides drop-offs at both the track start and finish on its Westport to Christchurch route, with services running daily only when seasonal demand dictates it. It's $44 from Christchurch to the track start, and $37 from Westport.

From Hanmer Springs, it may be possible to arrange transport to the trailheads with **Hanmer Springs Adventure Centre** (☑ 0800 368 7386, 03-315 7233; www.hanmeradventure.co.nz), depending on its workload.

Nelson Lakes Shuttles (p191) runs between Nelson and St Arnaud (Nelson Lakes National Park) to the St James (either trailhead) for $110 per person (minimum five people).

Trampers with their own vehicles can avail themselves of the services of Boyle River Outdoor Education Centre, near the southern end of the track. They will drop you off in your car at the track start ($26), then return your car to Boyle where it is stored until your return ($7 per day).

🏃 The Tramp

Day 1: Lewis Pass to Ada Pass Hut

5 HOURS, 10KM

Follow the Tarn Nature Walk from the car park, passing a beautiful tarn that, on a still day, reflects the surrounding mountains. The nature walk leads you right onto the St James Walkway, which heads northeast. You begin with a climb into beech forest, followed by a steep descent that drops 170m, and after 30 minutes reach a swing bridge over the **Maruia River Right Branch**. From the middle of the bridge you can peer into the start of **Cannibal Gorge**.

On the true right (west) bank of the gorge the track begins the longest climb of the day, topping out in 30 minutes at Phils Knob, where you can enjoy a sweeping view of the rugged valley below. You continue to sidle the side of the gorge, climbing in and out of numerous gullies, some posted as avalanche chutes.

Eventually you descend to a footbridge across the river, three hours (6km) from the car park, with Cannibal Gorge Hut (20 bunks) just another 15 to 20 minutes away. The hut is a nice facility on the edge of a grassy meadow and is a good choice if you arrive late at Lewis Pass.

Beyond the hut the track follows the Maruia River, and in 20 to 30 minutes you're rewarded with your first alpine scene when you emerge from the beech forest into a meadow dominated to the north by **Gloriana Peak** (2218m). To the south you can see much of the valley you just passed through. The track climbs a bush-clad terrace and stays above the Maruia River – now a rushing stream – for 30 minutes before descending into **Ada Pass Flats**, with peaks above it and a bridge at its end.

Cross the stream and within five minutes (1½ hours from Cannibal Gorge Hut) you arrive at Ada Pass Hut (14 bunks). This hut is not quite as roomy as Cannibal Gorge, but the mountain views from its porch and windows are much better.

Day 2: Ada Pass Hut to Christopher Hut

4–5 HOURS, 10.5KM

This is an easy and short day, but don't rush it. Linger if the weather is fine, for the alpine scenery is the best of any along the walkway.

The track departs from the eastern side of the hut, and after around 10 to 15 minutes it begins a gentle ascent to **Ada Pass** (1008m), fording the Maruia River Right Branch (by now more of a creek) along the way. The bush-clad pass is recognisable by the large sign announcing that the saddle is 998m – despite what maps list – and it marks the border between **Lewis Pass National Reserve** and **St James Conservation Area**. The walkway then proceeds to descend into **Ada Valley** along the true right (south) side of the Ada River, and within one hour breaks out into a large tussock grassland crowned by the craggy peak of **Faerie Queen** (2236m), which is often accented with freshly fallen snow. It is but one highlight of this valley track that affords breathtaking views as it passes in and out of the forest.

Orange-tipped poles lead you almost 2km across the grassland to where the track resumes in beech forest. You stay in the forest for one hour (3.5km) but three times break out into small meadows; the second one provides a view up rugged Camera Gully

to the north. Two hours from Ada Pass the track emerges from beech forest to reach the wide expanse of the St James Conservation Area. The flats (and the track) swing southeast at the confluence of the Ada River and Christopher River.

For the rest of the day the track switches between crossing grassy river flats and climbing onto the forested ridge to avoid slips along the river. If the day is nice and the water levels normal, you can simply follow the flats, crossing the river at will until you spot Christopher Hut.

About 1km (15 minutes) before reaching that hut, the track passes **Christopher (Ada) Cullers Hut** (four bunks), which is maintained as a historic hut. Built in 1956 for deer hunters, this hut is now more a monument to the old New Zealand Forest Service than a place to stay. The roomier Christopher Hut (14 bunks) has good views of the mountains surrounding the Waiau Valley. You may see a herd of wild horses grazing here.

Day 3: Christopher Hut to Anne Hut

4–5 HOURS, 13KM

This day is spent almost entirely on open river flats, which means lots of sun and very little shade in summer.

Leaving Christopher Hut, you cut across grassy flats along the true right bank of the Ada River for almost 2km, without getting close to any trees. Moving into some scrub you follow the river closely around Federation Corner as it heads for its confluence with the **Waiau River**. It takes 1½ hours (4km) to round the corner. Much of the time you're skirting the base of **Mt Federation** (1612m), occasionally climbing into the bush to avoid slips and steep drop-offs. Halfway around you can see the privately owned **Ada Homestead** complex on the opposite side of the river. This used to be St James Station's operational base.

Once in Henry Valley, you cross grassy terraces for the next 4km, at times following a 4WD track. The track keeps to the lower slopes of Mt Federation, through matagouri thickets, and eventually sidles up a bush-clad terrace before descending to a long swing bridge across the **Henry River**. Once on the true right (south) bank, the track merges again with the 4WD track and gently climbs to **Irishman Flats**, a long grassy terrace, and the site of Anne Hut (20 bunks).

From the flats, there are excellent views up the Henry Valley and into an amphitheatre in the **Spenser Mountains**. The best viewing spot is the top of a grassy knoll, which the track passes five minutes beyond the hut. Another herd of wild horses is often present in this area.

Day 4: Anne Hut to Boyle Flat Hut

6–7 HOURS, 17KM

The longest day of the walkway is split between tramping over grassy flats and climbing through beech forest. The day begins with a descent along a 4WD track to a footbridge across the **Anne River**. Crossing grassy flats, the track climbs a bush-clad spur to a second footbridge across Anne River, 4km from the hut. On the true right (east) side you return to more grassy meadows and follow the valley as it swings west towards Anne Saddle.

The climb to the saddle is remarkably mild, with only a steep pitch through the forest at the very end. Two to three hours (8km) from Anne Hut you reach **Anne Saddle** (1136m), which despite being the highest point of the tramp is a spot with no views. The 30-minute descent from the saddle is steep, dropping 210m over almost 2km. You bottom out at the **Boyle River** in a steep wooded valley. Follow Boyle River for the next 3.5km, remaining on its true left (east) side. At several points the track climbs high above the river to avoid flood conditions. If the water level is normal, it is far easier and quicker to ford the river and continue along its banks.

At one point, 6km from the saddle, you pass a 'Flood Track' sign that leads you up a steep embankment to a scenic grassy terrace and Rokeby Hut (three bunks). This hut is in the best shape of all the old ones, and has canvas cots. It would be a great place to stay if you're not in a hurry to catch the bus the next day.

Near the hut a bridge leads over Rokeby Stream, from where the flood track keeps you in the forest a bit longer before you descend to the grassy valley floor. You remain in open terrain for the final hour (3.5km), which ends with a swing-bridge crossing over the Boyle River, with Boyle Flat Hut (14 bunks) on the true right (west) side of an area that isn't actually that flat.

Day 5: Boyle Flat Hut to Boyle Village

4 HOURS, 14.5KM

This final section is along a well-benched track and is listed by DOC as 14.5km – though it seems much shorter. Most trampers have few problems reaching the SH7 in four hours, especially if they need to catch a bus elsewhere.

Even though there is a bit more climbing, the start of this day is a refreshing change from walking across the river flats. After recrossing the swing bridge you quickly enter cool forest and find yourself on the edge of the steep Boyle River Gorge, well above the river. Signposted **Dead Horse Gully** is reached within 15 minutes, where upon a peek over the edge justifies its name.

It takes one hour (3km) to traverse the gorge and descend to the river's edge at a swing bridge. If you ignore the bridge and continue along the true left (east) side of the river, a track leads to Magdalen Hut (six bunks), 1km away (20 minutes).

Cross the bridge instead, and follow the track on the true right (west) side down into **Magdalen Valley**. Within 1km you enter the valley to see the open pastoral land of Glenhope Station, and the **St Andrews Homestead** on the opposite side of the Boyle River. The next 8km stretch stays on the northern side of the Boyle, passing through patches of bush and climbing around a number of small gorges and slips. The walking is easy and fast, and eventually the track descends to a swing bridge.

From the other side of the bridge you have 2.5km to walk, starting with the day's longest climb. The track ends at a car park, where there are toilets and a gravel road leading past the Boyle River Outdoor Education Centre (p214). Just beyond the centre is SH7 and Boyle Shelter for those waiting for a bus.

ARTHUR'S PASS NATIONAL PARK

Arthur's Pass National Park lies 154km northwest of Christchurch, straddling both sides of the Southern Alps, known to Maori as Ka Tiritiri o te Moana ('steep peak of glistening white'). Of its 1148 sq km, two-thirds lie on the Canterbury side of the Main Divide and the rest is in Westland. It is a rugged, mountainous area, cut by deep valleys, and ranging in altitude from 245m at the Taramakau River to 2408m at Mt Murchison.

There are plenty of well-marked and popular day walks, especially around Arthur's Pass village. Longer trips, however, are largely confined to valley routes with saddle climbs in between. Cut tracks are usually provided only when necessary and much of the time you will be boulder-hopping along, or in, riverbeds. Most streams are unbridged, and the weather is changeable, so common sense is an essential companion in this territory.

The park's most famous one-day tramp, Avalanche Peak, offers views so staggering (on a clear day, that is) that the track seriously challenges the Tongariro Alpine Crossing as NZ's greatest day walk. Goat Pass Track is a good choice for trampers new to pass-hopping and following routes, while the Cass-Lagoon Saddles Track and Harper Pass are easier tramps at the edge of the national park.

History

Maori often made their way through this mountain pass on the way to mine the highly prized *pounamu* (greenstone) of the West Coast. On the return journey, however, they preferred alternative passes as they provided easier ascents and more favourably positioned food sources.

In September 1857 Edward Dobson travelled up the Hurunui River as far as Harper Pass, and possibly into the Taramakau Valley, before turning back. However, it was 20-year-old Leonard Harper who, in the same year, became the first European to cross the swampy saddle and descend the Taramakau River to reach the West Coast.

Edward Dobson didn't get a pass named after him but his son, Arthur, did. In March 1864 23-year-old Arthur Dobson and his 18-year-old brother Edward journeyed up the Bealey Valley, crossed what is now Arthur's Pass, and descended a short distance into Otira Gorge. Another of Arthur's brothers, George, was later commissioned to find the best route from Canterbury to the West Coast goldfields, and it was George who first referred to the pass as 'Arthur's Pass'.

After gold was gleaned from the West Coast, a rush saw around 4000 people pour over Harper Pass between February and April 1865. However, the poor condition of the pass intensified efforts of Christchurch citizens to build a dray road through the mountains. Work began on the Arthur's Pass road, and by 1866 the first coach drove from one side of the South Island to the other.

The Otira rail tunnel was completed in 1923. The next year alpine train excursions began, and became so popular that 1600 day-trippers from Christchurch poured into tiny Arthur's Pass village in a single day. Alarmed at visitors removing plants and cutting trees for firewood, residents began petitioning the government to turn the area into a national park. In 1929 Arthur's Pass became NZ's third national park, behind Tongariro and Egmont.

A most significant man-made feature of the park is undoubtedly the Otira Viaduct, opened in 1999. This impressive engineering feat soars above the steep gorge and tight zigzags of the old road called the Devils Staircase. Be sure to stop at the lookout if you can.

Environment

The Main Divide marks a sharp contrast in the park's ecology. The western side is very wet, with Otira averaging 5000mm of rain a year. Bealey Spur, on the eastern side, averages about 1500mm.

As one might imagine, this has quite some effect on the park's flora. The Westland slopes, with their higher rainfall and milder temperatures, are covered with lush forests of tall podocarp and, higher up, kamahi, rata and totara. On the eastern side is mountain beech forest with less understorey and drier conditions on the forest floor. The thick bush on the park's western side also contains more bird life; commonly seen are the tui, bellbird, tomtit, rifleman and grey warbler.

The bird to watch out for, literally, is the kea. This highly intelligent and naturally inquisitive alpine parrot searches huts for food, or just for amusement. Its most notorious traits are stealing food or shiny objects (including knives and car keys), dissecting boots and backpacks, and airing sleeping bags with its strong, curved bill. It's an entertaining bird, however, sighted often above the tree line and frequently in the village itself. Tempting as it may be, do not feed the kea as it encourages them to try new foods, often with fatal consequences.

ℹ Planning

WHEN TO TRAMP

The Arthur's Pass mountains not only attract bad weather, they create it, so expect to encounter conditions colder, windier and wetter than the lowlands either side. The most unsettled weather occurs in spring and autumn. Heavy rain is common in November and early December, resulting in impassable rivers. All but low-level tramps should be avoided in winter.

All the tramps in the area are best undertaken from November to March, with the best weather generally encountered in February and March. Note, though, that it's never going to get that hot, with an average maximum for Arthur's Pass in February of 17.5°C.

Be very wary of setting off before, after or during heavy rain, and in strong winds or when low cloud is hanging around. Check in at the DOC Arthur's Pass Visitor Centre to check the latest forecast and get a second opinion.

WHAT TO BRING

Pack rain gear and warm clothing whenever you embark on a tramp in the park, especially if you are heading above the bushline. The saddles and ridges will likely be cold and windy no matter how blue the sky.

MAPS & BROCHURES

With broad coverage and sufficient detail, NewTopo *Arthur's Pass* 1:55,000 is ideal for trip planning. For safe navigation you can purchase the requisite NZTopo50 maps at the Arthur's Pass Visitor Centre, where you can also obtain DOC's *Discover Arthur's Pass* brochure, an excellent and comprehensive guide to the park.

INFORMATION SOURCES

DOC Arthur's Pass Visitor Centre (☑ 03-318 9211; www.doc.govt.nz; SH73; ⊙ 8am-5pm Oct-Apr, 8.30pm-4.30pm May-Sep) houses the DOC field centre. It can advise on all park tramps, sells Topo maps and hut tickets, hires locator beacons and issues updates on the savagely changeable weather. It doesn't make onward bookings or reservations, but can help with local accommodation and transport. There are interesting information displays, including a 17-minute video on the history of the area.

If you're coming from Christchurch, the DOC Christchurch Visitor Centre (p214) also offers all necessary DOC services and resources, including track bookings, hut tickets, maps and advice. The DOC Waimakariri Area Office (p214), 29km north of Christchurch, is a handy stop if you're heading to the park from the north on SH1.

Avalanche Peak

Duration 6 to 8 hours

Distance 7km (4.3 miles)

Track Standard Tramping track

Difficulty Moderate

Start/End Arthur's Pass

Nearest Town Arthur's Pass (p235)

Transport None

Summary This popular loop track clambers to the 1833m summit of Avalanche Peak, which dramatically looms over Arthur's Pass village. On a clear day the views of the surrounding peaks, valleys and hanging glaciers are wonderful.

In this park of peaks, Avalanche Peak is without question the most popular one to climb. Its location is ideal, looming directly above the village and just south of Mt Rolleston. The route begins and ends right in the village, eliminating any need for special transport.

The alpine world experienced during this tramp is stunning on a clear day. Many experienced trampers will vouch that this is in fact NZ's best day tramp, outshining the dramatic volcanic peaks and steamy vents of the Tongariro Alpine Crossing.

Unequivocal is the fact that Avalanche Peak is an alpine climb that should only be attempted by the fleet of foot in good conditions. The total climb and descent is almost 1100m, and although the route is clearly marked and well trodden, it's still an arduous climb with a climax of 200m worth of narrow, crumbly ridge. People have died on Avalanche Peak when they failed to heed weather warnings.

Two routes, Avalanche Peak Track and Scotts Track, depart from SH73 and lead towards the peak, merging just before reaching it. Avalanche Peak Track is a much steeper climb, and at times you need to scramble up rock faces. Scotts Track is a more gradual and easier route. It's best to use Avalanche Peak Track to reach the summit and Scotts Track for the return, when your legs will be tired. Of course, the easiest return route to the peak is to simply use Scotts Track both ways, but you won't loop the loop.

Avalanche Peak & Goat Pass Track

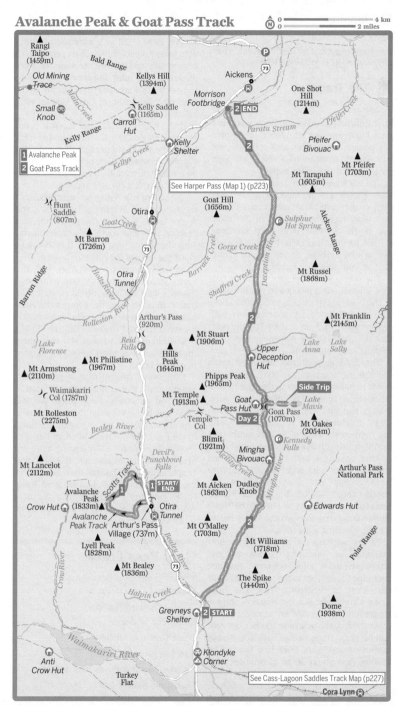

0 —————————— 4 km
0 —————————— 2 miles

Rangi Taipo (1459m)

Bald Range

Kellys Hill (1394m)

Aickens

P

73

Old Mining Trace

Main Creek

Kelly Saddle (1165m)

Carroll Hut

Morrison Footbridge

2 END

2

One Shot Hill (1214m)

Paratu Stream

PfeiferCreek

Small Knob

Kelly Range

Kelly Shelter

Pfeifer Bivouac

Mt Pfeifer (1703m)

1 Avalanche Peak
2 Goat Pass Track

Kellys Creek

See Harper Pass (Map 1) (p223)

Goat Hill (1656m)

Mt Tarapuhi (1605m)

Sulphur Hot Spring

Aicken Range

Hunt Saddle (807m)

Otira

Goat Creek

Gorge Creek

Deception River

Mt Barron (1726m)

73

Barrack Creek

Mt Russel (1868m)

Otira Tunnel

Holts River

Shaffrey Creek

Barron Ridge

Rolleston River

Arthur's Pass (920m)

Reid Falls

Mt Stuart (1906m)

2

Lake Anna

Mt Franklin (2145m)

Lake Florence

Mt Philistine (1967m)

Hills Peak (1645m)

Upper Deception Hut

Lake Sally

Mt Armstrong (2110m)

Waimakariri Col (1787m)

Phipps Peak (1965m)

Side Trip

Mt Rolleston (2275m)

Mt Temple (1913m)

Goat Pass Hut

Lake Mavis

Bealey River

Temple Col

Goat Pass (1070m)

Day 2

Mt Oakes (2054m)

Mt Lancelot (2112m)

Devil's Punchbowl Falls

Blimit (1921m)

Agility Creek

Mingha Bivouac

Kennedy Falls

Avalanche Peak (1833m)

Scotts Track

1

START/END

1

Mingha River

Arthur's Pass National Park

Crow Hut

Avalanche Peak Track

Otira Tunnel

Mt Aicken (1863m)

Dudley Knob

Edwards Hut

Arthur's Pass Village (737m)

Lyell Peak (1828m)

Mt O'Malley (1703m)

2

Polar Range

Mt Bealey (1836m)

73

Mt Williams (1718m)

Crow River

Bealey River

The Spike (1440m)

Halpin Creek

Dome (1938m)

Greyneys Shelter

2 START

Waimakariri River

Anti Crow Hut

Klondyke Corner

Turkey Flat

See Cass-Lagoon Saddles Track Map (p227)

Cora Lynn

CANTERBURY, ARTHUR'S PASS & AORAKI/MT COOK AVALANCHE PEAK

① Planning

MAPS

Your two map options are NewTopo *Arthur's Pass* 1:55,000 and NZTopo50 *BV20* (Otira).

🏃 The Tramp

6–8 HOURS RETURN, 7KM, ASCENT 1093M, DESCENT 1093M

First things first: make sure your water bottle is full before you set off as there is virtually none en route. That task complete, you will find the **Avalanche Peak Track** signposted at Arthur's Pass Chapel.

The track sets off along a gravel path that soon passes a waterfall-viewing site and then crosses over Avalanche Creek on historic Glasgow Bridge. Just beyond the bridge you begin climbing, and keep climbing. Within 10 minutes you're looking down at Arthur's Pass village, having already scrambled up your first rock face.

The climb is unrelenting, and the only time it levels out is just before you break out of the bushline, 1½ hours and 400m above the chapel. Yellow markers and a worn path replace the track here, and lead up the ridge that rises between the Avalanche Creek and Rough Creek catchments.

The climbing continues once you reach the tussock grass, and it takes one to 1½ hours to follow this ridge to the base of Avalanche Peak. In the first half the route skirts a large slip that leads down to the Rough Creek catchment; at times you're treading right on the edge of it. This would be a deathtrap in high winds and poor visibility.

After passing a pair of large cairns the climbing eases a bit and the views improve tremendously. **Mt Rolleston** (2275m) lies straight ahead, while to the east the Punchbowl Falls come into view. Should the *Tranz Alpine* train pass through the valley below, it's like watching a toy train.

At the northern end of the ridge, yellow markers lead you along its east side and around the tail of some rock scree. You then begin the final ascent to the prominent ridge that leads to Avalanche Peak. The ridge looks formidable, but the markers show a zigzag route up the side for an easier climb.

At the top, the yellow markers from Avalanche Peak Track merge with the orange markers from Scotts Track in a flat spot at 1680m; here you're 10 to 15 minutes from the summit.

The final leg is well poled, but you have to be careful. The ridge is narrow, falling sharply away to the McGrath Stream catchment at times, and the rock is loose. **Avalanche Peak** (1833m) is a rounded summit with enough space for about six people to sit comfortably and admire the views in every direction. The most impressive view is to the north, looking over towards Mt Rolleston with the icefall of Crow Glacier right below it.

If the wind is gentle and the sun is out you could spend the afternoon up here, enjoying the world at your feet. If you do stay a while, eventually a kea or two will arrive – do not feed them, and do not leave your daypack or anything else unattended.

The return trip begins by backtracking to the junction of Avalanche Peak Track and Scotts Track. Whereas the yellow markers descend the ridge south, this time you stay with the orange markers as they continue along the crest of the ridge to the east.

In the beginning Scotts Track will also have some narrow areas with steep drop-offs towards the McGrath Stream catchment, but 30 minutes from the summit the ridge eases up and the descent becomes a wonderful stroll through tussock. The bushline is reached in one to 1½ hours, at a spot where the track is well marked among the stunted mountain beech.

It's a 300m descent from here to SH73, along a track that is not nearly as steep or rugged as Avalanche Peak Track. You will also enjoy better views on the way down, as you are constantly passing small openings in the trees. Most of them are dominated by **Devil's Punchbowl Falls** leaping 131m out of a cleft in the mountains. It takes most people at least one hour to descend through the bush, longer if their legs are tired. Eventually you arrive at SH73, just north of Arthur's Pass village. Follow the road 200m south into the village.

Goat Pass Track

Duration 2 days

Distance 25km (15.5 miles)

Track Standard Route

Difficulty Moderate

Start Greyneys Shelter

End Morrison Footbridge

Nearest Town Arthur's Pass (p235)

Transport Shuttle bus

Summary This is a popular tramp that takes you over the 1070m Goat Pass, and along much of the easy-to-follow route that snakes beside the Mingha and Deception Rivers. The highlight is a night spent at Goat Pass Hut above the bushline.

Goat Pass Track – also referred to as the Mingha-Deception Route (the two rivers the route follows) – is an excellent introduction to tramping in Arthur's Pass. It is also one of the least complicated routes in the park, as long as the rivers run in your favour. Typical of the Southern Alps, the Bealey, Mingha and Deception Rivers can be very dangerous when in flood, and the Deception alone requires up to 30 compulsory crossings. This tramp should therefore not be attempted during periods of rain. Should the crossings start to look too difficult, backtrack or stay put – attempting a dicey crossing just isn't worth the risk.

This track forms the running leg of the Coast to Coast, NZ's most famous multisport race that crosses the South Island from the Tasman Sea to the Pacific Ocean by a gruelling combination of cycling, kayaking and running. On your travels, you may encounter some competitors training. With luck you'll also encounter whio, the nationally vulnerable and very cute blue duck.

The Goat Pass can be tramped in either direction, but the Mingha-Deception direction allows for a shorter day first.

ⓘ Planning

MAPS & BROCHURES

Your two map options are NewTopo *Arthur's Pass* 1:55,000, or NZTopo50 *BV20* (Otira).

HUTS

Goat Pass is a **Standard hut** (www.doc.govt. nz; $5); Upper Deception Hut and Mingha Bivouac are **Basic huts** (www.doc.govt.nz; free). There are no cooking facilities in any of them.

ⓘ Getting to/from the Tramp

The southern end of the track is at the confluence of the Bealey and Mingha Rivers, near Greyneys Shelter, 5km south of Arthur's Pass on SH73. The northern end is at the Morrison Footbridge at the confluence of the Otira and Deception Rivers, 19km north of Arthur's Pass on SH73.

You can be dropped off and collected by various passing bus services by prior arrangement. Try **Atomic Shuttles** (☑ 0508 108 359; www.

atomictravel.co.nz) and **West Coast Shuttle** (☑ 027 492 7000, 03-768 0028; www. westcoastshuttle.co.nz). **Mountain House Shuttle** (☑ 027 419 2354, 03-318 9258; www. trampers.co.nz), based at Mountain House YHA, provides tramper transport around the national park.

The Tramp

Day 1: Greyneys Shelter to Goat Pass Hut

4–5 HOURS, 9.5KM, 390M ASCENT

From Greyneys Shelter it's a 10-minute walk north along the road to the confluence of the **Bealey River** and **Mingha River**, which is easily spotted from SH73 as a huge gravel plain. Ford the Bealey at the safest-looking point, an instruction that applies throughout this tramp as the rivers are constantly changing course around here.

Once across, round the bend into the Mingha Valley and follow the riverbed, crossing the river as necessary. About 1½ hours from the shelter the bush comes down to meet the river here. Rock cairns mark both sides of the river here, indicating a ford back to the true right (west) side. Follow the Mingha along this side and across a huge rocky fan.

Continue following the river flat after the rock fan, to quickly arrive at a track signposted with an orange marker on the edge of the beech forest. At first the track runs level with the river but then it makes a steep ascent to the top of **Dudley Knob**. It's a good climb, and once on top you'll be able to see both sides of the river valley. The track descends the knob a short way and then begins a gentle climb towards Goat Pass. This stretch used to be very boggy but has been extensively planked. A little more than 2km from the knob the track passes Mingha Bivouac (two bunks).

For the next 1.5km you follow the track, fording the river at a sharp bend, where there is a large orange triangle marker on the true left (east) bank. This marks the final climb. The track passes the impressive bowl of **Mt Temple** (1913m), then follows the gorge to **Goat Pass** (1070m), although you rarely see it. This tussock slope is quite wet and boggy in places, with long sections of boardwalk. The climb is easy though, and from the pass you can look down on its northern side and spot the hut below.

Goat Pass Hut (20 bunks) is a great place to spend a night or two. It's a roomy hut, with a radio link to the Arthur's Pass Visitor Centre that can be used to receive the latest weather report. There is no fireplace in the hut because of the lack of firewood, and it can get chilly on cold nights – you'll need that fleece!

SIDE TRIP: LAKE MAVIS
3–4 HOURS, 2KM RETURN, 500M ASCENT

Those with time up their sleeve would do well to make the worthwhile climb to Lake Mavis, the national park's most accessible alpine lake. Ascend the spur track to the east of Goat Pass Hut, following the cairned ridge route.

Day 2: Goat Pass Hut to Morrison Footbridge
7–9 HOURS, 15.5KM, 770M DESCENT

The day begins at the stream behind the hut, where a couple of snow poles have been placed. Follow the small stream, stepping from boulder to boulder, and you'll soon emerge at **Deception River**. A huge rock cairn and a large pole alert trampers heading towards the pass to leave the river and avoid the gorge ahead.

Those heading down the valley continue boulder-hopping along the river, on the true right (east) side most of the time – although a series of cairns indicate when you should cross to the other bank. There are also short sections of unmarked track that can be used if found. After about 2km you pass Upper Deception Hut (six bunks), on the true right (east) bank, just before Good Luck Creek; look for it carefully because it's easy to miss.

Less than 2km from Upper Deception Hut you break out into a wide section of the valley. The walking becomes considerably easier and most of the track encountered will be on the true left (west) side of the Deception. Two hours from Upper Deception Hut you enter a gorge. Pass the junction of **Gorge Creek** at the gorge's northern end, and after another 2km enter another small gorge.

Between the two gorges lies the **sulphur hot spring**. It is located on the true right (east) side of the river, 350m down the valley from Spray Creek. It is easier to smell the sulphur than it is to find the spring, which emerges from a rock bank and forms a small, two-person pool of 38°C water.

At the end of the second gorge, 10km from Goat Pass, the Deception Valley swings to the northwest and begins to widen. It's about 5.5km from here to SH73, with the final 2km passing through open flats.

Eventually the Deception meets the **Otira River**, which can be crossed via **Morrison Footbridge**, just north of the confluence, on the true right side of Deception River.

Harper Pass

Duration 5 days

Distance 77km (48 miles)

Track Standard Tramping track and route

Difficulty Moderate

Start Aickens car park

End Windy Point

Nearest Towns Arthur's Pass (p235), Hanmer Springs (p234)

Transport Bus, shuttle bus

Summary A historic route followed by both early Maori and miners during the gold rushes, this track extends from Arthur's Pass National Park into Lake Sumner Forest Park, passing through beech forest and along wide river flats.

Maori often travelled this way over to the West Coast in search of *pounamu*, an experience that would eventually see them lead the first Europeans through this area, in 1857. Two guides, Wereta Tainui and Terapuhi, took Leonard Harper across the pass that now bears his name. By 1862, some three years after the first bridle paths were surveyed, the route was serving as the main gateway to the West Coast goldfields, with stores and liquor shops along the way. When the gold rush ended, however, the track fell into disrepair, until its reinvention as a tramping trail.

Today it is one of NZ's classic tramps, connecting Arthur's Pass to Lewis Pass. The track crosses the Main Divide over Harper Pass, a low saddle of only 963m. The segment in Arthur's Pass National Park is a valley route along the Taramakau River, but in Lake Sumner Forest Park the track is well cut and marked.

Trampers need to be cautious with the Taramakau. It is a large and unruly river in a high-rainfall area, making it prone to sudden flooding. The track can be walked in

Harper Pass (Map 1)

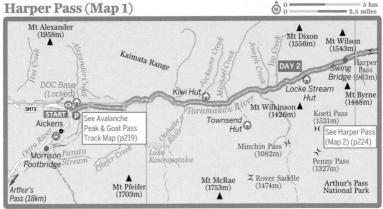

either direction, but a west to east crossing is recommended as you can be surer of good conditions as you cross the Otira, Otehake and Taramakau rivers – all of which are prone to flooding during rain. On the eastern side, the track is well defined along the Hurunui and Hope Rivers, and bridged at all major crossings.

🛈 Planning

MAPS

This tramp is covered by NZTopo50 maps *BU20* (Moana), *BU21* (Haupiri), *BU22* (Lake Sumner) and *BU23* (Boyle).

HUTS

Of the eight huts along the track, only Hope Kiwi Lodge is a **Serviced hut** (www.doc.govt.nz; $15). Locke Stream, Hurunui No 3 and Hurunui are **Standard huts** (www.doc.govt.nz; $5); and Kiwi, Harper Pass Bivouac, Camerons and Hope Shelter are **Basic huts** (www.doc.govt.nz; free).

🛈 Getting to/from the Tramp

The western end of the track is at Aickens on SH73, 30 minutes north of Arthur's Pass village.

You can arrange to be dropped off by various passing bus services, including Atomic Shuttles (p221) and West Coast Shuttle (p221). Mountain House Shuttle (p221), based at Mountain House YHA, provides tramper transport around the national park.

The eastern end of the track is Windy Point, on SH7, 7km west of the Hope Bridge and almost halfway between Maruia Springs and the turn-off to Hanmer Springs.

East West Coaches (p214) provides drop-offs at both the track start and finish on its Westport to Christchurch route, with services running daily only when seasonal demand dictates. It may be possible to arrange transport to the trailheads with Hanmer Springs Adventure Centre (p214), depending on its workload. Nelson Lakes Shuttles (p191) also stops at Windy Point, on demand, on its runs between the Lewis Pass, St Arnaud and Nelson.

Trampers with their own vehicles can avail themselves of the services of Boyle River Outdoor Education Centre, near the southern end of the track. They will drop you off in your car at the track start ($22), then return your car to Boyle where it is stored until your return ($7 per day).

The last day's walk takes most trampers five hours, so an early start is necessary if you hope to catch one of the buses. It is best to be at the highway, ready to flag down the bus, 30 minutes before it is due to arrive.

🥾 The Tramp

Day 1: Aickens Car Park to Locke Stream Hut

6 HOURS, 18KM

If the Otira River cannot be forded, postpone your trip, because you won't be able to cross the Taramakau later in the day. From the car park, follow the paddock fence to the Otira River, which you should ford, heading for the orange triangle marker in the gap in the trees on the other side.

A track leads through scrubby bush to grassy flats, which provide an easy walk to **Pfeifer Creek**. Near the creek is a junction with a track that leads south (right fork) to

Harper Pass (Map 2)

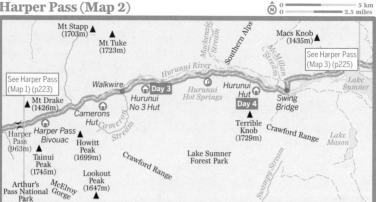

Lake Kaurapataka. The main route continues northeast, crossing first the **Otehake River**, followed by the **Taramakau River** to the true right (north) bank.

Continue along the true right for about a kilometre above the Otehake where the sign will indicate the short side track to Kiwi Hut (eight bunks), about 6km from Pfeifer Creek.

Above the hut, pick your own route, crossing and recrossing the river to take advantage of stable mossy flats. Towards Locke Stream the riverbed begins to narrow and eroded banks on the true right become steeper. Cross to the true left and continue on as far as Locke Stream, about 9km from Kiwi Hut. A short track (around 10 minutes) leads up through the bush to Locke Stream Hut (18 bunks).

Day 2: Locke Stream Hut to Hurunui No 3 Hut

6–7 HOURS, 15KM, 280M ASCENT

Above Locke Stream the valley continues to narrow and the Taramakau appears more like a mountain stream. Ongoing slips may slow your progress through this section.

From the hut, the track winds in and out of the forest as it climbs towards Harper Pass. Keep your eye on the markers as you go. This section is challenging, but within 1½ hours you should reach a swing bridge located 3km above Locke Stream.

Cross to the true right (north) side and follow the Taramakau (rarely seen through the bush) to the headwater gorges. Here the track begins a largely steep and sometimes rough 280m ascent through forest to **Harp-er Pass** (963m), marked by a sign around three hours into the day's journey.

The track drops quickly on the eastern side to the headwaters of the **Hurunui River**. Within 30 minutes you arrive at Harper Pass Bivouac (two bunks), located in a grove of ribbonwood above the stream on the true right (south) side.

Below the bivouac, walking becomes a lot easier as it drops down through beech forest. It's a steady 6.5km, two-hour descent from the bivouac to the first substantial flat, where you will find Camerons Hut (four bunks) on the edge of the forest. At **Cameron Stream** there's an emergency walkwire 100m up from the Hurunui riverbed. From here the track stays on the fringes of the forest for the next 1.5km until it opens onto a flat. Here you will find Hurunui No 3 Hut (16 bunks), which looks just like a deserted schoolhouse, standing in the middle of the grassy clearing. The old, two-roomed building has a large wooden porch and a wood stove.

Day 3: Hurunui No 3 Hut to Hurunui Hut

3–4 HOURS, 10KM

Below this hut, most of the tramping along the Hurunui Valley floor is through grassy flats. A 4WD track departs from the hut and crosses the flats, reaching a signposted junction after 1km. The main walking track veers to the southeast (right fork) and stays on the true right (south) side of the Hurunui River for the entire day.

The track undulates as it bypasses steep embankments cut into the hillsides. If you want flat and easy travel, veer north (left fork) at the junction and follow the 4WD vehicle track all the way along the true left (north) side. If you plan to stay at Hurunui Hut it's best to stick to the walking track.

From the junction the walking track is marked by a series of poles as it crosses the flats and enters forest. Sidle up and down along the forested hillsides for 2km, cross another flat and then make a long descent to the **Hurunui Hot Springs**, two hours from the hut. Keep an eye out for the side trail to the springs as it is easy to miss. The sulphurous thermal water emerges from rock 30m above the Hurunui and forms a cascade of hot water to the riverbed below. Depending on water levels it's possible for three or four people to soak chest deep in the pool.

The track leaves the hot springs and returns to the forest for 1km, before emerging onto a flat. Cut across the flat, return to manuka forest and, 1½ hours from the hot springs, arrive at Hurunui Hut (14 bunks).

Day 4: Hurunui Hut to Hope Kiwi Lodge

5–6 HOURS, 19KM

The track continues along the Hurunui River, and 1km below the confluence with McMillan Stream (about 30 minutes) arrives at a swing bridge. Cross over, and follow the vehicle track to where it swings sharply to the west. Here, a marked route heads east (right fork) and crosses the valley along the edge of the forest. To avoid some cliffs the

track dips into the bush once before reaching the head of **Lake Sumner**.

On the northern side of the lake, the track enters forest again for an easy climb to Three Mile Stream, crossed by a swing bridge. There's a junction here, with one track heading north towards Three Mile Stream Hut and another south to Charley's Point, on the lake. The main track departs east across the stream and begins the day's steepest climb, gaining 150m before levelling off and finally reaching bush-clad **Kiwi Saddle** (677m). Just before the saddle there is a short track to a **lookout**, which has a fine view across Lake Sumner.

From the saddle descend to the swampy grasslands of Kiwi Valley. Follow the track on your left to avoid the bogs and then pick up a 4WD track along the true right (east) side of the river. It's a one-hour walk through the cattle flats to Hope Kiwi Lodge (20 bunks), near the western edge of the forest. This hut is large, with five rooms and a wood stove.

Day 5: Hope Kiwi Lodge to Windy Point

5–6 HOURS, 15KM

Follow the poled route from the lodge through beech forest and grassy flats, and in around 30 minutes you will reach the Hope River swing bridge. Now on the true left (north) side of the river, the track immediately enters a large, open flat, and it's an easy walk for the next hour as you follow poles for 4km, until a bend in the river forces you to climb into the forest.

The track sidles between bush and more flats, and in 2km arrives at Hope Shelter (six bunks), marking the halfway point of the day. Little more than 7km of the journey remains.

The track stays in beech forest for the next two hours, until it breaks out onto a series of grassy terraces and crosses farmland for 2km to a swing bridge over the **Boyle River gorge**. On the other side the track leads past an outdoor education centre to a picnic area and a small shelter. An unsealed road covers the remaining 500m to Windy Point Shelter on SH7, the Lewis Pass Hwy.

Cass-Lagoon Saddles Track

Duration 2 days

Distance 30km (18.6 miles)

Track Standard Tramping track

Difficulty Moderate

Start Cass train station

End SH73 (Bealey Hut)

Nearest Town Arthur's Pass (p235)

Transport Bus, shuttle bus, train

Summary This track is just south of Arthur's Pass National Park, in Craigieburn Forest Park, and is one of the easiest alpine routes in the Arthur's Pass region. There are spectacular views from the two alpine saddles – Cass and Lagoon.

Established in 1967, the 4400-sq-km **Craigieburn Forest Park** extends from SH73 west of the Main Divide, and is bordered by Arthur's Pass National Park to the north and pastoral runs to the south and east. The park is typical of the Canterbury high country and includes river valleys, extensive beech forests and high peaks. The ranges are deeply dissected by streams, and the steep-sided mountains have large areas of rock and scree formed by uplift, glaciation and erosion. Two peaks within the park, Mt Greenlaw and Mt Avoca, exceed 2100m.

More than 35 species of bird have been sighted within the park, most of which are also seen in Arthur's Pass National Park. These include a good number of kea.

The area is also known for its caves. Cave Stream Scenic Reserve, just outside the forest park and south of Cass along SH73, offers experienced cavers an opportunity to explore a subterranean world. The stream disappears underground in the reserve, and can be followed for 30 to 45 minutes to a point where it re-emerges above ground.

A popular weekend trip for Canterbury trampers, part of this track is technically a 'route' but the entire walk is easy to follow and the alpine saddles are within the ability of any fit tramper. Note, though, that the Cass River is impassable in flood, so check the current status of the river with staff at the Arthur's Pass Visitor Centre. In normal conditions it is easily forded and its gravel beds make for a pleasant tramp. Heavy snowfalls and avalanches are common around the Cass Saddle in winter, so be wary of attempting it after April.

ⓘ Planning

MAPS

Between them, NZTopo50 maps *BV21* (Cass), *BV20* (Otira) and *BW20* (Lake Coleridge) cover the entire route.

HUTS

Hamilton Hut is a **Serviced hut** (www.doc.govt. nz; $15). Bealey and Cass Saddle are both **Basic huts** (www.doc.govt.nz; free), as are all other huts on this track.

ⓘ Getting to/from the Tramp

Both track entrances are along SH73 between Christchurch and Arthur's Pass. The Christchurch to Greymouth *TranzAlpine* train, operated by KiwiRail Scenic (p235), stops at Cass train station, where there is also a car park. At the Bealey Hut end you can be collected by various passing bus services (by prior arrangement), including Atomic Shuttles (p221) and West Coast Shuttle (p221). Mountain House Shuttle (p221), based at Mountain House YHA, provides tramper transport around the national park.

🚶 The Tramp

Day 1: Cass Train Station to Hamilton Hut

5–7 HOURS, 16KM, 706M ASCENT, 526M DESCENT

From the car park near the Cass train station, follow the road southwest to the signposted start of the track on SH73 (just south of the bridge over Cass River) and cross the stile into farmland. The route is well marked with poles, and travels along a 4WD track beside a pine-tree shelter break. **Cass River** is just beyond, and you head upstream along

Cass-Lagoon Saddles Track

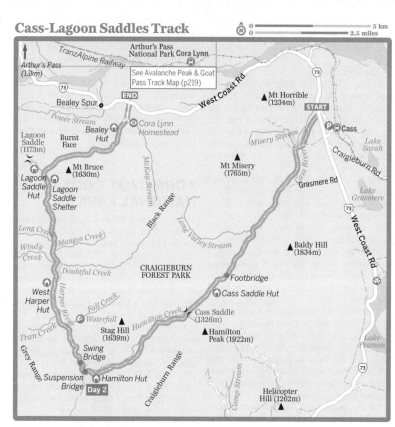

the gravel flats, fording from one side to the other as necessary.

After travelling up the riverbed for 4km (about 1½ hours), an orange marker appears on the true right (south) side; next to it is a well-defined track. You make an immediate climb, which is steep in parts, and after 3km cross Cass River on a bridge. The track then climbs another 90m in the next 1km to reach Cass Saddle Hut (three bunks). As far as bivvies go – most being little more than a mattress in a tin box – this one is not bad. It's near the bushline, with a small table, a stove and some space inside.

Within minutes of leaving the hut you begin climbing towards Cass Saddle. Once you break out of the trees there are great views. During winter this area is avalanche-prone, and in summer it's easy to see why – there are steep scree slopes on both sides of the alpine route. Poles and boardwalks lead through open tussock to **Cass Sad-**dle (1326m), 1.5km from the hut; the pass is marked by a large pole. You can look down into the Hamilton Valley and, on a clear day, even see the green roof of Hamilton Hut.

From the saddle the route veers off left for 100m, and then begins a quick descent into the bush and down a narrow ridge. The track drops more than 300m before it finally levels out in the upper portion of Hamilton Valley, where it crosses several streams.

About 1km from the hut the track emerges from the bush onto grassy terraces along Hamilton Creek. Impressive Hamilton Hut (20 bunks) sits on a ledge above the creek and has a commanding view of the valley.

Day 2: Hamilton Hut to SH73 (Bealey Hut)

8–9 HOURS, 14KM, 400M ASCENT, 520M DESCENT

The track heads west from the hut and almost immediately arrives at a suspension bridge across Hamilton Creek, from where you wander up Harper River on the true left (east) side and soon come to a swing bridge.

The track resumes on the true right (west) side, and follows the valley through forest and open flats for 4.5km to West Harper Hut (five bunks), an old-style hut built in the 1950s. West Harper Hut is 15 to 20 minutes beyond Tarn Creek and is strictly a hunter's bivvy, with a dirt floor, canvas bunks, a fireplace and even an impressive set of antlers mounted on the wall.

Keep in mind that the track is well marked with orange plastic triangles. Hunters' trails abound in the area, especially up side streams such as Tarn Creek, and it's easy to mistakenly take one, not noticing the main track resuming on the other bank.

From the hut the track soon arrives at a short gorge, which it bypasses with a steep climb. In fine weather it is easier to follow the river, fording it once or twice, to avoid the climb.

The track returns to Harper River, crosses Windy Creek and becomes more of a route along the river bed, with rock cairns marking the way. About 3km from West Harper Hut, ford the river to a cairn on the true left (east) bank and pass a signposted flood route before arriving at the confluence of Harper River and Long Creek.

At this point Long Creek usually looks like the major channel, so an orange marker has been erected slightly upstream of the confluence to point the way to Lagoon Saddle. Continue to follow the riverbed for another 500m, until a track on the true left (east) side leads into the bush and climbs to the saddle. The climb is steady but not steep, and 1½ to two hours from Long Creek you come to a sign pointing the way to Lagoon Saddle to the west and to the short spur track to Lagoon Saddle Shelter to the east. This classic A-frame provides welcome respite from the weather on cold, wet days. Across the river is Lagoon Saddle Hut (two bunks), the best place to stay, which has an outside fireplace.

The main track leaves the junction and climbs 120m through beech forest until it reaches the bushline. Above the trees there is an excellent view of Lagoon Saddle (1173m) and the tarn in its middle.

The climb continues over sometimes boggy ground, and the views of the snow-capped peaks of Arthur's Pass National Park to the north get better and better. It's about 3km across the alpine region, with snow poles marking the route around Mt Bruce (1630m), until you return to the forest edge at Burnt Face.

The final leg is a rapid 2.5km descent to Bealey Hut (six bunks). The hut is in good shape, considering its proximity to the road. It's a five-minute walk to the car park, and from there a road leads 1.5km through Cora Lynn Homestead to SH73.

AORAKI/MT COOK NATIONAL PARK

The spectacular 707-sq-km Aoraki/Mt Cook National Park is part of Te Wahipounamu – South West New Zealand World Heritage Area, which extends from Westland's Cook River down to Fiordland. Fenced in by the Southern Alps and the Two Thumb, Liebig and Ben Ohau Ranges, more than a third of the park has a blanket of permanent snow and glacial ice.

Of the 27 NZ mountains over 3050m, 22 are in this park. The highest is the mighty Aoraki/Mt Cook – at 3754m it's the tallest peak in Australasia. Known to Maori as Aoraki (Cloud Piercer), after an ancestral deity in Maori mythology, the mountain was named after James Cook by Captain Stokes of the survey ship HMS *Acheron*.

It's not surprising that, with so much rock and ice, this national park is not ideally suited for trampers. Although the scenery is phenomenal and the day walks to viewpoints are numerous, this is really a haven for climbers. Most valleys west of the divide are extremely rugged, with steep gorges and thick bush, while to the east they inevitably lead to glaciers requiring extensive experience and special equipment to traverse. Crossing the passes between the valleys is a major climbing feat.

Unsurprisingly for a place of such grandeur, the Aoraki/Mt Cook area has long been a magnet for visitors. The area around Mt Cook Village was set aside as a recreation reserve in the 1880s, with the national park formally gazetted in 1953. Aoraki/Mt Cook and Mt Sefton dominate the skyline around the village, with the Hooker and Tasman Glaciers also easily viewed. Satisfying short walks abound, frequented by hordes of visitors, some of whom will wait for days on end for Aoraki/Mt Cook to emerge from the cloud.

History

The first European to mention Aoraki/Mt Cook was Charles Heaphy. Travelling with Thomas Brunner along the West Coast in 1846, Heaphy made sketches of the mountain after learning about it from his Maori guides. In 1862 Julius von Haast and Arthur Dobson spent four months exploring the rivers, valleys and glaciers of what is now the park. Haast prepared a colourful account of their findings for the Canterbury Provincial Government. 'Nothing can be compared with the scenery, which certainly has not its equal in the European Alps,' he wrote.

In the early 1890s exploration of the area began in earnest when the Canterbury Provincial Government sent surveyors to explore passages through the Main Divide. In 1892 surveyor Charles Douglas ventured from the West Coast up the Copland Valley and explored several passes, finally deciding that Copland Pass offered the best possibilities.

Two years later, climbers Tom Fyfe, George Graham and Jack Clarke had their day in the sun when they finally summited Aoraki/Mt Cook in 1894. In doing so they pipped English climber Edward Fitzgerald and his Italian guide Mattias Zurbriggen at the post. As a consolation, however, the Euro-duo recorded the first east–west crossing in 1895, when they climbed what is now Fitzgerald Pass. They then spent three arduous days without supplies trying to find a way down the Copland Valley. Construction of the existing Copland Track began in 1910, and by 1913 the first Welcome Flat Hut was built. Its hot springs quickly made it a popular spot.

Environment

With only small patches of silver beech/tawhai left after early burnoffs, most of the native flora is found in the alpine shrublands and tussock grasslands. Over 300 species of plants are found in the park. Among the most spectacular are the daisy/tikumu (Celmisia), and the famed Mt Cook lily, the largest buttercup in the world. About 40 species of birds are found in the park, including the kea, the mischievous mountain parrot. Lucky bird-spotters may spy the native falcon (karearea). There are plenty of invertebrates, including large dragonflies, grasshoppers and butterflies. The rare jewelled gecko lives in the region but is

THE CONQUEST OF AORAKI/MT COOK

Inspired by photographs of Aoraki/Mt Cook viewed in a London exhibition, Irish parson William Spotswood Green mounted an expedition to summit the faraway mountain, accompanied by Swiss alpinists Emil Boss and Ulrich Kaufmann. In March 1882, having overcome numerous challenges en route such as treacherous river crossings and a fierce storm, they picked their way along Haast Ridge on the mountain's northern side. Just several hundred metres shy of the top they were halted by conditions and spent the night clinging to a narrow rock ledge at 3050m, listening to the boom of avalanches around them. The next morning they descended, having failed to reach the summit, although the glory of bagging the peak is often said to be theirs.

The gauntlet was picked up by local climbers Tom Fyfe, George Graham and Jack Clarke, who reached the summit proper on Christmas Day 1894. At one point expedition leader Fyfe (who would later become chief guide at the Hermitage in Mt Cook Village) dangled without footholds over the yawning abyss. He wrote, 'I'm afraid that the reckless way in which we romped over those last rocks was very foolhardy, but one would indeed need to be phlegmatic not to get a little excited on such an occasion.'

In 1913 Australian climber Freda du Faur became the first woman to reach the summit, much to the disdain of society ladies who considered such activity damaging to her 'reputation'. Fair enough, too. A lady in trousers? Out adventuring with the menfolk? Good grief!

In 1948 a young Auckland beekeeper named Edmund Hillary joined legendary local guide Harry Ayers in a party climbing the hitherto unconquered south ridge. Ayers would consider this climb his best ever feat, while Hillary lauded him for 'that subtle science of snow and ice craft that only experience can really teach.' It stood the young climber in good stead: just five years later he and Tenzing Norgay would summit the world's highest peak, Mt Everest.

very secretive. You may also see introduced mammals such as thar, chamois and red deer.

Planning

WHEN TO TRAMP
Aoraki/Mt Cook National Park does experience spells of fine weather, but it is long periods of foul weather for which it is most noted. The annual rainfall in Mt Cook Village is 4000mm and it rains an average of 160 days a year. The short tracks around Mt Cook Village can be done at any time of year, when conditions allow. The Mueller Hut Route, as with any alpine tramp, should be done during the traditional Aoraki/Mt Cook climbing season, from mid-November to late March, although trampers should closely monitor current conditions and heed forecasts.

WHAT TO BRING
Come prepared for strong winds, heavy rain and even snow in any season (then rejoice if the sky is clear and Aoraki/Mt Cook comes into view!). Some trampers take an ice axe, although crampons and rope are usually unnecessary during summer. Trekking poles are recommended and may be hired from Alpine Guides in the village.

MAPS & BROCHURES
The park is covered by NewTopo map *Aoraki Mt Cook* 1:65,000, which will prove helpful for trip planning. Numerous short walks from the village are covered in DOC's brochure *Walks in Aoraki/Mount Cook National Park*. The map covering the Mueller Route is NZTopo50 *BX15* (Aoraki/Mount Cook). See also DOC's detailed *Mueller Hut Route* brochure.

HUTS
There are 17 huts in the park, most of which can be accessed only by experienced alpinists. For overnight stays in Mueller Hut you need to sign in and out at the Aoraki/Mt Cook National Park Visitor Centre, where you can pay your hut fees. Annual hut passes are not valid. There are gas cookers in the hut.

INFORMATION SOURCES
The **Aoraki/Mt Cook National Park Visitor Centre** (☑ 03-435 1186; www.doc.govt.nz; 1 Larch Grove, Mt Cook Village) is first class. In addition to weather updates, hut bookings and personal advice, there are excellent displays on the natural and mountaineering history of the park. A fantastic place to while away a day in bad weather.

GUIDED TRAMPS
Resident in Mt Cook Village, **Alpine Guides** (☑ 03-435 1834; www.alpineguides.co.nz; Retail Centre, The Hermitage) offers guided climbs and mountaineering courses, as does **Southern Alps Guiding** (☑ 027 342 277, 03-435 1890; www.mtcook.com), also located in the village.

Mueller Hut Route

Duration 2 days

Distance 10km (6.2 miles)

Track Standard Route

Difficulty Demanding

Start/End Mt Cook Village

Nearest Town Mt Cook Village (p235)

Transport None

Summary This route offers a quintessential Southern Alps experience, achievable by those possessing sound tramping skills and fitness. The major highlight is the staggering view from Mueller Hut.

This route passes through a dynamic landscape, simultaneously uplifted and eroded in the neverending battle between powerful natural forces. Rock beds of schist, sandstone, siltstone and greywacke have been carved out by glaciation, dramatically illustrated on the climb to Mueller Hut. Hanging glaciers, moraines, and U-shaped valleys are all classic landmarks of icy geological transformation.

Populating this inhospitable environment are alpine flowers and herb fields, of which there are many to see during the 1000m climb to the rocky ridge and hut atop it.

Mueller Glacier was named by Julius Haast in 1862, after the Danish explorer and writer Ferdinand von Mueller. A series of Mueller Huts have perched above it since the first one was built between 1914 and 1915. The second, which replaced it in 1950, lasted only four months before being wiped out by an avalanche in its first winter. The scattered debris from the hut was hauled back up from the glacier and used to piece together temporary quarters (Mueller Hut, the third) until a totally new hut could be constructed in 1953. Mueller Hut IV was located higher on the Sealy Range and was the first alpine hut in NZ built with materials air-dropped onto the site, rather than packed in.

Number five came alive in 2003, 300m southwest of its predecessor, and required 130 helicopter loads of building materials. It was opened by the legend of NZ mountaineering, Sir Edmund Hillary.

Mueller Hut Route

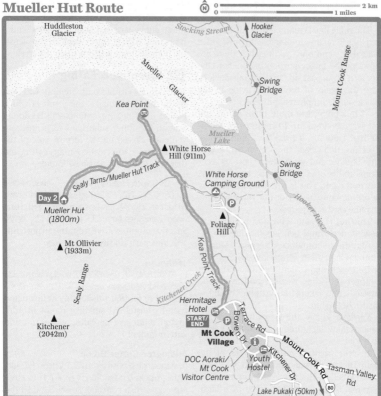

 The Tramp

Day 1: Mt Cook Village to Mueller Hut

4–5 HOURS, 5KM, 1040M ASCENT

The tramp begins at the Hermitage Hotel (near the DOC Visitor Centre) on Kea Point Track, a very level and well-maintained path that heads up the open scrub of Hooker Valley towards White Horse Hill. Within 30 minutes you pass Foliage Hill; you'll see two lodges and the campsite shelter near the base of White Horse Hill. The track begins to climb gently, moves into bush and comes to a signposted junction with Sealy Tarns Track. **Kea Point** is to the north (right fork), a 15-minute walk away. The side trip is worthwhile because the viewpoint is on moraine above Mueller Glacier, with Mt Sefton looming overhead.

The route to Mueller Hut heads west (left fork) on the **Sealy Tarns Track**. It's a

two-hour climb to the tarns, which is still a knee-bender at times, even though the track has been recently improved. As soon as you begin climbing you are greeted with excellent views of the lower Hooker Valley to the south, including Mt Cook Village. Higher still, there are views of the upper portions of the valley and Mueller Glacier. **Sealy Tarns**, a series of small pools, make a natural rest stop because they are on the ridge in a narrow meadow of alpine shrubs, grasses and herbs. They are also the only sight of water you are likely to pass during the climb.

Just south of the tarns, look for a huge rock cairn that marks the continuation to Mueller Hut. It begins as a well-worn track in tussock that involves a lot of scrambling, then eventually fades out altogether in a large boulder field. Follow the orange markers (every 200m) through the boulders, and finally up a steep and loose scree slope to the ridge. Take your time hopping from one boulder to the next to avoid any mishap.

The ridge line is marked by a large orange and black pole – impossible to miss on a clear day – and once you reach it there are views of the upper portion of Mueller Glacier as it flows past smaller hanging glaciers, with the peaks of the Main Divide in the background. Simply magnificent.

At this point, the route turns south and follows the ridge for 20 minutes to **Mueller Hut** (1800m), a bright red and orange structure that's easy to spot on a fine day. The boulder-and-scree slope here is very steep, and is often covered by snow all the way to the hut. This is where an ice axe may be useful, but whether or not you have one, extreme care is required.

This hut is a gem – big and roomy, with viewing decks and benches looking out towards the mountainous scenery. During summer a warden is stationed here, and at 7pm each night there's a radio call with a ranger providing weather and avalanche forecasts, and asking for the names of all the parties in the hut.

Needless to say, the views from the hut are excellent, including not only the namesake glacier below but, if you are blessed with clear weather, also the peaks of the Main Divide, crowned by Aoraki/Mt Cook. From Mueller Hut it's a 30-minute rock scramble to an outcrop, marked by a large cairn, just below **Mt Ollivier** (1933m). This was the first peak climbed by Sir Edmund Hillary, who trained in this area for his eventual summit of Everest.

Day 2: Mueller Hut to Mt Cook Village

3 HOURS, 5KM, 1040M DESCENT

Retrace your steps from Day 1. And this is the undersung joy of the return tramp – everything looks different in the other direction!

TOWNS & FACILITIES

Christchurch

☑ 03 / POP 380,900

Determinedly finding its feet after the earthquake of 22 February 2011 – one of NZ's worst natural disasters – this most English of NZ cities is adding a modern and innovative layer to its damaged heritage heart. Punts still glide

gently down the Avon River, and the Botanic Gardens and Hagley Park remain among NZ's finest public spaces, but an energetic entrepreneurial edge is also evident, cutting across the potholes and springing up in the cracks.

🛏 Sleeping & Eating

Much inner-city accommodation was lost in the 2011 earthquake, the result of which is that most of your options will be dotted around the inner suburbs, with some conveniently placed on the airport side of the city. Likewise, this is where many eating and drinking options can also be found.

North South Holiday Park   HOLIDAY PARK $
(☑ 0800 567 765, 03-359 5993; www.northsouth.co.nz; cnr John's & Sawyers Arms Rds, SH1, Harewood; campsites from $35, units $58-125; @ 🛜) Just five minutes' drive from the airport, this spacious park is leafy and low-key.

Jailhouse   HOSTEL $
(☑ 0800 524 546, 03-982 7777; www.jail.co.nz; 338 Lincoln Rd, Addington; dm/s/d $30/79/85; @ 🛜) Housed in an 1874 prison, this well-run and friendly hostel has smallish rooms in Addington, a hot spot for cafes, restaurants and entertainment.

Addington Coffee Co-op   CAFE $
(www.addingtoncoffee.org.nz; 297 Lincoln Rd, Addington; snacks & mains $6-20; 🛜 🍴) This modern and stylish coffeehouse serves splendid cafe fare (including brilliant baking) in bustling surrounds. Legendary big breakfasts, free wi-fi and an onsite laundry will be welcomed by trampers.

Cassels Brewery   PIZZERIA, CRAFT BEER $$
(www.casselsbrewery.co.nz; 3 Garlands Rd, Woolston) A fair schlep from the city, it's well worth making the effort to visit Cassels & Sons craft brewery where you can indulge in wood-fired pizza and a pint, and perhaps a night of live music. The tannery buildings out the back have been reincarnated into a very fine boutique shopping arcade.

🔒 Supplies & Equipment

Easily accessible Addington comes up trumps again, with the Tower Junction Mega Centre providing a great one-stop shop for travellers. There are several shops stocking outdoor adventure gear, including the tramper's friend **Bivouac Outdoor** (www.bivouac.co.nz; 81 Clarence St). There are also cafes and a pub, but for a wider selection head to Lincoln Rd.

Christchurch is a city of supermarkets, so you'll have no trouble stumbling across one. A good target is the centrally located **New World** (South City Centre, Colombo St).

ℹ Information

Christchurch i-SITE (☑ 03-379 9629; www.christchurchnz.com; Rolleston Ave, beside the Canterbury Museum; ⊙ 8.30am-5pm) Book transport and accommodation here, and purchase DOC hut passes or obtain general DOC information.

ℹ Getting There & Away

Christchurch is the main international gateway to the South Island, and has a rather beautifully improved airport to show for it. **Air New Zealand** (☑ 0800 737 000; www.airnewzealand.co.nz) services domestic and international destinations, as does **Jetstar** (☑ 0800 800 995; www.jetstar.com), although its domestic offering is limited to Auckland, Queenstown and Wellington.

InterCity (☑ 03-365 1113; www.intercity.co.nz; 118 Bealey Ave) is the main bus operator on the South Island, servicing major destinations such as Picton (5½ hours), Nelson (eight hours), Queenstown (eight hours), Dunedin (six hours) and Te Anau (10½ hours). Buses depart from 118 Bealey Ave, but that may change during the life of this book – check the website. **Naked Bus** (www.nakedbus.com; 70 Bealey Ave, cnr Montreal & Bealey Aves) heads north to Picton and Nelson, south to Dunedin and southwest to Queenstown, departing from outside the Canterbury Museum on Rolleston Ave. There are also myriad shuttle buses that run in various directions, generally at cheaper rates. Ask at the i-SITE where you can make bookings for most services.

For a bit of old-world charm, travel via train with **KiwiRail Scenic** (☑ 0800 872 467; www.kiwirailscenic.co.nz). The *Coastal Pacific* runs daily each way between Christchurch and Picton via Kaikoura and Blenheim, while the *TranzAlpine* has a daily route between Christchurch and Greymouth via Arthur's Pass.

Most major car- and campervan-rental companies have offices in Christchurch, as do numerous smaller local companies. Operators with national networks often want cars to be returned from Christchurch to Auckland because most renters travel in the opposite direction, so special rates may apply on this northbound route.

Akaroa

☑ 03 / POP 650

Akaroa ('Long Harbour' in Maori) was the site of the country's first French settlement. Today it is a charming, small town imbued with the feel of a low-key resort.

🛏 Sleeping & Eating

Akaroa Top 10 Holiday Park   HOLIDAY PARK $
(☑ 0800 727 525, 03-304 7471; www.akaroa-holidaypark.co.nz; 96 Morgans Rd; campsites from $35, units $70-118; @ ☜) On a terraced hillside above town and connected by a pathway to Woodhills Rd, this pleasant park has good harbour views and versatile options for every budget.

Chez la Mer   HOSTEL $
(☑ 03-304 7024; www.chezlamer.co.nz; 50 Rue Lavaud; dm $28-31, d with/without bathroom $83/73; @ ☜) A friendly backpackers with well-kept rooms and a shaded garden, complete with fish ponds, hammocks, barbecue and outdoor seating; it's also a TV-free zone. Free bikes and fishing rods are available.

Onuku Farm Hostel   HOSTEL $
(☑ 03-304 7066; www.onuku.co.nz; Onuku Rd; campsites per person from $12.50, dm/d from $28/66; ⊙ closed Jun-Aug; @ ☜) An eco-minded backpackers with basic huts, tent sites and a comfy house on a sheep farm near Onuku, 6km south of Akaroa and near the start of the Banks Peninsula Track.

L'Escargot Rouge   CAFE $
(www.lescargotrouge.co.nz; 67 Beach Rd; meals $8-14) Tasty gourmet pies, picnic fixings and French-accented breakfasts are the main attractions at the 'Red Snail'. Scrumptious homemade toasted muesli with fruit, yoghurt and honey will set you up for the day.

Akaroa Fish & Chips   FISH & CHIPS $
(59 Beach Rd; snacks & meals $6-15) No visit to Akaroa would be complete without a visit to this excellent fish-and-chip shop. Grab a table in the courtyard (or sit along the foreshore) and tuck into blue cod, scallops, oysters and other assorted deep-fried goodness.

Vangionis   ITALIAN $$
(www.vangionis.co.nz; Rue Brittan; tapas $8-18, pizzas $18-28) Thin-crust pizzas, tapas, pasta and Canterbury beers and wines all feature at this Tuscan-style trattoria. Secure an outside table and while away lunchtime, afternoon or evening. Takeaway pizzas are also available.

🛒 Supplies & Equipment

There's not much in the way of camping gear, but you'll do well for food supplies between **Akaroa Butchery & Deli** (67 Rue Lavaud), and the **Four Square Supermarket** (Rue Lavaud; ⊙ 8am-8pm) across the road.

CANTERBURY, ARTHUR'S PASS & AORAKI/MT COOK AKAROA

ℹ Information

Akaroa Information Centre (☎03-304 8600; www.akaroa.com; 80 Rue Lavaud; ☼9am-5pm) Akaroa Information Centre is opposite the ATM-equipped Bank of New Zealand and has information on tours, activities and accommodation.

ℹ Getting There & Away

Akaroa is only 82km from Christchurch. From November to April, **Akaroa Shuttle** (☎0800 500 929; www.akaroashuttle.co.nz) operates daily departing Christchurch at 8.30am and 2pm, returning from Akaroa at 10.30am, 3.35pm and 4.30pm. Bookings are recommended. **French Connection** (☎0800 800 575; www. akaroabus.co.nz) has a year-round daily departure from Christchurch at 9.15am, returning from Akaroa at 4pm.

Methven
☎03 / POP 1140

This small town is inland from Ashburton on the SH77, and during winter comes alive with skiers who use it as a base for Mt Hutt and other nearby ski areas. During summer it's much quieter.

🛏 Sleeping & Eating

Alpenhorn Chalet   HOSTEL $
(☎03-302 8779; www.alpenhorn.co.nz; 44 Allen St; dm $28, d $60-85; @🛜) Trampers are well catered for in this small, inviting home, complete with spa pool, log fire, free internet, complimentary espresso coffee, and an in-house massage therapist.

Flashpackers   HOSTEL $
(☎03-302 8999; www.methvenaccommodation. co.nz; cnr McMillan & Bank Sts; dm $25, d with/without bathroom $80/70; @🛜) This YHA-associated lodge has appealing dining and living areas, a large kitchen and indoor and outdoor spa pools. Prices include breakfast.

Supervalue Supermarket   SUPERMARKET $
(cnr The Mall & McMillan St) A more-than-adequate grocery shop.

Cafe Primo   CAFE $
(38 McMillan St; meals $10-18) Sandwiched in and around a raft of Kiwiana are tasty cakes and legendary bacon-and-egg sandwiches. This sunny cafe is also home to Methven's best coffee.

Blue Pub   PUB $$
(www.thebluepub.co.nz; Main St; mains $15-30) Drink at the bar crafted from a huge slab of native timber, challenge the locals to a game of pool, or tuck into robust meals such as sausage and mash.

ℹ Information

The Methven i-SITE (p209) stocks DOC brochures and hut tickets, and can advise on track transport.

Hanmer Springs
☎03 / POP 750

The main thermal resort on the South Island, Hanmer Springs is 10km off SH7, and 57km southeast of Boyle, the end of the St James Walkway. This makes the town an ideal place to pick up supplies before the tramp and to soak away those sore muscles afterwards. Head directly to **Hanmer Springs Thermal Pools** (☎03-315 0000; www.hanmersprings.co.nz; entry on Amuri Ave; adult/child $18/9; ☼10am-9pm) to experience your well-deserved bliss.

🛏 Sleeping & Eating

Le Gite   HOSTEL $
(☎03-315 5111; www.legite.co.nz; 3 Devon St; dm $28, d with/without bathroom $76/64; @🛜) This charming old converted home is a 10-minute walk from the centre and has large rooms and relaxing gardens.

**Hanmer Springs Top 10
Holiday Park**   HOLIDAY PARK $
(☎0800 904 545, 03-315 7113; www.mountain-viewtop10.co.nz; Bath St; campsites from $32, units $80-160; @🛜) A few minutes' walk from the Hanmer Springs Thermal Pools, this tidy camping ground has good facilities including basic cabins and motel units.

Powerhouse Cafe   CAFE $
(☎03-315 5252; www.powerhousecafe.co.nz; 6 Jacks Pass Rd; mains $12-20; 🛜🍽) Recharge your batteries with huge breakfasts, sophisticated lunch and dinner options, and fair-trade coffee. Sunny courtyard, wi-fi and plenty of gluten-free and vegetarian options.

🛠 Supplies & Equipment

For supplies to go, head to the excellent **Hanmer Springs Bakery** (16 Conical Hill Rd; ☼6am-4pm) or the **Four Square Supermarket** (Conical Hill Rd).

ℹ Information

Hanmer Springs i-SITE (☑ 03-315 0020, 0800 442 663; www.visithanmersprings.co.nz; 40 Amuri Ave; ⊙10am-5pm) Sells maps, DOC brochures and hut tickets.

ℹ Getting There & Away

Two shuttle-bus operators connect Hanmer Springs with Christchurch (1½ hours): **Hanmer Connection** (☑ 0800 242 663; www.atsnz. com) and **Hanmer Tours** (☑ 03-315 7418; www. hanmertours.co.nz). Shuttles depart from the Hanmer i-SITE. Check the websites of both companies for current departure points from Christchurch.

Arthur's Pass

☑ 03 / POP 50

As small as this hamlet is, Arthur's Pass still serves as the main centre for the national park and surrounding area. After a major tramp it's worth scheduling some extra days at this scenic mountain village to enjoy the numerous day walks that climb above the bushline.

🛏 Sleeping & Eating

Camping in the township is available at the basic **Arthur's Pass public shelter** ($6), opposite the DOC centre (p218), where there's running water, a sink, tables and toilets. There's more basic camping close to the start of the Goat Pass Track, 8km east of Arthur's Pass at **Klondyke Corner Campsite** (free).

Mountain House   HOSTEL $
(☑ 027 419 2354, 03-318 9258; www.trampers. co.nz; SH73; dm $27-29, s/d/tr/q $79/82/99/124, cottages d $140 plus $15 per person; @ 🤶) Excellent dorms and private rooms on one side of the highway, and older, but still comfortable, rooms across the road. The owners also provide transport to trailheads. Self-contained cottages with cozy open fires are also available. Bookings are recommended from November to April. You can sometimes camp ($20 per person) near the cottages. Phone ahead to check availability first.

Arthur's Pass Store & Tearooms   CAFE $
(SH73; 🤶) You don't want to be outfitting an expedition here, but this lone shop has some supplies, including stove fuel and adequate food to get you through a tramp. Slices a good sandwich, and serves up a good breakfast.

Wobbly Kea   CAFE $$
(www.wobblykea.co.nz; SH73; meals $15-32) This friendly cafe-bar serves steaks, pasta and pizza. Takeaway pizza ($28) is also available. Breakfast at the Wobbly Kea ($10 to $18) is a local tradition designed to set you up for the most active of days.

ℹ Information

The online directory of **Arthur's Pass Community Centre** (www.softrock.co.nz) is a mine of useful local information.

ℹ Getting There & Away

Arthur's Pass sees buses travelling between Christchurch (two hours) and Greymouth (2½ hours), a route serviced by Atomic Shuttles (p221) and West Coast Shuttle (p221). Bus tickets are sold at the Arthur's Pass Store.

The *TranzAlpine* – New Zealnd's most scenic train service – runs between Christchurch and Greymouth via Arthur's Pass, operated by **KiwiRail Scenic** (☑ 0800 872 467; www. kiwirailscenic.co.nz).

Mt Cook Village

☑ 03 / POP 234

This small hamlet is the access point for most visitors to Aoraki/Mt Cook National Park. The majority of accommodation options here are expensive because rooms are limited. The **DOC Aoraki/Mt Cook National Park Visitor Centre** (☑ 03-435 1186; www. doc.govt.nz; 1 Larch Grove; ⊙8.30am-6pm summer, 8.30pm-4.30pm winter) is the information hub of the village.

🛏 Sleeping & Eating

White Horse Hill Camping Area   CAMPSITE $
(☑ 03-435 1186; campsites $10; ⊙shelter 8am-7pm Oct-Apr, to 5pm May-Sep) This basic DOC campsite is 2km from the village centre. It has no electricity but boasts a pleasant shelter and diverting views. Note that campers and walkers can also use the **public shelter** (⊙8am-7pm Oct-Apr, to 5pm May-Sep) in the village, which has running water, toilets and coin-operated showers, but overnight stays are not permitted.

Unwin Hut   HOSTEL $
(☑ 0275 235 360, 03-435 1100; www.alpineclub.org. nz; SH80; dm $30) Located 3.5km before Mt Cook Village is basic Unwin Hut. This lodge belongs to the New Zealand Alpine Club but nonmembers are welcome to stay, space

permitting. There are basic bunks, a big common room with a fireplace and kitchen.

Mt Cook YHA
HOSTEL $$

(☑ 03-435 1820; www.yha.co.nz; cnr Bowen & Kitchener Drs; dm $37, d $118; @ ☎) This excellent hostel has a free sauna, drying room and log fires. Try to book a few days in advance.

Aoraki/Mt Cook Alpine Lodge
LODGE $$

(☑ 03-435 1860; www.aorakialpinelodge.co.nz; Bowen Dr; d $159-189, tr $164; @) Warmed up with Turkish rugs and underfloor heating, this lodge features a huge lounge and kitchen, and an alfresco barbecue area with superb mountain views.

Hermitage Aoraki/Mt Cook Hotel
INTERNATIONAL $$

(☑ 435 1809, 0800 686 800; www.hermitage.co.nz; Terrace Rd; meals $14-40) This sprawling complex has several dining options running the gamut from snacks and sandwiches to a dinner buffet. It is also home to the Sir Edmund Hillary Alpine Centre, with a theatre and museum dedicated to the climbing history of the area.

Old Mountaineers Cafe Bar
CAFE $$

(www.mtcook.com; Bowen Dr; lunch $17-24, dinner $22-35; ☎) Featuring mountain views, this cosy place delivers top-notch burgers, pizza, pasta and salad, and is a good-value alternative to the eateries at the Hermitage. Linger to study the old black-and-white pics and mountaineering memorabilia.

❶ Getting There & Away

The village's small airport only serves aerial sightseeing companies. Some of these may be willing to combine transport to the West Coast (ie Franz Josef) with a scenic flight, but flights are heavily dependent on weather.

InterCity (☑ 03-365 1113; www.intercity. co.nz) links Aoraki/Mt Cook to Christchurch (five hours), Queenstown (four hours) and Wanaka (with a change in Tarras; 4¼ hours). Buses stop at the YHA and the Hermitage, both of which handle bookings. The Cook Connection (☑ 0800 266 526; www.cookconnect. co.nz) has services to Twizel (one hour) and Lake Tekapo (two hours). Bus services in these towns link to Christchurch, Queenstown, Wanaka and Dunedin.

If you're driving, fill up at Lake Tekapo or Twizel. There is petrol at Aoraki/Mt Cook, but it's expensive and involves summoning an attendant from the Hermitage (for a fee).

West Coast

Includes ➡

The Old Ghost
Road Track 240
Inland Pack Track. . . . 244
Croesus Track. 247
Welcome Flat 251

Best Views

➡ Rocky Tor (p242)

➡ Specimen Point Hut (p243)

➡ Croesus Knob (p250)

➡ Douglas Rock Hut (p254)

Best Huts

➡ Ghost Lake Hut (p242)

➡ Ballroom Overhang (p247)

➡ Ces Clark Hut (p249)

➡ Welcome Flat (p253)

Why Go?

Hemmed in by the Tasman Sea and the Southern Alps, the wild and sparsely populated West Coast lays claim to three national parks and large tracts of three more, encompassed within a conservation estate covering nearly 90% of its land area.

Unsurprisingly, the Department of Conservation (DOC) is very active here, reworking existing tracks and helping to build new ones, such as the Old Ghost Road. This and many others follow the byways of pioneer-era miners and loggers, who left in their wake rusting relics and landmarks that bring their stories to life.

There are splendid tramps from one end of the coast to the other, not just through Kahurangi, Paparoa and Westland Tai Poutini National Parks, but also within the many parks and reserves that fill in the gaps.

While its remoteness and reputation for wet weather puts many trampers off, the West Coast stands as one of New Zealand's most rewarding tramping destinations.

When to Go

The West Coast is renowned for its rain, although the locals are liable to tell you that it falls mainly in big drops, and mostly at night. What is a fact is that the average rainfall in the lowlands is between 2000mm and 3000mm, 5000mm at the foot of the Alps, and in excess of 11,000mm a year in areas above 1200m. Much of it falls in late winter and spring. Flooded and impassable rivers, however, should be expected at any time of year.

Warm ocean currents sweep along the coast, resulting in a surprisingly mild climate. Midsummer to autumn can be exceptionally sunny, with long spells of settled weather. Westport and Punakaiki average almost 2000 hours of sunshine annually.

GATEWAY TOWNS

➡ Westport (p254)

➡ Punakaiki (p255)

➡ Greymouth (p255)

➡ Franz Josef Glacier (p256)

➡ Fox Glacier (p256)

Fast Facts

➡ The West Coat is NZ's most sparsely populated area. Its 32,000 residents make up less than 1% of NZ's population, spread throughout a disproportionate 9% of the country's area.

➡ The culinary star of the West Coast is whitebait, the young fry of a fish species called galaxiids, which are caught along rivers as they try and migrate from the ocean back upstream.

Top Tip

Encountering the infamous West Coast sandfly is a certainty. Keep them at bay by covering up when they are at their most active (dawn and dusk), and coating your exposed parts with a citronella-based repellent.

Resources

➡ www.buller.co.nz

➡ www.punakaiki.co.nz

➡ www.greydistrict.co.nz

➡ www.glaciercountry.co.nz

➡ www.foxglaciertourism. co.nz

Background Reading

Settlement of the West Coast was driven first by the gold rushes, which was followed quickly by the quest for its famously good coal. The birthplace of this industry – which continues (somewhat controversially) today – is Denniston, a once-isolated plateau perched above the narrow, coastal flats. Its apparent desolation belies its myriad fascinations, including its social history vividly re-imagined in Jenny Pattrick's best-selling novels, *The Denniston Rose* and *Heart of Coal*. Get your hands on the combined and illustrated edition if you can.

Many of the region's tramps follow old mining byways, which lend themselves equally well to gentle mountain biking. To discover the joys of the region's cycling trails, look for *Classic New Zealand Cycle Trails* by the Kennett Brothers, or *Mountain Biking South* by Dave Mitchell.

DON'T MISS

New Zealand's national bird, the kiwi, is a largely rare and elusive creature, more often heard than seen. On the West Coast, however, there are plenty of opportunities to encounter them if you know where to look.

Success is guaranteed at the **West Coast Wildlife Centre** (www.wildkiwi.co.nz; cnr Cron & Cowan Sts; admission $30, backstage pass $50; 🖱) in Franz Josef Glacier. This feel-good attraction ticks all the right boxes (exhibition, cafe and retail), then goes a whole lot further by actually breeding the rowi – the rarest kiwi in the world, along with another local species, the Haast tokoeka. It's worth visiting to view the conservation, glacier and heritage displays and mature kiwi in their ferny enclosure. However, the pièce de résistance is the 'backstage' incubating and chick-rearing area. You may well go ga-ga over the fluffy kiwi babies. Too cute!

You've got a very strong chance of seeing the rowi in the wild on a night-time expedition with **Okarito Kiwi Tours** (📞 03-753 4330; www.okaritokiwitours.co.nz; 2-3hr tours $75).

DOC Offices

➡ **Buller Area Office** (📞 03-788 8008; www.doc.govt.nz; 72 Russell St; ⊙ 8am-noon & 2-4.30pm Mon-Fri)

➡ **Paparoa National Park Visitor Information Centre and i-SITE** (📞 03-731 1895; www.doc.govt.nz; SH6; ⊙ 9am-5pm Oct-Nov, to 6pm Dec-Mar, to 4.30pm Apr-Sep)

➡ **Westland Tai Poutini National Park Visitor Centre & i-SITE** (📞 03-752 0796; www.doc.govt.nz; SH6, Franz Josef Glacier; ⊙ 8.30am-6pm summer, to 5pm winter)

➡ **DOC South Westland Weheka Area Office** (📞 03-751 0807; SH6, Fox Glacier; ⊙ 10am-2pm Mon-Fri)

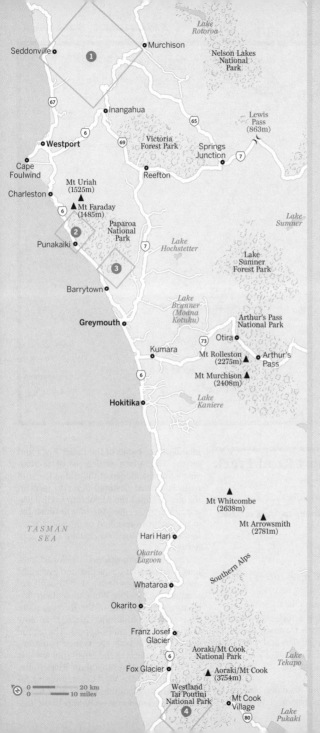

West Coast Tramps

1 The Old Ghost Road Track (p240)

2 Inland Pack Track (p245)

3 Croesus Track (p248)

4 Welcome Flat (p252)

The Old Ghost Road Track

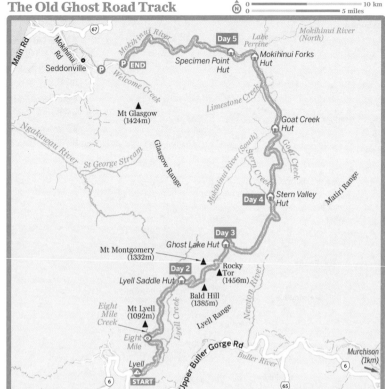

The Old Ghost Road Track

Duration 5 days

Distance 80km (50 miles)

Track Standard Tramping track & route

Difficulty Moderate

Start Lyell Campsite

End Seddonville

Nearest Towns Westport (p254), Punakaiki (p255)

Transport Bus, shuttle bus

Summary Following a historic byway, this spectacular new track traverses native forests, tussock tops, river flats and valleys with stunning views of the magnificent Mokihinui Gorge and surrounds.

The Lyell–Mokihinui Rd dates back to the 1870s, when it was begun at both ends – inland on the banks of the Buller River and on the West Coast settlement of Seddonville – but abandoned at the end of the gold rush. It seemed destined never to meet in the middle until the Mokihinui-Lyell Backcountry Trust secured funding to finish the job, creating an excellent tramp and a jewel in the crown of the New Zealand Cycle Trail network.

The Lyell campsite and walkway have long been popular for picnics and overnight stops, with visitors drawn in by readily accessible historic sites. While undeniably fascinating, the opening of the through-route means that gold-mining heritage is now only part of the trail's appeal. The alpine section takes in truly spectacular panoramas, but the valleys of the Mokihinui are just as captivating. The Mokihinui River is the third largest on the West Coast, draining no less than five mountain ranges as it wends through ancient forest on its way to the Tasman Sea. It's a rich habitat, home to numerous threatened species, including great spotted kiwi, whio (blue duck), longfin eels and the carnivorous snail called Powelliphanta.

The tramp can be completed in either direction, perhaps determined by the weather forecast to maximise views on the southern, alpine end. As described here it takes four nights and five days, resulting in a short second day's tramp to Ghost Lake Hut – a highlight of the journey and therefore a good place to pause and reflect. The track could be split several other ways, including combining the first two legs, resulting in a very long first day but saving one overall.

The first sections of the Old Ghost Road officially opened early in 2013. At the time of writing the full trail was due for completion in late 2014, at which point NZ will have got itself a very special new trail, one steeped in the flinty spirit of the pioneer era.

ⓘ Planning

WHEN TO TRAMP
Around a quarter of the Old Ghost Road is above 1000m, where snow may fall any time, but particularly from May to November, and bad weather may blow in at any time of year. In favourable weather, however, it's possible to tramp this track year-round. The best time is November through May.

MAPS
The best map for this track is NZTopo50 *BR22* (Lyell). The Mokihinui-Lyell Backcountry Trust (www.oldghostroad.org.nz) also produces an excellent map, useful for planning.

HUTS & CAMPING
There are six huts along the Old Ghost Road, two of which – Goat Creek and Mokihinui Forks – are **Basic huts** (www.doc.govt.nz; free). The other four – Lyell Saddle, Ghost Lake, Stern Valley and Specimen Point – are managed by the Mokihinui-Lyell Backcountry Trust (www.oldghostroad.org.nz) and must be booked in advance via its online booking system. Three of these Trust huts (Stern Valley excluded) have two four-person sleep-outs suitable for families and privacy-seekers. All huts have bunks, mattresses, toilets and rainwater supply, but no cooking facilities.

Camping is permitted anywhere along the track, as well as at Lyell, where there is a **Basic campsite** (www.doc.govt.nz; free) right on SH6. There's also pleasant camping at **Seddonville Holiday Park** (☑ 03-782 1314; campsites for 2 unpowered/powered $10/14, dm $10-15), which makes excellent use of an old schoolhouse and grounds.

INFORMATION SOURCES
The Old Ghost Road is managed in co-operation between DOC's Buller Area Office (p238) and Mokihinui-Lyell Backcountry Trust. Information is also available at the Westport or Murchison i-SITEs.

ⓘ Getting to/from the Tramp
Lyell campsite is 50 minutes' drive (62km) east of Westport, right on SH6 along the scenic Buller Gorge. Seddonville, at the northern end of the track, is 45 minutes' drive (50km) north of Westport, a walkable 1.5km off the main road, SH67.

Because this track is new, tramper transport services weren't yet bedded down at the time of writing. However, as both the Old Ghost Road trailheads are passed by tramper shuttles for the Heaphy Track you will have no trouble hooking on to their services, which are reasonably regular in season.

Trek Express (☑ 027-222 1872, 0800 128 735; www.trekexpress.co.nz) will drop you off at either trailhead, on demand (most economically tagging you on to a scheduled service), with sample fares of $40 from Westport to Lyell and $40 from Seddonville to Westport.

You can also be dropped off at Lyell by the bus operators running scheduled SH6 services to Westport from Nelson or Picton, the most regular of which are **InterCity** (☑ 03-365 1113; www.intercity.co.nz) and **Naked Bus** (www.nakedbus.com).

Scheduled daily shuttle services also pass Seddonville, run by **Karamea Express** (☑ 03-782 6757; info@karamea-express.co.nz).

🚶 The Tramp

Day 1: Lyell Campsite to Lyell Saddle Hut
4–6 HOURS, 16KM, 765M ASCENT
Located right on the highway on the scenic Buller Gorge, the Lyell campsite is a popular stop with both day visitors and overnighters attracted by its historic interest, in particular the gold-mining relics and the overgrown **Lyell Cemetery**, 10 minutes' walk from the campsite.

The Old Ghost Road is well signposted at the far end of the campsite, and the wooden gateway offers a good photo opportunity. Cross the bridge over **Lyell Creek** and follow the track as it begins its steady climb up what has long been a popular walkway, following the original miners' dray road.

Gentle, beech forest dominates as you head up the Lyell Valley. Around 45 minutes into the tramp you will reach the site of **Gibbstown**, where side tracks lead down to the site of the old alpine battery. It will take around an hour (3km) of gentle to reach **Eight Mile**, but it is only the odd rusty relic, stranded in the undergrowth, that betrays the existence of these settlements. Insightful interpretive displays will stir the imagination.

As you wind your way further up the valley, other interesting features come into view, such as the earthquake slips caused by the 1929 Murchison and 1968 Inangahua earthquakes. The damage is clearly visible in a series of gouges, still largely bald except for the odd tree clinging precariously to the loose, rocky slopes. Two such slips must be crossed around 2½ hours into the journey, where gates indicate that riders must dismount.

The track continues winding up the valley to **Lyell Saddle**, where a short spur track leads to **Lyell Saddle Hut** (20 bunks), clustered on a ridge overlooking the Mokihinui South Branch and the Glasgow Range.

Day 2: Lyell Saddle Hut to Ghost Lake Hut

3–5 HOURS, 12KM, 325M ASCENT

From Lyell Saddle Hut the track climbs steadily but gently towards the tops, with the occasional viewpoint out over the Glasgow Range and yonder as you wind hither and zither through the beech forest. The trees thin and become progressively stunted as you approach the bushline.

Around two hours (6km) from the hut you emerge on to the open tops of the **Lyell Range**, meandering along freshly benched track cut through the thick, golden tussock. Sweeping views take in an endless sea of peaks, all the way through to Ghost Lake Hut, around two hours (6km away). If you have plenty of time to dawdle, this is your cue to do so.

The trail remains more or less level as it continues up to **Mt Montgomery** (1332m), and sidles around its north side before passing beneath **Rocky Tor** (1456m), the highest peak along the route.

From here it is another hour of meandering along the ridge and side slopes before you reach **Ghost Lake Hut** (20 bunks), 1200m above sea level. Views abound in every direction; this is a fine spot to spend the night. Stay on the boardwalk when visiting the tarn, as it is a fragile environment.

Day 3: Ghost Lake Hut to Stern Valley Hut

4–5 HOURS, 11KM, 800M DESCENT

It's virtually all downhill from here – 800m over 10km, to be precise. Fortunately, the gradient is gentle, which means it's not as hard on the knees as some descents can be.

From Ghost Lake Hut, the route wiggles and winds its way through gorgeous meadows and scrub back down into mature bush. The track then undulates along the backbone of Stern Ridge on its journey to Stern Creek, with fine views of the Matiri Range to the east and the forested slopes of the Lyell Range to the west.

Around three hours from Ghost Lake Hut, you enter **Stern Valley**. There are two bridged crossings before you arrive in the valley meadows, and Stern Valley Hut (12 bunks) alongside the creek.

Day 4: Stern Valley Hut to Specimen Point Hut

7–10 HOURS, 25KM

The trail begins by meandering up through the north branch valley of **Stern Creek**, across strange but beautiful meadows. At twin lakes the route switches back into climbing mode for a short, sharp ascent towards the saddle leading over to the catchment of **Goat Creek**. Once over the saddle it's around one hour to Goat Creek Hut (four bunks), recently restored to its original 1958 design. It will take around four to five hours to cover the 12km from Stern Valley to Goat Creek Hut, which means you're around halfway through the day's journey.

The hut sits near the confluence of Goat Creek and the **Mokihinui River South** branch, which is then followed in the direction of Mokihinui Forks. The river must be forded en route, so choose your crossing carefully and sit it out if the conditions aren't right. A 90m bridge is planned for the South branch, although a completion date hadn't been set at the time of research.

As it follows the river downstream, the track passes through the magnificent podocarp **Mokihinui Forest**, in which reside whio, the karearea (NZ falcon) and pekapeka (native bats). Along the way you will also pass The Resurgence – a large spring that breaks the surface in a magical bubbling pool.

It's around two to three hours (9km) from Goat Creek to **Mokihinui Forks**, where the

South branch meets the **Mokihinui River North** branch, and the historic Mokihinui Forks Hut (10 bunks) is located.

Turning left at the forks, the trail continues for another 3km (less than an hour) to the head of the **Mokihinui River Gorge** and **Specimen Point Hut** (22 bunks). This hut sits atop a bluff over the Mokihinui with spectacular views down river.

Day 5: Specimen Point Hut to Seddonville

4–6 HOURS. 16KM

From Specimen Point, the Mokihinui Gorge leads the way as you follow the old miners' road for the largely flat walk out to Seddonville.

The Mokihinui River was the focus of a significant environmental stoush, when a government-owned electricity company was granted consent to dam the river and build a hydroelectric power station just upstream from Seddonville, in 2010. DOC, backed by other ardent conservationists Forest & Bird, lodged an appeal with the Environment Court and in 2012 the project was abandoned. At the time of writing Forest & Bird was lobbying for the river and its catchment to be added to Kahurangi National Park.

This section of track passes through old gold workings, with remnants to view along the way including a pelton wheel, drill rods, a stamping battery and, most significantly, the track itself.

It also crosses three suspension bridges spanning the infamous Suicide Slips. These slips were formed by the 1968 Inangahua earthquake and have posed a physical challenge to anyone wishing to travel up beyond the gorge.

About 45 minutes past the suspension bridges the track reaches the site of yet another mining ghost town – Seatonville. The clearing here is an excellent lunch spot.

Another hour on is a striking lookout point to Rough and Tumble Creek. The old iron bridge lying collapsed in the river shows that the track for the remainder of your journey was once the only land route to the northern town of Karamea.

The final kilometre of track broadens into a 4WD road before reaching civilisation. There are a series of small car parks along the way, although if you do have your car with you it is wiser to park close to the Seddonville pub.

PAPAROA NATIONAL PARK

Like the first explorers 170-odd years before them, most tourists travelling along the isolated West Coast between Westport and Greymouth are totally enthralled by the rugged seascape. Most famous are the Pancake Rocks, the limestone stacks at Dolomite Point, battered by huge ocean swells and punched through by blowholes. It is a truly awe-inspiring site, and a deserved 'must-do' for any West Coast visitor.

Inland are the rugged granite peaks of the Paparoa Range, lined by tramps rich with natural wonders and gold-mining history. Not until the creation and development of Paparoa National Park in 1987 did tracks such as the Inland Pack Track, and the Croesus Track that lies just outside the southern boundary, catch the attention of trampers. Even today, though, they remain somewhat underrated.

History

Middens (mounds of discarded shells and bone fragments) have been recorded at Barrytown, suggesting that Maori must have made many seasonal excursions to the nearby bays and rivers to gather food. The coastline, as rugged as it appears, was a trade route for Maori carrying Arahura River greenstone north.

The first European explorers through the area were probably Charles Heaphy and Thomas Brunner, who were led by Maori guide Kehu on a five-month journey down the coast in 1846. They passed a group of Maori heading north, but the first settlement seen was Kararoa, 20km south of Punakaiki.

Heaphy was greatly impressed by the Paparoa region, devoting 12 pages of his diary to it. He also wrote about 'incessant rain', delays caused by swollen rivers, and of climbing rotting rata and flax ladders up the steep cliffs of Perpendicular Point. Later that year Brunner and Kehu returned to the area. It was an epic journey, lasting 18 months, in which they completely circumnavigated the Paparoa Range, traced the Buller River from source to mouth and travelled as far south as Paringa.

Gold was discovered on the West Coast as early as 1864, but the hunt for the precious metal only really gained momentum two years later when famed prospector

William Fox chartered the SS *Woodpecker* and landed it on the lee side of Seal Island. The area just south of where the Fox River empties into the Tasman Sea became known as Woodpecker Bay, and miners by their thousands stampeded to this stretch of coast.

Reaching the areas along the 'beach highway' was extremely challenging for miners. Despite the Nelson Provincial Government replacing the Maori flax ladders at Perpendicular Point with chains, miners still journeyed inland for a safer route. In 1866 work began on the Inland Pack Track, which avoided the hazardous Perpendicular Point. It was cut through the western lowlands of the Paparoa Range, and in 1868 was used to extend the Christchurch–Greymouth telegraph line north to Westport.

After the miners left, tourism became the region's main activity. A coastal track being cut by the early 1900s eventually became SH6.

The Paparoa Range and lowlands were thrust into the consciousness of the nation in the 1970s, when there was interest in logging the area. This sparked a heated conservation campaign that led to the establishment, in 1987, of the 305-sq-km national park.

Environment

The Paparoa Range is composed mainly of granite and gneiss peaks, which have been carved by glaciers and weathered by rain, snow and wind into a craggy chain of pinnacles and spires. It is a low but very rugged range, between 1200m and 1500m in height, offering a true wilderness experience suitable only for experienced trampers with strong mental fortitude. Cloud and rain feature regularly in Paparoa's midst.

Between the mountains and the coast are the western lowlands, which are totally different in character. This is a karst landscape – a limestone region where the soft rock has been eroded by rivers and underground drainage. What remains are deep canyons and gorges, with limestone walls that rise up to 200m above the river. There are blind valleys, sinkholes, cliffs, overhangs, numerous caves and streams that disappear underground.

The nikau palms that line the coast and highway also extend inland. They combine with a profusion of black mamaku tree ferns, smaller ferns and supplejack vines to form a junglelike canopy. Still further inland, the lowland forest becomes a mixture of podocarp, beech and broad-leaved trees, with rimu and red beech often the most dominant species.

The size of the forest, and the fact that it's been left relatively untouched by humans, has led to the park's profusion of bird life. Commonly spotted along the tracks are bellbirds, tomtits, fantails, grey warblers, kereru (NZ pigeons), tui and the tiny rifleman. One of the favourites encountered is the western weka, a brown flightless bird often spotted in the Fossil Creek area along the Inland Pack Track, as well as in many other areas of the park. There are also many great spotted kiwi, but you'll hear them at night more often than you'll see them.

ⓘ Planning

Paparoa National Park Visitor Information Centre and i-SITE (p238), opposite the entrance to the Pancake Rocks, is a helpful centre providing a booking service for transport, accommodation and local activities, and selling maps, hut tickets and Great Walk passes. As many of the walks in the area involve river crossings, be sure to check in here for the latest weather and track conditions.

Inland Pack Track

Duration 2 days

Distance 27km (18 miles)

Track Standard Tramping track & route

Difficulty Moderate

Start Punakaiki

End Fox River bridge

Nearest Town Punakaiki (p255)

Transport Ask at Paparoa visitor centre

Summary This historic track, carved by gold-miners in 1866 to bypass the rugged coast, features an unusual landscape of steep gorges and interesting caves, as well as one of NZ's largest rock bivvies.

This track explores Paparoa National Park's otherwise hidden treasures, including river valleys lined by nikau palms and spectacular limestone formations. A major highlight is spending a night at the Ballroom Overhang, one of the largest rock bivvies in NZ. While there are no alpine passes to negotiate, nor any excruciating climbs above the tree line, the tramp is no easy stroll. There

Inland Pack Track

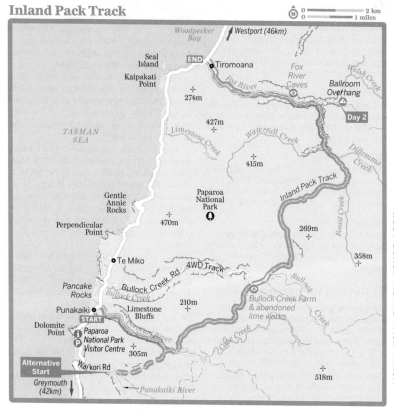

is plenty of mud to contend with, and numerous river crossings. It is suitable for well-equipped people with solid route-finding skills.

Dilemma Creek flows through a gorge so steep and narrow that trampers just walk down the middle of it. Occasionally you can follow a gravel bank, but much of the tramp involves sloshing from one pool to the next. When water levels are normal the stream rarely rises above your knees, and if it's a hot, sunny day this can be the most pleasant segment of the trip, but during heavy rain and flooding you should avoid this track at all costs. If the forecast is poor, wait another day or move down the coast to find another tramp. To be trapped by rising rivers with no tent makes for a very long night.

If you have a tent you can break the tramp more evenly over two days, or extend it to a leisurely three-day walk. It can be tramped in either direction, but starting at Punakaiki

makes navigating the Fox River beds much easier.

ⓘ WARNING

It cannot be stressed enough that the Inland Pack Track should not be attempted during or after periods of heavy rain. There are numerous river crossings and the route from Fossil Creek to Fox River/Dilemma Creek junction involves walking alongside and through the creek. These rivers and creeks can rise very quickly following rainfall – a swollen river should never be crossed.

Before departing, check with the Paparoa National Park Visitor Information Centre (p238), which posts daily weather forecasts. If heavy rain is forecast do not attempt the track.

ⓘ Planning

WHEN TO TRAMP

The Inland Pack Track is best tramped from December through March, when the rivers are at their lowest, but it is also possible to complete it in spring and autumn.

WHAT TO BRING

It is best to carry a tent in case you get stranded overnight by high river levels. If you're staying at the Ballroom Overhang, take a camp stove, as no fires are permitted.

MAPS & BROCHURES

This tramp is covered by NZTopo50 map *BS19* (Punakaiki) and *BS20* (Charleston). DOC's *Paparoa National Park* brochure details tramps of varying lengths around the Punakaiki area.

HUTS & CAMPING

There are no huts on this tramp. The **Bivvy** (www.doc.govt.nz; free) known as the Ballroom Overhang is the site of the only designated campsite.

ⓘ Getting to/from the Tramp

There are two places to start the tramp, both within a 15-minute walk of the National Park Visitor Information Centre in Punakaiki. The most scenic start is from Pororari River bridge, north on SH6. The alternative is off Waikori Rd, along the Punakaiki River, south on SH6.

The finish is at the Fox River bridge on SH6, 12km north of Punakaiki, from which there are no reliable transport options. However, this is the Coast, where almost anything can happen. You may well be able to sort out some ad hoc arrangement, including getting the InterCity bus to pick you up on its way past. This may be arranged through the visitor centre, who will have a handle on comings and goings.

🚶 The Tramp

Day 1: Punakaiki to the Ballroom Overhang

7–8 HOURS, 19.5KM

The track starts from the car park at the Pororari River bridge on SH6. It follows the river closely along its true left (south) bank, through a spectacular landscape of towering limestone bluffs graced by nikau palms and tree ferns. Keep an eye on the river's deep green pools: you may spot trout or eels in the morning, or perhaps you might feel inclined to take a dip. Stranger things have happened!

After 3.5km the track comes to a junction, with the right fork leading back to Punakaiki River and SH6 – a popular three-hour loop walk for day-trampers. Continue on the main track, which in 300m reaches a swing bridge across the Pororari River.

Heading northwards, the next 4km stretch works its way through silver beech forest. The track can become muddy in places, with fairly consistent scenery of thick bush and an occasional signposted sinkhole, but it is easy to follow.

After 1½ hours you enter a clearing where views of the Paparoas come into frame. Here you join a 4WD track across Bullock Creek Farm. The route passes the shacks of an abandoned lime works and a junction, the left fork of which leads back to SH6. Continue onwards to Bullock Creek, where large orange markers indicate the best place to ford it.

Once across the creek, the track follows a farm road for almost 1km and then re-enters the bush. The track stays in beech and rimu forest, but sidles an open area and passes some immense stands of flax. After 2km the track begins ascending to a low saddle (200m) on the main ridge dividing Bullock Creek and the catchment formed by Fox River. There's lots of mud here but the climb is easy, and views of Mt Fleming and flat-topped Mt Euclid are possible on a clear day. The descent on the other side is rapid.

The track remains fairly level until it emerges at Fossil Creek, 2½ hours from Bullock Creek, marked by a large rock cairn and a small sign. There is no track at this point – you simply follow the creek downstream for 1km or so, walking under a thick canopy of trees. The pools will be easy to wade through in normal conditions.

It takes 30 minutes to reach the confluence with Dilemma Creek, marked by another rock cairn and a small sign. This section of track, following Dilemma Gorge downstream, is the most spectacular part of the trip. Hemmed in by massive limestone walls, you will constantly ford the river, avoiding deep pools and following gravel bars. Keep in mind that if the first ford is a problem, the rest will be even more difficult. Fox River can be reached in well under an hour, but most trampers, revelling in the stunning scenery, take 1½ to two hours to cover this short stretch through the gorge.

A signpost on the true left side of Dilemma Creek, just before the confluence with Fox River, indicates where the track resumes. The confluence is easy to recognise because a sharp rock bluff separates the two canyons.

If you are heading to the Ballroom Overhang you need to assess the river levels carefully – do not assume that Fox River is safe to cross. There are deep pools at the confluence of Fox River and Dilemma Creek, and during high water this is not a good place to ford. If you follow the track west for 400m you come to a signposted junction for an alternative river crossing. This track drops to Fox River at a place where it may be forded. Again, assess your crossing carefully.

To reach the Ballroom Overhang, you will need to walk approximately 30 minutes upstream from the confluence along the Fox River. There is no formed track as you follow the riverbed, crossing the river numerous times. The Ballroom Overhang is located on the true right (north) side of the river.

The rock overhang is appropriately named. It's about 100m long, with a cavern and a towering arched ceiling, which is 20m high in the middle. The roof is a hanging garden of sorts, with grass, vines, rows of ferns and even small trees growing from it. There is plenty of sheltered space to pitch your tent; note that lighting fires is not permitted. You can freshen up in the Fox River, but remember: no soap!

ALTERNATIVE START: PUNAKAIKI RIVER TRACK

2 HOURS, 4KM

Purists who want to complete the whole, historic tramp should head south on SH6, and turn down Waikori Rd (east). This short gravel road (1.5km) leads to a parking area just before the suspension bridge over the Punakaiki River. After crossing the bridge, head northeast following the large orange track markers. The track passes through logged swamps to the base of the hill that separates the Punakaiki from the Pororari. A well-benched track climbs to a low saddle and then drops gently 80m to the Pororari. It levels off as it approaches the signposted branch track down the Pororari, one hour from the saddle. Head upstream to cross the swing bridge over the Pororari River, around 300m away.

Day 2: The Ballroom Overhang to Fox River Bridge

2–2½ HOURS, 7.5KM

Return to the track on the true left (south) side of Fox River. A benched track here follows the river west. It's a pleasant walk along the gorge, high above the river, and you pass scattered nikau palms and tangled kiekie. The track follows the valley for 3km before dropping to Fox River, where a wide ford to the true right (north) bank is marked.

On the other side is a junction, and the track heading east (right) goes to Fox River Caves. The 30-minute climb to the caves is gentle, with the exception of the final 100m. The entrances to the two impressive caves are inside a huge rock overhang. Only the upper, left (as you face them) cave can be entered. It is accessible on stone steps, and it's possible to walk 200m inside the main cave if you have a torch handy and a lack of claustrophobia. Failing that, even just a short foray inside will reveal some interesting stalagmites and stalactites.

After returning to the main track at the Fox River ford, stay on the true right (north) side and follow the track west along the river, crossing numerous gravel bars, and using the large orange trail markers designed to keep wandering trampers on course. This section takes about 45 minutes. You emerge at the car park off SH6 at Fox River bridge.

Croesus Track

Duration 2 days

Distance 18km (11 miles)

Track Standard Tramping track & route

Difficulty Moderate

Start Smoke-Ho Creek car park

End Barrytown

Nearest Towns Blackball (p249), Punakaiki (p255), Greymouth (p255)

Transport Shuttle bus

Summary This goldfields route links the Grey Valley with the West Coast at Barrytown. It takes in a variety of sights, including bushland, the tussock tops of the Paparoas and intriguing relics from the gold-mining era.

Croesus Track

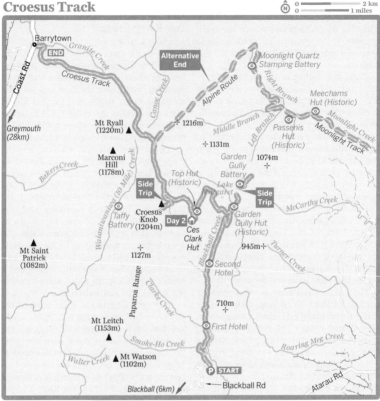

The history of the Paparoas is inextricably interwoven with the search for gold, and these mountains are criss-crossed with tracks made by miners. The Croesus Track is regarded as one of the best surviving 'pack tracks' in NZ.

When gold was found at Blackball Creek in 1864, miners formed a rough track up the creek, through what was known as 'some of the roughest country ever travelled by man' in the hopes of striking it rich. Over 18 years from 1881 to 1899, this early track was slowly replaced by a pack track which was eventually extended all the way across the Paparoas to the coast road.

This track is a pleasing blend of scenery and history, and is a great introduction to the windswept tops of the Paparoas. The views from the tramp's high points – Croesus Knob (1204m) and Mt Ryall (1220m) – are superb, with bald tussock tops stretching north and south. The track is also littered with gold-mining sites.

The tramp can be completed in one long day, but it is far more enjoyable with a stopover at a hut above the bushline.

Further exploration of this area can be had by joining the Croesus with the **Moonlight Track**, which intersect on the tops beyond Ces Clark Hut. This additional five- to six-hour, 15km tramp follows a tussocky ridgeline providing ever-changing views, east to the main divide, west to the Tasman Sea and north and south along the Paparoas. As it descends steeply and follows Moonlight Creek it passes a variety of historic artefacts, including tailings from gold claims, parts of the Moonlight quartz stamping battery dating to 1868, and the remains of a number of miners' huts. The track ends at Moonlight Valley Rd, leading to the village of Atarau.

ℹ Planning

WHEN TO TRAMP

Being an alpine crossing, this tramp is best done from November through March, but trampers do undertake it year-round, depending on weather conditions.

WHAT TO BRING

If you intend staying at Ces Clark Hut you will need to bring your own stove. Be sure, also, to come prepared for bad weather as conditions can change quickly in this area, any time of year.

MAPS

This track is covered by NZTopo50 *BT19* (Runanga) and *BT20* (Ahaura).

HUTS & CAMPING

Ces Clark is a **Serviced hut** (www.doc.govt. nz; $15), with a solid fuel heater but no cooking stove. Camping is also permitted, free except within 50m of the hut.

ℹ Getting to/from the Tramp

This track can be walked in either direction, but is more commonly completed from the backwater town of Blackball (25km inland from Greymouth), over to blink-and-you-miss-it Barrytown (16km south of Punakaiki). From Blackball, it's 6km up to the Smoke-Ho Creek car park on a rough and narrow but well-signposted road to Roa.

Blackball boasts a general store and a spectacularly good sausage shop, as well as the historic **Formerly the Blackball Hilton** (☑ 03-732 4705, 0800 452 2252; www.blackballhilton. co.nz; Hilton St; s/d incl breakfast $55/110, meals $12-34), where you can get food, lodging and transport to both trailheads as well as to and from Greymouth, on demand. Sample fares are $25 from Blackball to Smoke-Ho, and $50 from Barrytown to Blackball, with car storage available. **Kea Heritage Tours** (☑ 0800 532 868; www.keatours.co.nz) offers return-trip track transport from Greymouth ($50 per person, minimum two people).

At Barrytown the track is clearly signposted at the side of SH6, directly opposite the All Nations Hotel, which offers very limited services. You can arrange to be picked up from Barrytown by passing buses plying the Punakaiki to Greymouth route.

👣 The Tramp

Day 1: Smoke-Ho Creek Car Park to Ces Clark Hut

3–4 HOURS, 8KM, 640M ASCENT

At the car park you can climb the hill near the exposed coal seam for good views of the area, and then descend in a northwesterly direction through a mixed podocarp and beech forest towards the creek. The old pack track makes for easy walking, and within 10 minutes you pass the first set of mining artefacts – a pile of rusting rails. Within 1km you reach **Smoke-Ho Creek**, crossing it on a swing bridge.

The track then winds above **Blackball Creek** before descending to a grassy flat and **First Hotel site**, the location of a hotel in the late 1800s. The clearing is about 30 minutes from the car park.

Having crossed Clarke Creek on a swing bridge, the track to Ces Clark Hut continues north and in around 30 minutes reaches the signposted **Second Hotel site**, and if the weather permits you will be greeted with grand views of the **Paparoa Range**.

Follow the true left (east) bank of Blackball Creek as the track zigzags for one hour before reaching a junction where a side trail heads north to the last remaining battery, Garden Gully. The Croesus Track heads west, climbing steadily towards Ces Clark Hut, with glimpses of Lake Margaret below.

During the hour-long climb the track heads roughly west, then south, emerging through the bushline at **Top Hut**, a historic hut not suitable for overnight stops. Here you are greeted with fine views of the Grey Valley, past Lake Brunner to the Main Divide. You then round a spur to head north and quickly reach **Ces Clark Hut** (16 bunks), which enjoys splendid views of the Grey Valley.

This memorial hut, dedicated to a ranger who died on the track, is a fine place to spend a night. One of its many merits is that it's in great spotted kiwi (roa) territory. Occasionally kiwi can be heard from the hut, particularly the male, whose 'ki-wi' call is almost a shrill whistle. For those really keen to hear the bird, follow the track for 10 minutes above the hut to a small spur overlooking the Roaring Meg catchment. Kiwi are more active on dark nights than moonlit ones, and on such evenings it would be unusual not to hear a few calls from this spot in the first hour after sunset.

SIDE TRIP: GARDEN GULLY BATTERY TRACK

1 HOUR, 3KM RETURN

From the signposted Garden Gully junction, continue north to see **Garden Gully Hut** near the headwaters of Roaring Meg Creek (five minutes). Garden Gully is an old

WEST COAST CROESUS TRACK

miners' hut dating from the 1930s that has been recently restored for viewing (not overnight stops). Cross the creek on a swing bridge and the track soon forks. To the left, after 10 minutes, is the **Garden Gully Battery**, the only one in the area still standing. To the right, a route climbs for 15 minutes (30 minutes from Garden Gully junction) to the collapsed mine entrance.

Day 2: Ces Clark Hut to Barrytown

4–4½ HOURS, 10KM, 1160M DESCENT

The first stretch of this leg crosses the tops, marked by snow poles. Be warned that it may prove hard to follow if bad weather has rolled in.

The rough path heads northwest through tussock to the main ridge of the Paparoa Range; it is poled all the way to the bushline on the western side. Thirty minutes from the hut is a path striking off southwest to rocky **Croesus Knob** (1204m), which gives the track its name. The views are well worth the short burst of energy required to reach the summit.

Return to the main track and follow the poles to the northwest as they round the headwaters of **Waianiwaniwa (10 Mile) Creek**. Along the way there are views down

THE COAST TO COAST

Kiwis really are a mad bunch. Take, for instance, the annual **Coast to Coast** (www.coasttocoast.co.nz), the most coveted one-day multisport race in the country. Held in mid-February, the race starts in Kumara, 25km south of Greymouth. Intrepid racers start in the wee hours of the morning with a gentle 3km run, followed by a 55km cycle. Next it's a 33km mountain run over Goat Pass – you know any pass named after a goat isn't going to be flat. From there all there is to do is ride your bike another 15km, paddle your kayak 67km and get back on the bike for the final 70km to Christchurch.

The strong, the brave and the totally knackered will cross the finish line to much fanfare. The course is 243km long and the top competitors will dust it off in just under 11 hours – with slowpokes taking almost twice that.

the valley to Point Elizabeth, with Aoraki/Mt Cook and Mt Tasman visible further south on the horizon on especially clear days. Halfway across the tops you will pass a sign marking the alpine route to the Moonlight Valley and then come close to the summit of **Mt Ryall** (1220m). From Ces Clark Hut to this point, near the bushline, takes two hours – including the climb to Croesus Knob.

The well-marked track then plunges into the bush, which is predominantly subalpine species and beech, and drops steeply towards the West Coast. Further down, the gradient eases as you join an old miners' benched track, and the vegetation changes to nikau palms and other warm-climate species found along the Paparoa coastline.

About 2½ hours after reaching the bushline you emerge onto SH6, across the highway from the All Nations Hotel (which has limited services), where you can connect with passing bus services.

WESTLAND TAI POUTINI NATIONAL PARK

Around halfway down the South Island's West Coast, the 117-sq-km Westland Tai Poutini National Park extends from the highest peaks of the Southern Alps (Ka Tiritiri o te Moana) to the rugged and remote beaches of the wild West Coast. It is an area of magnificent primeval vistas – snow-capped mountains, glaciers, forests, tussock grasslands, lakes, rivers, wetlands and beaches. This world-class scenic landscape forms part of Te Wahipounamu – South West New Zealand World Heritage Area and is a treasure trove of amazing geology, rare flora and fauna and wonderful history.

The park is split by the Alpine Fault, creating a place of dramatic contrasts. East of the fault, mountains rise suddenly, and steep forested slopes are cut deeply with impassable gorges. High above, permanent snowfields feed myriad glaciers, including Fox Glacier (Te Moeka o Tuawe) and Franz Josef Glacier (Ka Roimata o Hine Hukatere), which descend right down to the lowlands.

On the west side are primeval rainforests – rata high up, and a profusion of ferns, shrubs and trees lower down. There are many lakes to explore on the narrow coastal plain, and the soaring ice-covered mountains provide a dramatic backdrop.

History

Early Maori settlements were situated near Westland Tai Poutini's lakes and lagoons, where food was plentiful. However, as they travelled up and down the coast in their pursuit of *pounamu* (greenstone), it is evident that they travelled widely through the forests and up into alpine areas.

It was gold, once again, that lured larger populations to the area. Indeed, in the year straddling 1864–65 at least 16,000 miners came to the rain-soaked wilderness in the hope of lining their pockets. The first prospectors headed for the rivers, but in the spring of 1865 gold was found glittering in the black-sand beaches. Townships sprung up, but the rushes didn't last. Just 18 months after their incredibly rapid emergence, the seaside settlements of Okarito, Five Mile and Gillespies were virtual ghost towns.

However, word was soon spread of the stunning landscape – Fox and Franz Josef glaciers, in particular. Determined visitors ventured to the remote coast to check it out for themselves, and by the start of the 1900s demand was such that the government was allocating funds for tracks and huts. Parties were guided up on to the ice and into the mountains by the Graham brothers, Peter and Alec, forerunners of the guiding enterprises that thrive to this day.

Suggestions that the snowfields and glaciers of the region should be added to Aoraki/Mt Cook National Park united West Coast support for its own national park. Westland Tai Poutini National Park was subsequently gazetted on 29 March 1960.

During the 1970s the focus of conservation shifted to the lowland forests of the West Coast, resulting in the 1982 addition of the southern part of Okarito State Forest and Waikukupa State Forest. The park was further extended in 1983 to incorporate the complete catchment of the Upper Karangarua Valley, thus establishing more natural boundaries and securing an area with distinctive ecological and scenic values. Other additions were made to the park in 2002, namely North Okarito and Saltwater State Forests.

Environment

Westland Tai Poutini has a very wet climate, the prevailing westerly pushing storms laden with huge amounts of moisture across the Tasman Sea, and when they hit the high peaks of the Southern Alps the resulting storms and rainfall can be impressive. The result is plenty of snow and ice near the tops. In all, the park contains 60 named glaciers, two of which – Franz Josef and Fox – are among the West Coast's best-known tourist attractions.

The lowlands are covered in dense rainforest, while nearer the coast are scenic lakes, wetlands and wide river mouths. Wading birds and other water-loving creatures thrive among the wetlands. The threatened kamana (crested grebe) can be found on Lake Mapourika, and Okarito Lagoon is famous for the stunning kotuku (white heron). In the heart of lowland forest lives the only population of the endangered rowi – NZ's rarest kiwi. Kea are common throughout the park, and the forest is filled with bird life.

🛈 Planning

INFORMATION SOURCES

The national park is attended by two DOC offices, the biggest of which is Westland Tai Poutini National Park Visitor Centre & i-SITE (p238), located in Franz Josef, the larger of the two glacier towns. The other is South Westland Weheka Area Office (p238) in Fox Glacier. Both stock maps and brochures, assist with hut bookings, and hold current weather forecasts. The former doubles as an i-SITE, and so offers a broader range of general travel services.

Welcome Flat

Duration 3 days

Distance 50km (31 miles)

Track Standard Easy tramping track

Difficulty Easy to moderate

Start/End Karangarua River bridge

Nearest Towns Fox Glacier (p256), Franz Josef Glacier (p256)

Transport Bus, shuttle bus

Summary A tramp along the Karangarua and Copland Rivers to open alpine areas with epic mountain scenery, plus a soothing soak in the Welcome Flat hot springs.

This tramp up the Copland Valley to Welcome Flat Hut is a popular overnight return trip for visitors to the Glacier Region. It offers a window into Westland Tai Poutini's spectacular forest, river and mountain scenery, while natural hot pools at Welcome Flat are an added attraction for weary adventurers.

Welcome Flat

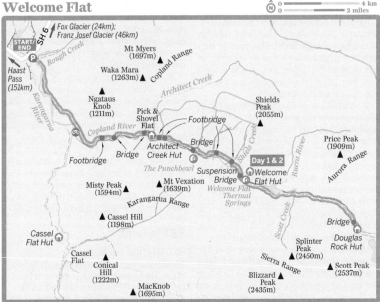

ⓘ WARNING

Heed the weather warnings before departing on a tramp to Welcome Flat! Although the track is well benched, with flood bridges at major crossings, even small streams can become raging torrents during and after heavy rain – a common occurrence on the West Coast. Be sure to check the latest weather forecast at the DOC offices in either Franz Josef Glacier, Fox Glacier or Haast, and leave your intentions via Adventuresmart (www.adventure smart.org.nz).

The forests of the Copland Valley are visually dominated by a healthy canopy of southern rata, a spectacular sight during the summer flowering season. The forest gives way at higher altitudes to the upper montane vegetation of tree daisies and *Dracophyllums,* which in turn give way to the truly alpine habitats of tussock grasslands and native herbs.

Regular possum control has been undertaken since the mid-1980s and as a result the forest damage is significantly less than in the neighbouring Karangarua Valley, which has extensive canopy dieback.

The only real drawback of this tramp is that you must eventually turn around and backtrack to SH6.

ⓘ Planning

WHEN TO TRAMP

This half of the Copland Track can be tramped year-round if the creeks are fordable. The high season is from November through April.

MAPS

This tramp is covered by NZTopo50 maps *BX14* (Gillespies Beach) and *BX15* (Fox Glacier).

HUTS & CAMPING

The recommended overnight stop for this tramp is Welcome Flat, a **Serviced hut** (www.doc. govt.nz; $15), and the adjacent Sierra Room, a self-contained space (the old warden's quarters) with a gas cooker, cooking utensils and a hot shower ($100 per night). There are also **Standard huts** (www.doc.govt.nz; $5) along this route: Architect Creek and Douglas Rock. None have cookers, so bring your own stove.

In recent years Welcome Flat has become an extremely popular tramp, a result of which is that the huts and campsite must be booked all year round, either online or in person at DOC visitor centres and local i-SITEs.

❶ Getting to/from the Tramp

The start of the track, Karangarua River bridge, is right on SH6, 48km from Franz Josef Glacier, and 26km from Fox Glacier. There is a bus stop at the bridge, from where you can flag down the passing daily **InterCity bus** (☑ 03-365 1113; www.intercity.co.nz), which heads past going south to Haast at around 9.10am, and north to Fox and Franz around 2.55pm.

Franz Josef–based **Glacier Valley Eco Tours** (☑ 0800 999 739; www.glaciervalley.co.nz) will run you to the bridge for a $100 minimum charge. Fox-based **Fox Glacier Shuttles** (☑ 0800 369 287) will get you there from Fox for $30 per person (minimum two people).

 The Tramp

Day 1: Karangarua River Bridge to Welcome Flat Hut

7 HOURS, 18KM

From the bus shelter, just northeast of the bridge on SH6, a vehicle track leads 200m to Rough Creek and a car park. The tramp begins by fording **Rough Creek** – a swing bridge 30 minutes upstream is only needed during floods. You can usually rock-hop across the creek without getting your feet wet. Remember, if you need to use the flood bridge, you're going to encounter impassable rivers further up the valley and should not continue.

Beyond Rough Creek the track stays in the bush along the **Karangarua River**, although the track is out of view of the river most of the time until it breaks out onto an open river flat within 1km. Orange triangle markers lead you across the flat and back into the totara and rimu bush. About 4km from the car park the track passes the confluence of the Karangarua and the **Copland River**, where there is a five-minute side track (right) to a lookout over the rivers.

The track then swings almost due east to head up the Copland Valley. Eventually you descend to the water and begin boulder-hopping along the banks of the Copland River. Trail markers direct you back into the forest to cross a bridge over an unnamed stream, which drains the Copland Range to the north. Within 2km you cross another bridge over **McPhee Creek**, and then arrive at the long bridge over **Architect Creek**, the halfway point to Welcome Flat Hut. Here you will find Architect Creek Hut (two bunks).

 WARNING

There are two active landslide areas to be crossed on the track to Welcome Flat Hut. The landslide areas are approximately 30 minutes upstream of Architect Creek, and on the true left of Shiels Creek. Both are signposted. Due to unstable slopes care is required during and just after heavy rain.

At Architect Creek you begin an ascent (totalling 300m) to the hut. About 30 minutes beyond the creek is a landslide area. If conditions are wet, use caution and care when traversing these unstable slopes. At first the climb is gradual, and within 2km you reach the flood bridge over **Palaver Creek**. After **Open Creek** the track steepens until you cross **Shiels Creek** and reach the day's high point (500m). You're now 1km from the hot springs, with most of the tramp a descent through ribbonwood forest.

Welcome Flat thermal springs were first noted by Charles Douglas in 1896. The water emerges from the ground at around 60°C and flows through a series of three shallow pools towards Copland River. The hottest pool – knee-deep and the size of a tennis court – is still 55°C, so most bathers prefer the second pool. Sandflies can be thick here in the day, but a midnight soak on a clear evening is a trip highlight; lie back in the warm water and count the falling stars.

The excellent **Welcome Flat Hut** (31 bunks), a short stroll from the pools, is popular and must be booked in advance. It has a potbelly stove, coal and a radio. A warden is usually stationed here.

Day 2: Welcome Flat Hut to Douglas Rock Hut (Return)

5 HOURS RETURN, 14KM

The track up to Douglas Rock Hut is a 7km tramp, often done in less than three hours. Despite being a rougher track than that to Welcome Flat, it is an ideal day trip from Welcome Flat, especially without the burden of a heavy backpack.

From Welcome Flat Hut, cross the suspension bridge to the south side of Copland River. Head east along the river, and after 30 minutes you break out at the open tussock of **Welcome Flat**. This pleasant area along the river is surrounded by peaks and snowfields, including Mt Sefton (3151m), the

WEST COAST WELCOME FLAT

Footstool (2764m) and Scott Peak (2537m). The flats are marked with rock cairns that lead more than 2km to **Scott Creek** at their eastern end. Scott Creek is not bridged, but under normal conditions is easy to ford. In bad weather it is extremely hazardous.

From Scott Creek the track climbs out of the flats and sidles above the **Copland River Gorge**, crossing two major stream washouts. The well-defined track can be slippery, so be careful if it's wet. The track crosses a suspension bridge over **Tekano Creek**, 1½ hours from Scott Creek, then immediately arrives at **Douglas Rock Hut** (eight bunks) in the first patch of forest below the bushline, at 700m.

Built in 1931–32, this hut originally had two rooms (one for men, one for women). In 1979 it was modified to one room, and platforms replaced the bunks. The only shelter between Copland Pass and Welcome Flat, the hut has a radio link to the DOC offices in Fox Glacier and Haast, providing weather reports at times notified inside the hut.

Mt Sefton towers over Douglas Rock Hut, and beyond the hut a marked route continues towards the Copland Pass. Marked by cairns and poles the route ascends through subalpine vegetation with improving views of the high mountain peaks. The route ends at the alpine basin. Do not attempt to go further unless you have a high level of mountaineering experience and appropriate equipment.

Return to Welcome Flat Hut, reversing the day's route.

Day 3: Welcome Flat Hut to Karangarua River Bridge

6 HOURS, 17KM

Retrace your Day 1 steps to the Karangarua River bridge on SH6.

TOWNS & FACILITIES

Westport

📞 03 / POP 4850

The port of Westport made its fortune in coal mining, the same industry that keeps it stoked today. It boasts few features of prolonged interest, but has all the necessary facilities and services to set you on your merry way.

🛏 Sleeping & Eating

Westport Holiday Park   HOLIDAY PARK **$$**

(📞 03-789 7043; www.westportholidaypark.co.nz; 31 Domett St; campsites from $32, d $98-150) This back-street park has decent tenting areas and A-frame 'chalets' as well as adequate amenities and a mini-golf course.

Buller Court Motel   MOTEL **$$**

(📞 03-789 7979; www.bullercourtmotel.co.nz; 253 Palmerston St; d $120-170, q $195-215; 🖥) One of many main-road options, this older-style complex is tastefully maintained and impresses with an away-from-the-road aspect and small but private grassy gardens.

PR's Cafe   CAFE **$**

(124 Palmerston St; meals $12-19; ⊙ 8am-4.30pm Mon-Fri, 8am-3pm Sat & Sun; 🖥) Amid a competitive cafe scene, PR's stands out not only for its first-prize pastries, cakes and sharp club sandwiches, but for its modern take on daytime cafe fare. Salmon omelette with dill aioli and spanakopita join seasonal specials on a blackboard menu, to be enjoyed perusing the daily papers either inside the smart interior or street-side.

Porto Bello   BAR, RESTAURANT **$$**

(📞 03-789 5570; 62 Palmerston St; meals $12-29; ⊙ 5pm-late) Roman columns and renaissance artwork give this place a Colosseum feel, but the food has its roots firmly in the US of A. Six local craft beers on tap, $16.50 steak specials and occasional live music keep the locals happy.

🛒 Supplies & Equipment

Habitat Sports   OUTDOOR EQUIPMENT

(📞 03-788 8002; www.habitatsports.co.nz; 234 Palmerston St; ⊙ 9am-5pm Mon-Fri, 9am-1pm Sat) This all-rounder stocks all the necessary gear within reasonable expectations.

New World   SUPERMARKET

(244 Palmerston St; ⊙ 8am-8.30pm) Once again, the New World supermarket comes to the rescue in style, offering a great range of food.

ℹ Information

Westport i-SITE (📞 03-789 6658; www.buller. co.nz; 113 Palmerston St; ⊙ 9am-5pm Nov-Mar, 10am-4.30pm Apr-Oct) provides general and DOC-related visitor information and booking services for huts and Great Walks.

ℹ Getting There & Away

Westport is a stop on the daily Nelson to Fox Glacier runs of **InterCity** (☑ 03-365 1113; www.intercity.co.nz). Naked Bus (p241) runs the same route three times a week. **Trek Express** (☑ 027-222 1872, 0800 128 735; www.trekexpress.co.nz) passes through Westport on its frequent high-season Wangapeka and Heaphy Track runs (Nelson to Westport $95). Buses leave from the i-SITE.

Punakaiki

☑ 03 / POP 70

On the edge of Paparoa National Park, almost halfway between Westport and Greymouth, this small settlement has decent accommodation but lacks many other services. There is no bank, dairy or petrol station. **Punakaiki Promotions** (www.punakaiki.co.nz) is a good source of visitor information.

🛏 Sleeping & Eating

Punakaiki Beach Camp HOLIDAY PARK $
(☑ 03-731 1894; beachcamp@xtra.co.nz; 5 Owen St; campsites $32, d $42-58) With a backdrop of sheer cliffs, this salty park with good grass is studded with clean, old-style cabins and shipshape amenities.

Punakaiki Beach Hostel HOSTEL $
(☑ 03-731 1852; www.punakaikibeachhostel.co.nz; 4 Webb St; campsites per person $20, dm/s/d $27/53/71; @ 🛜) This clean, canary-yellow hostel has a sea-view veranda, comfy beds, great communal facilities and courteous staff.

Punakaiki Tavern PUB $$
(www.punakaikitavern.co.nz; SH6; mains $19-32; ☉8am-late) This pub does decent portions of honest food served in comfortable surrounds. Most nights the punters are a mix of local and international, conducive to friendly conversation.

ℹ Getting There & Away

InterCity (☑ 03-365 1113; www.intercity.co.nz) runs daily to Westport (three hours), Greymouth (45 minutes) and Franz Josef (four hours). **Naked Bus** (www.nakedbus.com) runs the same route three times a week.

Greymouth

☑ 03 / POP 10,000

This is the largest town on the West Coast, sitting with its back to the sea at the mouth of the Grey River. On the main road and rail route through Arthur's Pass and across the Southern Alps from Christchurch, Greymouth sees its fair share of travellers, for whom it is well set up.

🛏 Sleeping & Eating

Global Village Travellers' Lodge HOSTEL $
(☑ 03-768 7272; www.globalvillagebackpackers.co.nz; 42 Cowper St; campsites per person $18, dm/d/tr/q $28/70/96/120; @ 🛜) A collage of African and Asian infuses this hostel with energy and warmth, as do free kayaks, mountain bikes, spa, sauna, barbecue and fire pit.

Greymouth Seaside Top 10 Holiday Park HOLIDAY PARK $
(☑ 0800 867 104, 03-768 6618; www.top10greymouth.co.nz; 2 Chesterfield St; campsites $40-46, cabins $60-125, motel r $110-374; @ 🛜) This well-appointed beachside park is 2.5km south of town. The facilities are a little worn, but there are plenty of accommodation options, and a jumping pillow and go-karts to keep the kids amused.

DP:One Cafe CAFE $
(104 Mawhera Quay; meals $7-23; ☉8am-8pm Mon-Fri, 9am-5pm Sat & Sun; 🛜) A stalwart of the Greymouth cafe scene, this hip place cups up the best espresso in town, along with good-value grub. Groovy NZ tunes, wi-fi, a relaxed vibe and quayside tables make this a great place for a meet-up to while away a grey day.

Speight's Ale House PUB $$
(130 Mawhera Quay; lunch $12-29, dinner $19-35; ☉11am-late) Housed in the imposing 1909 'Brick House' building, one of the big brands of NZ beer stands its ground with a well-stocked bar, generous meals and several airy but ambient rooms.

🔒 Supplies & Equipment

Coll Sportsworld OUTDOOR EQUIPMENT
(53 Mackay St; ☉8am-5pm Mon-Fri, 9am-1pm Sat) Greymouth's sports shop stocks all basic tramping supplies, including stove fuel.

Countdown SUPERMARKET
(174 Mawhera Quay; ☉7am-9pm) Centrally located; one of several supermarkets around town.

ℹ Information

The **Greymouth i-SITE** (☑ 03-768 5101, 0800 473 966; www.greydistrict.co.nz; Railway

Station, 164 Mackay St; ⊙ 9am-5pm Mon-Fri, 9.30am-4pm Sat & Sun; 🛜) inside the railway station houses a very helpful crew, and an abundance of local and DOC information.

❶ Getting There & Away

Sharing the old railway station with the i-SITE, the **West Coast Travel Centre** (☎ 03-768 7080; www.westcoasttravel.co.nz; Railway Station, 164 Mackay St; ⊙ 9am-5pm Mon-Fri, 10am-4pm Sat & Sun; 🛜) books all forms of transport, including buses, trains and interisland ferries, and has luggage-storage facilities. It also serves as the bus depot.

InterCity (☎ 03-365 1113; www.intercity. co.nz) stops in Greymouth on its daily West Coast service from Nelson to Queenstown, heading north to Westport (two hours) and Nelson (six hours), and south to Franz Josef Glacier (3½ hours) and Fox Glacier (4¼ hours). **Naked Bus** (www.nakedbus.com) also runs between Nelson and Queenstown, stopping at all major West Coast towns en route.

You can get across SH73 (Arthur's Pass) between Greymouth and Christchurch with **Atomic Shuttles** (☎ 0508-108 359; www.atomictravel. co.nz) and **West Coast Shuttle** (☎ 03-768 0028, 027 492 7000; www.westcoastshuttle. co.nz).

The other way to travel between Greymouth and Christchurch is on one of the world's most scenic train journeys, the *TranzAlpine,* operated by **KiwiRail Scenic** (☎ 0800 872 467; www. kiwirailscenic.co.nz), which calls in at Arthur's Pass National Park.

Franz Josef Glacier

☑ 03 / POP 330

Franz Josef Glacier is more action-packed than Fox Glacier, but heavy tourist traffic often swamps both towns from December to February.

🛏 Sleeping & Eating

**Franz Josef Top 10
Holiday Park**   HOLIDAY PARK $
(☎ 0800 467 897, 03-752 0735; www.franz-joseftop10.co.nz; 2902 Franz Josef Hwy; sites from $40, d $65-165; @🛜) This spacious holiday park, 1.5km from the township, has tip-top facilities and more sleeping options than you can shake a stick at.

Glow Worm Hostel   HOSTEL $
(☎ 0800 151 027, 03-752 0172; www.glowwormcottages.co.nz; 27 Cron St; dm $24-26, d $65-100; @🛜) Relax at this quiet haven with homely communal areas and a nice nod to local

history in the bedrooms. If you are back by 6pm, there's free vegie soup on offer. If the rain settles in, chill out with a good DVD.

Alice May   MODERN NZ $$
(cnr Cowan & Cron Sts; mains $18-33; ⊙ 4pm-late) Resembling an old staging post, this sweet spot serves up meaty, home-style meals in its character-filled dining room and outside where there are mountain views.

The Landing   BAR, RESTAURANT $$
(www.thelandingbar.co.nz; SH6; mains $19-39; ⊙ 7.30am-late) A bustling, well-run pub serving up megaportions of crowd-pleasing food; think big burgers, steaks and pizzas. The patio – complete with heaters and umbrellas – is a sociable hangout.

🔒 Supplies & Equipment

Four Square   SUPERMARKET
(SH6; ⊙ 7.45am-9.30pm) The only game in town, Four Square steps up to the plate, big time.

❶ Getting There & Away

Buses leave from outside the Four Square supermarket. InterCity (p241) has daily buses south to Fox Glacier (35 minutes) and Queenstown (eight hours), and north to Greymouth (five hours) and Nelson (10 hours). Book at the DOC visitor centre (p238) or YHA.

Fox Glacier

☑ 03 / POP 260

Fox Glacier is 23km from Franz Josef Glacier, around halfway between Franz and the trailhead for the Welcome Flat track. It is the quieter of the two towns, and a gateway to the extremely photogenic **Lake Matheson** (www.lakematheson.com), with its gorgeous walkway and delightful cafe.

For non-DOC related information, including transport bookings, visit the folks at **Fox Glacier Guiding** (☎ 03-751 0825, 0800 111 600; www.foxguides.co.nz; 44 Main Rd).

🛏 Sleeping & Eating

Fox Glacier Holiday Park   HOLIDAY PARK $$
(☎ 0800 154 366, 03-751 0821; www.fghp.co.nz; Kerrs Rd; campsites from $38, cabins $58-60, d $94-199; @🛜) This park has a range of different sleeping options to suit all budgets. Renovations, including a swanky facilities block, playground and barbecues, have improved what was already a good choice.

Lake Matheson Motels
MOTEL **$$**

(☏ 03-751 0830, 0800 452 2437; www.lakemath-eson.co.nz; cnr Cook Flat Rd & Pekanga Dr; d $139-155, q $190; ☏) From the outside this place looks pretty ordinary, but inside the rooms are immaculate, and have upmarket furnishings.

Hobnail Cafe
CAFE **$**

(44 Main Rd; meals $11-19; ⊘ 7.30am-3pm) Cabinets full of high-quality stodge include stuffed spuds, pastries, panini, biscuits and cake, plus there are hearty breakfasts such as bubble and squeak. Located in the same building as Fox Glacier Guiding.

Last Kitchen
CAFE **$$**

(cnr Sullivan Rd & SH6; mains $22-28; ⊘ 11am-late) A modern cafe with a cosy fire indoors, and a pleasant alfresco deck, this place dishes up healthy portions of contemporary fare with a primarily Mediterranean bent. A good place to savour a glass of fine New Zealand wine.

🔒 Supplies & Equipment

Fox Glacier General Store
SUPERMARKET

(⊘ 8am-8pm) This store has adequate supplies at prices commensurate with its size and location.

❶ Getting There & Away

Franz Josef buses also service Fox Glacier.

Mt Aspiring National Park & Around Queenstown

Includes ➡

Routeburn Track 261

Greenstone Caples
Track 265

Mavora–Greenstone
Walkway. 269

Rees-Dart Track 272

Matukituki Valley
Tracks 275

Gillespie Pass
Circuit 278

Best Views

➡ Harris Saddle (p264)

➡ Key Summit (p265)

➡ McKellar Saddle (p267)

➡ Rees Saddle (p274)

➡ Cascade Saddle (p278)

Best Huts

➡ Routeburn Falls
Hut (p264)

➡ Greenstone Hut (p269)

➡ Aspiring Hut (p277)

➡ French Ridge Hut (p278)

➡ Siberia Hut (p281)

Why Go?

Mt Aspiring National Park is a fitting end to New Zealand's Southern Alps. It has wide valleys with secluded flats, more than 100 glaciers, and mountain ranges with peaks higher than 2700m – including 3033m Mt Aspiring/Tititea, NZ's tallest mountain outside Aoraki/Mt Cook National Park.

The park stretches from the Haast River in the north to the Humboldt Mountains in the south, where it borders Fiordland National Park. The park is now part of the Te Wahipounamu – South West New Zealand World Heritage Area, which includes Aoraki/Mt Cook, Westland Tai Poutini and Fiordland National Parks.

At more than 3555 sq km, Aspiring is the country's third-largest national park, with the majority of tramping activity taking place around Glenorchy, where trailheads for the famous Routeburn, Rees-Dart and Greenstone Caples tracks can be found. The tramping territory to the north, through the Matukituki and Wilkin-Young valleys, provides more mountain solitude.

When to Go

The weather varies greatly across Aspiring, with the mountains dictating the terms. Glenorchy is dry, notching up around 1140mm of rain each year, with the lower Rees, Matukituki and Wilkin not much wetter at around 1500mm. Head into the Route Burn and Dart valleys, and the western half of the Greenstone and Caples, and you can multiply that by around five. Snow may fall above 1000m in almost any month, and spring and early summer are high risk for avalanches.

The weather is generally settled from late December to March, with February often suggested best for tramping. However, being an alpine region you must be prepared for sudden changes in weather and unexpected storms at any time of year.

Background Reading

Although much of the Queenstown area was originally settled in the quest for gold, this enterprise was quickly usurped by farming, with high-country stations scattered throughout the region. Many of today's tramping tracks pass through them and follow old stock droving routes along the valleys – such as the Greenstone, the Caples, and Mavora. *High Country Legacy* by Alex Hedley recalls the life and times of four generations of farmers at Mt Aspiring Station, while Iris Scott's similarly titled *High Country Woman* tells the autobiographical tale of a widow (with three children) running the 180,000-hectare Rees Valley Station near Glenorchy. Such stories retold will certainly put the odd blister and sandfly bite into perspective.

DON'T MISS

It would be a shame to come all this way to NZ's southern lakes without actually getting out on the water. Fortunately Queenstown's 'Lady of the Lake' will happily oblige.

The stately, steam-powered **TSS Earnslaw** (☑0800 656 503; www.realjourneys.co.nz; Steamer Wharf, Beach St, Queenstown; tours from $55) plies the waters of Lake Wakatipu on lake tours and excursions to the high-country Walter Peak Farm, where you can see sheep-shearing and deft dog demonstrations.

Built in 1912 (the same year as the *Titanic*), the *Earnslaw* started life transporting sheep, cargo and passengers to surrounding high-country stations, but now is one of the oldest tourist attractions in Central Otago and the only remaining passenger-carrying, coal-fired steamship in the Southern Hemisphere. Despite her age, the old girl still works 14-hour days in the summer months and cruises for 11 months of the year.

DOC Offices

➡ **Queenstown Visitor Centre** (☑03-442 7935; www.doc.govt.nz; 36 Shotover St; ⊙8.30am-5.30pm)

➡ **DOC Mt Aspiring National Park Visitor Centre** (☑03-443 7660; www.doc.govt.nz; Ardmore St, Wanaka; ⊙8am-5pm daily Nov-Apr, 8.30am-5pm Mon-Fri, 9.30am-4pm Sat May-Oct)

➡ **Makarora Visitor Centre** (☑03-443 8365; www.doc.govt.nz; SH6, Makarora; ⊙8am-5pm daily Dec-Mar, 8am-5pm Mon-Fri Apr & Nov, closed May-Oct)

➡ **Fiordland National Park Visitor Centre** (☑03-249 7924; www.doc.govt.nz; cnr Lakefront Dr & Te Anau-Manapouri Rd; ⊙8.30am-4.30pm, to 6pm 9 Dec-16 Mar)

GATEWAY TOWNS

➡ Queenstown (p282)

➡ Glenorchy (p283)

➡ Te Anau (p316)

➡ Wanaka (p283)

Fast Facts

➡ Such is the popularity of the Queenstown area that at peak times (ski season and midsummer), visitors can outnumber locals by as many as three to one.

➡ The Queenstown and Wanaka townships lie on NZ's third- and fourth-largest lakes, respectively. Lake Wakatipu is 283 sq km, and Lake Wanaka is 192 sq km.

➡ NZ's second-most-popular Great Walk, the 32km Routeburn Track is normally walked in three days. The 2013 winner of the Routeburn Classic race completed it in a tad over three hours!

Top Tip

If at all possible, try to schedule an extra night in one of the huts, enabling you to do day walks without a full pack, and with plenty of time to dawdle and smell the honeysuckle.

Resources

➡ www.queenstownnz.co.nz

➡ www.lakewanaka.co.nz

➡ www.glenorchy-nz.co.nz

➡ www.fiordland.org.nz

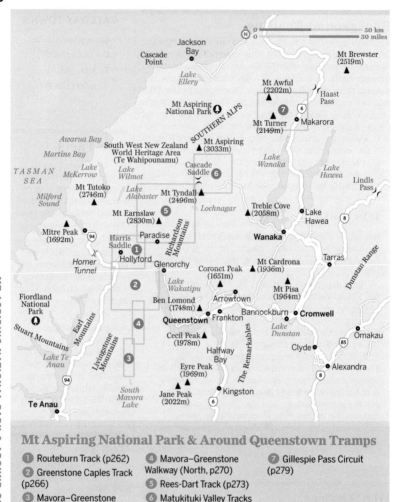

Mt Aspiring National Park & Around Queenstown Tramps

1 Routeburn Track (p262)
2 Greenstone Caples Track (p266)
3 Mavora–Greenstone Walkway (South, p271)
4 Mavora–Greenstone Walkway (North, p270)
5 Rees-Dart Track (p273)
6 Matukituki Valley Tracks (p276)
7 Gillespie Pass Circuit (p279)

History

Although there are traces of early settlement in this area, it is thought that Maori primarily passed through on their way between Central Otago and South Westland where they sourced pounamu (greenstone), highly valued for its use in tools, weapons and taonga (treasure). Maori expeditions in search of greenstone are said to have been conducted as late as 1850 – about the same time the first Europeans began exploring the region.

In 1861 David McKellar and George Gunn, part explorers and part pastoralists, shed some light on the Greenstone Valley when they struggled up the river and climbed one of the peaks near Lake Howden. What they saw was the entire Hollyford Valley, which they mistakenly identified as George Sound in central Fiordland. The great Otago gold rush began later that year, and by 1862 miners were digging around the lower regions of the Dart and Rees Rivers, as well as in the Route Burn Valley.

A prospector called Patrick Caples made a solo journey up the Route Burn from Lake

Wakatipu in 1863, and discovered Harris Saddle, before descending into the Hollyford Valley and Martins Bay. Caples returned through the valley that now bears his name, ending a three-month odyssey in which he became the first European to reach the Tasman Sea from Wakatipu.

It was not until late in the 19th century that the first European crossed the Barrier Range from Cattle Flat on the Dart to a tributary of the Arawata River. William O'Leary, an Irish prospector better known as Arawata Bill, roamed the mountains and valleys of this area and much of the Hollyford Valley for 50 years, searching out various metals and enjoying the solitude of these open, desolate places.

Mountaineering and a thriving local tourist trade began developing in the 1890s, and by the early 1900s it was booming, even by today's standards. Hotels sprang up in Glenorchy, along with guiding companies that advertised horse-and-buggy trips up the Rees Valley. Sir Thomas Mackenzie, Minister of Tourism, pushed for the construction of the Routeburn Track and hired Harry Birley of Glenorchy to establish a route. In 1912 Birley 'discovered' Lake Mackenzie and the next year began cutting a track.

The famous track had reached Lake Howden by the outbreak of WWI, but the final portion wasn't completed until the road from Te Anau to Milford Sound was built by relief workers during the Depression – until then a tramp on the Routeburn meant returning on the Greenstone.

The first move to make Mt Aspiring a national park came in 1935, but for all its beauty and popularity with trampers and tourists, the park wasn't officially gazetted until 1964.

Its legendary beauty landed the park and surrounds starring roles in the *Lord of the Rings* trilogy. The Mavora Lakes area, in particular, stole the limelight, being the scene of Silverlode and Anduin rivers, Nen Hithoel, the edge of Fangorn Forest and south of Rivendell.

Environment

The landscape of Mt Aspiring National Park is largely glacial in origin. During the ice ages, massive glaciers carved into the metamorphic and sedimentary rock. As they retreated they left a sculpted landscape of U-shaped valleys, small hanging valleys and rounded cirques and ridges. The park still contains more than 100 glaciers, ranging from the large Bonar Glacier on the flank of Mt Aspiring to the smaller ones that hang from the sides of the Matukituki Valley.

Beech forests dominate below the bushline, with each beech species favouring different growing conditions. The red beech thriving in the sunny valleys makes for semi-open forests and easy tramping, unlike the Fiordland forests with their dense, close understorey. Look out for ribbonwoods – one of NZ's few deciduous trees. These are the first to colonise open areas caused by slips and avalanches. At higher altitudes you will find silver or mountain beech, while west of the Divide there are rainforests of rimu, matai, miro and kahikatea.

In between the valleys are blooming mountain meadows that support one of the greatest ranges of alpine plants in the world. In alpine areas there are beautiful clusters of snow berry and coprosma in subalpine turf. In the Route Burn Valley, look for mountain daisies, snow grasses and veronica. Another beautiful plant of this region is the NZ edelweiss.

The forests are alive with native birds, including fantail, rifleman, bellbird, pigeon and cute South Island robin and tomtits. Along the rivers you may see whio (blue ducks) and paradise shelducks, and towards evening moreporks and native bats, NZ's only native land mammal. In alpine areas look out for the threatened rock wren and unmistakable kea.

Introduced animals include whitetail and red deer in lower areas and chamois about the mountaintops. Unfortunately, possums, rats and stoats are widespread. Introduced brown and rainbow trout are found in the lower Route Burn and brown trout are present in Lake Howden.

Routeburn Track

Duration 3 days

Distance 32km (20 miles)

Track Standard Great Walk

Difficulty Moderate

Start Routeburn Shelter

End The Divide

Nearest Towns Queenstown (p282), Glenorchy (p283), Te Anau (p316)

Transport Shuttle bus

MT ASPIRING NATIONAL PARK & AROUND QUEENSTOWN ROUTEBURN TRACK

Routeburn Track

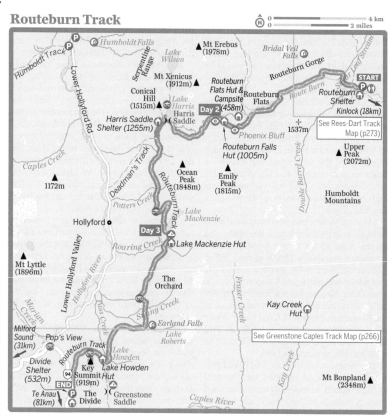

Summary This renowned alpine crossing includes a breathtaking day above the bushline as you cross Harris Saddle.

The Routeburn, one of NZ's best-known tracks, is a tramp over the Southern Alps' Main Divide, linking Mt Aspiring and Fiordland National Parks. Much of it is through thick rainforest, where red, mountain and silver beech form the canopy, and ferns, mosses and fungi cover everything below like wall-to-wall carpet. However, it's the alpine sections that appeal most to trampers. Views from Harris Saddle (1255m) and the top of nearby Conical Hill take in waves breaking far below in Martins Bay, while from Key Summit there are panoramic views of the Hollyford Valley and the Eglinton and Greenstone River Valleys.

The tranquillity of forest and meadow and dramatic views of entire valleys and mountain ranges are ample rewards for the steep hikes and frequent encounters with other trampers. Indeed, the track's overwhelming popularity resulted in the introduction of one of the first booking systems in NZ in 1995. Independent walkers need to reserve hut passes before embarking on the tramp.

In summer, be prepared for huts that are full, a constant flow of foot traffic, and a small gathering of people admiring the views at Harris Saddle. You must put up with the large number of people because the mountain scenery is truly exceptional.

The considerable amount of climbing is tempered by the well benched and graded track. A strong tramper could walk this track in less than three days, but considering all the expense and hassle of booking the huts, why would you want to?

The track can be hiked in either direction, but most trampers begin on the Glenorchy side and end at the Divide. The trip can be made into a circuit by returning via either the Greenstone or Caples Tracks.

❶ Planning

The four huts on the Routeburn Track are well serviced from late October to April. Outside this period the track is a winter crossing that should only be attempted by experienced trampers.

MAPS & BROCHURES
There are many maps for the Routeburn, but the best is the NZTopo50 *CB09* (Hollyford). The track is also covered by NewTopo *Routeburn, Greenstone* 1:40,000. DOC's *Routeburn Track* brochure includes a useful directory.

HUTS, CAMPING & BOOKINGS
Because of the Routeburn's popularity, you must now book all accommodation passes for huts and campsites in advance for any tramp from late October to April. You must then tramp on the days booked, with rangers on duty to check that you've done so.

Bookings are available through Great Walks Bookings (p291), and in person at DOC visitor centres nationwide.

There are four huts on the Routeburn Track – Routeburn Flats, Routeburn Falls, Lake Mackenzie and Lake Howden – the most popular of which are Routeburn Falls and Lake Mackenzie, both near the bushline. All have gas rings for cooking. Outside the Great Walks season, bookings are not required and the huts ($15) are not serviced.

Camping ($18) is permitted at Routeburn Flats and Lake Mackenzie, and at Greenstone Saddle (20 minutes from Lake Howden Hut) where it's free.

Overnight use of Harris Shelter and the track-end shelters is not permitted.

INFORMATION SOURCES
DOC Queenstown Visitor Centre (p273), upstairs in Outside Sports, is the place to arrange logistics, obtain maps, passes and track updates and hire personal locator beacons.

DOC Fiordland National Park Visitor Centre (p259) is close to the shores of Lake Te Anau and has friendly staff who can help with tramping arrangements, weather forecasts and info on track conditions.

GUIDED TRAMPS
Ultimate Hikes (☑ 03-450 1940, 0800 659 255; www.ultimatehikes.co.nz) runs guided tramps of the Routeburn. Its three-day tramp features comfortable lodge accommodation, meals and expert interpretation. The trip costs $1370 in high season (1 December to 31 March), and $1225 in the shoulder (all November and the first two weeks of April). It also offers the 'Grand Traverse', which is a six-day combination of the Greenstone and Routeburn (high/shoulder sea-

son $1865/1660), with smaller groups and more rustic accommodation but including a welcome rest day to soak up the wilderness atmosphere. You're best to book early, but it isn't always necessary.

❶ Getting to/from the Tramp

Kiwi Discovery (☑ 03-442 7340, 0800 505 504; www.kiwidiscovery.com; 37 Camp St, Queenstown) services the Routeburn all year round. Sample sector fares are Queenstown to Routeburn Shelter ($45, two hours), via Glenorchy; the Divide to Queenstown ($78, four hours); and $116 for a return trip. It also offers a package that combines return-trip track transport to and from Queenstown with a cruise on Milford Sound ($116).

Te Anau–based **Tracknet** (☑ 03-249 777, 0800 483 262; www.tracknet.net) runs frequent services from the Divide to Te Anau ($38, 1¼ hours), with onward connections to Queenstown ($45, four hours).

Glenorchy Journeys (☑ 0800 495 687; www.glenorchyjourneys.co.nz) offers on-demand, flexible transport services to Routeburn Shelter from Queenstown/Glenorchy ($45/25).

Buckley Transport (☑ 03-442 8215; www.buckleytransport.co.nz) provides on-demand track transport from Queenstown to Routeburn Shelter ($45) and from the Divide back to Queenstown ($90).

Info & Track Centre (☑ 03-442 9708; www.infotrack.co.nz; 37 Shotover St; ⊘ 7am-9pm) plies the Routeburn Shelter to Queenstown route ($45).

Trackhopper (☑ 021 187 7732; www.trackhopper.co.nz; from $230 plus fuel costs) offers a handy car-relocation service from either end of the Routeburn Track, so you don't have to backtrack over parts of the country you've already seen. Similar services are available for the Greenstone Caples Track and the Rees-Dart Track.

🏃 The Tramp

Day 1: Routeburn Shelter to Routeburn Falls Hut
4 HOURS, 8.8KM, 560M ASCENT

The track begins with a crossing of **Route Burn** on a swing bridge to its true left (north) bank, before winding for 1km through a forest of red, silver and mountain beech to a footbridge over **Sugar Loaf Stream**. The forest here is magnificent, with red beech trees towering overhead. Once across the stream the track climbs gently for 20 minutes until it reaches the swing bridge over the small gorge carved by **Bridal Veil Falls**. More impressive rock scenery follows as the track sidles Routeburn Gorge, providing ample opportunities to peer at the deep pools at the bottom. The dramatic views end at Forge Flats, a gravel bar along a sharp bend in the Route Burn and a popular place to linger in the sun.

Just beyond the flats the track uses a long swing bridge to cross to the true right (south) side of the Route Burn and heads back into the bush where it skirts the grassy flats. It's an easy 30-minute stroll along a level track through the bush to a signposted junction, where the right fork leads to Routeburn Flats Hut (20 bunks), five minutes away. The hut overlooks the river, the wide grassy flats, and the mountains to the north. Two hundred metres on is Routeburn Flats Campsite.

The main track (left fork) begins a steady ascent towards Routeburn Falls Hut. The track climbs 270m over 3km (about 1½ hours) before reaching the hut above the bushline. Emily Creek footbridge is the halfway point of this climb, and just beyond it the track sidles a steep rock face called Phoenix Bluff. The track soon crosses a huge slip, where a massive 1994 flood sent trees crashing towards the flats below. The resultant forest clearing affords magnificent views of the valley and surrounding peaks.

From the slip you resume the steady but rocky climb to Routeburn Falls Hut (48 bunks), the scene of many comings and goings. The hut is right at the tree line (1005m) and its long veranda offers views of the flats and the surrounding Humboldt Mountains. Right behind the hut is a private lodge for guided trampers. There is no camping around this hut and wardens are strict about enforcing this rule.

Day 2: Routeburn Falls Hut to Lake Mackenzie

4–6 HOURS, 11.3KM, 215M ASCENT, 355M DESCENT

From the hut it's a short climb to the impressive Routeburn Falls, which tumble down a series of rock ledges. Once on top of the falls the track cuts across an alpine basin towards the outlet of Lake Harris. The walk is fairly level at first – it crosses a couple of bridges and then begins a steady climb. You pass beneath a pair of leaning boulders, ascend more sharply and then arrive at Lake Harris. Sore legs and aching muscles are quickly forgotten as the stunning view of the lake materialises, especially on a clear day, when the water reflects everything around

it. Carved by a glacier, Lake Harris is 800m long and 500m wide. In winter it freezes over and chunks of ice are often seen floating on the lake when the Routeburn Track opens for the season in October.

The track works its way around the lake along bluffs and moraines. You get a second jolt 1½ to two hours from the hut, when entering the grassy meadows of Harris Saddle. From this 1255m vantage point, part of the Hollyford Valley comes into view, almost to Martins Bay if the weather is clear. If you are blessed with such weather, drop your packs and climb the steep side track to Conical Hill (one hour return). The 360-degree view from the 1515m peak includes the Darran Mountains, Richardson Range (in Otago) and the entire Hollyford Valley.

The Harris Saddle emergency shelter is a popular stopping place on the boundary between Mt Aspiring and Fiordland National Parks. The track begins its descent towards the Hollyford Valley via wooden steps and then turns sharply south. For the most part the track here is narrow but level, clinging to the Hollyford face of the ridge, high above the bushline. A strong tramper could probably walk from the saddle to Lake Mackenzie in less than two hours, but why rush? This is the best part of the trip, a stretch where you need to stop often and soak up the incredible alpine scenery.

After 30 minutes the track arrives at the signposted junction with Deadman's Track, an extremely steep route to the floor of the Hollyford Valley (five hours). The immense views continue, and 2km from the junction with Deadman's Track the route crosses a swing bridge over Potters Creek. In another 30 minutes you can see the cabins of Gunn's Camp at the bottom of the Hollyford Valley, directly below you.

Two hours from the saddle the track rounds a spur to the east side of the ridge and comes within view of Lake Mackenzie, a jewel set in a small green mountain valley. The DOC hut is clearly visible on the far shore. The track zigzags down to the lake, dropping sharply for the final 300m. It then skirts the bush and arrives at Lake Mackenzie Hut (50 bunks), a two-storey building overlooking the southern end of the lake. There are bunks on the 2nd floor of the hut, and additional beds are in a separate bunk room.

Because of the fragile nature of the lakeshore and the alpine plants, the Lake Mackenzie Campsite is a small facility, but it does have toilets, a water supply and a cooking shelter. The lake doesn't have a conventional outlet, so please don't wash or bathe in it.

Day 3: Lake Mackenzie to the Divide

4–5 HOURS, 12KM, 380M DESCENT

The track begins in front of the hut, passes the lodge for guided trampers and enters the bush. You begin with a level walk, crossing several swing bridges over branches of **Roaring Creek**, and within 15 minutes begin climbing. The climb regains the height lost in the descent to Lake Mackenzie, and is steady but not steep.

About 40 minutes to one hour from the hut, the track breaks out at a natural clearing, known as the orchard, where a handful of ribbonwoods resemble fruit trees. The view of the Darran Mountains is excellent.

More alpine views are enjoyed for the next hour or so, as the track passes through several avalanche clearings in the forest. Eventually you descend to **Earland Falls**, a thundering cascade that leaps 174m out of the mountains. On a hot day this is an ideal spot for an extended break, as the spray will quickly cool you off. If it's raining the falls will be twice as powerful and you might have to use the flood route, which is signposted along the main track.

The track steadily descends and after 3km emerges at **Lake Howden**. This is a major track junction and during the peak season it resembles Piccadilly Circus, with trampers and guided walkers going every which way. The Routeburn Track is the right fork (west); the Greenstone Track is the left fork (south). If you're planning to spend an extra night on the track, you can either stay at Lake Howden Hut (28 bunks) on the shores of the beautiful lake, or camp near the south end of the lake by following the Greenstone Track for 20 minutes to **Greenstone Saddle**.

The Routeburn Track swings past the flanks of **Key Summit** and in 15 minutes comes to a junction. If you're not racing to catch a bus, the 30-minute side trip (left fork) to the top is worth it on a clear day – from the 919m summit you can see the Hollyford, Greenstone and Eglinton Valleys, and there are some crazy stunted beech trees and sphagnum bogs to marvel at.

From the junction the Routeburn Track descends steadily to the bush, where thick rainforest resumes, before reaching the Divide, the lowest east–west crossing in the

Southern Alps. It's 3km (one hour) from Lake Howden to the Divide, where there is a huge shelter with toilets and a car park. Buses and vans are constantly pulling in here on their way to either Milford Sound or Te Anau. Welcome back to civilisation.

Greenstone Caples Track

Duration 4 days

Distance 59km (36.7 miles)

Track Standard Tramping track

Difficulty Moderate

Start/End Greenstone car park

Nearest Towns Glenorchy (p283), Te Anau (p316)

Transport Shuttle bus

Summary These two tracks provide a return trip between the Divide and Greenstone car park close to the shores of Lake Wakatipu, passing through World Heritage Area wilderness of considerable renown.

Although no Maori archaeological sites have been found in the Greenstone and Caples Valleys, it is known that the Greenstone, as the name suggests, was widely used by Maori during their travels in pursuit of highly prized *pounamu*. Europeans would later traverse the valleys in search of grazing sites, with farming commencing in the Caples in 1880. The Greenstone and Pass Burn were utilised as stock routes.

The Greenstone Valley is wide and open with tussock flats and beech forest. The Caples is narrower and more heavily forested, interspersed with grassy clearings; many consider the Caples to be more scenic, with its pretty parklike appearance.

The two tracks link at McKellar Saddle near the Divide, and near Greenstone car park on the Lake Wakatipu shore where the road links to Glenorchy and on to Queenstown.

Trampers can choose to walk just one track in one direction, or traverse both as a thereand-back journey of four or five days. Routeburn trampers planning to continue on the Greenstone can easily walk from Mackenzie Hut to McKellar Hut, which takes from five to seven hours. It's also possible to link the Greenstone with the Mavora Walkway.

ⓘ Planning

WHEN TO TRAMP

The Greenstone is a low-level route and can be tramped year-round. The Caples, however,

Greentone Caples Track

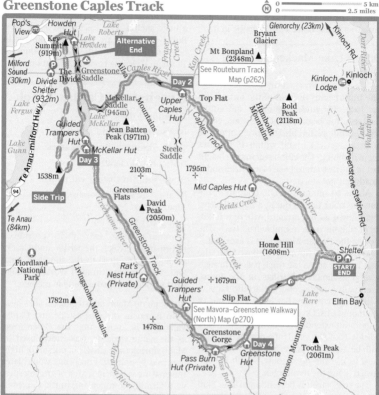

climbs over an alpine saddle and therefore should be avoided in winter, except by those with experience and equipment for cold, snow and ice. The ideal time to tramp this route is November to April.

MAPS & BROCHURES

Maps required for the entire loop are NZTopo50 CB9 (Hollyford), CB10 (Glenorchy) and CC9 (North Mavora Lake). The track is also covered by NewTopo Routeburn, Greenstone 1:40,000. DOC's brochure is entitled The Greenstone Caples Track.

HUTS, CAMPING & BOOKINGS

There are four **Serviced huts** (www.doc.govt. nz; $15) between the two tracks: McKellar and Greenstone on the Greenstone, and Mid Caples and Upper Caples on the Caples. All have heating, but no stoves, and rangers are likely to be in the vicinity from late October until mid-April to keep things in check. Camping ($5) is permitted next to the huts. Obtain hut tickets from DOC visitor centres nationwide.

INFORMATION SOURCES

DOC Queenstown Visitor Centre (p273), upstairs in Outside Sports, is the place to arrange logistics, obtain maps, passes and track updates and hire personal locator beacons.

DOC Fiordland National Park Visitor Centre (p259) is close to the shores of Lake Te Anau and has friendly staff who can help with all tramping arrangements, weather forecasts and info on track conditions.

ℹ Getting to/from the Tramp

Buckley Transport (p263) provides on-demand track transport between Queenstown and the Divide ($90). The Divide is also serviced in summer by Kiwi Discovery (p263) and Te Anau–based Tracknet (p263).

Glenorchy Journeys (p263) offers on-demand, flexible transport services to Greenstone car park from Queenstown/Glenorchy ($55/35).

Info & Track Centre (p263) services Greenstone car park from Queenstown/Glenorchy ($50/35).

Trackhopper (p263) offers handy car-relocation services.

MT ASPIRING NATIONAL PARK & AROUND QUEENSTOWN GREENSTONE CAPLES TRACK

🏃 The Tramp

Day 1: Greenstone Car Park to Upper Caples Hut

3½–5½ HOURS, 16KM

The track departs the car park and in a few minutes passes a junction where the left fork leads to a bridge across the Greenstone River. Remain on the true left (north) side of the Greenstone River, pass the confluence with the Caples River and, 30 minutes from the car park, arrive at a signposted junction. Here, the Greenstone Track heads southwest, quickly crossing a swing bridge over the Caples.

The Caples Track continues along the true left side of the Caples River, but stays in beech forest above the valley to avoid crossing Greenstone Station. At one point the woolshed of an old homestead may be spotted on the far bank.

It's 2½ hours along the east bank before the well-marked track descends past an impressive gorge and crosses a bridge over the Caples to Mid Caples Hut (12 bunks) on an open terrace above the river. From the hut the track remains on the true right (west) side of the river and crosses open grassy flats for the first hour. You then ascend into beech forest to round a small gorge before quickly returning to the flats.

Eventually the track turns into bush before it emerges at the southern end of Top Flat. It takes about 25 minutes to cross the flat and cut through more beech forest to Upper Caples Hut. Just before the hut is a signposted junction with the Steele Saddle route south to the Greenstone Track, an extremely difficult tramp (10 to 12 hours). Upper Caples Hut (12 bunks) is on a grassy flat where the valley begins to narrow, 1½ to 2½ hours from Mid Caples Hut. It's a scenic location to spend the night, with the Ailsa Mountains rising directly behind the hut.

Day 2: Upper Caples Hut to McKellar Hut

6–7 HOURS, 13KM, 520M ASCENT, 380M DESCENT

The track leaves the valley floor and climbs gently to McKellar Saddle, two hours from the hut. At first it is quite rough with exposed tree roots and rocks, but becomes easier after an hour as it sides up towards the bush edge.

ⓘ WARNING

The upper Caples River can rise extremely fast during periods of heavy rain. You cross a number of unbridged side streams along the track between the Upper Caples Hut and the Greenstone Track, and caution should be used when travelling this stretch during foul weather.

Two hours from the hut it reaches Mc Kellar Saddle (945m), an extremely wet and boggy area crossed by boardwalks built to protect the fragile subalpine vegetation. The views are good from the saddle – on a clear day the peaks and hanging valleys of Fiordland can be seen to the west.

Leaving the saddle, the track descends at an easy grade for about 1½ hours to the point where you break out of the bush near the head of Lake McKellar. Here, the track swings north to bypass swampy lowlands, then crosses a bridge to the signposted Greenstone Track.

The Greenstone Track heads south (left fork) and crosses the grassy flat, where you are treated to views of Lake McKellar. It then gently climbs the forested edges of the lake, a couple of times dipping close enough for you to scout for cruising trout, but mostly skirting the hillsides, where views are but brief glimpses through the trees. Within one hour of passing Caples Track (2.5km) you arrive at McKellar Hut (24 bunks), in a small clearing next to the Greenstone River. The rocky face of Jean Batten Peak (1971m) looms overhead.

ALTERNATIVE FINISH: LAKE MCKELLAR TO THE DIVIDE

2–3 HOURS, 6.5KM

If you are not completing the loop on the Greenstone Track, this is your cue to head to the Divide. Take the right fork, north. After 45 minutes to one hour, you will reach beautiful Lake Howden then Lake Howden Hut (28 bunks). At the hut you will see a major track junction. Head west (left) along the Routeburn Track, passing the flanks of Key Summit and another trail junction. The 30-minute side trip (left fork) around the top of Key Summit is worthwhile on clear days – when, from the 919m summit, you should be able to see the Hollyford, Greenstone and Eglinton Valleys. From the

MT ASPIRING NATIONAL PARK & AROUND QUEENSTOWN GREENSTONE CAPLES TRACK junction the Routeburn Track descends steadily to the bush and thick rainforest, before reaching the Divide, the lowest east–west crossing in the Southern Alps. It is 3km (one hour) from Lake Howden Hut to the Divide, where there is a car park and a shelter with toilets and water.

SIDE TRIP: PEAK 1538
6–8 HOURS, 17KM, 918M ASCENT

If you have a spare day at McKellar Hut, an interesting day walk is to climb Peak 1538 just southwest of the hut. Departing from the 'McKellar Hut' sign on the way to Howden Hut, is a track that climbs to the bushline. From there it's a steep climb through the alpine tussock to the top of Peak 1538. You can then follow the ridge to Key Summit (919m), descend to Howden Hut, and follow the first leg of the Greenstone Track back to McKellar Hut.

Day 3: McKellar Hut to Greenstone Hut
4½–6½ HOURS, 18KM

This day is spent tramping through the heart of the Greenstone Valley, where you'll see lots of cattle and, if you're wearing polarising sunglasses, a few of the river's famous trout.

The track immediately crosses the Greenstone River on a bridge in front of the hut to the true left (east) side. You then cut through beech forest for 30 minutes (1.5km), emerging at the northern end of Greenstone Flats, which are dominated by Jean Batten Peak.

The track cuts across bullrush grass and then returns to bush for almost 2km, skirting the Greenstone River, which boasts many beautiful pools. After crossing a large grassy flat the track moves higher onto the forested bluffs.

For the next three hours the track stays predominantly in the bush above the open valley. There is an occasional stretch of rocks and roots, but for the most part the track is a straightforward tramp with little climbing. When you emerge into a large open flat you can soon spot private Rat's Nest Hut on the opposite bank of the river.

You remain in grassy flats until the track ascends around a gorge. Short side trails allow you to peer down between the rock walls at the roaring Greenstone River, before the track descends to Steele Creek and a major swing bridge. Just before the bridge is a signposted junction with a track heading north (left fork) to Steele Saddle and Upper Caples Hut, a demanding tramp (10 to 12 hours). On the other side you break out of the trees and cross a grassy terrace to a signposted junction. The left fork heads off to a

FISHING FOR TROUT

Early European settlers to NZ, wishing to improve the country's farming, hunting and fishing opportunities, were responsible for the introduction of such ghastly wreckers as possums and rabbits. One of their more successful introductions was that of trout – brown and rainbow – released into NZ rivers in the second half of the 19th century.

Today they are much prized by sports anglers, whom you may stumble across flicking their flies thigh-deep in limpid rivers or on the edge of deep green pools. While this pastime, nay obsession, remains a mystery to the authors of this book, it is apparent that it brings much unbridled joy and satisfaction to the lives of its patrons. To quote NZ author and poet Kevin Ireland in his wonderful book *How to Catch a Fish*, 'It has as much to do with simple stubbornness and personal compulsion as it does with any complex notions of happiness and mystical fulfilment. The last thing to which it has any reasonable relationship is success.'

The Greenstone River is one of NZ's most-lauded trout fisheries. Accessible only on foot via the Greenstone Track (or by helicopter), the luminous green river boasts plentiful fish of legendary size – both brown and rainbow – averaging between 1.5kg and 3kg. As you tramp alongside the river, keep an eye on the pools – you may well spot a few swaying around in the clear water.

Trout fishing is highly regulated, with licences required to fish anywhere in NZ. Licences and information can be obtained from Fish & Game New Zealand (www.fishandgame.org.nz). However, your best bet will be to go with a local guide; i-SITEs can help you find one. Otherwise, peruse the helpful online guide, NZ Fishing (www.nzfishing.com).

private hut for guided trampers. Right above you is the closed Mid Greenstone Hut, formerly the second stop along the track before being replaced by the current Greenstone Hut, 1½ hours east along the valley.

The right-hand fork descends to open flats for the next 3km. Re-enter the bush across from the confluence of the Greenstone River and Pass Burn; the hut on the other side of the river is private. The track now begins to skirt around **Greenstone Gorge**, and after 2km comes to a junction with a track to Greenstone Hut. It's a five-minute descent to the bridge across the Greenstone River, from where there's a good view of the narrow rock walls of the gorge. Another 10 minutes from the swing bridge is **Greenstone Hut** (20 bunks) and the northern end of the Mavora–Greenstone Walkway. This is a great hut with a huge kitchen and wraparound deck that takes in the surrounding mountains.

Day 4: Greenstone Hut to Greenstone Car Park

3–5 HOURS, 12KM

Begin the day by recrossing the bridge over the gorge and returning to the Greenstone Track. Head right on the main track as it continues on the true left (north) side of the river. You climb high above the gorge, and then swing left with the valley before crossing Slip Creek on a bridge and entering the western end of **Slip Flat**, 40 minutes to one hour after leaving Greenstone Hut.

It takes 1km to cross the flats and re-enter the bush close to the river. After 20 to 30 minutes the track crosses a stream and comes to a signposted junction. The track to the east (right fork) stays close to the river before crossing a stock bridge and heading for **Lake Rere** (one hour). Take the main track to the north (left fork), which remains on the true left (north) side of the river and climbs through the rest of the gorge.

About 1½ to two hours from the gorge the track reaches a swing bridge over the **Caples River**, after which you will see a signposted junction. If you started this walk at the Divide, take the left fork on to the Caples Track to complete the loop.

If you are finishing at the Greenstone car park, take the right fork and follow the track along the true left bank of the Greenstone River. It will take 30 minutes to reach the trailhead.

Mavora–Greenstone Walkway

Duration 3 days

Distance 50km (31 miles)

Track Standard Tramping track

Difficulty Easy

Start Mavora Lakes Campsite

End Greenstone car park

Nearest Towns Te Anau (p316), Glenorchy (p283)

Transport Shuttle bus, plane

Summary Part of the national Te Araroa Walkway (www.teararoa.org.nz), this tramp features alpine scenery of considerable splendour with the bonus of a lot less trampers than the nearby Greenstone, Caples or Routeburn Tracks.

Mavora Lakes Park, in the Snowdon State Forest, lies within the Te Wahipounamu – South West New Zealand World Heritage Area. The heart of the park is the sublime Mavora Lakes camping area, huge golden meadows sitting alongside two lakes – North and South Mavora – fringed by forest and towered over by the impressive Thomson and Livingstone Mountains with peaks rising to more than 1600m.

The Mavora Lakes Walkway follows the Mararoa River for much of its length before peeling off to meet the Greenstone. This route was once used to drive cattle from Martins Bay on the West Coast through to Mossburn, so many segments are the breadth of a road. The first day, in fact, is along a 4WD track open to mountain bikers and motorists; vehicles are prohibited beyond Boundary Hut as the track enters privately owned Elfin Bay Station.

The tramp as described here is a three-day trip, but many trampers choose to do it in four, spending a night at Greenstone Hut. The walkway can be tramped in either direction, but as transport connections are easier to arrange from the Greenstone end, it is described here from south to north.

Environment

The Mavora Lakes Walkway winds through a much more gentle topography than the Routeburn or Caples Tracks, making the tramp ideal for families and others not up to a major alpine crossing. Parklike tussock grasslands and beech forests dominate the

MT ASPIRING NATIONAL PARK & AROUND QUEENSTOWN

Mavora–Greenstone Walkway (North)

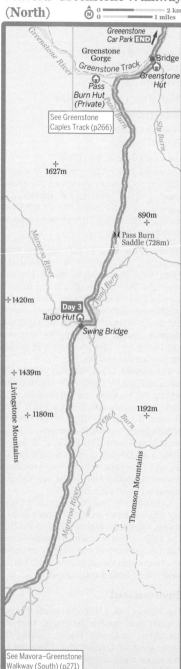

See Greenstone Caples Track (p266)

1627m

890m

Pass Burn Saddle (728m)

Day 3 Taipo Hut

Swing Bridge

1420m

1439m

1180m

1192m

Livingstone Mountains

Mavora River

Trench Burn

Thomson Mountains

See Mavora–Greenstone Walkway (South) (p271)

broad valley, which is up to 2km wide in places and is enclosed by 2000m peaks. Bird life is plentiful along the track and includes riflemen, parakeets, tomtits and robins in the open forests, and paradise shelducks in the wetland ponds.

❶ Planning

WHEN TO TRAMP

This track can be tramped at any time of year. As some sections are exposed to mountain weather, however, adequate equipment and good judgement are required.

MAPS & BROCHURES

The tramp is covered by NZTopo50 *CC09* (North Mavora) and *CB10* (Glenorchy). DOC's *Mavora Lakes Park* brochure provides information on various recreational activities including camping – an unsurprisingly popular pastime in the spectacular area around the lakes.

HUTS & CAMPING

Careys, Boundary and Taipo are all **Standard huts** (www.doc.govt.nz; $5). Greenstone is a **Serviced hut** (www.doc.govt.nz; $15). Hut tickets can be purchased from any DOC visitor centre nationwide. Idyllic Mavora Lakes Campsite, at the start of the walkway, is a **Standard campsite** (www.doc.govt.nz; $6) with barbecues, water taps, toilets and sandflies on standby.

INFORMATION SOURCES

DOC Queenstown Visitor Centre (p273), upstairs in Outside Sports, is the place to arrange logistics, obtain maps, passes and track updates and hire personal locator beacons.

DOC Fiordland National Park Visitor Centre (p259) is close to the shores of Lake Te Anau and can help with all tramping arrangements, local weather forecasts and information on track conditions.

❶ Getting to/from the Tramp

By car from SH94, between Mossburn and Te Anau, turn north at Centre Hill or Burwood Station and follow Mt Nicholas Rd and then Mavora Lakes Rd (both unsealed) for 39km to the camping area. In summer this area is popular with locals, so catching a bus to the turn-off on SH94 and hitching to the trailhead is not out of the question. **InterCity** (☑ 03-442-4922; www.intercity.co.nz) buses pass the turn-off on their daily Queenstown to Te Anau run. From Te Anau, Tracknet (p263) will take tramping parties to the trailhead on demand for a minimum fare of $200.

Another option from Te Anau is with **Wings & Water Te Anau** (☑ 03-249 7405; www.wingsandwater.co.nz), which will fly into North

Mavora Lake in a floatplane that holds four passengers plus gear, for $805 per flight.

Transport services for the Greenstone car park are offered by Buckley Transport (p263), Kiwi Discovery (p263), Glenorchy Journeys (p263) and Info & Track Centre (p263).

🥾 The Tramp

Day 1: Mavora Lakes Campsite to Boundary Hut

4–5 HOURS, 16KM

The track is signposted at the southern end of **North Mavora Lake** and immediately enters beech forest following a rough 4WD track along the lake, which can be seen through the trees. After one hour (3km) the track departs the forest for good, swinging up and away from it. The next two hours are in open territory and incredibly scenic, with the **Livingstone Mountains** rising steeply to the west beyond the lake.

Just before reaching the head of the lake, 9km (two to three hours) from the camping ground, the walkway passes Careys Hut (seven bunks). Perched above the lake overlooking a gravelly beach, this is an ideal spot for a dip on a hot day.

The walkway stays on the 4WD track, climbing above the head of the lake and passing a junction. The left fork, along a 4WD track that is rougher than the one you're following, is the route up the Windon Burn to Basic Forks Hut (three hours). Take the right fork, which leads you up to a terrace above the **Mararoa River**. This is probably the steepest climb of the tramp, and it rewards with good views of the valley and surrounding mountains.

After sidling the hill for 30 minutes, you drop back to the river and enter grassy flats bordering its banks. It takes one hour to cross the flats before a sign pops up pointing the way to Boundary Hut (eight bunks), on the true left (east) side of the river.

Day 2: Boundary Hut to Taipo Hut

4–5 HOURS, 12KM

How long this section of track takes you is heavily weather-dependent, as foul weather will slow you down as you search for subsequent marker poles. The alternative option for this second leg is to skip Taipo Hut and push on to Greenstone Hut – a 22km, seven- to eight-hour day.

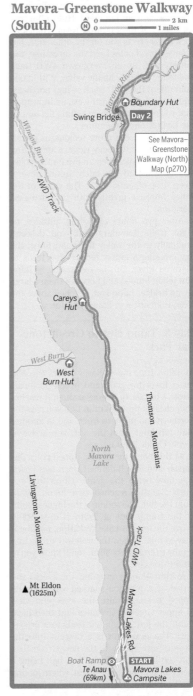

Mavora–Greenstone Walkway (South)

See Mavora–Greenstone Walkway (North) Map (p270)

MT ASPIRING NATIONAL PARK & AROUND QUEENSTOWN

The morning begins by crossing the swing bridge seen from Boundary Hut to the true right side of the Mararoa River. High tussock grass greets you on the other side, but orange-tipped poles keep you on course. You quickly pick up an overgrown 4WD track and follow it easily up the valley. Within one hour (3km) the 4WD track swings northeast and the poles head northwest, an indication that you're about to begin sidling the base of the Livingstone Mountains.

This section can prove tedious, as you sidle around the tussocky ridge, leapfrogging from pole to pole. Keep an eye on the poles, as they will lead you safely around several steep drop-offs and cliffs. The views of the valley improve greatly with the increased elevation.

After two hours of sidling hillsides, or 11km from Boundary Hut, you descend gradually to the valley floor and finish the day crossing a grassy terrace that leads to Mararoa River. On the other side is Taipo Hut (eight bunks) and between them a large swing bridge. Taipo Hut, perched above the river, is identical to Boundary Hut.

Day 3: Taipo Hut to Greenstone Car Park

7–10 HOURS, 22KM

At Taipo Hut, the walkway leaves the Mararoa River for good and heads northeast across a terrace of tussock so high it reaches your chest at times. Within 1km you pass the northern end of **Pond Burn** and in another 2km (an hour from the hut) you arrive at scenic Upper Pond Burn.

At this point the orange-tipped poles disappear and a well-defined track takes over. You now begin the gentle climb to **Pass Burn Saddle**, reached two hours (6km) from the hut. The saddle is the highest point of the tramp, but at 728m is only 400m above the level of Lake Wakatipu, making it easy to miss. When the walkway drops into a gully to cross Pass Burn, you'll know you're on the descent.

Within 1km of crossing the creek, you arrive at a junction marked with orange-tipped poles. Admire the sweeping view of upper Greenstone Valley and then head right (the fork to the left leads to a private hut). The next 2km is a descent into the **Greenstone Valley** to the new Greenstone Hut (20 bunks), with the first half being a steep drop through the forest, where footing can be tricky at times.

You reach the hut in four to five hours, about 10km from Taipo Hut, making it the ideal stop for lunch if you're pushing on. The hut is in a clearing above the confluence of **Sly Burn** and the **Greenstone River**, and under the rocky pinnacles of Tooth Peak. It's a five-minute descent to the swing bridge across Greenstone River and its impressive gorge. On the other side you quickly climb out of the gorge to a junction with the Greenstone Track.

From Greenstone Hut it is around four hours (11km) to the Greenstone car park. If your plan is to return to Te Anau, you can head west on the **Greenstone Track**. It's 4½ to 6½ hours to McKellar Hut and then three hours out to the Divide, where you can catch a bus along with all the Routeburn Track trampers.

Rees-Dart Track

Duration 4 days

Distance 62km (38.5 miles)

Track Standard Tramping and easy tramping tracks

Difficulty Moderate

Start Muddy Creek car park

End Chinamans Flat

Nearest Town Glenorchy (p283)

Transport Shuttle bus, jetboat

Summary Alpine scenery, wild rivers and a possible day trip to Dart Glacier have made the Rees-Dart one of the most popular tracks in Mt Aspiring National Park.

The Rees-Dart Track connects two splendid schist-lined valleys shaped by glaciation. Indeed, the relatively small Dart Glacier was once part of an enormous system that terminated at Kingston, 135km away at the southern end of Lake Wakatipu.

As it winds up one valley and back down the other, this track takes in a variety of scenery, such as meadows of flowering herbs, and mighty bluffs and moraine walls.

Demand on the Routeburn has had a flow-on for the Rees-Dart, which is now extremely popular and has undergone upgrades to suit. It is, however, longer and definitely more challenging than the Routeburn or Greenstone Caples, and has several stream crossings, which can be hazardous in heavy rain or snowmelt.

The most common approach is to tramp up the Rees Valley and return down the

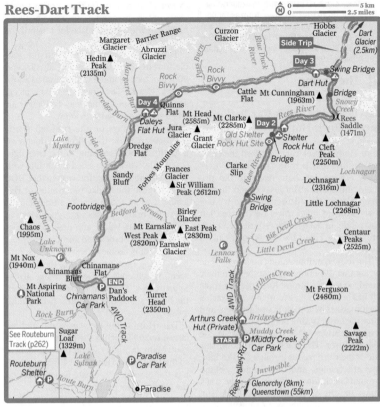

Rees-Dart Track

Dart – the easiest direction in which to climb Rees Saddle and the way the tramp is described here. Plan an extra night at Dart Hut if you want to include a day trip to Cascade Saddle to view Dart Glacier.

ⓘ Planning

WHEN TO TRAMP

The high sections of the Rees-Dart are subject to avalanches in late winter and early summer, with snow often lingering as late as December. The best time to tramp is December to April.

MAPS & BROCHURES

This tramp is covered by NZTopo50 maps CA10 (Lake Williamson) and CB10 (Glenorchy), as well as NewTopo Rees-Dart Track 1:40,000. DOC's brochure is The Rees Dart Track.

HUTS & CAMPING

There are three **Serviced huts** (www.doc.govt. nz; $15) on this trip – Shelter Rock, Dart and Daleys Flat. Each has a solid-fuel fire and water

but no cooking facilities. You can camp next to the huts for $5, and elsewhere on the route with the exception of the fragile alpine and subalpine areas between Shelter Rock and Dart Huts. Be sure to purchase your hut tickets in advance from any DOC visitor centre.

INFORMATION SOURCES

Queenstown Visitor Centre (☏ 03-442 7935; www.doc.govt.nz; 36 Shotover St, Queenstown; ☺ 8.30am-5.30pm), upstairs in Outside Sports, is the place to arrange logistics, obtain maps, passes and track updates and hire personal locator beacons.

ⓘ Getting to/from the Tramp

Glenorchy Journeys (p263) offers on-demand, flexible transport services to and from Muddy Creek and Chinamans Flat from Queenstown ($55) and Glenorchy ($35). Each trailhead is also serviced on demand for around $50 by Buckley Transport (p263) and Info & Track Centre (p263).

The track can be finished with an exhilarating jetboat ride down the Dart River, from as far upstream as Sandy Bluff (depending on river flows) to Glenorchy with **Dart River Jet Safaris** (03-442 9992, 0800 327 8538; www.dartriver.co.nz; adult/child $219/119).

🏃 The Tramp

Day 1: Muddy Creek Car Park to Shelter Rock Hut

6–8 HOURS, 19KM

From Muddy Creek car park, ford the creek and head across private farmland of Rees Valley Station for 2km, reaching the private Arthurs Creek Hut just beyond Bridges Creek. Grassy flats lie beyond, and it's one hour (4km) of open travel on the true left (east) side of **Rees River** until the track fords Twenty Five Mile Creek; poles mark the route.

The route continues along open river flats for another 1½ hours and can be extremely muddy at times – almost knee-deep in spots if it has been raining. Eventually you reach a track marked by a park boundary sign, and enter the bush. Within 500m the track crosses a swing bridge to the true right (west) side of Rees River. The track continues on this side of the river, passes through **Clarke Slip**, over grassy flats, and then begins a climb through beech forest. Within 2km the track passes the site of the old Shelter Rock Hut, now used occasionally as a campsite. From here it's 1km along the true right (west) bank of the Rees, through stands of stunted beech, before the track crosses a swing bridge back to the true left (east) bank to arrive at the new Shelter Rock Hut (22 bunks).

Day 2: Shelter Rock Hut to Dart Hut

4–6 HOURS, 10KM, 487M ASCENT

The climb over the alpine pass of Rees Saddle begins by following the river on the true left (east) side for a short time, to pick up a well-marked track that rises through alpine scrub. The track gradually sidles up the valley until it reaches a tussock basin below the saddle, about 4km from the hut.

Rees Saddle is the obvious low point to the northeast, and you keep to the streambed before climbing up the steep slope to the top. The final ascent is marked with orange poles and a well-beaten path, but is still a steep climb of 100m. As you would

expect, **Rees Saddle** (1471m) provides great views of the surrounding peaks and valleys, making it the natural place for lunch if the weather is clear.

Follow the orange poles from the saddle towards Dart Hut. You quickly descend 90m to a terrace and a group of tarns above Snowy Creek. The track traverses steep, snow-grass slopes, which can be dangerous when wet or covered with snow.

The route stays on the true left (west) of **Snowy Creek**, then drops suddenly to a footbridge and crossing to the true right (east) side. This steep-sided creek fills with so much snow during the winter that DOC must remove the bridge in advance, or risk losing it to an avalanche. The track climbs above the bridge, passes some good views of the upper Dart Valley, and descends across broken slopes of rock and shrub.

Dart Hut is visible on the true left (south) bank of the Dart River during the final descent, which ends at a swing bridge across Snowy Creek. The camping spots just before the bridge signal that the hut is five minutes away.

Dart Hut (32 bunks) was rebuilt and enlarged in 2003, such is the popularity of this spot. Many trampers spend two nights here so they can hike to view **Dart Glacier**, which has the tendency to create a bottleneck at the height of the tramping season.

SIDE TRIP: DART GLACIER

4–6 HOURS RETURN, 14KM

The rewarding side trip to view Dart Glacier is strenuous and challenging and should only be attempted in good weather, by those confident navigating unmarked routes over steep terrain. Cross Snowy Creek Bridge and follow the poles and rock cairns along the Dart River and the edge of Dart Glacier. After about three hours you will begin to climb moraine and tussock slopes with increasingly impressive views of the glacier and the Snowdrift Range to the west. If conditions are ideal and you have the energy, you can push on to Cascade Saddle (eight to 10 hours return from Dart Hut, 20km).

Day 3: Dart Hut to Daleys Flat Hut

5–7 HOURS, 18KM

The track climbs west, away from the hut and along a bluff above the **Dart River**, offering an occasional view of the rushing water below or the valley in front as it passes through thick forest.

Around 6km into the day, the track climbs sharply, but then drops into a rocky stream clearing near the eastern end of **Cattle Flat**. The track quickly emerges from forest onto the flat, an almost-endless grassy area where the trail appears as a path of trampled grass marked occasionally by a rock cairn. The Dart River is seen as you cross the flat, as is a portion of **Curzon Glacier**, high in the mountains across the river. The track follows the middle of the flat and in 3km passes a sign to a rock bivvy. The bivvy, a three-minute walk up a side track, is a huge overhanging rock that can easily hold at least six people. If it's raining this is an excellent place for lunch.

The track continues across Cattle Flat for another 1.5km and finally returns to the bush. From here it's another 1½ to two hours to Daleys Flat Hut. You begin with a steady drop towards the river, and reach the banks of the Dart in 2.5km. Along the way you pass another rock bivvy, much smaller than the one at Cattle Flat. Eventually the track breaks out at **Quinns Flat**, a beautiful stretch of golden grass surrounded by mountains, and then returns to the bush.

The track crosses a few more streams and, in 30 minutes, arrives at Daleys Flat. Follow the trampled grass across the flat to reach Daleys Flat Hut (20 bunks).

Day 4: Daleys Flat Hut to Chinamans Flat

4–6 HOURS, 16KM

As the Chinamans Flat trailhead is fairly well serviced by transport operators, you should arrange a pick-up time that suits your level of tramping speed. Fast trampers can make it out in four hours, but it pays to allow a full six hours if you want to minimise your chances of missing your ride.

The morning begins in forest, but within 15 minutes the track comes to a small grassy flat, only to return to the bush on a high bank above the river. About 4km from the hut the track breaks out onto **Dredge Flat**. Use the markers to locate where the track re-enters the bush in the middle of the flat. At the lower end of the flat, Sandy Bluff looms overhead.

As soon as the track enters the forest it begins a gradual climb to **Sandy Bluff**. At one time, trampers used a ladder and steel cables to scale the rock face of this steep

bluff, but in 2000 a new track was blasted out, and handrails and steps were added to make the climb considerably safer, not to mention easier. At the top you are rewarded with a fine view of Dredge Flat and the valley beyond.

The track immediately descends to a grassy flat, crosses it and then stays close to the river for the next 7km. Eventually the track enters an open flat, with **Chinamans Bluff** straight ahead and an impressive waterfall from **Lake Unknown** visible high in the mountains across the Dart River.

The track skirts the bluff, requiring only a fraction of the climbing endured at Sandy Bluff, and descends onto **Chinamans Flat**. Skirt yet another bluff, this one along a new segment of track that provides access around a washed-out area to the start of a 4WD track where you will find a shelter, toilets and an information panel. If you haven't arranged a pick-up, it's still another 6km to the end of Glenorchy Paradise Rd, a good two-hour tramp along the 4WD track through **Dan's Paddock**.

Matukituki Valley Tracks

Duration 2 to 5 days

Distance 18km (11 miles) minimum

Track Standard Tramping track and route

Difficulty Easy to demanding

Start/End Raspberry Creek car park

Nearest Town Wanaka (p283)

Transport Shuttle bus

Summary Besides the obvious physical splendours, the beauty of the Matukituki Valleys is the range of tramps that can be completed, often as day walks, from the homebase of Aspiring Hut.

An hour's drive from Wanaka, the West and East Matukituki Valleys offer enjoyable day walks as well as access to a number of demanding tramping and climbing routes in Mt Aspiring National Park. The valley walks cross private farmland (with grazing stock) and beech forest flats and the higher-altitude routes negotiate alpine tussock grasslands and snowfields.

The East Matukituki is well worth exploring, and can in fact be traversed through to the Wilkin Valley over the 1430m Rabbit Pass – a challenging five- to six-day route.

Matukituki Valley Tracks

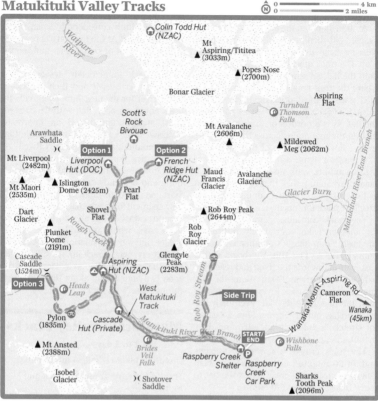

However, it is the West Matukituki that is the star of the show. An easy tramp up the valley leads to the splendid Aspiring Hut, a fantastic base from which to head off on myriad other return tramps – you could easily while away a week here day-walking and just soaking up the spectacular mountain scenes. Aspiring Hut is also the first stop en route to Glenorchy via the challenging Cascade Saddle, a somewhat notorious alpine crossing. A hut warden will be present from November to mid-April, jollying everyone along and providing updates on conditions and sterling advice.

ⓘ Planning

WHEN TO TRAMP
The lower lands of the East and West Matukituki Valleys may be tramped all year round in favourable conditions. During winter and spring there is avalanche danger on the Rob Roy Track, Shovel Flat, above Pearl Flat and Cascade Saddle. The Saddle is a high alpine crossing and should only be attempted when the pass is free of snow, normally from December to March. Even then, sudden cold fronts can sweep through and bring snow at any time; it is also infamous for cloud, which has left trampers hopelessly lost.

MAPS & BROCHURES
The following Matukituki Valley tramps are covered by NZTopo50 map CA11 (*Aspiring Flats*); for Cascade Saddle you will also need CA10 (*Lake Williamson*). DOC's *Matukituki Valley Tracks* brochures details the East Matukituki tramps that are not described here.

HUTS
Aspiring Hut (www.doc.govt.nz; $25) is a New Zealand Alpine Club (NZAC) facility that is administered by DOC. The fee can be paid at the Mt Aspiring National Park Visitor Centre in Wanaka (p259), or to the warden who is stationed at the hut from November through to mid-April. French Ridge and Colin Todd huts are also **NZAC huts** (www.doc.govt.nz; $20); Liverpool Hut is a **Serviced hut** (www.doc.govt.nz; $15).

INFORMATION SOURCES

DOC Mt Aspiring National Park Visitor Centre (p259), on the eastern edge of Wanaka, provides all the usual information and services as well as museum-style displays on local geology, flora and fauna.

ℹ️ Getting to/from the Tramp

The tramp begins at a car park at Raspberry Creek, 54km from Wanaka. **Alpine Shuttles** (📱 03-443 7966; www.good-sports.co.nz) makes the run from Wanaka to Raspberry Creek at 9.15am and 2pm, from November to April, with pick up at various Wanaka hostels for $35 per person.

🚶 The Tramp

Day 1: Raspberry Creek Car Park to Aspiring Hut

2–2½ HOURS, 9KM

Cross the bridge over **Raspberry Creek** to a 4WD track on the other side; the track cuts across the open valley of grassy flats on the true right (south) bank of the **Matukituki River West Branch**. The scenery up the river includes Shotover Saddle and Mt Tyndall to the left (south), Cascade Saddle straight ahead (west), and occasional sheep and cattle. Within 2km the track passes the swing bridge that provides access across the river to the **Rob Roy Glacier Track**, and on a good day the hanging glacier can be clearly seen above it.

The 4WD track continues up the valley to Aspiring Hut on the true right (west) side of the river. At one point, near Wilsons Camp, the track climbs to the left to bypass a small bluff hidden in a clump of beech trees. Less than 4km from the bridge the track climbs away from the river again, passing **Brides Veil Falls**. The private Cascade Hut can be seen from the ridge. At this point the track swings northwest, passes Cascade Hut, and in another 30 minutes reaches Aspiring Hut (38 bunks).

Built by the Alpine Club in 1949, this stone-and-wood hut is a classic climbers' lodge with an atmosphere of high adventure. The views are impressive, especially of the mountains at the head of the valley, including **Mt Aspiring/Tititea** (3033m) – try to nab a bunk under the big windows. A warden is stationed here in summer to collect fees and to relay weather reports. A designated camping area adjacent to Aspiring Hut is equipped with a shelter and toilet for campers.

SIDE TRIP: ROB ROY GLACIER

3–4 HOURS RETURN, 10KM

This is one of the most popular day tramps in the Wanaka area. Fifteen minutes after setting off from the Raspberry Creek car park, a swing bridge crosses the West Matukituki River. On the other side, the track climbs through a small gorge into beech forest, then into alpine vegetation at the head of the valley, where good views of the **Rob Roy Glacier** can be enjoyed.

Option 1: Aspiring Hut to Liverpool Hut

3–4 HOURS, 6KM, 635M ASCENT

This makes a great overnight excursion from Aspiring Hut, or a grand day out taking up to seven hours return. The track is rated moderate during good conditions, but the tussocky tops can be treacherous and slippery when covered in snow. It requires some physical exertion as you clamber up to Liverpool Hut from the flats, but the views from the top are well worth the effort.

From Aspiring Hut, follow the well-signposted track up the valley. After 10 minutes a bridge crosses Cascade Creek, and a 1km bush section emerges on to an open terrace leading to **Shovel Flat**. From the head of Shovel Flat there's 400m of bush before you reach **Pearl Flat**, around 1½ hours from Aspiring Hut. From Pearl Flat you can continue up to the head of the valley, a rewarding pilgrimage for those psyched out by the climb to Liverpool Hut. It's another two hours (3.2km) to the valley head.

However, the Liverpool Hut contingent should cross the swing bridge at Liverpool Stream and perhaps pause to fortify themselves for a climb of a couple of hours or so. It's steep, and slippery, particularly below the bushline, so expect to put those arms into action as you pull yourself up and onward.

Above the bush the track initially leads across steep exposed shingle, rock and tussock terrain before reaching easier tussock-covered terrain and a knoll overlooking the hut. When the hut is first sighted, *do not* sidle across to the hut below this knoll. Liverpool Hut (10 bunks), at its 1100m vantage, enjoys majestic views of Mt Aspiring/Tititea and surrounding peaks.

Option 2: Aspiring Hut to French Ridge Hut

4–5 HOURS, 7.2KM, 1035M ASCENT

The French Ridge Track holds significant allure for mountain-lovers, but has been the downfall of numerous trampers over the years. Although rated moderate, the upper part of this route is very exposed and treacherous, so should be attempted only by the fit, experienced and well equipped. It's no wonder this is a popular tramp, though, with French Ridge Hut perched high on the flanks of its namesake mountain and the opportunity to venture further up the ridge if desired.

Follow the track to **Pearl Flat** as described under Option 1. Cross the swing bridge at Liverpool Stream, then continue 10 minutes further up the valley where a second swing bridge provides access across the river. The track enters the bush and climbs steeply all the way to the ridge, with narrow guts and creek beds to negotiate in the subalpine zone. Follow the gentle tussock slopes for about 1km and you will reach **French Ridge Hut** (20 bunks), just below the normal summer snowline of approximately 1500m.

If you wish to venture beyond the hut to the Quarterdeck and **Bonar Glacier** and onward to Colin Todd Hut (12 bunks), you will need to be an experienced climber and have the necessary equipment. If you don't, then enjoy the views you have from the hut or hire a guide. The vista from the top of the **Quarterdeck** is one of the best in the national park, with Mt Aspiring/Tititea, the 'Matterhorn of the South', as a backdrop.

Option 3: Aspiring Hut to Cascade Saddle

4½ HOURS, 6KM, 1370M ASCENT

Cascade Saddle is one of the most beautiful alpine passes in NZ, and in good summer weather it can be tramped without the aid of mountaineering gear. It is the crossing point between the West Matukituki and the Dart Valley, via the **Cascade Saddle Route**, which links with the Rees-Dart Track.

It makes for a spectacular return day tramp from Aspiring Hut. But be warned: it is a steep and difficult climb partially smothered in super-slippery snow grass, and trampers have fallen to their deaths here. It should not be attempted by inexperienced trampers nor in adverse conditions. If you

have any doubts, seek advice from the hut warden, who will also have current weather forecasts on hand.

The track is signposted behind the hut and heads southwest into mixed beech forest. Within an hour there are views of Mt Aspiring/Tititea to the north, and the rest of the valley to the east.

The track makes a steady ascent, and after two to three hours from the hut breaks out above the bushline. For most trampers this is a glorious moment. If the day is clear there will be stunning views the minute you leave the last few stunted beech trees.

The next section is very difficult. The route is marked by snow poles and follows a steep snow-grass and tussock ridge upwards. Sometimes you're on all fours working from one pole to the next, because the route sidles a few ledges and rocky outcrops, and at times becomes very steep. You are never more than 100m from the left of the spur. From the bushline it's a good two hours before the track swings to the left and then, veering right again, climbs an easy slope to the **Pylon**, the marker at 1835m. Take a break here – the views are wonderful.

From the marker, the track skirts the ridge to the south and then descends steadily through rock and scree to Cascade Creek (follow the standards). The route crosses the stream to its true left (west) side and climbs some easy slopes towards **Cascade Saddle** to the north. The route to the Rees-Dart veers left just before the saddle, but you can continue to the low point (at 1524m), where you can look from its edge straight down a sheer 1000m rock face to a small valley below – but be careful! It's an incredible feeling looking at so much scenery, with Mt Aspiring/Tititea to one side and the Dart Glacier to the other.

So, with that under your belt, it's time to return to Aspiring Hut via the same route, which would afford an entirely different perspective were it not for the fact that you'll be looking at your feet the entire time. The tramp back down is interminable!

Gillespie Pass Circuit

Duration 3 days

Distance 54km (33.5 miles)

Track Standard Tramping track

Difficulty Moderate to demanding

Start/End Makarora, SH6

ℹ Information

Queenstown i-SITE (☎ 0800 668 888, 03-442 4100; www.queenstownnz.co.nz; cnr Shotover & Camp Sts; ⊗ 8am-6.30pm) offers booking and accommodation services and information on Queenstown, Arrowtown and Glenorchy.

ℹ Getting There & Away

Air New Zealand (☎ 0800 737 000; www.airnz. co.nz) has daily direct flights between Queenstown and Auckland and Christchurch, with onward domestic connections.

There are myriad bus options, most of which can be booked at the i-SITE, including **InterCity** (☎ 03-442 4922; www.intercity.co.nz), NZ's largest bus network servicing all significant South Island destinations. **Naked Bus** (www. nakedbus.com) travels to the West Coast, Te Anau, Christchurch, Dunedin, Cromwell, Wanaka and Invercargill. **Atomic Shuttles** (www. atomictravel.co.nz) connects Queenstown with Christchurch, Dunedin, Wanaka and Greymouth. Smaller transport operators include **Bottom Bus** (www.bottombus.co.nz), which does a loop of the south of the South Island; and **Wanaka Connexions** (www.alpinecoachlines.co.nz), which links Queenstown with Wanaka, as does twice-daily **Connectabus** (☎ 0800 405 066; cnr Beach & Camp Sts).

Glenorchy

☎ 03 / POP 215

A picturesque hamlet at the head of Lake Wakatipu, about 47km from Queenstown, Glenorchy has a limited choice of places to stay and eat. You can get supplies, but the choice is restricted to what is sold at the camping grounds and hotel. Better to outfit your tramp and hire necessary equipment in Queenstown.

🛏 Sleeping & Eating

Glenorchy Holiday Park   HOLIDAY PARK $
(☎ 03-441 0303; www.glenorchyaccommodation. co.nz; 2 Oban St; campsites $28, dm $20, units $32-80; @) This spread-out park is well set up for trampers, with a small store and information centre.

Kinloch Lodge   LODGE $
(☎ 03-442 4900; www.kinlochlodge.co.nz; Kinloch Rd; dm $33, d $82-132) Across Lake Wakatipu from Glenorchy, this is a great place to unwind or prepare for a tramp. It has comfy, colourful rooms, a hot tub, and on-site restaurant and bar. Also on offer is secure parking and track transport.

Glenorchy Cafe   CAFE $
(Mull St; ⊗ 8am-5pm, dinner Nov-Apr) You'll find plenty of hearty fare here, including pizza and breakfast stacks, perennial favourites of the locals.

ℹ Information

Glenorchy visitor information centre (☎ 03-409 2049; www.glenorchy-nz.co.nz; Oban St), inside the Glenorchy Hotel, is an excellent provider of local information and hires out mountain bikes and fishing rods.

ℹ Getting There & Away

Glenorchy is serviced by numerous operators, to-ing and fro-ing between the trailheads. Your best bets for Queenstown to Glenorchy services ($20) are Glenorchy Journeys (p263) and Buckley Transport (p263).

Wanaka

☎ 03 / POP 3500

Presenting a sharp contrast to the hype of Queenstown, laid-back, lakeside Wanaka offers an alluring combination of stunning scenery, a sweet little township, and outdoor activities galore.

🛏 Sleeping & Eating

Aspiring Campervan & Holiday Park   HOLIDAY PARK $
(☎ 0800 229 8439, 03-443 6603; www.campervanpark.co.nz; Studholme Rd; campsites from $37, units $65-160; @ 🖙) Grassy tent sites, cosy cabins, a spa pool and sauna make this a welcoming spot for the visiting tramper.

Matterhorn South   HOSTEL $
(☎ 03-443 1119; www.matterhornsouth.co.nz; 56 Brownston St; dm $26-30, d $68-95; @ 🖙) Right at the edge of central Wanaka, this friendly spot has good-value dorms and studios, a sunny TV and games room, and a relaxing garden.

Wanaka Bakpaka   HOSTEL $
(☎ 03-443 7837; www.wanakabakpaka.co.nz; 117 Lakeside Rd; dm/d $27/64; @ 🖙) This friendly hostel high above the lake has inspiring views, top-notch amenities and good-value rooms.

Wanaka Lakeview Holiday Park   HOLIDAY PARK $
(☎ 03-443 7883; www.wanakalakeview.co.nz; 212 Brownston St; campsites $34, units $55-100) A short walk from the town centre, this park

has grassy sites set amid the pines, basic cabins and en-suite flats.

Kai Whakapai CAFE $
(cnr Helwick & Ardmore Sts; meals $10-30; 🛜) A Wanaka institution, Kai (the Maori word for food) is the place for massive sandwiches and pizzas, great coffee and local beer. A great spot on a sunny day.

Relishes Cafe CAFE $$
(99 Ardmore St; breakfast & lunch $12-20, dinner $27-34) A cafe by day with good breakfast and lunch options, this place whips out the white tablecloths at night and becomes a classy restaurant. Toast the lake views with a glass or two of Central Otago's finest.

🎒 Supplies & Equipment

Outside Sports OUTDOOR EQUIPMENT
(17-23 Dunmore St; ⊙ 8.30am-6pm) Buy or hire tramping gear here.

New World SUPERMARKET
(Dunmore St; ⊙ 7.30am-9pm) Good for food on the track.

❶ Information

Lake Wanaka i-SITE (☑ 03-443 1233; www.lakewanaka.co.nz; Ardmore St) can be found in the log cabin on the lakefront.

❶ Getting There & Away

InterCity has a daily bus to Queenstown (two hours), which connects to the glaciers via Haast Pass, as well as daily services from Christchurch (eight hours). **Atomic Shuttles** (www.atomictravel.co.nz) goes to Christchurch (seven hours), Greymouth (eight hours), Dunedin (four hours) and Te Anau (four hours). **Naked Bus** (www.nakedbus.com) services similar routes. Queenstown and Wanaka are linked by many bus services, including the twice-daily **Connectabus** (☑ 0800 405 066) and **Wanaka Connexions** (☑ 03-443 9120; www.alpinecoachlines.co.nz).

Air New Zealand (p283) has daily flights to Christchurch.

Fiordland & Stewart Island/Rakiura

Includes ➡

Milford Track 290
Hollyford Track 295
Kepler Track 300
Hump Ridge Track . . 303
Rakiura Track 308
North West Circuit . . . 312

Best Huts

➡ Martins Bay Hut (p300)
➡ Luxmore Hut (p302)
➡ Okaka Lodge (p306)
➡ Long Harry Hut (p314)

Best Views

➡ Mackinnon Pass (p294)
➡ Sutherland Falls (p295)
➡ Martins Bay (p300)
➡ Mt Luxmore (p302)
➡ Trig F (p306)
➡ Big Sandhill (p315)

Why Go?

Welcome to the deep green deep south, home to one of New Zealand's finest outdoor treasures – Fiordland National Park. At 12,607 sq km it is the country's largest national park and one of the largest in the world, and makes up half of Te Wahipounamu – South West New Zealand World Heritage Area. Stretching from Martins Bay in the north to Te Waewae Bay in the south, the park is bordered by the Tasman Sea on one side and a series of deep lakes on the other. Between lie more than 500km of tracks, with 60-odd huts dotted along them.

Across Foveaux Strait to the south is Stewart Island, NZ's 'third' island. It's relatively small, just 1722 sq km, but 85% of that area falls within Rakiura National Park, lined with 280km of tracks.

Such stats may be impressive, but the reality is almost beyond belief. The overuse of superlatives such as 'staggering', 'stunning' and 'spectacular' is almost impossible.

When to Go

Fiordland is synonymous with waterfalls, lakes and fiords... and rain. Prevailing winds from the Tasman Sea dump up to 8000mm annually around the park's western parts, although Te Anau averages just 1200mm, sheltered by mountains. Overall, the park averages 200 rainy days annually, with lowland summer temperatures around 18°C.

Similarly, Stewart Island's rainfall has been known to wreak tramping havoc. The annual measure at Halfmoon Bay may be a relatively low 1600mm, but it occurs over 275 days of the year. At higher altitudes and along the south and west coasts, the gauge hits a lofty 5000mm. Considering the latitude, though, the overall climate is surprisingly mild, with reasonable temperatures most of the year.

GATEWAY TOWNS

➡ Te Anau (p316)

➡ Tuatapere (p317)

➡ Invercargill (p317)

➡ Oban (p318)

Fast Facts

➡ The mighty Fiordland National Park covers almost 5% of NZ's total land area.

➡ At 580m, the Sutherland Falls, accessible from the Milford Track, are NZ's loftiest cascade.

➡ With a healthy population of around 20,000, kiwi outnumber humans on Stewart Island by around 50 to one.

Top Tip

Dodge the Kepler and Milford Track crowds and save yourself some money at the same time by tramping either side of the Great Walks season.

Resources

➡ www.fiordland.org.nz

➡ www.hikesouth.com

➡ www.southlandnz.com

➡ www.westernsouthland.co.nz

➡ www.visitinvercargillnz.com

➡ www.stewartisland.co.nz

Background Reading

Take the momentous Gondwanaland bust-up and biodiversity backstory out of the equation, and you'll find Fiordland dominated by pioneer history – much of it involving isolation, deprivation and occasional insanity. Allow us to recommend two books to illustrate this point: *The Land of Doing Without: Davy Gunn of the Hollyford,* by Julia Bradshaw, brings to life the legendary backcountry hero; and *Pioneers of Martins Bay* – Alice McKenzie's memoir of growing up in a wild and remote extremity of Fiordland. For excellent illustrated regional histories, look for anything by John Hall-Jones.

DON'T MISS

There's no getting around it: no visit to Fiordland is complete without a trip to Milford Sound, the first sight of which will likely knock your socks off (if the drive there hasn't already). Sheer rocky cliffs rise from still, dark waters, while forests clinging to the slopes sometimes relinquish their hold, causing a 'tree avalanche' into the waters. The spectacular, photogenic 1692m-high Mitre Peak rises dead ahead. A postcard will never do it justice, and a big downpour will only add to the drama. The average annual rainfall of 7m is more than enough to fuel cascading waterfalls and add a shimmering moody mist to the scene.

A cruise on Milford Sound is Fiordland's most accessible experience, complete with seals, dolphins and excellent interpretation. These cruises are incredibly popular, and you will encounter busloads of other visitors. But don't worry. Out on the water all this humanity seems tiny compared to nature's vastness.

But we're getting ahead of ourselves, because getting there is half the fun – especially if you have your own transport allowing you to stop at every DOC signpost you see. The 119km Te Anau–Milford Highway (SH94) is a veritable dot-to-dot of short nature walks and lookout points. DOC's *Fiordland National Park Day Walks* will set you on your way.

DOC & Track Offices

➡ **Fiordland National Park Visitor Centre** (☎03-249 7924; www.doc.govt.nz; Lakefront Dr)

➡ **Tuatapere Hump Ridge Track Office** (☎03-226 6739, 0800 486 774; www.humpridgetrack.co.nz; 31 Orawia Rd, Tuatapere; ☺7.30am-6.30pm, limited hours in winter)

➡ **Rakiura National Park Visitor Centre** (☎03-219 0009; www.doc.govt.nz; 15 Main Rd, Oban; ☺8am-5pm Oct-Mar, shorter hours in winter)

FIORDLAND NATIONAL PARK

NZ's largest national park is a truly great wilderness, and you don't have to look too hard to see why it buddies up with the Egyptian pyramids and the Grand Canyon in the list of World Heritage sites. It is jagged and mountainous, densely forested and cut through by numerous deeply recessed sounds (technically fiords) that reach inland like crooked fingers from the Tasman Sea.

It remains formidable and remote, with the rugged terrain, rainforest-like bush and abundant waterways having kept progress and people out of much of the park. The fringes of Fiordland are easily visited, but most of the park is impenetrable to all but the hardiest trampers, making it a true wilderness in every sense. The most intimate way to experience Fiordland is on foot.

It is not the only way, though, as more than 500,000 annual visitors to Milford Sound can tell you. Of that number – many of whom flock in during the peak months of January and February – some 14,000 arrive by foot via the Milford Track. This isn't just Fiordland's most famous track: it is often labelled the 'finest walk in the world'. The rest of Milford Sound's visitors arrive via the 119km Te Anau–Milford Highway (SH94), an intensely scenic byway passing through the sheer-sided and beautiful Eglinton Valley, and the Divide, the lowest east–west pass in the Southern Alps. Prepare to be amazed.

Indeed, one of the first impressions trampers gain of the park is of the almost overpowering steepness of the mountains, an impression accentuated by the fact that they are usually separated only by narrow valleys. The rocks and peaks of Fiordland are very hard and have eroded slowly, compared to the mountains of Mt Aspiring and Arthur's Pass, which are softer. Gentle topography this is not. It is raw and hard-core all the way.

History

In comparison with other regions, little is known of the pre-European history of the Maori in Fiordland. There is evidence of a permanent settlement at Martins Bay, and possibly of summer villages throughout Fiordland, which were used for seasonal hunting expeditions. The most significant archaeological find in the region was made in 1967, when mid-17th-century burial remains were discovered in a cave in Lake Hauroko.

In 1770 Captain Cook worked his way up the west coast in the *Endeavour,* but was unsuccessful in landing: it was too dusky in one instance, and doubtful in another. He returned three years later, bringing the *Resolution* into Dusky Sound, where the crew recuperated after three months at sea. Recorded in his log in 1773 was probably the first written description of sandflies: 'most mischievous animals that cause a swelling not possible to refrain from scratching'.

In 1792 a 12-strong sealing gang arrived. Left in the sound for 10 months, they reaped a harvest of 4500 skins, and constructed one of NZ's first European buildings. By 1795 there were 250 settlers in Dusky Sound.

Whaling briefly followed sealing, with the first significant shore-based South Island whaling station built in 1829 at Preservation Inlet. The industries devastated seal and whale populations, but encouraged exploration of the coast. In 1823, Welsh sealing captain John Grono was the first to record sailing into Milford Sound, naming it after his hometown of Milford Haven.

Fiordland was explored from the sea until 1852, when a party reached Te Anau from the Waiau Valley. Nine years later two cattle drivers, David McKellar and George Gunn, climbed to the top of Key Summit and became the first Europeans to view the Hollyford Valley. This set off more explorations, resulting in myriad firsts commemorated in the names of major landmarks.

As usual, it was gold-mining that encouraged deeper delving into the wilderness. In 1868, the Otago Provincial Government attempted to stimulate further growth by starting a settlement at Martins Bay. Some lots at Jamestown (as it was known) were sold, but the settlers who moved there found life hard and lonely. By 1870 there were only eight houses in Jamestown. Nine years later the settlement was deserted, leaving only a handful of people living at Martins Bay.

A couple of legendary hermits settled in Fiordland around this time, one of whom was Donald Sutherland, a colourful character who sailed single-handedly from Dunedin into Milford Sound in 1877 and became known as the 'Hermit of Milford'. In 1880, Sutherland and John Mackay struggled up the Arthur Valley from Milford Sound in search of precious minerals. The fine waterfall they found was named after Mackay

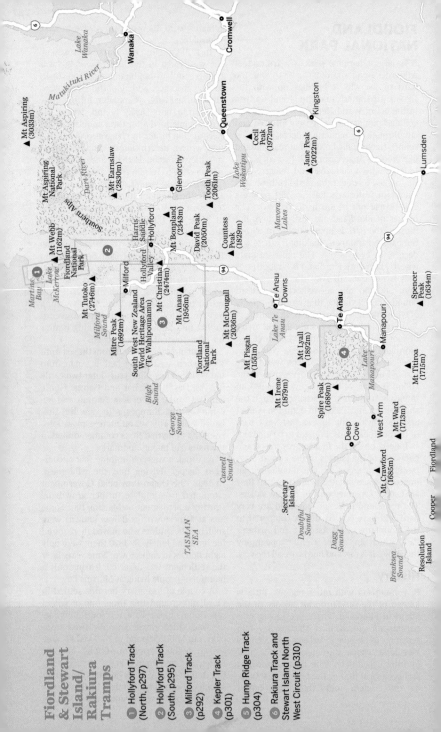

Fiordland & Stewart Island/ Rakiura Tramps

1 Hollyford Track (North, p297)

2 Hollyford Track (South, p295)

3 Milford Track (p292)

4 Kepler Track (p301)

5 Hump Ridge Track (p304)

6 Rakiura Track and Stewart Island North West Circuit (p310)

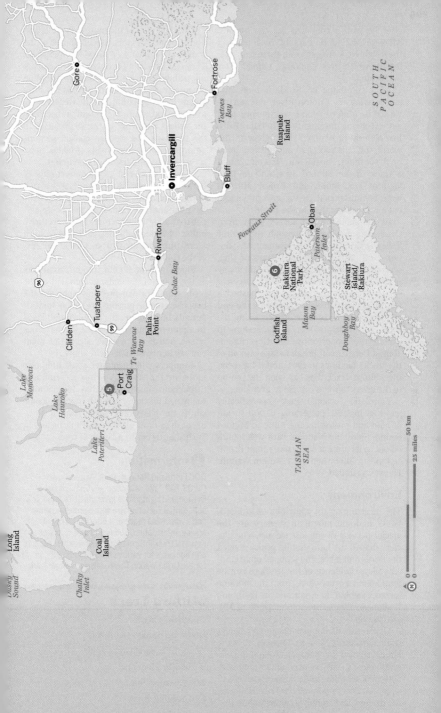

after he won a coin toss for the honour. After several more days of bush-bashing they sighted a magnificent three-leap waterfall, which was equitably named after Sutherland.

After stumbling on to Mackinnon Pass and viewing the Clinton River, the pair returned by Milford Sound, where word soon got out about the mighty Sutherland Falls. Erroneously proclaimed the highest in the world, the falls soon had adventurers lined up to see them. The pressure was on to build a track to the Milford area, and in 1888 Quintin Mackinnon and Ernest Mitchell were commissioned by the government to cut a route along the Clinton River.

At the same time, a survey party from Otago was moving up through the Arthur Valley. Hearing of this development, Mackinnon and Mitchell stopped track-cutting, scrambled over the pass and made their way past the present site of Quintin Hut to meet Adams. A rough trail was thus established, a few flimsy huts thrown up, and by the end of the year tourists were already using the route, with Mackinnon as guide. Seeking to exploit this opportunity, the Government Tourist Department began to take over all of the track's facilities in 1901, and it has been the Milford Track that has been the pin-up of the area's tourism campaign ever since.

Fiordland National Park was officially gazetted in 1952, preserving 10,000 sq km of land and protecting the route to Milford Sound. Fiordland National Park was rounded out to its present size – more than 12,000 sq km – in 1999 when the 22-sq-km Waitutu Forest was added.

Environment

The most important contributors to Fiordland's majestic mountain scenery are the glacial periods of the last ice age. The glaciers shaped the hard granite peaks, gouged the fiords and lakes, and scooped out rounded valleys. Evidence of the ice floes can be found almost everywhere, from the moraine terraces behind Te Anau and in Eglinton's U-shaped valley to the pointed peaks of Milford Sound.

One result of the glaciers is Fiordland's trademark lakes, such as Te Anau. It is the largest lake on the South Island and the second largest in the country, 66km long with 500km of shoreline and a surface area of 342 sq km. Another major lake is Lake Hauroko, the deepest lake in NZ, plunging 463m.

The sheerness of the mountain walls and fiords (some sea cliffs rise 1.5km out of the water) allow plenty of scope for waterfalls. They can be seen all over the place – cascading, tumbling, roaring or simply dribbling down a green mossy bluff. All this moisture means lush vegetation. On the eastern side, forests of red, silver and mountain beech fill the valleys and cling to the steep faces. In the northern and western coastal sections ,impressive podocarp forests of matai, rimu, southern rata and totara can be found.

Much of the forest grows on a surface of hard rock covered by only a thin layer of rich humus and moss, a natural retainer for the large amounts of rain. It is this peaty carpet that allows thick ground flora to thrive under towering canopies, and sets western Fiordland bush apart from that of the rest of the country.

Fiordland is well known to bird-watchers as the home of the endangered takahe. The birds trampers will probably spot are the usual kereru (NZ pigeons), riflemen, tomtits, fantails, bush robins, tui, bellbirds and kaka. In alpine regions you may see kea and rock wrens, and if you wander around at night you might occasionally hear a kiwi.

Trampers will encounter something else in the air: the sandfly. The insect is common throughout much of NZ but Fiordland is renowned for them. A much more welcome site is the glowworm, easily spotted glowing at dusk or at night beneath ferns and in bush sharply cut by a benched track.

ℹ Information

DOC Fiordland National Park Visitor Centre (☎ 03-249 7924; www.doc.govt.nz; Lakefront Dr), located right on the lakeside at Te Anau, is a substantial visitor centre with a small museum and audiovisual theatre. It offers an array of advice, information, books and maps, as well as regional track information, daily weather reports and bookings for various huts including those for the Great Walks. There's also a free car park.

Milford Track

Duration 4 days

Distance 53.5km (33 miles)

Track Standard Great Walk

Difficulty Moderate

Start Glade Wharf

End Sandfly Point

Nearest Town Te Anau (p316)

Transport Shuttle bus, boat

Summary The best-known track in NZ, with towering peaks, deep glaciated valleys, rainforests, alpine meadows and spectacular waterfalls.

The Milford Track is popular. Popular but still not overrun, despite an annual click-rate of more than 7000 independent trampers. For this you can thank a regulation system that – while keeping people moving through in significant volume – still ensures some level of tranquillity.

During the Milford tramping season, the track can only be walked in one direction, starting from Glade Wharf. You must stay at Clinton Hut the first night, despite it being only one hour from the start of the track, and you must complete the trip in the prescribed three nights and four days. This is perfectly acceptable if the weather is kind, but if it goes sour you'll still have to push on across the alpine Mackinnon Pass and may miss some rather spectacular views. It's all down to the luck of the draw.

During the Great Walk season, the track is also frequented by guided tramping parties, who stay at cosy, carpeted lodges with hot showers and proper food. Unsurprisingly, such trips are in hot demand for soft-core trampers and those with cash to spare. Clever timetabling means you may only stumble across them here and there – unless of course, you are one of them.

Also drawn to the Milford honeypot is a swarm of small aeroplanes that buzz through the valleys and over the peaks. A scenic flight is undoubtedly a fantastic way to appreciate the grandeur, and *perhaps* almost as satisfying as walking the track.

Yes, the Milford Track is busy, but it's hardly Piccadilly Circus. And at the end of the day, this is one of the greatest and most accessible of NZ's wilderness adventures.

ⓘ Planning

WHEN TO TRAMP
The season for the Milford is late October to late April. Outside this period there is no scheduled transport on or off the track and it is a winter crossing that should only be attempted by experienced trampers. New Zealanders, inclined to kvetch about how busy and expensive it is, commonly embark on the Milford Track just before or just after the Great Walks season when both prices and number of trampers drop.

WHAT TO BRING
Pack insect repellent. You will encounter sandflies along most of the trail; depending on the time of year and weather conditions they will range from mildly bothersome to horrible. At times they can be so thick it is hard to stop for a scenic view.

The huts have gas cookers, but some trampers still take their own stoves so they can enjoy hot soup for lunch and not wait in the evening until a stove is available. You will also need your own cooker in the off-season, when the gas cookers are removed.

MAPS & BROCHURES
The track is covered by NewTopo map *Milford Track* 1:55,000, and 1:70,000 Parkmap 335-01 *(Milford Track)*.

HUTS & BOOKINGS
The Milford Track is a Great Walk and between late October and mid-April you'll need a Great Walk pass ($162) to cover your three nights in the huts – Clinton, Mintaro and Dumpling. Each has gas cookers, cold running water and heating in the main kitchen/dining hut, plus communal bunk rooms with mattresses. Ablution blocks have flush toilets and washbasins, although in the off-season facilities are reduced to a long drop and tap only. In season, a DOC ranger is resident at each hut and is able to pass on information about the environment and weather, or help you should an emergency arise.

Hut passes must be obtained in advance. Book early! You must begin the track on the day for which your booking is made, and you must walk the track in the prescribed four days. Bookings can be made beginning 1 July for the following season.

For further information and bookings, contact **Great Walks Bookings** (☑ 0800 694 732; www.greatwalks.co.nz) or visit any DOC visitor centre. If you are alone or in a pair, and can wait a few days, there is a *slight* possibility of spaces becoming available due to cancellations. Check for cancellations at www.doc.govt.nz or any major DOC office.

In the off-season there is no requirement to tramp the track with prescribed stops, and the huts revert to **Serviced huts** (www.doc.govt.nz; $15).

GUIDED TRAMPS
Ultimate Hikes (☑ 03-450 1940, www.ultimate-hikes.co.nz) is the only operator permitted to run guided tramps of the Milford Track. Its five-day tramp features comfortable lodge accommodation, meals and expert interpretation. The trip costs $2095 in high season (1 December to 31 March), and $1930 in the shoulder (all November and the first two weeks of April). You're best to book early, but it isn't always necessary.

Milford Track

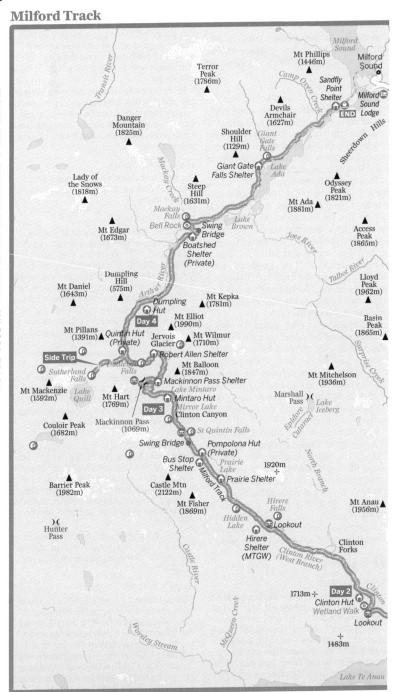

Milford Sound

Mt Phillips
(1446m)

Camp Oven Creek

Sandfly
Point
Shelter

Milford
Sound

Terror
Peak
(1786m)

Milford
Sound
Lodge

END

Devils
Armchair
(1627m)

Danger
Mountain
(1825m)

Shoulder
Hill
(1129m)

Giant
Gate
Falls

Sheerdown Hills

Giant Gate
Falls Shelter

Lake
Ada

Odyssey
Peak
(1821m)

Lady of
the Snows
(1818m)

Mackay Creek

Steep
Hill
(1631m)

Mt Ada
(1881m)

Access
Peak
(1865m)

Mt Edgar
(1673m)

Mackay
Falls

Bell Rock

Swing
Bridge

Lake
Brown

Joes River

Talbot River

Lloyd
Peak
(1962m)

Boatshed
Shelter
(Private)

Arthur River

Basin
Peak
(1865m)

Mt Daniel
(1643m)

Dumpling
Hill
(575m)

Dumpling
Hut

Mt Kepka
(1781m)

Day 4

Mt Pillans
(1391m)

Quintin Hut
(Private)

Mt Elliot
(1990m)

Jervois
Glacier

Mt Wilmur
(1710m)

Robert Allen Shelter

Surprise Creek

Side Trip

Dudleigh
Falls

Sutherland
Falls

Mt Balloon
(1847m)

Mackinnon Pass Shelter

Mt Mitchelson
(1936m)

Mt Mackenzie
(1592m)

Lake
Quill

Mt Hart
(1769m)

Lake Mintaro

Mintaro Hut

Marshall
Pass

Lake
Iceberg

Mirror Lake

Epidore
Cataract

Day 3

Clinton Canyon

Mackinnon Pass
(1069m)

St Quintin Falls

North Branch

Couloir Peak
(1682m)

Swing
Bridge

Pompolona Hut
(Private)

Mt Anau
(1956m)

Bus Stop
Shelter

Prairie
Lake

1920m

Milford Track

Barrier Peak
(1982m)

Prairie Shelter

Castle Mtn
(2122m)

Hirere
Falls

Mt Fisher
(1869m)

Hidden
Lake

Lookout

Clinton
Forks

Hunter
Pass

Castle River

Hirere
Shelter
(MTGW)

Clinton River
(West Branch)

Clinton

1713m

Day 2

Clinton Hut
Wetland Walk

McQueen Creek

Lookout

Worsley Stream

1483m

Lake Te Anau

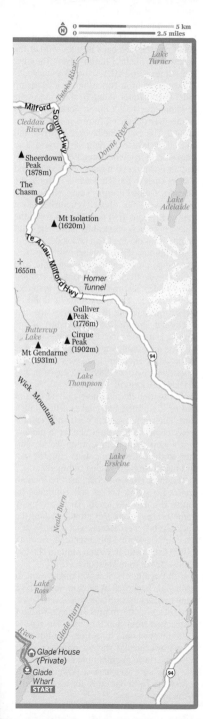

ℹ Getting to/from the Tramp

TO THE START

The track starts at Glade Wharf, which lies at the head of Lake Te Anau and is accessed by a scheduled, twice-daily 1½-hour boat trip from Te Anau Downs. Te Anau Downs is 27km from Te Anau on the road to Milford Sound and has a car-parking area if you wish to leave your vehicle.

Scheduled bus services from Te Anau to meet the boat at Te Anau Downs are run by **Tracknet** (☑ 0800 483 262; www.tracknet.net), which of-fer a return-trip bus-boat-bus transfer leaving Te Anau at 9.45am and 12.15pm ($25). It is based at Te Anau Lakeview Kiwi Holiday Park, where there is secure parking.

Other buses passing through Te Anau Downs on the way to Milford Sound are **InterCity** (☑ 03-442 4922; www.intercity.co.nz) and **Kiwi Discovery** (☑ 03-442 7340, 0800 505 504; www.kiwidiscovery.com).

The boat service from Te Anau Downs to Glade Wharf is run by **Real Journeys** (☑ 03-249 7416, 0800 656 501; www.realjourneys.co.nz; $79; ☉ 10.30am & 1pm).

Transport can be booked at the **Fiordland National Park Visitor Centre** (☑ 03-249 7924; www.doc.govt.nz; Lakefront Dr), or online at www.doc.govt.nz when you purchase your hut pass.

Another way to reach the start of the track from Te Anau is with **Wings & Water Te Anau** (☑ 03-249 7405; www.wingsandwater.co.nz), which will fly you to Glade Wharf in a floatplane that holds three passengers plus gear, for $690 per flight.

FROM THE END

The Milford Track finishes at Sandfly Point, a 15-minute boat trip from Milford Sound village. The boat departs at 2pm, 3pm and 4pm and is usually booked as part of a track transport package.

From Milford Sound village, there are daily bus services to the Divide (the start of the Route-burn Track, 45 minutes), Te Anau Downs (two hours), Te Anau (2½ hours) and Queenstown (five hours). You will be given options to book the above connecting transport online, at the same time as you book your hut tickets.

You may wish to linger a while, or even over-night, in Milford, perhaps taking a kayak trip or cruise. Accommodation is available at **Milford Sound Lodge** (☑ 03-249 8071; www.milford lodge.com; SH94; campsites from $18, dm $30-33; @), where there's a tiny shop/cafe/bar.

As you leave Milford you will pass through the amazing Homer Tunnel. The tunnel began as a relief project in the 1930s, and was finally opened to motor traffic in 1954.

🏃 The Tramp

Day 1: Glade Wharf to Clinton Hut

1 HOUR, 5KM

The track from Glade Wharf is a wide 4WD trail once used by packhorses to carry supplies to the huts. In 15 minutes it passes Glade House, the official start of the Milford Track. The track crosses the Clinton River on a large swing bridge, and continues along the river's true right (west) side as a gentle, well-trodden path.

At one point the track offers an impressive view of the peaks next to Dore Pass to the east, but most of the tramp along the river is through beech forest. Look out for the short side track leading to the wetland boardwalk that takes you into a fascinating sphagnum moss swamp, home to all sorts of unusual plant life.

From Glade Wharf, it takes only one hour to reach Clinton Hut (40 bunks), the first hut for independent trampers. Situated in a clearing alongside a wetland, this facility is actually three huts, built after the Clinton Forks Hut was removed in 1997 after the river threatened to carry it away. There are now two sleeping huts with 20 beds each, and a communal dining room, all facing onto a large deck.

Once you've offloaded your packs and had a refreshing cuppa, stroll down to the river to catch some sunshine. It's a beautiful spot to reflect.

Warden talks at this (and every) Milford Track hut during the Great Walk season are given at 7.30pm. They include a weather forecast and track condition update, and are a great opportunity to ask questions and share a few yarns.

Day 2: Clinton Hut to Mintaro Hut

5–6 HOURS, 16.5KM

This day is another easy, level walk, until the final two hours, when you climb to Mintaro Hut – the first step in crossing Mackinnon Pass. The track continues beside the Clinton River to Clinton Forks.

Keep an eye out for blue ducks around this stretch of river. Endemic to NZ, the whio (blue duck) has no close relatives anywhere in the world. It is in fact bluish-grey, with a pale pink bill and a reddish-brown spotted breast. The males whistle and the females produce a guttural rattle-like call. Back in 2004, a whio recovery program saw ducklings released back into the wild at the headwaters of the Clinton River. They are sometimes seen in the Arthur River, also.

Beyond Clinton Forks the track heads up the Clinton River West Branch. A couple of kilometres past Clinton Forks the track climbs over debris left from a major landslip in 1982. The avalanche blocked the river and created the lake to the right of the track; dead trees emerge from the water. Wispy waterfalls feather down on both sides of the valley and a short walk to the left leads to views of the cascades. Guided trampers have a lunch stop near Hirere Falls, about 1km further along the track. About 4km past Clinton Forks the valley becomes noticeably narrower, with granite walls closing in on both sides.

Mackinnon Pass, further up the valley, comes into view for the first time, and a short side track curves west to Hidden Lake, which features a towering waterfall on its far side. The track remains in beech forest until it comes to the prairies, the first grassy flat. Prairie Lake, at the start of this stretch, is a good place for a swim, since the water is marginally warmer than other lakes in the valley. There are good views from here towards Mt Fisher (1869m) to the west, and Mackinnon Pass to the northwest. A new shelter (with toilet) has been built at the top end of the prairie and makes a nice lunch stop. The track re-enters bush and begins a rocky climb to Bus Stop Shelter, a gloomy lunch stop 9km from Clinton Forks, and then to the deluxe Pompolona Hut, the second night's stop for guided trampers.

The track crosses Pompolona Creek on an impressive swing bridge and continues its course through low scrub. There are many frame bridges along this stretch, before the track ascends more steeply as it passes a side track to St Quintin Falls, eventually working its way to Lake Mintaro and Mintaro Hut (40 bunks), 3.5km from Pompolona Hut.

If the weather is clear you might want to stash your backpack at the hut and make a foray to Mackinnon Pass (1069m) to be assured of seeing the impressive views without obstruction from clouds or rain. The pass is a 1½- to two-hour climb from the hut, and offers a spectacular view at sunset on clear evenings. If you are planning to catch a sunset, make sure you have a powerful headlamp (with fresh batteries) for a safe return to the hut.

Day 3: Mintaro Hut to Dumpling Hut

6–7 HOURS, 14KM, 489M ASCENT, 969M DESCENT

The track leaves the hut, swings west with the valley and resumes its climb to Mackinnon Pass. Crossing the Clinton River for a second time it follows a series of almost a dozen switchbacks out of the bush and into alpine territory. This is a stiff climb at a knee-bending angle, but after 4km the track reaches the large memorial cairn that honours the discovery of this scenic spot by Quintin Mackinnon and Ernest Mitchell in 1888.

The track then levels out and crosses Mackinnon Pass, with impressive views all around the Clinton and Arthur Valleys and several nearby peaks. The two most prominent peaks from the pass are Mt Hart (1769m) and Mt Balloon (1847m). If the weather is fair, you'll want to spend some extra time at the pass; if it isn't, you won't be able to get off it fast enough. The track passes several tarns, ascends to the highest point of the tramp at 1154m, and reaches Mackinnon Pass Shelter – a good place for a restorative break on cold days – before swinging north for the descent.

From the pass to Dumpling Hut the track drops 870m in 7km. Soon, it arrives at Roaring Burn, crosses it and re-enters the bush. The stream, with its many beautiful waterfalls and rapids, is an impressive sight, but the long series of wooden and pierced-metal stairways and lookout platforms that trips down the valley beside it is almost as eye-catching. Their construction in 1996–97 is testimony to the Milford's popularity among soft-core trampers. There are fine views of Dudleigh Falls on Roaring Burn shortly before Quintin Hut. Quintin is actually a series of lodge buildings for guided trampers, but there's also a day-use shelter for independent trampers. Nearby is historic Beech Hut, a reconstruction of a primitive hut from the early days of the Milford Track.

The awesome Sutherland Falls can be reached from Quintin Hut shelter, where you can leave your pack before following the spur track. It's well worth making the 1½-hour return trip. Dropping a total of 580m in three spectacular leaps, this is one of the loftiest waterfalls in the world.

The track leaves Quintin Hut and descends Gentle Annie Hill, re-entering thick forest, which is often slippery and wet underfoot. Within 3km (one hour) of Quintin Hut, the track arrives at Dumpling Hut (40 bunks), a welcome sight after a long day over the pass.

Day 4: Dumpling Hut to Sandfly Point

5½–6 HOURS, 18KM

The track descends back into bush and soon the roar of Arthur River is heard as the trail closely follows the true right (east) bank. About two hours (6km) from the hut, the track reaches the private Boatshed Shelter (a morning-tea stop for guided trampers) and crosses Arthur River on a large swing bridge.

Just beyond the bridge the track crosses another bridge over Mackay Creek, and comes to a very short side track to Mackay Falls and Bell Rock. This is your cue to lift the weight off your back for a bit while you take a gander at these amazing natural wonders. It's well worth the scrabble into the tiny cave under Bell Rock, where the water has eroded a space underneath large enough to stand in. Mackay Falls may not be a patch on Sutherland Falls, but they're still a nice feature for Mackay to have his name on!

The track begins to climb a rock shoulder of the valley, laboriously cut with pick-axes a century ago, above Lake Ada. At one point there is a view of the lake all the way to Joes Valley. From here the track descends to Giant Gate Falls, passing them on a swing bridge before continuing along the lakeshore. The shelter just before Giant Gate Falls is a popular lunch stop.

It takes about one hour to follow the lake past Doughboy Shelter (a private hut for guided trampers) through wide, open flats at the end of the valley to the Sandfly Point Shelter, the end of the tramp.

Hollyford Track

Duration 5 days

Distance 56.8km (35 miles)

Track Standard Tramping and easy tramping tracks

Difficulty Easy to moderate

Start Lower Hollyford Rd

End Martins Bay

Nearest Town Te Anau (p316)

Transport Shuttle bus, jetboat, plane

Hollyford Track (South)

0 ——— **2 km**
0 ——— **1 miles**

Demon Trail Hut

Lake Speden

Lake Alabaster

Lookouts

Lake Mantle

Hollyford Track (North) (p297)

Demon Trail

Pyke–Big Bay Route

Suspension Bridge

Day 3

Lake Alabaster Hut

Chair Creek

Pyke Lodge (Private)

Fiordland National Park

Swing Bridge

Rainbow Creek

Swing Bridge

Homer Creek

Little Homer Saddle (168m)

Glacier Creek

Prospector Peak (1549m)

Darran Mountains

Hidden Falls Hut

Day 2

Hidden Falls Creek

Sunshine Hut (Private)

Swing Bridge

Cleft Creek

1521m

Lake Hyslop

Hollyford Track

Chasm Creek

Swamp Creek

Bridge

Eel Creek

Swing Bridge

Mt Tuhawaiki (2092m)

Korako Glacier

START

Swing Bridge

Rainbow Lake

Shelter

Humboldt Track

Humboldt Creek

Moraine Creek

Lower Hollyford Rd

Caples Creek

Gunn's Camp (Hollyford) (1.7km); SH94 (9.2km)

Summary A forest tramp to isolated and historic Martins Bay, with no alpine crossings but some excellent mountain scenery, plus opportunities for trout and coastal fishing, and a seal colony.

The Hollyford is the longest valley in Fiordland National Park, stretching 80km from the Darran Mountains to remote Martins Bay. The upper portions of the valley are accessible by Lower Hollyford Rd, which extends 18km from Marian Corner (on Milford Rd) to the start of the track. The track is generally recognised as extending from the road end to Martins Bay.

In recent years portions of the route have been upgraded, new transport services have emerged and more trampers have discovered the lush rainforest, extensive bird life and unique marine fauna (seals and penguins) at Martins Bay. The track now averages about 4000 trampers a year – both guided parties and independent trampers – which is still far less than the numbers using the Routeburn or Milford Tracks.

One reason the Hollyford will always lag behind its two famous counterparts is its length. The track is basically a one-way tramp, unless the Pyke-Big Bay Route is taken. Combined with the Hollyford, this challenging and strenuous route loops from Martins Bay along the coast to Big Bay, heads inland to Pyke River, and then goes down the shore of Lake Alabaster to return to the Hollyford at Lake Alabaster Hut. A strong, experienced tramper could cover the walk from Martins Bay to Lake Alabaster along this route in three days, with nights spent at Big Bay and Olivine Huts. The second day, however, would be a nine- to 12-hour tramp. As we say, it is strenuous and challenging. Contact the local DOC office if you want to investigate this possibility.

The majority of trampers turn tail at Martins Bay and retrace their steps to the road end, or arrange to be flown out. If possible, spend an extra day by the bay. It offers superb coastal scenery and saltwater fishing, as well as good views of a seal colony and penguins. But be prepared for the attentions of swarms of sandflies and mosquitoes, who will quickly introduce themselves.

ⓘ Planning

WHEN TO TRAMP

The Hollyford is the only major low-level track in Fiordland and can be tramped year-round. Summer is the most popular season.

WHAT TO BRING

Pack a stove and some fuel; there are no stoves in the huts along the track.

MAPS & BROCHURES

The best maps for this tramp are NZTopo50 CB09 (Hollyford), CA09 (Alabaster) and CA08 (Milford Sound). DOC produces a *Hollyford Track* brochure.

HUTS, CAMPING & BOOKINGS

Trampers have the use of six DOC huts on the track. Five are **Serviced huts** (www.doc.govt. nz; $15): Hidden Falls, Lake Alabaster, Demon Trail, Hokuri and Martins Bay, with mattresses, heating, water and toilet facilities. McKerrow Island is a **Standard hut** (www.doc.govt.nz; $5). Camping ($5) is permitted next to the huts, although the sandflies will prevent this being even remotely enjoyable. Obtain your hut passes online from DOC (www.doc.govt.nz).

To reach the trailhead, trampers will pass **Gunn's Camp** (www.gunnscamp.org.nz; Lower Hollyford Valley Rd; camping per person $12, dm $20), a good place to head out from, especially if you've just completed the Milford or Routeburn. A small store stocks tramping food, but the highlight of the camp is undoubtedly the small museum dedicated to Davy Gunn (see p298) and the history of the valley. It's a two-hour walk from the camp to the road end and the start of the tramp, although the camp also offers transfers (by donation) and car storage for $2 per day.

GUIDED TRAMPS

Hollyford Track (☑ 03-442 3000, 0800 832 226; www.hollyfordtrack.com) offers three-day guided tramps, staying at private huts/lodges, including a three-day tramp to Martins Bay ($1895) that ends with a scenic flight to Milford Sound.

ⓘ Getting to/from the Tramp

A number of buses on the Te Anau–Milford Sound run will drop off or pick up trampers at Marian Corner, or even at Gunn's Camp, but the latter still leaves you about 10km short of the start of the track.

Some operators do service the Hollyford Rd end, including **Tracknet** (☑ 0800 483 262; www.tracknet.net), which runs Monday, Wednesday and Friday on demand (two hours). **Trips & Tramps** (☑ 03 249 7081; www.trips andtramps.com) also runs to the Hollyford Rd end via Milford Sound, and organises return-trip plane and bus transport packages between Te Anau, Milford Sound and the Hollyford Track.

Many trampers will avoid backtracking all or a portion of the track by either flying or catching the jetboat. **Fly Fiordland** (☑ 0800 359 346;

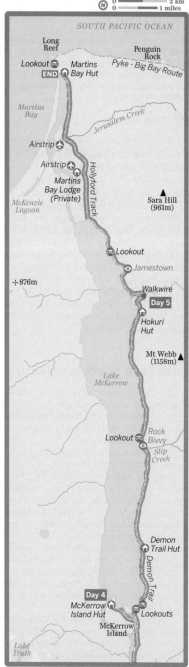

Hollyford Track (North)

www.flyfiordland.com) flies between Martins Bay and Milford Sound for $160 per person (minimum two people).

Hollyford Track (03-442 3000, 0800 832 226; www.hollyfordtrack.com) also runs a jet-boat along Lake McKerrow, between Martins Bay to the Pyke confluence near McKerrow Island Hut ($110). This saves a day and eliminates walking the Demon Trail, by far the most arduous portion of the track. This service must be booked in advance.

🏃 The Tramp

Day 1: Lower Hollyford Road to Hidden Falls Hut

2–3 HOURS, 9KM

After floods washed out a road bridge in 1994, the Hollyford became 1km longer and it now begins at a swing bridge over Humboldt Creek. Within 1km, the track sidles along a rock bluff on a raised boardwalk that clings to the bluff's face and then descends to cross a swing bridge over Eel Creek.

Less than one hour from the car park you reach a bridge over Swamp Creek. The force of the 1994 floods is clearly seen here, with one side of this stream completely cleared of bush and trees.

The track remains level and dry, skirting Swamp Creek for a spell before emerging at the banks of the **Hollyford River** for the first time. At this point the track closely follows the true right (east) bank of the river and offers an occasional view of the snow-capped **Darran Mountains** to the west. It's about 4.5km from Swamp Creek to a point where the track emerges onto the open flat of **Hidden Falls Creek**, quickly passing the signposted junction to Sunshine Hut, a private shelter for guided trampers.

Just beyond the hut, a side track leads to Hidden Falls, two minutes upstream from the swing bridge. The waterfall is stunning and aptly named, as a rock cleft partially blocks the view. You can boulder hop along the stream to get a better view of the cascade.

Hidden Falls Hut (12 bunks) is 15 to 20 minutes away, on the northern side of the swing bridge, along the edge of a large river flat. There is a fine view of **Mt Madeline** (2536m) to the west.

Day 2: Hidden Falls Hut to Lake Alabaster Hut

3–4 HOURS, 10.5KM

The track departs from behind the hut, and passes through a forest of ribbonwood

---

THE LAND OF DOING WITHOUT

Davy Gunn is one of the great legends of the NZ back country. He was born in 1887 in Waimate, Canterbury, the son of a shepherd. Gunn was a chip off the old block from the get-go, working as a stock agent and farmer, and then in 1926 buying the McKenzie family farm in remote Martins Bay. He eventually held the lease of more than 25,000 acres in the Hollyford Valley.

It was here that legend was born, as Gunn became the ultimate bushman. From his base at Deadmans Hut on the banks of the Hollyford River, Gunn lived on the sniff of an oily rag, calling the Hollyford 'The Land of Doing Without'. He set to improving the stock-droving track to facilitate his annual four-month-long, 175-mile cattle drive to the Invercargill sale yards. Talk about a hard row to hoe!

It's not surprising then that Davy looked for alternative sources of income. Having constructed huts through the valley, he gradually went from running cattle to guiding tourists, beginning in 1936.

This was to be the year of Gunn's greatest achievement: the emergency dash he undertook to get help for victims of an aircraft crash in Big Bay in 1936. Gunn tramped from Big Bay to Lake McKerrow, rowed up the lake and then rode his horse more than 40km to a construction camp, where he telephoned for help. The trip would take an experienced tramper three days – Gunn did it in 21 hours. And that's how you become a *legend*.

Having slipped over a bluff in 1950, aged 63, Gunn began to lose much of his strength and vigour. On Christmas Day in 1955, as he was attempting to cross the Hollyford River with a 12-year-old boy in the saddle behind him, his horse stumbled and fell. Both Gunn and the boy were swept to their deaths; Gunn's body was never found.

and podocarps for 2km before beginning its climb to **Little Homer Saddle** (168m). It's about a 30- to 45-minute climb through beech forest to reach the saddle. The march up is steady but not steep, and along the way there are views through the trees of Mt Madeline and **Mt Tutoko** (2723m) – Fiordland's highest mountain and one of NZ's most inaccessible peaks – to the west.

The descent is noticeably steeper than the climb, and it includes a short series of switchbacks before finally reaching a swing bridge across Homer Creek. From the middle of this bridge you get a good view of **Little Homer Falls** thundering 60m into a pool in the stream. The track remains level until, after around 30 minutes, it swings back to the Hollyford and crosses a swing bridge over Rainbow Creek.

The track stays with the Hollyford for 2km before it meets the **Pyke River**. You never really see the confluence of the rivers, but you'll know you've reached the Pyke when the water flows in the opposite direction to the Hollyford. The track passes Pyke Lodge, which serves as accommodation for guided trampers. After crossing Chair Creek you come to a suspension bridge over Pyke River.

If you're planning to stop for the night, skip the Pyke bridge and continue up the true left (east) side of the river for 20 minutes to Lake Alabaster Hut (26 bunks), on the shore of scenic **Lake Alabaster**, where a skinny dip could be had if you move like lightning to outwit the sandflies. The track continuing northeast along the shore of Lake Alabaster is part of the **Pyke-Big Bay Route**.

Day 3: Lake Alabaster Hut to McKerrow Island Hut

3–4 HOURS, 10.5KM

Backtrack for 20 minutes to the suspension bridge over Pyke River and, after crossing it, continue beneath the rocky bluffs along the lower section of the river. Here the track enters a lush podocarp forest, and all sights and sounds of the two great rivers are lost in the thick canopy of trees. The stretch of track from Pyke Bridge to the south end of Lake McKerrow can be rough, uneven and very muddy at times of wet weather.

The track works its way through the bush for two hours before breaking out into a clearing next to Hollyford River, now twice

as powerful as it was above the Pyke River junction.

Before reaching **Lake McKerrow** the river swings west around **McKerrow Island**; another channel (usually dry) rounds the island to the east. Near the dry river bed there is a sign pointing up the main track to Demon Trail Hut. This is also the start of a marked route across the eastern channel to a track on McKerrow Island. Follow this track around the northern side of the island to reach McKerrow Island Hut (12 bunks), pleasantly situated near the mouth of the main channel and partially hidden by bush.

If the rain has been heavy it may be impossible to cross the eastern river bed, in which case you can continue on the Demon Trail, and in about 1½ hours reach Demon Trail Hut (12 bunks). If you're at McKerrow Island Hut when it rains, there's little you can do but wait until the channel can be safely forded.

The mouth of the main channel is popular for trout fishing, although in recent years the growing seal colony at Martins Bay has been venturing further and further into Lake McKerrow to feast on trout, much to the dismay of anglers. Seals have even been spotted as far inland as Pyke Lodge.

Day 4: McKerrow Island Hut to Hokuri Hut

6½–7½ HOURS, 13.8KM

From the signpost on the main track it's a 20-minute tramp to the start of the Demon Trail, which begins in a clearing that was once a hut site. This leg used to have a reputation as one of the most exhausting nonalpine tracks in NZ. Although it has been upgraded in recent years it is still demanding, especially in the wet. Spare a thought for the Martins Bay settlers who built it in the 1880s as a cattle track – if they hadn't, it's likely the Hollyford Track wouldn't exist.

It's 3km (one hour) from the start of the trail to Demon Trail Hut, which sits in a pleasant spot overlooking Lake McKerrow.

At **Slip Creek**, considered the halfway point for the day, a nearby rock bivvy will shelter six people in inclement weather. But most trampers try to cover the section from McKerrow Island to Hokuri Hut as quickly as possible. Hokuri Hut (12 bunks) is on the shore of Lake McKerrow at Gravel Cove and was rebuilt in 2005.

Day 5: Hokuri Hut to Martins Bay

4–5 HOURS, 13KM

It's about a 10-minute tramp beyond the hut to Hokuri Creek, which can usually be forded near its mouth on Gravel Cove; if it can't be crossed here, there is a three-wire bridge 20 minutes upstream. From the other side of the creek begins one of the most scenic stretches of the tramp, following the gravel lakeshore for almost two hours, providing views of the lake and the surrounding mountains on a clear day.

The track dips into a small bay, where a sign announces the short spur track inland to the site of the historic township of **Jamestown**. A plaque marks the spot, but all that remains of the settlement are apple trees planted by the early settlers. Less than one hour from Jamestown you reach a signposted turn-off, where the track leaves the lake for good and heads inland.

Here the track cuts through a lush podocarp forest with many impressive kahikatea trees. About 3km (one hour) from the lakeshore you break out into the grassy clearing of the **Hollyford Valley airstrip**. A sign points to Martins Bay Lodge, which provides accommodation for guided walkers, while poles lead across the clearing and around one end of the airstrip. The track re-enters the bush of tall tutu and scrub and, just before emerging at **Jerusalem Creek**, passes a signposted junction to the **Air Fiordland airstrip**.

After the Jerusalem Creek ford (normally easy) the track continues through forest and climbs a bluff. Within 45 minutes you pass a sign for the Lower Hollyford boat launch, and just beyond that the track breaks out to a view of the river near its mouth. **Martins Bay Hut** (24 bunks) overlooks the river mouth and is a few minutes up the track (2½ hours from the shoreline of Lake McKerrow). This hut is an excellent place to whittle away an extra day, viewing the seal colony or looking for penguins.

The seals use the large boulders of **Long Reef** for basking during the day. It's a 30-minute walk from the hut, beginning with a track that skirts the bluffs around the mouth of the river. After passing a sign for the Pyke-Big Bay Route, the track breaks out at the rocky shore.

Boulder hop across the shore towards **Long Reef seal colony**, one of the biggest in NZ. There are usually seals on both sides of the point. They are used to trampers, but do not approach too closely; adults will chase you away from their pups and it's amazing how fast they can move across the rocks. There is fascinating rock-pool examination to be had here, too.

An old cattle track continues north then east of Long Reef; this is the track to Big Bay and the circular route to Lake Alabaster.

Kepler Track

Duration 4 days

Distance 60km (37 miles)

Track Standard Great Walk

Difficulty Moderate

Start/End Lake Te Anau control gates

Nearest Town Te Anau (p316)

Transport Shuttle bus, boat

Summary Built in 1988 to reduce the pressure on the Milford and Routeburn Tracks, this tramp rivals both in terms of alpine scenery.

The Kepler Track was first conceived in 1986 and opened in 1988, during NZ's centennial celebration of its national park system. The Kepler is one of the best-planned tracks in NZ: a loop beginning and ending near the control gates where the Waiau River empties into the southern end of Lake Te Anau. DOC staff can actually show you the start of this Great Walk from a window inside the Fiordland National Park Visitor Centre.

Like the Routeburn, the Kepler is an alpine crossing and includes an all-day tramp across the tops taking in incredible panoramas of Lake Te Anau, its South Fiord arm, the Jackson Peaks and the Kepler Mountains. Along the way it traverses rocky ridges, tussock lands and peaceful beech forest. It's no wonder the Kepler has become one of the most popular tracks in NZ.

The route can be covered in four days, spending a night at each of three huts. It is also possible to reduce the tramp to three days by continuing past Moturau Hut and leaving the track at Rainbow Reach swing bridge. However, spending a night at Moturau Hut on the shore of Lake Manapouri is an ideal way to end this tramp. The track can be walked in either direction, although the most popular is the anticlockwise option described here.

Kepler Track

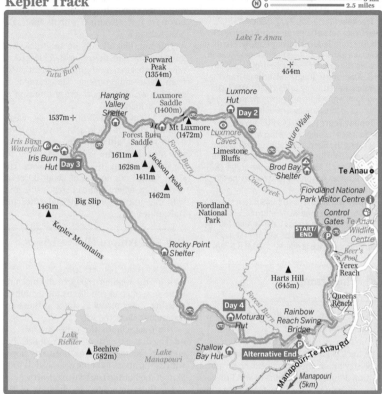

ⓘ Planning

WHEN TO TRAMP

The season is late October to late April.

MAPS

The 1:60,000 Parkmap 335-09 (Kepler Track) is sufficient for this track.

HUTS, CAMPING & BOOKINGS

The Kepler Track is a Great Walk and between late October and mid-April, you need a Great Walk pass (hut per night $54) for the three DOC huts – Luxmore, Iris Burn and Moturau. Each hut has gas cookers, cold running water and heating in the main kitchen/dining hut, plus communal bunk rooms with mattresses. Ablution blocks have flush toilets and washbasins. In season, a DOC ranger is resident at each hut and is able to relay information about the environment and weather, or help you should an emergency arise. Hut passes must be obtained in advance, and it will pay to book early. Bookings can be made from July for the following season. For further

information and bookings, contact **Great Walks Bookings** (☎ 0800 694 732; www.greatwalks. co.nz) or visit any DOC visitor centre.

At Brod Bay and near Iris Burn Hut you will find **Serviced campsites** (www.doc.govt.nz; $15) with cooking shelters.

In the off-season, the huts revert to backcountry **Serviced huts** (www.doc.govt.nz; $15), with facilities reduced to a long-drop toilet and tap water only.

ⓘ Getting to/from the Tramp

The start of the track is 4km (a one-hour walk) from the DOC Fiordland National Park Visitor Centre via the Lakeside Track. This track skirts the southern end of Lake Te Anau and passes through the interesting Te Anau Wildlife Centre before reaching the control gates, where the Kepler Track begins.

If you are driving to the track, follow Manapouri–Te Anau Rd (SH95) south from the park visitor centre and take the first right turn, which is clearly marked by a yellow AA sign.

Continue past the golf course and take another right-hand turn to a car park.

Tracknet (☎ 03-249 7777, 0800 483 262; www.tracknet.net) operates the Kepler Track Shuttle from Te Anau Holiday Park, where there is secure parking. During the tramping season the shuttle departs for the control gates ($6) at 8.30am and 9.30am, and picks up from the Rainbow Reach swing bridge ($10) at 9.30am and 3pm, with a 5pm pick-up by arrangement. There is secure parking available.

Topline Tours (☎ 03-249 8059; www.top linetours.co.nz) also runs a bus to the Kepler, departing the Fiordland National Park Visitor Centre at 9am for the control gates ($5), and 10.30am and 2.15pm for the swing bridge ($8). Their services run on demand only in the off-season.

Kepler Water Taxi (☎ 03-249 8364; stevsaun ders@xtra.co.nz; one-way/return $25/50) offers a boat service across Lake Te Anau to Brod Bay ($25), slicing 1½ hours off the first day's tramp. The service is offered daily at 8.30am and 9.30am.

🏃 The Tramp

Day 1: Lake Te Anau Control Gates to Luxmore Hut

5–6 HOURS, 13.8KM, 883M ASCENT

The track begins by skirting the lake to Dock Bay, staying on the fringe of a beech forest. Within 30 minutes it begins to wind through an impressive growth of tree ferns, with crown ferns carpeting the forest floor. The track continues to skirt the lake's western shore and crosses a footbridge over Coal Creek.

After a further 3km the track crosses another stream and arrives at Brod Bay, a beautiful sandy beach on the lake. There are toilets, a table and a barbecue here, and for those who started late and have a tent it's a scenic campsite.

The track to Mt Luxmore is signposted near the beach and you now begin the steepest climb of the tramp. The track ascends steadily and in 3km (two hours) reaches a set of towering limestone bluffs, an ideal lunch spot. At the bluffs the track swings due west, skirts the rock, then turns north and resumes climbing through stunted mountain beech.

Within 1km the track breaks out of the bush and you get the tramp's first glorious panorama, of Lake Te Anau, Lake Mana-pouri and the Takitimu, Snowdon and Earl Mountains. The track climbs a couple of small rises, and within one hour of leaving

the bush skirts a small bluff. On the other side, at a commanding elevation of 1085m, is Luxmore Hut (55 bunks), with its namesake peak behind it.

This hut, like all huts on the track, was built in 1987 and then quickly enlarged. It now features two levels and has great views from the common room. The warden receives a weather report every morning at around 8.30am.

Mt Luxmore (1472m) can be easily climbed without backpacks (two to three hours return), although you can also save this mission for the following day and instead venture out to Luxmore Caves. The short track leads to one of about 30 caves in the area, where you can step inside and, with the aid of a torch, view stalactites and stalagmites.

Day 2: Luxmore Hut to Iris Burn Hut

5–6 HOURS, 14.6KM, 588M DESCENT

Wait for the weather report in the morning to be sure of good conditions for the alpine crossing. Carry plenty of water as there are no streams along the way.

The track climbs the ridge towards the unnamed peak east of Mt Luxmore, but ends up sidling along its northern slopes with Mt Luxmore looming overhead. Within 3km of the hut the track swings north.

For those interested in climbing to the peak of Mt Luxmore, easily distinguished by its large trig, it's best to follow the track to Luxmore Saddle (1400m) and drop your backpacks. From here it's an easy 15- to 20-minute climb along a rocky ridge to the top. If the weather is clear, the view is perhaps the finest of the tramp – a 360-degree panorama that includes the Darran Mountains, 70km to the north.

After crossing the ridge to the north of Mt Luxmore, the track skirts a bluff on steep-sided slopes for 3km, until it reaches a high-point on the ridge beyond Luxmore Saddle. Here, the track swings away from the ridge and sidles along the slopes before descending to Forest Burn Shelter. This is close to Forest Burn Saddle, which is reached two hours from Luxmore Hut. Beware of strong wind gusts when crossing the saddle.

From the shelter the track skirts the bluffed end of a ridge, with great views of Lake Te Anau's South Fiord. About 3.5km from the shelter, the track rounds the bluffs onto a ridge crest and the tramp becomes considerably easier. Follow the ridge, skirt two knobs and then climb another one. Once on this high point you can see Hanging Valley Shelter.

The shelter sits on a ridge at 1390m and is usually reached two hours from Forest Burn Shelter. The views are great, so spend some extra time here if your timing allows. It takes most trampers less than two hours to reach Iris Burn Hut from here, and because most of the tramp is through bush, this view is much more inspiring than anything else you'll see along the way.

The track leaves the shelter and follows a ridge to the south for 2km. The ridge crest is sharp, and at times you feel as though you're on a tightrope. Eventually the track drops off the ridge with a sharp turn to the west, and descends into the bush. The descent is a quick one, down a seemingly endless series of switchbacks, and the track drops 390m before crossing a branch of Iris Burn.

The track levels out as it skirts the side of this hanging valley, at one point becoming a boardwalk across the steep face. The views of Iris Burn are excellent, and there's even a seat, so lean back and take it all in.

The final segment of the day is over more switchbacks, with the track dropping 450m. Just when it levels out, Iris Burn Hut (50 bunks) comes into view – a welcome sight. For a pleasant evening walk, head up the valley for 20 minutes to view the impressive Iris Burn waterfall.

Day 3: Iris Burn Hut to Moturau Hut

5–6 HOURS, 16.2KM

The main track begins behind the hut with a short climb, before levelling out in beech forest. Within 3km it crosses a branch of the Iris Burn and breaks out into a wide, open area. Evidence of the cause of this clearing – a huge 1984 landslide called the Big Slip – is to your right, where piles of rocks, now covered in regenerating vegetation, and fallen trees can be seen everywhere. The track returns to the bush across the clearing and continues down the valley, at times following the river.

The track crosses several branches of Iris Burn, and remains almost entirely in the bush (one section is through an incredibly moss-laden stand of trees) until it reaches a rocky clearing called Rocky Point, where some of the boulders are bright orange (the result of a healthy growth of red algae). At this point, 11km from Iris Burn Hut, the track climbs over Heart Hill.

Having passed a view of Lake Manapouri at the mouth of Iris Burn, the track swings east, and in 1km returns within sight of the lake. On its final leg the track skirts the shore of Shallow Bay until it arrives at Moturau Hut (40 bunks). This is a pleasant hut with a view of Lake Manapouri from the kitchen.

Day 4: Moturau Hut to Lake Te Anau Control Gates

4½–5 HOURS, 15.5KM

For the first 2km, the track heads southeast through bush until it reaches a junction with a short track to Shallow Bay Hut (six bunks). The main track heads east (left fork) and within 1km comes to a wetland known as Amoeboid Mire. This wetland is crossed on a boardwalk, which includes a viewing platform. After skirting the southern side of the grassy swamp, the track reaches an old river terrace that overlooks Balloon Loop, which is 5km from Moturau Hut.

A swing bridge crosses Forest Burn, which meanders confusingly before emptying into Balloon Loop. From here it's 30 minutes along the river terrace to the swing bridge at Rainbow Reach, 1½ hours from the hut. There is an option to leave the track here, and catch a shuttle back to Te Anau.

It's three hours (11km) to the control gates, with the track continuing in an easterly direction. Within one hour it swings due north to pass Queens Reach, climbing onto a river terrace. There are views through the trees of a set of rapids, before the track moves into an area of manuka scrub. At Yerex Reach, two hours from the Rainbow Reach swing bridge, the track passes a few old posts and a quiet segment of the river known as Beer's Pool. At this point you're only 30 to 45 minutes from the control gates.

Hump Ridge Track

Duration 3 days

Distance 58km (36 miles)

Track Easy tramping track

Difficulty Moderate

Start/End Rarakau car park

Nearest Town Tuatapere (p317)

Transport Shuttle bus

Hump Ridge Track

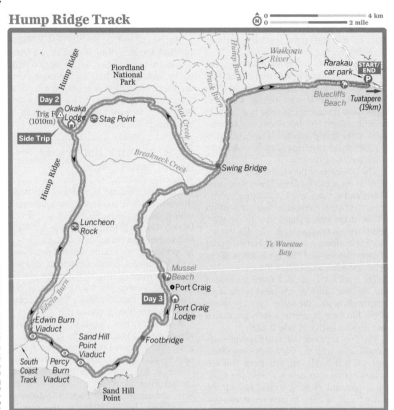

Summary Climbing over the crest of Hump Ridge, this community-run track is rich in natural and cultural history – from spectacular coastal and alpine scenery to the intriguing relics of a historic timber town.

Tuatapere Hump Ridge Track, although not classified as a Great Walk, has all the qualities of one. The track winds across some of NZ's wildest land – both public and private – leading trampers through parts of Fiordland National Park, along an alpine ridge, through forest, across Maori land and beside the south coast.

Unlike almost all major NZ tracks, this one doesn't fall within DOC's remit. It was conceived and built by the local community, under the umbrella of the Tuatapere Hump Ridge Track Charitable Trust, formed in 1995. Not only did this community group need to raise $3.5 million for the project, they needed to secure the cooperation and permission of private landowners. An amazing effort on all fronts saw the track open in 2001, as NZ's first and only privately operated independent tramp on public land.

If you want to complete the entire circuit and stay in both huts, the track must be tramped anticlockwise, with the first night at Okaka Lodge. If you are not interested in climbing Hump Ridge, a night at Port Craig Village makes a wonderful and easy coastal walk.

History

The Waitutu – on the south coast between Fiordland and Tuatapere – was first visited by early Maori in their search for food, and then later by Captain Cook. In 1770, while anchored off the mouth of the Waiau River, Cook wrote in his log: 'The face of the country bears a very rugged aspect being full of high craggy hills.' This was the first recorded description of Fiordland, and it is thought that Cook was observing the Hump Ridge. The first coastal track was cut by the government in 1868, to provide an alternative to the unreliable shipping service to the gold-rush towns in Preservation Inlet.

In 1910, John Craig and Daniel Reese of the Marlborough Timber Company walked this area, assessing the forest for its commercial timber viability. The volumes were staggering, estimated at more than 152 million cubic metres. The question was, how to get the timber out? It was decided to build a mill, wharf and tramway system at Mussel Point (Port Craig) to extract and ship the timber. Despite the drowning of Craig in 1917, the new mill was built and was in operation three years later. At the time it was the largest in the country. The mill was closed for the first time in 1929, a result of the Depression, and then permanently closed in 1932. It was dismantled during WWII, along with the wharf, by the NZ Navy, which feared a Japanese invasion.

With much of the Waitutu forest still uncut and its logging rights up for grabs, the area became the object of one of NZ's greatest environmental campaigns. In 1938, the Royal Forest and Bird Protection Society was the first group to push for the land to be added to the adjacent Fiordland National Park. In 1972, the Nature Conservation Council was successful in removing the Waitutu State Forest from a logging proposal for the area, and in 1981 the former National Parks and Reserves Authority again urged the government to add the forest to the national park.

After reaching a settlement on compensation for Maori land claims in the area, the Waitutu State Forest – comprising 460 sq km of virgin forest – was added to NZ's largest national park in 1998.

🛈 Planning

WHEN TO TRAMP

This tramp is possible year-round, but operates in three seasonal modes. During shoulder (early November to mid-December) and high (mid-December to early April) seasons, the lodges are fully serviced and a manager will be in residence. In winter (mid-April to late October), the hot water is turned off and the gas cookers are removed.

WHAT TO BRING

Good raingear is a necessity. Gaiters may also prove useful. Along with gas cookers, all cooking equipment, crockery and cutlery are provided in the huts during the summer season. Pillows are also provided.

MAPS

The most detailed map is the NZTopo50 CG07 (Sand Hill Point). DOC also produces a map for the coastal track, which you can purchase from the information centre in Tuatapere; you will also be given a detailed map when you make your track booking.

LODGES, GUIDED TRAMPS & BOOKINGS

The track is managed by the trust like a Great Walk would be: advance bookings are essential and you must pick up accommodation passes before beginning the tramp.

Independent walking passes cost $175 and cover two nights' accommodation at two lodges: Okaka and Port Craig. These huts are very well serviced, with heating, gas cookers, running water, flush toilets and a drying room. Also included in the cost is hot porridge for breakfast. Optional extras include 'helipacking' ($80), where your pack is transferred between lodges; lodge room upgrades ($100 per person in twin or double beds, linen provided, plus a hot shower); and hot showers ($10; bring your own towel). A Prime Package ($450) is also available, which includes a pre-trip night's accommodation, a pack transfer for the first day, sleeping bags and a freeze-dried evening meal.

Guided tramps (four days, $1595 share twin) are also available, which include a pre-trip night's accommodation, helicopter flight, private lodge rooms and all meals.

Note that in winter, the independent walking pass reduces to $25.

Bookings should be made through Tuatapere Hump Ridge Track Office (p317).

🛈 Getting to/from the Tramp

The trailhead is at Rarakau, 19km from Tuatapere. The track trust operates its own transport, available every day during high season, on scheduled days during the shoulder season, and on demand during winter. Shuttles depart at 7.30am with local accommodation pick-ups available. Shuttles leave Rarakau at 3pm for the return journey to Tuatapere.

Those with their own vehicle can leave it at the Rarakau car park. The car-park area is on private land, is fenced and is overlooked by the farmhouse. A $5 donation is appreciated.

🚶 The Tramp

Day 1: Rarakau Car Park to Okaka Lodge

8–9 HOURS, 19KM, 940M ASCENT

From the car park, follow the signs to the beginning of the track, which leads you through the forest, away from the stony beach, and within 2km descends to the Waikoau River footbridge. Nearby is a cluster of private holiday homes or, as they are known in Southland, cribs. Once across the Waikoau River, the next hour is a walk along a beautiful beach to **Hump Burn**. Keep an eye on the surf – you may see Hector's dolphins frolicking in small groups.

From the beach you enter forest and follow a former logging road, passing some old logging equipment along the way and two more cribs nestled in the forest. The one nearest the **Track Burn** bridge kindly offers shelter and water, making it an ideal place for a break when it's raining.

The logging road ends at the Track Burn bridge, and on the other side is a well-graded benched track that takes you high above the rocky shore. About 2.5km from the bridge (two to three hours from the car park) you reach a swing bridge in the Flat Creek ravine. On the other side is a signposted junction – the left fork is the walk to Port Craig Village and the right fork leads to Okaka Lodge, 9km away on Hump Ridge.

Heading right (west), the first 2.5km is easy, as you make your way up and over high river terraces and through mixed podocarp and beech forest. The track then crosses a steep-sided stream and begins the climb up a long spur. In places the climb is quite strenuous.

Eventually you come to **Stag Point**, a narrow steep-sided ridge with a view to the east. It's another hour, and more steady climbing, until you reach a trail junction. At the signposted junction, head right and follow the boardwalk through stunted silver beech forest and open alpine clearings to **Okaka Lodge** (40 bunks). Built in 2001, the hut is magnificently located on the side of a glacial cirque, overlooking Te Waewae Bay and the Waiau basin, and the Takitimu Mountains to the north.

SIDE TRIP: TRIG F
30 MINUTES, 1KM RETURN, 50M ASCENT

It is well worth the extra effort to climb **Hump Ridge** itself and explore this alpine wonderland. The track to the crest of the ridge is a boardwalk that forms a loop around **Trig F**, a 1010m highpoint.

Hump Ridge consists of sandstones, mudstones and conglomerated rocks of the Tertiary period. A striking series of rock towers among the tussock, herb fields and alpine tarns have been left after years of weathering. From Trig F the views to the west include the rugged mountains of Fiordland National Park, Lake Hauroko and Lake Poteriteri. To the south you can see Solander Island in Foveaux Strait and Stewart Island.

Day 2: Okaka Lodge to Port Craig Lodge

7–9 HOURS, 19KM, 920M DESCENT

Be sure to check the weather forecast, and fill your water bottles before heading out; this day is along an exposed section of track and should be treated with respect.

Return to the main loop at the junction, and head south along the right fork towards Luncheon Rock. For the next 4.5km the track traverses the subalpine crest of Hump Ridge. For the most part it is an undulating tramp along the top of the ridge. On a nice day this is a section to be savoured for its spectacular views and interesting subalpine flora. A boardwalk is provided to protect the delicate plant life.

Within two hours you reach **Luncheon Rock**, site of a toilet, water and the last good views before the descent to the coast. For the next 2½ hours the track descends steeply to the coastal marine terraces, passing some interesting, ghostly rock outcrops.

Once you bottom out it is 2km to the Edwin Burn Viaduct, with the track passing through the Rowallan Maori Lands. In 1906 this land was given to the southern Maori in compensation for land taken in Otago and Canterbury by the government in the 1840s. All trampers should respect the access given by the owners and keep to the track.

At the **Edwin Burn Viaduct** the trail emerges at the original South Coast Track, an old logging road. Edwin Burn is the first of three viaducts crossed or viewed on the way to Port Craig Village. Constructed from Australian hardwood, they were built to carry tramlines across the deep ravines.

The track follows the tramway all the way to Port Craig, and within 30 minutes the second and largest of the viaducts is reached. At 36m high and 124m long, the **Percy Burn Viaduct** is thought to be the largest wooden viaduct still standing in the world. The best point to view this immense structure is from the track below it.

From here it is 6km (two hours) to Port Craig Village, crossing the **Sand Hill Point Viaduct** along the way. Sand Hill Point is one Fiordland's most historic places, as it was used for centuries as a resting spot for

Maori hunting parties. Unfortunately, a side trip to the point is strictly prohibited.

The monotony of the tramway is suddenly broken when you arrive at the open grassy area where Port Craig Lodge (40 bunks) is located. The old logging wharf at Port Craig – or what's left of it – makes for an interesting walk, to view the machinery and other relics still lying about. Also keep your eyes peeled for dolphins and possibly even a whale in Te Waewae Bay.

Day 3: Port Craig Lodge to Rarakau Car Park

6–8 HOURS, 20KM

After leaving the lodge the track enters the bush near the old school, before winding through large stands of podocarp forest and over a series of bluffs. It used to be possible to follow the coast around this section, but what the sea wants the sea shall have, and coastal erosion now makes the coastal route impassable, even at a very low tide.

After about 1¾ hours, the track emerges onto the coastline at **Breakneck Creek**. From here it climbs over the headland before dropping back to the coast again at Blowholes Beach.

At the end of the beach a post marked with a fishing buoy indicates the track over another headland to the next beach. The track leaves this beach and enters one final small cove before climbing back up onto the coastal terrace and past the junction of the track to Okaka. Continue to the swing bridge over **Flat Creek** and retrace your steps from day one back to Track Burn and on to Rarakau car park. It's about two hours to the car park from Track Burn.

STEWART ISLAND/ RAKIURA

The southernmost part of NZ and its 'third' island, Stewart Island/Rakiura is remote, comprising vast tracts of wilderness and populated by just several hundred people and a *lot* of birds, including the national icon, the kiwi.

Around 85% of the 1722-sq-km island was gazetted as Rakiura National Park in 2002. It is bounded by 755km of coastline, punctuated by long beaches, impressive sand dunes and crystal-clear bays fringed by lush rainforest. The interior is mostly bush, broken up by steep gullies and ridges, several of which emerge above the bushline. The highest point on Stewart Island – Mt Anglem/ Hananui – is only 980m and sees the occasional dusting of snow.

Add fascinating human history to this sleepy and unique end-of-the-line island, and you've got a fine prospect for trampers. There are more than 280km of tracks, and while much of it is quite challenging – with indecisive weather and widespread mud being notable features – the birds, views and peacefulness are ample rewards.

History

Rakiura, the Maori name for Stewart Island, means 'land of the glowing sky', referring perhaps to the aurora australis (Southern Lights), which is often seen in this southern sky, or maybe to the spectacular blood-red sunrises and sunsets. Excavations in the area provide evidence that, as early as the 13th century, tribes of Polynesian origin migrated to the island to hunt moa. However, Maori settlements were thin and scattered, because the people were unable to grow kumara (sweet potato), the staple food of settlements to the north. They did make annual migrations to the outer islands to seek muttonbird (titi), a favourite food, and to the main island to search for eel, shellfish and certain birds.

The first European visitor was Captain Cook, who sailed around the eastern, southern and western coasts in 1770 but couldn't figure out if it was an island or a peninsula. Deciding it was attached to the South Island, he called it South Cape. In 1809 the sealing vessel *Pegasus* circumnavigated Rakiura and named it after its first officer, William Stewart. Stewart charted large sections of the coast during a sealing trip in 1809, and drafted the first detailed map of the island.

Sealing ended by the late 1820s, to be replaced temporarily by whaling, but the small whaling bases on the island were never profitable. Other early industries were timber milling, fish curing and shipbuilding. A short-lived gold rush towards the end of the 19th century brought a sufficient influx of miners to warrant building a hotel and a post office.

The only enterprise that has endured is fishing. Initially those doing the fishing were few in number, but when a steamer service from Bluff began in 1885 the industry expanded, resulting in the construction of cleaning sheds on Ruapuke Island and a refrigerating plant in the North Arm of Port Pegasus.

Today, tourism and, to a much lesser extent, fishing are the occupations of most of the island's 400 or so residents.

Environment

Birds previously hunted, or at least take, for granted, by humans are now conserved and treasured, and NZ's 'third island' is establishing itself as a bird haven of international repute. With an absence of mustelids (ferrets, stoats and weasels) and with large areas of intact forest, Stewart Island has one of the largest and most diverse bird populations of any area in NZ, and offers more opportunities to spot kiwi in the wild. The Rakiura tokeka (local brown kiwi) population is estimated to be around 20,000.

A great place to see lots of birds in one place is Ulva Island/Te Wharawhara, a quick water-taxi ride from Oban. Established as a bird sanctuary in 1922, it remains one of Rakiura's wildest corners – 'a rare taste of how NZ once was and perhaps could be again', according to DOC. As the result of an extensive eradication program, the island was declared rat-free in 1997 and three years later was chosen as the site to release endangered South Island saddlebacks. The air resonates with the song of tui and bellbirds, which share their island home with many other birds including kaka, weka, kakariki and Rakiura tokeka/kiwi.

There are also plenty of seabirds, including blue penguins, shags, mollymawks, prions, petrels and albatross, as well as the sooty shearwater, which is seen in large numbers during breeding season.

Exotic animals include two species of deer, the red and the Virginia (whitetail), which were introduced in the early 20th century, as were brush-tailed possums, which are now numerous throughout the island and destructive to the native bush. Rakiura also has NZ fur seals, NZ sea lions, elephant seals and, occasionally, leopard seals that visit the beaches and rocky shores.

Beech, the tree that dominates much of NZ, is absent from Rakiura. The predominant lowland bush is podocarp forest, with exceptionally tall rimu, miro, totara and kamahi forming the canopy. Because of mild winters, frequent rainfall and porous soil, most of the island is a lush forest, thick with vines and carpeted in deep green ferns and moss.

ℹ Information

WHEN TO TRAMP

It is possible to tramp year-round on Rakiura. At the summer solstice there are 17 hours of daylight; in winter this decreases to about nine.

WHAT TO BRING

Pack a stove for use in the huts. Also pack gaiters, to help combat the mud, although it's probably best that you accept that your boots will never be the same again.

A personal locator beacon is also highly recommended and available from the National Park Visitor Centre in Oban.

MAPS & BROCHURES

The National Park Visitor Centre holds maps specially tailored to the Rakiura and North West Circuit tracks. As well as DOC's brochures *Rakiura Track* and *North West and Southern Circuit Tracks*, obtain the excellent *Rakiura Short Walks* brochure, which details 13 shorter adventures you might like to fit in around longer tramps.

INFORMATION

Rakiura National Park Visitor Centre (☑ 03-219 0009; www.doc.govt.nz; 15 Main Rd, Oban; ☺ 8am-5pm Oct-Mar, shorter hours in winter) has useful information on the island and good displays on flora and fauna, and you can store gear here while you're tramping ($10 for a small locker, $20 for a large one).

Rakiura Track

Duration 3 days

Distance 39km (24 miles)

Track Standard Great Walk

Difficulty Moderate

Start/End Oban (p318)

Transport None required

Summary Connecting the beginning and the end of the North West Circuit, this Great Walk provides a shorter and easier loop, and features the sheltered shores of Paterson Inlet and the beautiful beaches on the way to Port William.

Built in 1986, the Rakiura Track is a peaceful and leisurely loop offering a rewarding combination of coastal scenery, native forest, historical interest and diverse bird life including forest songbirds, soaring seabirds and beaky waders.

Rakiura Track is actually only 32km long, but adding the road sections at either end bumps it up to 39km, conveniently forming a circuit from Oban. As it provides the only short loop in Rakiura National Park (all the others require seven to 10 days), the track is the most popular Stewart Island tramp, with around 3500 people walking it annually. Also, because it is a Great Walk, it has been gravelled to eliminate most of the mud for which the island is famous.

This tramp is described here as crossing from Port William to North Arm, the easiest direction to walk it, especially if starting later in the day.

ⓘ Planning

HUTS, CAMPING & BOOKINGS

As this is a Great Walk, all huts and campsites need to be booked in advance, either online or in person at the National Park Visitor Centre in Oban. Make sure you print the confirmation letter of your booking and carry it with you.

There are two **Great Walk huts** (www.doc.govt. nz; $22), at Port William and North Arm, which have wood stoves for heat (firewood provided), but no gas rings for cooking, so pack a stove and some form of lighting. There's a limit of two consecutive nights in one hut and pre-booking ensures that you have a bunk for the night. Note that standard hut tickets and Backcountry Hut Passes cannot be used on the Rakiura Track.

There are **Standard campsites** (www.doc. govt.nz; $6) in the vicinity of both huts, along with another one at Maori Beach. Camping is not permitted elsewhere along the track.

Leave your intentions with a trusted friend; visit the website of **Adventure Smart** (www. adventuresmart.org.nz) for details.

🥾 The Tramp

Day 1: Oban to Port William

4–5 HOURS, 13KM

Leave the DOC Visitor Centre and turn right to walk down Main Rd. Turn left into Elgin Tce past the Ship to Shore store, and up the hill. Follow this main coast road over a series of hills to **Horseshoe Bay**, then on to **Lee Bay**, the official entrance to Rakiura National Park.

At beautiful Lee Bay, walk through the **Anchorstone/Te Puka**, a giant chain-link sculpture symbolising what the Maori believe was a spiritual connection between Stewart Island/Rakiura (the anchor) and Bluff/Motu Pohue (the stern post of the South Island, which is the canoe).

The track enters the bush and crosses a bridge over Little River to skirt the coast.

You then follow the coast around Peters Point to Maori Beach. Within 2km the track descends onto the southern end of **Maori Beach**, where you immediately come to a creek that can easily be waded at low tide. If the tide is in, stay on the track to quickly reach a footbridge inland. North of the creek is a campsite with a toilet and shelter, in a grassy clearing near the beach.

A sawmill began operating at Maori Beach in 1913, and at one time a large wharf, a second sawmill and a network of tramways were constructed to extract rimu. By 1920 there were enough families living here to warrant opening a school. The onset of the Depression led to the closure of Rakiura's last mill in 1931, but a rusting steam boiler from that logging era can still be seen down a short track near the footbridge.

Continue north along the smooth sand of Maori Beach to reach a bridge at the far end, one hour from Little River. The track then climbs a small hill and continues to the intersection with the track to North Arm. To reach Port William, turn right and you will gradually drop to the Port William campsite, nestled just above the shores of **Magnetic Beach**.

Just a few minutes beyond the campsite at the beach's northern end you'll find Port William Hut (24 bunks). In 1876, the government had grand plans for a settlement here, offering 50 families free land to develop the timber resources and offshore fisheries. The settlement was a dismal failure, as the utopia the government had hoped to foster was plagued by isolation and loneliness. All that remains of the settlement are the large gum trees next to the hut.

Day 2: Port William to North Arm Hut

6 HOURS, 13KM

It will take around 45 minutes to backtrack to the turn-off on the hill between Port William and Maori Hill. Here the Rakiura Track departs west (right fork) and heads inland. Say farewell to the east coast as you make your way through beautiful regenerating podocarp forest, as well as lush and dense virgin forest. Take a breather at the log haulers, massive machines that were used to drag forest giants from the depths of the gullies.

The walk settles into a pattern of climbing over a number of hills as it heads south, passing through a variety of vegetation including previously milled and virgin podocarp forest.

Rakiura Track & Stewart Island North West Circuit

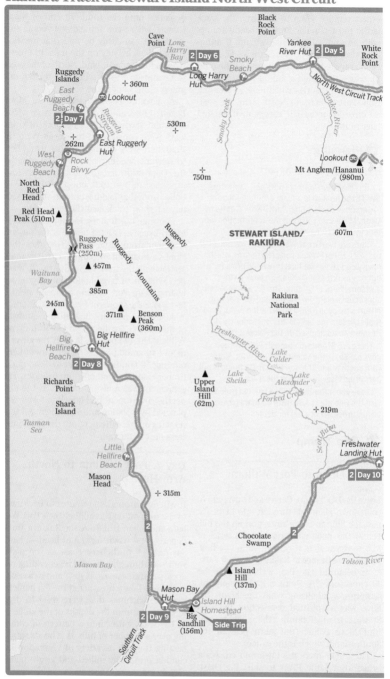

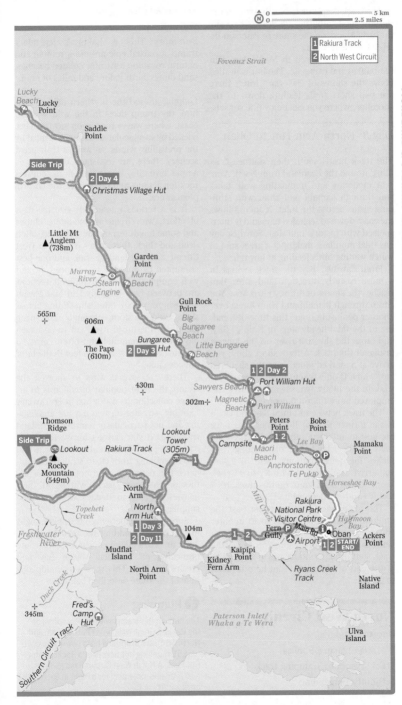

The track descends to North Arm, an important food-gathering *(mahinga kai)* site for early Maori, on the shore of Paterson Inlet/Whaka a Te Wera.

The track leads you to North Arm Hut (24 bunks) and campsite. The hut is nestled above the shores of **Paterson Inlet**; there are two short trails leading down to the shoreline, where you can enjoy fine sunsets.

Day 3: North Arm Hut to Oban

4–5 HOURS, 13KM

The track heads south then southeast, sidling around the headland from North Arm.

A moderate and undulating walk takes you through kamahi and rimu with stunning vistas across the inlet. It then follows the coast down to secluded bays and is interspersed with historic mill sites. Sawdust Bay has tidal mudflats, making it a great spot to watch wading birds feeding at low tide.

From Sawdust Bay the track swings in a more easterly direction, and after 1km reaches the shores of **Kidney Fern Arm**. You climb through kamahi and rimu forest over another peninsula ridge, this time descending to the tidal headwaters of **Kaipipi Bay**, and cross the sluggish river on the longest bridge of the track. After a short climb you arrive at a marked junction to the sheltered bay, which is only two minutes down a side trail. In the 1860s, two sawmills at this bay employed more than 100 people.

The track between Kaipipi Bay and Oban is the former Kaipipi Rd, which was once the best-maintained and most heavily used road on the island. The old logging road makes for quick tramping, and in 2.5km you arrive at a junction with **Ryan's Creek Track**. If you head south on this track, it's a scenic two-hour detour into Oban.

The main track continues east past the junction as an old road, and in 10 minutes you reach a signposted junction to Fern Gully car park. From the junction, follow the track southeast, soon arriving at a car park at the end of Main Rd. From here it's 2km to Oban.

North West Circuit

Duration 11 days

Distance 125km (78 miles)

Track Standard Tramping track

Difficulty Demanding

Start/End Oban (p318)

Transport Boat, plane

Summary This is Rakiura's legendary tramp, a coastal epic around a remote and natural coastline featuring isolated beaches, sand dunes, birds galore and miles of mud.

Looping around the northern half of Rakiura, the tramp takes in the wild western coast, where waves roar in on stormy days, backed by spectacular sand dunes formed by the prevailing winds. As well as truly great scenery, there are constant diversions – ample bird life, interesting flora, curious rock formations and relics from the island's pioneer era.

It is a serious mission: 11 sizeable days of effort, with frequent, moderate climbs and some tough terrain. But it's mud, often deep and thick, that makes the North West Circuit such a legendary trail, and one best attempted by only the experienced, fit and well equipped. The most difficult sections are between East Ruggedy Hut and Mason Bay, where you are often slip-sliding across slicks and sloshing through knee-deep gloop. On the upside, you get to end each day with a communal and often convivial washing of boots, socks and feet in the huts' outside sinks.

There are several ways to shorten the tramp, the most popular of which is to arrange collection by water taxi at Freshwater Landing, shaving off two days of challenging and not particularly scintillating inland tramping. If you can get away reasonably early it is possible to combine days one and two by walking from Oban straight to Bungaree Hut (seven to eight hours). Be aware, though, that your packs will be at their heaviest with 10 to 11 days' worth of food supplies.

Super-eager, experienced trampers might like to consider adding the **Southern Circuit**, an extra 56km, a challenging route branching off between Mason Bay and Freshwater Hut. This means you skip day nine of the route described below.

ⓘ Planning

The huts on this tramp, with the exception of the Rakiura Great Walk huts (Port William and North Arm), are **Standard huts** (www.doc.govt.nz; $5), requiring hut tickets or a Backcountry Hut Pass. A North West Circuit Pass ($35) is also available, providing for a night in each of the backcountry huts.

The two **Great Walk huts** (www.doc.govt.nz; $22) need to be booked in advance, either online at www.greatwalks.co.nz or in person at the National Park Visitor Centre in Oban. Make sure you print the confirmation letter of your booking and carry it with you.

ⓘ Getting to/from the Tramp

The North West Circuit begins and ends in Oban. It can be shortened with water-taxi transport, dropping off or picking up at various huts along the way. **Stewart Island Water Taxi** (☏ 03-219 1394, 0800 469 283; www.portofcall.co.nz) takes trampers to Port William Hut ($50), North Arm Hut ($50), Freshwater Landing ($55), Bungaree Hut ($65), Christmas Village Hut ($95) and even Yankee River Hut ($145). Other water-taxi operators are **Rakiura Water Taxi** (☏ 03-219 1014; www.seaviewwatertaxi.co.nz) and **Aihe Eco Charters & Water Taxi** (☏ 03-219 1066; www.aihe.co.nz).

🧍 The Tramp

Day 1: Oban to Port William

4–5 HOURS, 13KM

Follow day one of the Rakiura Track, to Port William Hut (p309).

Day 2: Port William to Bungaree Hut

3–4 HOURS, 6KM

Return along the trail over the small hump to the main track, and head north. Climb a small saddle, cross a bridge to **Sawyers Beach** and then head inland. The famous mud-bashing of Rakiura now begins.

After 40 minutes of slipping and sliding you are rewarded with a view of the Titi (Muttonbird) Islands to the east. It's 3km through the bush before the track begins a steady drop to **Little Bungaree Beach**.

From the beach you cross a small headland and descend to **Big Bungaree Beach**, following the golden curve of sand for 1km to the hut at the far end. Bungaree Hut (16 bunks) is a splendid spot to rest after a relatively short tramping day.

Day 3: Bungaree Hut to Christmas Village Hut

6 HOURS, 11.5KM

The track resumes climbing from the hut, crossing a series of hills and gullies as it works its way inland across **Gull Rock**

Point. After 3km the track descends sharply onto **Murray Beach** for a 2km stretch of golden sand. This is a good spot for a swim, although the sandflies will likely prevent any languid sunbathing.

Sawmilling was undertaken in the 1900s and a number of tramways were built to remove timber. The main track heads along one of them for 1km, then undulates and crosses numerous streams.

In 3.5km you pass a spur track which you should climb over to the bridged stream on the northern side. Near the pebbled beach just north of Christmas Village Bay is Christmas Village Hut (12 bunks). From this point on the track gets progressively harder – if you have concerns then this is a good point to return to Oban.

SIDE TRIP: MT ANGLEM/HANANUI
6–7 HOURS, 11KM RETURN, 800M ASCENT

Some trampers pause a day at Christmas Village Hut in order to climb **Mt Anglem/Hananui** (980m), the highest point on Rakiura. The junction to the well-defined summit track is 500m beyond the hut. The track starts out muddy and pretty much stays that way most of the climb. Less than 30 minutes from the top you reach a subalpine meadow where you can view a large tarn, and from there the tramp to the peak is easier. On a clear day the views from the top are excellent – you can see the northern half of Rakiura all the way to Mason Bay, as well as the South Island.

Day 4: Christmas Village Hut to Yankee River Hut

5–6 HOURS, 12KM

It's a steep climb from the hut to the junction with the Mt Anglem/Hananui Track (left fork). The main track heads north as it works its way through a rimu forest, and remains dry for 5km until it descends to a swing bridge and onto **Lucky Beach**. There is little sand and a lot of sandflies, so you won't be enticed to linger.

Follow the beach briefly and then pick up the track again at the western end, where it climbs steeply through dense ferns and bush. For 4km (two hours) you cover undulating terrain, then begin a long descent to the sluggish **Yankee River**. It's only a few more minutes to Yankee River Hut (16 bunks), a good place for wildlife spotting. If you're lucky you may see kiwi and

FIORDLAND & STEWART ISLAND/RAKIURA NORTH WEST CIRCUIT

penguins, and seals often take a dip at the mouth of the river.

Day 5: Yankee River Hut to Long Harry Hut

4–5 HOURS, 8.5KM

Backtrack to the main trail, which crosses a bridge over the Yankee River and rises steadily for 200m over the ridge of Black Rock Point. It then descends to Smoky Beach, reached two hours from the hut. The climb is a knee-bender and the track is often muddy, but the beach and the interesting sand dunes are ample compensation.

The track continues along the beach for 2km to its western end, before heading inland to cross Smoky Creek on a swing bridge. If the tide isn't too high and the creek isn't in flood, you can skip the bridge and simply ford the stream.

On leaving the creek, the track ascends high above the beach and begins a tough stretch. You actually see Long Harry Hut 30 minutes before you reach it, because the track then descends into and climbs out of a deep gully. Less than 3km from Smoky Beach you reach the new Long Harry Hut (12 bunks), high above the ocean.

Day 6: Long Harry Hut to East Ruggedy Hut

6 HOURS, 9.5KM

The tough tramping continues as you climb in and out of four more bush-clad gullies and streams for 1.5km, until descending near the northern end of Long Harry Bay.

From Long Harry Bay, the track follows a terrace for a short distance, then climbs along Cave Point Ridge, along which there are good views. The track then descends to the rocky coastline, reaching it around one hour from Long Harry Bay. Follow the coast for 30 minutes, then enter the low scrub at a signpost. The track makes a steep 200m climb over a ridge, topping out at a lookout over East Ruggedy Beach and the islands offshore.

Drop to Ruggedy Stream, with scenic East Ruggedy Beach beyond it. The track moves inland from the beach, and is marked by poles through the sand dunes and scrub. About 1km (15 minutes) from the beach you reach East Ruggedy Hut. Patches of soft sand are often found close to the creek and some care is required while crossing them.

A sign outside East Ruggedy Hut (12 bunks) calls it 'the Ritz' and, as far as most trampers are concerned, it is. Bunks are separated into two rooms, while its large veranda is a good place to soak up the afternoon sun.

Day 7: East Ruggedy Hut to Big Hellfire Hut

7–8 HOURS, 14KM

From East Ruggedy Hut follow the track west, reaching West Ruggedy Beach in 40 minutes to an hour. This is one of the circuit's most scenic beaches – a long stretch of coarse sand, framed to the east by the Ruggedy Mountains and to the north by the Ruggedy Islands.

The track follows the beach. At extreme high tide it may be necessary to take the high-tide detour over a steep rocky outcrop halfway down the beach, but at mid to low tide this won't be necessary. At the southern end of the beach the track re-enters bush and begins climbing, working its way to the eastern side of the Ruggedy Mountains.

The track sidles around the eastern side of the range, around Red Head Peak (510m), and climbs to Ruggedy Pass (250m) before descending to Waituna Bay. Boulders line the shore of this remote bay, which is about three hours from West Ruggedy Beach.

The final segment of the day is a two-hour, steady climb to Hellfire Pass, from where there are views of the interior of the island. Brace yourself for mega-mud on this particular section.

Big Hellfire Hut (12 bunks) is an excellent place to spend the night. Situated 200m above sea level, it has incredible views of the Ruggedy Mountains and the Freshwater Flats. A sand dune right outside the door stretches all the way down to Big Hellfire Beach, a scenic stretch of shoreline well worth the 30-minute climb back to the hut.

Day 8: Big Hellfire Hut to Mason Bay Hut

7 HOURS, 15KM

Despite what some maps show, there are no creeks near the track between Big Hellfire and Little Hellfire Beaches, so make sure your water bottles are full when you depart the hut.

From Big Hellfire Hut the track follows the crest of the ridge, affording grand views.

The track sidles off the ridge, crosses a number of gullies, and three to four hours from Hellfire Pass emerges at **Little Hellfire Beach**. Both the ascent of the ridge and the descent can be extremely muddy at times.

Follow the beach for 1km to its southern end, where the track moves inland to climb a bush-and-scrub saddle around **Mason Head**, before descending to the northern end of **Mason Bay**. The climb to the saddle is very steep, and if it's been raining it will also be very muddy. It is slow going and the majority of people need two hours to climb around Mason Head to Mason Bay.

If the tide is right, you can follow the hard sandy beach for one of the most scenic walks on the island. At high tide or with big seas it may be necessary to take the high-tide detour over a steep rocky outcrop partway down the beach. Your best bet is to plan your trip around the tides or take a break and wait for it to recede if daylight allows.

After a 4.5km (two-hour) beach stroll, you cross the mouth of Duck Creek and arrive at a large pole with orange triangles, which marks the track to Mason Bay Hut (20 bunks). The track skirts the stream all through the sand dunes and arrives at the hut in 15 to 20 minutes.

Built in 1968, the hut received a major facelift in 2006, due to the growing popularity of Mason Bay, and now features three bunk rooms and a large kitchen/dining area. The scenic sand dunes of Mason Bay, and the opportunity at night to look (or just listen) for kiwi, has many visitors spending an extra day here.

SIDE TRIP: BIG SANDHILL
1 HOUR, 2KM RETURN

At 156m, **Big Sandhill** is the tallest sand dune along Mason Bay and is an easy climb for great views or to watch the sunset. Just east of the hut on the main track is a bridge over Duck Creek; on the other side you take a side trail that winds through the scrub. Within minutes you'll be on the open sand of the giant dune, where a route to its grassy peak is easy to see.

Day 9: Mason Bay Hut to Freshwater Landing Hut
3–4 HOURS, 15.5KM

To the east of Mason Bay Hut, the track is an old tractor path all the way to Freshwater Landing, making for easy and fast travel during normal conditions. But keep in mind that Freshwater Valley is very flat and can flood quickly when it rains, with waist-deep water in places.

Within 30 minutes of leaving Mason Bay Hut you reach **Island Hill Homestead**: a centre of farming activity in the 1880s, it is now a highly valued historic building. The track continues through red tussock and flax, and in 2km skirts the base of **Island Hill** (137m), the only slight bit of elevation in this otherwise flat landscape.

Beyond the hill you begin cutting across the famed **Chocolate Swamp**, where the track is one long boardwalk. Despite the planks, you'll still be sloshing your way through during rainy periods. Within 30 minutes (or two hours from Mason Bay Hut) you cross the swamp and move into a forest of manuka and scrub where, for the next 3km, the track parallels a ditch – an extension of Scott Burn.

Eventually you cross Scott Burn on a footbridge, and from here it's less than one hour to Freshwater Landing Hut (16 bunks). You arrive on the south side of **Freshwater River**, where there's a jetty for water taxis, and cross a swing bridge to reach the hut on the north side. Many trampers opt to take the water taxi instead of walking the last sections of track, as the trip down the river by boat is quite spectacular.

SIDE TRIP: ROCKY MOUNTAIN
3 HOURS, 5KM RETURN, 539M ASCENT

Starting behind Freshwater Landing Hut, this track passes through forest and sub-alpine vegetation to the rocky top of the appropriately named **Rocky Mountain** (549m), from where there are panoramic views over the Freshwater Flats and Paterson Inlet.

Day 10: Freshwater Landing Hut to North Arm Hut
6–7 HOURS, 11KM

This day is a difficult tramp, with a fair clump of climbing up muddy slopes. Three unbridged creeks are crossed at the Freshwater Landing end, which may be impassable during periods of heavy rain.

The track begins by skirting Freshwater River for a spell, and then swings east to climb Thomson Ridge. After 2.5km the climb becomes considerably steeper, wetter and more slippery. At the top, boggy areas are extensive and for the effort spent getting there, the views are disappointing.

The descent off the ridge is just as steep. After one hour the track reaches a swing bridge and begins sidling around the head of **North Arm**. Looking at a map you'd think this would be a scenic stretch, but in reality it's a constant up-and-down trudge, during which you never see the bay through the thick bush. This continues until you reach **North Arm Hut** (24 bunks) at the end of what is a long day for many.

Day 11: North Arm Hut to Oban

4–5 HOURS, 13KM

Follow day three of the Rakiura Track (p312).

TOWNS & FACILITIES

Te Anau

📞 03 / POP 3000

Peaceful, lakeside Te Anau is a good base for tramping, having a sufficiency of necessities and an invigorating, inspiring outlook.

🛏 Sleeping & Eating

This is a trampers' town and the accommodation options reflect that. Book early from late December to early February.

Te Anau Lakeview Holiday Park
HOLIDAY PARK $

(📞 03-249 7457, 0800 483 262; www.teanau holidaypark.co.nz; 77 Te Anau–Manapouri Rd; sites from $20, dm $35, s $40, units from $84-270; @ 🛜) This large complex across the road from the lake, 1km from Te Anau township, is well equipped and has multiple accommodation options including a backpacker lodge. Besides tramper-friendly facilities like vehicle and gear storage, it's also the home base for Tracknet shuttles.

Te Anau YHA Hostel
HOSTEL $

(📞 03-249 7847; www.yha.co.nz; 29 Mokonui St; dm $33-42, d $90-120; @ 🛜) This centrally located hostel is bright and breezy and well set up for trampers, with gear storage, track information and a barbecue in the grassy backyard.

Te Anau Top 10 Holiday Park
HOLIDAY PARK $

(📞 0800 249 746, 03-249 7462; www.teanautop10.co.nz; 128 Te Anau Tce; sites $38, units $72-160; @ 🛜) Close to town, this small but delightful holiday park has a good range of motel-style units as well as campsites (nice tenting area), a sauna, bike hire, barbecue area and modern communal kitchen.

Fiordland National Park Lodge
LODGE $

(📞 03-249 7811, 0800 500 805; www.teanau-milfordsound.co.nz; d/md $28/65-75; 🛜) Located at Te Anau Downs, just 600m from the wharf where boats depart for Glade Wharf and the start of the Milford Track, this large-capacity lodge has luggage storage and secure parking.

Sandfly Cafe
CAFE $

(9 The Lane; breakfast & lunch $7-17) This is a lovely, chilled-out cafe in which to fuel up or restore yourself after a tramp. Enjoy excellent coffee and cruisy music, all-day breakfasts and yummy home-baking.

Miles Better Pies
PIES $

(cnr Town Centre & Mokonui St; pies $4-6) This irresistible little pie shop offers everything from traditional mince to gourmet venison and Thai curry pies. There are a few pavement tables, but sitting beside the lake is more pleasant.

Red Cliff
RESTAURANT $$

(12 Mokonui St; ⊙4pm-10pm) Redcliff offers Te Anau's finest dining and coolest bar. The cottage cafe has loads of character, a garden bar, and a Poet's Corner featuring live entertainment during summer.

🎒 Supplies & Equipment

Bev's Tramping Gear Hire
OUTDOOR EQUIPMENT

(www.bevs-hire.co.nz; 16 Homer St; ⊙9am-noon & 5.30-7pm) One of two standout options for tramping gear (buy and hire).

Te Anau Outside Sports
OUTDOOR EQUIPMENT

(www.outsidesports.co.nz; 38 Town Centre; ⊙9am-5pm) A great option for buying or hiring tramping and camping equipment.

Fresh Choice Supermarket
SUPERMARKET

(1 The Lane) For groceries.

ℹ Information

Fiordland i-SITE (📞 03-249 8900; www.fiordland.org.nz; 85 Lakefront Dr; ⊙8.30am-5.30pm) Advice and bookings for activities, accommodation and transport.

ℹ Getting There & Away

InterCity (✆ 03-442 4922; www.intercity.co.nz) has daily bus services between Te Anau and Queenstown (2½ hours), Invercargill (2½ hours) and Dunedin (4¾ hours). Buses depart outside Kiwi Country on Miro St. **Naked Bus** (www.nakedbus.com) links Te Anau with Queenstown, Invercargill and Milford Sound, as does **Tracknet** (✆ 0800 483 262; www.tracknet.net).

Safer Parking (✆ 025 260 9032, 03-249 7198; www.saferparking.co.nz; 48 Caswell Rd) has secure parking.

Tuatapere

✆ 03 / POP 650

On the banks of the Waiau River, this former timber-milling town is now a sleepy farming centre, although the Hump Ridge Track has woken things up a bit.

🛏 Sleeping & Eating

Waiau Hotel   HOTEL $
(✆ 03-226 6409; www.waiauhotel.co.nz; 49 Main St; s $30-45, d $90-100) This classic rural-town hotel offers simple and friendly hospitality including clean rooms and home-cooked meals featuring famous Tuatapere sausage.

Shooters
Backpackers   HOLIDAY PARK, BACKPACKERS $
(✆ 027 222 2612, 0800 009 993; www.tuatapere accommodation.co.nz; 73 Main St; sites from $30, dm $28, units $80-120; @ 🖥) In the centre of town, this tidy complex with a farmy feel has a modern backpacker wing with a spacious and sociable communal kitchen area.

Last Light Lodge   HOLIDAY PARK, CAFE $
(✆ 03-226 6667; www.lastlightlodge.com; 2 Clifden Hwy; sites from $15, dm $30, units $56-66) A funky spot in Tuatapere with plenty of simple overnight options including camping, dorms and cabins. The in-house cafe serves robust breakfasts and yummy snacks amid cool retro furniture.

Yesteryears Cafe   CAFE $
(3a Orawia Rd; light meals $10-15) Rip into Aunt Daisy's sugar buns and a quintessentially Kiwi milkshake, and buy homemade jam for on-the-road breakfasts at this cafe-cum-museum with displays of quirky jumble.

🔒 Supplies & Equipment

A few basic tramping supplies (to buy and hire) can be found in the Tuatapere Hump Ridge Track Office.

Tuatapere
Service Station   OUTDOOR EQUIPMENT
(20 Orawia Rd) Best in town for camping and tramping supplies. Across the road from the track office.

Four Square   SUPERMARKET
(75 Main Rd) A mini supermarket in the village.

Tuatapere Sausages   FOOD
(75 Main Rd) The famous butchery.

ℹ Information

Tuatapere Hump Ridge Track Office (✆ 03-226 6739, 0800 486 774; www.humpridge track.co.nz; ☺ 7.30am-6.30pm, limited hours in winter) For information and bookings of almost any description. Also houses the Tuatapere visitor information centre.

Western Southland (www.westernsouthland. co.nz) The online tourism directory for the area.

ℹ Getting There & Away

Tuatapere is 100km south of Te Anau, a drive of around 1¼ hours. Invercargill, to the southeast, is 85km away, which takes just over an hour.

Being somewhat off the beaten track, the town is currently only serviced by **Trips & Tramps** (✆ 03-249 7081, 0800 305 807; www.tripsand tramps.co.nz), which runs twice weekly between Te Anau and Tuatapere during the peak tramping season (mid-December to late April; one way/ return $50/95).

Invercargill

✆ 03 / POP 49,300

Any trip to Stewart Island/Rakiura inevitably includes a stopover in Invercargill, the southernmost city in NZ. Although not as tourism-oriented as many other South Island towns, Invercargill can meet your needs for accommodation, restaurants, transport and a cold beer at the end of a tramp. This is where you'll want to stock up on supplies before heading to Rakiura.

🛏 Sleeping & Eating

Invercargill Top 10
Holiday Park   HOLIDAY PARK $
(✆ 03-218 9032, 0800 486 873; www.invercargill top10.co.nz; 77 McIvor Rd; sites from $19, units $78-150; @ 🖥) This quiet leafy place 6.5km north of town has private sites and good communal facilities. Modern, comfortable studios and self-contained cabins have en suites.

Southern Comfort Backpackers HOSTEL $
(☑03-218 3838; coupers@xtra.co.nz; 30 Thomson St; dm/s/d $28/65/66) This mellow, comfortable house has a TV-free lounge, colourful rooms, a modern, well-equipped kitchen and lovely gardens. Free luggage storage for trampers.

388 Tay MOTEL $$
(☑03-217 3881, 0508 388 829; www.388taymotel. co.nz; 388 Tay St; d $120-160; ☎) Modern and spacious units and a friendly welcome are standard at this well-run spot that's a stand-out along Invercargill's Tay St motel alley.

The Batch CAFE $
(173 Spey St; snacks & mains $8-15) A relaxed beachy ambience and top-notch coffee and smoothies add up to this cafe being regularly voted Southland's best. Delicious counter food includes bagels and brownies, and a smallish wine and beer list partners healthy lunch options. Open later on Friday nights, until 7.30pm.

Louie's Café CAFE $$
(142 Dee St; ⊙Wed-Sat) This cosy cafe-bar specialises in tapas-style snacks ($12), and there's also a concise blackboard menu (mains $20 to $30). Relax near the fireside, tuck yourself away in various nooks and crannies, or spread out on a comfy padded sofa and enjoy the chilled-out music.

🛒 Supplies & Equipment

Southern Adventure OUTDOOR EQUIPMENT
(www.southernadventure.co.nz; 31 Tay St; ⊙8.30am-5.30pm Mon-Thu, to 7pm Fri, 10am-3pm Sat) For tramping equipment and stove fuel.

Pak 'n Save SUPERMARKET
(95 Tay St; ⊙8am-9pm) For food supplies.

ℹ️ Information

DOC Southland Conservancy (☑03-211 2400; www.doc.govt.nz; 7th fl, 33 Don St; ⊙8.30am-4.30pm Mon-Fri) Sells hut tickets, maps and brochures for tracks around Rakiura and Southland.

Invercargill i-SITE (☑03-214 6243; www. invercargillnz.com; Queens Park, 108 Gala St; ⊙8am-5pm) In the same building as the Southland Museum & Art Gallery, this centre offers loads of friendly advice and a pleasant coffee shop.

ℹ️ Getting There & Away

Air New Zealand (☑0800 737 000; www. airnz.co.nz) has several daily flights between Invercargill and Christchurch (from $89), with connections to most other cities in NZ. The main way to reach the airport is by taxi ($8 to $10).

For those taking the ferry to Rakiura, **Stewart Island Experience** (☑03-212 7660, 0800 000 511; www.stewartislandexperience.co.nz; 12 Elgin Tce; ⊙8.30am-6pm) runs a shuttle between Bluff and Invercargill ($25) with pick-up and drop-off in Invercargill at the i-SITE and airport.

Buses leave from the Invercargill i-SITE, where you can also book your tickets. Companies serving the town are **InterCity** (☑03-365 1113; www.intercity.co.nz) and **Naked Bus** (www. nakedbus.com), which provide links to major southern destinations and beyond, while Te Anau–based **Tracknet** (☑0800 483 262; www. tracknet.net) plies the Te Anau–to–Queenstown route. The **Catlins Coaster** (☑03-477 9083; www.catlinscoaster.co.nz) runs along the Southern Scenic Route through to Dunedin.

Oban
☑03 / POP 400
Most of Rakiura's small and close-knit population lives in the settlement of Oban on Halfmoon Bay. Most trampers spend a night in town before heading into the bush.

🛏️ Sleeping & Eating

Stewart Island Backpackers HOSTEL $
(☑03-219 1114; www.stewartislandbackpackers. com; Dundee & Ayr Sts; sites $20, dm/d $35/70; @) This brightly painted hostel has a sociable atmosphere and three-bed dorms, many of which open onto a courtyard. There are also tent sites.

Jo & Andy's B&B B&B $
(☑03-219 1230; jariksem@clear.net.nz; cnr Morris St & Main Rd; s $60, d/tw $90; @ ☎) An excellent option for budget travellers, this cozy blue home squeezes in twin, double and single rooms and proffers a big breakfast of muesli, fruit and homemade bread. There are hundreds of books if the weather packs up.

South Sea Hotel HOTEL, RESTAURANT $
(☑03-219 1059; www.stewart-island.co.nz; cnr Argyle St & Elgin Tce; s $65-100, d $85-110) This is a welcoming spot at the end of a long tramp, with comfortable rooms and an on-site bar and restaurant.

Church Hill Restaurant & Oyster Bar CAFE, BAR $$
(☑03-219 1323; www.churchill.co.nz; 36 Kamahi Rd; ⊙noon & dinner) During summer this heritage villa's sunny deck provides hilltop views,

and in cooler months you can get cosy inside beside the open fire. Food highlights include local smoked salmon and old-fashioned desserts. Book early for a dinner spot.

 Supplies & Equipment

Ship to Shore   SUPERMARKET
(Elgin Tce; ⊙ 7.30am-7.30pm) This mini-mart has a good selection of groceries and other tramper needs, including white spirits and freeze-dried meals, but as you might expect, prices are higher on this side of Foveaux Strait.

❶ Information

Stewart Island Experience (☑ 03-212 7660, 0800 000 511; www.stewartislandexperience. co.nz; 12 Elgin Tce; ⊙ 8.30am-6pm) In the big red building. Books accommodation and activities, handles sightseeing tours and rents scooters and cars.

❶ Getting There & Away

Stewart Island Flights (p356) links Invercargill and Rakiura (one way/return $115/195, 20 minutes, three daily); ask about stand-by fares. It runs a minibus between the Rakiura airstrip and Oban, which is included in the airfare. The baggage allowance is only 15kg per person – not much if you're carrying tramping gear – and if you exceed that weight the excess may have to come on a later flight.

Stewart Island Experience (☑ 0800 000 511, 03-212 7660; www.stewartislandexperience. co.nz; Main Wharf) operates the passenger-only ferry from Bluff to Rakiura ($69, one hour) around three times daily, with additional runs during the summer, when you should definitely book ahead. Foveaux Strait is often stormy, so carry some seasickness pills. Cars and camper-vans can be stored in a secure car park at Bluff for an additional cost.

Note that a visitor levy ($2.50) is charged each way on all transport on and off the island, added to your airfare or ferry fare when you book.

Understand New Zealand

NEW ZEALAND TODAY 322

The Christchurch earthquake, Pike River mine tragedy, a challenge to NZ's 'clean green' image, and the government's response.

HISTORY 324

Tread a New Zealand timeline from Maori and Pakeha settlement, through the fast-paced evolutionary stages of one of the world's youngest countries.

ENVIRONMENT 334

Get the lowdown on the land, flora, fauna, national parks and environmental issues.

New Zealand Today

Historically considered a tough, nimble little country with bankable primary industries and a resilient economy, New Zealand has proven as susceptible as any first-world country to the downturn in global financial trading. It may have been able to take this challenge in its stride were it not for a devastating series of earthquakes and a mining tragedy, and frequent, costly storms and floods. Pressure is on to keep the economic wheel turning, but at what cost to its '100% Pure' environment?

Best on Film

Lord of the Rings trilogy (Dir: Sir Peter Jackson; 2001–03) The three-instalment adaptation of Tolkien's work that cleaned up at the Oscars.
The Hobbit trilogy (Dir: Sir Peter Jackson; 2012–14) Having practised on *LOTR*, director Jackson goes all out on the prequel.
The Piano (Dir: Jane Campion; 1993) Erotica, an unforgettable axe scene and a youthful Sookie Stackhouse from *True Blood*.
Whale Rider (Dir: Niki Caro; 2002) Allegorical battle of the sexes set in a small, Maori village; cameo from whale.
Boy (Dir: Taika Waititi; 2010) Funny, affectionate portrayal of a young Maori boy reconnecting with his father.

Best in Print

The Luminaries (Eleanor Catton; 2013) Gold-rush tales in epic form; winner of the 2013 Man Booker.
The Collected Stories of Katherine Mansfield (Penguin; 2007) The essential anthology of NZ's most famous short-story writer.
Mister Pip (Lloyd Jones; 2007) Charles Dickens changes a girl's expectations during the Bougainville civil war.
The Carpathians (Janet Frame; 1988) The beloved NZ writer's last novel; magical happenings in a rural town.
Potiki (Patricia Grace; 1986) A Maori community faces mortal danger in this poignant novel by a revered writer.

Shaky Isles

There's no denying it, NZ has had it tough over the last few years. It may be a long way away from just about everywhere but it is not immune to the vagaries of the global economy. In September 2010, just as the country was edging out of its worst recession in 30 years, a magnitude 7.1 earthquake struck near Christchurch, the nation's second-largest city. The damage was extensive but miraculously no lives were lost, partly because the earthquake occurred in the early hours of the morning when people were in their beds.

Then, in the early afternoon of 22 February 2011, a magnitude 6.3 earthquake struck Christchurch. This time the city wasn't so lucky and 185 people lost their lives. Numerous buildings, already weakened by the September 2010 quake and its aftershocks, were damaged beyond repair and had to be demolished completely.

The city's rebuild has been slow: the centre of the city didn't reopen fully until mid-2013. Cantabrians, however, have displayed admirable resilience and innovation, helping Christchurch to re-emerge as one of NZ's most exciting cities. With the city centre still somewhat 'munted', fringe suburbs have been reinvigorated, such as Woolston ('Coolston') and Addington, while an innovative cardboard (yes cardboard!) cathedral has been brought into the fold. The city was named by Lonely Planet as one of the world's top 10 cities in its *Best in Travel 2013*.

Christchurch isn't the only place to be awarded such a plaudit, with the South Island's West Coast named as one of the world's must-visit regions in *Best in Travel 2014*. Increasing recognition of its extensive conservation estate and unique ecological values sits uncomfortably alongside continual interest in exploiting the area's natural resources. But mining has always been part of the Coast way of life, as is the danger so often associated with it. In November 2010 29 men lost their lives when a series of explosions ripped through the Pike River coalmine near Greymouth in another widely felt tragedy that further pushed the bounds of the country's emotional and economic resilience.

The Economic Environment

With estimates for the Christchurch rebuild having ballooned to more than $40 billion, it could take decades for NZ to recover fully. The pressure is on to keep the economic wheel turning, with dairy farming and tourism the main grist to the mill.

These two earners are proving somewhat at odds. NZ's '100% Pure' tourism campaign employs images of beautiful landscapes in pristine condition. The country, however, has been repeatedly rumbled in recent years as environmentalists – and the media – turn their spotlight on the country's 'clean green' credentials. Controversial proposals for open cast mines on conservation land, extensive offshore oil and gas exploration, evidence of dirty dairy farming, river pollution levels, Department of Conservation (DOC) budget cuts, and questionable urban planning – there have been endless hooks for a bad news story, and plenty of reasons to protest.

One of the latest controversies is over the 1991 *Resource Management Act,* which regulates environmental management and development. Under fire from parliamentarians seen to be in cahoots with big business, this landmark legislation is set to be softened, further opening the door to development at the cost of the environment. Already disgruntled by recent state asset sales and the passing of an Act that permits increased personal surveillance, the NZ public is decidedly twitchy.

POPULATION: **4.5 MILLION**

AREA: **268,680 SQ KM**

GDP GROWTH: **0.8%**

INFLATION: **1.7%**

UNEMPLOYMENT: **6.4%**

TOTAL NUMBER OF SNAKES: **0**

DISTANCE BETWEEN NORTH AND SOUTH ISLANDS: **23KM**

if New Zealand were 100 people

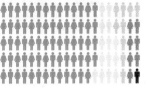

69 would be European
14 would be Maori
9 would be Asian
7 would be Pacific Islanders
1 would be Other

where they live
(% of New Zealanders)

63 — North Island
20 — South Island
10 — Australia
5 — Rest of the World
2 — Travelling

population per sq km

NEW ZEALAND   AUSTRALIA   USA

 ≈ 3 people

History

James Belich
One of New Zealand's foremost modern historians, James Belich has written a number of books on NZ history and hosted the TV documentary series *The New Zealand Wars*.

New Zealand's history is not long, but it is fast. In less than a thousand years these islands have produced two new peoples: the Polynesian Maori and European New Zealanders. The latter are often known by their Maori name, 'Pakeha' (though not all like the term). NZ shares some of its history with the rest of Polynesia, and with other European settler societies, but has unique features as well. It is the similarities that make the differences so interesting, and vice versa.

Making Maori

Despite persistent myths, there is no doubt that the first settlers of NZ were the Polynesian forebears of today's Maori. Beyond that, there are a lot of question marks. Exactly where in east Polynesia did they come from – the Cook Islands, Tahiti, the Marquesas? When did they arrive? Did the first settlers come in one group or several? Some evidence, such as the diverse DNA of the Polynesian rats that accompanied the first settlers, suggests multiple founding voyages. On the other hand, only rats and dogs brought by the founders have survived, not the more valuable pigs and chickens. The survival of these cherished animals would have had high priority, and their failure to be successfully introduced suggests fewer voyages.

NZ seems small compared with Australia, but it is bigger than Britain, and very much bigger than other Polynesian islands. Its regions vary wildly in environment and climate. Prime sites for first settlement were warm coastal gardens for the food plants brought from Polynesia (kumara or sweet potato, gourd, yam and taro); sources of workable stone for knives and adzes; and areas with abundant big game. NZ has no native land mammals apart from a few species of bat, but 'big game' is no

'Kaore e mau te rongo – ake, ake!' (Peace never shall be made – never, never!) War chief Rewi Maniapoto in response to government troops at the battle of Orakau, 1864

TIMELINE	AD 1000 –1200	1642	1769
	Possible date of the arrival of Maori in NZ. Solid archaeological evidence points to about AD 1200, but much earlier dates have been suggested for the first human impact on the environment.	First European contact: Abel Tasman arrives on an expedition from the Dutch East Indies (Indonesia) to find the 'Great South Land'. His party leaves without landing, after a sea skirmish with Maori.	European contact recommences with visits by James Cook and Jean de Surville. Despite some violence, both manage to communicate with Maori. This time NZ's link with the outside world proves permanent.

exaggeration: the islands were home to a dozen species of moa (a large flightless bird), the largest of which weighed up to 240kg, about twice the size of an ostrich. There were also other species of flightless birds and large sea mammals such as fur seals, all unaccustomed to being hunted. For people from small Pacific islands, this was like hitting the jackpot. The first settlers spread far and fast, from the top of the North Island to the bottom of the South Island within the first 100 years. High-protein diets are likely to have boosted population growth.

By about 1400, however, with big-game supply dwindling, Maori economics turned from big game to small game – forest birds and rats – and from hunting to gardening and fishing. A good living could still be made, but it required detailed local knowledge, steady effort and complex communal organisation, hence the rise of the Maori tribes. Competition for resources increased, conflict did likewise, and this led to the building of increasingly sophisticated fortifications, known as *pa*. Vestiges of *pa* earthworks can still be seen around the country (on the hilltops of Auckland, for example).

The Maori had no metals and no written language (and no alcoholic drinks or drugs). But their culture and spiritual life was rich and distinctive. Below Ranginui (sky father) and Papatuanuku (earth mother) were various gods of land, forest and sea, joined by deified ancestors over time. The mischievous demigod Maui was particularly important. In legend, he vanquished the sun and fished up the North Island before meeting his death between the thighs of the goddess Hine-nui-te-po in an attempt to conquer the human mortality embodied in her.Maori traditional performance art, the group singing and dancing known as *kapa haka,* has real power, even for modern audiences. Visual art, notably woodcarving, is something special – 'like nothing but itself', in the words of 18th-century explorer-scientist Joseph Banks.

For a thorough overview of NZ history from Gondwanaland to today, visit history-nz.org.

Rumours of late survivals of the giant moa bird abound, but none have been authenticated. So if you see a moa in your travels, photograph it – you have just made the greatest zoological discovery of the last 100 years.

THE MORIORI & THEIR MYTH

One of NZ's most persistent legends is that Maori found mainland NZ already occupied by a more peaceful and racially distinct Melanesian people, known as the Moriori, whom they exterminated. This myth has been regularly debunked by scholars since the 1920s, but somehow hangs on.

To complicate matters, there were real 'Moriori', and Maori did treat them badly. The real Moriori were the people of the Chatham Islands, a windswept group about 900km east of the mainland. They were, however, fully Polynesian, and descended from Maori – 'Moriori' was their version of the same word. Mainland Maori arrived in the Chathams in 1835, as a spin-off of the Musket Wars, killing some Moriori and enslaving the rest. But they did not exterminate them. The mainland Moriori remain a myth.

1772	1790s	1818–36
Marion du Fresne's French expedition arrives; it stays for some weeks at the Bay of Islands. Relations with Maori start well, but a breach of Maori *tapu* (sacred law) leads to violence.	Whaling ships and sealing gangs arrive in the country. Relations are established with Maori, with Europeans depending on the contact for essentials such as food, water and protection.	Intertribal Maori 'Musket Wars' take place: tribes acquire muskets and win bloody victories against tribes without them. The war tapers off in 1836, probably due to the equal distribution of weapons.

PAUL KENNEDY / GETTY IMAGES ©

» Statue of James Cook

Enter Europe

NZ became an official British colony in 1840, but the first authenticated contact between Maori and the outside world took place almost two centuries earlier in 1642, in Golden Bay at the top of the South Island. Two Dutch ships sailed from Indonesia, to search for southern land and anything valuable it might contain. The commander, Abel Tasman, was instructed to pretend to any natives he might meet 'that you are by no means eager for precious metals, so as to leave them ignorant of the value of the same'.

When Tasman's ships anchored in the bay, local Maori came out in their canoes to make the traditional challenge: friends or foes? Misunderstanding this, the Dutch challenged back, by blowing trumpets. When a boat was lowered to take a party between the two ships, it was attacked. Four crewmen were killed. Tasman sailed away and did not come back; nor did any other European for 127 years. But the Dutch did leave a name: 'Nieuw Zeeland' or 'New Sealand'.

Contact between Maori and Europeans was renewed in 1769, when English and French explorers arrived, under James Cook and Jean de Surville. Relations were more sympathetic, and exploration continued, motivated by science, profit and great power rivalry. Cook made two more visits between 1773 and 1777, and there were further French expeditions.

Unofficial visits, by whaling ships in the north and sealing gangs in the south, began in the 1790s. The first mission station was founded in 1814, in the Bay of Islands, and was followed by dozens of others: Anglican, Methodist and Catholic. Trade in flax and timber generated small European–Maori settlements by the 1820s. Surprisingly, the most numerous category of European visitor was probably American. New England whaling ships favoured the Bay of Islands for rest and recreation; 271 called there between 1833 and 1839 alone. To whalers, 'rest and recreation' meant sex and drink. Their favourite haunt, the little town of Kororareka (now Russell) was known to the missionaries as 'the hellhole of the Pacific'. New England visitors today might well have distant relatives among the local Maori.

One or two dozen bloody clashes dot the history of Maori–European contact before 1840 but, given the number of visits, interracial conflict was modest. Europeans needed Maori protection, food and labour, and Maori came to need European articles, especially muskets. Whaling stations and mission stations were linked to local Maori groups by intermarriage, which helped keep the peace. Most warfare was between Maori and Maori: the terrible intertribal 'Musket Wars' of 1818–36. Because Northland had the majority of early contact with Europe, its

Similarities in language between Maori and Tahitian indicate close contact in historical times. Maori is about as similar to Tahitian as Spanish is to French, despite the 4294km separating these island groups.

The Ministry for Culture & Heritage's history website (www.nzhistory.net.nz) is an excellent source of info on NZ history.

1837	1840	1844	1858
Possums are introduced to New Zealand from Australia. Brilliant.	Starting at Waitangi in the Bay of Islands on 6 February, around 500 chiefs countrywide sign the Treaty of Waitangi to 'settle' sovereignty once and for all. NZ becomes a nominal British colony.	Young Ngapuhi chief Hone Heke challenges British sovereignty, first by cutting down the British flag at Kororareka (now Russell), then by sacking the town itself. The ensuing Northland war continues until 1846.	The Waikato chief Te Wherowhero is installed as the first Maori King.

CAPTAIN JAMES COOK *TONY HORWITZ*

If aliens ever visit earth, they may wonder what to make of the countless obelisks, faded plaques and graffiti-covered statues of a stiff, wigged figure gazing out to sea from Alaska to Australia, from NZ to North Yorkshire, from Siberia to the South Pacific. James Cook (1728–79) explored more of the earth's surface than anyone in history, and it's impossible to travel the Pacific without encountering the captain's image and his controversial legacy in the lands he opened to the West.

For a man who travelled so widely, and rose to such fame, Cook came from an extremely pinched and provincial background. The son of a day labourer in rural Yorkshire, he was born in a mud cottage, had little schooling, and seemed destined for farm work – and for his family's grave plot in a village churchyard. Instead, Cook went to sea as a teenager, worked his way up from coal-ship servant to naval officer, and attracted notice for his exceptional charts of Canada. But Cook remained a little-known second lieutenant until, in 1768, the Royal Navy chose him to command a daring voyage to the South Seas.

In a converted coal ship called *Endeavour,* Cook sailed to Tahiti, and then became the first European to land at NZ and the east coast of Australia. Though the ship almost sank after striking the Great Barrier Reef, and 40% of the crew died from disease and accidents, the *Endeavour* limped home in 1771. On a return voyage (1772–75), Cook became the first navigator to pierce the Antarctic Circle and circle the globe near its southernmost latitude, demolishing the myth that a vast, populous and fertile continent surrounded the South Pole. Cook crisscrossed the Pacific from Easter Island to Melanesia, charting dozens of islands between. Though Maori killed and cooked 10 sailors, the captain remained sympathetic to islanders. 'Notwithstanding they are cannibals,' he wrote, 'they are naturally of a good disposition.'

On Cook's final voyage (1776–79), in search of a northwest passage between the Atlantic and Pacific, he became the first European to visit Hawaii, and coasted America from Oregon to Alaska. Forced back by Arctic pack ice, Cook returned to Hawaii, where he was killed during a skirmish with islanders who had initially greeted him as a Polynesian god. In a single decade of discovery, Cook had filled in the map of the Pacific and, as one French navigator put it, 'left his successors with little to do but admire his exploits'.

But Cook's travels also spurred colonisation of the Pacific, and within a few decades of his death, missionaries, whalers, traders and settlers began transforming (and often devastating) island cultures. As a result, many indigenous people now revile Cook as an imperialist villain who introduced disease, dispossession and other ills to the Pacific (hence the frequent vandalising of Cook monuments). However, as islanders revive traditional crafts and practices, from tattooing to *tapa* (traditional barkcloth), they have turned to the art and writing of Cook and his men as a resource for cultural renewal. For good and ill, a Yorkshire farm boy remains the single most significant figure in the shaping of the modern Pacific.

Tony Horwitz is a Pulitzer-winning reporter and nonfiction author.
In researching Blue Latitudes (or Into the Blue), Tony travelled the Pacific –
'boldly going where Captain Cook has gone before'.

1860–69	1861	1863–64	1868–72
First and Second Taranaki wars, starting with the controversial swindling of Maori land by the government at Waitara, and continuing with outrage over the confiscation of more land as a result.	Gold discovered in Otago by Gabriel Read, an Australian prospector. As a result, the population of Otago climbs from less than 13,000 to over 30,000 in six months.	Waikato Land War. Up to 5000 Maori resist an invasion mounted by 20,000 imperial, colonial and 'friendly' Maori troops. Despite surprising successes, Maori are defeated and much land is confiscated.	East Coast war. Te Kooti, having led an escape from his prison on the Chatham Islands, leads a holy guerrilla war in the Urewera region. He finally retreats to establish the Ringatu Church.

Ngapuhi tribe acquired muskets first. Under their great general Hongi Hika, Ngapuhi then raided south, winning bloody victories against tribes without muskets. Once they acquired muskets, these tribes saw off Ngapuhi, but also raided further south in their turn. The domino effect continued to the far south of the South Island in 1836. The missionaries claimed that the Musket Wars then tapered off through their influence, but the restoration of the balance of power through the equal distribution of muskets was probably more important.

Europe brought such things as pigs (at last) and potatoes, which benefited Maori, while muskets and diseases had the opposite effect. The negative effects have been exaggerated, however. Europeans expected peoples like the Maori to simply fade away at contact, and some early estimates of Maori population were overly high – up to one million. Current estimates are between 85,000 and 110,000 for 1769. The Musket Wars killed perhaps 20,000, and new diseases did considerable damage too (although NZ had the natural quarantine of distance: infected Europeans usually recovered or died during the long voyage, and smallpox, for example, which devastated native Americans, did not make it here). By 1840, the Maori had been reduced to about 70,000, a decline of at least 20%. Maori bent under the weight of European contact, but they certainly did not break.

Abel Tasman named NZ Stateland, assuming it was connected to Staten Island near Argentina. It was subsequently named after the province of Zeeland in Tasman's Holland.

Making Pakeha

By 1840, Maori tribes described local Europeans as 'their Pakeha', and valued the profit and prestige they brought. Maori wanted more of both, and concluded that accepting nominal British authority was the way to get them. At the same time, the British government was overcoming its reluctance to undertake potentially expensive intervention in NZ. It too was influenced by profit and prestige, but also by humanitarian considerations. It believed, wrongly but sincerely, that Maori could not handle the increasing scale of unofficial European contact. In 1840, the two peoples struck a deal, symbolised by the treaty first signed at Waitangi on 6 February that year. The Treaty of Waitangi now has a standing not dissimilar to that of the Constitution in the US, but is even more contested. The original problem was a discrepancy between British and Maori understandings of it. The English version promised Maori full equality as British subjects in return for complete rights of government. The Maori version also promised that Maori would retain their chieftainship, which implied local rights of government. The problem was not great at first, because the Maori version applied outside the small European settlements. But as those settlements grew, conflict brewed.

In 1840, there were only about 2000 Europeans in NZ, with the shanty town of Kororareka (now Russell) as the capital and biggest settlement.

'God's own country, but the devil's own mess.' Prime Minister Richard (King Dick) Seddon, speaking on the source of NZ's self-proclaimed nickname 'Godzone'.

1886–87
Tuwharetoa tribe gifts the mountains of Ruapehu, Ngauruhoe and Tongariro to the government to establish the world's fourth national park.

1893
NZ becomes the first country in the world to grant the vote to women, following a campaign led by Kate Sheppard, who petitioned the government for years.

JOHN ELK III / GETTY IMAGES ©

» Mt Ngauruhoe (p89), Tongariro National Park

By 1850, six new settlements had been formed with 22,000 settlers between them. About half of these had arrived under the auspices of the New Zealand Company and its associates. The company was the brainchild of Edward Gibbon Wakefield, who also influenced the settlement of South Australia. Wakefield hoped to short-circuit the barbarous frontier phase of settlement with 'instant civilisation', but his success was limited. From the 1850s, his settlers, who included a high proportion of upper-middle-class gentlefolk, were swamped by succeeding waves of immigrants that continued to wash in until the 1880s. These people were part of the great British and Irish diaspora that also populated Australia and much of North America, but the NZ mix was distinctive. Lowland Scots settlers were more prominent in NZ than elsewhere, for example, with the possible exception of parts of Canada. NZ's Irish, even the Catholics, tended to come from the north of Ireland. NZ's English tended to come from the counties close to London. Small groups of Germans, Scandinavians and Chinese made their way in, though the last faced increasing racial prejudice from the 1880s, when the Pakeha population reached half a million.

Much of the mass immigration from the 1850s to the 1870s was assisted by the provincial and central governments, which also mounted large-scale public works schemes, especially in the 1870s under Julius Vogel. In 1876, Vogel abolished the provinces on the grounds that they were hampering his development efforts. The last imperial governor with substantial power was the talented but Machiavellian George Grey, who ended his second governorship in 1868. Thereafter, the governors (governors-general from 1917) were largely just nominal heads of state; the head of government, the premier or prime minister, had more power. The central government, originally weaker than the provincial governments, the imperial governor and the Maori tribes, eventually exceeded the power of all three.

The Maori tribes did not go down without a fight, however. Indeed, their resistance was one of the most formidable ever mounted against European expansion, comparable to that of the Sioux and Seminole in the US. The first clash took place in 1843 in the Wairau Valley, now a wine-growing district. A posse of settlers set out to enforce the myth of British control, but encountered the reality of Maori control. Twenty-two settlers were killed, including Wakefield's brother, Arthur, along with about six Maori. In 1845, more serious fighting broke out in the Bay of Islands, when Hone Heke sacked a British settlement. Heke and his ally Kawiti baffled three British punitive expeditions, using a modern variant of the traditional *pa* fortification. Vestiges of these innovative earthworks can still be seen at Ruapekapeka (south of Kawakawa). Governor Grey claimed victory in the north, but few were convinced at the time. Grey

HISTORY MAKING PAKEHA

Maurice Shadbolt's *Season of the Jew* (1987) is a semifictionalised story of bloody campaigns led by warrior Te Kooti against the British in Poverty Bay in the 1860s. Te Kooti and his followers compared themselves to the Israelites who were cast out of Egypt.

To find out more about the New Zealand Wars, visit www.newzealandwars.co.nz.

'I believe we were all glad to leave New Zealand. It is not a pleasant place. Amongst the natives there is absent that charming simplicity...and the greater part of the English are the very refuse of society.' Charles Darwin, referring to Kororareka (Russell), in 1860.

1901	1908	1914–18	1931
NZ politely declines the invitation to join the new Commonwealth of Australia.	NZ physicist Ernest Rutherford is awarded the Nobel Prize in chemistry for 'splitting the atom', investigating the disintegration of elements and the chemistry of radioactive substances.	NZ's contribution to WWI is staggering for a country of just over one million people: about 100,000 NZ men serve overseas. Some 60,000 become casualties, mostly on the Western Front in France.	Napier earthquake kills 131 people.

had more success in the south, where he arrested the formidable Ngati Toa chief Te Rauparaha, who until then wielded great influence on both sides of Cook Strait. Pakeha were able to swamp the few Maori living in the South Island, but the fighting of the 1840s confirmed that the North Island at that time comprised a European fringe around an independent Maori heartland.

In the 1850s, settler population and aspirations grew, and fighting broke out again in 1860. The wars burned on sporadically until 1872 over much of the North Island. In the early years, a Maori nationalist organisation, the King Movement, was the backbone of resistance. In later years, some remarkable prophet-generals, notably Titokowaru and Te Kooti, took over. Most wars were small-scale, but the Waikato war of 1863–64 was not. This conflict, fought at the same time as the American Civil War, involved armoured steamships, ultramodern heavy artillery, telegraph and 10 proud British regular regiments. Despite the odds, the Maori won several battles, such as that at Gate Pa, near Tauranga, in 1864. But in the end they were ground down by European numbers and resources. Maori political, though not cultural, independence ebbed away in the last decades of the 19th century. It finally expired when police invaded its last sanctuary, the Urewera Mountains, in 1916.

The Six o'clock Swill referred to the frantic after-work drinking at pubs when men tried to drink as much as possible from 5.05pm until strict closing time at 6pm.

Welfare & Warfare

From the 1850s to the 1880s, despite conflict with Maori, the Pakeha economy boomed on the back of wool exports, gold rushes and massive overseas borrowing for development. The crash came in the 1880s, when NZ experienced its Long Depression. In 1890, the Liberals came to power, and stayed there until 1912, helped by a recovering economy. The Liberals were NZ's first organised political party, and the first of several governments to give NZ a reputation as 'the world's social laboratory'. NZ became the first country in the world to give women the vote in 1893, and introduced old-age pensions in 1898. The Liberals also introduced a long-lasting system of industrial arbitration, but this was not enough to prevent bitter industrial unrest in 1912–13. This happened under the conservative 'Reform' government, which had replaced the Liberals in 1912. Reform remained in power until 1928, and later transformed itself into the National Party. Renewed depression struck in 1929, and the NZ experience of it was as grim as any. The derelict little farmhouses still seen in rural areas often date from this era.

In 1935, a second reforming government took office: the First Labour government, led by Michael Joseph Savage, easily NZ's favourite Austral-

Wellington-born Nancy Wake (codenamed 'The White Mouse') led a guerrilla attack against the Nazis with a 7000-strong army. She had the multiple honours of being the Gestapo's most-wanted person and being the most decorated Allied servicewoman of WWII.

1935–49	1936	1939–45	1948
First Labour government in power, under Michael Savage. This government creates NZ's pioneering version of the welfare state, and also takes some independent initiatives in foreign policy.	NZ aviatrix Jean Batten becomes the first aviator to fly solo from Britain to NZ.	NZ troops back Britain and the Allied war effort during WWII; from 1942 a hundred thousand or so Americans arrive to protect NZ from the Japanese.	Maurice Scheslinger invents the Buzzy Bee, NZ's most famous children's toy.

ian. For a time, the Labour government was considered the most socialist government outside Soviet Russia. But, when the chips were down in Europe in 1939, Labour had little hesitation in backing Britain.

NZ had also backed Britain in the Boer War (1899–1902) and WWI (1914–18), with dramatic losses in WWI in particular. You can count the cost in almost any little NZ town. A central square or park will contain a memorial lined with names – more for WWI than WWII. Even in WWII, however, NZ did its share of fighting: a hundred thousand or so New Zealanders fought in Europe and the Middle East. NZ, a peaceful-seeming country, has spent much of its history at war. In the 19th century it fought at home; in the 20th, overseas.

LAND WARS *ERROL HUNT*

Five separate major conflicts made up what are now collectively known as the New Zealand Wars (also referred to as the Land Wars or Maori Wars). Starting in Northland and moving throughout the North Island, the wars had many complex causes, but *whenua* (land) was the one common factor. In all five wars, Maori fought both for and against the government, on whose side stood the Imperial British Army, Australians and NZ's own Armed Constabulary. Land confiscations imposed on the Maori as punishment for involvement in these wars are still the source of conflict today, with the government struggling to finance compensation for what are now acknowledged to have been illegal seizures.

Northland war (1844–46) 'Hone Heke's War' began with the famous chopping of the flagpole at Kororareka (now Russell) and 'ended' at Ruapekapeka (south of Kawakawa). In many ways, this was almost a civil war between rival Ngapuhi factions, with the government taking one side against the other.

First Taranaki war (1860–61) Starting in Waitara, the first Taranaki war inflamed the passions of Maori across the North Island.

Waikato war (1863–64) The largest of the five wars. Predominantly involving Kingitanga, the Waikato war was caused in part by what the government saw as a challenge to sovereignty. However, it was land, again, that was the real reason for friction. Following defeats such as Rangiriri, the Waikato people were pushed entirely from their own lands, south into what became known as the King Country.

Second Taranaki war (1865–69) Caused by Maori resistance to land confiscations stemming from the first Taranaki war, this was perhaps the war in which the Maori came closest to victory, under the brilliant, one-eyed prophet-general Titokowaru. However, once he lost the respect of his warriors (probably through an indiscretion with the wife of one of his warriors), the war too was lost.

East Coast war (1868–72) Te Kooti's holy guerrilla war.

1953	1973	1974	1981
New Zealander Edmund Hillary, with Tenzing Norgay, 'knocks the bastard off'; the pair become the first men to reach the summit of Mt Everest.	Fledgling Kiwi prog-rockers Split Enz enter a TV talent quest... finishing second to last.	Pacific Island migrants who have outstayed visas ('overstayers') are subjected to Dawn Raids by immigration police under Robert Muldoon and the National government. These raids continue until the early 1980s.	Springbok rugby tour divides the nation. Many New Zealanders show a strong anti-apartheid stance by protesting the games. Others feel sport and politics shouldn't mix, and support the tour going ahead.

Better Britons?

British visitors have long found NZ hauntingly familiar. This is not simply a matter of the British and Irish origin of most Pakeha. It also stems from the tightening of NZ links with Britain from 1882, when refrigerated cargoes of food were first shipped to London. By the 1930s, giant ships carried frozen meat, cheese and butter, as well as wool, on regular voyages taking about five weeks one way. The NZ economy adapted to the feeding of London, and cultural links were also enhanced. NZ children studied British history and literature, not their own. NZ's leading scientists and writers, such as Ernest Rutherford and Katherine Mansfield, gravitated to Britain. This tight relationship has been described as 'recolonial', but it is a mistake to see NZ as an exploited colony. Average living standards in NZ were normally better than in Britain, as were the welfare and lower-level education systems. New Zealanders had access to British markets and culture, and they contributed their share to the latter as equals. The list of 'British' writers, academics, scientists, military leaders, publishers and the like who were actually New Zealanders is long. Indeed, New Zealanders, especially in war and sport, sometimes saw themselves as a superior version of the British – the Better Britons of the south. The NZ–London relationship was rather like that of the American Midwest and New York.

'Recolonial' NZ prided itself, with some justice, on its affluence, equality and social harmony. But it was also conformist, even puritanical. Until the 1950s, it was technically illegal for farmers to allow their cattle to mate in fields fronting public roads, for moral reasons. The 1953 American movie, *The Wild One,* was banned until 1977. Sunday newspapers were illegal until 1969, and full Sunday trading was not allowed until 1989. Licensed restaurants hardly existed in 1960, nor did supermarkets or TV. Notoriously, from 1917 to 1967, pubs were obliged to shut at 6pm. Yet the puritanical society of Better Britons was never the whole story. Opposition to Sunday trading stemmed, not so much from belief in the sanctity of the Sabbath, but from the belief that workers should have weekends too. Six o'clock closing was a standing joke in rural areas, notably the marvellously idiosyncratic region of the South Island's West Coast. There was always something of a Kiwi counterculture, even before imported countercultures took root from the 1960s.

There were also developments in cultural nationalism, beginning in the 1930s but really flowering from the 1970s. Writers, artists and filmmakers were by no means the only people who 'came out' in that era.

The Waitangi Treaty Grounds, where the Treaty of Waitangi was first signed in 1840, is now a tourist attraction for Kiwis and non-Kiwis alike. Each year on 6 February, Waitangi hosts treaty commemorations and protests

TREATY OF WAITANGI

1985

Rainbow Warrior is sunk in Auckland Harbour by French government agents to prevent the Greenpeace protest ship from making its intended voyage to Moruroa, where the French are conducting nuclear tests.

1992

Government begins reparations for the Land Wars, and confirms Maori fishing rights in the 'Sealord deal'. Major settlements follow, including, in 1995, reparations for the Waikato land confiscations.

» Memorial to the sunken ship, *Rainbow Warrior*

JENNY & TONY ENDERBY / GETTY IMAGES ©

Coming In, Coming Out

The 'recolonial' system was shaken several times after 1935, but managed to survive until 1973, when Mother England ran off and joined the Franco-German commune now known as the EU. NZ was beginning to develop alternative markets to Britain, and alternative exports to wool, meat and dairy products. Wide-bodied jet aircraft were allowing the world and NZ to visit each other on an increasing scale. NZ had only 36,000 tourists in 1960, compared with more than two million a year now. Women were beginning to penetrate first the upper reaches of the workforce and then the political sphere. Gay people came out of the closet, despite vigorous efforts by moral conservatives to push them back in. University-educated youths were becoming more numerous and more assertive.

From 1945, Maori experienced both a population explosion and massive urbanisation. In 1936, Maori were 17% urban and 83% rural. Fifty years later, these proportions had reversed. The immigration gates, which until 1960 were pretty much labelled 'whites only', widened, first to allow in Pacific Islanders for their labour, and then to allow in (East) Asians for their money. These transitions would have generated major socioeconomic change whatever happened in politics. But most New Zealanders associate the country's recent 'Big Shift' with the politics of 1984.

In 1984, NZ's third great reforming government was elected – the Fourth Labour government, led nominally by David Lange and in fact by Roger Douglas, the Minister of Finance. This government adopted an antinuclear foreign policy, delighting the left, and a more-market economic policy, delighting the right. NZ's numerous economic controls were dismantled with breakneck speed. Middle NZ was uneasy about the antinuclear policy, which threatened NZ's ANZUS alliance with Australia and the US. But in 1985, French spies sank the antinuclear protest ship *Rainbow Warrior* in Auckland Harbour, killing one crewman. The lukewarm American condemnation of the French act brought middle NZ in behind the antinuclear policy, which became associated with national independence. Other New Zealanders were uneasy about the more-market economic policy, but failed to come up with a convincing alternative. Revelling in their new freedom, NZ investors engaged in a frenzy of speculation, and suffered even more than the rest of the world from the economic crash of 1987.

The early 21st century is an interesting time for NZ. Food, wine, film and literature are flowering as never before, and the new ethnic mix is creating something very special in popular music. There are continuities, however – the pub, the sportsground, the quarter-acre section, the bush, the beach and the bach – and they too are part of the reason people like to come here. Realising that NZ has a great culture, and an intriguing history, as well as a great natural environment, will double the bang for your buck.

Scottish influence can still be felt in NZ, particularly in the south of the South Island. NZ has more Scottish pipe bands per capita than Scotland itself.

HISTORY COMING IN, COMING OUT

NZ's staunch antinuclear stance earned it the nickname 'The Mouse that Roared'.

1995	2004	2010	2011
Peter Blake and Russel Coutts win the Americas Cup for NZ, sailing *Black Magic*; red socks become a matter of national pride.	Maori TV begins broadcasting – for the first time, a channel committed to NZ content and the revitalisation of Maori language and culture hits the small screen.	A cave-in at Pike River coalmine on the South Island's West Coast kills 29 miners.	A severe earthquake strikes Christchurch, killing 185 people and badly damaging the central business district. NZ hosts (and wins!) the Rugby World Cup.

Environment

A small chip off the very old block of Gondwanaland, which broke away 85 million years ago, New Zealand's natural world is full of strange creatures, unique plants and peculiar landforms. Although it has been greatly altered during 1000 years of human occupation, it remains a wild and deeply intriguing place to visit, most notably in its national parks and marine reserves that enjoy a high level of protection. Environmentalists, however, have plenty to keep them occupied.

NZ is one of the most spectacular places in the world to see geysers. Rotorua's short-lived Waimangu geyser, formed after the Mt Tarawera eruption, was once the world's largest, often gushing to a dizzying height of 400m.

GEYSERS

The Land

NZ is a young country – its present shape is less than 10,000 years old. Having broken away from the supercontinent of Gondwanaland (which included Africa, Australia, Antarctica and South America) in a stately geological dance some 85 million years ago, it endured continual uplift and erosion, buckling and tearing, and the slow fall and rise of the sea as ice ages came and went. Straddling the boundary of two great colliding slabs of the earth's crust – the Pacific plate and the Indian/Australian plate – to this day NZ remains the plaything of nature's strongest forces.

The result is one of the most varied and spectacular series of landscapes in the world, ranging from snow-dusted mountains and drowned glacial valleys to rainforests, dunelands and an otherworldly volcanic plateau. It is a diversity of landforms you would expect to find across an entire continent rather than a small archipelago in the South Pacific.

A by-product of movement along the tectonic plate boundary is seismic activity – earthquakes. Not for nothing has NZ been called 'the Shaky Isles'. Most quakes only rattle the glassware, but one was indirectly responsible for creating an internationally celebrated tourist attraction...

In 1931 an earthquake measuring 7.9 on the Richter scale levelled the Hawke's Bay city of Napier, causing huge damage and loss of life. Napier was rebuilt almost entirely in the then-fashionable art-deco architectural style, and walking its streets today you can relive its brash exuberance in what has become a mecca for lovers of art deco.

However, the North Island doesn't have a monopoly on earthquakes. In September 2010 Christchurch was rocked by a magnitude 7.1 earthquake. Less than six months later, in February 2011, a magnitude 6.3 quake destroyed much of the city's historic heart and claimed 185 lives, making it the country's second-deadliest natural disaster.

The Great Southern Alps

Evidence of NZ's tumultuous past is everywhere. The South Island's mountainous spine – the 650km-long ranges of the Southern Alps – is a product of the clash of the two plates; the result of a process of rapid lifting that, if anything, is accelerating. Despite NZ's highest peak, Aoraki/Mt Cook, losing 10m from its summit overnight in a 1991 landslide, the Alps are on an express elevator that, without erosion and landslides, would see them 10 times their present height within a few million years.

The South Island also sees some evidence of volcanism – if the remains of the old volcanoes of Banks Peninsula weren't there to repel the sea, the vast Canterbury Plains, built from alpine sediment washed down the rivers from the Alps, would have eroded away long ago.

It is, however, the Southern Alps that dominate the landscape, dictating settlement patterns, throwing down engineering challenges and offering outstanding recreational opportunities. The island's mountainous backbone also helps shape the weather, as it stands in the path of the prevailing westerly winds that roll in, moisture-laden, from the Tasman Sea. As a result, bush-clad lower slopes of the western Southern Alps are among the wettest places on earth, with an annual precipitation of some 15,000mm. Having lost its moisture, the wind then blows dry across the eastern plains towards the Pacific coast.

An Island of Volcanoes

On the North Island, the most impressive changes have been wrought by volcanoes. Auckland is built on an isthmus peppered by scoria cones, on many of which you can still see the earthworks of *pa* (fortified villages) built by early Maori. The city's biggest and most recent volcano, 600-year-old Rangitoto Island, is just a short ferry ride from the downtown wharves. Some 300km further south, the classically shaped cone of snowcapped Mt Taranaki/Egmont overlooks tranquil dairy pastures.

But the real volcanic heartland runs through the centre of the North Island, from the restless bulk of Mt Ruapehu in Tongariro National Park

---

NEW ZEALAND ENVIRONMENTAL CARE CODE

Toitu te whenua (leave the land undisturbed). To support this approach, the Department of Conservation (DOC) has developed an Environmental Care Code that includes the following directives:

Protect plants & wildlife Treat forests and birds with care and respect; they are unique and often rare.

Remove rubbish Litter is unattractive, harmful to wildlife and can increase vermin and disease. Plan to reduce rubbish on your visit and carry out what you carry in.

Bury toilet waste In areas without toilet facilities, bury your toilet waste in a shallow hole well away from waterways, tracks, campsites and huts.

Keep streams & lakes clean When cleaning and washing, take the water and wash well away from the water source. Because soaps and detergents are harmful to water life, drain used water into the soil so it can be filtered.

Take care with stoves & fires Portable fuel stoves are less harmful to the environment and are more efficient than campfires. If you use a fire, keep it small, use only dead wood, put it out by dousing it with water and checking the ashes.

Camp carefully When camping, leave no trace of your visit.

Keep to the track By keeping to the track (where one exists) you lessen the chance of damaging fragile plants.

Consider others People visit the back country and rural areas for many reasons. Be considerate of others who also want to enjoy the environment.

Respect the country's cultural heritage Many places in NZ have a spiritual and historical significance. Treat these places with consideration and respect.

Enjoy your visit Take a last look before leaving an area; will the next visitor know you have been there?

Protect the environment This is important, for your own sake, for the sake of those who come after you and for the environment itself.

northeast through the Rotorua lake district out to NZ's most active volcano, White Island, in the Bay of Plenty. Called the Taupo Volcanic Zone, this great 250km-long rift valley – part of a volcano chain known as the 'Pacific Ring of Fire' – has been the seat of massive eruptions that have left their mark on the country physically and culturally.

Most spectacular were the eruptions that created Lake Taupo. Considered the world's most productive volcano in terms of the amount of material ejected, Taupo last erupted 1800 years ago in a display that was the most violent anywhere on the planet within the past 5000 years.

You can explore the North Island's volcanic landscapes on numerous tramps in the Tongariro and Egmont national parks. The former is home to three of the country's most famous volcanoes – Mt Ruapehu, Tongariro and Ngauruhoe (Mt Doom in the *Lord of the Rings* films), the peak of which can be bagged via a side trip on the world-famous Tongariro Alpine Crossing.

Egmont National Park is centred upon the near-symmetrical cone of Mt Taranaki, laced with tracks that go up, down and around the relatively young, quiescent volcano. To the northwest, within the park's bounds, you can also traverse the Pouakai and Kaitake ranges, deeply eroded volcanic stumps that were active between 250,000 and 600,000 years ago.

The North Island has a much more even rainfall than the South, and is spared the temperature extremes of the South, which can plunge when a wind blows in from Antarctica. The important thing to remember, especially if you are tramping at high altitude, is that NZ has a maritime climate. This means weather can change with lightning speed, catching out the unprepared.

Wildlife

NZ may be relatively young, geologically speaking, but its plants and animals go back a long way. The tuatara, for instance, an ancient reptile unique to these islands, is a Gondwanaland survivor closely related to the dinosaurs, while many of the distinctive flightless birds (ratites) have distant African and South American cousins.

B Heather and H Robertson's *Field Guide to the Birds of New Zealand* is a comprehensive guide for bird-watchers and a model of helpfulness for anyone even casually interested in the country's remarkable bird life.

Due to its long isolation, the country is a veritable warehouse of unique and varied wildlife, most of which is found nowhere else. And with separation of the landmass occurring before mammals appeared on the scene, birds and insects have evolved in spectacular ways to fill the gaps.

The now extinct flightless moa, the largest of which grew to 3.5m tall and weighed over 200kg, browsed open grasslands much as cattle do today (skeletons can be seen at Auckland Museum), while the smaller kiwi still ekes out a nocturnal living rummaging among forest leaf litter for insects and worms much as small mammals do elsewhere. One of the country's most ferocious-looking insects, the mouse-sized giant weta, meanwhile, has taken on a scavenging role elsewhere filled by rodents.

As one of the last places on earth to be colonised by humans, NZ was for millennia a safe laboratory for such risky evolutionary strategies, but with the arrival first of Maori and soon after Europeans, things went downhill fast.

Many endemic creatures, including moa and the huia, an exquisite songbird, were driven to extinction, and the vast forests were cleared for their timber and to make way for agriculture. Destruction of habitat and the introduction of exotic animals and plants have taken a terrible environmental toll and New Zealanders are now fighting a rearguard battle to save what remains.

Birds

The first Polynesian settlers found little in the way of land mammals – just two species of bat – but forests, plains and coasts alive with birds. Largely lacking the bright plumage found elsewhere, NZ's birds – like its endemic plants – have an understated beauty that does not shout for attention.

Many of NZ's bird species have been lost since the arrival of humans. However, conservation projects – governmental, NGO and community-run – operate from one end of the country to the other. Smaller projects involve initiatives such as pest-trapping and habitat

ENVIRONMENTAL ISSUES IN AOTEAROA NEW ZEALAND

Aotearoa New Zealand likes to sell itself as clean and green. We have the NZ Forest Accord to protect native forests. National parks and reserves now cover a third of the country. Marine reserves continue to pop up around the coast. Our antinuclear legislation seems unassailable. A closer look, however, reveals a dirtier picture.

NZ is one of the highest per-capita emitters of greenhouse gases. We are one of the most inefficient users of energy in the developed world. Public transport is negligible in most places. Add the ongoing battle in many communities to stop the pumping of sewage and toxic waste into waterways, a conflict often spearheaded by *tangata whenua* (Maori), and the 'clean and green' label looks a bit tarnished.

One of our challenges is that our biggest polluting sector is also our biggest export earner. Pastoral farming causes half of our greenhouse-gas emissions. Clearing forests to grow cows and sheep has left many hillsides scoured by erosion. Grazing animals damage stream edges and lake margins, and farm run-off has left many waterways unsafe for swimming or drinking. The worse culprit is dairy farming, and while regional councils and farming groups are fencing and planting stream banks to protect water quality, their efforts are outstripped by the sheer growth in dairying. Meanwhile, governments are reluctant to take on the powerful farming lobby.

Our other major challenge is around mining and drilling. The state-owned company Solid Energy plans to expand coalmining on the West Coast and convert lignite (the dirtiest form of coal) into fertiliser and diesel. The government is also encouraging overseas companies to prospect for offshore oil in what would be some of the deepest and most difficult waters for drilling in the world. Once again local *iwi* (tribes) such as Te Whanau a Apanui are in the front lines alongside environmental groups like Greenpeace, fighting to prevent the marine ecosystems of the East Coast being put at risk.

Despite these things, NZ has some good things going on. A high proportion of our energy is from renewable sources. Farm animals, except for pigs and chickens, are mostly grass fed and free range. We are getting better with waste minimisation and resource recovery. Like most countries, though, we need to make a stronger effort to develop not just sustainable, but regenerative economic systems.

Our biggest saving grace is our small population. As a result, Aotearoa is a place well worth visiting. This is a beautiful land with enormous geographical and ecological diversity. Our forests are unique and magnificent, and the bird species that evolved in response to an almost total lack of mammalian life are spectacular, although now reduced in numbers from introduced predators such as rats, stoats and hedgehogs.

Visitors who want to help protect our ecological integrity can make the biggest impact by asking questions of their hosts: every time you ask where the recycling centre is; every time you question wasteful energy use, car use and water use, and every time you ask for organic or free-range food at a cafe or restaurant, you affect the person you talk to.

Aotearoa New Zealand has the potential to be a world leader in ecological wisdom. We have a strong tradition to draw from – the careful relationship of reciprocity that Maori developed with the natural world over the course of many, many generations. We live at the edge of the Pacific, on the Rim of Fire, a remnant of the ancient forests of Gondwanaland. We welcome conscious travellers.

Nandor Tanczos is a social ecologist based in Ngaruawahia.
He was a Member of Parliament for the Green Party from 1999 to 2008.

restoration in urban parks and reserves. Larger projects (such as nation-wide possum-control measures) are usually managed by the Department of Conservation (DOC) or local authorities, with business and volunteer groups sometimes chipping in to help. A major contributor to the protection of birds is Forest & Bird, NZ's largest independent conservation organisation. For a selection of some of the birds you may encounter on the tracks and elsewhere, refer to our bird-spotting guide (p34).

National Parks

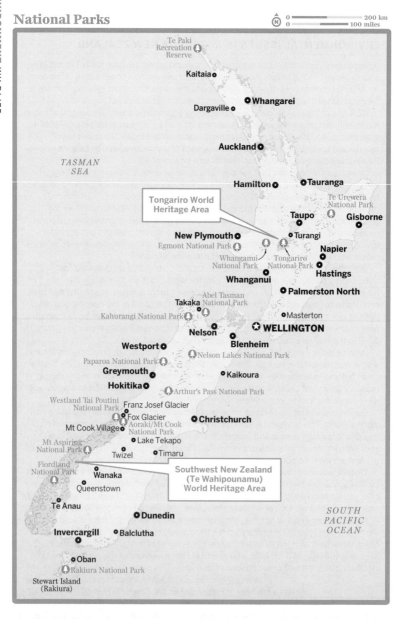

NZ'S NATIONAL PARKS & RESERVES

NZ has 14 national parks covering a total of 30,858 sq km, or just under 12% of the country's landmass. They embrace almost every conceivable landscape: from sparkling bays and lagoons to snow-topped volcanoes, and from thickly forested wildernesses to majestic mountains, glaciers and fiords.

According to *The National Parks Act* (1980), they 'contain scenery of such distinctive quality, ecological systems, or natural features so beautiful, unique, or scientifically important that their preservation is in the national interest.' We couldn't agree more, and Unesco seem to concur too, bestowing the honour of World Heritage status to five of them: Tongariro on the North Island, and Fiordland, Westland Tai Poutini, Aoraki/Mt Cook and Mt Aspiring that make up the South Island's Te Wahipounamu.

NZ's national parks, from north to south:

➡ Te Urewera

➡ Tongariro

➡ Whanganui

➡ Egmont

➡ Kahurangi

➡ Abel Tasman

➡ Nelson Lakes

➡ Paparoa

➡ Arthur's Pass

➡ Westland Tai Poutini

➡ Aoraki/Mt Cook

➡ Mt Aspiring

➡ Fiordland

➡ Rakiura

Joining these national parks are three marine parks, more than 30 marine reserves, 19 forest parks and hundreds of regional parks and reserves, together offering huge scope for wilderness experiences, ranging from climbing, snow skiing and mountain biking to tramping, kayaking and trout fishing.

Plants

No visitor to NZ (particularly Australians!) will go for long without hearing about the damage done to the bush by that bad-mannered Australian import, the brush-tailed possum. The long list of mammal pests introduced to NZ accidentally or for a variety of misguided reasons includes deer, rabbits, stoats, pigs and goats. But the most destructive by far is the possum, 70 million of which now chew through millions of tonnes of foliage a year despite the best efforts of the DOC to control them.

Among favoured possum food are NZ's most colourful trees: the kowhai, a small-leaved tree growing to 11m, that in spring has drooping clusters of bright-yellow flowers (NZ's national flower); the pohutukawa, a beautiful coastal tree of the northern North Island that bursts into vivid red flower in December, earning the nickname 'Christmas tree'; and a similar crimson-flowered tree, the rata. Rata species are found on both islands; the northern rata starts life as a climber on a host tree (that it eventually chokes).

The few remaining pockets of mature centuries-old kauri are stately emblems of former days. Their vast hammered trunks and towering, epiphyte-festooned limbs, which dwarf every other tree in the forest, are reminders of why they were sought after in colonial days for spars and building timber. The best place to see the remaining giants is Northland's Waipoua Kauri Forest, home to three-quarters of the country's surviving kauri. You can also get up close to these behemoths of the botanical world along the Aoetea Track on Great Barrier Island and in Coromandel's Kauaeranga Valley.

Now the pressure has been taken off kauri and other timber trees, including the distinctive rimu (red pine) and the long-lived totara (favoured for Maori war canoes), by one of the country's most successful imports – *Pinus radiata*. Pine was found to thrive in NZ, growing to maturity in just 35 years, and plantation forests are now widespread through the central North Island – the Southern Hemisphere's biggest, Kaingaroa Forest, lies southeast of Rotorua.

You won't get far into the bush without coming across one of its most prominent features – tree ferns. NZ is a land of ferns (more than 80 species) and most easily recognised are the mamaku (black tree fern) – which grows to 20m and can be seen in damp gullies throughout the country – and the 10m-high ponga (silver tree fern), with its distinctive white underside. The silver fern is equally at home as part of corporate logos and on the clothing of many of the country's top sportspeople.

The only native palm in NZ is the nikau, with its spiky, geometric fronds and bulbous seed pods. A profusion of these attractive plants can be seen on the Heaphy Track in Kahurangi National Park.

NZ's alpine zones support a wide range of plant species, of which a high proportion is endemic. The bushline, usually marked by the upper limit of beech trees, varies from 1500m on Mt Ruapehu down to about 900m in Fiordland. Above the bush, alpine scrub merges into snow tussock, which in turn merges, in wetter areas, into alpine herb fields. In drier regions tussock grassland is often found almost unmixed with other plant types. Higher still, plant cover becomes sparse and a number of specialised communities are found, including fellfield, scree, cushion vegetation and, near high ridges and summits, snow-bank vegetation.

For a comprehensive history of NZ conservation and insight into 'where to from here', you can't go past the landmark tome *New Zealand's Wilderness Heritage*, written and photographed by three pre-eminent fellows of the realm: Les Molloy, Craig Potton and Rod Morris.

Survival Guide

DIRECTORY A–Z....342

Accommodation........ 342

Children 346

Climate................ 346

Customs Regulations ... 347

Electricity 347

Embassies &
Consulates 347

Food & Drink........... 348

Health................. 348

Insurance.............. 349

Internet Access......... 349

Money................. 349

Opening Hours 350

Post................... 350

Public Holidays......... 350

Safe Travel............351

Telephone 351

Time 352

Visas.................. 352

Visitor Information
Centres 352

Women Travellers....... 353

Work.................. 353

TRANSPORT.......354

GETTING THERE &
AWAY 354

Entering the Country.... 354

Air 354

Sea 355

GETTING AROUND.......356

Air 356

Bicycle 356

Boat 357

Bus 357

Car & Motorcycle.......357

Hitching &
Ride-Sharing........... 360

Local Transport......... 360

Train 360

GLOSSARY 361

Directory A–Z

Accommodation

Across New Zealand, you can bed down in historic guesthouses, facility laden hotels, uniform motel units, beautifully situated campsites, and hostels that range in character from clean-living to tirelessly party-prone.

If you're travelling during peak tourist seasons, book your bed well in advance. Accommodation is most in demand (and at its priciest) during the summer holidays from Christmas to late January, at Easter, and during winter in snowy resort towns such as Queenstown.

Visitor information centres provide reams of local accommodation information, and most can make bookings on your behalf.

For online listings, visit **Automobile Association** (AA; ☑ 0800 500 444; www.aa.co.nz) and **Jasons** (www.jasons.com). The **Department of Conservation** (DOC; www.doc.govt.nz) is the best re-

source for on-the-track accommodation.

B&Bs

Bed-and-breakfast (B&B) accommodation is popular, popping up in the middle of cities, in rural hamlets and on stretches of isolated coastline. Rooms can be in everything from suburban bungalows to stately manors owned by the same family for generations.

Breakfast may be 'continental' (cereal, fruit, toast and tea or coffee), or a stomach-loading cooked meal including eggs, bacon and sausages. Some B&B hosts may also cook dinner for guests and advertise dinner, bed and breakfast (DB&B) packages.

B&B tariffs are typically in the $120 to $180 bracket (per double), though some places charge upwards of $300 per double.

Online resources:

Bed & Breakfast Book (www.bnb.co.nz)

Bed and Breakfast Directory (www.bed-and-breakfast.co.nz)

Camping & Campervans

FREEDOM CAMPING

Never just assume it's OK to camp somewhere. Check at the local i-SITE or DOC office, or with commercial holiday parks. If you are freedom camping, ensure you are fully self-contained and treat the area with respect. Instant fines can apply for camping in prohibited areas, or for irresponsible disposal of waste. For more freedom camping info see www.camping.org.nz.

HOLIDAY PARKS

Campers and campervan drivers alike converge upon NZ's hugely popular 'holiday parks', slumbering peacefully in powered and unpowered sites, cheap bunk rooms (dorm rooms), cabins and self-contained units that are often called motels or tourist flats. Well-equipped communal kitchens, dining areas and games and TV rooms often feature. In cities, holiday parks are usually a fair way from the action, but in smaller towns they can be impressively central or near lakes, beaches, rivers and forests.

The nightly cost of holiday-park camping is usually between $15 and $20 per adult, with children charged half price; powered sites are a couple of dollars more. Cabin/unit accommodation normally ranges from $60

SLEEPING PRICE RANGES

The following price ranges refer to a double room in high season. Price ranges generally increase by 20% to 25% in the nation's largest cities (Auckland, Wellington and Christchurch) and some busy tourist areas.

$ less than $100

$$ $100–200

$$$ more than $200

DEPARTMENT OF CONSERVATION (DOC) HUTS & CAMPSITES

Huts

DOC maintains a network of more than 950 huts in its national parks, conservation areas and reserves. The majority of these operate on a first-come, first-served basis and fall into three categories, paid for with Backcountry Hut Passes or hut tickets (which you purchase before your trip):

Serviced Huts (www.doc.govt.nz; $15) Equipped with mattresses, water supply, toilets, hand-washing facilities and heating with fuel available; may have gas cooking facilities, and a warden.

Standard Huts (www.doc.govt.nz; $5) Mattresses, water supply and toilets; wood heaters are provided at huts below the bushline.

Basic Huts (www.doc.govt.nz; free) Or 'Bivvy' – very basic enclosed shelter with limited facilities.

There are two other categories of huts. **Great Walk Huts** ($15-52, varies by season) are the most comfortable, with mattresses, water supply, toilets, hand washing facilities and heating with fuel available. They may have solar lighting, gas cooking facilities and a hut warden. Bookings are essential and can be made via **Great Walks Bookings** (☏0800 694 732; www.greatwalks.co.nz; per night $54) or in person at any DOC Visitor Centre. Most of these huts revert to Serviced or Standard Huts out of the Great Walk season.

There are also private club huts that are open to the public, such as those owned by the New Zealand Alpine Club (NZAC). These have mattresses, a water supply, toilets and hand-washing facilities. They may have heating and cooking facilities. Backcountry Hut Passes and hut tickets are generally not valid at club huts and bookings may be required.

Campsites

There are also plenty of campsites throughout the DOC estate, which are either paid for in cash when you arrive at the campsite, or to a camp warden, or in some cases when you book via www.doc.govt.nz. They fall into the following categories:

Backcountry campsites (free) – with toilets and a water supply, which may be from a stream. They may have picnic tables, cooking shelters or fireplaces.

Basic campsites (free) – very limited facilities so you need to be fully self-sufficient. There are basic toilets and water from a tank, stream or lake. Access may be by road or boat.

Standard campsite ($6) – with toilets (usually the composting or pit variety), water supply (tap, stream or lake) and vehicle or boat access. Wood barbecues and fireplaces, showers (cold), picnic tables, a cooking shelter and rubbish bins may be provided.

Scenic campsite ($10) – located in high-use locations, these have toilets, tap water supply and vehicle or boat access. Wood barbecues and fireplaces, cold showers, picnic tables, a cooking shelter and rubbish bins may be provided.

Serviced campsite ($15) – with flush toilets, tap water, kitchen/cooking bench, hot showers, rubbish collection and road access for all types of vehicles. Laundry facilities, barbecues, fireplaces, cookers and picnic tables may be available.

In addition, all Great Walks (except Milford) have **Great Walk Campsites** (www.doc. govt.nz; $6-18) near huts or in designated areas. There are nearly 60 Great Walk Campsites offering basic facilities including toilets, handwashing sinks and a water supply. Some have picnic tables and cooking shelters. These are very popular and must be booked in advance.

Backcountry camping where there are no facilities is permitted on most tracks (excluding Great Walks). You can also camp near huts, and use their water and toilet facilities, although camping outside a Serviced Hut costs $5.

HUT ETIQUETTE

Located everywhere from deep forest to mountain high, DOC's backcountry huts are a very special part of the NZ tramping experience. Using them is a privilege and a pleasure – as long as everyone follows a few simple guidelines.

Share the Bunks

When huts are crowded, everybody needs to shift across on the platform bunks and share the mattresses. Nobody wants to sleep on the bare floor. It's important to remember that purchasing a hut ticket does not guarantee you a bunk.

Be Quiet in the Evening & Early Morning

Huts in the middle of the bush are not places for blaring radios, excessive drinking or all-night partying. Be considerate of trampers who hit the sack early or sleep in late. Try to minimise your use of torches at night and early in the morning.

Pack Out Rubbish

Carry out your rubbish and do not leave half-burnt trash in the fireplace. In almost every hut, signs urge trampers to 'pack it in and pack it out'.

Replace Firewood

Wood stoves in huts are primarily for heat on cold nights. If you must light a fire, make sure to restock the wood box with both kindling and logs for the next party, who may arrive wet and cold.

Conserve Water

Most huts are equipped with rainwater tanks, which can run dry during hot summers. Use water sparingly and do not use soap to bathe in nearby rivers and lakes.

Keep Huts Clean

Leave muddy boots and gaiters outside. Before leaving in the morning, clean the counters and tables and sweep the floor.

Pack Ear Plugs

In larger huts along popular tracks, somebody will inevitably snore at night. If you're a light sleeper, pack earplugs.

Pay Your Hut Fees!

Huts in NZ are extremely affordable. But to maintain the system, everybody – locals and overseas visitors alike – needs to pay for the privilege either with hut tickets or a pass.

to $120 per double. Unless noted otherwise, the prices we list for campsites, campervan sites, huts and cabins are for two people during the summer months. The 'big three' holiday park operators around NZ – Top 10, Kiwi Parks and Family Parks – all offer discount cards for loyal visitors. Most decent commercial camping grounds are members of the **Holiday Parks Association of New Zealand** (www.holidayparks. co.nz).

Farmstays

Farmstays open the door on the agricultural side of NZ life, with visitors encouraged to get some dirt beneath their fingernails at orchards, and dairy, sheep and cattle farms. Costs can vary widely, with B&Bs generally ranging from $80 to $120. Some farms have separate cottages where you can fix your own food, while others offer low-cost, shared, backpacker-style accommodation.

Farm Helpers in NZ (FHINZ; www.fhinz.co.nz) produces a booklet ($25) that lists around 350 NZ farms providing lodging in exchange for four to six hours' work per day. **Rural Holidays NZ** (www.ruralholidays. co.nz) lists farmstays and country homestays throughout NZ on its website.

Hostels

NZ is packed to the rafters with backpacker hostels, both independent and part of large chains, ranging from small, homestay-style affairs with a handful of beds to refurbished hotels and towering modern structures in the big cities. Non-member rates for a hostel bed usually range between $25 and $35 per night.

Online, www.hostelworld. com is useful for pre-trip planning.

Budget Backpacker Hostels (www.bbh.co.nz) NZ's biggest hostel group, with almost 300 hostels on its books, including homestays and farmstays. Membership costs $45 and entitles you to stay at member hostels at rates listed in the annual (free) *BBH World Traveller Accommodation* booklet. Nonmembers pay an extra $3 per night, though not all hostel owners charge the difference. Pick up a membership card from any member hostel, or have one mailed to you overseas for $50 (see the website for details).

YHA New Zealand (Youth Hostels Association; www. yha.co.nz) YHA has around 50 hostels in prime NZ locations. It's part of the Hostelling International (HI; www.hihostels.com) network, so if you're already an HI member in your own country, membership entitles you to use NZ hostels. You can buy a year-long membership card at major NZ YHA hostels for $42 (free for under-18s), or book online and have your card mailed to you overseas for the same price. Hostels also take non-YHA members for an extra $3 per night. NZ YHA hostels also supply bed linen.

Nomads Backpackers (www.nomadsworld.com) Eight franchises throughout NZ: Auckland (two), Rotorua, Waitomo, Taupo, Wellington, Kaiteriteri and Queenstown. Membership costs AUD$37 for 12 months and gives you various discounts and one free night's accommodation.

Base Backpackers (www. stayatbase.com) A chain with eight hostels around NZ. Expect clean dorms, women-only areas and party opportunities aplenty. Offers a 10-night 'Base Jumping' accommodation card for $239, bookable online.

BOOK YOUR STAY ONLINE

For more accommodation reviews by Lonely Planet authors, check out http://lonelyplanet.com/new-zealand/hotels. You'll find independent reviews, as well as recommendations on the best places to stay. Best of all, you can book online.

Hotels, Motels & Pubs
HOTELS

At the top end of the hotel scale are five-star international chains, resort complexes and architecturally splendorous boutique hotels, all of which charge a hefty premium for their mod cons, snappy service and/or historic opulence. We quote 'rack rates' (official advertised rates) for such places, but discounts and special deals often mean you won't have to pay these prices.

MOTELS

NZ's towns have a glut of nondescript, low-rise motels and 'motor lodges', charging between $80 and $180 for double rooms. They tend to be squat structures congregating just outside CBDs, or skulking by highways on the edges of towns. Most are modernish (though decor is often mired in the '90s) and have similar facilities, namely tea- and coffee-making equipment, fridge and TV. Prices vary with standards.

PUBS

The least expensive form of NZ hotel accommodation is the humble pub. As is often the case elsewhere, some of NZ's old pubs are full of character (and characters), while others are grotty, ramshackle places that are best avoided, especially by women travelling solo. Also check whether there's a band cranking out tunes the night you plan to be in town, as you could be in for a sleepless night. In the cheapest pubs, singles/doubles might cost as little as $30/60 (with a shared bathroom down the hall), though $50/80 is more common.

Rental Accommodation

The basic Kiwi holiday home is called a 'bach' (short for 'bachelor', as they were often used by single men as hunting and fishing hideouts); in Otago and Southland they're known as 'cribs'. These are simple self-contained cottages that can be rented, in rural and coastal areas, often in isolated locations. Prices are typically $80 to $130

BACKCOUNTRY HUT PASSES & TICKETS

With some exceptions (Great Walk huts and campsites, huts owned by the NZ Alpine Club, and vehicle-accessible Serviced, Scenic and Standard campsites), huts and campsites are paid for with Backcountry Hut tickets and passes. These should be purchased in advance online, or at DOC offices, visitor centres or outdoor supplies shops.

It costs $5 per hut ticket. You simply deposit the appropriate number of ticket butts in the box at the hut when you arrive. If you plan to do a lot of tramping, a Backcountry Hut Pass (one year/six months $122/92), valid for Serviced and Standard Huts, might prove a wise investment.

PRACTICALITIES

→ **DVDs** Kiwi DVDs are encoded for Region 4, which includes Mexico, South America, Central America, Australia, the Pacific and the Caribbean.

→ **Electricity** To plug yourself into the electricity supply (230V AC, 50Hz), use a three-pin adaptor (the same as in Australia; different from British three-pin adaptors).

→ **News** Leaf through Auckland's *New Zealand Herald*, Wellington's *Dominion Post* or Christchurch's *The Press* newspapers, or check out www.stuff.co.nz.

→ **Radio** Tune in to Radio National for current affairs and Concert FM for classical and jazz (see www. radionz.co.nz for frequencies). Kiwi FM (www.kiwifm. co.nz) showcases NZ music; Radio Hauraki (www. hauraki.co.nz) cranks out classic rock (the national appetite for Fleetwood Mac is insatiable...).

→ **TV** Watch one of the national government-owned TV stations (TV One, TV2, TVNZ 6, Maori TV and the 100% Maori language Te Reo) or the subscriber-only Sky TV (www.skytv.co.nz).

→ **Weights and measures** NZ uses the metric system.

per night, which isn't bad for a whole house or self-contained bungalow.

For more upmarket holiday houses, the current trend is to throw rusticity to the wind and erect luxurious cottages on beautiful nature-surrounded plots. Expect to pay anything from $130 to $400 per double.

Online resources:

→ www.holidayhomes.co.nz

→ www.bookabach.co.nz

→ www.holidayhouses.co.nz

→ www.nzapartments.co.nz

Children

Thanks in part to its hut system and range of tracks, NZ is well suited for a tramping holiday with children. Along some tracks, such as the Heaphy, Routeburn and Lake Waikaremoana, it would be unusual not to have kids in the huts each night.

The huts mean that children (and parents) can carry less gear and start each day with dry clothes, ensuring a comfortable experience in the bush. DOC also encourages families to go tramping by not charging children under the age of 11 for huts or campsites, and offering a 50% discount to older kids.

The key to a successful tramp with kids is to carefully select the track to match their level of endurance. Children younger than 10 years do best on tracks that are well benched and bridged, and where the next hut is only four or five hours away at most. An alternative for parents with very young children (ages four to six) not up for the rigours of tramping every day is to use a hut as a base camp, taking them on day walks.

The other important thing about tramping with children is to make sure you pack enough food. After a day outdoors, parents are often shocked to see their children consume twice as much as they would at home.

For helpful general tips, see Lonely Planet's *Travel with Children*.

Climate

Lying between 34°S and 47°S, NZ is squarely in the 'Roaring Forties' latitude – meaning it has a prevailing and continual wind blowing over it from west to east, ranging from gentle freshening breezes to occasional raging winter gales. Coming across the Tasman Sea, this breeze is relatively warm and moisture-laden. When it hits NZ's mountains the wind is swept upwards, where it cools and dumps its moisture. When the wind comes from the south (from Antarctica) it's icy cold – a southerly wind always means cold weather.

Rainfall The South and North Islands, because of their different geological features, have two distinct patterns of rainfall. On the South Island the Southern Alps act as a barrier for the moisture-laden winds coming across the Tasman Sea. This creates a wet climate on the western side of the mountains and a dry climate on the eastern side; annual rainfall is more than 7500mm in parts of the west but only about 330mm across some of the east, even though it's not far away. On the North Island, the western sides of the high volcanoes also get a lot more rain than the eastern sides, although since there's no complete barrier (as there is in the Southern Alps) the rain shadow is not as pronounced. Rainfall is more evenly distributed over the North Island, averaging around 1300mm per year. On the North Island rain falls throughout the year; typically, rainy days alternate with fine days, which is enough to keep the landscape perennially green.

Snow Snow is mostly seen in the mountains, and it can snow above the bushline any time of year. However, in the South Island there can also be snowfalls at sea level in winter, particularly in the far south.

Regional variations The South Island is a few degrees cooler than the North Island. It's quite warm and pleasant in Northland (the far north of the North Island) at any time of year; it's almost always a few degrees warmer than the rest of the country. Higher altitudes are always considerably cooler, and it's usually windy in Wellington, which catches winds blowing through Cook Strait in a sort of wind tunnel from the Tasman Sea to the Pacific Ocean.

Unpredictability One of the most important things trampers need to know about NZ's climate is that it's a maritime climate, rather than the continental climate typical of larger land masses. This means the weather can change with amazing rapidity.

Customs Regulations

For the low-down on what you can and can't bring into NZ, see the **New Zealand Customs Service** (www.customs.govt.nz) website. Per-person duty-free allowances:

➡ Three bottles of spirits or liqueur (each containing not more than 1125mL)

➡ 4.5L of wine or beer

➡ 200 cigarettes (or 50 cigars or 250g of tobacco)

➡ Dutiable goods up to the value of $700.
Customs are serious about bio-security and keeping out any diseases that may harm NZ's agricultural industry. Tramping gear such as boots and tents will be checked and may need to be cleaned before being allowed in. You must declare any plant or animal products (including anything made of wood), and food of any kind. You'll also come under greater scrutiny if you've arrived via Africa, Southeast Asia or South America. Weapons and firearms are either prohibited or require a permit and safety testing.

Electricity

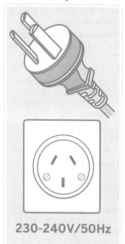

230-240V/50Hz

Embassies & Consulates

Most principal diplomatic representations to NZ are in Wellington, with a few in Auckland.

Remember that while in NZ you are bound by NZ laws. Your embassy will not be sympathetic if you end up in jail after committing a crime locally, even if such actions are legal in your own country.

In genuine emergencies you may get some assistance, but only if other channels have been exhausted. For example, if you need to get home urgently, a free ticket is unlikely as the embassy would expect you to have insurance. If you have

Auckland

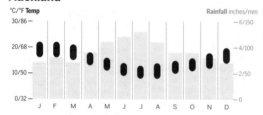

Christchurch

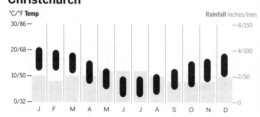

Queenstown

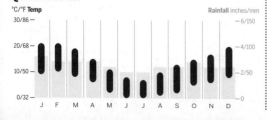

all your money and documents stolen, it might assist with getting a new passport, but a loan for onward travel is out of the question.

Embassies, consulates and high commissions include the following:

Australian High Commission (☑04-473 6411; www. australia.org.nz; 72-76 Hobson St, Thorndon, Wellington)

Canadian High Commission (☑04-473 9577; www. newzealand.gc.ca; L11, 125 The Terrace, Wellington)

Chinese Embassy (☑04-4742 9631; www.chinaembassy. org.nz; 2-6 Glenmore St, Kelburn, Wellington)

Fijian High Commission (☑04-473 5401; www.fiji.org. nz; 31 Pipitea St, Thorndon, Wellington)

French Embassy (☑04-384 2555; www.ambafrance-nz.org; 34-42 Manners St, Wellington)

German Embassy (☑04-473 6063; www.wellington. diplo.de; 90-92 Hobson St, Thorndon, Wellington)

Irish Consulate (☑09-977 2252; www.ireland.co.nz; L3, National Bank Tower, 205 Queens St, Auckland)

Israeli Embassy (☑04-439 9500; http://embassies.gov.il/ wellington; L13, Bayleys Building, 36 Brandon St, Wellington)

Japanese Embassy (☑04-473 1540; www.nz.emb-japan. go.jp; L18, The Majestic Centre, 100 Willis St, Wellington)

Netherlands Embassy (☑04-471 6390; http:// newzealand.nlembassy.org; L10, Cooperative Bank Building, cnr

---

EATING PRICE RANGES

The following price ranges refer to the cost of a main meal:

$ less than $15

$$ $15 to $32

$$$ more than $32

Featherston & Ballance Sts, Wellington)

UK High Commission (☑04-924 2888; www.gov.uk; 44 Hill St, Thorndon, Wellington)

US Embassy (☑04-462 6000; http://newzealand. usembassy.gov; 29 Fitzherbert Tce, Thorndon, Wellington)

Food & Drink

The NZ foodie scene once slavishly reflected Anglo-Saxon stodge, but nowadays the country's restaurants and cafes are adept at throwing together traditional staples (lamb, beef, venison, green-lipped mussels) with Asian, European and pan-Pacific flair.

Eateries themselves range from fry-'em-up fish-and-chip shops and pub bistros, to cafes drowned in faux-European, grungy or retro stylings, to restaurant-bars with full à-la-carte service, to fine-dining establishments with linen so crisp you'll be afraid to prop your elbows on it

On the liquid front, NZ wine is world class (especially sauvignon blanc and pinot noir), and you'll be hard-pressed to find a NZ town of any size without decent espresso. NZ's craft beer scene (www.soba.org. nz) is also riding a wave of popularity.

Most large urban centres have at least one dedicated vegetarian cafe or restaurant. See the **New Zealand Vegetarian Society** (www.vegsoc. org.nz) restaurant guide for listings. Beyond this, almost all restaurants and cafes offer vegetarian menu choices (although sometimes only one or two). Many eateries also provide gluten-free and vegan options.

Most small and medium-sized NZ towns will have at least one supermarket (New World, Pak 'n Save or Count-down, for example) with a wide selection of reasonably

priced food. When planning for a tramp try to make sure you stock up where there is a decent supermarket rather than relying on a small corner shop or dairy.

There are more than 50 farmers markets held around NZ, usually at weekends. These are excellent places to meet local producers and source fresh regional produce. Check out www. farmersmarkets.org.nz for details.

Health

NZ is one of the healthiest countries in the world in which to travel. Diseases such as malaria and typhoid are unheard of, and the absence of poisonous snakes or other dangerous animals makes this a very safe region to get off the beaten track and out into the beautiful countryside.

Before You Go
MEDICATIONS

Bring medications in their original, clearly labelled containers. A signed and dated letter from your physician describing your medical conditions and medications, including generic names, is also a good idea. If carrying syringes or needles, be sure to have a physician's letter documenting their medical necessity.

VACCINATIONS

NZ has no vaccination requirements for any traveller, but the World Health Organization recommends that all travellers be covered for diphtheria, tetanus, measles, mumps, rubella, chickenpox and polio, as well as hepatitis B, regardless of their destination. Ask your doctor for an International Certificate of Vaccination (or 'the yellow booklet'), which will list all the vaccinations you've received.

In New Zealand

Health insurance is essential for all travellers. While health care in NZ is of a high quality and not overly expensive by international standards, considerable costs can be built up and repatriation can be extremely expensive.

NZ does not have a government-funded system of public hospitals. But all travellers are covered for medical care resulting from accidents that occur while in NZ (eg motor-vehicle accidents, adventure-activity accidents) by the Accident Compensation Corporation (ACC; www.acc.co.nz). Costs incurred due to treatment of a medical illness that occurs while in NZ will only be covered by travel insurance. For more details, see www.moh.govt.nz.

The 24-hour, free-call **Healthline** (☑0800 611 116; www.healthline.govt.nz) offers health advice throughout NZ.

Insurance

A watertight travel-insurance policy covering theft, loss and medical problems is essential. Some policies specifically exclude designated 'dangerous activities' such as scuba diving, parasailing, bungy jumping, white-water rafting, motorcycling, skiing and even tramping. If you plan on doing any of these things (a distinct possibility in NZ), make sure the policy you choose covers you fully.

You may prefer a policy that pays doctors or hospitals directly rather than you having to pay on the spot and claim later. If you have to claim later, make sure you keep all documentation. Some policies ask you to call back (reverse charges) to a centre in your home country where an immediate assessment of your problem is made. Check that the policy covers ambulances and emergency medical evacuations by air.

It's worth mentioning that under NZ law, you cannot sue for personal injury (other than exemplary damages). Instead, the country's Accident Compensation Corporation administers an accident compensation scheme that provides accident insurance for NZ residents and visitors to the country, regardless of fault. This scheme does not cancel out the necessity for your own comprehensive travel-insurance policy, as it doesn't cover you for such things as loss of income or treatment in your home country or ongoing illness.

Internet Access

Getting online in NZ is easy in all but the most remote locales. You will still find internet cafes in the bigger urban centres but they are generally on the wane. Your best bet for connecting without your own device is at your accommodation or the local public library.

Wi-fi is popping up all over the country, from hotel rooms to pub beer gardens to hostel dining rooms. Usually you have to be a guest or customer to access the internet at these locations – you'll be issued with a code, a wink and a secret handshake to enable you to get online. Sometimes it's free; sometimes there's a charge.

The country's main telecommunications company is Telecom New Zealand (www.telecom.co.nz) which has wireless hotspots around the country. If you have a wi-fi-enabled device, you can purchase a Telecom wireless prepaid card from participating hot spots. Alternatively, you can purchase a prepaid number from the login page at any wireless hotspot using your credit card. See the website for hotspot listings.

If you've brought your palmtop or notebook computer, you might consider buying a prepay USB modem (a 'dongle') with a local SIM card: both Telecom and Vodafone (www.vodafone.co.nz) sell these from around $80.

Money

ATMs & EFTPOS

Branches of the country's major banks, including the Bank of New Zealand, ANZ, Westpac and ASB, have 24-hour ATMs that accept cards from other banks and provide access to overseas accounts. You won't find ATMs everywhere, but they're widespread across both islands.

Many NZ businesses use electronic funds transfer at point of sale (EFTPOS), a convenient service that allows you to use your bank card (credit or debit) to pay directly for services or purchases, and often withdraw cash as well. EFTPOS is available practically everywhere, even in places where it's a long way between banks.

Bank Accounts

We've heard mixed reports on how easy it is for non-residents to open a bank account in NZ. Some sources say it's as simple as flashing a few pieces of ID, providing a temporary postal address (or your permanent address) and then waiting a few days while your request is processed. Other sources say that many banks won't allow visitors to open an account unless they're planning to stay in NZ for at least six months, or unless the application is accompanied by some proof of employment. Bank websites are also rather vague on the services offered to short-term visitors. If you think you'll need to open an account, do your homework before you arrive in the country and be prepared to shop around to get the best deal.

Credit & Debit Cards

Perhaps the safest place to keep your NZ travelling money is inside a plastic card! The most flexible option is to carry both a credit and a debit card.

CREDIT CARDS

Credit cards (Visa, MasterCard etc) are widely accepted for everything from a hostel bed to a bungy jump. Credit cards are pretty much essential if you want to hire a car. They can also be used for over-the-counter cash advances at banks and from ATMs, depending on the card, but be aware that such transactions incur charges. Diners Club and Amex cards are not as widely accepted.

DEBIT CARDS

Apart from losing them, the obvious danger with credit cards is maxing out your limit and going home to a steaming pile of debt. A safer option is a debit card, with which you can draw money directly from your home bank account using ATMs, banks or Eftpos machines. Any card connected to the international banking network (Cirrus, Maestro, Visa Plus and Eurocard) should work, provided you know your PIN. Fees for using your card at a foreign bank or ATM vary depending on your home bank; ask before you leave. Companies such as Travelex offer debit cards (Travelex calls them Cash Passport cards) with set withdrawal fees and a balance you can top up from your personal bank account while on the road – nice one!

Currency

NZ's currency is the NZ dollar, comprising 100 cents. There are 10c, 20c, 50c, $1 and $2 coins, and $5, $10, $20, $50 and $100 notes. Prices are often still marked in single cents and then rounded to the nearest 10c when you hand over your money.

Moneychangers

Changing foreign currency or travellers cheques is usually no problem at banks throughout NZ or at licensed moneychangers such as Travelex in the major cities. Moneychangers can be found in all major tourist areas, cities and airports.

Taxes & Refunds

The Goods and Services Tax (GST) is a flat 15% tax on all domestic goods and services. Prices include GST. There's no GST refund available when you leave NZ.

Tipping

Tipping is completely optional in NZ – the total at the bottom of a restaurant bill is all you need to pay (note that sometimes there's an additional service charge). That said, it's totally acceptable to reward good service – between 5% and 10% of the bill is fine.

Travellers Cheques

Amex, Travelex and other international brands of travellers cheques are a bit old-fashioned these days, but they're easily exchanged at banks and moneychangers. Present your passport for identification when cashing them; shop around for the best rates/lowest fees.

Opening Hours

Note that most attractions close on Christmas Day and Good Friday.

Shops and businesses 9am to 5.30pm Monday to Friday, and 9am to 12.30pm or 5pm Saturday. Late-night shopping (until 9pm) in larger cities on Thursday and/or Friday nights. Sunday trading in most big towns and cities.

Supermarkets 8am to 7pm, often 9pm or later in cities.

Banks 9.30am to 4.30pm Monday to Friday; limited number of city branches also open Saturday mornings.

Post offices 8.30am to 5pm Monday to Friday; larger branches also 9.30am to 1pm Saturday. Postal desks in newsagents open later.

Restaurants Food served until 9pm, often until 11pm on Fridays and Saturdays.

Cafes 7am to 4pm or 5pm.

Pubs Noon until late; food from noon to 2pm and from 6pm to 8pm.

Post

The services offered by **New Zealand Post** (✆0800 501 501; www.nzpost.co.nz) are reliable and reasonably inexpensive. Within NZ, standard postage is 70c for regular letters and postcards, and $1.40 for larger letters.

International destinations are divided into two zones: Australia and the South Pacific, and the rest of the world. The standard rate for postcards is $1.90 worldwide, and for letters it's $1.90 to Australia and the South Pacific and $2.40 elsewhere. Express rates are also available. Check out the incredibly precise calculator on the website for more details, including info on parcels.

Public Holidays

NZ's main public holidays:

New Year 1 and 2 January

Waitangi Day 6 February

Easter Good Friday and Easter Monday; March/April

Anzac Day 25 April

Queen's Birthday First Monday in June

Labour Day Fourth Monday in October

Christmas Day 25 December

Boxing Day 26 December

In addition, each NZ province has its own anniversary-day holiday. The dates of these vary – when they fall on Friday to Sunday, they're usually observed the following Monday; if they fall on Tuesday to Thursday, they're held on the preceding Monday. See www.dol.govt.nz for a list.

The Christmas holiday season, from mid-December

to late January, is part of the summer school vacation. It's the time you're most likely to find transport and accommodation booked out, and the odd long, grumpy queue at tourist attractions. There are three shorter school-holiday periods during the year: from mid- to late April, early to mid-July, and mid-September to early October. For exact dates see www. minedu.govt.nz.

Safe Travel

Violent crime Although it's no more dangerous than other developed countries, violent crime does happen in NZ, so it's worth taking sensible precautions on the streets at night or if staying in remote areas. Gang culture permeates some parts of the country; give any black-jacketed, insignia-wearing groups a wide berth.

Theft Theft from cars is a problem around NZ – travellers are viewed as easy targets. Avoid leaving valuables in your vehicle, no matter where it's parked. The safest way to get to and from trailheads is with local transport operators. If you have your own car, think carefully about whether you're prepared to leave it unattended in a car park for any length of time. It is usually very easy to find secure parking and gear storage in nearby towns, with transport operators running you from there to the track and back again. This will drastically reduce your chances of being a victim of theft or vandalism.

Environmental hazards NZ has been spared the proliferation of venomous creatures found in neighbouring Australia (spiders, snakes, jellyfish...). Sharks patrol NZ waters, but rarely nibble on humans. Much greater ocean hazards are rips and undertows, which can quickly drag swimmers out to sea: heed local warnings. Don't underestimate the dangers posed by the NZ back country and its unpredictable, ever-changing climate, especially in high-altitude areas.

Road safety Kiwi roads are often made hazardous by speeding locals, wide-cornering campervans and traffic-ignorant sheep. Set yourself a reasonable itinerary and keep your eyes on the road. Cyclists take care: motorists can't always overtake easily on skinny roads.

Sandflies In the annoyances category, NZ's sandflies are a royal pain. Your best defence is to cover up or slather yourself with insect repellent.

Telephone

Telecom New Zealand
(www.telecom.co.nz) The country's key domestic player, with a stake in the local mobile (cell) market.

Vodafone (www.vodafone. co.nz) Telecom's main rival.

2degrees
(www.2degreesmobile.co.nz) Alternative mobile network option.

International Calls

Payphones allow international calls, but the cost and international dialling code for calls will vary depending on which provider you're using. International calls from NZ are relatively inexpensive and subject to specials that reduce the rates even more, so it's worth shopping around.

To make international calls from NZ, you need to dial the international access code (✆00), the country code and the area code (without the initial 0). So for a London number, you'd dial ✆00-44-20, then the phone number.

If dialling NZ from overseas, the country code is ✆64, followed by the appropriate area code minus the initial zero.

Local Calls

Local calls from private phones are free! Local calls from payphones cost $1 for the first 15 minutes, and 20c per minute thereafter, though coin-operated payphones are scarce – you'll need a phone-

card. Calls to mobile phones attract higher rates.

Long Distance Calls & Area Codes

NZ uses regional two-digit area codes for long-distance calls, which can be made from any payphone. If you're making a local call (ie to someone else in the same town), you don't need to dial the area code. But if you're dialling within a region (even if it's to a nearby town with the same area code), you do have to dial the area code.

Information & Toll-Free Calls

Numbers starting with ✆0900 are usually recorded information services, charging upwards of $1 per minute (more from mobiles); these numbers cannot be dialled from payphones.

Toll-free numbers in NZ have the prefix ✆0800 or ✆0508 and can be called free of charge from anywhere in the country, though they may not be accessible from certain areas or mobile phones. Telephone numbers beginning with ✆0508, ✆0800 or ✆0900 cannot be dialled from outside NZ.

Mobile Phones

Local mobile phone numbers are preceded by ✆021, ✆022, ✆025 or ✆027. Mobile phone coverage is good in cities and towns and most parts of the North Island, but can be patchy away from urban centres on the South Island.

If you want to bring your own phone and use a prepaid service with a local SIM card, Vodafone is a practical option. Any Vodafone shop (found in most major towns) will set you up with a SIM card and phone number (about $40); top-ups can be purchased at newsagents, post offices and petrol stations practically anywhere.

Alternatively, if you don't bring your own phone from home, you can rent one from

Vodafone Rental (www.vodarent.co.nz) from $5 per day (for which you'll also need a local SIM card), with pick-up and drop-off outlets at NZ's major airports. We've also had some positive feedback on **Phone Hire New Zealand** (www.phonehirenz.com), which hires out mobile phones, SIM cards, modems and satellite phones.

Remember, you're unlikely to get any mobile coverage in large areas of the backcountry.

Phonecards

NZ has a wide range of phonecards available, which can be bought at hostels, newsagents and post offices for a fixed dollar value (usually $5, $10, $20 and $50). These can be used with any public or private phone by dialling a toll-free access number and then the PIN number on the card. Shop around – rates vary from company to company.

Time

NZ is 12 hours ahead of GMT/UTC and two hours ahead of Australian Eastern Standard Time. The Chathams are 45 minutes ahead of NZ's main islands.

In summer, NZ observes daylight-saving time, where clocks are wound forward by one hour on the last Sunday in September. Clocks are wound back on the first Sunday of the following April.

Visas

Visa application forms are available from NZ diplomatic missions overseas, travel agents and **Immigration New Zealand** (☑09-914 4100, 0508 558 855; www.immigration.govt.nz). Immigration New Zealand has more than a dozen offices overseas; consult the website.

Visitor's Visa

Citizens of Australia don't need a visa to visit NZ and can stay indefinitely (provided they have no criminal convictions). UK citizens don't need a visa either and can stay in the country for up to six months.

Citizens of another 57 countries that have visa-waiver agreements with NZ don't need a visa for stays of up to three months provided they have an onward ticket and sufficient funds to support their stay. Nations in this group include Canada, France, Germany, Ireland, Japan, the Netherlands and the USA.

Citizens of other countries must obtain a visa before entering NZ. Visas come with three months' standard validity and cost $130 if processed in Australia or certain South Pacific countries (eg Samoa, Fiji), or around $165 if processed elsewhere in the world.

A visitor's visa can be extended for stays of up to nine months within one 18-month period, or to a maximum of 12 months in the country. Applications are assessed on a case-by-case basis; visitors will need to meet criteria such as proof of ongoing financial self-support. Apply for extensions at any Immigration New Zealand office.

Work Visa

It's illegal for foreign nationals to work in NZ on a visitor's visa, except for Australians who can legally work without a visa or permit. Non-Australians who wish to work in NZ will need to apply for a work visa, which translates into a work permit after arrival and is valid for up to three years. You can apply for a work permit after you're in NZ, but its validity will be backdated to when you entered the country. The fee for a work visa ranges from $230 to $360, depending on where and how it's processed (paper or online) and the type of application.

Working Holiday Scheme

Eligible travellers who are only interested in short-term employment to supplement their travels can take part in one of NZ's working-holiday schemes (WHS). Under these schemes citizens aged 18 to 30 years from 40 countries – including Canada, France, Germany, Ireland, Japan, Malaysia, the Netherlands, Scandinavian countries, the UK and the USA – can apply for a visa. For most nationalities the visa is valid for 12 months. It's only issued to those seeking a genuine working holiday, not permanent work, so you're not supposed to work for one employer for more than three months.

Most WHS-eligible nationals must apply for this visa from within their own country; residents of some countries can apply online. Applicants must have an onward ticket, a passport valid for at least three months from the date they will leave NZ and evidence of sufficient funds to meet their living costs. The application fee is $165 regardless of where you apply, and isn't refunded if your application is declined.

The rules vary for different nationalities, so make sure you read up on the specifics of your country's agreement with NZ at www.immigration.govt.nz/migrant/stream/work/workingholiday.

Visitor Information Centres

Almost every Kiwi city or town seems to have a visitor information centre. The bigger centres stand united within the outstanding **i-SITE** (www.newzealand.com/travel/i-sites) network, affiliated with Tourism New Zealand (the official national tourism body). i-SITEs have trained staff, information on local activities and attractions, and free brochures and maps. Staff can also book activities, transport and accommodation.

Bear in mind that many information centres only promote accommodation and tour operators who are paying members of the local tourist association, and that sometimes staff aren't supposed to recommend one activity or accommodation provider over another.

There's also an excellent network of Department of Conservation visitor centres to help you plan activities, make bookings and buy maps – and generally pick the brains of knowledgeable DOC staff for local track conditions and recommendations. Visitor centres also usually have displays on local lore, flora and fauna.

From abroad, a good place for pre-trip research is the official website of **Tourism New Zealand** (www.newzealand.com). It has information in several languages, including German and Japanese.

Women Travellers

NZ is generally a very safe place for women travellers, although the usual sensible precautions apply. If you're out on the town, for example, always keep enough money aside for a taxi back to your accommodation. Lone women should also be wary of staying in basic pub accommodation unless it looks safe and well managed.

The real dangers in the NZ wilderness are associated with weather, terrain and bad preparation, all of which can be countered with good sense. It is outside the wilderness areas where the greater risks lie: travel with recommended operators and stay at reputable accommodation; travel with a friend or in a group; avoid walking alone late at night; and never, ever hitchhike alone.

Work
Finding Work

There's plenty of casual work around, mainly in agriculture (fruit picking, farming, wineries), hospitality or ski resorts. Office-based work can be found in IT, banking, finance and telemarketing. Register with a local office-work agency to get started.

Seasonal fruit picking, pruning and harvesting is prime short-term work for visitors. More than 300 sq km of apples, kiwifruit and other fruit and veg are harvested from December to May. Rates are around $10 to $15 an hour for physically taxing toil – turnover of workers is high. You're usually paid by how much you pick (per bin, bucket or kilogram). Prime North Island picking locations include the Bay of Islands (Kerikeri and Paihia), rural Auckland, Tauranga, Gisborne and Hawke's Bay (Napier and Hastings); on the South Island try Nelson (Tapawera and Golden Bay), Marlborough (around Blenheim) and Central Otago (Alexandra and Roxburgh).

Winter work at ski resorts and their service towns includes bartending, waiting, cleaning, ski-tow operation and, if you're properly qualified, ski or snowboard instructing.

Backpacker publications, hostel managers and other travellers are good sources of info on local work possibilities. **Base Backpackers** (www.stayatbase.com/work) runs an employment service via its website, while the Notice Boards page on **Budget**

Backpacker Hostels (BBH; www.bbh.co.nz) lists job vacancies in BBH hostels and a few other possibilities.

Kiwi Careers (www.kiwicareers.govt.nz) lists professional opportunities in various fields (agriculture, creative, health, teaching, volunteer work and recruitment), while **Seek** (www.seek.co.nz) is one of the biggest NZ job-search networks, with thousands of jobs listed.

Income Tax

Death and taxes – no escape! For most travellers, Kiwi dollars earned in NZ will be subject to income tax, deducted from payments by employers – a process called Pay As You Earn (PAYE). Standard NZ income tax rates are 10.5% for annual salaries up to $14,000, then 17.5% up to $48,000, 30% up to $70,000, then 33% for higher incomes. A NZ Accident Compensation Corporation (ACC) scheme levy (1.7%) will also be deducted from your pay packet. Note that these rates tend to change slightly year to year.

If you visit NZ and work for a short time (eg on a working holiday scheme), you may qualify for a tax refund when you leave. Complete a *Refund Application – People Leaving New Zealand IR50* form and submit it with your tax return, along with proof of departure (eg air-ticket copies) to the **Inland Revenue Department** (www.ird.govt.nz).

Travellers undertaking paid work in NZ must obtain an IRD number. Download the *IRD Number Application – Individual IR595* form from the Inland Revenue Department website. IRD numbers normally take eight to 10 working days to be issued.

Transport

Getting There & Away

Flights, tours and rail tickets can be booked online at lonelyplanet.com/bookings.

Entering the Country

Disembarkation in New Zealand is generally a straightforward affair, with only the usual customs declarations to endure and the uncool scramble at the luggage carousel. Recent global instability has resulted in increased security in NZ airports, in both domestic and international terminals, and you may find customs procedures more time-consuming. One procedure has the Orwellian title Advance Passenger Screening, a system whereby documents that used to be checked after you touched down in NZ (passport, visa etc) are now checked before you board your flight – make sure all your documentation is in order so that your check-in is stress-free.

There are no restrictions when it comes to foreign citizens entering NZ. If you have a current passport and visa (or don't require one), you should be fine.

Air

There's a number of competing airlines servicing NZ and a wide variety of fares to choose from if you're flying in from Asia, Europe or North America, though ultimately you'll still pay a lot for a flight unless you jet in from Australia. NZ's popularity and abundance of year-round activities mean that almost any time of year airports can be swarming with inbound tourists – if you want to fly at a particularly popular time of year (eg over the Christmas period), book well in advance.

High season for flights into NZ is summer (December to February), with slightly less of a premium on fares over the shoulder months (October/November and March/April). The low season generally tallies with the winter months (June to August), though this is still a busy time for airlines ferrying ski bunnies and powder hounds.

AIRPORTS

A number of NZ airports handle international flights, with Auckland receiving most traffic.

Auckland International Airport (AKL; ☑0800 247 767, 09-275 0789; www.aucklandairport.co.nz; Ray Emery Dr)

Christchurch Airport (CHC; ☑03-358 5029; www.christchurchairport.co.nz; Memorial Ave)

Dunedin Airport (DUD; ☑03-486 2879; www.dnairport.co.nz; Miller Rd)

Hamilton International Airport (HIA; ☑07-848 9027; www.hamiltonairport.co.nz; Airport Rd)

Queenstown Airport (ZQN; ☑03-450 9031; www.queenstownairport.co.nz; Sir Henry Wrigley Dr)

Rotorua International Airport (☑07-345 8800; www.rotorua-airport.co.nz)

Wellington Airport (WLG; ☑04-385 5100; www.wellingtonairport.co.nz; Stewart Duff Dr)

AIRLINES FLYING TO & FROM NEW ZEALAND

Winging in from Australia, Virgin Australia, Qantas and Air New Zealand are the key players. Air New Zealand also flies from North America, or you can head south with Air Canada and American Airlines. From Europe, the options are a little broader, with British Airways, Lufthansa and Virgin Atlantic entering the fray, and several others stopping in NZ on broader round-the-world routes.

NZ's own overseas carrier is **Air New Zealand** (NZ; ☑0800 737 000, 09-357 3000; www.airnewzealand.co.nz), which flies to runways across Europe, North America, eastern Asia and the Pacific. Other airlines that connect NZ with international destinations include the following (note that ☑0800 and ☑0508 phone numbers mentioned here are for dialling from within NZ only):

Aerolineas Argentinas (AR; ☑09-969 7607; www.aerolineas.com.ar)

CAMPING STOVES & AIRLINES

You cannot take stove fuel, in any form, on an aeroplane. In the past, trampers have also run into problems flying with white-spirit stoves, even when the fuel tanks and bottles are empty. However, most airlines will allow you to check in camping stoves and fuel containers provided the fuel tanks and/or containers have been completely drained of all liquid and action has been taken to nullify the danger. This may involve taking the following steps:

➡ Completely drain all fuel from the fuel tank and bottle, and then leave it uncapped for at least six hours to allow any residual fuel to evaporate, or add cooking oil to the fuel bottle (to elevate the flash point of any residual liquid) and then empty it.

➡ Securely fasten the cap of the fuel bottle and wrap the stove in an absorbent material, such as paper towel. Place it in a plastic bag, close it with an elastic band or twine, and pack it in checked-in baggage.

➡ At check-in, declare that you are carrying these restricted items; you may have to sign a declaration form to confirm that you have cleaned and drained your equipment.

Requirements and restrictions do vary between airlines and airports; check with your airline *before* travelling.

Air Canada (AC;☑0508 747 767, 09-969 7470; www. aircanada.com)

Air China (CA;☑09-379 7696; www.airchina.com.cn)

Air Tahiti Nui (YN;☑09-972 1217; www.airtahitinui.com.au)

Air Vanuatu (NF;☑09-373 3435; www.airvanuatu.com)

Aircalin (SB;☑09-977 2238; www.aircalin.com)

American Airlines (AA; ☑09-912 8814; www.aa.com)

British Airways (BA;☑09-966 9777; www.britishairways. com)

Cathay Pacific (CX;☑0800 800 454, 09-379 0861; www. cathaypacific.com)

China Airlines (CI;☑09-977 2288; www.china-airlines.com)

China Southern (CZ;☑09-302 0666; www.csair.com)

Emirates (EK;☑0508 364 728, 09-968 2208 ; www.emirates.com)

Etihad Airways (EY;☑09-977 2207; www.etihad.com)

Fiji Airways (FJ;☑0800 800 178, 09-379 2404; www. fijiairways.com)

Jetstar (JQ;☑0800 800 995, 09-975 9426; www.jetstar. com) Joins the dots between key tourism centres: Auckland, Wel-lington, Christchurch, Dunedin and Queenstown (and flies Queenstown–Sydney).

Korean Air (☑09-914 2000; www.koreanair.com)

LAN (LA;☑0800 451 373, 09-308 3352; www.lan.com)

Lufthansa (LH;☑0800 945 220, 09-303 1529 ; www. lufthansa.com)

Malaysia Airlines (MH; ☑0800 777 747, 09-379 3743; www.malaysiaairlines.com)

Qantas (QF;☑0800 808 767, 09-357 8900; www.qantas. com.au)

Singapore Airlines (SQ; ☑0800 808 909, 09-379 3209; www.singaporeair.com)

South African Airways (SA;☑09-977 2237; www. flysaa.com)

Thai Airways International (TG;☑09-377 3886; www.thaiairways.com)

Virgin Australia (DJ;☑0800 670 000; www.virginaustralia. com)

TICKETS

Automated online ticket sales work well if you're doing a simple one-way or return trip on specified dates, but are no substitute for a travel agent with the low-down on special deals, strategies for avoiding layovers and other useful advice.

Round-the-world (RTW) tickets If you're flying to New Zealand from the other side of the world, RTW tickets can be bargains. They're generally put together by the big airline alliances, and give you a limited period (usually a year) in which to circumnavigate the globe. You can go anywhere the participating airlines go, as long as you stay within the prescribed kilometre extents or number of stops and don't backtrack when flying between continents. Ticket providers include the following:

Oneworld (www.oneworld. com)

Skyteam (www.skyteam.com)

Star Alliance (www.staralliance.com)

Circle Pacific tickets This is similar to a RTW ticket but covers a more limited region, using a combination of airlines to connect Australia, NZ, North America and Asia, with stopover options in the Pacific islands. As with RTW tickets, there are restrictions on how many stopovers you can take.

Sea

It's possible (though by no means easy or safe) to make your way between NZ and

Australia, and some smaller Pacific islands, by hitching rides or crewing on yachts. Try asking around at harbours, marinas, and yacht and sailing clubs. Popular yachting harbours in NZ include the Bay of Islands and Whangarei (both in Northland), Auckland and Wellington. March and April are the best months to look for boats heading to Australia. October to November is a peak departure season in Fiji to beat the cyclones that soon follow in that neck of the woods.

There are no passenger liners operating to/from NZ, and finding a berth on a cargo ship (much less enjoying the experience) is no easy task.

Getting Around

Air

Those who have limited time to get between NZ's attractions can make the most of a widespread network of domestic flights.

AIRLINES IN NEW ZEALAND

The country's major domestic carrier, Air New Zealand, has a network covering most of the country. Australia-based **Jetstar** (JQ; ☑0800 800 995, 09-975 9426; www.jetstar.com) also flies between five major destinations (Auckland, Wellington, Christchurch, Dunedin and Queenstown). Between them, these two airlines service the main routes and carry

the vast majority of domestic passengers in NZ. Beyond this, several small-scale regional operators provide essential transport services to outlying islands such as Great Barrier Island in the Hauraki Gulf, Stewart Island and the Chathams.

Domestic operators include the following:

Air Chathams (☑03-305 0209; www.airchathams.co.nz) Services to the remote Chatham Islands from Wellington, Christchurch and Auckland.

Air Fiordland (☑03-249 6720, 0800 107 505; www.airfiordland.com) Services around Milford Sound, Te Anau and Queenstown.

Air New Zealand (NZ; ☑0800 737 000, 09-357 3000; www.airnewzealand.co.nz) Offers flights to almost 30 domestic destinations.

Air West Coast (☑0800 247 937, 03-738 0524; www.airwestcoast.co.nz) Charter and scenic flights ex-Greymouth, over the West Coast glaciers and Aoraki/Mt Cook, and stopping in Milford Sound, Queenstown and Christchurch.

Air2there.com (☑0800 777 000, 04-904 5130; www.air2there.com) Connects destinations across Cook Strait, including Paraparaumu, Wellington, Nelson and Blenheim.

Fly My Sky (☑09-256 7025; www.flymysky.co.nz) At least three flights daily from Auckland to Great Barrier Island.

Golden Bay Air (☑0800 588 885, 03-525 8725; www.goldenbayair.co.nz) Flies

regularly between Wellington and Takaka in Golden Bay. Also connects to Karamea for Heaphy Track trampers.

Great Barrier Airlines (☑0800 900 600, 09-275 9120; www.greatbarrierairlines.co.nz) Plies the skies over Great Barrier Island, Auckland, Whangarei and Whitianga.

Soundsair (☑03-520 3080, 0800 505 005; www.soundsair.co.nz) Numerous flights each day between Wellington and Picton, Blenheim and Nelson.

Stewart Island Flights (☑03-218 9129; www.stewartislandflights.com) Flies between Invercargill and Stewart Island.

Sunair (☑0800 786 247, 07-575 7799; www.sunair.co.nz) Flies to Whitianga from Auckland, Great Barrier Island, Hamilton, Rotorua and Tauranga. Has other North Island routes too.

Bicycle

Touring cyclists proliferate in NZ, particularly over summer. NZ is clean, green and relatively uncrowded, and has lots of cheap accommodation (including camping) and abundant fresh water. The roads are mostly in good nick, and the climate is generally not too hot or cold. Road traffic is the biggest danger: trucks overtaking too close to cyclists are a particular threat. Bikes and cycling gear (to rent or buy) are readily available in the main centres, as are bicycle repair shops.

Road rules By law all cyclists must wear an approved safety helmet (or risk a fine); it's also

---

CLIMATE CHANGE & TRAVEL

Every form of transport that relies on carbon-based fuel generates CO_2, the main cause of human-induced climate change. Modern travel is dependent on aeroplanes, which might use less fuel per kilometre per person than most cars but travel much greater distances. The altitude at which aircraft emit gases (including CO_2) and particles also contributes to their climate change impact. Many websites offer 'carbon calculators' that allow people to estimate the carbon emissions generated by their journey and, for those who wish to do so, to offset the impact of the greenhouse gases emitted with contributions to portfolios of climate-friendly initiatives throughout the world. Lonely Planet offsets the carbon footprint of all staff and author travel.

vital to have good reflective safety clothing. See www.nzta.govt.nz/traffic/ways/bike for more bike safety and legal tips.

Transporting bikes Cyclists who use public transport will find that major bus lines and trains only take bicycles on a 'space available' basis and charge up to $10. Some of the smaller shuttle bus companies, on the other hand, make sure they have storage space for bikes, which they carry for a surcharge. If importing your own bike or transporting it by plane within NZ, check with the relevant airline for costs and the degree of dismantling and packing required.

Rental The rates offered by most outfits for renting road or mountain bikes range from $10 to $20 per hour and $30 to $50 per day. Longer-term rentals are often available by negotiation.

Boat

NZ may be an island nation but there's virtually no long-distance water transport around the country. Obvious exceptions include the boat services between Auckland and various islands in the Hauraki Gulf, the inter-island ferries that chug across Cook Strait between Wellington and Picton, and the passenger ferry that negotiates Foveaux Strait between Bluff and the town of Oban on Stewart Island.

Bus

Bus travel in NZ is relatively easy and well organised, with services transporting you to the far reaches of both islands (including the start/end of various walking tracks), but it can be expensive, tedious and time-consuming.

NZ's one-stop-shop bus company is **InterCity** (📞03-442-4122; www.intercity.co.nz), who can drive you to just about anywhere on the North and South Islands. They also offer discounts for YHA, BBH and VIP backpacker members. **Naked Bus** (📞0900 625 33; www.nakedbus.com) is the main competition, a

budget operator with fares as low as $1 (!). The best prices are generally available online, booked a few weeks in advance.

Many provincial routes are serviced by smaller, local bus and shuttle bus operators, some of which provide scheduled and on-demand tramper transport services, as detailed for each tramp within this book.

NATIONWIDE PASSES

Flexipass A hop-on, hop-off InterCity pass, allowing travel to pretty much anywhere in NZ, in any direction. The pass is purchased in blocks of travel time: minimum 15 hours ($117), maximum 60 hours ($449). The average cost of each block becomes cheaper the more hours you buy. You can top up the pass if you need more time.

Flexitrips An InterCity bus-pass system whereby you purchase a specific number of bus trips (eg Auckland to Tauranga would count as one trip) in blocks of five, with or without the north–south ferry trip included. Including the ferry, 5/15/30 trips cost $210/383/550 (subtract $54 if you don't need the ferry).

Aotearoa Adventurer, **Kiwi Explorer**, **Kia Ora New Zealand** and **Tiki Tour New Zealand** Hop-on, hop-off, fixed-itinerary nationwide passes offered by InterCity. These passes link tourist hot spots and range in price from $645 to $1219. See www.travelpass.co.nz for details.

Naked Passport (www.nakedpassport.com) A Naked Bus pass that allows you to buy trips in blocks of five, which you can add to any time, and book each trip as needed. For 5/15/30 trips it's $157/330/497. An unlimited pass costs $597 – great value if you're travelling NZ for many moons.

NORTH ISLAND PASSES

InterCity also offers 13 hop-on, hop-off, fixed-itinerary North Island bus passes, ranging from short $43 runs between Rotorua and Taupo, to $249 trips from Auckland to Wellington via the big

sights. See www.travelpass.co.nz for details.

SOUTH ISLAND PASSES

On the South Island, InterCity offers 11 hop-on, hop-off, fixed-itinerary passes, ranging from $43 trips between Christchurch and Kaikoura, to $583 loops around the whole island. See www.travelpass.co.nz for details.

BACKPACKER BUSES

If you feel like clocking up some kilometres with like-minded fellow travellers, the following operators run fixed-itinerary bus tours, nationwide or on the North or South Island. Accommodation and hop-on/hop-off flexibility are often included.

Adventure Tours New Zealand (📞+61 3 8102 7800; www.adventuretours.com.au)

Flying Kiwi (📞0800 693 296, 03-547 0171; www.flyingkiwi.com)

Haka Tours (📞03-980 4252; www.hakatours.com)

Kiwi Experience (📞09-336 4286; www.kiwiexperience.com)

Stray Travel (📞09-526 2140; www.straytravel.com)

Car & Motorcycle

The best way to explore NZ in depth is to have your own wheels. It's easy to hire cars and campervans at good rates; alternatively, consider buying your own vehicle.

AUTOMOBILE ASSOCIATION (AA)

NZ's **Automobile Association** (AA; 📞0800 500 444; www.aa.co.nz/travel) provides emergency breakdown services, maps and accommodation guides (from holiday parks to motels and B&Bs).

Members of overseas automobile associations should bring their membership cards – many of these bodies have reciprocal agreements with the AA.

DRIVING LICENCES

International visitors to NZ can use their home country's driving licence – if your licence isn't in English, it's a good idea to carry a certified translation with you. Alternatively, use an International Driving Permit (IDP), which will usually be issued on the spot (valid for 12 months) by your home country's auto-mobile association.

FUEL

Fuel (petrol, aka gasoline) is available from service stations across NZ. LPG (gas) is not always stocked by rural suppliers; if you're on gas, it's safer to have dual-fuel capability. Aside from remote locations like Milford Sound and Mt Cook, petrol prices don't vary too much from place to place (very democratic): per-litre costs at the time of research were around $2.20. It's good to remember that outside of main towns it can be a long way between service stations. Don't run out of fuel!

CAMPERVAN HIRE

Check your rear-view mirror on any far-flung NZ road and you'll probably see a shiny white campervan (aka mobile home, motor home, RV) packed with liberated travellers, mountain bikes and portable barbecues cruising along behind you.

Most towns of any size have a holiday park or camping ground with powered sites for around $35 per night. There are also 250-plus vehicle-accessible **Department of Conservation** (DOC; www.doc.govt.nz) camp-sites around NZ, ranging in price from free to $15 per adult: check the website.

You can hire campervans from dozens of companies, prices varying with season, vehicle size and length of rental.

A small van for two people typically has a mini-kitchen and foldout dining table, the latter transforming into a double bed when dinner is done and dusted. Larger 'superior' two-berth vans include shower and toilet. Four- to six-berth camper-vans are the size of trucks (and similarly sluggish) and, besides the extra space, usually contain a toilet and shower.

Over summer, rates offered by the main rental firms for two-/four-/six-berth vans start at around $160/260/300 per day, dropping to as low as $45/60/90 per day in winter.

Major operators include the following:

Apollo (☐0800 113 131, 09-889 2976; www.apollocamper.co.nz)

Britz (☐0800 831 900, 09-255 3910; www.britz.co.nz)

Kea (☐0800 520 052, 09-448 8800; www.keacampers.com)

Maui (☐0800 651 080, 09-255 3910; www.maui.co.nz)

United Campervans (☐0800 759 919, 09-275 9919; www.unitedcampervans.co.nz)

Budget players in the campervan industry offer slick deals and funky, well-kitted-out vehicles for back-packers. Rates are competitive (from as low as $25 per day May to September; from $95 per day December to February). Operators include the following:

Backpacker Sleeper Vans (☐0800 321 939, 03-359 4731; www.sleepervans.co.nz) The name says it all.

Escape Rentals (☐0800 216 171; www.escaperentals.co.nz) Loud, original paintwork, plus outdoor barbecues for hire.

Hippie Camper (☐0800 113 131; www.hippiecamper.co.nz) Think Kombi vans for the new millennium.

Jucy (☐0800 399 736, 09-374 4360; www.jucy.co.nz) Bright green and purple livery, smart vans.

Mighty (☐0800 422 267, 09-255 3985; www.mightycampers.co.nz) Reliable operator, affiliated with the Britz/Maui/Kea empire.

Spaceships (☐0800 772 237, 09-526 2130; www.spaceshipsrentals.co.nz) The customised 'Swiss Army Knife of campervans' that folds out for extra space.

CAR HIRE

Competition between car-rental companies in NZ is torrid, particularly in the big cities and Picton. Remember that if you want to travel far, you need unlimited kilometres. Some (but not all) companies require drivers to be at least 21 years old – ask around.

Most car-hire firms suggest (or insist) that you don't take their vehicles between

FREEDOM CAMPING

NZ is so photogenic, it's tempting to just pull off the road at a gorgeous viewpoint and camp the night. But always ask a local or check with the local i-SITE, DOC office or commercial camping ground, as rules and regulations differ from region to region. If you are free-dom camping, treat the area with respect – if your van isn't fully self-contained you can't stay in designated camping sites that don't have toilets. Legislation allows for $200 instant fines for camping in prohibited areas, or improper disposal of waste (in cases where dumping waste could damage the environment, fees are up to $10,000). See www.camping.org.nz for more freedom camping tips, and www.tourism.govt.nz for info on where to find dump stations.

islands on the Cook Strait ferries. Instead, you leave your car at either Wellington or Picton terminal and pick up another car once you've crossed the strait. This saves you paying to transport a vehicle on the ferry, and is a pain-free exercise.

International rental companies
The big multinational companies have offices in most major cities, towns and airports. Firms sometimes offer one-way rentals (eg collect a car in Auckland, leave it in Wellington), but there are often restrictions and fees. On the other hand, an operator in Christchurch may need to get a vehicle back to Auckland and will offer an amazing one-way deal (sometimes free!).

The major companies offer a choice of either unlimited kilometres, or 100km (or so) per day free, plus so many cents per subsequent kilometre. Daily rates in main cities typically start at around $45 per day for a compact, late-model, Japanese car, and around $75 for medium-sized cars (including GST, unlimited kilometres and insurance).

Avis (☎0800 655 111, 09-526-2847; www.avis.co.nz)

Budget (☎0800 283 438, 09-529 7784; www.budget.co.nz)

Europcar (☎0800 800 115; www.europcar.co.nz)

Hertz (☎0800 654 321, 03-358 6789; www.hertz.co.nz)

Thrifty (☎0800 737 070, 03-359 2721; www.thrifty.co.nz)

Local rental companies Local rental firms dapple the *Yellow Pages* (www.yellow.co.nz). These are almost always cheaper than the big boys – sometimes half the price – but the cheap rates may come with restrictions: vehicles are often older, and with less formality sometimes comes a less protective legal structure for renters.

Rentals from local firms start at around $30 per day for the most compact option. It's obviously cheaper if you rent for a week or more, and

there are often low-season and weekend discounts.

Affordable independent operators with national networks include the following:

a2b Car Rentals (☎0800 545 000; www.a2b-carrentals.co.nz)

Ace Rental Cars (☎0800 502 277, 09-303 3112; www.acerentalcars.co.nz)

Apex Rentals (☎0800 939 597, 03-379 6897; www.apex-rentals.co.nz)

Go Rentals (☎0800 467 368, 09-525 7321; www.gorentals.co.nz)

Jucy Rentals (☎0800 399 736, 09-374 4360; www.jucy.co.nz)

Omega Rental Cars (☎0800 525 210, 09-377 5573; www.omegarentalcars.com)

Pegasus Rental Cars (☎0800 803 580, 03-548 2852; www.rentalcars.co.nz)

MOTORCYCLE

Born to be wild? NZ has great terrain for motorcycle touring, despite the fickle weather in some regions. Most of the country's motorcycle-hire shops are in Auckland and Christchurch, where you can hire anything from a little 50cc moped (aka nifty-fifty) to a throbbing 800cc touring motorcycle and beyond. Following are recommended operators (who also run guided tours) with rates from around $85 to $320 per day:

New Zealand Motorcycle Rentals & Tours (☎09-486 2472; www.nzbike.com)

Te Waipounamu Motorcycle Tours (☎03-377 3211; www.motorcycle-hire.co.nz)

INSURANCE

Rather than risk paying out wads of cash if you have an accident, you can take out your own comprehensive insurance policy, or (the usual option) pay an additional fee per day to the rental company to reduce your excess. This brings the amount you must pay in the event of an accident

down from around $3000 to nil or around $300, depending on how much you pay.

Most insurance agreements won't cover the cost of damage to glass (including the windscreen) or tyres unless you take out extra cover, and insurance coverage is often invalidated on beaches and certain rough unsealed roads – read the fine print.

PURCHASE

Buying a car then selling it at the end of your travels can be one of the cheapest and best ways to see NZ. Auckland is the easiest place to buy a car, followed by Christchurch: scour the hostel notice boards and check out **Trade Me** (www.trademe.co.nz). **Turners Auctions** (☎09-525 1920, 03-343 9850; www.turners.co.nz) is NZ's biggest car-auction operator, with 10 locations.

Legalities Make sure your prospective vehicle has a Warrant of Fitness (WoF) and registration valid for a reasonable period: see www.nzta.govt.nz for details.

Buyers should also take out third-party insurance, covering the cost of repairs to another vehicle in an accident that is your fault: try the **Automobile Association** (AA; ☎0800 500 444; www.aa.co.nz). NZ's no-fault Accident Compensation Corporation scheme covers personal injury, but make sure you have travel insurance too.

Various car-inspection companies inspect cars for around $170; find them at car auctions, or they will come to you. Try **Vehicle Inspection New Zealand** (VINZ; ☎0800 468 469, 09-573 3230; www.vinz.co.nz) or the AA.

Before you buy it's wise to confirm ownership of the vehicle, and find out if there's anything dodgy about the car (eg stolen, or outstanding debts). **LemonCheck** (☎0800 536 662, 09-420 3090; www.lemoncheck.co.nz) offers this service.

Buy-back deals You can avoid the hassle of buying/selling a vehicle privately by entering into a buy-back arrangement with a dealer. Predictably, dealers often find sneaky ways of knocking down the return-sale price, which may be 50% less than what you paid. Hiring or buying and selling a vehicle yourself (if you have the time) is usually a better bet.

ROAD HAZARDS

NZ traffic is usually pretty light, but it's easy to get stuck behind a slow-moving truck or campervan – pack plenty of patience. There are also lots of narrow wiggly roads, one-way bridges and plenty of gravel roads, all of which require a more cautious driving approach. And watch out for sheep!

ROAD RULES

Kiwis drive on the left-hand side of the road; cars are right-hand drive. Give way to the right at intersections.

At single-lane bridges (of which there are a surprisingly large number), a smaller red arrow pointing in your direction of travel means that *you* give way.

Speed limits on the open road are generally 100km/h; in built-up areas the limit is usually 50km/h. Speed cameras and radars are used extensively.

All vehicle occupants must wear a seatbelt or risk a fine. Small children must be belted into approved safety seats.

Always carry your licence when driving. Drink-driving is a serious offence and remains a significant problem in NZ, despite widespread campaigns and severe penalties. The legal blood alcohol limit is 0.08% for drivers over 20, and 0% (zero!) for those under 20.

Hitching & Ride-Sharing

NZ is no longer immune from the perils of solo hitching (especially for women). Those who decide to hitch are taking a small but potentially serious risk. That said, it's not unusual to see hitchhikers along country roads.

LOCAL TRANSPORT TO/FROM THE TRACKS

Local transport to and from tramps is generally pretty good, and it's possible to spend a season tramping without ever having to rent a car or stick out your thumb. For each tramp we have identified the best ways, and operators, for getting to and from the tracks.

The most common way of reaching a trail is with the tramper buses, vans or mini-buses that service tracks around Mt Aspiring, Fiordland, Abel Tasman, Kahurangi, Egmont, Tongariro and Whanganui National Parks, and Great Barrier Island. Many have regular routes and scheduled stops, while others are on-demand. During the summer tramping season you can often arrange to split the fare with another party.

There are also several places where water transport is more convenient than travelling on land. Regular launch and water-taxi services operate along the Abel Tasman Coast Track, departing from Marahau and Kaiteriteri. Water transport is also available to tracks in the Marlborough Sounds, Lake Te Anau, Doubtful Sound, Lake Hauroko, Lake Waikaremoana and Stewart Island.

Alternatively, check hostel notice boards for ride-share opportunities, or have a look at www.carpoolnz.org or www.nationalcarshare.co.nz.

Local Transport
BUS, TRAIN & TRAM

NZ's larger cities have extensive bus services but, with a few honourable exceptions, they are mainly daytime, weekday operations; weekend services can be infrequent or nonexistent. Negotiating inner-city Auckland is made easier by the Link and free City Circuit buses. Christchurch has a free city shuttle service and the historic tramway. The main cities have late-night buses on boozy Friday and Saturday nights.

The only city with a decent train service is Wellington, with five suburban routes.

TAXI

The main cities have plenty of taxis and even small towns may have a local service.

Train

NZ train travel is about the journey, not about getting anywhere in a hurry or par-

---

ticularly cheaply. **KiwiRail** (☑0800 872 467, 04-495 0775; www.kiwirailscenic.co.nz) operates four routes:

Capital Connection Weekday commuter service between Palmerston North and Wellington.

Coastal Pacific Summer service between Christchurch and Picton.

Northern Explorer Between Auckland and Wellington.

TranzAlpine Over the Southern Alps between Christchurch and Greymouth.

Reservations can be made through KiwiRail; directly, or at most train stations (notably *not* at Palmerston North or Hamilton), travel agents and visitor info centres.

TRAIN PASSES

KiwiRail's **Scenic Rail Pass** (www.tranzscenic.co.nz) allows unlimited travel on all of its rail services, including passage on the Wellington–Picton Interislander ferry. One-/two-/three-week passes cost $599/699/799 per adult. Freedom Passes give three to nine days' travel, are valid for 12 months, and cost between $417 and $1161.

Glossary

bach – holiday home

backcountry – anywhere away from roads or other major infrastructure

benched track – a trail cut and levelled to create even terrain

billy – small pot

bivouac, bivvy – rudimentary shelter under a rock ledge, or a small hut

bluff – steep or precipitous land feature, cliff

bouldering – hopping from one boulder to the next, often along a river where there is no trail

bridle – a track that also accommodates horses

burn – small river

bush – forest

bushline – boundary between the last patches of forest and the alpine area

cairn – stack of rocks marking a track, *route* or *fork*

cirque – rounded, high ridge or bowl formed by glacial action

contour – a line on a map connecting land points with the same elevation

dairy – small convenience store/newsagent

DOC – Department of Conservation (or Te Papa Atawhai); government department that administers conservation estate

flat – open, level area of grass or gravel

ford – to cross a stream or river where there is no bridge

fork – an alternative track leading off from a junction

gorge – narrow ravine, where a river or stream often flows

graded – levelled track for easier tramping

Great Walks – a set of nine of NZ's most popular outdoor adventures

head – uppermost part of a valley

iwi – tribe

longdrop – outdoor toilet or privy

moraine – an accumulation of debris deposited by a glacier

pa – fortified Maori village, usually on a hilltop

Pakeha – European settler

permolat – metal disks nailed to trees to aid navigation

pounamu – greenstone or jade

ridgeline – crest of a ridge, which is often used for travel above the *bushline*

route – unformed track requiring significant *backcountry* and navigational skills and experience

saddle – low point on a ridge or between two peaks providing passage from one catchment to another

scree – slope of loose stones found in alpine areas

scroggin – trail mix

slip – an area where large volumes of earth and rocks have 'slipped' from the hillside

snow pole – post used to mark a *route* above the *bushline*

spur – side trail; small ridge that leads up from a valley to the main ridge

swing bridge – bridge over a river or creek, held by heavy wire cables

switchback – zigzagging track that is designed to reduce the steepness of a climb or descent

tarn – small alpine lake

terrace – raised flat area often featuring a bluff-like edge

torch – flashlight

tramp – bushwalk, trek, hike

trig – triangular marker used by surveyors; also called trig point or trig station

true left/right – the left/right side of a waterway as seen when facing downstream

walkwire – cable set-up for crossing streams and rivers

white spirits – white gas that is used in camping stove

Behind the Scenes

SEND US YOUR FEEDBACK

We love to hear from travellers – your comments keep us on our toes and help make our books better. Our well-travelled team reads every word on what you loved or loathed about this book. Although we cannot reply individually to postal submissions, we always guarantee that your feedback goes straight to the appropriate authors, in time for the next edition. Each person who sends us information is thanked in the next edition – the most useful submissions are rewarded with a selection of digital PDF chapters.

Visit **lonelyplanet.com/contact** to submit your updates and suggestions or to ask for help. Our award-winning website also features inspirational travel stories, news and discussions.

Note: We may edit, reproduce and incorporate your comments in Lonely Planet products such as guidebooks, websites and digital products, so let us know if you don't want your comments reproduced or your name acknowledged. For a copy of our privacy policy visit lonelyplanet.com/privacy.

OUR READERS

Many thanks to the travellers who used the last edition and wrote to us with helpful hints, useful advice and interesting anecdotes: Anja Bialkowski, Andrew Clark, Rose & John Dudley, Kate Hebblethwaite, Rich Jenkins, Shanna Jowers, Mike Mackaplow, Corinne Mercadie, Richard Nottage, Rob Philip, Joe Rowing, Frank Stocksiefen, Alison Webb and Michel Wyss.

AUTHOR THANKS

Sarah Bennett & Lee Slater

First and foremost, a huge thank you to Errol Hunt, former commissioning editor and exemplary Kiwi responsible for this and many other Lonely Planet New Zealand guidebooks. Thanks also to the other Melbourne staff who provided vital assistance and encouragement along the way, especially Martine Power, Diana Von Holdt and Andrea Dobbin. We also wish to acknowledge Jim DuFresne's excellent work on previous editions. Finally, our thanks – as always – to all of the people who have provided information and advice in compiling this epic. The majority of such people work for the Department of Conservation/Te Papa Atawhai, but we also wish to acknowledge the staff of Forest & Bird, Mountain Safety Council, and visitor information centres throughout the country. *Kia ora e hoa ma.*

ACKNOWLEDGMENTS

Climate map data adapted from Peel MC, Finlayson BL & McMahon TA (2007), 'Updated World Map of the Köppen-Geiger Climate Classification', *Hydrology and Earth System Sciences*, 11, 163344.

Cover photograph: Bushwalker on Routeburn Track, South Island, New Zealand. Grahame McConnell/Getty

THIS BOOK

This 7th edition of Lonely Planet's *Hiking & Tramping in New Zealand* guidebook was researched and written by Sarah Bennett & Lee Slater. The previous edition was written by Jim DuFresne. This guidebook was commissioned in Lonely Planet's Melbourne office and produced by the following:

Commissioning Editor
Errol Hunt

Coordinating Editors
Andrea Dobbin, Elizabeth Jones

Cartographer
Julie Dodkins

Book Designer
Katherine Marsh

Managing Editors
Sasha Baskett, Barbara Delissen, Angela Tinson

Senior Editor
Catherine Naghten

Senior Cartographer
Diana Von Holdt

Assisting Editors
Carolyn Bain, Carolyn Boicos, Kirsten Rawlings

Assisting Cartographers
Jeff Cameron, James Laversha, Gabriel Lindquist

Cover Research
Naomi Parker

Thanks to Anita Banh, Ryan Evans, Samantha Forge, Larissa Frost, Genesys India, Jouve India, Indra Kilfoyle, Alison Lyall, Kate Mathews, Virginia Moreno, Darren O'Connell, Trent Paton, Alison Ridgway, John Taufa, Ross Taylor, Juan Winata.

Thanks also to the following members of NZ's Department of Conservation, who assisted the authors in verifying information in this guide: Peter Blaxter, Dale Chittenden, Robyn Cormack, Kay Davies, Helen Ough Dealy, Jake Downing, Toni Ellis, Sarah Ensor, Margot Ferrier, Annette Grieve, Shana Harding, Katrina Henderson, Claire Hill, Sorrel Hoskin, Carolyn Knight, Ian McClure, Kiersten McKinley, John Mason, Rachael Mason, Earl Rewi, Elena Sedouch, Shirley Slatter, Michael Smeaton, Carolyn Smith, Kelly Stratford, Murray Thomas, Paul Thornton, Keri Tuna, Kaja Vetter, Jill Wainwright, Elaine Warr, Dave Westcott and John Wotherspoon

BEHIND THE SCENES

Index

A

Abel Tasman Coast Track 8, 166, 169-74, **170**
  accommodation 171
  guided tramps 171
  maps 171
  planning 169, 171
  travel to/from 171
Abel Tasman, Kahurangi & Nelson Lakes (region) 51, 165-201, **167**
  accommodation 165
  climate 165
  Department of Conservation offices 166
  gateway cities & towns 197-201
  highlights 165, 166
  internet resources 166
  planning 165-6
  travel seasons 165
Abel Tasman National Park 168-74, **8**
  environment 168
  history 168
  packing 169
  travel seasons 168-9
accommodation 342-6, see also individual accommodation types, individual tracks
activities 28-33, see also individual activities
Ada Homestead 215
Ada Pass 215
Ada Pass Flats 215
Ahu Ahu Track 74
Ahukawakawa Swamp 115
Ahukawakawa Track 115
air travel
  airlines 354-5, 356
  airports 354

Map Pages **000**
Photo Pages **000**

camping stove air travel regulations 355
  to/from New Zealand 354-5
  within New Zealand 356
Akaroa 233-4
altimeters 41
Amoeboid Mire 303
Anderson Track 75
animals 336-8, see also individual animals
Anne Saddle 216
Antimony Mine Track 150
Aoraki/Mt Cook 228, 229
Aoraki/Mt Cook National Park 228-32
  accommodation 230
  environment 229-30
  guided tramps 230
  history 229
  maps 230
  packing 230
  planning 230
  travel seasons 230
Aotea Track 64-9, **66-7**
  accommodation 67
  environment 65
  history 65
  maps 67
  packing 66
  planning 64-7
  travel seasons 65
  travel to/from 67
area codes 351
Around the Mountain Circuit 119-21, **116-17**
  accommodation 114
  guided tramps 114
  maps 114
  planning 113-14, 119
  travel seasons 113
  travel to/from 114
Arthur's Pass (village) 235
Arthur's Pass National Park 216-28
  environment 217
  history 217

maps 218
  packing 218
  planning 218
  travel seasons 218
ATMs 349
Auckland 80-1
Auckland City Walk 75
Auroa Track 120
Avalanche Peak 218-19, **219, 19**
  maps 218, 220
  packing 218
  planning 218, 218-19
  travel seasons 218
avalanches 41

B

B&Bs 342
backpacks 46-7
bank accounts 349
Banks Peninsula Track 204-8, **207**
  accommodation 205-6
  environment 205
  history 205
  maps 205
  planning 204-6
  travel seasons 205
  travel to/from 206
Barn Paddock Campground 73
Batten, Jean 330
Battleship Bluff 128
Bay of Many Coves Saddle 151
bays 18
  Anapai Bay 173
  Bark Bay 172
  Bottle Bay 152
  Brod Bay 302
  Camp Bay 150
  Duncan Bay 154
  Goat Bay 173
  Horseshoe Bay 309
  Kaipipi Bay 312
  Kerr Bay 196, 197

  Lee Bay 309
  Long Harry Bay 314
  Mason Bay 315, **12**
  Ngawhakawhiti Bay 154
  Nydia Bay 154
  Otanerito Bay 207
  Sleepy Bay 207
  Stony Bay 207
  Torrent Bay 172
  Waiharakeke Bay 173
  Waituna Bay 314
beaches 18
  Anchorage Beach 172
  Big Bungaree Beach 313
  Big Bush Beach 161
  Big Hellfire Beach 314
  Big Rock Beach 180
  Blowholes Beach 307
  East Ruggedy Beach 314
  Huia Beach 73
  Karekare Beach 74
  Koura Beach 180
  Little Bungaree Beach 313
  Little Hellfire Beach 315
  Lucky Beach 313
  Magnetic Beach 309
  Maori Beach 309
  Murray Beach 313
  Nettle Beach 180
  Ninety Mile Beach 58, **17**
  Onetahuti Beach 173, **8**
  Paterson Inlet 312
  Sawyers Beach 313
  Scotts Beach 180
  Smoky Beach 314
  Te Horo Beach 60
  Te Werahi Beach 58-9
  Twenty Minute Beach 180
  Twilight Beach (Te Paengarehia) 58
  Twin Beach 180
  West Ruggedy Beach 314
Beer's Pool 303
Bettjeman's House 128
bicycle travel, see cycling, mountain biking

Big Sandhill 315
Billygoat Basin 79
Billygoat Track 79
birds 34-7, 122-3, 337-8
  bellbird, see korimako
  blue duck, see whio
  falcon, see karearea
  fantail, see piwakawaka
  grey warbler, see riroriro
  kaka 36, **36**
  kakariki 36, **37**
  karearea 36, **36**
  kea 36, **37**
  kereru 34, **35**
  kiwi 34, 336, **35**
  korimako 34, **35**
  miromiro 36, **36**
  moa 336
  morepork, see ruru
  paradise shelduck 34, **35**
  piwakawaka 34, **34**
  pukeko 34, **34**
  rifleman, see tititi pounamu
  riroriro 34, **35**
  robin 34, **35**
  ruru 36, **37**
  silvereye, see tauhou
  tauhou 34, **34**
  tititi pounamu 34, **35**
  tomtit, see miromiro
  tui 36, **37**
  weka 34, **35**
  whio 36, 294, **37**
  woodhen, see weka
bird watching 28, 34-7
Blackburn Mine 211
Blue Pools 280
boat travel
  to/from New Zealand 355-6
  within New Zealand 357
boating 103
books 322, see also individual regions
  animals & plants 336, 340
  history 329
  tramping 55, 85, 111, 145, 166, 203, 259, 286
Boomerang Slip 115
Boulder Bay Track 64
Brames Falls Track 119-20
Bridge to Nowhere 129
budget 15
Buller Gorge 241
bungy-jumping 32

Buntings Bush Gully 162
Buried Forest 161
bus travel
  regional services 357
  local services 360
business hours 350

C
campervans 342-4, 358
camping 16, 342-4, 358
camping stove air travel regulations 355
campsites 343
  Anapai Bay Campsite 173
  Bark Bay Campsite 172
  Bay of Many Coves Campsite 151
  Black Rock Campsite 151
  Brook Valley Holiday Park 159
  Camp Bay Campsite 150
  Davies Bay (Umungata) Campsite 152
  Green Campsite 69
  Harvey Bay Campsite 154
  Heaphy River Campsite 179
  James Mackay Campsite 178
  Korokoro Campsite 100
  Lake Mackenzie Campsite 264-5
  Lyell Campsite 241
  Mangapurua Trig Campsite 127
  Mangatepopo Campsite 91
  Moss Creek Campsite 79
  Mutton Cove Campsite 173
  North Arm Campsite 312
  Nydia Bay Campsite 154
  Onetahuti Campsite 173
  Pandora Campsite 60
  Pelorus Bridge Campground & Cafe 157
  Perry Saddle Campsite 177
  Port William Campsite 309
  Routeburn Flats Campsite 264
  Saxon Campsite 178
  Scotts Beach Campsite 180
  Tapotupotu Campsite 60

  Tapuaenui Campsite 101
  Te Pukatea Bay Campsite 172
  Totaranui Campsite 173
  Twilight Campsite 58
  Waiharakeke Campsite 173
  Waiopaoa Campsite 99
  Watering Cove Campsite 172
  Young Forks Campsite 280
Cannibal Gorge 214-15
canoeing 33
Canterbury, Arthur's Pass & Aoraki/Mt Cook (region) 51, 202-36, **204**
  accommodation 202
  books 203
  climate 202
  Department of Conservation offices 203
  gateway cities & towns 232-6
  highlights 202-3
  internet resources 203
  planning 202-3
  travel seasons 202
Cape Maria van Diemen 58
Cape Reinga (Te Rerenga Wairua) 55, 60
Cape Reinga Lighthouse 58, 60
Caples Track 267
car travel 357-60
  car hire 358-9
  driving licences 358
  road safety 351
Cascade Kauri 75
Cascade Saddle 278
Cascade Track 193
Cass Saddle 227
Cass-Lagoon Saddles Track 226-8, **227**
  accommodation 226
  maps 226
  packing 218
  planning 218, 226
  travel seasons 218
  travel to/from 226
Cattle Flat 275
Cave Point Ridge 314
caves 186
  Cave Stream Scenic Reserve 226
  Fox River Caves 247
  Heaphy Track caves 178
  Lava Caves 64

  Luxmore Caves 302
  Ngarua Caves 186
  Rawhiti Cave 186
  Water Caves 210
  Whirinaki caves 106
caving 106
cell phones 14, 351-2
children, travel with 346
Chinamans Flat 275
Chocolate Swamp 315
Christchurch 232-3
  earthquakes 322, 334
Cleopatra's Pool 172
climate 14, 41-2, 346-7, see also individual regions
climbing 16-17, see also rock climbing
Clinton Forks 294
clothing 45-6
Coast to Coast Race 250
Coffins Creek 68
communications 44
compasses 40
Cone Saddle Track 137
Connect Track 74
consulates 347-8
Cook, Captain James 112, 146, 149, 205, 287, 304-5, 324, 327, **325**
Coopers Castle Route 68
Coppermine Saddle 158
Coromandel Forest Park 75
Coromandel Peninsula 79
costs 15
Cotterell, John 190
Craigieburn Forest Park 226
Craters of the Moon 85
Craw Campground 75
credit cards 349-50
creeks
  Architect Creek 253
  Avalanche Creek 220
  Blackball Creek 249
  Blue Duck Creek 178
  Breakneck Creek 307
  Bullock Creek 246
  Captain Creek 157
  Chime Creek 183
  Coal Creek 302
  Crayfish Creek 180
  Deception Creek 178
  Dilemma Creek 246
  Flat Creek 307
  Fossil Creek 246
  Goat Creek 242
  Gorge Creek 177
  Hamilton Creek 227, 228
  Hidden Falls Creek 298
  Hokuri Creek 300

creeks continued
Hopeless Creek 194
Humboldt Creek 298
Jerusalem Creek 300
Katipo Creek 180
Long Creek 228
Lyell Creek 241
Mackay Creek 295
Makaka Creek 137
McPhee Creek 253
Murray Creek 179
Palaver Creek 253
Potters Creek 264
Raspberry Creek 277
Roaring Creek 265
Roebuck Creek 158
Rough Creek 253
Scott Creek 254
Shiels Creek 253
Slip Creek 299
Smoke-Ho Creek 249
Smoky Creek 314
Snowy Creek 274
Speargrass Creek 196
Stag Creek 280
Steele Creek 268
Stern Creek 242
Swamp Creek 298
Tarn Creek 228
Tekano Creek 254
Totara Creek 137
Waianiwaniwa (10 Mile) Creek 250
Webb Creek 78
Weka Creek 178
Wekakura Creek 180
Windy Creek 228
Woolshed Creek 210
crime 351
Croesus Knob 250
Croesus Track 247-50, **248**
accommodation 249
maps 249
packing 249
planning 247-9
travel seasons 249
travel to/from 249
culture 333
currency 350
Curtis Falls Track 121
customs regulations 347
cycling 148, 150, 356-7, see also mountain biking

D
Dancing Camp Dam 78-9
dangers 360, see also safety
Darwin, Charles 329
day tramps
Avalanche Peak 218-20
Pouakai Crossing 118-19
St Arnaud Range Track 196-7
Tongariro Alpine Crossing 91
day walks 18
daylight-saving time 352
Dead Horse Gully 216
Deadmans Track 132
debit cards 349-50
Department of Conservation campsites & huts 343, see also individual regions
Dieffenbach Cliffs 115
Dieffenbach, Ernest 112
dolphin watching 29, 2
Donnelly Flat 136
Dredge Flat 275
drinks
alcoholic 348
water 49
driving, see car travel
driving licences 358
Dry Rock Shelter 187
du Faur, Freda 229
d'Urville, Dumont 168
DVDs 346

E
earthquakes 322, 329, 333, 334
Eatwells Lookout 151
economy 323, 330, 333
Edwin Burn Viaduct 306
eels 190
EFTPOS 349
Egmont National Park 112-21
accommodation 114
environment 112-13
guided tramps 114
maps 114
planning 113-14
travel seasons 113
travel to/from 114
Eight Mile 242
electricity 346, 347
embassies 347-8
Emerald Lakes 92, 2
Emerald Pool 157, 210

emergencies 43-4
Endeavour Inlet 149
environment 334-40
environmental hazards 351
environmental issues 323, 337
equipment 40
etiquette, tramping 335
exchange rates 15
extreme sports 32

F
Fanthams Peak Track 120
farm accommodation
Hawkswood Farm 162
Medina Farm 161
Ngaroma Farm 161
farmers markets 348
farmstays 344
films 322
film locations
Hobbit, The 87, 157
Last Samurai, The 112
Lord of the Rings trilogy, the 87, 203, 261
Piano, The 74
Fiordland & Stewart Island/Rakiura (region) 52, 285-320, **288-9**
accommodation 285
books 286
climate 285
Department of Conservation offices 286
gateway cities & towns 316-20
highlights 285-6
internet resources 286
travel seasons 285
Fiordland National Park 287, 290-307
environment 290
history 287, 290
planning 290
first aid 44
fishing 29, 268
Flanagan's Corner 177
Flea Bay Cottage 206
Flora Saddle 185-6, 187
flowers 339
food 48-9, 138, 348
footwear 46
Forest Burn Saddle 302
forest parks
Coromandel Forest Park 75
Craigieburn Forest Park 226

Kaimanawa Forest Park 93-96
Mt Richmond Forest Park 154
Ruahine Forest Park 129-32
Tararua Forest Park 132-9
Fox Glacier (glacier) 250, 251
Fox Glacier (town) 256-7
Franz Josef Glacier (glacier) 250, 251
Franz Josef Glacier (town) 256
freedom camping 358
French Ridge Track 278

G
gaiters 46
Gentle Annie Track 135, 137
geography 334-6
geology 334-6
Gibbons Track 74
Gibbs Hill Track 174
Gibbstown 242
Gillespie Pass 281
Gillespie Pass Circuit 278-81, **279**
accommodation 279
guided tramps 280
maps 279
planning 278-80
travel seasons 279
travel to/from 280
Gilmor Clearing 184
glaciers
Bonar Glacier 278
Crow Glacier 220
Curzon Glacier 275
Dart Glacier 274
Fox Glacier 250, 251
Franz Josef Glacier 250, 251
Mueller Glacier 232
Rob Roy Glacier 277
Glenorchy 283
global positioning system (GPS) 40
glowworms 106
Goat Pass 221
Goat Pass Track 220-2, **219**
accommodation 221
maps 218, 221
packing 218
planning 218, 220-1
travel seasons 218
travel to/from 221
Gouland Downs 177

GPS, see global positioning system (GPS)
Great Southern Alps 334-5
Great Walks, the 8-13
  Abel Tasman Coast Track 8, 166, 169-74, **170**
  Heaphy Track 11, 175-80, **176-7, 178, 11**
  Kepler Track 11, 300-3, **301, 11**
  Lake Waikaremoana Great Walk 10, 98-101, **100-101, 10**
  Milford Track 13, 290-5, **292-3, 13**
  Rakiura Track 13, 308-12, **310-11**
  Routeburn Track 13, 261-5, **262**
  Tongariro Northern Circuit 8, 89-94, **90**
  Whanganui Journey 10, 128
greenhouse gas emissions 337
Greenstone Caples Track 265-9, **266**
  accommodation 266
  maps 266
  planning 265-6
  travel seasons 265-6
  travel to/from 266
Greenstone Valley 268, 272
Greymouth 255-6
Gridiron Gulch 187
guided tramps
  Aoraki/Mt Cook National Park 230
  Coromandel Peninsula 78
  Gillespie Pass Circuit 280
  Hollyford Track 297
  Hump Ridge Track 305
  Lake Waikaremoana Great Walk 98
  Milford Track 291
  Mueller Hut Route 230
  Routeburn Track 263
  Tableland Circuit 185
  Tongariro Alpine Crossing 89
  Tongariro Northern Circuit 89
  Whirinaki tramps 104
Gull Rock Point 313
Gunn, Davy 298

H
Hamilton Track 73
Hamilton Valley 227

Hanmer Springs 234-5
Harper Pass 222-6, **223, 224, 225**
  accommodation 223
  maps 223
  packing 218
  planning 218, 222-3
  travel seasons 218
  travel to/from 223
Harris Saddle 264
Havelock 163-4
Hawkswood Range 162
health 42-3, 348-9
Heaphy Track 11, 175-80, **176-7, 178, 11**
  accommodation 176
  guided tramps 175
  maps 176
  packing 176
  planning 175-7
  travel seasons 175
  travel to/from 176-7
heatstroke 42-3
Hellawell's 128
Hellfire Pass 314
Herangi Hill 58
hiking etiquette 335
hiking tours, see guided tramps
Hillary Trail 69-75, **70-1**
  accommodation 73
  environment 72
  history 72
  maps 72
  packing 72
  planning 69-73
  travel seasons 72
  travel to/from 73
Hillary, Sir Edmund 30, 229, 232, 331
Hinewai Reserve 207-8
historic sites 54, 332
history 18, 324-33
  books 329
  European settlement 326-8, 328-30
  internet resources 325, 326
  Land Wars 331
  Maori people 324-5
  Musket Wars 326, 328
  WWI 329
  WWII 330, 331
historical sites 18
hitching 360
Holdsworth-Kaitoke Track 136-9, **136-7**
  accommodation 136-7
  maps 136

planning 136-7
travel seasons 136
travel to/from 133-4
holiday parks 342, 344
holidays 350-1
Holly Hut Track 115
Hollyford Track 295-300, **296, 297**
  accommodation 297
  guided tramps 297
  maps 297
  packing 297
  planning 295-8
  travel seasons 296
  travel to/from 297-8
homestays 151, 344
Hone Heke 326
Hongi Valley 121
horse trekking 29
Horseshoe Basin 186
hostels 344-5
hot springs
  Goat Pass springs 222
  Hanmer Springs Thermal Pools 234
  Hurunui Hot Springs 225
  Kaitoke Hot Springs 67-8
  Tongariro springs 90
  Welcome Flat Thermal Springs 253
hotel accommodation 345
Houghton Track 75
Howard Saddle 196
Hump Ridge 306
Hump Ridge Track 303-7, **304**
  accommodation 305
  guided tramps 305
  maps 305
  packing 305
  planning 303-5
  travel seasons 305
  travel to/from 305
huts 15, 343, 344, 345, see also regional planning sections
  Ada Pass Hut 215
  Anchorage Hut 172
  Angelus Hut 192
  Anne Hut 215
  Architect Creek Hut 253
  Aspiring Hut 277
  Atiwhakatu Hut 136
  Awaroa Hut 173
  Bark Bay Hut 172
  Bealey Hut 228
  Beech Hut 295
  Belltown Manunui Hut 184

Big Hellfire Hut 314
Blue Lake Hut 195
Boundary Hut 271
Boyle Flat Hut 216
Brown Hut 177
Browning Hut 158
Bungaree Hut 313
Camerons Hut 224
Cannibal Gorge Hut 215-16
Captain Creek Hut 157
Careys Hut 271
Cass Saddle Hut 227
Cecil King's Hut 182
Central Whirinaki Hut 106
Ces Clark Hut 249
Christmas Village Hut 313
Christopher Hut 215
Christopher (Ada) Cullers Hut 215
Clinton Hut 294
Coldwater Hut 193, 194
Colin Todd Hut 278
Cone Hut 138
Daleys Flat Hut 275
Dart Hut 274
Demon Trail Hut 299
Douglas Rock Hut 254
Dumpling Hut 295
D'Urville Hut 195
East Ruggedy Hut 314
Flora Hut 187
French Ridge Hut 278
Freshwater Landing Hut 315
Garden Gully Hut 249-50
Ghost Lake Hut 242
Goat Creek Hut 242
Goat Pass Hut 222
Gouland Downs Hut 177
Greenstone Hut 269, 272
Hacket Hut 159
Hamilton Hut 227
Harper Pass Bivouac 224
Heaphy Hut 179
Helicopter Flat Hut 183
Hidden Falls Hut 298
Hokuri Hut 299
Hurunui Hut 225
Hurunui No 3 Hut 224
Iris Burn Hut 303
James Mackay Hut 178
John Tait Hut 194
Jumbo Hut 135
Kaiaraara Hut 68
Kerin Forks Hut 281
Kings Creek Hut 182

huts *continued*
Kiwi Hut 224
Kiwi Saddle Hut 182
Lagoon Saddle Hut 228
Lake Alabaster Hut 299
Lake Dive Hut 120
Lake Howden Hut 265, 267
Lake Mackenzie Hut 264
Lakehead Hut 193
Lewis Hut 179
Liverpool Hut 277
Locke Stream Hut 224
Long Harry Hut 314
Luxmore Hut 302
Lyell Saddle Hut 242
Magdalen Hut 216
Maketawa Hut 121
Mangamate Hut 106
Mangatepopo Hut 91
Marauiti Hut 100
Martins Bay Hut 300
Mason Bay Hut 315
McKellar Hut 267
McKerrow Island Hut 299
Mid Caples Hut 267
Mid Waiohine Hut 135
Middy Creek Hut 157
Mingha Bivouac 221
Mintaro Hut 294
Moerangi Hut 106
Mokihinui Forks Hut 243
Moturau Hut 303
Mt Arthur Hut 186
Mt Heale Hut 68
Mueller Hut 232
Ngapurua Hut 125
North Arm Hut 312, 316
Old Waihohonu Hut 93
Omaru Hut 125
Oturere Hut 92
Panekire Hut 99
Perry Saddle Hut 177
Pinnacles Hut 78, 210
Port William Hut 309
Pouakai Hut 117, 118
Pouri Hut 125
Powell Hut 135
Puketotara Hut 126
Quintin Hut 295
Rangiwahia Hut 131
Rocks Hut 158
Roebuck Hut 158

Rokeby Hut 216
Routeburn Falls Hut 264
Routeburn Flats Hut 264
Sabine Hut 195
Sandy Bay Hut 102-3
Saxon Hut 178
Sayers Hut 137
Shelter Rock Hut 274
Siberia Hut 281
Speargrass Hut 196
Specimen Point Hut 243
Stern Valley Hut 242
Stone Hut 183
Syme Hut 120
Taipo Hut 183, 272
Top Hut 249
Totara Flats Hut 137
Trevor Carter Hut 183
Triangle Hut 132
Tutuwai Hut 138
Upper Caples Hut 267
Upper Deception Hut 222
Upper Gridiron Hut 187
Upper Te Hoe Hut 106
Upper Travers Hut 194
Upper Whirinaki Hut 106
Waiaua Gorge Hut 119
Waiharuru Hut 100-1
Waihohonu Hut 92-3
Waingongoro Hut 120
Waiopaoa Hut 99, 100
Waipakihi Hut 96
Wangapeka Bivvy 184
Welcome Flat Hut 253
West Harper Hut 228
West Sabine Hut 195
Whariwharangi Hut 174
Woolshed Creek Hut 210, 211
Yankee River Hut 313-14
Young Hut 280
Hydrocamp 78, 79
hypothermia 42

I
Ihaia Track 119
immigration 331, 354
Inland Pack Track 244-7, **245**
accommodation 246
maps 246
packing 246
planning 244-6
travel seasons 246
travel to/from 246
insurance
car 359

health 349
travel 349
internet access 349
internet resources 15, *see also individual regions*
Invercargill 317-18
Irishman Flats 215
Island Hill Homestead 315
Islington Bay 64
itineraries 20-7, **20, 21, 22, 23**
Iwituaroa Reserve 152

J
Jamestown 300
Johnson's 128

K
Kahui Track 119
Kahurangi National Park 174-87, **11**
environment 174-5
guided tramps 175
history 174
planning 175
travel seasons 175
Kaiaraara Track 68
Kaiauai Shelter 118
Kaiauai Track 118
Kaikoura 145, 164
Kaikoura Coast Track 159-62, **160**
accommodation 160
environment 159-60
history 159
maps 160
packing 160
planning 159-61
travel seasons 160
travel to/from 161
Kaikoura Peninsula Walkway 145
Kaimanawa Forest Park 93-6
Kaipo Lagoon 103
Kaitaia 81-2
Kaitoke Hot Springs 67-8
Kaitoke Wetlands 67
Kaiuma Saddle 153-4
Kaiwhakauka Track 126-9, **127**
accommodation 126
maps 126
planning 126-7
travel to/from 127
Kapoaiaia Track 119
Kapowairua 60-1
Karamatura Campground 73

Karamatura Track 73
Karamea 200
Kauaeranga Gorge & Dam 79
Kauaeranga Kauri Trail 75-80, **76-7**
accommodation 78
environment 77
history 77
maps 78
planning 75-8
travel seasons 77-8
travel to/from 78
Kauaeranga Valley 78
kauri 68, 75, 80, 339-40
Kauri Timber Company Sawmill 69
kayaking 29, 166
Kea Point 231
Kenepuru Saddle 151
Kepler Track 11, 300-3, **301, 11**
accommodation 301
maps 301
planning 300-2
travel seasons 301
travel to/from 301-2
Ketatahi Track 92
Kidney Fern Arm 312
King, Cecil 182
kiwi 34, 238, 249, **35**
Kiwi Saddle 225
Kiwiriki Track 68
Knutzen Track 74
Kuataika Track 75
Kuataika Trig Lookout 75

L
Lagoon Saddle 228
Lake Angelus Track 191-3, **188-9**
accommodation 191
maps 191
packing 191
planning 190-1, 191-2
travel seasons 190
travel to/from 191
Lake Dive Track 120
Lake Waikaremoana Great Walk 10, 98-101, **100-1, 10**
accommodation 99
guided tramps 98
maps 97
planning 98-9
travel seasons 97
Lakehead Track 193
lakes
Blue Lake 195

Crucible Lake 281
Emerald Lakes 92, **2**
Hidden Lake 294
Lake Alabaster 299
Lake Angelus 192, 196
Lake Constance 195
Lake Harris 264, **12**
Lake Howden 265, 267
Lake Kaurapataka 224
Lake Mackenzie 264
Lake Manapouri 303
Lake Mavis 222
Lake McKellar 267
Lake McKerrow 299
Lake Mintaro 294
Lake Rere 269
Lake Rotoiti 193
Lake Rotoroa 195
Lake Ruapani 103
Lake Sumner 225
Lake Tekapo 203
Lake Waikareiti 102
Lake Waikaremoana 98-100
Lake Wainamu 75
Lake Wakatipu 259
North Mavora Lake 271
Saddle Lakes 184
Tama Lakes 93
Land Wars 88, 331
landforms 54
languages 14
Lava Caves Track 64
Leslie-Karamea Track 183
lighthouses
Cape Maria van Diemen Lighthouse 58
Cape Reinga Lighthouse 58, 60
Farewell Spit Lighthouse 179
Line W Track 68
Little Homer Saddle 299
Little Wanganui Saddle 183-4
local transport 360
lodges
Awaroa Lodge 173
Bridge to Nowhere Lodge 126
Furneaux Lodge 149-50
Holdsworth Lodge 134-5, 136
Hope Kiwi Lodge 225
Konini Lodge 120
Lochmara Lodge 152
Mahana Lodge 150-1
Okaka Lodge 306
Port Craig Lodge 307

Salisbury Lodge 187
Tahurangi Lodge 121
Long Reef 300
Long Road Track 75
Long Trestle Bridge 79
loop walks 18-19
Lord of the Rings film locations 87, 157, 203, 261
Lost Valley Track 183
Lower Lake Dive Track 120

M
Mackay Downs 178
Mackinnon Pass 294, 295, **5**, **13**
Magdalen Valley 216
Mangahuia Trig 132
Mangapurua Landing 129
Mangapurua Track 126-8, **127**
accommodation 126
maps 126
planning 126-7
travel to/from 127
Mangapurua Trig 127
Mangatepopo Track 90
Mangorei Track 118
Manukau Harbour 74
Maori guides (historical)
Kehu 190, 243
Tainui, Wereta 222
Terapuhi 222
Maori history 324-5
Maori legends 86, 112, 122
Maori tribes 96, 97, 103, 212
Ngai Tahu 205, 212
Ngati Apa 129
Ngati Kahungungu 129
Ngati Mamoe 205
Ngati Ruapani 96
Ngati Tumatakokiri 212
Ngati Tuwharetoa 86, 88
Rangitane 129
Tainui 62
Te Kawerau a Maki 72
Tuhoe 96-7, 103
Waitaha 205
Maori Wars, see Land Wars
maps 40, see also individual tracks
Marahau 199
Maraunui Bay 100
Marawhara Walk 74
Marchant Ridge 139
marine mammals 29, see also individual animals
Masterton 142

Matemateaonga Range 125
Matemateaonga Track 123-6, **124**
accommodation 123
maps 123
planning 123, 125
travel to/from 123, 125
Matukituki Valley Tracks 275-8, **276**
accommodation 276
maps 276
planning 275-7
travel seasons 276
travel to/from 277
Mavora-Greenstone Walkway 269-72, **270**, **271**
accommodation 270
environment 269-70
maps 270
planning 269-71
travel seasons 270
travel to/from 270-1
McClimonts Mine 210
McKellar Saddle 267
McKenzie Bay 64
McKerrow Island 299
measures 346
medications 348
Medina Conservation Area 161
Mercer Bay Loop Walk 74
Methven 234
Milford Sound 286
Milford Track 13, 290-5, **292-3**, **5**, **13**
accommodation 291
guided tramps 291
maps 291
packing 291
planning 290-3
travel seasons 291
travel to/from 293
warden talks 294
Minginui 104
moas 325
mobile phones 14, 351-2
Mokihinui Forest 242
Mokihinui River Gorge 243
money 15, 349-50
moneychangers 350
Moonlight Track 248
Moriori people 325
Moss Creek 79-80
motels 345
motorcycle travel 357-60
Motuara Island 149
Motueka 198-9
mountain biking 19, 28, 29-30, 150, 175-6

Mountain House Shelter 135
mountain passes 18
mountaineering 30
mountains
Aoraki/Mt Cook 228, 229
Avalanche Peak 220
Biggs Tops 183
Conical Hill 264
Conical Knob 157
Dome 119
Dun Mountain 158
Faerie Queen 215
Fanthams Peak 120
Flagtop 192
Footstool 254
Gloriana Peak 215
Gordons Pyramid 186
Henry Peak 118
Hirakimata (Mt Hobson) 68
Jean Batten Peak 267
Julius Summit 192
Key Summit 265, 267-8
Maude Peak 117
Maungamahue 131
Maungapiko 68-9
Mt Alba 281
Mt Angelus 192
Mt Anglem/Hananui 313
Mt Arthur 185-6, 187
Mt Aspiring/Tititea 277
Mt Awful 281
Mt Balloon 295
Mt Bruce 228
Mt Cook, see Aoraki/Mt Cook
Mt Cupola 195
Mt Donald McLean 73-4
Mt Federation 215
Mt Fell 157
Mt Hart 295
Mt Holdsworth 135
Mt Humphries (Whakaihuwaka) 125
Mt Hutt 234, **31**
Mt John 203
Mt Luna 183
Mt Luxmore 302
Mt Madeline 298
Mt Montgomery 242
Mt Ngauruhoe 86-8, 90, 91-2, 92, **3**, **328**
Mt Ollivier 232
Mt Pouakai 117, 118
Mt Pukekaikiore 90-1
Mt Rolleston 220
Mt Ryall 250

mountains continued
  Mt Ruapehu 86-8, 93
  Mt Sefton 253
  Mt Somers 210, 212
  Mt Taranaki 112-13,
    121, **17**
  Mt Temple 221
  Mt Tongariro 86-7, 88, 92
  Mt Travers 194
  Mt Tutoko 299
  Mt Vernon 208
  Mt Wilson 161-2
  Mt Young 68
  Peak 1538 268
  Photographic Peak 119
  Pinnacles 79
  Pipipi Peak 125
  Red Head Peak 314
  Rocky Mountain 315
  Rocky Tor 242
  Scott Peak 254
  Skull Peak 162
  Te Paki 60
  Tirikawa Pa 60
  Wooded Peak 158
Mt Arthur Summit Track 186
Mt Aspiring National Park
  & Around Queenstown
  (region) 52, 258-84, **260**
  accommodation 258
  books 259
  climate 258
  Department of
    Conservation offices
    259
  environment 261
  gateway cities & towns
    282-4
  highlights 258-9
  history 260-1
  internet resources 259
  planning 258-9
  travel seasons 258
Mt Cedric Track 196
Mt Cook, see Aoraki/Mt Cook
Mt Cook Village 235-6
Mt Holdsworth-Jumbo
  Circuit 134-6, **134**
  accommodation 134-5
  maps 134
  planning 134-5
  travel seasons 134
  travel to/from 133-4
Mt Ngauruhoe 86-8, 90,
  91-2, 92, **3**, **328**

Mt Pukekaikiore 90-1
Mt Richmond Forest Park 154
Mt Robert Circuit 192
Mt Ruapehu 86-8, 93
Mt Somers Track 208-12,
  209
  accommodation 209
  environment 208-9
  gateway towns 209
  history 208
  maps 209
  planning 208-9
  travel seasons 209
  travel to/from 209
Mt Taranaki 112-13, 121, **17**
Mt Taranaki Summit 121,
  116-17
  guided tramps 114
  maps 114
  planning 113-14, 121
  travel seasons 113
  travel to/from 114
Mt Tongariro 86-7, 88, 92
Mueller Hut Route 230-2,
  231
  accommodation 230
  guided tramps 230
  maps 230
  packing 230
  planning 230
  travel seasons 230
Muir Track 74
Muriwai 75
Murupara 108-9
Musket Wars 326, 328
Mutton Cove 173

N

National Park (town) 107-8
national parks 339, **338**
  Abel Tasman National
    Park 168-74, **8**
  Aoraki/Mt Cook National
    Park 228-32
  Arthur's Pass National
    Park 216-28
  Egmont National Park
    112-21
  Fiordland National Park
    287, 290-307
  Kahurangi National Park
    174-87, **11**
  Mt Aspiring National
    Park 258-82
  Nelson Lakes National
    Park 187-97, **188-9**
  Paparoa National Park
    243-50

Te Urewera National Park
  96-103
Tongariro National Park
  8, 86-93, **9**
Westland Tai Poutini
  National Park 250-4
Whanganui National
  Park 121-9
natural formations, see
  also caves
  Arch Point 173
  Ballroom Overhang 247
  Bell Rock 295
  Bus Stop 211
  Dudley Knob 221
  Duke Knob 210
  Hookey Knob 211
  Lookout Rock 211
  Luncheon Rock 306
  Parachute Rocks 197
  Rocky Point 303
navigation 39-41
Nelson 197-8
Nelson Lakes National Park
  187-97, **188-9**
  accommodation 191
  environment 190
  history 190
  maps 191
  packing 191
  planning 190-1
  travel seasons 190
  travel to/from 191
New Plymouth 139
New Zealand Cycle Trail/
  Nga Haerenga 29-30,
  31
New Zealand
  Environmental Care
  Code 335
New Zealand Long Trail 61
New Zealand Wars (Land
  Wars) 88, 331
newspapers 346
North Arm 312, 316
North Egmont Visitor
  Centre 111
North West Circuit 312-16,
  310-11
  accommodation 312-13
  maps 308
  packing 308
  planning 308, 312-13
  travel seasons 308
  travel to/from 313
Northland, Auckland &
  Coromandel (region)
  50, 54-83, **57**
  books 55
  climate 54

Department of
  Conservation
  offices 55
gateway cities & towns
  80-3
highlights 54, 55
internet resources 55
planning 54-5
travel seasons 54
Nydia Saddle 154
Nydia Track 152-4, **153**
  accommodation 153
  maps 153
  planning 152-3
  travel seasons 153
  travel to/from 153

O

Oaonui Track 119
Oban 318-19
Ohinepango Springs 93
Old Ghost Road Track
  240-3, **240**
  accommodation 241
  maps 241
  planning 240-1
  travel seasons 241
  travel to/from 241
Old Mill Track 69
Omanawanui Track 74
Omanawanui Trig 74
Onahau Lookout Track 152
opening hours 350
Orakei Korako 85
Oreville Stamping
  Battery 69
Oroua Valley 131
Otago Central Rail Trail **31**
Otanerito Farmhouse 207
Otaraheke Clearing 125
outdoor activities 28-33

P

Pack Track 69
packing 45-8, see also
  individual tracks
Palmerston North 141
Pandora Bay 60
Pandora Track 60
Panekiri Bluff 99
Paparoa National Park
  243-50
  environment 244
  history 243-4
  planning 244
paragliding 32
parks & reserves, see
  national parks, forest
  parks

Pass Burn Saddle 272
passports 354
Patekaha Island 100
Peach Tree Track 68
Pelorus Bridge Scenic
  Reserve 156, 157
Pelorus Track 154-9, **155**
  accommodation 156
  environment 156
  facilities 156
  history 156
  maps 156
  planning 154, 156-7
  travel seasons 156
  travel to/from 156-7
Percy Burn Viaduct 306
Peripatus Track 75
personal locator
  beacons (PLBs) 43, 44
phonecards 352
Picton 162-3
Pike River Coalmine
  disaster 323, 333
Pinchgut Track 192
Pipeline Track 73
planning, see also
  individual regions,
  individual tracks
  budgeting 14-15
  clothing 45-6
  equipment 46-8
  food 48-9
  internet resources 14-15
  itineraries 20-7
  New Zealand basics
    14-15
  New Zealand's regions
    50-2
  outdoor activities 28-33
  safety 38-44
  travel seasons 14
  water 49
  weather 14, 41-2, 346-7
plants 339-40
podocarp forests 104, 122
Pohutukawa Glade Walk 74
Point Kean 145
politics 323, 330, 333
population 323
possums 339
postal services 350
Pouakai Circuit 115-19, **116-17**
  accommodation 114
  maps 114
  planning 113-5
  travel seasons 113
  travel to/from 114
Pouakai Crossing 118-9,
  116-17

guided tramps 114
  planning 113-5, 118
  travel seasons 113
  travel to/from 114
Pouakai Tarns 117, 118, **17**
Pouakai Track 117
pub accommodation 345
public holidays 350-1
Puffer Saddle 138
Pukenui Trig 99
Punakaiki 255
Puniho Track 119
Puriri Ridge Track 74
Purple Peak Saddle 208

Q
Queen Charlotte &
  Marlborough (region)
  51, 144-64, **147**
  books 145
  climate 144
  Department of
    Conservation offices
    145
  environment 146
  gateway cities & towns
    162-4
  highlights 145
  history 146
  internet resources 145
  planning 144-5
  travel seasons 144
Queen Charlotte Track 146,
  148-52, **148-9**
  accommodation 148
  maps 148
  mountain biking 150
  packing 148
  planning 146, 148-9
  travel seasons 148
  travel to/from 149
Queenstown 282-3
Quinns Flat 275

R
radio stations 346
radios 44
rafting, see white-water
  rafting
Rahui Island 103
rail passes 360
Rain Gauge Spur 135
Rainbow Warrior 332,
  333
rainfall 346
Rakiura, see Stewart
  Island/Rakiura
Rakiura Southern Circuit
  312

Rakiura Track 13, 308-12,
  310-11, 12
  accommodation 309
  maps 308
  packing 308
  planning 308-9
  travel seasons 308
Ram Track 118
Rangitoto Coastal Track 64
Rangitoto Crater
  Lookout 64
Rangitoto Island Loop 61-4,
  62-3
  accommodation 63
  environment 63
  history 62
  maps 63
  packing 63
  planning 61-4
  travel seasons 63
  travel to/from 63-4
Rangitoto Rim Track 64
Rangitoto Summit Track 64
Rangitoto Wharf 64
Rangiwahia & Deadmans
  Loop 130-2, **130**
  accommodation 131
  maps 130-1
  packing 130
  planning 130-1
  travel seasons 130
  travel to/from 131
Red Crater 92
Redcliffe Point 206
Rees Saddle 274
Rees-Dart Track 272-5, **273**
  accommodation 273
  maps 273
  planning 272-4
  travel seasons 273
  travel to/from 273-4
renewable energy 337
rental accommodation
  345-6
rescue 43-4
Resolution Bay 149
resorts
  Bay of Many Coves
    Resort 151
  Endeavour Resort 150
  Portage Resort Hotel 151
  Punga Cove Resort 150
  Te Mahia Bay Resort 152
river crossings 42-3, 114,
  245
rivers 17, 42-3
  Ada River 215
  Anne River 216
  Aorere River 177

Arthur River 295
Bealey River 221
Big River 178
Boyle River 216, 226
Brown River 177
Caples River 267, 269
Cass River 226-7
Clinton River 294
Copland River 253
Dart River 274-5
Deception River 222
East Branch Sabine
  River 195
Falls River 172
Forest Burn 303
Fox River 247
Freshwater River 315
Greenstone River 268,
  272
Gunner River 179
Harper River 228
Heaphy River 179
Henry River 215
Hollyford River 298,
  299
Hope River 225
Hurunui River 224
Iris Burn 303
Karamea River 183
Karangarua River 253
Kauaeranga River 78
Kohaihai River 180
Makarora River 280, 282
Mararoa River 271, 272
Maruia River 214-15
Matukituki River 277
Mingha River 221
Mokihinui River 242, 243
Oroua River 132
Otehake River 224
Otira River 222, 223
Pelorus River 157, 158
Pond Burn 272
Pororari River 246, 247
Punakaiki River 246,
  247
Pyke River 299
Rees River 274
Roaring Burn 295
Rolling River 182
Route Burn 263
Saxon River 178
Scott Burn 315
Stony River 119
Taipo River 183
Taramakau River 224
Tauherenikau River 138
Travers River 193, 194
Waikoau River 306

rivers continued
Waiohine River 137
Waipakihi River 96
Waiwhakaiho River 118
Wangapeka River 182
Whanganui River 121-2, 126
Whirinaki River 106
Wilkin River 281
Yankee River 313-14
Young River 280
road safety 351
Robert Ridge 192
rock climbing 30
Rocky Lookout 135
Round-the-Mountain Track 93
Routeburn Gorge 264
Routeburn Track 13, 261-5, **262**
accommodation 263
guided tramps 263
maps 263
planning 261-3
travel seasons 263
travel to/from 263
Ruahine Forest Park 129-32
Ruapani Circuit 101-3, **102**
accommodation 101-2
maps 97
planning 97-8, 101-2
travel seasons 97
travel to/from 98
Rutherford, Ernest 329

S
safety 38-44, 351
hitching 360
Salisbury's Open 187
Sand Hill Point Viaduct 306-7
sandflies 351
Sandy Bay (Ngatangawhiti) 60
Sandy Bluff 275
satellite phones 44
Scott Point 58
Scotts Hill Lookout 180
scuba-diving 30, 32
Seal Cove 206
seal watching 29, 206, 300
Sealy Tarns 231
search-and-rescue 44
Separation Point 173
Sharp Cone 96

Ship Cove 149
shopping 48
Siberia Experience 281
skiing 32-3
Skinner Point Lookout 173
skydiving 32
Slaughterhouse Gully 210
sleeping bags & mats 47
Slip Track 73
Slippery Creek 128
snow 346
snowboarding 32-3
socks 46
Soda Springs 91
Somers Saddle 210
Sooty Shearwater Conservation Project 207
South Fork Track 68
Spirits Bay 60-1
St Arnaud 201
St Arnaud Range Track 196-7, **188-9**
maps 191
packing 191
planning 190-1, 196
travel seasons 190
travel to/from 191
St James Walkway 212-16, **213**
accommodation 214
environment 213-15
history 212
maps 214
planning 212-14
travel seasons 214
travel to/from 214
Stag Point 306
star-gazing 203
Staveley Hill 211
Stern Valley 242
Stewart Island/Rakiura 285-6, 307-16, **289**
environment 308-9
history 307-8
maps 308
packing 308
planning 308
travel seasons 308
Stony Bay Cottage 207
stoves 47, 355
Stratford 140
Stratford Plateau 120
streams
Atiwhakatu Stream 135, 137
Bowyers Stream 210
Browning Stream 159
Cameron Stream 224

Caves Stream 211
Cedric Stream 196
Hukere Stream 193
Kai Auahi Stream 118
Kaiaraara Stream 68
Kaiwhakauka Stream 127
Kakanui Stream 106
Kiwiriki Stream 68
Marchant Stream 138
Minarapa Stream 115
Omahakie Stream 153
Pararaha Stream 74
Pony Stream 210
Siberia Stream 281
Sugar Loaf Stream 263
Taumutu Stream 106
Te Paki Stream (Kauaeparaoa) 58
Te Werahi Stream 58-9
Three Mile Stream 225
Trifalls Stream 211
Waihohonu Stream 92
Waihoroihika Stream 101
Wairere Stream 93
Waitahora Stream 61
sunburn 42
supermarkets 348
surfing 28, 33
Sutherland, Donald (explorer) 287, 290
Swanson 75
Swanson Pipeline Track 75
swimming 144

T
Tabernacle Lookout 183
Tableland Circuit 184-7, **185**
accommodation 184-5
guided tramps 185
maps 184
planning 184-5
travel seasons 175
travel to/from 185
Takaka 199-200
Tapotupotu Bay 60
Taranaki, Whanganui & Around Wellington (region) 50, 110-43, **113**
books 111
climate 110
Department of Conservation offices 111
gateway cities & towns 139-43
highlights 110-11
internet resources 111
planning 110-11
travel seasons 110

Tararua biscuits 138
Tararua Forest Park 132-9
Tarawamaomao Point 60
Tasman, Abel 146, 168, 324
Taungatara Track 120
Tawari Bay 102-3
taxes & refunds 350
taxis 360
Te Anau 316-17
Te Araroa 61
Te Henga Walkway 75
Te Horo Bay 60
Te Kooti 97
Te Kopua Bay 100
Te Paki Coastal Track 56-61, **59**
accommodation 57
environment 56
history 56
maps 57
packing 57
planning 56-8
travel seasons 56-7
travel to/from 58
Te Paki Recreation Reserve 58
Te Urewera National Park 96-103
accommodation 97-8
environment 97
gateway cities & cities 98
guided tramps 98
history 96-7
maps 97
planning 97-8
travel seasons 97
travel to/from 98
Te Whaiti-nui-a-toi Canyon 106
Te Wherowhero 326
telephone services 351-2
tents 47
Tester House 128
Thames (town) 83
theft 351
Thomson Ridge 315-16
Three Kings Islands 60
time 352
tipping 350
Tonga Island Marine Reserve 172
Tonga Quarry 172
Tonga Saddle 173
Tongariro Alpine Crossing 91
Tongariro National Park 8, 86-93, **9**
accommodation 89

Map Pages **000**
Photo Pages **000**

environment 87-8
guided tramps 89
history 86-7, 88, 93
maps 88-9
packing 88
travel seasons 88
travel to/from 89
Tongariro Northern Circuit 8, 89-94, **90**
accommodation 89
guided tramps 89
maps 88-9
packing 88
travel seasons 88
travel to/from 89
Tongariro, Urewera & Central North Island (region) 50, 84-109, **87**
books 85
climate 84
Department of Conservation offices 85
gateway cities & towns 98, 104, 107-9
highlights 85, 87
internet resources 85
planning 84-5
travel seasons 84
Top Flat 267
Torea Saddle 151
Totara Flats 137
Totara Saddle 158
tourist information 352-3
tours, see also guided tramps
bus 357
motorcycle 359
track ratings 15
train travel 360
Tramline Track 68, 69
tramping etiquette 335
trams 360
travel to/from New Zealand 354-6
travel within New Zealand 356-60
travellers cheques 350
Travers Saddle 194
Travers-Sabine Circuit 193-6, **188-9**
accommodation 191
maps 191
packing 191
planning 190-1, 193
travel seasons 190
travel to/from 191
tree ferns 340
trees 339-40

Treaty of Waitangi 326, 328, 332
Trig F 306
Trig GG 206
Trig R 211
trout 268
Tryphena 82-3
TSS *Earnslaw* 259
Tuai 98
Tuatapere 317
Turangi 108
Tutakakahikura Scenic Reserve 206
TV 346

U
Umukarikari Range 95-6
Umukarikari Trig 96
Umukarikari-Urchin Circuit 94-6, **95**
accommodation 95
maps 95
packing 94
planning 94-5
travel seasons 94
travel to/from 95
Unity Saddle 211
Upper Kauri Track 75
Upper Lake Dive Track 120
Urchin Track 96
Urchin Trig 96
Ussher Track 74

V
vacations 350-1
vaccinations 348
vegetarian travellers 348
Vern's Camp 106
visas 352, 354
visitor information centres 352-3
Volcanic Activity Centre 85
volcanoes 16, 85, 335-6
Mt Ngauruhoe 86-8, 90, 91-2, 92, **3, 328**
Mt Ruapehu 86-8, 93
Mt Taranaki 112-13, 121, **17**
Mt Tongariro 86-7, 88, 92
Pukekaikiore 90-1
Pukeonake 90-1
Rangitoto 63, 64

W
Waikareiti Track 102
Wainui 174
Wairoa 109
Waitangi Treaty Grounds 332

Wake, Nancy 330
walking poles 47
Wanaka 283-4
Wangapeka Saddle 183
Wangapeka Track 180-4, **181**
accommodation 182
maps 182
packing 182
planning 180, 182
travel seasons 175
travel to/from 182
wars
New Zealand Wars (Land Wars) 88, 331
WWI 329
WWII 330, 331
water 49
waterfalls 18
Bells Falls 115, 119
Billygoat (Atuatumoe) Falls 79
Bridal Veil Falls 263
Brides Veil Falls 277
Cascade Falls 172
Dawson Falls 120
Devil's Punchbowl Falls 220
Dudleigh Falls 295
Earland Falls 265
Giant Gate Falls 295
Hidden Falls 298
Hidden Lake Falls 294
Hirere Falls 294
Howden Falls 211
Iris Burn Falls 303
Kauri Falls 69
Kitekite Falls 74
Korokoro Falls 100
Little Homer Falls 299
Mackay Falls 295
Maidens Relief 210
Routeburn Falls 264
Saxon Falls 183
Spa Pool Waterfall 210
St Quintin Falls 294
Sutherland Falls 295
Taranaki Falls 93, **9**
Travers Falls 194
Whirinaki Falls 106
weather 14, 41-2, 346-7, see also individual regions
websites, see internet resources
weights 346
Welcome Flat 251-4, **252**
accommodation 252
maps 252
planning 251-3

travel seasons 252
travel to/from 253
Wellington 142-3
West Coast (region) 51, 237-57, **239**
accommodation 237
books 238
climate 237
Department of Conservation offices 238
gateway cities & towns 254-7
highlights 237-8
internet resources 238
planning 237-8
travel seasons 237
West Coast Wildlife Centre 238
Westland Tai Poutini National Park 250-4
environment 251
history 251
planning 251
Westport 254-5
weta 336
Whakapapa Village 107
whale watching 29, 145
Whanahuia Range 131
Whanganui 140-1
Whanganui Journey 10, 128, **10**
Whanganui National Park 121-9
environment 122-3
history 122
planning 123
travel seasons 123
Whanganui River 10, 121, 122, 126, **10**
Whatipu 74
Whatipu Scientific Reserve 74
Whirinaki Te Pua a Tane Conservation Park 103-6
accommodation 104
environment 103-4
gateway towns & facilities 104
guided tramps 104
history 103
maps 104
planning 104
travel seasons 104
Whirinaki Track 104-6, **105**
accommodation 104
guided tramps 104
maps 104
planning 104-6

Whirinaki Track
  continued
  travel seasons 104
  travel to/from 106
White Horse Hill 231
Whites Track 74

white-water rafting 28, 33
wildlife 16, 34-7, 336-40,
  *see also individual
  species*
wildlife conservation 337
Wilkies Pools Track 120

Windy Point 158
wine 348
women travellers 353
work 353
WWI 329
WWII 330, 331

Y
Yellow Point 172

Map Legend

Sights
- Beach
- Bird Sanctuary
- Buddhist
- Castle/Palace
- Christian
- Confucian
- Hindu
- Islamic
- Jain
- Jewish
- Monument
- Museum/Gallery/Historic Building
- Ruin
- Sento Hot Baths/Onsen
- Shinto
- Sikh
- Taoist
- Winery/Vineyard
- Zoo/Wildlife Sanctuary
- Other Sight

Activities, Courses & Tours
- Bodysurfing
- Diving
- Canoeing/Kayaking
- Course/Tour
- Skiing
- Snorkelling
- Surfing
- Swimming/Pool
- Walking
- Windsurfing
- Other Activity

Sleeping
- Sleeping
- Camping

Eating
- Eating

Drinking & Nightlife
- Drinking & Nightlife
- Cafe

Entertainment
- Entertainment

Shopping
- Shopping

Information
- Bank
- Embassy/Consulate
- Hospital/Medical
- Internet
- Police
- Post Office
- Telephone
- Toilet
- Tourist Information
- Other Information

Geographic
- Beach
- Hut/Shelter
- Lighthouse
- Lookout
- Mountain/Volcano
- Oasis
- Park
- Pass
- Picnic Area
- Waterfall

Population
- Capital (National)
- Capital (State/Province)
- City/Large Town
- Town/Village

Transport
- Airport
- Border crossing
- Bus
- Cable car/Funicular
- Cycling
- Ferry
- Metro station
- Monorail
- Parking
- Petrol station
- Subway station
- Taxi
- Train station/Railway
- Tram
- Underground station
- Other Transport

Note: Not all symbols displayed above appear on the maps in this book

Routes
- Tollway
- Freeway
- Primary
- Secondary
- Tertiary
- Lane
- Unsealed road
- Road under construction
- Plaza/Mall
- Steps
- Tunnel
- Pedestrian overpass
- Walking Tour
- Walking Tour detour
- Path/Walking Trail

Boundaries
- International
- State/Province
- Disputed
- Regional/Suburb
- Marine Park
- Cliff
- Wall

Hydrography
- River, Creek
- Intermittent River
- Canal
- Water
- Dry/Salt/Intermittent Lake
- Reef

Areas
- Airport/Runway
- Beach/Desert
- Cemetery (Christian)
- Cemetery (Other)
- Glacier
- Mudflat
- Park/Forest
- Sight (Building)
- Sportsground
- Swamp/Mangrove

OUR STORY

A beat-up old car, a few dollars in the pocket and a sense of adventure. In 1972 that's all Tony and Maureen Wheeler needed for the trip of a lifetime – across Europe and Asia overland to Australia. It took several months, and at the end – broke but inspired – they sat at their kitchen table writing and stapling together their first travel guide, *Across Asia on the Cheap*. Within a week they'd sold 1500 copies. Lonely Planet was born.

Today, Lonely Planet has offices in Melbourne, London and Oakland, with more than 600 staff and writers. We share Tony's belief that 'a great guidebook should do three things: inform, educate and amuse'.

OUR WRITERS

Sarah Bennett & Lee Slater

Coordinating Authors Sarah and Lee live in hilly Wellington, but spend many months on the road each year in their small campervan, boots on board, bikes on the back, living like kings on morsels of cheese, craft beer and fresh air. Specialists in 'soft-core adventure' (tramping without crampons, kayaking without capsize), they relive their journeys in magazine features and guidebooks including *Let's Go Camping* and Lonely Planet's *New Zealand*. For more information, visit www.bennettandslater.co.nz.

Jim DuFresne

Author of the previous edition Jim first came to New Zealand more than 20 years ago in search of high peaks and wild places. He found both, along with some fine trout fishing, and has been returning ever since with his backpack and fly rod in hand. Jim began his writing career as the sports and outdoors editor of the *Juneau Empire* and was the first Alaskan sportswriter to win a national award from Associated Press. Today he lives in Michigan and feeds his appetite for the alpine world with frequent trips to Alaska and New Zealand, having authored Lonely Planet's *Alaska*, *Hiking in Alaska* and the previous editions of this guidebook.

Read more about Jim at:
lonelyplanet.com/members/kidven

Contributing Authors

Professor James Belich wrote the History chapter (p324). James is one of NZ's pre-eminent historians and the award-winning author of *The New Zealand Wars*, *Making Peoples* and *Paradise Reforged*. He has also worked in TV – *New Zealand Wars* was screened in NZ in 1998.

Tony Horwitz wrote the Captain James Cook boxed text (p327) in the History chapter. Tony is a Pulitzer-winning reporter and nonfiction author. His fascination with James Cook, and with travel, took him around NZ, Australia and the Pacific while researching *Blue Latitudes* (alternatively titled *Into the Blue*), part biography of Cook and part travelogue.

Published by Lonely Planet Publications Pty Ltd
ABN 36 005 607 983
7th edition – April 2014
ISBN 978 1 74179 017 7
© Lonely Planet 2014 Photographs © as indicated 2014
10 9 8 7 6 5 4 3 2 1
Printed in China

32953012527158